Population Change and Economic Development in East Asia

EAST-WEST CENTER SERIES ON

CONTEMPORARY ISSUES IN ASIA AND THE PACIFIC

Series Editor, Muthiah Alagappa

Population Change and Economic Development in East Asia

CHALLENGES MET, OPPORTUNITIES SEIZED

Edited by Andrew Mason

STANFORD UNIVERSITY PRESS

Stanford University Press
Stanford, California
© 2001 by the Board of Trustees of the
Leland Stanford Junior University

Printed in the United States of America

Library of Congress Cataloging-in-Publication Data
Population change and economic development in East
    Asia : challenges met, opportunities seized / edited by
    Andrew Mason.
        p.   cm. — (Contemporary issues in Asia and the
    Pacific)
    Includes bibliographical references and index.
    ISBN 0-8047-4303-7
    ISBN 0-8047-4322-3 (pbk.)
        1. East Asia—Population—Economic aspects—
    Congresses.   2. East Asia—Economic conditions—
    Congresses.   3. East Asia—Population policy—
    Congresses.   I. Mason, Andrew, 1947–   II. Series.

    HB3650.5.A3 P66   2002
    304.6'2'095—dc21   2001049156

Original printing 2001

Last figure below indicates year of this printing:
09 08 07 06 05 03 02 01

Typeset by G&S Typesetters in 10/14 Sabon

CONTEMPORARY ISSUES IN ASIA AND THE PACIFIC

Series Editor, Muthiah Alagappa

A collaborative effort by Stanford University Press and the East-West Center, this series addresses contemporary issues of policy and scholarly concern in Asia and the Pacific. It focuses on political, social, economic, demographic, environmental, and technological change and the problems related to such change. Books in this series are comparative or regional studies or are works on a single country that address issues in a comparative or regional context.

The East-West Center, located in Honolulu, Hawai'i, is a public, nonprofit educational and research institution established by the US Congress in 1960 to foster understanding and cooperation among the governments and peoples of the Asia Pacific region, including the United States.

Also available in this series:

Political Legitimacy in Southeast Asia: The Quest for Moral Authority
Edited by Muthiah Alagappa

Chiefs Today: Traditional Pacific Leadership and the Postcolonial State
Edited by Geoffrey M. White and Lamont Lindstrom

Making Majorities: Constituting the Nation in Japan, Korea, China, Malaysia, Fiji, Turkey, and the United States
Edited by Dru C. Gladney

Capital, Coercion, and Crime: Bossism in the Philippines
John T. Sidel

Contents

Figures

Tables

Contributors

DENNIS A. AHLBURG is a professor of industrial relations at the University of Minnesota, Minneapolis, and at the university's Center for Population Analysis and Policy.

JOHN BAUER is a research manager for the Workforce Training and Education Coordinating Board, State of Washington, and a former fellow at the East-West Center.

GRIFFITH FEENEY is an adjunct fellow at the East-West Center, Honolulu.

YUJIRO HAYAMI is a professor of international economics at Aoyama-Gakuin University, Tokyo.

MATTHEW HIGGINS is vice-president of Merrill Lynch Global Economics.

FUNG-MEY HUANG is an assistant research fellow at the Institute of Economics, Academia Sinica, Taipei.

ERIC R. JENSEN is a professor of economics, the Department of Economics, College of William and Mary, Williamsburg, Virginia.

RONALD D. LEE is a professor of demography and economics, University of California, Berkeley.

PHILIP MARTIN is a professor of agricultural economics at the University of California, Davis; chair of the University of California's Comparative Immigration and Integration Program; and editor of *Migration News*.

ANDREW MASON is a professor, Department of Economics, University of Hawai'i, and a senior fellow at the East-West Center, Honolulu.

TIMOTHY MILLER is a research scientist, Department of Demography, University of California, Berkeley.

YOSHIO OKUNISHI is a professor of economics, Hosei University, Tokyo.

HARRY OSHIMA is a former visiting fellow at the East-West Center, Honolulu.

MUN HENG TOH is a professor of economics, Department of Business Policy, Faculty of Business Administration, National University of Singapore.

AMY ONG TSUI is a professor of population and family health sciences and director of the Bill and Melinda Gates Institute for Population and Reproductive Health, Johns Hopkins University Bloomberg School of Public Health. At the time that she conducted the research in this volume, she was a professor, Department of Maternal and Child Health and the Carolina Population Center, University of North Carolina at Chapel Hill.

JEFFREY G. WILLLAMSON is Laird Bell Professor of Economics at Harvard University, Cambridge, Massachusetts.

Preface

THIS VOLUME is the result of a project initiated by the East-West Center. Papers were presented at three meetings held in 1997: the Conference on Population and the Asian Economic Miracle, East-West Center, Honolulu, HI, January 7–10, 1997; a Learning Forum on Demographic Momentum and Macroeconomics, the World Bank Institute and the East-West Center, Washington, DC, July 21–22, 1997; and the Policy Seminar on Asian Economic Development: Long Term Perspectives, Nihon University, East-West Center, and the World Bank Institute, Tokyo, October 20–21, 1997. A second volume, *Population Policies and Programs in East Asia* (Mason 2001), has been published and documents how policies contributed to demographic change in East Asia.

Many individuals, in addition to the authors, contributed to this project by participating in the conferences, by discussing papers, and by providing valuable input. I would like to acknowledge Muthiah Alagappa, Mahluddin Khan Alamgir, Sajeda Amin, Nancy Birdsall, David Bloom, Colin Bradford, Jeff Brown, Lee-Jay Cho, Minja Kim Choe, Julie DaVanzo, Angus Deaton, Phil Estermann, Jacques van der Gaag, David Horlacher, Ponciano Intal Jr., Andrew Kantner, Mitsuaki Kojima, Toshio Kuroda, Sumner LaCroix, Karen Mason, Thomas Merrick, Duck Woo Nam, Naohiro Ogawa, Mathana Phananiramai, Catherine Pierce, Lant Pritchett, Robert Retherford, Gerard Russo, Joanne Salop, T. Paul Schultz, Sara Seims, Yukiyasu Sezai, R. Paul Shaw, Young-Soo Shin, Hananto Sigit, Steven Sinding, Kenji Sumida, Krishnamurthy Sundaram, Ann Takayesu, Noreen Tanouye, Pravin Visaria, Michael Ward, Sidney Westley, John Williamson, Peter Xenos, and Sharon Yamamoto. Two individuals contributed to this effort in special ways. Sandra Ward spent endless hours copy editing these papers. Burnham O. Campbell helped to initiate this project and would have served as coeditor had it not been for his untimely death.

Support for this project was provided by the United States Agency for International Development (USAID), the Rockefeller Foundation, the William and Flora Hewlett Foundation, the World Bank, and the Ministry of Foreign Affairs (MOFA) of Japan. Support from USAID and MOFA was provided as part of the Common Agenda for Cooperation in Global Perspectives.

Population Change and Economic Development in East Asia

Population and Economic Growth in East Asia

ANDREW MASON

THE TWENTIETH CENTURY was a period of unprecedented demographic change. The global population increased nearly fourfold, growing from 1.6 billion in 1900 to 6 billion in 2000 (Cohen 1995, app. 2: 400–401; UN DESIPA 1998). Population growth rates accelerated, particularly in the developing world, during the first part of the twentieth century, reaching a peak in the late 1960s. The response to rapid population growth was also unprecedented. Motivated by concerns about the environmental and economic effects of population growth, the United Nations convened three international conferences to develop a global population strategy. Bilateral foreign aid agencies, multilateral institutions such as the World Bank, and private foundations invested billions of dollars in population programs. Many developing-country governments, especially in Asia, vigorously pursued policies aimed at slowing population growth. They launched antinatalist media campaigns, established and subsidized family planning programs, and devised wide-ranging incentive programs. A few countries resorted to highly coercive methods, sacrificing the reproductive rights of their citizens.

The countries of East Asia [1] were among the first and most active proponents of policies aimed at reducing fertility. Beginning in the 1960s or earlier, East Asian developing countries abandoned pronatalist policies, identified population stabilization as a national development objective, and adopted comprehensive programs intended to slow population growth. At first glance the East Asian experience appears to provide strong support for the efficacy of antinatalist population policies. Childbearing and population growth rates dropped more rapidly there than in any other region of the developing or industrialized world. During the same period, the countries of East Asia achieved unparalleled economic success. Within three decades, 1960–90, they were transformed from an economic backwater to the most dynamic region in the world economy. Countries that were impoverished in 1960 joined the ranks of developed countries, and in some respects surpassed the high-income countries of the West.

In this book the connections between demographic change and economic development in East Asia are examined. The goal is to determine whether demographic change in general and population policy in particular played an important role in East Asia's economic success. Two broad sets of issues are addressed. First, did rapid demographic change contribute to East Asian economic development? Specifically, what aspects of the region's development were influenced by demographic trends? What were the mechanisms through which demographic trends influenced the East Asian economies? What institutional, political, social, and economic features conditioned the influence of population on development? Second, what was the role of population policy in East Asia? What policies and programs were implemented and at what cost? What evidence is there that East Asia's population policies achieved their demographic goals? Is it possible or likely that demographic outcomes were a product only of the region's rapid economic development, or did population policies accelerate the transition to low fertility and slower population growth?

The issues addressed in this book are important ones. First, many of the demographic changes examined here are persistent in nature and will influence the economies of East Asia for many decades. When East Asia's recent financial crisis has become a distant memory, demographic forces will still be exerting a deep and fundamental influence. Second, East Asia potentially holds important lessons for many other countries in the developing world. The countries examined here accelerated their economic growth and slowed their population growth with speeds unmatched elsewhere in the developing world.

These issues are addressed in this volume through a detailed examination of the experience between 1960 and 1990 of six East Asian economies: Japan, South Korea, Taiwan, Singapore, Thailand, and Indonesia. These countries were selected for several reasons.

First, they are the first group of developing countries to achieve low fertility—low enough to produce zero or negative population growth. Because their fertility transition has been so compressed, we have a detailed record of the entire transition and accompanying economic changes. Other demographic features, including life expectancy and age structure, have also changed rapidly. Hence, if demographic variables influence development, their effects will surely be evident in East Asia.

Second, the East Asian experience is instructive because the countries got so many things right. Numerous studies of population and development have concluded that rapid population growth exacerbates the costs of poor economic policy. Less clear has been the impact of population variables in an environment of outstanding policy formulation and implementation. Of course, the countries of East Asia have made mistakes, but few countries have matched their record over the post–World War II era.

Third, a regional approach provides a different perspective from that of national or global studies. The fact that this group of successful countries is drawn from a relatively small geographic region suggests that spillovers may have played an important role. The possibility that demographic change in one country has an important bearing on economic conditions in a neighboring country has received little attention in the literature. A study of East Asia may provide new insights in this area.

Finally, the countries of the study relied on voluntary population programs. They made use of incentives and disincentives to encourage couples to bear fewer children. They urged their citizens to adopt small family norms. They did not, however, systematically resort to coercive programs that sacrificed personal freedom at the altar of economic growth.

Although the shared experience of the six economies is a focus of this study, their differences are also instructive. The economies span a wide range of development and demographic circumstances. Income levels in Japan and Singapore in 1960 were substantially higher than those in Thailand and Indonesia. By 1960 women in Japan were bearing only two children each, whereas in Indonesia fertility did not begin to decline until the late 1960s. The populations of Indonesia and Japan are among the largest in the world; Singapore's population is among the smallest. Immigration was an important component of demographic change in Singapore but not elsewhere. Regional variation in the populations and economies of Thailand and Indonesia are critical to an understanding of development in those countries, much more so than in Taiwan or South Korea. The countries of Northeast Asia were densely populated by 1960 and had limited natural resources. Thailand, on the other hand, was still bringing land under cultivation in 1960, and Indonesia's development during the 1970s was aided by vast petroleum reserves.

Although our focus is on six countries, we introduce the experience of other countries in the region at appropriate points. Three other Asian economies also enjoyed high rates of economic growth during the post–World War II era: Hong Kong, Malaysia, and China. Neither Hong Kong nor China receives primary attention in this study because of the unusual nature of their economies. China, of course, had a command economy rather than a market economy. Moreover, China has relied heavily on coercive population policies. The predominance of trade and financial services in Hong Kong's economy and its symbiotic relationship with mainland China distinguish it from other East Asian economies and those elsewhere in the world. Malaysia's demographic experience is also different from that of the other countries examined here. Although its population policies and demographic trends were similar to those of the other countries during the 1960s and the 1970s, Malaysia abandoned population stabilization as a development objective in the early 1980s and adopted policies designed to maintain relatively high birth rates and population growth.

Rapid population growth in East Asia presented two major challenges: feeding a rapidly growing population and productively employing a rapidly growing labor force. Although birth rates dropped precipitously in East Asia, populations have enormous built-in momentum that makes large increases in their size inevitable. East Asia's food problem seemed acute because the region was densely populated and Northeast Asia was lacking in natural resources compared with other regions of the world. Similarly, the employment problem seemed acute because such a large share of the region's labor force was employed in an agricultural sector that could surely not absorb additional workers at an adequate wage.

Both of these challenges were met with spectacular success. Growth in food production outpaced population increase by a substantial margin. Rapid, labor-intensive industrialization led to growth in employment opportunities that was more than sufficient to meet the needs of large cohorts of young adults. This experience demonstrates that *given the right conditions and the right policies*, described in detail in this volume, rapid population growth is not impoverishing. The difficult question to answer is whether the conditions and policies that favored East Asian development can be replicated elsewhere.

Although the countries of East Asia continued to experience substantial population increase between 1960 and 1990, growth rates did slow. Moreover, the countries of East Asia experienced substantial declines in childbearing, increases in life expectancy, and changes in age structure. These demographic changes created opportunities for more rapid economic growth. They led to the emergence of a substantial gap between labor force growth and population growth, to high rates of saving and investment, and to more favorable conditions for human resource investment. The evidence presented in this volume shows that through these mechanisms demographic change had a substantial favorable impact on economic growth.

Again, the connection between demography and economy was not automatic. The countries of East Asia accelerated their rates of economic growth by maximizing the potentially beneficial effects of demographic change. Success depended on the development of strong institutions and effective policies, including those that governed research and innovation, labor and capital markets, and educational and health care systems, and on favorable external conditions, such as the strengthening of the global trading system.

The East Asian experience confirms that population policy can have an important demographic impact. The full development benefits can be realized, however, only if countries adopt sound development policies that encourage innovation, saving and investment, the efficient allocation of labor, rapid growth in industrial and manufacturing employment, investment in human resources, and the elimination of gender bias.

That demographic factors do not operate independently of other forces has been demonstrated, once again, by East Asia's recent financial crisis. So long as the crisis persists, many of the potential benefits of favorable demographic conditions will not be realized. A large labor-population growth gap is advantageous only if job growth keeps pace with growth in the supply of workers. High rates of saving are advantageous only if sound investment opportunities are available. In the absence of successful financial reform, a new era of rapid economic growth will be unattainable, favorable demographics or not.

The Population Debate

Thomas Malthus, with the publication of his *First Essay*, may forever be viewed as the originator of the "population problem," but he was by no means the first to express alarm about rapid population growth. Cohen (1995) documents writings about the dangers of population growth as early as 1600 B.C. With the emergence of rapid population growth in the 1950s and 1960s, renewed concern was reflected in both scholarly and popular writings. Coale and Hoover (1958), in their comprehensive study of India, identified many of the important issues that are still the subject of scholarly debate. The US National Academy of Sciences initiated three efforts (US NRC, Committee on Science and Public Policy 1963; US NAS 1971; US NRC, Working Group on Population Growth and Economic Development 1986; Johnson and Lee 1987). The World Bank undertook its own influential study (World Bank 1984). Several other studies have also affected current thinking about the role of population in development (Simon 1981; Kelley 1988a; Cassen and contributors 1994; Ahlburg, Kelley, and Mason 1996; ADB 1997). Despite these and other efforts, the implications for society of population growth remain an issue of considerable dispute.

As Amy Ong Tsui discusses in Chapter 16, modern concern about rapid population growth reached its zenith in the 1960s and 1970s, when world population growth was peaking. United Nations Secretary-General U Thant issued his *Statement on Population* in 1966, recognizing the importance of the "population problem" and establishing "that the opportunity to decide the number and spacing of children is a basic human right" (Nortman 1970: 37). Alarmist writings by Ehrlich (1968), Meadows et al. (1972), and Brown (1974) influenced popular perceptions about the dangers of rapid population growth. The US National Academy of Sciences recommended that action be taken "to limit population growth now" (US NAS 1971: vi). The view that rapid population growth was a major obstacle to economic development received mixed support by governments in the Third World but was

embraced by the governments of developing countries in East Asia (as discussed in Chapter 16).

A revisionist view of population and development emerged during the
1980s. The more alarmist positions advanced during the 1960s and 1970s
in particular were discounted. The World Bank (1984: 79), for example,
concluded that "rapid population growth . . . acts as a brake on development" while noting that moderate population growth might have beneficial
development effects. Other scholars, for example, Kelley (1988a), emphasized the complexity of the links between population and development, arguing that the impact of population on development depends on context and
that in some circumstances population growth might be favorable. The influential US National Academy of Sciences study (US NRC, Working Group
on Population Growth and Economic Development 1986) was decidedly
more cautious than many earlier studies when it summed up its findings as
follows (p. 90): "On balance, we reach the qualitative conclusion that slower
population growth would be beneficial to economic development for most
developing countries. A rigorous quantitative assessment of these benefits is
difficult and context-dependent."

Debate over the links between population and development has been less
heated during the 1990s, but several recent studies have challenged the consensus reached in the 1980s. *Emerging Asia: Changes and Challenges* (ADB
1997) advances the view that changing demographic conditions are likely
to favor economic growth in Asia. Drawing on analyses of international
cross-sectional data, Radalet, Sachs, and Lee (1997), Bloom and Williamson
(1998), and Kelley and Schmidt (2001) concluded that changing demographic conditions have had a major impact on economic growth. Why recent empirical analysis points to a stronger relationship than earlier work
does is not entirely resolved. Perhaps events during the 1970s masked any
relationships among the variables. Perhaps improvements in data quality,
particularly better measurement of cost-of-living differences among countries, account for the change. Or perhaps the connections between population and development evolve so slowly that the experience of a decade or two
is insufficient to assess the connections. The East Asian experience lends cre-
dence to the view that population change can have a significant development
impact.

Overview of Economic and
Population Trends in East Asia

In 1960 the countries of East Asia were poor. Income in Japan was higher
than in the rest of the region but well below incomes in the United States and
other Western countries. Moreover, prospects for achieving economic growth

did not seem promising. The countries were largely agrarian and traditional. Histories of foreign domination, except in Japan and Thailand, had undermined the development of strong political and economic institutions. Rates of saving and investment were low. One of the few bright spots was the relatively high level of literacy.

From 1960 to 1990 the region's economic success was remarkable. Japan became the world's second largest economy. By 1990 per capita income in Singapore exceeded that in the United Kingdom, Canada, Italy, or Australia. Standards of living had greatly improved in South Korea, Taiwan, Thailand, and Indonesia. Adding to these remarkable accomplishments is the fact that many of the East Asian countries maintained relatively equal income distributions during the high-growth era.

An enormous literature provides detailed and often conflicting explanations of the region's economic success. Drawing on recent studies, John Bauer (Chapter 2) points to several conclusions that are virtually indisputable. First, rates of saving and investment that rose to high levels were essential to the region's growth. Experience elsewhere has shown that high investment rates do not guarantee economic growth, but East Asian countries maintained high rates of return to capital while rapidly expanding their industrial sectors. Second, the countries managed a rapid structural transformation from agricultural to industrial and service-oriented economies. Third, the region enjoyed a relatively well-educated labor force that grew rapidly, ensuring the availability of a large pool of skilled workers. Women played an especially important role in human resource trends, because both their educational attainment and their participation in the labor force increased substantially during the high-growth era.

There is less consensus among economists about the extent to which East Asian growth reflects productivity gains that arose with improvements in the underlying efficiencies of their economies. Some studies have concluded that growth in total factor productivity (TFP) has been low; other studies have found TFP growth rates similar to or higher than those of other industrial economies.

The policies implemented in East Asia clearly contributed to the region's economic success. In Chapter 2 Bauer delineates the most important of these. Governments encouraged domestic enterprises to be outward looking and to compete in the global marketplace. Stable macroeconomic policies ensured low rates of inflation, which are essential to achieving efficient, competitive firms. Government policies were market oriented in some important respects but interventionist in others. They made considerable use of financial incentives, subsidies, and access to credit to promote the growth of particular industries. Labor markets were relatively flexible and efficient, as emphasized by Yoshio Okunishi in Chapter 12. Agricultural policies, highlighted by Yujiro Hayami in Chapter 4, included land reform, investment in rural infrastructure, and research and development efforts. Governments were relatively stable, strong, and committed to economic development. Finally, external conditions were helpful. Ironically, it appears that both the Korean War and the Vietnam War may have benefited the economies of the region. Liberalization of the world economy was a fortuitous development.

In the 1960s demographic conditions in East Asia did not seem conducive to rapid economic development. As Griffith Feeney and I discuss in Chapter 3, mortality rates were high. Many children did not survive to their first birthday, and life expectancy was well below that of countries in the West. Typically, women had an average of six births or more. Health conditions were improving, but with declining death rates the countries began to experience rates of population growth that reached historically high levels shortly after the end of World War II.

After peace was restored to the region with the end of World War II, the Chinese revolution, and the Korean War, East Asia began to experience rapid demographic change. The most remarkable feature of that change was the rapid transition to low fertility. Partly in response to social and economic development and partly in response to government programs, couples began having fewer children. In Taiwan during the early 1950s, for example, women were averaging about six births during their reproductive span. By 1985, however, they were averaging only two births. In Taiwan and the other countries in East Asia childbearing was completely transformed with the passing of a single generation or less.

Countries of East Asia were the first in the developing world to complete the transition to low fertility. Of all the countries in the world with high fertility in 1960, in only six were women averaging two or fewer births by 1990: Taiwan, South Korea, Thailand, Singapore, Hong Kong, and China. Of 36 countries with a per capita income of less than US$1,000 and a population in excess of 2 million in 1960, only 5 countries had achieved a total fertility rate of 3 births or less per woman by 1990: China, South Korea, Thailand, Indonesia, and Romania (see Chapter 3).

Mortality conditions also improved rapidly in East Asia during the second half of the twentieth century. Japan achieved the longest life expectancy of any country in the world. In Singapore and Taiwan life expectancy reached levels comparable to those found in the more developed countries. South Korea, Thailand, and Indonesia experienced substantial gains as well.

Immigration has played an idiosyncratic role in East Asia, a topic that is described in more detail by Philip Martin in Chapter 13. Taiwan and South Korea both experienced large population inflows. More than a million Chinese nationalists fled to Taiwan from the mainland in 1949 and 1950. South Korea's population experienced two large-scale migrations: first, a repatriation of Koreans after the defeat of Japan in World War II and, second, an influx from North Korea when China entered the Korean War. South Korea and Thailand both sent significant numbers of workers to the Middle East during the 1980s. Indonesia has actively promoted the export of labor and the remittance of earnings. In Singapore government policy actively encouraged immigration by skilled workers and their families and by unskilled workers in areas of critical shortage (Yap 2001). For the most part, however, the governments of East Asia have restricted immigration, and foreign-born workers constitute a small portion of the work force in every country but Singapore (see Table 13.1).

Relatively closed borders and declining rates of childbearing produced slower population growth. By the early 1990s Japan's population was growing at only 0.2% per annum, whereas the populations of South Korea, Taiwan, Singapore, and Thailand were growing at about 1% per annum. Population growth in Indonesia had dropped to 1.6% per annum. Despite the emergence of slower population growth, however, the populations of East Asia have grown substantially since the end of World War II. Japan's population has increased by 50%, and the populations of other East Asian countries have increased by two to three times.

Changes in fertility and mortality in East Asia led to a second important demographic phenomenon: changing age structure. In Chapter 3 Feeney and Mason discuss in detail how and why age structure changes during the demographic transition. Most important is a large swing in the proportion of the population in the working ages. This phenomenon, called the demographic bonus by some and the demographic gift by others, has been especially pronounced in East Asia. Between 1960 and 1990 the proportion of population of working age (15–64 years) increased by 10 percentage points in Thailand, 14 percentage points in South Korea, 15 percentage points in Taiwan, and 17 percentage points in Singapore. Japan's working-age population proportion increased by only 8 percentage points during the 1960–90 period because much of its rise occurred during the 1950s. Only Indonesia has not yet experienced a large increase in the proportion of the working-age population. In contrast to the East Asian experience, Africa's working-age population proportion declined by 2 percentage points, Europe's increased by 3 percentage points, and Latin America's increased by 4 percentage points between 1960 and 1990 (see Chapter 3). Some individual countries experienced greater increases, but changes of the magnitude occurring in East Asia are rare. Understanding the economic impact of changing age structure is key to assessing the role of population in East Asia's economic development.

Rapid Population Growth: East Asia's Challenge

When population growth rates accelerated in the 1950s and 1960s, the threat to development efforts appeared self-evident to most observers of the time. Relative to its population, Asia was poorly endowed in land and natural resources. Measured by either total surface area or agricultural area, land per capita was one-seventh of that in Africa or Latin America (see Chapter 4). The first challenge in Asia was to feed its rapidly growing population.

The agricultural sector was also a primary source of employment, but one with apparently limited growth prospects. In Japan a third of the labor force earned its livelihood from agriculture in 1960. In four of the other countries considered in this volume the agricultural labor force in 1960 ranged from 56% of the total in Taiwan to 84% in Thailand (Table 1.1). The situation in the city-state of Singapore was quite different, with only 7% of its labor force employed in agriculture in 1960. The second challenge, then, was to provide productive jobs for rapidly growing labor forces.

As documented throughout this volume, East Asia responded with spectacular success. Food output per capita rose by 36% in Asia (47% in East Asia) between 1963 and 1992. During the same period, food production per capita increased by only 13% in Latin America and declined by 7% in Africa (see Chapter 4). Unemployment and stagnation did not result from the combination of limited land and rapid labor force growth.

How were these challenges met? In Chapter 4 Hayami describes the essential features of East Asia's success at feeding its growing population. Land productivity increased rapidly as agricultural innovation responded to two

TABLE 1.1

Summary of Agricultural Statistics: Six East Asian Countries, 1960–90

Statistic and period	Japan	South Korea	Taiwan[a]	Singapore	Thailand	Indonesia
Percentage of total labor force in agriculture						
1960	33.1	61.3	56.1	7.4	83.7	74.8
1990	7.3	18.1	12.6	0.4	64.1	55.2
Value added in agriculture (percentage of total GDP)						
1960	13.1	35.8	28.9	3.8	36.4	51.5
1990	2.5	8.7	4.1	0.3	12.5	19.4
Annual labor force growth, 1960–90 (%)						
Combined	1.2	2.9	3.1	3.5	2.9	2.5
Agriculture	−3.9	−1.2	−1.9	−6.5	2.0	1.5
Nonagriculture	2.3	5.4	5.4	3.7	5.5	4.5
Annual growth in GDP per worker, 1960–90 (%)						
Combined	4.9	5.0	5.7	4.8	4.5	3.4
Agriculture	4.5	4.4	4.1	5.9	1.8	1.2
Nonagriculture	4.2	3.7	4.4	4.6	2.9	3.2
Arable land per agricultural worker (hectares per worker)						
1970	0.47	0.38	0.54	0.18	0.88	0.61
1990	0.88	0.55	0.84	0.20	0.86	0.47

SOURCES: World Bank (1999). For Taiwan, ROC DGBAS (1986); ROC DGBAS (various years), *Statistical Yearbook of the Republic of China* for 1996; and Summers and Heston (1991).
[a]Labor force statistics for Taiwan are based on employment rather than on the labor force.

factors: substantial decline in the price of fertilizer and increased demand for food as a result of population growth. The innovative process was a complex one. It required developing grains that were more responsive to fertilizer inputs, establishing research institutions that could adapt modern grain varieties to local conditions, and creating a new agricultural infrastructure— irrigation in particular—to utilize modern grain varieties successfully.

The innovation process was neither smooth nor automatic. Increases in productivity came in spurts and with substantial regional differences. The complexity of the innovation process, particularly the slow evolution of institutions, is apparent in the experience of individual countries and regions within Asia. The dramatic development and diffusion of modern rice and wheat varieties in tropical Asia, known as the Green Revolution, illustrates the point. Even before the mid-1960s, population growth was substantial and the price of fertilizer had declined substantially. High-yielding varieties were available for temperate zones, and major advances were possible with a relatively modest effort. Yet gains in yield per hectare were unimpressive. Success was possible only with a social decision to invest in research that otherwise would not have taken place (see Chapter 4).

Hayami (Chapter 4) identifies several features of Asia that explain its successful adaptation, raising the possibility that its experience may not be easily replicated elsewhere, particularly in Africa. Because of its dense population, Asia has long been dominated by settled agriculture and has a relatively well-developed infrastructure. Both an adequate transportation system and an irrigation system were essential elements of the Green Revolution. These features are lacking in Africa, where shifting cultivation and nomadic grazing are commonly practiced (and are sufficient in the absence of population pressure). A more important consideration may be the ability of the political system to respond to public needs by providing physical infrastructure and supporting research efforts that are critical to agricultural innovation. The rulers of settled agrarian Asian societies may have taxed peasants heavily, but those rulers also maintained an infrastructure that would support the agricultural system. This tradition appears to be lacking in Africa, where "politicians and citizens continue to have a stronger sense of belonging to their local and rural communities than to their nations" (Chapter 4).

East Asia's second challenge was to provide employment for its rapidly growing labor forces in economies that were short on land and predominantly agricultural. The economic policies and the favorable external conditions that accounted for the region's success are summarized and discussed in more detail in Chapters 2 and 12. The success of economic restructuring warrants particular attention.

In Japan, Taiwan, and South Korea, where the supply of land was particularly limited, labor force growth was accommodated entirely through changes in industrial and employment structure. Between 1960 and 1990 Taiwan and South Korea achieved rates of growth of nonagricultural employment of 5.4% per year. Their agricultural labor forces declined annually by 2% and 1%, respectively. Japan's agricultural labor force declined by 4% per year.

Thailand and Indonesia adjusted somewhat differently to rapid labor force growth. Both countries experienced significant growth in their agricultural labor forces. They responded differently, in part, because neither country faced land shortages as severe as those found in Northeast Asia. In both countries land under cultivation increased during this period. Between 1970 and 1990, arable land increased by about 10% in Indonesia and by about 50% in Thailand (World Bank 1999). Arable land per agricultural worker declined only slightly in Thailand. Of the countries in our study, only Indonesia experienced a significant decline in arable land per agricultural worker.

The shift of the labor forces of Indonesia and Thailand out of agriculture also occurred more slowly because their industrial sectors were smaller and less developed than those of Northeast Asia. Nonagricultural employment grew as rapidly in Thailand, at 5.5% annually between 1960 and 1990, as in South Korea or Taiwan. Nonagricultural employment also grew rapidly, if somewhat more slowly, in Indonesia (see Table 1.1). But because the nonagricultural sectors in Thailand and Indonesia were so small, even their rapid growth was insufficient to absorb the large numbers of new workers.

The importance of the structural transformation of the economies of East Asia is reinforced by comparing the performance of output per worker in agriculture and nonagriculture between 1960 and 1990 (Table 1.1). In every country output per worker overall grew more rapidly than output per worker in either the agricultural or nonagricultural sector because of the shift of workers into the more productive nonagricultural sector. In Thailand the impact of the shift was particularly great because the productivity gap between agriculture and nonagriculture was, and remains, so large. In Northeast Asia, where employment in agriculture actually declined, output per worker grew as rapidly in the agricultural sector as in the nonagricultural sector, further contributing to overall economic growth. But in both Thailand and Indonesia, continued growth of the agricultural labor force appears to have exacted a price. In these two countries, output per worker grew significantly more slowly in the agricultural sector than in the nonagricultural sector.

The East Asian experience shows that, even in the face of a limited supply of land, rapid population growth does not necessarily lead either to a decline in per capita food production or to slow economic growth. Lower fertilizer prices and public policies that led to agricultural innovation and investment in infrastructure allowed the countries of East Asia to increase their food production much more rapidly than their populations. In Northeast Asia this was accomplished despite a significant decline in the agricultural labor force.

Development of the agricultural sector contributed to overall economic growth, but the extraordinary growth of the nonagricultural sector and the policies that made it possible were critical. Any potentially adverse effect of employment growth on labor productivity in agriculture was circumvented in Northeast Asia. In Southeast Asia, where the industrial sectors were less developed, growth in the agricultural labor force was unavoidable and labor productivity in agriculture lagged, accounting for part of the differences in economic growth between the newly industrialized economies (NIEs) and the less developed economies of Southeast Asia.

Demographic Change and East Asia's Opportunities

At the same time that the challenges of rapid population growth were being met in East Asia, other demographic changes were creating opportunities for more rapid economic growth. Chief among these was changing age structure. Because of declining rates of childbearing, the total number of children in East Asia quickly stabilized, whereas the working-age population continued to grow rapidly. This led to an unusually high concentration of the population in the productive ages or, stated conversely, to an usually low dependency ratio. The implications for labor force, saving and investment, and human resource investment are addressed in sections II and III of this volume.

The emergence of a substantial gap between labor force growth and population growth contributed to high rates of economic growth and was a consequence of rapid demographic transition in East Asia (ADB 1997). The rate of labor force growth exceeded the rate of population growth by 0.8% per annum between 1960 and 1990. In Latin America the gap averaged 0.4% annually, and in Western industrialized countries the gap was 0.3% annually. In Africa and South Asia labor forces grew more slowly than populations (Table 1.2).

Why did East Asia's labor forces grow so much more rapidly than their populations? The increased concentration of the working-age population is primarily responsible. Analysis by Okunishi in Chapter 12 shows that essentially all the increase in the proportion of males in the labor force was a consequence of changing age structure. Changes in age-specific participation rates among males, influenced by higher rates of school enrollment, actually depressed labor force growth.

The situation for women was quite different. Changes in age structure had a similar, although somewhat smaller, effect on female labor force growth. These changes were reinforced by rising rates of female labor force participation in Taiwan, South Korea, Singapore, and Indonesia. As discussed in more detail in Chapters 12 and 14, the number of women in the labor force

TABLE 1.2

Population and Labor Force Growth: Average Annual Growth Rates in Major World Regions, 1960–90[a]

Region	Rate of growth (%)	
	Population	Labor force
Africa	2.6	2.3
Latin America	2.3	2.7
Asia		
South Asia	2.6	2.5
High performers	1.9	2.7
Europe and North America	0.8	1.1

SOURCE: ILO Bureau of Statistics (1997).
[a]Values are unweighted averages of country values.

grew so rapidly because more women entered the labor force when they completed school, postponed marriage to work for more years as single adults, and remained in the labor force after marrying, both during and after completing their childbearing. These changes were more than sufficient to offset lower rates of participation among young women.

The pattern for Japan and Thailand with respect to female employment differs from that of the other countries because female labor force participation rates were already high in 1960. In Japan more than 40% of the labor force consisted of women, and in Thailand the amount was nearly 50%. Participation rates among urban women rose substantially in both countries, but in both countries the gains among urban women were offset by the shift out of agriculture, where female participation rates have been traditionally high (see Chapter 14; Phananiramai 1997).

Domestic conditions determined the supply of labor in most of the countries because their borders were largely closed to immigration (see Chapter 13). Singapore, which has actively encouraged labor migration, is an exception to this generalization. By the mid-1990s one in five workers in Singapore was an immigrant. In the other countries less than 5% of the work forces consisted of migrant workers, and in Japan and South Korea less than 1% (see Table 10.1). Singapore's increasing reliance on immigrant workers contributed to a population–labor force growth gap that was the largest among the rapid-transition countries of East Asia.

Changes in the supply of workers are only part of the story. In some countries with stagnant economies rapid growth of the working-age population has produced unemployment, withdrawals from the labor force, and slower labor force growth. In East Asia successful economic policies, described in Chapter 2, and effective labor policies, described in Chapter 12, led to rapid growth in the demand for workers. Employment in manufacturing and services grew so rapidly that jobs for new entrants to the labor force were read-ily available, workers could be pulled out of the agricultural sector, and low unemployment rates could be sustained. Thus East Asia effectively capital-ized on the rapid growth in the working-age population and the increased availability of women.

This phenomenon, noted in other recent studies of the interaction be-tween demographics and economic growth, has been referred to as the de-mographic bonus or the demographic gift because of its contribution to eco-nomic growth (Bloom and Williamson 1998; Kelley and Schmidt 2001). Given a specified level of output per worker, an increase in the number of workers relative to population translates directly into higher per capita out-put. The average population–labor force growth gap of 0.8% per annum for East Asia augments the growth rate of per capita income by 0.8% per annum. Between 1960 and 1990 the bonus accounted for as much as 19% of Taiwan's growth in per capita income and as little as 7% of Japan's (see Table 8.2).

Saving, Capital Deepening, and Growth in Output per Worker

Although output or income per capita is widely used to measure the mate-rial standard of living, output per worker measures more directly the perfor-mance of an economy. Analyses of economic performance, many of which are summarized in Chapter 2, identify two broad explanations for growth in output per worker. The first is the accumulation of productive factors, namely, human and physical capital. The second is the increase in factor pro-ductivity. Demographic variables bear directly on factor accumulation, and how they do so is the focus of several chapters in this volume. Considerably less is known about the effects of population variables on factor productiv-ity, although Bauer discusses the issue in Chapter 2. Studies of East Asia con-sistently point to the importance of factor accumulation, especially the in-crease in physical capital per worker, called *capital deepening.*

As I discuss in more detail in Chapter 8, capital deepening is caused by ei-ther a decrease in the rate of growth of the labor force or an increase in sav-ing and investment rates. In Japan labor force growth declined substantially between 1960 and 1990, but other East Asian countries did not experience substantially slower labor force growth. In these countries capital deepening occurred because saving and investment rates increased substantially from the low levels that prevailed in 1960 (see Table 2.2).

Three chapters in this volume investigate the extent to which demo-graphic factors contributed to the large increases in saving and investment experienced by the East Asian economies. In Chapter 5 Jeffrey Williamson

and Matthew Higgins analyze a cross-section of time series of aggregate saving and investment data. In Chapter 6 Ronald Lee, Timothy Miller, and I present a simulation model with parameters based, in part, on detailed microeconomic data from Taiwan. In Chapter 7 Toh Mun Heng analyzes a time
series of aggregate saving rates for Singapore, a particularly interesting case
because of Singapore's large mandatory pension program.

Williamson and Higgins find that changes in demographic factors between the early 1970s and the early 1990s led to an increase in gross national
saving by 13.6 percentage points in Northeast Asia and by 11.5 percentage
points in Southeast Asia. Toh finds saving effects for Singapore that are similarly large. Lee, Mason, and Miller find an effect of demographic factors on
the net saving rate, from trough to peak, that is substantial but well below
the estimates obtained by Williamson and Higgins or Toh from analyzing
aggregate saving data.

Table 1.3 compares the results reported in this volume with those from
two other recent studies of population and saving: Kelley and Schmidt (1996)
and Deaton and Paxson (2000). To facilitate comparison, I have combined
Taiwan's demographic characteristics with the saving models estimated in
each of these studies to obtain saving forecasts.[2] The results presented in
Table 1.3 address two points. The first is the total rise in saving that can be
attributed to demographic factors over the entire demographic transition.
The second is the change in saving between 1960 and 1990 that can be attributed to demographic factors. These two calculations differ primarily because the estimated models imply that changes in demographic factors after
1990 will lead to further increases in saving rates.

All the analyses find that demographic factors exert an upward influence
on saving rates. Williamson and Higgins (Chapter 5), Toh (Chapter 7), and
Kelley and Schmidt (1996) all find large effects based on their statistical
analyses of gross national saving rates. In these studies the rise from trough

TABLE 1.3

Predicted Saving Rates (%), 1960–90, Based on Taiwan's Demographics:
Five Alternative Models

	Over demographic transition			1960–90		
Model	Minimum	Maximum	Change	1960	1990	Change
Williamson and Higgins						
(Chapter 5)	1.6	44.7	43.0	1.6	36.8	35.1
Kelley and Schmidt (1996)	8.3	33.4	25.1	9.9	30.9	21.0
Toh (Chapter 7)	8.7	53.7	45.0	9.1	46.2	37.1
Lee, Mason, and Miller						
(Chapter 6)	5.1	19.6	14.5	9.3	16.0	6.7
Deaton and Paxson (2000)	18.2	24.6	6.5	19.3	22.4	3.1

to peak ranges from 25 percentage points (Kelley and Schmidt 1996) to 45 percentage points (Chapter 7). The swing in net national saving implied by the Lee, Mason, and Miller simulations (Chapter 6) is 14 percentage points. Deaton and Paxson (2000) estimated a swing in household saving rates of 6 percentage points, a demographic effect that is more modest but still of consequence.

The second set of figures in Table 1.3 shows the increase in saving rates between 1960 and 1990 that can be attributed to demographic factors. The estimates range from 3 percentage points for Deaton and Paxson (2000) and 7 percentage points for Lee, Mason, and Miller (Chapter 6) to 21, 35, and 37 percentage points for the three models estimated from gross national saving data.

There are a number of possible explanations for the wide range of these estimates. Definitional differences are partly responsible. The cross-national studies analyze broad measures of saving; the Deaton and Paxson analysis is of a much narrower saving measure. The studies also use different methods. Deaton and Paxson (2000) used household survey data to estimate age profiles of consumption and earning. They analyzed the effect of demographics by holding these profiles constant and by allowing population age structure to vary. Thus their model does not capture the effect of changing age profiles on aggregate saving. In the Lee, Mason, and Miller analysis (Chapter 6) age profiles of saving are influenced by the decline in fertility and the rise in life expectancy. Thus the Lee, Mason, and Miller approach gives a more complete accounting of the impact of demographic variables on aggregate saving. The cross-national studies of aggregate saving may capture the effects of changing life expectancy to the extent that life expectancy and age structure variables are highly correlated. The Lee, Mason, and Miller simulation analysis indicates, however, that the effects of changing demographic variables cannot be as large as the effects found in aggregate analyses if saving is governed by the conventional life-cycle saving model. If the effect of population on saving is so large, then some yet-to-be-identified behavioral model must be at work.

Despite the great variation in the estimates of the size of the effects, these studies do agree that demographic factors have influenced saving rates and hence the rate of capital deepening. In Chapter 8 I use growth-accounting techniques to assess the impact of population change on Taiwan's economic growth, incorporating the effects of demography on saving from Lee, Mason, and Miller simulations. The conclusion is that output per worker grew faster by 0.9% per annum between 1965 and 1990 because of changing demographic conditions. The combined effect of demography, including saving effects and the gap between population and labor force growth, was to increase growth in output per capita by 1.8%, accounting for 28% of Taiwan's growth between 1965 and 1990 (see Table 8.2).

Human Resources

Human resources—education and health—are often cited as a critical element of East Asian economic success [see Chapters 2 and 9 and World Bank (1993a)]. To some extent the East Asian countries began the high-growth era with a human resources advantage. Compared with other countries at similar levels of development, their life expectancies and rates of primary school enrollment were high in 1960 (see Chapters 2, 3, and 9). In some respects, however, East Asia was not very different from other developing countries of the time. The shares of gross national product (GNP) devoted to public education were similar to levels found elsewhere in the developing world. The gender gaps in education were substantial. In Singapore nearly one-quarter of the adult population was illiterate in 1970 (World Bank 1999). In Thailand relatively few students went beyond the required four years of schooling.

East Asia's high-growth era was marked by substantial gains in human resources. Life expectancy, school enrollment, and educational attainment all increased rapidly. Spending per student rose much faster in East Asia than elsewhere. The gender gap in education was greatly reduced. Private resources devoted to education also increased rapidly, especially in Japan and South Korea, as parents responded to highly competitive education systems (Tsuya and Choe 1999).

Although gains in education and health are widely believed to have contributed to the region's economic success, estimates of the magnitude of that contribution vary widely. Many studies reviewed by Fung-Mey Huang in Chapter 11 find that the returns to investment in education are high. Econometric estimates of growth models, reviewed by Dennis Ahlburg and Eric Jensen in Chapter 9, yield mixed results about the contribution of education to economic growth. Recent research based on endogenous growth models stresses that "investment in human capital produces spillover benefits that can lead to higher sustained rates of economic growth" (Huang, Chapter 11). On the other hand, growth-accounting studies, reviewed in Chapter 2, indicate that improved educational attainment contributed much less to the region's economic growth than did conventional investment. The contribution of health to rapid economic growth has been studied less, although a few recent studies have identified health as an important determinant of growth [for example, Radalet, Sachs, and Lee (1997) and Jamison, Lau, and Wang (1998)].The studies presented here do not provide new estimates of the effects of human resources on economic development. Rather, they examine in detail the extent to which demographic factors have facilitated or impeded the growth of human resources.

Public Spending on Human Resources

East Asia's fertility decline had a fairly immediate and direct impact on educational programs and budgets. Before the decline began, the number of children reaching school age each year was growing rapidly, requiring a matching expansion of school systems just to maintain educational standards. Fertility fell so rapidly, however, that within a few years the number of children reaching school age each year stabilized. The effect of this demographic shift depended on the policy response. If countries responded by maintaining the share of GNP devoted to education, expenditures per school-age child would necessarily have increased. Alternatively, the more favorable demographics could have led to a reallocation of resources to alternative public purposes or to a reduction in the size of government. The development effect of these possible responses would depend, in turn, on the returns to spending on education at the margin, compared with alternative uses of the increased resources. If countries were underinvesting in education because of resource mobilization problems, then more favorable demographics would have had a positive development effect.

Although the response in public spending is inherently a policy decision, several studies (described in more detail in Chapter 9) have investigated the response of education policy to changing demographics. Those studies generally conclude that favorable shifts in demographics result in a rise in spending per student, have no effect on the share of GNP devoted to education, and have an uncertain effect on the proportion of school-age children enrolled in school (Schultz 1987, 1996; Tan and Mingat 1992; Kelley 1996; others cited by Ahlburg and Jensen in Chapter 9).

Ahlburg and Jensen provide a more complete accounting of the response of education to East Asian demographics. The region's experience seems broadly consistent with more general evidence about the developing world. By and large, East Asian countries maintained educational budgets as demographic circumstances improved, producing a rapid rise in investment per school-age child.

Household-Level Investment in Children

East Asian families faced much the same issue as their governments—the trade-off between the number of children and expenditures per child. Mirroring trends in the support ratio, the number of children declined in relation to the number of adults in the average family. Over a period of 25–30 years, the average number of surviving children dropped from 4 or 4.5 children to about 2 children in Japan, Taiwan, South Korea, and Singapore. Similar declines were under way in Thailand and Indonesia but were not completed by 1990. Dating the timing of the decline in completed family size is somewhat problematic, but it probably began around 1940 in Japan, around 1970 in South Korea, Taiwan, and Singapore, later in the 1970s in Thailand, and around 1980 in Indonesia (see Chapter 3).

Preceding the decline in family size in East Asia was a sustained rise resulting from improvements in infant and child mortality. In South Korea, for example, the average number of surviving children to women age 35–39 increased from 3.0 in 1930 to 4.5 in 1960. Similar changes are documented for Japan and Indonesia and surely occurred in the other East Asian countries as well (see Chapter 3).

The speed and complexity of the changes in family size make it difficult to assess the human resource implications of East Asia's demographic transition. Adding to this difficulty are the variety and complexity of mechanisms by which demographics may influence human resources at the family level. The available evidence indicates that declining fertility may have important favorable physiological effects related to the mother's age at childbirth, the average birth interval, and the birth order of the child. (Ahlburg and Jensen review the recent literature in Chapters 9 and 10.)

One key issue at the family level is whether an increase in the number of children in the family reduces the investment in each child. In principle, families can avoid this trade-off and base their investment decisions without reference to the number of children they are supporting. As Ahlburg and Jensen point out, families can behave like profit-maximizing firms and invest in their children so long as the returns on that investment exceed the cost of their capital. For several reasons, however, parents may not follow this strategy. First, constraints on the availability of credit may deter parents. Typically, capital is not readily available for investment in education, in part because human capital cannot be offered as collateral. Second, investment in education involves a transfer of resources from parents to children. If parents have insufficient means of ensuring what they perceive to be an equitable distribution of resources between themselves and their children, they may choose to underinvest in them.

The decline in family size in East Asia was accompanied by a rise in expenditures per child. Numerous cross-sectional studies have established that a child raised in a small family will receive, on average, a larger share of family resources, will more likely be enrolled in school, and have higher educational attainment and health status than a child raised in a large family. Interpreting causal relationships based on these empirical findings, however, is fraught with difficulties. When we observe a decline in the number of children accompanied by a rise in expenditures per child, we cannot easily rule out the possibility, for example, that a rise in the returns to education are leading parents to spend more on their children and, as a consequence, reduce their childbearing. On balance, however, the evidence reviewed by

Ahlburg and Jensen indicates that declining family size in East Asia has led parents to invest more in their children's education.

The principles and the complexities that govern educational outcomes also influence health outcomes. Jensen and Ahlburg's analysis in Chapter 10 provides an innovative policy perspective on this issue by distinguishing the effect of unwanted births from that of wanted births. The policies and programs implemented in East Asia had two distinctive features. Through public campaigns governments attempted to influence views about the desirable number of children. They also provided couples with the means to avoid births that the couples did not want to have. The question that Jensen and Ahlburg seek to answer is how enabling couples to achieve their fertility goals influences investment in human capital.

Jensen and Ahlburg compare the experiences of the Philippines and Indonesia, which at the time of the available surveys were much poorer than other, more successful East Asian economies and had higher birth rates and higher rates of unwanted fertility. It is in such a context that they expect to see harsher trade-offs that would measurably influence child health. They find that unwantedness did indeed lead to substantial increases in morbidity among children in these two relatively poor economies.

What can we conclude? First, at the beginning of East Asia's high-growth era the demographics were not particularly favorable to human resource investment. The relatively high levels of educational attainment and health around 1960 cannot be attributed to declining fertility or declining family size, except possibly in Japan. Second, the rapid rise in the support ratio and the corresponding decline in average family size beginning in the early 1970s in South Korea, Taiwan, and Singapore and later in Thailand and Indonesia had clear advantages for human resource investment. Third, quantifying the effects of the demographic changes on human resource investment is difficult, but the effects were probably positive and may have been substantial. Finally, the demographic changes have occurred so recently that their impact on the quality of the labor force and on economic growth could have been felt only toward the end of East Asia's high-growth era, but favorable effects on family welfare may have been enjoyed from the outset of the decline.

Income Inequality

East Asia's high-growth era was all the more impressive because it was relatively inclusive. As a group, the countries of East Asia had more equal distributions of income than the developing countries of Africa or Latin America. Moreover, rapid economic growth was not for the most part accompanied by deteriorating income distributions. East Asia's inequality experience was, however, more varied than many other features of its economic development. Japan, Taiwan, and South Korea had particularly low degrees of income inequality. Levels of income inequality in Southeast Asia, on the other hand, did not differ greatly from levels found in Latin America and Africa. Trends in inequality also varied in the region. Some countries experienced rising inequality, others declining inequality, and still others relatively unchanging inequality (see Chapter 5).

Two chapters in this volume examine the changes in inequality during East Asia's high-growth era and identify the major factors, particularly demographic factors, that contributed to these changes. Harry Oshima and I (Chapter 15) consider major hypotheses and evidence that inequality was influenced by changes in age structure, changes in factor proportions that were influenced by demographics, and changes in the economic role of women. Bauer (Chapter 14) looks more intensively at the substantial changes in the economic lives of women during this period.

The differences in income inequality within the region reflect complex factors, including history, culture, climate, economic structure, and policy, making it difficult to isolate demographic factors. Oshima and I begin our analysis of the role of demographics by considering the implications of the rapid decline in child dependency. One possibility, along the lines proposed by Kuznets (1966), is that the initial decline in child dependency would have a disequalizing effect. Suppose that before the decline in child dependency, family size is uniformly high in all segments and hence not an important source of inequality in per capita household income. When fertility begins to decline, the urban, educated elite are the first to opt for smaller families. This would exacerbate differences in per capita income between the urban elite and the rest of society and would raise the overall degree of inequality. This disequalizing effect would be reversed as lower income families began to opt for smaller families.

There is ample evidence that rates of childbearing declined first among urban, educated, high-income couples. But low rates of childbearing quickly spread to all segments of East Asian societies. Moreover, the available evidence indicates that variation in family size is an important source of inequality in populations with high dependency rates. The widespread availability of modern, effective, and inexpensive contraceptives may have allowed even low-income women to regulate their childbearing. Although the evidence is limited to a few countries and relatively short time periods, it appears that the decline in child dependency has had an equalizing effect on per capita household income.

Oshima and I also consider three possible influences of changing demographics on the variation in income per adult: changes in the age composition of the adult population, changes in factor proportions and factor prices, and changes in the monetary contribution of women to household income.

The age composition of the adult population can lead to a rise in income inequality if the population becomes more concentrated in an age group with highly variable income or in an age group whose average income differs substantially from the average income of the entire population. Between 1960 and 1990 the most significant change in adult age structure was a decline in the relative size of the young adult and teenage groups. In some countries this shift has reduced inequality; in others it has not (Lam 1997b). The only evidence for East Asia comes from Taiwan (Schultz 1997) and shows that changes in age structure there led to a modest increase in inequality between 1976 and 1995.

A shift in factor proportions, that is, a rise in the capital-labor ratio, over the demographic transition can reduce income inequality by inducing a rise in wages relative to returns on capital. This reduces income inequality if the ownership of capital is concentrated among high-income individuals. In East Asia the capital-labor ratio rose because of higher saving rates, not because of slower labor force growth. The effect on inequality depends on how changes in saving rates have influenced the distribution of wealth. This is an issue about which little is known. Consequently, no conclusion can be drawn about the overall distributional effect.

The effect of women's increased earnings, the final mechanism explored in Chapter 15, is an issue that has been considered in numerous empirical studies, including several of East Asian economies. With few exceptions, those studies conclude that the contribution of women to household income reduces inequality. Oshima and I also find this to be the case in Taiwan. However, we also find that the effect on inequality was no greater when women contributed 25% to household income, as they did in 1993, than when they contributed 15% to household income, as they did in 1976. In Taiwan the decline in the gender gap in earnings after 1976 did not reduce inequality in household income. Unfortunately, other studies of East Asia do not address the important possibility that the effect of women's earnings on inequality varies substantially as their contribution rises.

The assessments of the economic status of women undertaken by Bauer (Chapter 14) differs from the approach taken by Oshima and me (Chapter 15) because Bauer focuses on differences between men and women rather than on variation among spending units. His study examines the dramatic changes in the lives of women that occurred during the high-growth era. The decline in women's traditional roles was evident in reduced childbearing and substantial increases in the age at marriage. The rise in modern economic roles was evident in the gains in schooling, increased labor force participation, and higher wages and earnings. In many respects, gender roles became blurred between 1960 and 1990, and the gender gap declined. The effect of these changes on inequality in household income is uncertain, but they surely raised the autonomy of women, increased their control over economic resources, and elevated their power with the family.

Bauer's overview of the changing status of women in East Asia identifies many important changes in the lives of women that bear on their economic and social position relative to men. School enrollment and educational attainment increased much more rapidly among women than among men. While labor force participation rates among men declined modestly, female labor force participation rates rose. Women were working more, in part because they were marrying later and in part because they were remaining in the labor force after marriage, during childbearing years, and after childbearing was completed. Perhaps as important was the shift in the nature of female employment. Women were much more likely to be employed in the formal sector outside the home than as unpaid family workers. However, employment continued to be heavily stratified along gender lines in most East Asian settings.

At least in some East Asian countries for which reliable data are available, wage differentials between men and women declined. It is not entirely clear, however, that the wage gap declined as rapidly as women's relative gains in education and experience warranted. Phananiramai (1997), for example, presented evidence that this is not the case in Thailand and that some important discriminatory practices remain. Likewise, women in Northeast Asian countries have made few inroads into positions of leadership in either the public or the private sector.

Major changes in the economic roles of women in East Asia could not have occurred in the absence of rapid demographic change. The mean age at first marriage rose substantially. By 1990 Japan, South Korea, Taiwan, and Singapore were among the latest-marrying populations in the world. Labor force growth in these countries was fueled to a great extent by growth in the number of single women in their 20s in the work force. Likewise, the decline in the number of births and in the number of years devoted to rearing young children has encouraged women to abandon traditional roles in favor of working outside the home. Clearly identifying the causal mechanisms is almost an impossible task, however, because of their complexity. For example, to some extent the structural changes in the economies of East Asia created new opportunities for women, thereby inducing changes not only in their economic behavior but also in their demographic behavior. To some extent the decline in infant and child mortality allowed women to fulfill their reproductive responsibilities at a much reduced cost. And to some extent the development and increased availability of modern contraception allowed women to control their reproduction and pursue nontraditional goals.

The increased role of women in the formal economic sector has come with costs for many women. Working away from home has added long commutes, particularly in congested urban areas. Although the decline in the number of children has eased their child-rearing responsibilities, demanding educational systems in Japan, South Korea, and some other East Asian countries have greatly increased the amount of time that women spend helping school-age children. Available time-use studies indicate that husbands have not assumed much more responsibility at home as women's responsibilities outside the home have grown. Among women who were employed 42 to 48 hours per week in 1994, Japanese women spent an additional 28 hours doing housework compared with their husbands' 3.2 hours. South Korean men were more helpful: Working women spent 32 hours doing housework, whereas their husbands spent 12 hours. In the United States the housework hours were 24 and 10 for wives and husbands, respectively (Tsuya and Bumpass 1998).

Population Programs and Policies

The countries of East Asia were pronatalist in their views and policies until the second half of the twentieth century. Japan's Meiji government prohibited not just infanticide and abortion but also the manufacture and distribution of contraceptives because it viewed a large population as important to its military and economic power (Inoue 2001). Sun Yat-Sen, the founder of the Republic of China, believed that slower population growth would undermine his nation's power (Liu 2001). Thailand's government was providing bonuses for large families as late as 1956 (Gullaprawit 2001). In Indonesia President Soekarno was unconcerned about rapid population growth, and family planning efforts were unpopular with community and religious leaders (Pasay and Wongkaren 2001).

In the late 1950s and early 1960s positive views toward larger populations began to give way to concern about rapid population growth. Despite opposition from some political groups, governments cautiously initiated efforts to slow the rates of growth. They began to dismantle legal obstacles to fertility reduction. Japan led this trend by legalizing, in 1947, the manufacture and distribution of most contraceptive drugs and devices by private companies. (It legalized oral contraceptives only recently, however.) In 1948 Japan essentially legalized abortion, allowing it if a pregnancy threatened a woman's physical or economic well-being (Inoue 2001). In 1961 South Korea set aside its law prohibiting the importation or production of contraceptives. In Indonesia in the 1960s the Ministry of Health ended its prohibition against the distribution of contraceptives. Governments also supported efforts by nongovernmental family planning organizations that had recently been established in the region. Private organizations such as the Population and Community Development Association of Thailand, the Indonesian Planned Parenthood Foundation, and the Planned Parenthood Federation of Korea played a particularly important role during this transitional period.

In more economically advanced Japan rapid fertility decline occurred during the 1950s with only indirect government involvement. Other East Asian governments became increasingly involved in population policies and programs. Key political and religious groups were persuaded to recognize the importance of slowing population growth. The governments adopted national development plans with specific targets for population growth reduction. They initiated public campaigns to persuade couples to bear fewer children. They launched education programs about modern contraceptive methods both in the communities and in the schools. Family planning clinics and distribution systems, many of them heavily subsidized, were established to increase the availability of contraceptive supplies and services.

The earliest efforts focused on education, persuasion, and increased access to modern contraceptives. Beginning in the 1970s, however, some governments implemented "beyond family planning" policies. Singapore adopted a comprehensive set of incentives and disincentives (Yap 2001), and similar efforts were pursued elsewhere in the region. Many of these efforts relied on financial incentives, but other initiatives were designed to attack some of the social underpinnings of high fertility. In South Korea, for example, legislative action addressed gender bias in the hope that reducing a preference for sons would lead to lower birth rates (Kwon 2001). In the countries examined in this study, however, population measures stopped well short of coercive programs, such as India's ill-fated sterilization campaigns during the 1970s and China's one-child policy.

East Asia's family planning programs were among the best run of any in the world. In a short period of time they greatly expanded the supply of modern contraceptive services at relatively modest cost. Programs in Taiwan, South Korea, Thailand, and Indonesia have served as models for other countries. Tsui (Chapter 16) attributes their success to four factors. First, despite the governments' primary objective of curbing rapid population growth, their programs and policies emphasized family planning and health objectives. Second, religious or other politically powerful groups did not mount strong opposition to the programs. Third, the governments maintained a significant and sustained effort, which included considerable financial support. Finally, the governments willingly and successfully worked with nongovernmental entities.

Population programs came at a cost. The best available information suggests that annual per capita funding of family planning was approximately US$0.20 or less in the mid-1970s and rose to around US$1.00 by the early 1990s. In Singapore and South Korea spending peaked during the 1980s and declined thereafter as more and more couples turned to private family planning sources (see Chapter 16). Family planning expenditures were a small portion of government budgets. In Thailand, for example, the peak demand on public coffers occurred in 1977, when 0.38% of total government expenditures went to family planning (Gullaprawit 2001, Table 6). In Indonesia family planning expenditure reached 0.6% of the government's budget in 1986–87 (Pasay and Wongkaren 2001, Table 8).

Family planning programs clearly met programmatic goals, such as increased use of contraceptive methods, but their impact on demographic outcomes is uncertain. The study countries were all experiencing rapid social and economic development. Reductions in child mortality, higher wages, greater employment and educational opportunities for women, and a host of other development factors contributed to changing childbearing patterns. In an analysis of the determinants of fertility decline, Tsui (Chapter 16) estimates the contribution of family planning and development factors. She concludes that the total fertility rate in other countries of the developing world would have been lower by one birth per woman from 1982 onward had they implemented family planning programs similar to those in the study countries of East Asia.

That population policies and programs were a success in East Asia is an inescapable conclusion. Commitments to reducing rates of childbearing and slowing population growth rates led to unprecedented declines in fertility. Rapid social and economic development drove the region's demographic transformation, but government action accelerated the process.

Conclusion

In 1960 the countries of East Asia faced difficult economic problems. In the view of many at the time, the emergence of rapid population growth was one of the most serious of those problems. No one anticipated how effectively the problems would be handled nor how successful development efforts would be over the ensuing three decades. This study attempts to explain how the countries of East Asia not only overcame the problems associated with population growth but also turned demographic change to their advantage. How this was accomplished is an important story because of its potential value to other developing countries that are experiencing the same kinds of demographic changes and struggling with similar development problems. Moreover, for the East Asian countries themselves, understanding the past is essential to understanding the future and the likely implications of continued demographic change there.

The East Asian experience offers many important lessons. First, with effective policies and adequate institutions, food production can keep pace with rapid population growth. Despite their dense populations, the countries of East Asia managed to increase their per capita production of grains substantially. They achieved these gains through innovations that allowed more effective use of fertilizers and greatly increased output per hectare.

Second, whether rapid labor force growth impedes the structural transformation from an agricultural economy to a modern, industrial economy appears to depend on initial conditions. The labor forces grew at similarly rapid rates in both Northeast Asia and Southeast Asia. In Northeast Asia, however, the nonagricultural sector absorbed all additional workers. The countries of Southeast Asia were less successful. The nonagricultural sectors were so small in Indonesia and Thailand in 1960 that even rapid growth could absorb only a portion of new workers. As a consequence, labor productivity grew more slowly in the agricultural sector than the nonagricultural sector and the shift of the labor force out of the low-productivity agricultural sector came more slowly.

Third, fertility decline led to an increase in the relative size of the working population and, consequently, more rapid growth in output per capita. In East Asia the favorable swing in age structure was unusually large because fertility declined so rapidly.

Fourth, rapid demographic change contributed to high rates of saving and investment, rapid capital deepening, and more rapid growth in output per worker and per capita. Estimates of the impact of demographic change vary, but even conservative estimates indicate an important effect.

Fifth, fertility decline and a decline in unwanted births had an important influence on health status and educational attainment. Rapid fertility decline led to smaller families and to a reduced fiscal burden of publicly funded programs for children. Later childbearing, longer birth intervals, and a decline in the percentage of unwanted births all had positive effects on child health. These gains directly enhanced the welfare of children and their parents and, with a substantial lag, may result in higher labor productivity and incomes. The productivity benefits are more likely to be felt in the future than they were before 1990 because of the lags involved.

Sixth, changes in the economic roles of women, which depend in part on the availability of modern birth control methods and reduced rates of childbearing, played an important role in rapid economic growth. Women made a disproportionately important contribution to economic growth in East Asia. Their educational attainment, their labor force participation, their average wages, and their incomes grew more rapidly than those of their male counterparts.

Seventh, demographic change had an uncertain impact on income inequality. Although East Asia has been noted for growth with equity, the trends and levels of income inequality are varied and are influenced by a wide range of idiosyncratic factors. The influence of demographic change is difficult to ascertain given the currently available research, and no general conclusions about the links between population and inequality are warranted.

Eighth, the speed of the demographic transition matters. East Asia's rapid demographic transition led to accelerated economic growth in two ways. First, it led to large swings in the age structure and a particularly large gap between labor force growth and population growth. Second, fertility decline, changes in age structure, and increases in life expectancy caused saving and investment to rise to higher levels because the demographic changes were so rapid.

Ninth, the economic impact of the demographic transition is important. Demographic change influences the economy in myriad ways and over sustained periods of time. Any individual effect may be small in any particular year, but taken in their entirety over a sustained period, East Asia's favorable demographic changes had a substantial impact on standards of living.

Tenth, increased integration of the global economy has had an important bearing on the economic impact of demographic change in East Asia. That impact has not been limited to the domestic economies. To some extent, changing demographics influenced labor force migration, trade patterns, and international capital flows. As a consequence, changing demographic conditions, particularly in Japan, influenced rates of economic growth elsewhere in East Asia.

Eleventh, an accelerated demographic transition is possible. The demographic transition usually evolves slowly compared with many other social and economic phenomena. East Asia's experience demonstrates, however, that demographic behavior can change rapidly. The transition from high to low fertility took 30 years or less in the countries of East Asia, whereas it took 100 years in the United States and 2 centuries in France.

Twelfth, there are different paths to low fertility, but population policies and programs often influence the timing and pace of fertility decline. In the West and in Japan low fertility rates were reached as a consequence of social and economic development. Government policy sometimes impeded and sometimes facilitated fertility decline, but at most it played a secondary role. On the other hand, in East Asia's developing countries governments actively promoted reduced childbearing and slower population growth. Rapid fertility decline occurred there in part because of the region's rapid social and economic development but also in part because effective and comprehensive public programs were established that encouraged couples to reduce their childbearing and provided them with effective and low-cost means to regulate their fertility.

Perhaps the most important lesson from the East Asian experience is that the effects of population depend on the social, economic, and policy context in which those changes occur. In the 1960s rapid population growth presented a number of potentially important impediments to East Asia's economic development. The adverse effects were avoided or minimized because of effective policies and institutions that were only indirectly related to population. The rapid growth of population did not lead to a decline in per capita production of grains because research institutions were established that could develop the high-yield varieties so essential to economic success. Rapid labor force growth in Northeast Asia did not lead to unemployment or underemployment in the agricultural sector because labor markets were flexible and because economic policies so successfully promoted growth of labor-intensive manufacturing and service sectors.

Likewise, subsequent demographic changes created *opportunities* for more rapid economic growth. Favorable outcomes depended as well on a variety of features of the countries in the region. The gap between labor force and population growth was advantageous only because development policies (for example, effective export promotion) provided gainful employment to a rapidly growing labor force. Demographic change led to high rates of saving because macroeconomic stability and the development of financial institutions encouraged saving and also because governments avoided large-scale transfer systems that could have undermined saving incentives. High rates of saving and investment led to more rapid economic growth because political stability and responsible macroeconomic policies created an economic environment in which firms could operate efficiently and maintain high rates of return to capital. Changes in the population age structure led to greater spending on education because public policy and parents attached a high priority to education. Changes in the childbearing responsibilities of women had a favorable economic effect because governments eliminated laws and administrative policies that discriminated against women. In short, rapid demographic change was a necessary but by no means sufficient condition for rapid economic growth. Demographic changes created opportunities that East Asian countries seized by pursuing economic and social policies and by strengthening institutions that supported development efforts.

I. THE POPULATION–ECONOMIC GROWTH NEXUS IN EAST ASIA

2

Economic Growth and Policy in East Asia

JOHN BAUER

EAST ASIAN ECONOMIES grew at unprecedented rates between 1960 and 1990. Eight of them in particular were highly successful: Japan, South Korea, Taiwan, Singapore, Hong Kong, Thailand, Indonesia, and Malaysia (World Bank 1993a). The literature suggests that rapid increases in physical capital, human capital, and employment—that is, factor accumulation—played the critical role in their success. Moreover, the strongest effects of declining birth rates and changing age structure on the region's economic growth appear to have operated through factor accumulation, with the effects on saving being especially important. Factor accumulation alone, however, is not the whole story. The high rates of investment that sustained growth in physical capital were critical to economic growth. But how were these economies able to efficiently allocate massive increases in the capital stock? As Harberger (1997: 34) noted, the "real surprise with respect to the East Asian countries concerns their capacity to simultaneously achieve such high rates of investment on the one hand, and such high rates of return on the other. It is this combination, together with rates of total factor productivity (TFP) improvement that are significantly above world standards, that form the basis of the East Asian miracle."

To provide a broad perspective on economic development in East Asia, in this chapter I review recent growth-accounting studies, discuss the controversies surrounding East Asian economic policies, and examine the potential channels through which demographic change may have contributed to the

I thank Jeff Brown for very capable research assistance. I also thank the participants of the Conference on Population and the Asian Economic Miracle for their valuable comments. I am especially indebted to Sumner LaCroix, Andrew Mason, Dennis Ahlburg, Yujiro Hayami, and Harry Oshima.

region's success. I consider the debate over the controversial role played by TFP growth in the region. TFP growth could be the result of technological innovation, increases in efficiency, or scale economies. Although the debate continues, the emerging consensus is that TFP improvements have made a substantial contribution to output growth. That contribution, however, tends to be dwarfed by the contribution made by the extremely rapid factor accumulation. The ways in which demographic change might have affected productivity growth in these economies is also discussed.

Next, I examine several other factors that are believed to have promoted growth in the region, in part by encouraging the efficient allocation of resources. These factors include the successful economies' outward orientation, their sound macroeconomic policies, their market orientation versus interventionist policies, their relatively equal income distributions, their labor market policies and agricultural policies, and political factors. Demographic change may have played a role in promoting greater income equality in the region, and it has affected technological innovation in agriculture.

Two points should to be noted at the outset. First, whereas the successful East Asian economies share many common characteristics, they also exhibit significant differences. Some generalizations are therefore inappropriate. Second, although consensus views have emerged on the important contributions made by some factors to the region's success, the contributions of others are still being debated. I outline these debates in my discussion.

Economic Growth in East Asia

Table 2.1 summarizes the rapid growth in real gross domestic product (GDP) per capita achieved by the eight highly successful economies. For comparison, Table 2.1 also presents the growth rates for eight other major developing countries.

Table 2.1 suggests two main observations. First, average annual growth rates were exceptionally high in East Asia from 1960 to 1990. Growth was especially rapid in the newly industrializing economies (NIEs)—Hong Kong, South Korea, Singapore, and Taiwan—in excess of 6% per annum. Second, the growth rates for these East Asian economies remained, in general, consistently high over time. The region's growth is extraordinary not only because of its rapid rate but also because it has been sustained for such a long period. Such sustained growth has not been true for most developing countries. Brazil and Mexico, for example, achieved rapid growth in the 1960s and 1970s, only to experience negative growth during the debt crisis of the 1980s.

Dramatic structural changes have accompanied East Asia's rapid GDP growth. As one would expect, changes in the sectoral compositions of out-

TABLE 2.1

Average Annual Economic Growth in Real GDP per Capita (%):
16 Countries, 1960–90[a]

Country	1960–90	1960–70	1970–80	1980–90
Selected East Asian countries				
Japan	5.26	9.06	3.21	3.53
South Korea	6.66	6.20	6.10	7.69
Taiwan	6.20	5.55	7.12	5.92
Singapore	6.52	5.99	8.49	5.07
Hong Kong	6.29	6.95	6.61	5.32
Thailand	4.45	4.81	3.56	4.97
Indonesia	3.76	1.14	5.83	4.32
Malaysia	4.28	4.17	5.67	2.99
Comparison countries				
Egypt	2.87	3.63	3.47	1.50
China	2.83	2.05	3.34	3.09
Brazil	2.73	3.11	5.70	−0.63
Mexico	2.40	3.41	4.18	−0.38
Nigeria	1.87	3.02	6.29	−3.68
India	1.67	0.46	0.95	3.60
Philippines	1.47	2.14	2.92	−0.64
Bangladesh	1.26	2.96	−1.65	2.48

SOURCE: Summers et al. (n.d.).
[a]Real income is estimated by means of the Chain index.

put and employment have been dramatic. For example, between 1960 and 1990 the industrial share of GDP rose from 19% to 45% in South Korea, from 18% to 37% in Singapore, from 19% to 39% in Thailand, and from 14% to 40% in Indonesia (World Bank 1980, 1992).

Rapid growth has also generated substantial declines in poverty rates (World Bank 1990). Indonesia's poverty rate fell from 58% in 1970 to 17% by 1987. Malaysia's dropped from 37% in 1973 to 15% by 1987. Singapore's declined from 31% in 1972 to only 10% by 1982, and Thailand's declined from 59% to 26% between 1962 and 1986. These figures are based on the head-count index, using country-specific poverty lines.

Factor Accumulation

The successful East Asian economies have been able to generate dramatic growth in physical capital, human capital, and employment. I discuss the importance of each of these in turn, beginning with the stock of physical capital, which grew rapidly in response to high rates of saving and investment.

Physical Capital, Saving, and Investment

The disparity in saving rates among developing countries increased between 1960 and the early 1990s. The East Asian economies achieved substantial increases in saving and investment rates. Gross domestic saving as a share of GDP more than doubled, rising from 14% to more than 35%. In contrast, saving rates stagnated in Latin America and collapsed in sub-Saharan Africa (Schmidt-Hebbel, Serven, and Solimano 1996).

Table 2.2 shows saving rates for East Asian economies in detail. Saving rates, although uniformly high by international standards, have varied substantially across the successful East Asian economies, ranging from 28% to 47% in 1993. Whereas saving rates were already high in Japan and Malaysia by 1960, this was not true in the other economies. Saving rates in Singapore, Hong Kong, and South Korea were low in the early 1960s but then rose dramatically thereafter. Indonesia's rates rose dramatically in the 1970s, as did Thailand's in the 1980s.

High rates of saving have supported unusually high rates of investment. Japan's investment rate (that is, investment as a percentage of real GDP) rose fairly steadily during the 1960s. It fluctuated during the 1970s and 1980s but remained over 30%. Singapore's investment rate shot up from just over 10% in 1960 to about 40% in the early 1970s. Its rates have fluctuated in the 30–40% range since then. South Korea's investment rate climbed from just over 5% in the early 1950s to 20% in the late 1960s to almost 40% by 1991. Taiwan's investment rate, which was under 15% in the early 1960s, rose rapidly in the late 1960s, reaching a peak of more than 30% in the mid-1970s. Hong Kong is the exception among the NIEs. Its investment rate has fluctuated but has not risen dramatically over this period [investment rates calculated from the Penn World Table; see Summers and Heston (1991)].

TABLE 2.2

Gross Domestic Savings as a Percentage of GDP:
Eight East Asian Countries, 1960–93

Country	1960	1965	1970	1980	1993
Japan	34	28	40	31	33
South Korea	1	8	15	23	35
Taiwan	18	21	26	32	28
Singapore	−3	10	18	30	47
Hong Kong	6	29	25	24	31
Thailand	14	19	21	22	36
Indonesia	8	8	14	30	31
Malaysia	27	24	27	32	38

SOURCES: For all countries except Taiwan, World Bank, *World Development Report* (various years). For Taiwan, ROC CEPD (various years), *Taiwan Statistical Data Book.*

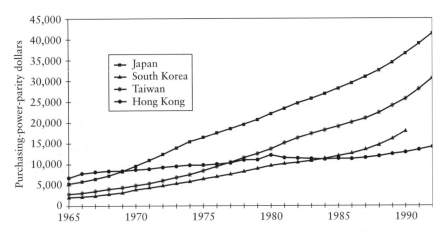

Source: Summers et al. (n.d.).

FIGURE 2.1. Capital per Worker: Four Asian Countries, 1965–92. All currencies are converted into US dollars, taking account of differences in purchasing power resulting from price differentials among countries.

Investment rates in Southeast Asian countries also have increased substantially. Thailand's investment rate rose during the 1960s, fluctuated in the 15–20% range during the 1970s and early 1980s, and has risen sharply since the late 1980s. The rate in Indonesia rose rapidly from the late 1960s to the early 1980s and has fluctuated above 25% since then. Malaysia's investment rates increased rapidly during the 1970s and early 1980s and declined during the mid-1980s, only to climb again during the late 1980s and early 1990s.

These high rates of investment caused East Asian capital stocks to grow rapidly. For example, according to estimates by Kim and Lau (1994), average annual growth rates of the capital stock over the study period 1960–1990 were in the range of 9.0–12.4% in Japan and the NIEs. (The rate for the United States, by comparison, was only 2.9% from 1948 to 1990.) Capital accumulation was so rapid that, despite substantial employment growth, capital-labor ratios increased dramatically. Figure 2.1 presents the trends in capital per worker for Japan, South Korea, Taiwan, and Hong Kong. Capital per worker rose by a factor of 6.9 in Japan and by a factor of 8.6 in South Korea and Taiwan from 1965 to 1990. The increase in Hong Kong was more modest, but even there capital per worker almost doubled over the same period. These figures should be regarded as approximations, because data on capital stocks are difficult to estimate with accuracy.

Impact of Saving and Investment on Growth

To what extent do East Asia's high rates of saving and investment explain the region's rapid economic growth? Growth-accounting studies provide one answer. These studies attempt to estimate the relative contributions to GDP growth made by changes in labor supply, the accumulation of physical and human capital, and changes in TFP. Increases in output that cannot be linked to changes in capital or labor are attributed to increases in TFP.

A number of growth-accounting studies are available for East Asia [for example, Young (1992, 1995), Kim and Lau (1994), and Harberger (1996)]. There is debate over the methods used by these researchers and concern over the quality of the data [see Harberger (1996) for a discussion]. Despite their different methods, different data, and different estimates, they all conclude that capital accumulation has played a dominant role in East Asian growth. Kim and Lau (1994), for example, attributed 48–72% of the growth in the NIEs and Japan to increases in the capital stock. Young (1992) estimated that 83% of Singapore's growth between 1971 and 1990 was due to capital accumulation alone. In examining the reasons for the dramatic narrowing of the output gap between Japan and the United States between 1960 and 1974, Nishimizu and Jorgenson (1995) concluded that it was due largely to Japan's much greater capital accumulation. Recent growth-accounting studies for Indonesia, Malaysia, and Thailand also suggest that capital accumulation was the most important factor (Abimanyu 1995; Limskul 1995; Tham 1995).

The consensus view is that capital accumulation has played a vital role in East Asia's growth. Moreover, high rates of domestic saving have been important because domestic savings have provided most of the funds for domestic investment (Carliner 1995; Schmidt-Hebbel, Serven, and Solimano 1996). In a closed economy, of course, domestic saving must equal investment. This need not be true in an open economy, because capital inflows there could finance a saving-investment gap. Nevertheless, a strong positive correlation exists between domestic saving and investment rates (Feldstein and Horioka 1980; Feldstein and Bacchetta 1991). Why this should be the case is a matter of debate.

Whatever the reason, domestic saving has funded most of the investment in East Asia. Some countries have benefited from flows of foreign capital. The relative importance of foreign and domestic savings in the region's financing of investment has varied among countries and over time (Riedel 1988). In the 1950s foreign savings, mainly aid from the United States, financed a high proportion of investment in Taiwan and South Korea. US aid declined in the 1960s, but South Korea continued to rely on foreign capital, although to a lesser extent. Taiwan, on the other hand, stopped relying on foreign savings altogether and became a net international investor. Singapore relied heavily on foreign capital, mainly in the form of direct investment. Japan did not rely on foreign capital. Its current account was close to being balanced until the 1980s, when sizable capital outflows began (Krueger 1995).

A common view of East Asian growth, therefore, is that high rates of investment were the principal engine of growth and that high rates of saving made the high rates of investment possible. Not everyone accepts this view, however. Perkins (1994) argued that Asian saving and investment rates were not especially high in the early years of high growth, although they became so later. He concluded that large savings may be more an outcome of high growth than a cause. Other recent studies have challenged the view that investment generates growth (Blomstrom, Lipsey, and Zejan 1993; King and Levine 1994; Schmidt-Hebbel, Serven, and Solimano 1996).

Stiglitz and Uy (1996) performed tests to see whether income determines savings or, more accurately, saving determines income in East Asian economies. Their results suggest that income growth has been a predictor of saving in Indonesia, Japan, South Korea, Taiwan, and Thailand, but their results are ambiguous for Hong Kong and Malaysia. In Singapore income growth was not a predictor of the increases in saving rates. Stiglitz and Uy argued that these results support the idea of a virtuous cycle, in which high growth leads to high rates of saving and high saving rates lead to high growth.

Although the causality studies raise important questions, capital accumulation appears to be critical to growth. It is difficult to find countries that have grown rapidly for long periods without relatively high rates of investment (Riedel 1988; Schmidt-Hebbel, Serven, and Soliano 1996). Of course, capital accumulation alone is not sufficient. For one thing, accumulation must be efficient. I shall return to this point later.

Factors Responsible for High Saving Rates

Numerous factors have been proposed to explain the rise in East Asian saving rates. Many analysts have noted that stable macroeconomic policies have kept inflation rates relatively low, and low inflation has helped to promote positive real interest rates (World Bank 1993a; Stiglitz and Uy 1996). Governments in the region are also thought to have promoted saving by ensuring the security of banking systems and improving access by small savers (World Bank 1993a). Stiglitz and Uy (1996) asserted that the postal saving systems in Japan, Malaysia, Singapore, and Taiwan were the most important of the institutions that their governments created to promote savings.

High rates of public saving also contributed substantially to aggregate savings in the region. For example, in Taiwan saving by the government and public enterprises typically accounted for 30% of total savings (Dessus, Shea, and Shi 1995). Public saving was achieved largely through expenditure restraint, as evidenced by low public consumption to GDP ratios. Public saving does not appear to have fully crowded out private saving in these economies (World Bank 1993a; Stiglitz and Uy 1996).

Stiglitz and Uy (1996) noted that most of the East Asian governments also imposed restrictions on consumer credit. The governments discouraged consumption by preventing mortgage markets and other consumer credit instruments from developing. Forced saving schemes (provident funds and other mandatory pension schemes) do not appear to have been an important factor in general. Japan, Malaysia, and Singapore have such schemes, but their effect on saving is not clear (World Bank 1993a).

Singh (1995) argued that it is high corporate saving that distinguishes the East Asian countries. He claimed that an essential aim of East Asian governments has been to encourage corporate profits and savings. High corporate profits have generated higher corporate saving and investment, rather than just higher dividends, for two reasons. First, fiscal measures encourage corporations to retain earnings. Second, the structure of share ownership insulates corporations from the pressure for greater dividend distributions (UNCTAD 1994). In Taiwan, for example, savings by private enterprises account for almost a quarter of total savings on average (Dessus, Shea, and Shi 1995). Fiscal policy seems to have had a large influence on corporate saving in Taiwan. Tax policies in particular have encouraged private enterprises to accumulate their own savings (Chang 1992).

Factors Promoting High Rates of Investment

Several additional factors have been proposed to explain the high rates of investment in the region. East Asian governments have promoted investment by providing good infrastructure. Some analysts argue that these governments have also created a favorable investment climate by adopting stable macroeconomic policies and by providing political stability, secure property rights, and good industrial relations. The governments have used a variety of tax policies to encourage investment by raising the retained earnings of companies. At one extreme, South Korea and Taiwan have used complicated tax codes to promote investment in certain industries; at the other extreme, Hong Kong has had a largely neutral tax structure with low corporate tax rates (World Bank 1993a: 228). The East Asian governments have also used tax, tariff, and exchange rate policies to keep the relative prices of capital goods below those in other low- and middle-income countries (World Bank 1993a).

The governments of Japan, South Korea, and Taiwan attempted to reduce some of the risks to the private sector through bailouts, signaling their policy intentions by directing credit and credit guarantees to small firms. The World Bank (1993a) claimed that in Northeast Asia these efforts were apparently successful, or at least not a failure, whereas in some Southeast Asian countries the attempts to limit risk were less successful.

The role played by financial repression is also controversial. Some observers have argued that by keeping interest rates below market-clearing levels, governments were able to promote investment by lowering the costs of borrowing. Stiglitz and Uy (1996) maintained that financial repression does not appear to have discouraged saving and that moderate repression may actually encourage saving by increasing profits and corporate saving. The World Bank (1993a), however, tended to play down the role of financial repression in the region. It asserted that, although most of the East Asian governments have controlled interest rates, they have not used repression as a consistent policy. According to this perspective, repression does not seem to have played a major role, either positive or negative, in the region, although it may have contributed to growth in Japan, South Korea, and Taiwan. The potential problem with keeping interest rates artificially low is that it creates a need to ration credit and raises the potential for misallocation of capital. Lee and Haggard (1995) adopted an alternative view, arguing that in some Asian countries during certain periods government interventions and financial repression have promoted efficiency and rapid growth. Financial repression, they argued, is not always inefficient because the alternative is not always a well-functioning private capital market.

East Asian governments created development banks to help provide long-term credit for industrialization. Development banks have been major lenders in Indonesia, Japan, South Korea, and Taiwan but not in the other successful East Asian economies (World Bank 1993a: 226). Stiglitz and Uy (1996) argued that development banks have some advantages over markets, particularly at early stages of development. One advantage is their institutional capacity to monitor borrowers closely.

The industrial policies of the region are a subject of intense debate, which I discuss later. Here, I focus on directed credit policies. Stiglitz and Uy (1996) claimed that among the East Asian governments Japan and South Korea have most aggressively attempted to direct credit to specific firms and industries. Indonesia and Malaysia apparently had little success with directing credit and abandoned such schemes. Thailand avoided credit programs directed at specific firms and industries.

Stiglitz and Uy (1996) noted that it is extremely difficult to evaluate the success of credit interventions and that the results in Northeast Asia have been mixed. However, they took a fairly favorable view of these interventions in Japan and South Korea, arguing that those governments directed credit to areas with high social returns. Other economists take a more negative view of such policies. Perkins (1994), for example, argued that much of South Korea's and Taiwan's success was due to informal mechanisms that were developed to get around the limitations imposed by their state-controlled banking systems.

Demographic Change and Physical Capital per Worker

Growth-accounting studies along with the broader literature on investment in East Asia suggest that the most substantial effects of demographic change on economic growth should be demographic effects on capital accumulation. Studies identify two such potential effects of slower population growth and changing age structure: (1) with the saving rate held fixed, they can promote capital deepening, and (2) they can promote saving.

Fertility declines in East Asia have contributed to rapid capital deepening in the region. Solow's (1956) neoclassical growth model makes the role of population growth clear: Given a fixed rate of saving, a higher population growth rate results in a lower steady-state ratio of capital to labor and therefore lower per capita income. This is capital dilution.

Mankiw, Romer, and Weil (1992), surveying a large cross-section of countries, provided an estimate of the capital dilution effect from higher population growth. They reported that the traditional Solow model does not correctly predict the magnitudes of the effects of changes in saving and population growth rates on per capita income across countries. The model does much better when the accumulation of human capital and physical capital is added. By using regression analysis, they estimated the effects of the average rate of growth of the working-age population, the average share of real investment in GDP, and the percentage of the working-age population that is in secondary school (their proxy for human capital accumulation) on real GDP per worker. These three variables explain almost 80% of the cross-country variation in income per worker. Moreover, the analysis reveals a significant and substantial *negative* effect of population growth on GDP per working-age person. The elasticity of income per capita with respect to population growth is -2. Population growth has a larger effect in Mankiw, Romer, and Weil's (1992) augmented model than in the traditional Solow model. The reason is that more rapid population growth causes human capital dilution as well as physical capital dilution. In criticizing this augmented model, King and Levine (1994) noted that there are no strong reasons to treat physical or human capital accumulation as exogenous.

In fact, the effect of population growth on capital per worker could be even greater because saving rates are not fixed. In addition to the capital dilution effect, fertility declines may further affect capital per worker by facilitating increases in saving rates. Slower population growth may have favorable, although transitory, effects on saving rates by reducing the proportion of young people in a population and by increasing the proportion of those of high-saving, prime working ages. Several studies in this volume suggest that demographic change has contributed substantially to the rise in saving rates in East Asia over the study period 1960–1990 [see Chapters 5, 6, and 7 and Mason (1987, 1988)].

Human Capital and Economic Growth

New theories about economic growth place a major emphasis on human capital. Lucas (1993), for example, asserted that the main engine of growth is the accumulation of human capital and that human capital is the main source of differences in living standards among countries. He also argued that human capital investment has important spillover effects (Lucas 1988). According to this argument, the acquisition of skills by a worker not only increases the worker's own productivity but also improves the productivity of other workers by raising the average level of skills in the economy [see Srinivasan and Robinson (1995) for a recent discussion]. Recent empirical work, such as that by Mankiw, Romer, and Weil (1992), also suggests that human capital is important for growth.

Education and Human Capital

The literature on East Asian development stresses the strong commitment to human capital investment in the region and the favorable effects of high educational attainment in several countries. Ogawa, Jones, and Williamson (1993) noted that East Asia has higher levels of literacy and educational attainment and invests more in education than does Latin America, even after levels of development in the two regions are held constant. East Asian governments have received high marks for their education policies. These policies, which focused on primary and secondary schooling, generated rapid improvements in labor force skills (World Bank 1993a). The successful Asian economies moved quickly to achieve universal primary education and then to expand secondary education. Universities and other tertiary institutions received a lower share of resources than elsewhere (Perkins 1994).

Human capital accumulation was especially rapid in the NIEs, adding to growth in effective labor supply. Between 1966 and 1990 the percentage of the working population with secondary or higher education, for example, rose from 27% to 71% in Hong Kong, from 26% to 75% in South Korea, from 16% to 66% in Singapore, and from 26% to 68% in Taiwan (Young 1995: 642).

The emphasis on human capital has apparently paid off. Barro and Sala-I-Martin (1995) analyzed GDP growth using more than a dozen variables and a large cross-section of countries.[1] In one exercise they examined nine fast-growing East Asian economies (China, Hong Kong, Indonesia, Japan, South Korea, Malaysia, Singapore, Taiwan, and Thailand) and concluded that the initially high levels of human capital (educational attainment and life expectancy) in these countries contributed substantially to their growth during the 1965–75 period. Kim and Lau (1995) estimated that increases in educational attainment have accounted for 11–14% of the growth in the NIEs.

Human Capital and Demographic Change

An influential study by Schultz (1987) using cross-national data found no effect of population growth on enrollment rates. Schultz did find adverse effects of rapid growth on expenditures per child, teachers' salaries, and teacher-student ratios, and this result focused attention on the potential beneficial effects of lower fertility on the quality of schooling. Pritchett (1996) argued that these variables are not good proxies for quality of schooling, citing studies that call into question the effect of expenditures per child and teacher-pupil ratios on educational outcomes [see Harbison and Hanushek (1992) and Hanushek (1995)].

Some scholars have argued that declining fertility rates have contributed to human capital accumulation in East Asia. Williamson (1993) reported that decreases in the relative size of school-age populations made it possible to deepen expenditures per child and to raise educational quality. He estimated that the decline in East Asian secondary-school-age cohorts accounted for 3–4% of the enrollment rate rise and 10–13% of the increase in expenditures per child between 1970 and 1990. Cassen and contributors (1994) also argued that lower fertility rates helped East Asian countries to afford human capital investments. They cited the example of South Korea. If fertility there had stayed at its 1960 level through 1980, the number of primary-school children would have been one-third larger and expenditure on primary education would have been higher by 1% of GDP. The fertility declines, however, allowed South Korea to improve both the extent and the quality of its education (see Chapter 9 for an extensive discussion of these issues).

Labor Supply and GDP Growth

Employment growth has been impressive in East Asia. In the NIEs, for example, employment growth ranged from 2.8% to 4.4% per year from the early 1960s to 1990 (Kim and Lau 1994).

Substantial increases in labor force participation helped to fuel rapid labor force growth. Between 1966 and 1990 aggregate labor force participation rates rose from 38% to 49% in Hong Kong, from 27% to 51% in Singapore, from 27% to 36% in South Korea, and from 28% to 37% in Taiwan (Young 1995) (see Chapter 14 for a discussion of the important role played by rising female labor force participation in East Asia).

Growth-accounting studies suggest that rapid employment growth made substantial contributions to GDP growth. Kim and Lau (1994), for example, estimated that increases in the labor supply account for 15–32% of the growth in the NIEs. Young (1992) attributed about one-quarter of the GDP growth in Singapore and Hong Kong to labor.

Rapid labor force growth during the 1960s and 1970s helped to moderate wage growth in the NIEs. The large cohorts of youth coming of working age, the large numbers of migrants from rural areas to urban areas, and the rising numbers of young women entering the labor market helped to moderate wage growth during the initial labor-intensive industrialization drives (Bauer 1990). The fertility declines in East Asia began to reduce labor force growth rates in the 1980s, and this contributed to the labor scarcity that has emerged in Japan and the NIEs.

Labor Supply and GDP per Worker

It is important to distinguish among GDP, GDP per worker, and GDP per capita when discussing the effects of changes in labor supply. In the preceding discussion, for example, I argued that rapid labor force growth in the 1960s and 1970s contributed to rapid GDP growth in the NIEs. Nevertheless, more rapid labor force growth may actually slow growth in GDP *per worker*. Slower labor force growth during the 1980s in East Asia should have acted to encourage growth in labor productivity.

Labor productivity (GDP per worker) has increased dramatically in East Asia. The increases are generally attributed to increases in capital per worker, and the favorable effects of slower population growth in this regard have already been discussed. A related channel through which demographic change has affected labor productivity is industrial restructuring. Slower labor force growth has contributed to increasing labor scarcity and rising labor costs in Japan and the NIEs. These developments in turn have hastened changes in these economies from labor-intensive manufacturing to higher value-added, more capital- and skill-intensive manufacturing. This restructuring has allowed for increases in labor productivity. Restructuring may also promote more rapid growth of TFP, a topic I address later.

Labor Force Participation and GDP per Capita

Increases in physical and human capital generate increases in output *per worker*. Lower fertility can also affect output *per capita* through favorable effects on aggregate labor force participation rates. Ogawa, Jones, and Williamson (1993) noted that an obvious implication of rapid fertility decline in East Asia is that during the later stages of the demographic transition, labor force participation rises, allowing per capita income to rise as workers become a greater proportion of the population. Some of the increase in partici-

TABLE 2.3

Growth in Real GDP per Capita Relative to Real GDP per Worker
(Growth Rate of GDP per Capita/Growth Rate of GDP per Worker):
Eight East Asian Countries

Country	1960–90	1960–70	1970–80	1980–90
Japan	1.05	1.08	0.93	1.07
South Korea	1.12	1.12	1.15	1.11
Taiwan	1.10	1.05	1.11	1.12
Singapore	1.24	1.10	1.49	1.08
Hong Kong	1.11	0.99	1.29	1.09
Thailand	1.04	0.96	1.10	1.10
Indonesia	1.01	0.82	0.97	1.14
Malaysia	1.15	0.96	1.30	1.21

SOURCE: Summers et al. (n.d.).

pation is due to changes in the population's age distribution, and some of it is due to increases in the number of women entering the labor market as child-bearing declines.

Table 2.3 compares growth in real GDP per capita with GDP per worker for the eight East Asian economies. The comparison is done for the period 1960–1990 and for each of the three decades separately. The growth rate of GDP per capita is the sum of the growth rate of GDP per worker and the growth in aggregate labor force participation. A comparison of per capita and per worker growth rates, therefore, reveals the effect of changing participation on income per person. Although not all the increase in participation is due to demographic change alone, this exercise allows us to gauge roughly the potential effect of reduced fertility through this channel.

Table 2.3 suggests that the effect has varied considerably among the eight countries. It is large for the NIEs, where the growth of GDP per capita was 10–24% higher than the growth of GDP per worker. Among the countries in the Association of Southeast Asian Nations (ASEAN) the effect of increasing participation was also large in Malaysia during the 1970s and 1980s. Rising participation contributed to per capita income growth in Thailand during the 1970s and 1980s and in Indonesia during the 1980s.

Total Factor Productivity

The growth-accounting studies mentioned so far have sparked a lively debate about the nature of growth in East Asia. The main controversy concerns estimates for growth in TFP in the NIEs. As already noted, increases in output that are not associated with factor accumulation are attributed to increases in TFP. The studies by Kim and Lau (1994) and Young (1992, 1995) have been interpreted to suggest that TFP growth in the NIEs has been modest and that productivity increases have contributed relatively little to output growth. Kim and Lau (1994), for example, estimated that increases in TFP accounted for only 14–35% of the growth in the NIEs, whereas it generated 46–71% of growth in the G-5 countries (France, West Germany, Japan, the United Kingdom, and the United States).[2] They argued that productivity growth has been relatively low because until recently there has been little investment in research and development, software development, market development, or on-the-job training in the NIEs. Young (1992) found that TFP change accounted for 35% of the growth in Hong Kong but made no contribution in Singapore. Recent studies suggest that TFP growth in Malaysia, Indonesia, and Thailand has also been modest (Abimanyu 1995; Limskul 1995; Tham 1995).

Krugman (1994b), noting the modest TFP growth in those countries, argued that economic growth in East Asia, although remaining high by world standards, will slow substantially in the future. According to his argument, because growth in East Asia has been based largely on factor accumulation rather than on technological innovation, it will run into diminishing returns and must slow. Much of the region's growth has been due, for example, to increases in saving and investment rates. The Solow growth model demonstrates that an increase in the saving rate brings about only a temporary increase in the rate of economic growth. In some endogenous growth models factor-driven growth can continue indefinitely, but there is little support for such models. Young (1992) argued that his results for East Asia support the neoclassical (Solow) growth model. Those results do not support the endogenous growth models, which reject the assumption of diminishing returns.

Growth rates in East Asia will undoubtedly decline. Nevertheless, the concern over TFP growth seems to be overblown, for several reasons.

First, there is still room for factor-driven growth in the region. Lau (1996), for example, argued that the NIEs are still far behind the G-5 countries in their physical and human capital per worker.

Second, the belief that TFP growth in East Asia is relatively low is based largely on a misinterpretation of the estimates from these studies. A major problem is the focus on the percentage contributions of increases in capital, labor, and TFP to economic growth. Harberger (1996) pointed out that the problem with looking at percentage contributions is that the TFP contribution is bound to look small as a fraction of growth in countries that save 30% or 40% of GDP.

Increases in TFP have been important, but the TFP contribution to output growth has been dwarfed by the rapid factor accumulation in the region. Studies using conventional growth-accounting methods generally find TFP growth in East Asia to be about average. For example, Young (1995) estimated annual TFP growth rates to have been 1.7% for South Korea, 2.3% for Hong Kong, and 2.6% for Taiwan over the period 1960–1990. He concluded that "while, with the exception of Singapore, productivity growth in the NICs [newly industrializing countries] is not particularly low, it is also, by postwar standards, not extraordinarily high" (Young 1995: 671).

Third, recent studies have obtained more robust estimates for TFP growth in the region. For example, Harberger (1996) reported somewhat higher estimates for TFP growth in the region than do earlier studies. Moreover, he interpreted his results in a way that highlights the importance of TFP growth. Harberger (1996) derived a two-deflator approach to growth accounting. The method uses a GDP deflator to deflate nominal flows and a standard worker as the basic unit for measuring labor. Although Harberger's approach still attributes growth to a labor contribution, capital contribution, and residual, there are conceptual differences between it and the traditional growth-accounting approach.

Harberger (1997) analyzed economic growth in Japan, South Korea, Malaysia, Taiwan, Thailand, and several Latin American countries. His median estimates for TFP growth over time were 2.5% per year in South Korea, 1.2% in Malaysia, 4.0% in Taiwan, and 3.0% in Thailand. He also carried out his growth accounting for high- and low-growth periods. In all periods TFP growth was considerably more robust in East Asia than in Latin America. Harberger (1997) estimated that TFP grew at more than 4% per annum for East Asian countries in their periods of rapid growth, compared with 3% or less for his sample of Latin American countries in their periods of rapid growth. During the periods of slow growth, TFP rose by 1% per year in East Asia and *declined* by an average of 1% in Latin America.

Harberger's (1997) estimates for average annual TFP growth are about one percentage point higher than those of Young (1995) for South Korea and Taiwan, the two countries for which both have estimates. Harberger did not think that his estimates were all that much higher, but he interpreted his results in a different way. He concluded, for example, that one main factor that distinguishes episodes of high growth from low growth is the difference in rates of TFP improvement. In both East Asian and Latin American countries differences in TFP growth were major factors contributing to differences in GDP growth among countries and over time.

A fourth reason the concern over East Asia's growth in TFP seems to be exaggerated is that many observers believe that the rate of technical progress in the region has been accelerating or will accelerate in the future. There is some evidence that TFP growth has recently become more rapid. Young (1995), who provided estimates for the NIEs in various periods, found, for example, that average annual TFP growth in Taiwan was more rapid in the 1980s than in the 1970s. The TFP growth rate in South Korea also improved over time, rising from 1.3% per annum in the late 1960s to 2.6% per annum in the late 1980s. Rao and Lee (1995) reported that TFP growth has accelerated in Singapore since 1987. Liang (1995) suggested that TFP growth has accelerated in Taiwan since the early 1980s. He concluded that the more rapid TFP growth occurred because of industrial restructuring, educational improvements of the work force, and increased spending on research and development. Abimanyu's (1995) estimates suggest that TFP growth in Indonesia increased after 1985, in large part because of deregulation and other policy reforms.

Demographic Change and Total Factor Productivity

Declining fertility may promote TFP growth. One way that it can do so is through its effects on labor force growth. Many observers have argued that slower labor force growth and rising labor scarcity create incentives to innovate and increase the rate of technical change [for example, Habakkuk (1971), David (1975), Cutler et al. (1990), and Romer (1994)]. Romer (1994) speculated that more abundant labor has a negative effect on TFP growth because it lowers the incentives to discover and adopt labor-saving innovations that have positive spillover effects.

The recent declines in labor force growth rates in the NIEs, therefore, may promote faster TFP growth. Oshima (1995: 111) argued that the faster TFP growth in Taiwan and South Korea may be sustained as the surplus labor from agriculture disappears and technological progress becomes increasingly labor saving. In previous decades the availability of cheap labor from the large agricultural sector lessened the need to install the more costly, sophisticated labor-saving technologies, especially among the many small and medium-size establishments.

Lau's (1996: 26) discussion of the prospects for TFP growth in East Asia outlines a broad channel through which demographic change could affect productivity in the region. Lau argued that after a threshold capital-labor ratio is reached, diminishing marginal productivity of capital will set in. When this occurs, the desirability of intangible capital (research and development, human capital, and technological change) increases. The benefits of intangible capital are also increased as a result of complementarities among physical capital, human capital, research and development, and technical progress. Lau concluded that these forces will propel future TFP growth in East Asia. I would argue, therefore, that demographic change, to the extent that it accelerates the rise in capital-labor ratios and promotes human capital accumulation, should promote TFP growth in East Asia.

Development Strategies, Government
Policies, and Other Factors

A number of other factors are believed to have promoted economic growth in East Asia, in part by encouraging the efficient allocation of resources. They include the outward orientation of the East Asian economies, stable macroeconomic policies, a market orientation rather than interventionist policies, relatively equal income distributions, labor market policies, agricultural policies, and the political actions of their governments.

Outward Orientation

The successful East Asian economies are distinguished by their rapid growth in exports. During the 1970s, exports grew at an average annual rate of 9.5% in East Asia, compared with only 3.9% for all low- and middle-income countries. From 1980 to 1992 East Asian exports grew at 10.5% per year, compared with only 4.4% per year for all low- and middle-income countries.

It is the growth in *manufactured* exports that has been most impressive. Manufactured exports accounted for only 6% of South Korea's exports in 1960. A full 90% of the country's exports were manufactured exports by 1980. The industrial share of exports for Taiwan rose from 32% in 1960 to 91% by 1980 (ROC CEPD 1997). The importance of manufactured exports increased dramatically only in the 1980s for the ASEAN countries (World Bank, *World Development Reports*, various years).

Exports and Economic Growth

Many observers believe that openness to international trade has been the most important factor underlying the region's rapid economic growth (Naya 1988; Balassa 1991; Hughes 1992; Edwards 1993; Krueger 1993, 1995; Perkins 1994; Carliner 1995). International trade is important in all the successful East Asian economies and is the factor most consistently correlated with their success (World Bank 1993a: 292).

Although all the successful East Asian economies except Hong Kong passed through an import substitution phase, these phases ended earlier than in other developing countries. A common reason for moving away from import substitution strategies was the need for foreign exchange (World Bank 1993a). Growth accelerated in several countries after they abandoned import substitution policies and adopted outward-oriented policies. As Krueger (1995) reported, this happened in South Korea, Singapore, and Taiwan. Taiwan's policy reforms began in the early 1950s, and rapid growth started five years earlier there than in South Korea. South Korea's policies changed dramatically between 1958 and 1963, shifting the economy from an inward to an outward orientation, and rapid growth ensued. Since 1965 Singapore's growth has also been export led.

In general, developing economies that adopt an outward orientation grow considerably faster than economies that focus on import substitution (Carliner 1995). Why should export orientation promote growth? There may be substantial static and dynamic gains from trade. Trade can permit countries to achieve economies of scale and to benefit from specialization. Competition in world markets should force domestic producers to become more efficient and to learn new technologies. Moreover, exports generate foreign exchange, which may facilitate imports of raw materials and capital goods. It has also been argued that export orientation encouraged higher saving in the NIEs (World Bank 1987). According to this argument, there is a higher marginal propensity to save export income, and capital markets are less distorted in export-oriented economies.

Despite these observations, some scholars question the impact of exports on growth. Although empirical studies show a strong positive relationship between economic growth and export growth, correlation does not necessarily imply causation. Chowdhury and Islam (1993: 79–80) cited studies that attempt to test whether export growth causes economic growth. Their results were mixed for Asian countries, and they concluded that, instead of exports causing growth, growth may cause exports or some third factor may cause both. Young (1994), using data from the Penn World Table, found the evidence on the relationship between manufacturing export shares and the growth of output per capita to be weak.

Policies to Promote Export Growth

Policies to promote exports have varied over time and among countries. Such policies include export credits, duty-free imports for export producers, tax incentives, subsidized infrastructure, preferential financing, foreign-investment incentives, and exchange rate management that prevents real exchange rates from becoming overvalued (World Bank 1993a). Stiglitz and Uy (1996) added that governments have promoted the development of export markets and have adopted licensing and other regulations designed to enhance the reputation of their countries' exports.

Two issues have provoked debate in the literature: the extent to which these export promotion activities were applied uniformly across exporters and the extent to which exporting economies have been open to imports. Balassa (1991), Hughes (1992), Krueger (1993, 1995), and others have argued that exports were promoted with largely neutral incentives (World Bank 1993a). For example, Krueger (1995) argued that the policy measures adopted to stimulate export growth were largely uniform and across the board. She also noted that as export levels grew, policymakers found that it was too costly to rely on tax credits, credit rationing, or export subsidies. They turned increasingly to exchange rate policy as the principal means of promoting exports. "The broad picture, then, is that all East Asian exporters had fairly uniform incentives for exporting across virtually all industries and activities. Although occasional episodes of intervention can be found, some of them proved to be major policy mistakes, and in any event the degree of intervention was small contrasted with that in inner-oriented developing countries" (Krueger 1995: 21).

Others argue that incentives were not neutral across sectors or firms during periods of rapid growth. Amsden (1989) and Wade (1990) claimed that the Northeast Asian governments intervened to gain a comparative advantage (World Bank 1993a). The World Bank study seems to take an intermediate view, arguing that these governments implemented their export promotion strategies in three distinct ways. In Japan, South Korea, and Taiwan incentives were essentially neutral on average, divided between import substitutes and exports. But within the export sector incentives were not neutral among industries or firms; rather, there was an effort to promote specific exporting industries. Hong Kong and Singapore had free trade regimes and made export credit available but did not subsidize it. Singapore concentrated its efforts on attracting foreign investment to its exporting firms. The more recent export drives in Southeast Asia have relied less on specific incentives and more on gradual trade liberalization and institutional support for exporters. The recent efforts to attract foreign direct investment in Indonesia, Malaysia, and Thailand have also been export-oriented (World Bank 1993a: 358–60).

Foreign Direct Investment

Foreign direct investment in East Asia has received considerable attention. Direct investments, as opposed to portfolio investments, are purchases of factories, land, and capital goods. The investor retains some degree of control over the investment [for discussions, see James, Naya, and Meier (1989), Hill (1990), Riedel (1991), Chowdhury and Islam (1993), and Ramstetter (1993)]. Foreign investment policies have varied widely among countries and over time. Japan practically prohibited foreign direct investment, and South Korea and Taiwan have been hostile to it. Hong Kong has had liberal foreign investment policies, and Singapore has actively promoted it (Perkins 1994; Carliner 1995). Thailand has also had a relatively liberal investment regime. Indonesia's policies have had dramatic swings, from being hostile in the early 1960s to being liberal during the 1967–72 period to becoming restrictive in the late 1970s and early 80s and becoming liberal once again since 1985 (Hill 1990).

The importance of foreign direct investment, in the overall transfer of capital, is generally minor. Singapore and South Korea are extreme cases. Singapore is the only country in which foreign direct investment has accounted on average for more than 10% of gross capital formation; this was in 1965–84. During the same period, foreign direct investment represented less than 2% of gross capital formation in South Korea (James, Naya, and Meier 1989). Foreign direct investment has played a more important role in Indonesia, Malaysia, Singapore, and Thailand than in either Japan or South Korea (Singh 1995). It has made substantial contributions to the export drives in these countries, where multinational corporations account for large shares of manufactured exports (Hill 1990).

Stable Macroeconomic Policies

Many economists argue that sound macroeconomic management is important for growth. In a recent study Fischer (1993) presented cross-sectional and longitudinal regressions that suggest that inflation, large budget deficits, and distorted foreign exchange markets have negative effects on growth. Moreover, he found evidence that causation runs from macroeconomic policy to growth. Higher inflation and budget deficits inhibit growth by reducing investment and productivity growth. Harberger (1997) examined periods of major inflation in several countries and found that GDP per capita decreases as inflation moves to its peak, then recovers as inflation is brought under control. He argued that during inflationary periods prices do not rise uniformly. Inflation distorts relative prices and impairs the operation of an economy.

Many observers claim that macroeconomic policies have contributed to East Asia's growth. Macroeconomic management has been generally sound: Fiscal deficits have been kept under control, inflation has been relatively moderate, and real interest rates have been stable (World Bank 1993a). Of course, there have been lapses in macroeconomic management, even among the successful countries. Dowrick (1994) noted the double-digit inflation in Indonesia and South Korea and a fiscal deficit in Malaysia. Perkins (1994), however, argued that when countries have deviated from sound macroeconomic policies, it has usually not been for long. For example, in South Korea budgetary reforms led to smaller fiscal deficits beginning in the mid-1960s and inflation fell (Krueger 1995).

Market Orientation versus Interventionist Policies

The relative importance of market orientation and interventionist policies is a subject of considerable debate. The conventional view is that East Asian governments have been largely market-oriented and that this orientation has promoted the region's growth. However, some economists subscribe to a revisionist, or heterodox, view that growth has been due largely to strong and selective government interventions.

The Conventional and Revisionist Views

According to the conventional view, successful economies have relied largely on markets to allocate resources. Four factors are emphasized: limited price distortions, competition, limited size of the public sector, and limited market-friendly government interventions.

The World Bank (1993a: 298) argued that the orientation toward trade and the absence of price controls and other distortionary policies led to relatively low price distortions in East Asia. There is some debate on this point, which I discuss later. Here, I will just mention that the extent to which prices are distorted seems to vary considerably among countries in the region (Perkins 1994).

Competition, both international and domestic, is believed to have promoted growth. Domestic markets were protected but apparently less so than in most developing countries (World Bank 1993a). Singh (1995), a revisionist, argued that, whereas competition in domestic markets did exist, it was managed. For example, in Japan Singh asserted that the government discouraged competition in young industries, but that when those industries became technologically mature, competition was allowed. In South Korea competition among the *chaebol*, the large conglomerates that dominate that economy, is intense.

A third market-related factor in the success of East Asian economies is the limited size of their public sectors (Kuznets 1988). Barro and Sala-I-Martin (1995) found that the low levels of government consumption in East Asian countries made notable positive contributions to growth in real per capita GDP.

The fourth factor, limited government intervention, is perhaps the most controversial. According to the World Bank's market-friendly view, government interventions in the region were limited mostly to cases where markets failed. Moreover, market forces were allowed to discipline interventions. The direct and indirect costs of intervention were not allowed to become excessive. When interventions have threatened macroeconomic stability, governments have consistently come down on the side of prudent macroeconomic management (World Bank 1993a: 6–7).

Boltho (1985), Amsden (1989), Wade (1990), Singh (1995), and others have challenged this view. The revisionist, or heterodox, view is that governments actively guided investments to promote growth. Rather than limiting price distortions, they altered prices to promote certain industries. Wade (1990), for example, claimed that East Asia's success is due to a higher level and different composition of investment than that of less successful economies and that the differences in investment are due to government actions.

The Debate over Industrial Policy in Northeast Asia

The most intense debate is over industrial policy—the use of financial incentives, subsidies, and access to credit to alter industrial structure for the purpose of promoting growth and productivity. Two main issues dominate the debate: the extent to which East Asian governments have actually intervened selectively and the extent to which industrial policies have affected growth.

The literature focuses on Northeast Asia, where interventions have been most extensive. In Southeast Asia government interventions have played a less prominent role (World Bank 1993a). Wade (1990) presented detailed descriptions of industrial policies in Japan, South Korea, and Taiwan. He wrote that the objective of early Japanese industrial policy was to encourage sectors that faced income-elastic demand in international markets and exhibited economies of scale. In later years Japan's industrial policy has had a narrower focus on technology. Promoted industries included steel, automobiles, textiles, shipbuilding, and later, electronics and semiconductors. The government used a long list of measures: directed credit, protection of domestic markets, allocation of foreign exchange to targeted firms, exchange rate controls, controls on direct foreign investment, export promotion, and selective government leadership in investment and technology. The Korean government promoted heavy and chemical industries (iron, steel, metal products, machinery, electronics, and industrial chemicals). Wade claimed that the government altered investment patterns by allocating credit, controlling exchange and interest rates, limiting foreign competition and foreign investment, promoting exports, and exercising leadership in certain industries. He also argued that the government of Taiwan intervened aggressively by setting agricultural prices, protecting some domestic industries, and using tax incentives and subsidized credit to push investment into selected industries.

Were these interventions effective? The conventional view is that selective interventions were not beneficial. Policy failures are often cited. For example, Krueger (1995: 24) referred to studies by Yang (1993) and Yoo (1990) that suggest that interventions in Taiwan and South Korea were harmful. Yang found TFP growth across industries in Taiwan to be negatively correlated with levels of government support. Yoo concluded that the Korean government's support for heavy and chemical industries during the 1970s acted to slow growth.

Some scholars argue that the interventions have been merely market conforming and that the targeted industries would have prospered in any case because of their comparative advantage. The World Bank (1993a) found little evidence that industrial policies have altered the industrial composition of the high-performing East Asian economies in ways that would not have been predicted on the basis of factor intensities and factor prices. Other studies have reached similar conclusions.

Revisionist scholars, on the other hand, argue that industrial policies were fundamental to Northeast Asia's economic success. Their argument has two parts.

First, they claim that pervasive market failures created a need for government intervention. Stiglitz (1989) discussed several potential failures. He claimed that capital markets in East Asia were weak, leading governments to create financial institutions and to allocate capital. He also asserted that spillover effects were important. He cited the example of technological spillovers, that is, benefits of technological innovations that accrue to parties not involved in the development. Private markets provided inadequate incentives for investing in the production and acquisition of technology because they had difficulty appropriating the benefits. Stiglitz (1989) also thought that the East Asian economies had coordination failures. Underdeveloped markets meant that prices could not perform their coordination role.

Second, the revisionists argue that the conventional emphasis on policy mistakes is misplaced in studies that have found that governments have not always picked the winners very well. In response to these studies, Wade (1990: 334) made the following assertion: "The governments of Taiwan, South Korea, and Japan have *not so much picked winners as made them*. They have made them by creating a larger environment conducive to the viability of new industries—especially by shaping the social structure of investment so as to encourage productive investment and discourage unproductive investment, and by controlling key parameters on investment decisions so as to make for greater predictability."

Relatively Equal Income Distributions

The average income disparity for East Asia, as measured by the Gini coefficient, is low relative to that for Latin America and Africa. Moreover, the average disparity for East Asia was only marginally higher during the 1990s than it was in the 1960s (Deininger and Squire 1996). There has been no apparent general increase in inequality. Rapid economic growth in the region did not take place at the expense of equity. Oshima and Mason provide a more detailed assessment in Chapter 15.

Recent cross-national studies suggest that greater income equality promotes economic growth (Persson and Tabellini 1994; Deininger and Squire 1996; Perotti 1996). After accounting for other factors that influence growth, Deininger and Squire (1996) reported that countries with unequal income distributions have grown more slowly than countries with more equal distributions. They believed that the link between high inequality and low growth lies largely in the inability of the poor to borrow. Perotti (1996) also concluded that reducing inequality can stimulate growth. He found evidence to support the following linkages between income distribution and economic growth: First, greater inequality is associated with less education, especially at the secondary level; second, inequality is linked to higher fertility rates, and third, greater inequality is associated with political instability. Schmidt-Hebbel, Serven, and Solimano (1996) also claimed that income distribution affects capital accumulation by influencing public policies and political stability. A high degree of inequality may incite labor militancy and increase political conflict.

The emerging consensus is that the relatively equal income distributions in East Asia have contributed to the region's growth (Carliner 1995). Stiglitz (1989) argued that land reform in Northeast Asia caused rural productivity and incomes to rise, that it resulted in increased savings and domestic demand, and that the redistribution of income contributed to political stability. Rising wages reduced inequality, made workers satisfied and productive, and promoted good relations between workers and employers. Perkins (1994) added that low levels of income inequality help to explain why there was so much emphasis on primary and secondary education in the region. In less equal societies there tends to be a greater concern with providing higher education to the elite.

Efficient Labor Markets and Labor Market Policies

Wage determination in East Asia was apparently left largely to flexible labor markets, and the relatively low wage differentials among skill groups and across regions are cited as evidence of efficient markets (Fields 1992; World Bank 1993a). Flexible labor markets are believed to have promoted the efficient allocation of labor. They may have also facilitated export growth. Krueger (1995: 22) argued that, given the region's reliance on labor-intensive manufactured exports, growth rates would have been lower had artificially high wages or regulations driven up labor costs. Kuznets (1988) proposed that one reason for strong export growth in East Asia has been its competitive labor markets, which facilitated the transfer of labor from agriculture to industry.

Freeman (1992) claimed that wage repression, or restraint on wage growth, did not appear to have played an important role in East Asia. Wages were determined largely by supply and demand, and they rose rapidly. Labor repression, or restraints on organized labor, certainly occurred. Government control over labor movements varied from country to country (Frenkel 1993). Labor policies have also changed over time, most notably in South Korea and Taiwan after they underwent political liberalization during the late 1980s. A common intervention has been to promote the establishment of enterprise-level unions while discouraging the development of the potentially more powerful industry- and economy-wide unions. Some observers argue that government intervention has contributed to low incidences of labor unrest, a factor that many believe has promoted industrialization. These arguments ignore the potentially beneficial effects of unions. According to the collective-voice view, for example, unions promote productivity by facilitating communication between workers and employers and by establishing seniority and other work rules (Freeman and Medoff 1984).

Agricultural Policies

Another important factor, which I mention only briefly, is the adoption of favorable agricultural policies. Although the agricultural shares of employment and GDP declined rapidly in East Asia, agricultural output and productivity grew rapidly. Important factors in this success included land reform, agricultural extension services, the provision of infrastructure, investment in rural areas, and relatively low levels of direct and indirect taxation on agriculture (World Bank 1993a).

The impact of demographic factors on innovation in agriculture has received much attention (Hayami and Kikuchi 1982; Hayami and Ruttan 1987). In Chapter 4 of this volume, Hayami concludes that the increasing scarcity of land resulting from population pressure is a basic force in East Asia, driving research for the transfer of agricultural technology across different environments. It also encourages investment in land infrastructure.

Political Factors

Little (1979) stated that much of the success of Japan and the NIEs was due to governments and their economic policies. East Asian governments have been praised for their strength, stability, and commitment to economic development. An interesting question is, Why have these governments been able to adopt sound policies while others have failed? Perkins (1994: 660) asked rhetorically where the "honest bureaucracies and economic technocrats insulated from narrow political pressures" came from. His answer for South Korea, Taiwan, and Singapore was that they faced the critical problem of survival. They could not afford to fail economically. Moreover, these economies were largely free from the landlord elites that plague the Philippines and parts of Latin America. Little (1979) asserted that Indonesia, Malaysia, and to a lesser degree Thailand have the same kinds of political and social structures that are found in so many other parts of the world, but he did not explain how these societies managed to support policies conducive to sustained growth.

Mackie (1988) analyzed the political underpinnings of growth in the ASEAN countries. He concluded: "A high degree of consensus within the elite on the basic objectives of economic policy seems to be a crucially important condition of successful economic performance. Where the elite is seriously fragmented, as in Indonesia before 1965 (and also initially in Malaysia and Singapore), governments have to be primarily concerned with power-maintenance strategies rather than longer-term economic objectives" (p. 325).

Exogenous Factors

Finally, some argue that success in East Asia has been partly a result of good luck. Robinson (1993) noted that many factors underlying the success of the region were exogenous. The Korean War sparked a commodity boom from which the East Asian economies benefited. The Vietnam War channeled American spending into the region. Perhaps most important was the massive expansion in world trade that followed liberalization by the developed economies in the 1970s and 1980s.

Conclusion

Capital accumulation allowed East Asia's economies to grow rapidly for more than three decades. High rates of investment, sustained by high rates of saving, played the dominant role in the region's success. Increases in TFP also contributed to economic growth, but this contribution was dwarfed by the effect of capital accumulation. Government policies induced households and firms to save more, and other policies promoted the efficient absorption and allocation of the massive increases in capital stocks. Students of East Asia's economic development tend to agree on the importance of several of these policies: the strong emphasis on outward-oriented growth and export promotion, the relatively disciplined macroeconomic policies, the willingness to invest in needed infrastructure, the high rates of public saving, the promotion of financial-sector development, and education policies that generated rapid increases in primary and secondary school enrollments. There is less agreement on other policies, such as financial repression and industrial policy.

The demographic transition in East Asia, characterized by rapid declines in fertility and concomitant changes in population age structure, contributed to the growth process. Demographic change made its strongest economic contribution through its effects on capital accumulation. Fertility declines and changes in age composition promoted the rise in saving rates among East Asian households. Lower fertility, after a lag, also caused labor force growth to slow. This facilitated the dramatic increases in capital-labor ratios, and output per worker grew more quickly because of this capital deepening. Demographic change also made other contributions. Fertility declines made it easier for governments to increase school expenditures per pupil, and this may have helped to increase the quality of schooling. During the later stages of the demographic transition in East Asia, fertility declines and changes in age composition also facilitated the rise in labor force participation rates. This allowed per capita income to increase even more rapidly as workers became a great proportion of the population.

3

Population in East Asia

GRIFFITH FEENEY AND ANDREW MASON

DURING THE SECOND HALF of the twentieth century, the world's developing countries experienced population growth at unprecedented rates. The populations of Africa and Latin America essentially tripled. Between 1950 and 1995 Asia's population increased from 1.4 billion to 3.5 billion. To many observers Malthus's warnings about uncontrolled population growth two centuries earlier seemed prescient. In South Korea, Japan, Taiwan, and the island of Java, home to most of Indonesia's population, high population densities and limited natural resources exacerbated fears of unchecked population growth. Asian leaders, among others, were gravely concerned about the implications of rapid population growth for the development of their own countries (see Chapter 16).

The era of rapid population growth seems almost certain to end during the twenty-first century. Population growth rates in Asia, Latin America, and the world peaked during the 1960s and are declining slowly but steadily. Change came somewhat later to Africa, but population growth has slowed there as well. In most countries population growth is gradually declining, although within major world regions there is considerable variation in the rate of decline (Table 3.1).[1]

Declining population growth rates do not, of course, imply declining population size. Every country in Asia is experiencing some population growth. Japan will be the first to experience zero population growth and then population decline, probably within this decade. All other countries in Asia will experience population growth for many years. By the middle of the twenty-first century Asia's population is expected to exceed 5 billion and Latin America and Africa will experience even more growth in percentage terms (UN DESIPA 1995b).

We thank Jeff Brown and Noreen Tanoue for their able assistance.

TABLE 3.1

*Population Size and Population Growth: Six Asian Countries
and Major Regions of the World, 1950–95*

Country/region	Population (millions)			Maximum population growth rate[a]		1990–94 growth rate (%)
	1950	1995	Percentage increase	Rate	Year	
Japan	83.6	125.1	49	1.4	1950–54	0.2
South Korea	20.4	45.0	123	3.1	1955–59	1.0
Taiwan	7.6	21.4	182	3.7	1950–54	1.1
Singapore	1.0	2.8	196	4.9	1950–54	1.0
Thailand	20.0	58.8	195	3.1	1965–69	1.1
Indonesia	79.5	197.6	148	2.4	1970–74	1.6
Africa	224	728	225	2.9	1980–84	2.8
Asia	1,403	3,458	147	2.4	1965–69	1.6
Europe	549	727	32	1.0	1950–54	0.1
Latin America and Caribbean	166	482	191	2.8	1960–64	1.8
North America	166	293	77	1.8	1950–54	1.1
More developed regions	809	1,167	44	1.2	1950–54	0.4
Less developed regions	1,711	4,550	166	2.5	1965–69	1.9
World	2,520	5,716	127	2.0	1965–69	1.6

SOURCES: UN DESIPA (1995b) and ROC DGBAS (various years), *Statistical Yearbook.*
[a]Maximum growth rate is for the five-year periods between 1950 and 1995.

The six countries that are the focus of this volume are experiencing, in broad terms, the same demographic changes that are occurring elsewhere in the developing world, but they are on the leading edge. Population growth rates in East Asia peaked relatively early and have declined relatively fast. Changes in Thailand and Indonesia have come somewhat later than in the more developed economies of Japan, South Korea, Taiwan, and Singapore, but compared with countries at similar development levels, Thailand and Indonesia have progressed rapidly toward an end to substantial population growth.

In this chapter we explore the demographic experience of these six countries with two objectives in mind. The first objective is to examine the underlying processes that led to the era of rapid population growth and are leading to its end. The second objective is to explore in more detail the demographic changes that have occurred and will continue. Demographic changes exert an influence at both the aggregate and the family levels. In the next section we take a macrodemographic perspective, examining changes in the size, growth, and age structure of the population. The following section focuses on the household or family level, examining how demographic changes are influencing the lives of three key groups: prime-age adult women, children, and the elderly.

Aggregate Processes of the Demographic Transition

In traditional societies the risk of death is high throughout life. Women bear many children, but many of them die in infancy and childhood. Population grows slowly or not at all. High mortality risks and low growth rates produce a young age distribution, with relatively many young people and relatively few old people. Fertility, mortality, and age distribution are in approximate long-term equilibrium. Numbers of births and deaths may fluctuate sharply from year to year, but long-term averages are reasonably stable.

In modern societies women bear on average about two children each and almost everyone survives to old age. Population again grows slowly or not at all. Under modern demographic conditions, however, slow growth combines with low mortality to produce an old age distribution, with much larger numbers of elderly persons. Fertility, mortality, and age distribution are again in approximate equilibrium.[2]

Between the traditional and modern regimes comes the demographic transition. In the simplest account death rates begin to decline while birth rates remain high, resulting in a surge in population growth. After a time birth rates decline as well, and population growth eventually subsides.

The process is complicated, however, by changes in a population's age distribution. Figure 3.1 shows birth, death, and growth rates in a simulated demographic transition modeled loosely on the experience of Taiwan. At the beginning of the twentieth century birth and death rates were nearly equal, yielding a population growth rate near zero. As is conventional among demographers, rates are expressed as annual births, deaths, and net increase per 1,000 persons in a population. The transition begins with declining death rates. Birth rates do not change initially, and so population growth rates rise. The birth rates in Figure 3.1 begin to decline after about 40 years, but growth rates continue to rise for another 10 years or so until declining birth rates outpace declining death rates.

In our simulation life expectancy at birth rises from 25 years in 1900 to 73 years in 1990 and remains constant thereafter. The level of fertility declines from 5.5 children per woman in 1955 to 2.0 children per woman in 1990 and remains constant thereafter. As is apparent from Figure 3.1, however, the transition does not end with the stabilization of mortality risks and the average number of children born per woman.[3] Although the population growth rate declines substantially from its peak 90 years after the beginning of the transition, it continues to decline for another 40 years, during which time population growth continues. The birth rate continues to decline dur-

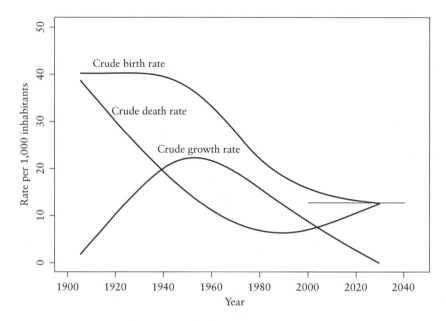

FIGURE 3.1. Stylized Demographic Transition.

ing this period, but the death rate rises. This unexpected rise in the death rate
is explained by changes in the population age distribution. Ninety years into
the transition, changes in fertility and mortality have resulted in an age distribution that is much younger than the equilibrium age distribution for the
current levels of fertility and mortality. The age distribution has not caught up
with changes in fertility and mortality. The catching-up process takes about
40 more years, during which the population age distribution grows steadily
older. This aging pushes more and more people into the oldest age groups,
where mortality risks are highest, and the death rate therefore rises. Population aging lowers the birth rate as well, but the effect here is less pronounced.[4]

The population growth that occurs during the last 40 years of this modeled
demographic transition is a manifestation of *population momentum*. The
term, adopted by analogy from the physics of moving bodies, refers most often to a tendency for population size to continue to grow after fertility rates
have reached replacement level. More generally, population momentum refers to population change that results from an imbalance between the current age distribution and current levels of fertility and mortality (Preston and
Guillot 1997). In the demographic literature momentum often refers only to
the impact of a population's age structure on its birth rates. The impact of
age structure on death rates is neglected. Here, the impact of age structure
on death rates is as important as its impact on birth rates.

The demographic transition model provides a useful point of departure for a more detailed assessment of demographic changes in East Asia. In the following sections we examine mortality and fertility change with an eye to assessing whether East Asia's demographic experience is distinctive.

Mortality Decline

From the perspective of the modern world mortality risks in the premodern world were almost unimaginably high. Reducing mortality risks and improving health surely rank among humanity's greatest accomplishments. Improvements in mortality came first to the West. Life expectancy rose gradually during the nineteenth century and more rapidly during the twentieth century as living standards improved and scientific advances increased our understanding of health and infectious disease. The gains in the United States during the first half of the twentieth century illustrate that success: Average life expectancy rose from 47 years in 1900 to 68 years by 1950.

Improvements in mortality risks were by no means confined to the more developed countries, but in the early 1950s the gap between the developed and the developing countries was enormous. Persons born in more developed countries could expect to live to their mid-60s; those born in less developed countries could expect to reach age 40. Mortality conditions were worst in Africa and little better in Asia. Latin American countries had a decided advantage within the developing world (Table 3.2).

The post–World War II era has seen a rapid decline in mortality risks throughout the developing world and a continued decline in the developed world. The gap in life expectancy between developing and developed areas remains large: 12.1 years for 1990–94, but this gap is less than half the 25.5-year gap of 1950–54. The greatest gains have been made in Asia, where life expectancy increased by 23.2 years and the infant mortality rate dropped from 180 to 65 infant deaths per 1,000 live births between 1950–54 and 1990–94.

Two survival curves, one for Taiwan in 1906 and the other for Japan in 1996, illustrate the significance of the extremes of East Asia's twentieth-century experience (Figure 3.2). Both curves show the proportion of a group of persons just born that will survive to any age given prevailing age-specific mortality risks. In early twentieth-century Taiwan about 35% of all children died before reaching their fifth birthday. From age 5 proportions surviving declined nearly linearly through age 80, indicating an approximately uniform distribution of deaths from late childhood through very old age. Few people survived long enough to reach old age. In contrast, virtually all children born in contemporary Japan survive to adulthood. Few people die until well into their 50s, and half of all persons survive to age 80.

TABLE 3.2

Life Expectancy and Infant Mortality: Six Asian Countries
and Major Regions of the World, Early 1950s to Early 1990s

Country/region	Life expectancy			Infant mortality rate		
	1950–54	1990–94	Change	1950–54	1990–94	Change
Japan	63.9	79.5	15.6	51	4	−47
South Korea	47.5	71.1	23.6	115	11	−104
Taiwan[a]	62.5	74.4	11.9	36	6	−30
Singapore	60.4	74.8	14.4	66	6	−60
Thailand	47.0	69.0	22.0	132	37	−95
Indonesia	37.5	62.7	25.2	160	58	−102
Africa	37.8	53.0	15.2	186	93	−93
Asia	41.3	64.5	23.2	180	65	−115
Europe	63.4	72.9	9.5	72	12	−60
Latin America and Caribbean	51.4	68.5	17.1	125	45	−80
North America	66.3	76.1	9.8	29	9	−20
More developed regions	66.5	74.4	7.9	59	11	−48
Less developed regions	41.0	62.3	21.3	178	70	−108
World	46.4	64.4	18.0	156	64	−92

SOURCES: UN DESIPA (1995b) and ROC DGBAS (various years), *Statistical Yearbook*.
[a]For Taiwan the values for 1950–54 are for 1956; the values for 1990–94 are the averages from annual data.

Japan's life expectancy of 80 years in 1996 was the highest of any nation in the world, but no country, no matter how impoverished or deprived, had a life expectancy in the 1990s as low as Taiwan's 28 years in 1906. Advances in life expectancy have been sufficiently rapid during the twentieth century that most countries have mortality conditions much closer to Japan's at the end of the twentieth century than to Taiwan's at the beginning of it.

Given their level of development, the East Asian countries considered here began the era of high economic growth with relatively high life expectancies. In a scatter plot of life expectancy against per capita gross national product (GNP) for 1960–64 Japan, Taiwan, Singapore, South Korea, and Thailand are clearly along the upper envelope (Figure 3.3). Indonesia is the only country with a life expectancy that can be characterized as typical for its income level. [Unless noted to the contrary, our income data come from the Penn World Tables, Version Mark 5.6a, updated (Summers and Heston 1991).]

These six countries are not sharply distinguished from other countries by the speed of their mortality decline. For the world as a whole, life expectancy rose by 18 years between 1950–54 and 1990–94. Japan, Taiwan, and Singapore experienced smaller gains; South Korea, Thailand, and Indonesia saw larger gains. However, mortality conditions did improve more rapidly in

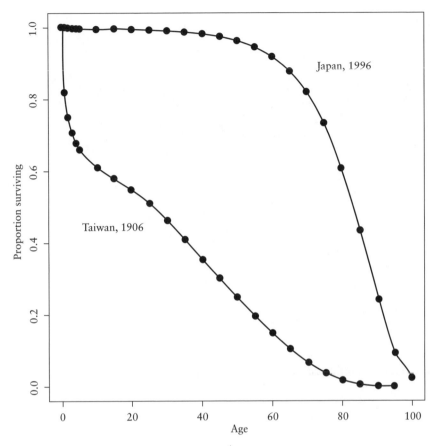

FIGURE 3.2. Extremes of Human Survivorship.

East Asian countries than was typical in other countries at similar initial levels of mortality. Japan illustrates the point with a life expectancy equal to Europe's in 1950–54, but almost seven years greater than Europe's in 1990–94 (Table 3.2).

That mortality risks fell rapidly in the six countries is hardly surprising. They were among the most rapidly developing in the world, and one would expect gains in life expectancy to be among the benefits of development. Yet the same plot of life expectancy against per capita GNP for 1990–94 reveals an interesting phenomenon (Figure 3.4). With the exception of Japan, life expectancy in these countries is clearly low in relation to income. The gains in life expectancy have been substantial, but they have not kept pace with the gains in income.

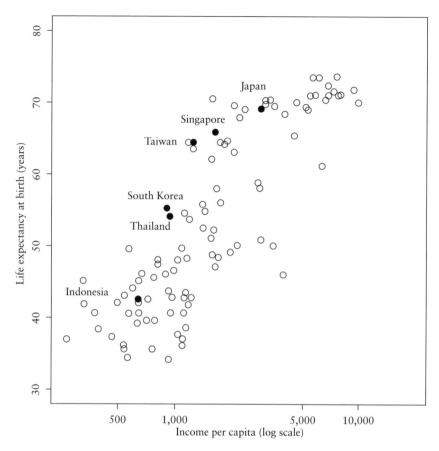

FIGURE 3.3. Life Expectancy and Income: 113 Countries, 1960–64.

As the six countries were entering their era of high economic growth, then, they were further along in their mortality transition than other developing countries, and they proceeded more rapidly through their mortality transition than have other countries. The gains in life expectancy did not quite keep pace, however, with the gains in per capita income.

Fertility Decline

In 1960 the more populous countries of the world belonged to one of two groups. Of the 113 countries with populations of 2 million or more, 81 were high-fertility countries in which women had an average of 6.7 births over their reproductive life span. In the remaining 32 countries women averaged only 2.8 births. Many of the latter group of countries had experienced lower

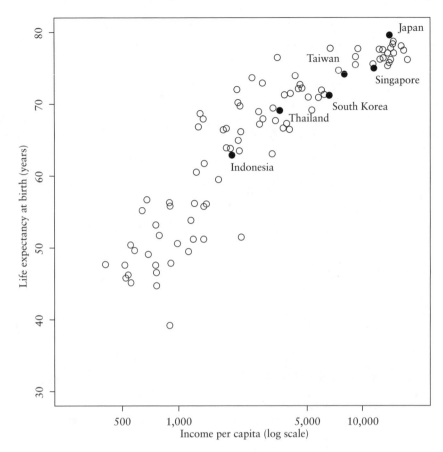

FIGURE 3.4. Life Expectancy and Income: 113 Countries, 1990–94.

levels of fertility in their recent past but were in the midst of the post–World War II baby boom. The dividing line between high-fertility and low-fertility countries, clearly indicated in Figure 3.5, is 4.5 children per woman.[5]

Most low-income countries belonged to the high-fertility group, and most high-income countries belonged to the low-fertility group. Annual per capita income of the high-fertility countries averaged $1,260, compared with $5,100 for the low-fertility countries (1985 US dollars). There was substantial overlap, however. For example, Venezuela, a member of the high-fertility group, had a per capita income of $6,300, and Romania, a member of the low-fertility group, had a per capita income of $480. Within the high- and low-fertility groups the level of per capita income bears strikingly little relationship to the level of fertility.

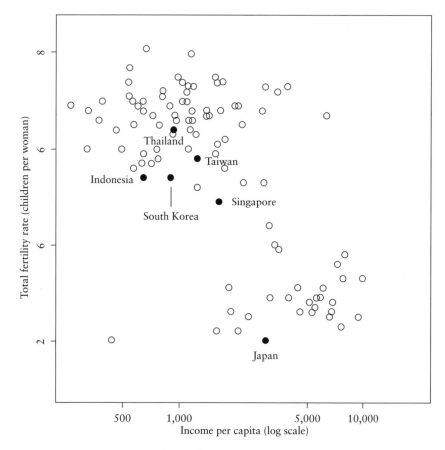

FIGURE 3.5. Fertility and Income: 113 Countries, 1960–64.

Locating the six countries in Figure 3.5 is a simple way to identify their distinctive features in the early 1960s. Japan was the only Asian country to have joined the low-fertility group by then. Indeed, Japan was one of only three countries to have achieved replacement-level fertility. Japan, however, was a relatively new member of that group. Its total fertility rate (TFR) had dropped below 4 births per woman by 1940, rebounded to 4.5 births per woman in the aftermath of World War II, and then dropped precipitously, reaching replacement level in the late 1950s.

The other five countries that are the focus of this study all belonged to the high-fertility group, but in 1960–64 their fertility was low in relation to other high-fertility countries. In Singapore women were averaging just under five births. South Korea, Indonesia, and Taiwan belonged to a relatively small group of countries in which women were averaging 5.5 births. Only

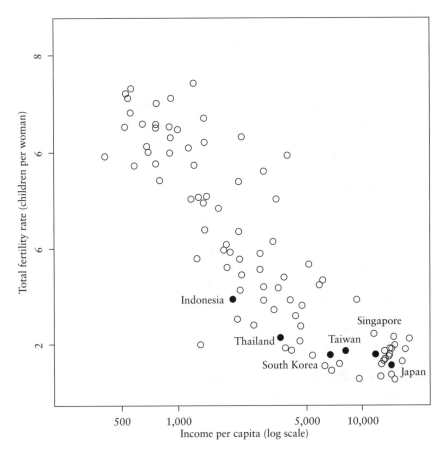

FIGURE 3.6. Fertility and Income: 113 Countries, 1990–94.

women in Thailand were averaging six or more births. By contrast, women in 67 of the 81 high-fertility countries were averaging 6 or more births.

Why were fertility rates relatively low among the six East Asian countries? In Taiwan, Singapore, and South Korea fertility decline was under way by the 1960s. During the 1950s, women in each of these countries had been bearing children at about the same rate as women in Thailand. In contrast, Indonesian fertility was at or near its peak in the early 1960s. So far as has been documented, however, Indonesian women never averaged six births over the reproductive span. In any event, as a group the high-fertility countries in our study had less distance to travel than many other countries to complete the transition to replacement fertility.

By the early 1990s six of the high-fertility countries of the 1960s had achieved replacement fertility (Figure 3.6). All are located in East or Southeast Asia: Taiwan, South Korea, Thailand, Singapore, Hong Kong, and China. Indonesian women were averaging just under three births, a very low level compared with countries at similar development levels in 1960. Of the 36 countries with per capita incomes of $1,000 or less in 1960, only 4 (China, South Korea, Thailand, and Romania) had completed the fertility transition by the early 1990s and only 1 of the remaining countries (Indonesia) had a TFR below 3 births per woman. After Indonesia, India had achieved the lowest fertility, with a TFR of 3.7.[6]

The difference between the fertility-income relationship and the mortality-income relationship is striking. In 1960 the six study countries were, in relation to their level of development, far along in their fertility and mortality transitions. But mortality changes, although impressive, did not keep pace with economic growth, whereas fertility changes did.

Although few of the high-fertility countries of the 1960s had completed their fertility transitions by the 1990s, many experienced large and rapid declines in their rates of childbearing. Nearly half of them experienced a drop in the TFR of two or more births. Rapid fertility decline thus appears to have been a widespread phenomenon.

To analyze the pace of fertility decline further, we estimated the time at which fertility began to drop and the rate of decline for all countries that had experienced a sufficient fertility decline by 1990 for a rate of decline to be reliably estimated.[7] The median rate of fertility decline for the 42 countries was slightly more than 1 child (1.04 child) per woman per decade. Twenty-three countries had rates of decline greater than one child and a TFR in 1990–94 of less than four children per woman. Table 3.3 shows data for these countries and also for Malaysia, which had a decline of slightly less than 1 (0.94) child per woman per decade.

Examination of these estimates leads to two conclusions. First, among the countries with rates of fertility decline over the median the countries of East and Southeast Asia had slightly more rapid rates of decline than countries in other regions, but the differences are small. The median rates shown in the last column of Table 3.3 indicate that rapid rates of fertility decline have been by no means unique to Asia. Fertility declined nearly as quickly in many other parts of the world. Second, the rate of fertility decline does not bear a close relationship to economic growth. The countries of Latin America that experienced a substantial drop in fertility did not have high rates of economic growth. None grew as rapidly as the high-growth economies of Asia, nor was their economic performance as a group notably distinguished from other countries of the world.

The high-performing economies of East Asia are distinctive, however, with respect to the *duration* of their fertility transitions—the number of years required to reach replacement fertility once decline has begun. For the East and Southeast Asian countries the median duration of the transition is only

TABLE 3.3

*Total Fertility Rates: Six Asian Countries and
Selected Comparison Countries, Selected Periods[a]*

Region and country	Total fertility rate		Fertility decline			Rate of decline
	1960–64	1990–94	Onset	Level	Duration	
East and Southeast Asia						
Japan	2.0	1.5	1934	4.9	39	1.0
South Korea	5.4	1.7	1961	5.6	23	1.5
Taiwan	5.5	1.8	1954	6.5	31	1.5
Singapore	4.9	1.7	1954	6.4	23	2.0
Thailand	6.4	2.1	1964	6.4	28	1.7
Indonesia	5.4	2.9	1968	5.5	25	1.0
China	5.6	2.0	1968	5.8	22	2.4
Hong Kong	5.3	1.2	1963	4.8	16	1.6
Malaysia	6.7	3.6	1957	6.8	55	0.9
Latin America and Caribbean						
Brazil	6.2	2.9	1958	6.2	58	1.0
Chile	5.3	2.5	1962	5.2	60	1.4
Colombia	6.8	2.7	1960	6.8	61	1.3
Costa Rica	6.9	3.1	1955	6.9	77	1.1
Dominican Republic	7.3	3.1	1960	7.4	72	1.4
Ecuador	6.7	3.5	1967	6.6	55	1.2
Jamaica	5.6	2.4	1970	5.2	27	1.3
Mexico	6.8	3.2	1969	6.7	50	1.4
Panama	5.9	2.9	1963	5.8	53	1.0
Peru	6.9	3.4	1966	6.8	61	1.4
Venezuela	6.7	3.3	1960	6.5	62	1.0
Middle East						
Egypt	7.1	3.9	1962	6.9	49	1.0
Kuwait	7.3	3.1	1969	7.3	48	1.7
Morocco	7.2	3.8	1970	7.1	42	1.5
Tunisia	7.2	3.2	1966	7.0	46	1.4
Median						
East and Southeast Asia	5.4	1.8	1961	5.8	25	1.5
Latin America and Caribbean	6.7	3.1	1962	6.6	60	1.3
Middle East	7.2	3.5	1968	7.1	47	1.4

SOURCE: UN DESIPA (1995b).

[a]See text for explanation of fertility decline parameters. Rate of decline is expressed as the number of children per woman per decade in the total fertility rate.

25 years. Elsewhere, the transition is projected to take twice as long. Only in Jamaica is the shift from high to replacement fertility projected to occur as quickly as in East and Southeast Asia.

Several factors account for the shorter duration of the fertility transition in East Asia. First, initial fertility levels were lower there than elsewhere by almost one child per woman. Second, the rate of decline was somewhat faster there than in Latin America. Third, East Asian countries sustained rapid fertility decline until replacement or below-replacement fertility was achieved. The pattern for many countries and for UN projections is that fertility decline slows before replacement fertility is reached. For example, in Chile fertility declined rapidly during the 1960s and 1970s, but it has declined much more gradually since.[8]

Estimates of the duration of the fertility transition may prove to be inaccurate for countries that have not yet achieved replacement fertility. Recently available data (PRB 1998) indicate that Mexico may complete the transition more quickly than projected. In contrast, Jamaica will not achieve replacement fertility as rapidly as projected. Despite the uncertainties, fertility transitions accomplished in less than 30 years are clearly beyond the reach of any of the countries outside East Asia.

Despite the considerable variation in the duration of fertility decline among the developing countries, they are proceeding through the transition much more rapidly than countries in the West. For example, in the United States nearly 120 years was required to bring the TFR from nearly 7 children per woman in 1820 to 2.1 children per woman in 1937, a rate of decline of 0.4 children per woman per decade. Fertility began to decline in France in the late eighteenth century and continued declining well into the nineteenth century, with an average rate of decline of only 0.2 children per woman per decade. In the late-developing Scandinavian countries declines were somewhat more rapid, but in no case were they higher than 0.7 children per woman per decade.[9]

Population Momentum and Changing Age Structure

Achieving a long life expectancy and replacement fertility is an important milestone, but the demographic transitions in the study countries are far from over. All continue to experience population growth, and all are experiencing substantial changes in their age structures. In this section we explain why population growth is continuing, how long it is likely to last, how much additional growth is likely to occur, and how population age structures will change.

The changes in population age distribution that occur during the demographic transition are a key feature of the demographic landscape in the six countries included in our study, arguably as important as the changes in mortality, fertility, and population growth. They are important demographically because age structure is responsible for continued rapid population growth, even when mortality risks and childbearing behavior are consistent with zero population growth. They are important economically because economic activities vary substantially with age.

To describe what happens to age distribution during the demographic transition, we introduce a simple model. We begin with a pretransition population in equilibrium. The number of births each year (B) is constant and

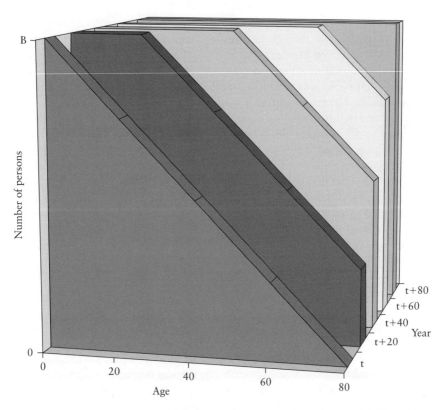

FIGURE 3.7. Changes in a Model Age Distribution over the Demographic Transition.

equal to the number of deaths. The population growth rate is zero. Life expectancy is 40 years, with deaths uniformly distributed over an 80-year life span. Given these fertility and mortality conditions, the age distribution declines linearly from the number of births B at age 0 (that is, at birth) to zero at age 80, as shown by the plotted distribution for year t in Figure 3.7. The total population is given by $40B$.

Suppose that in year t mortality declines instantaneously to a post-transition regime in which everyone survives to age 80. Suppose further that childbearing declines in such a way as to maintain the annual number of births at B. After 20 years, in year $t + 20$, the age distribution of persons under age 20 will be uniform and the number of persons over age 20 will decline linearly as before. The number reaching age 80 will equal the number age 60 in year t (the "$t + 20$ years" line in Figure 3.7). After 60 years the age distribution of all persons under age 60 will be uniform, and after 80 years there will be equal numbers of persons at every age. At the end of 80 years the transition is complete. Population growth is zero, the numbers of births and deaths are equal, and the age distribution does not change from the uniform distribution achieved at year $t + 80$.

This representation abstracts from many of the details of any particular country's demographic transition, but it demonstrates several key features of the transition. First, the shift to a modern mortality regime produces a substantial but circumscribed increase in the total population. The population increases to fill out the older ages. In the particular illustration provided here, the population doubles, increasing from $40B$ to $80B$ (life expectancy times the annual number of births). Second, the duration of the transition reflects the human life span. In the stylization the number of years that the transition lasts is determined exactly by the life span. If the shift from a traditional to a modern mortality regime is not instantaneous, as of course it is not, the transition's duration will exceed the life span by an amount that depends on how rapidly mortality and fertility decline. Third, the transition is accompanied by enormous changes in the population age distribution. The population under age 20 increases by only 14%. The population aged 20–60 doubles. The population age 60 and older increases in size by 800%. Finally, the shifts in age structure during the transition are sequenced in a particular manner. Population growth slows from the youngest age groups up. At the outset the population under age 20 grows more slowly than the adult population and ceases to grow entirely 20 years into the transition. Only after 20 years does growth in the adult population begin to slow. Sixty years into the transition, the population under age 60 has stopped growing and the population age 60 and older is just beginning to slow.

The changes described by this highly stylized model are surprisingly consistent with the experience of the study countries. In every case we see large increases in population numbers, declining population growth rates, a filling-out of the population age distribution sequenced as described here, and a prolonged period during which approximate equilibrium between population age distribution and levels of fertility and mortality is reestablished. There is, however, one important aspect of age distribution change during the demographic transition that the model does not capture. As mortality risks fall and life expectancy increases at the beginning of the transition, population age distributions become younger, not older. Because mortality risks in infancy and childhood are extremely high, as illustrated by the Taiwan survival schedule in Figure 3.2, survivorship of children tends to increase more than survivorship of older persons.

The initial impact of mortality decline is a younger population. In the simulated demographic transition shown in Figure 3.1 the portion of the population age 0–14 rises from 35.2% at the beginning of the transition to 41.5% 55 years into the transition. Only when fertility decline begins does the proportion of youth turn downward, although the decrease proceeds

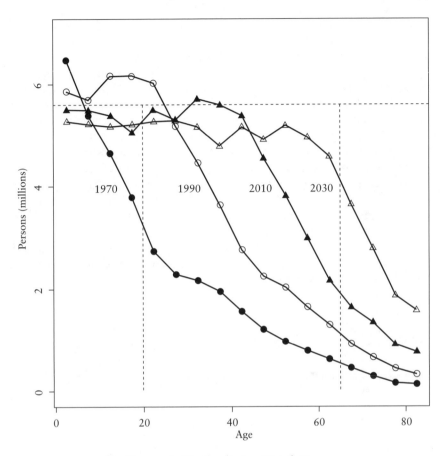

FIGURE 3.8. Changes in Thailand's Age Distribution, 1970–2030.

much more rapidly than the increase. The dramatic rise of the youthful portion of the population in the early stages of the demographic transition has
potentially important implications for economic growth and development
(see Chapter 5).

The example of Thailand shows how closely our highly stylized model of
changing age distribution approximates the empirical experience of the six
study countries (Figure 3.8). Thailand's age distribution in 1970 was young,
the consequence both of rapid population growth in earlier decades and high
mortality in more remote decades. Fertility fell sharply in the 1970s and
1980s, however, so that numbers of births were roughly constant during
those decades and the number of persons in the 0–4 age group in 1990 was
not much different from the number in 1970 (slightly less, in fact).

Note that each point of the 1970 distribution is moved to the right by
20 years, because everyone who survives gets 20 years older, and downward,

because some people do not survive. When mortality is low, however, nearly all persons survive until reaching the older age groups, so that most movement is to the right rather than downward.

It is of course possible that demographic developments in Thailand over the next 40 years will not unfold so neatly as these projections suggest. Fertility may fall to and remain at levels substantially below 2 children per women, as has happened in many developed countries over the past 50 years. In that case there will be fewer young persons than are shown in Figure 3.8. Increases in fertility are less likely but would have the opposite effect.

At present and in future decades, this population momentum inherent in current age distributions will be the primary driver of population growth in five of the six study countries (Indonesia being the exception). Those five countries have achieved replacement fertility, but birth rates and death rates have not yet converged because of the populations' age structures. Japan's population is currently growing slowly, and its population size is projected to peak in this decade. At that point Japan will enter a period of depopulation. By 2050 Japan's population is projected to be 11% smaller than in 1990 (Table 3.4).

Populations of the other five high-performing economies will be substantially larger in 2050 than in 1990. The populations of South Korea, Taiwan, and Singapore are projected to increase by 20–30%, Thailand's by nearly

TABLE 3.4

Population Growth in Six Asian Countries and Major Regions of the World, 1990–2050

Country/region	Population (millions)			Population growth rate	
	1990	2050	Percentage change	1990–95	2045–50
Japan	124	110	−11	0.2	−0.4
South Korea	43	56	30	1.0	0.0
Taiwan	20	25	25	0.7	−0.4
Singapore	3	3	22	1.0	−0.1
Thailand	56	82	46	1.1	0.3
Indonesia	183	319	74	1.6	0.4
Africa	632	2,141	239	2.8	1.2
Asia	3,186	5,741	80	1.6	0.4
Europe	722	678	−6	0.4	−0.3
Latin America and Caribbean	440	839	91	1.8	0.5
North America	278	389	40	1.0	0.2
Oceania	26	46	77	1.6	0.4
More developed regions	1,143	1,208	6	0.4	−0.1
Less developed regions	4,141	8,626	108	1.9	0.6
World	5,285	9,833	86	1.6	0.5

SOURCES: UN DESIPA (1995b). Taiwan projections based on estimates provided by Timothy Miller; for details, see Chapter 6.

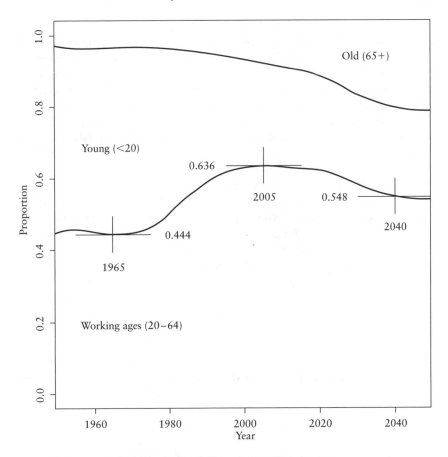

FIGURE 3.9. Changes in South Korea's Age Distribution, 1950–2050.

50%, and Indonesia's by almost 75%. By the middle of the twenty-first century population growth is projected to be negligible, zero, or negative, depending on the country.

Changing age structure has important implications for economic analyses. Of particular interest to broad assessments is the dependency structure of the population. Any human population consists of three broad age groups: (1) those of working age (often defined as ages 20–64), whose efforts are primarily responsible for economic production; (2) children (ages 0–19); and (3) the elderly (ages 65 and older), who are economically dependent on prime-age adults. (We have used the years 0–19 instead of 0–14 to define the youngest age group because of the large high school enrollments in these countries.) South Korea's experience illustrates the evolution of the dependency structure over the demographic transition (Figure 3.9).

Two important changes in dependency structure characterize South Korea and other countries going through the demographic transition. The first
is the long swing in the relative size of the working-age population. Over the
demographic transition the percentage of South Korea's population in the
working ages increases from 44% in the mid-1960s to an anticipated peak
of 64% in 2005. This change represents an enormous increase in the productive potential of the South Korean population over a period of 40 years.
This high level is not permanent, but the projected level in 2040 is still well
above the pretransition level. If the projection were extended beyond 2050,
the decline in the working-age population would continue until about half
of the population was of working age.

The second change apparent in Figure 3.9 is a shift in the dependency
structure from one in which youths dominate to one in which youths and the
elderly are roughly in balance. In 1960 more than 94% of dependents were
under the age of 20. By 1990 this figure had fallen to 88%. By 2050 the number of elderly dependents will nearly equal the number of young dependents.

The changes in age structure in the six study countries are summarized in
Table 3.5. Between 1960 and 1990 four of the high-performing economies
experienced substantial increases in the concentration of their populations at
the working ages. The increases for Singapore, South Korea, Taiwan, and
Thailand ranged from 10 to 17 percentage points. The smaller increase for
Japan reflects the particular time span selected. Japan experienced a substantial increase during the 1950s. The increase in Indonesia has been modest to
this point, because Indonesia's transition is occurring somewhat later than
in the other countries.

Values for the world's regions provide some comparative context for the
East Asian experience. Many countries in Africa are sufficiently early in their
demographic transitions that the proportion of the population under age
20 is rising and the proportion of the working-age population is declining.
Other countries of the world, on average, experienced modest increases in
the percentages of the working-age population. Even in Europe the growth
of the elderly population was insufficient to reverse the trend. The increase
in North America was relatively large and can be traced to the entry of baby
boomers into the working ages. Comparing the country values of East Asia
with regional averages overstates the extent to which the large increases in
working-age populations were confined to East Asia. Thirty-three countries,
about 20% of the 150 countries with populations of 1 million or more in
1990, experienced increases in their working-age populations of 5 percentage points or more. Nine, including several non-Asian countries, had increases of 10 percentage points or more.

The shift in dependency away from a population dominated by youths
is readily apparent in Table 3.5. The percentages of people under age 20
have declined steeply in all study-group countries except Indonesia. The

TABLE 3.5

Age Structure: Six Asian Countries and Major World Regions, 1960 and 1990

	Percentage in specified age group								
	20–64			Under 20			65 and older		
Country/region	1960	1990	Change	1960	1990	Change	1960	1990	Change
Japan	54	62	8	40	27	−14	6	12	6
South Korea	45	59	14	51	36	−15	3	5	2
Taiwan	43	58	15	54	36	−18	3	6	4
Singapore	46	63	17	52	31	−21	2	6	4
Thailand	43	53	10	54	43	−11	3	4	2
Indonesia	47	49	3	50	47	−3	3	4	1
Africa	44	42	−2	53	55	2	3	3	0
Asia	46	49	3	50	47	−3	4	4	0
Europe	56	59	3	35	29	−7	9	12	4
Latin America and Caribbean	44	48	4	52	47	−5	4	5	1
North America	52	60	8	40	28	−12	8	12	4
Oceania	50	54	3	43	38	−5	7	8	2

SOURCE: UN DESIPA (1995b).

percentages of people age 65 and older have begun to rise, but, as we have noted, most of the relative growth in the older population comes late in the demographic transition. Japan is much further along than the other countries, with 12% of its population age 65 and older in 1990. Moreover, the increase in the percentage of elderly in Japan between 1960 and 1990 was greater than in any other country in the world.

Changes at the Household or Family Level

The macrodemographic perspective we have maintained thus far identifies important changes in the size, growth, and age structure of the population that have clear and potentially important links to the macroeconomy. Other important aspects of the demographic transition are not easily described at the aggregate level. In the following sections we undertake a more microdemographic approach, looking at demographic changes as they relate to three important groups: prime-age adult women, children, and the elderly.

Women

Demographic changes over the transition are of fundamental importance to the lives of women. Little more than a generation ago, women in many East Asian countries were averaging six or more births during their lifetime. Childbearing began in the teens and early 20s and extended into the late 30s and 40s. Given the short life expectancies that prevailed then, women could expect to devote a major portion of their adult lives to bearing and rearing children. Today, young women in many East Asian countries are averaging two or fewer births during their lifetime. Many of them are delaying marriage and childbearing to their late 20s and their 30s. Instead of early marriage they are opting for more schooling and for work, changes that John Bauer explores more fully in Chapter 14 of this volume.

A substantial delay in marriage and childbearing in all six countries accompanied the decline in childbearing during the transition. On average, women are marrying about two years later in Japan and Thailand, three years later in South Korea and Indonesia, five years later in Taiwan, and nearly seven years later in Singapore (Table 3.6). There is persuasive evidence that increasing percentages of East Asian women may never marry (Jones 1997).

Consensual unions and childbearing outside marriage are relatively rare in East Asia, and thus delayed childbearing has closely matched the delay in marriage. Because women are bearing fewer children, childbearing has become increasingly concentrated. In Japan, Taiwan, and South Korea most women are bearing their children in their late 20s and early 30s (Table 3.7).

TABLE 3.6

Singulate Mean Age at Marriage for Females:
Six Asian Countries, 1960 and 1990[a]

Country	ca. 1960	1990	Change (years)
Japan	24.9	26.7	1.8
South Korea	22.6	25.4	2.9
Taiwan	21.1	25.9	4.8
Singapore	20.3	27.1	6.7
Thailand	21.7	23.2	1.5
Indonesia	18.6	21.6	3.1

SOURCES: Population censuses for two census years.
[a]For a description of how singulate mean age at marriage is measured, see Hajnal (1953).

TABLE 3.7

Percentage of Women who were Mothers, by Age Group:
Four Asian Countries, 1970s and Early 1990s[a]

Women's age	Japan 1970	Japan 1990	Taiwan 1976	Taiwan 1993	South Korea 1970	South Korea 1990	Indonesia 1971	Indonesia 1990
15–19	u	u	14.3	3.3	1.2	0.2	24.2	8.3
20–24	15.6	9.5	47.7	22.1	29.5	11.3	71.4	51.4
25–29	68.5	44.4	85.5	62.1	81.9	65.5	89.2	82.0
30–34	86.4	77.7	97.5	87.1	95.6	90.8	93.3	91.2
35–39	88.4	87.2	98.8	92.8	97.4	95.3	94.0	93.5
40–44	88.0	88.5	98.1	92.3	97.8	97.3	93.2	93.6
45–49	88.6	83.7	96.0	90.1	97.3	98.0	92.8	93.9

SOURCES: For Japan, South Korea, and Indonesia we used population censuses for the respective years. For Taiwan we used our tabulations from data collected in National Family Income and Expenditure Surveys.

u, data are unavailable.

[a]Values for Japan (1970), South Korea, and Indonesia represent women who had given birth. Values for Japan (1990) and Taiwan are estimates of the percentages of women living with their own children.

Of women age 25–29 in the early 1990s more than one-third in South Korea and Taiwan and more than one-half in Japan had not begun childbearing. Indonesian women commence bearing children at younger ages; one-half of all women in their early 20s were mothers in 1990. Nonetheless, the shift to later childbearing ages is unmistakable, even in Indonesia.

All six countries have experienced a rapid decline in the number of births, but trends in the number of surviving children differ considerably among them. In the early stages of a demographic transition, child mortality rates are so high that women have few surviving children. Depending on the speed

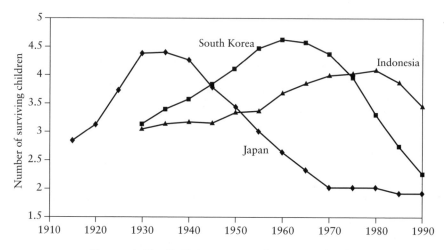

FIGURE 3.10. Changes in Family Size: Japan, South Korea, and Indonesia, 1915–90.

of mortality and fertility decline, the number of surviving children may increase substantially. Only when child mortality rates reach low levels will the trend in the number of surviving children necessarily follow the trend in childbearing.

The number of surviving children in a family rises in the early childbearing years, during which children are born more rapidly than they die. As the mother passes through her 30s, deaths of children already born in high-mortality settings tend to outnumber new births and the number of surviving children declines [see Bongaarts (1987b) for simulation results]. Because there is no fixed number of surviving children for a woman, it is necessary to devise a suitable index. In Figure 3.10 we show the average number of surviving children for women, age 35–39, in Indonesia, Japan, and South Korea, the three countries for which we have data. In contrast to the downward trend in fertility emphasized earlier, all three countries experienced an extended period during which the average number of surviving children was rising.

For example, in Japan the number of surviving children rose during the first half of the twentieth century, reaching a peak for women who were completing their childbearing during the 1930s. Over a period of 30 years family size dropped from more than four children per woman to two children per woman. Since 1970 five successive cohorts of women have averaged close to two children each. The trends in South Korea and Indonesia are similar. Both countries experienced an extended period during which the number of surviving children increased; that period was followed relatively recently by a decline.

The timing varies considerably among the three countries. In South Korea family size began to decline from about 4.5 children per woman in the 1960s, but even as late as 1975 women who were completing their childbearing had an average of 4 children. Only women who were about to complete their childbearing in 1990 had close to two surviving children. The Indonesian experience shows an even longer period during which family size was rising, although the increase was more gradual than in either South Korea or Japan. The decline in family size among women who have completed their childbearing is in its early stages in Indonesia, having dropped only 0.5 child from the 1980 peak [Feeney and Mason (1998) provide more details on methods used to construct these figures].

To summarize and to extrapolate to the experience of the region as a whole, working-age women in South Korea (and probably in Taiwan and Singapore as well) experienced a substantial decline in child-rearing responsibilities during the era of high economic growth, 1960–90. Change in Indonesia has been more recent. Thailand's experience, no doubt, falls somewhere between that of South Korea and that of Indonesia. In Japan the child-rearing responsibilities of women were already substantially diminished by 1960 and have continued to decline.

Children

Investment in human capital is widely regarded to have been an essential element of Asian economic success. At the outset of the high-growth era the countries in our study had relatively healthy and well-educated populations. Moreover, health status and rates of educational attainment improved rapidly during the high-growth era. The linkages between population and human capital formation are examined in some detail in this volume (Chapters 9–11) and elsewhere by Montgomery and Lloyd (1996), among others.

Identifying changes in demographic characteristics of the family that may bear on human capital or the quality of children requires a shift in perspective from that of the mother to that of the child. In the process of making that shift, we consider several key questions: Has there been a significant decline in the average size of the families in which children are being raised? How recently did that decline begin? Was it preceded by a period during which the average family size increased? Are there other important aspects of the family in East Asian countries that might have a bearing on their economic success?

Answering these questions is more difficult than one might at first suppose for several reasons. If, for example, we follow a birth cohort through childhood, its average family size changes as siblings are born and die. For some purposes, such as assessing competition among siblings for the mother's time, family size at young ages is of particular interest. For other purposes, such as assessing competition among siblings for financial resources, family size at older, more costly ages is of greater relevance. Because of the limited availability of data, we rely on measures of family size for older children whose mothers have completed their childbearing. Data available for the United States suggest, however, that family size at older ages is highly correlated with family size at younger ages.[10]

Another complication is that examining demographic variables from the point of reference of children involves different calculations and different results from those obtained by examining the same variables from the reference point of the mother. In determining the average number of children in a family from a mother's perspective, each number, large or small, carries equal weight. When children are the unit of analysis, however, each child carries equal weight. Because there are more children in larger families, the average size of the sibset, as demographers refer to sibling set, is greater. In a population with high variance in childbearing the average sibset size will substantially exceed the average number of children. A simple example illustrates this. Consider a population consisting of three families with zero, two, and four children. The average family has two children, but children are being raised in families with an average of $[(2 \times 2) + (4 \times 4)]/6 = 3.33$ children. However, in a population in which all women bear two children, sibset size will also be two.

Average sibset size can be calculated for South Korea and Indonesia by using published data reporting the number of ever-married women by their age and the number of surviving children [for similar data for Latin America and sub-Saharan Africa, see Lloyd and Desai (1992)]. The values for South Korea and Indonesia are plotted in Figure 3.11. Sibset size substantially exceeds the average number of surviving children, but the trend is consistent with the changes in the number of surviving children.

Taken together, the Indonesian and South Korean results show that the decline in sibset size is so recent that any significant effect on the human capital or quality of the labor force before 1990 is unlikely. The average sibset size of entering workers in Indonesia is much greater than the sibset size of departing workers (those who entered the labor force in the 1950s). Hence the size of the family of origin of the working-age population is rising, not declining.

South Korea is further along in the transition to smaller families. But even in South Korea the average quality of the labor force so far has not been influenced in any important way by the decline in sibset size. The average working-age adult in 1990 had 5.0 siblings in his or her family, compared with 5.2 siblings in 1980 and 4.8 siblings in 1970.[11]

Perhaps in Japan, but probably nowhere else in Asia, changes in sibset size

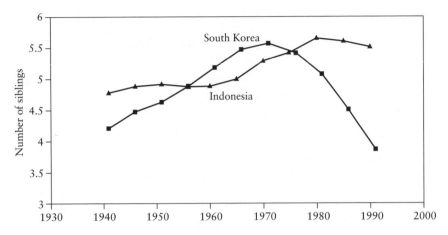

FIGURE 3.11. Trends in Sibset Size: South Korea and Indonesia, 1940–92.

have influenced the overall quality of the labor force in important ways. Of course, there may be other channels by which demographic changes influence human capital formation. Changes in age structure may have affected educational budgets, for example. Delayed or reduced childbearing may have influenced decision making by women about their own schooling.

Demographic features of the family, other than the number of children present, also may have an important bearing on human resource development. Women's age at marriage and age at first birth are relatively high and increasing, so that few children are born to young women. In East Asia births outside marriage are rare and rates of divorce are low; children are therefore more likely to be members of intact and possibly more economically viable family units. Many children are raised in extended households and so are less subject to swings in available resources that otherwise naturally arise over the life cycle.

Of these factors the adverse health impact for mother and child of either early or late childbearing has been most extensively investigated (Lloyd 1994; Montgomery and Lloyd 1996). Much less is known about the direct human capital impact of the other demographic features. There are clearly identifiable ways, however, that the resources available to children are enhanced when they are raised in intact or extended households. Because these conditions may have contributed to the human resource advantage enjoyed by many countries in East Asia, a brief review is warranted.

As discussed, women have delayed marriage and childbearing so that relatively few children are born to young women. For example, by 1995 in Taiwan only one-twentieth of all births were to women under the age of 20 and only one-quarter were to women age 20–24. Nearly two-thirds were to women age 25–34 [ROC DGBAS, various years (1996), *Statistical Yearbook of the Republic of China*]. In India in 1991–92 nearly one-quarter of all births were to teenagers and nearly 40% were to women in their early 20s (IIPS 1995). Of the six countries included in our study only in Indonesia are young women engaged in childbearing to any significant extent. About 15% of all births there were to teenagers in 1988–91, compared with 18% in 1967–70.

Several demographic forces ensure that a high percentage of children in the six countries live with both parents. Few children are born to unmarried women, parents are unlikely to divorce, and, given high rates of life expectancy, both parents usually survive until their children are grown. In recent years the percentage of female children under the age of 15 living in a household headed by a lone parent ranged between 5% and 6% in Japan, South Korea, Singapore, Thailand, and Indonesia; for male children the percentages ranged between 5% and 8% in those same countries. A somewhat higher percentage of boys (12%) than of girls (10%) lived with one parent in Taiwan in 1990 (our calculations, based on primary census data). In contrast, 28% of American children under the age of 18 in 1990 did not live with both parents (including stepparents) and 49% did not live with both birth parents (Hogan and Lichter 1995: 99).

A final issue is how changes in the extended family system may have influenced the resources—time and financial resources—available to East Asian families engaged in child rearing. The extended multigeneration family potentially serves an important role in human capital formation. Childbearing and human resource investment is heavily concentrated within the life cycle and, in a nuclear family system, falls most heavily on young parents whose income and wealth may be low compared with what they can expect later in life. In the absence of constraints on indebtedness, parents can accumulate debt in order to invest in their children. However, imperfections of capital markets may lead parents to underinvest in their children if there are no other institutional arrangements (Becker and Tomes 1976). The extended multigeneration family has historically been the institution that makes resources available to children without relying on capital markets (Mason and Miller 2000).

The extent to which children in the six countries are living in three-generation rather than nuclear households has been relatively stable. In Japan the proportion of children under age 15 living in nuclear households increased modestly, from 65% in 1970 to 69% in 1990. In South Korea children are also somewhat more likely to live in nuclear households than previously (Feeney and Mason 1998). By contrast, in Taiwan the proportion of children under the age of 15 living with grandparents increased from 24% to 28% between 1976 and 1993 (our calculations, based on Family Income and Expenditure Surveys). In other respects the Asian household is under-going substantial change, but when it comes to child rearing, it is the re-silience of the extended family rather than its deterioration that is most note-worthy. Low mortality, by increasing the survivorship of grandparents, and low fertility, by reducing the number of siblings who must share grand-parents, may be contributing to the continuation of the extended family in Asia by facilitating the accommodation of three-generation stem families.

The Elderly

The rapid growth of the elderly population is one of the key features of the demographic transition that we emphasized in our description of macro-demographic change in East Asia. The demographic transition has impor-tant implications for the life circumstances of the elderly that bear on their economic welfare, income inequality, saving rates, and rates of economic growth (see Chapters 5–8).

The decline in mortality over the demographic transition ensures that a much larger portion of the population survives to old age and that those who do so will live longer. The survival curves for Taiwan in 1906 and for Japan in 1996, charted in Figure 3.2, show the extremes in the chances of surviv-ing to old age. In a high-mortality population fewer than 1 in 5 survive to age 60; in a low-mortality population more than 9 in 10 reach old age.

Until the later stages of the transition the increases in the expected years of life for those who survive to old age are more modest than may be ap-preciated. Most of the early gains in life expectancy lead to more years lived at young ages, not at old ages. For example, in Taiwan life expectancy at birth for females rose from 65.4 years in 1956 to 77.8 years in 1994, an increase of 12.4 years. Only a little more than one-third of that increase, 4.5 years, came from a rise in the number of years lived at old age. In 1956 women who survived to age 60 could expect to live an additional 16.9 years, compared with 21.4 years by 1994. As life expectancy reaches higher levels, the gains are much more heavily concentrated at the older ages. For example, 80% of the increase in female life expectancy in Taiwan between 1990 and 1994 was concentrated at ages 60 and older.

With population aging the institutional arrangements by which the elderly gain access to resources become increasingly important to their well-being. Family support systems are dominant in traditional societies, but in modern settings new institutions evolve that supplement or, to some extent, supplant the family. Demographic forces influence the family support system in direct ways. In a traditional setting an elderly person is likely to have no surviving spouse and must rely on his (or, more likely, her) few surviving children or grandchildren. During the demographic transition, an elderly person is more likely to have a surviving spouse and more surviving adult children; and in

a modern setting he or she is much more likely to have a surviving spouse
and as many surviving children as in a pretransition setting.

The elderly in East Asia were less likely to be widowed and more likely to
be married in 1990 than earlier. Between 1970 and 1990 Singapore had the
smallest gain in the percentage of currently married women, 3 percentage
points; and Taiwan and Japan had the largest gains, 20 and 9 percentage
points, respectively (Table 3.8). The especially large increase in Taiwan is
probably a consequence of its unusual sex ratio, which resulted from heavy
male immigration from the Chinese mainland around 1950. Even with these
gains, however, a minority of elderly women in all six countries were married in 1990.

Elderly men were two to three times more likely than elderly women to
have a surviving spouse in 1970. Except in Taiwan, between 70% and 80%
of men age 65 and older were married. In Singapore the percentage of elderly
men who were married declined slightly between 1970 and 1990, but elsewhere the percentage increased. The gains were somewhat smaller for men
than for women except in South Korea.

Adult children play an important role in any viable family support system
for the elderly and for elderly women in particular. Confucian traditions
heavily influence family obligations in Japan, South Korea, Taiwan, Singapore, and, to some extent, Thailand. Filial piety, the obligation of a son to
his father, is an important organizing principle that guides many family relationships, including living arrangements, lines of authority, inheritance,
and transfers between living family members. A woman marries into the
family of her husband, and her position within the family is defined by the
position of her husband, even after his death (Cho and Moto 1994; Fricke,
Chang, and Yang 1994).

TABLE 3.8

*Percentage of Elderly Currently Married: Six Asian Countries,
1970 and 1990[a]*

Country	Males		Females	
	1970	1990	1970	1990
Japan	76.0	80.6	31.4	40.1
South Korea	73.5	82.6	21.7	28.1
Taiwan	60.2	66.7	25.5	45.5
Singapore	75.9	74.7	30.8	33.6
Thailand	72.0	73.1	34.2	38.3
Indonesia	78.6	80.1	23.0	28.3

SOURCES: Population censuses (respective years).
[a]Values are for persons 65 and older, except in Singapore, where they are for
persons 60 and older.

The elderly are experiencing an enormous rise and fall in the number of surviving adult children, as can be inferred for Japan, South Korea, and Indonesia from Figure 3.10. In South Korea demographic changes from 1960 to 1990 led to a large increase in the number of elderly women's surviving children. In 1960 women who were age 65–69 had, on average, 3 surviving children (the value plotted for women age 35–39 in 1930 in Figure 3.10). By 1990 women age 65–69 had an average of 4.5 surviving children, the largest number in South Korea's history. In the coming years, however, the number of surviving children will be declining, and by 2020 women in their early 60s will have about 2 surviving children.[12] Elderly Japanese women, those age 65–69, experienced an increase in the number of surviving children until the 1960s and early 1970s. Since then, the number of surviving children has declined. Women reaching their 65th birthday between 1995 and 2000 are the first cohort in this century to average only two surviving children. Indonesia represents the other extreme among the six study countries. There the trend in the number of surviving children is upward for the elderly and will continue to be so until early in the twenty-first century.

It is difficult to assess the extent to which demographic changes and other social and economic forces are affecting the family support system in Asia. Data on living arrangements, however, suggest that the family continues to play an important role, but one that is slowly eroding. Typically, the elderly live in a family household. Roughly, at least 9 out of 10 elderly men and at least 8 out of 10 elderly women are living with family members. The sole exception to this generalization is Taiwan, with its large elderly male immigrant population. Rates of institutionalization are relatively low. Elderly persons living outside family households typically live alone. In 1990 women in Indonesia, South Korea, and Japan were most likely to be living by themselves, but much less so than in the United States, where 37% of elderly women lived alone (US BOC 1992).[13]

In some Asian countries a shift toward nonfamilial living arrangements for the elderly has emerged during the last few decades. In South Korea and Japan the percentages of elderly living in family households have declined. The changes for men have been rather modest, but for women they have been more substantial. In both countries a rise in the proportion living alone and, to a lesser extent, in the proportion living in institutions is responsible for the decline in family living arrangements.

The elderly in Japan and Taiwan are also moving away from multigenerational living arrangements. In Japan the percentage of elderly males living with children declined from 72% in 1970 to 54% in 1990. The percentage of elderly women living with their children declined from 70% to 52% during the same period. In Taiwan the percentage of elderly men living with children or any family member from a younger generation declined from 80%

to 62% between 1976 and 1993. For elderly women the percentage declined from 87% to 72%.

Likewise, elderly South Koreans are shifting away from multigenerational living arrangements. Between 1970 and 1990 the proportion of elderly men and women who were parents of a household head declined, whereas the proportion of such men and women who were the head or spouse of the head increased. Moreover, the average number of children (age 0–19) and prime-age adults (age 20–64) living in households headed by the elderly declined precipitously in South Korea over the same period.

In neither Thailand nor Indonesia do we find evidence of a shift away from multigenerational living arrangements. In Thailand the proportion of elderly who lived in a household headed by one of their children increased between 1970 and 1990, whereas the proportion who headed their own households declined. The average number of prime-age adults living in households headed by the elderly rose between 1970 and 1990. In Indonesia the proportion of elderly heading households increased modestly during the 1980s, whereas the proportion who lived in a household headed by a child declined by about 5 percentage points. The number of prime-age adults in households headed by the elderly did not change (Table 3.9).

For now, the extended family remains an important source of support for the elderly in Asia. Many elderly continue to live with their children. Many live near their children and often receive financial and personal support. However, a shift away from the extended family is clearly under way in the eco-

TABLE 3.9

Age Composition of Households Headed by the Elderly:
Five Asian Countries, Recent Decades[a]

Household characteristic	Japan		South Korea		Taiwan	Thailand		Indonesia	
	1970	1990	1970	1990	1990	1970	1990	1980	1990
Number of members	3.36	2.62	5.05	2.72	3.75	4.86	4.20	2.92	2.86
Children	0.78	0.37	2.06	0.56	0.93	1.94	1.18	0.81	0.69
Prime-age adults	1.11	0.72	1.49	0.76	1.34	1.59	1.68	0.79	0.81
Elderly	1.47	1.53	1.50	1.40	1.48	1.33	1.34	1.32	1.36
Dependency ratio									
Old age	1.32	2.13	1.01	1.84	1.10	0.84	0.80	1.67	1.68
Combined	2.03	2.64	2.39	2.58	1.80	2.06	1.50	2.70	2.53

SOURCE: Tabulated from primary population census data.

[a]Elderly households are defined as those with a female householder age 65 or older or, if no female householder is present, a male householder age 65 or older. Children are those under age 20; prime-age adults are those age 20–64.

nomically more developed East Asian countries. Changes in living arrangements are most evident in Japan and South Korea. In Taiwan the changes are coming at a somewhat slower pace. In the least developed of the high-performing economies, Thailand and Indonesia, there is little evidence of a shift away from a family-based support system.

Conclusion

The demographic experience of the East Asian countries is of special interest because they were the first countries to make the transition from high fertility to replacement fertility during the post–World War II era. That experience is much more thoroughly documented by censuses, surveys, and vital statistics than the demographic transitions that occurred much earlier in the West. Thus East Asia provides the first real opportunity for detailed study of the first two phases of the demographic transition.

The broad outlines of the demographic transition are similar across countries, but there are great differences in the timing, speed, and magnitude of change. Demographic events in the developing world are different from earlier changes experienced in the West. In the developing world mortality rates dropped much more rapidly, population growth rates reached much higher levels, the swings in age structure have been much more dramatic, and in many countries the rates of childbearing dropped much more precipitously. Post–World War II baby booms were modest and short-lived compared with the experience of the United States and many other Western countries. Because of these differences, the effects of population changes in the West may be a poor guide to what can be expected elsewhere.

Differences between East Asia and other countries of the developing world are also considerable. East Asia held an advantage in the 1950s. Life expectancy was already higher than in other developing regions, and rates of childbearing were lower. Moreover, East Asia proceeded more rapidly to the high levels of life expectancy that currently prevail. Rapid economic growth combined with equity, declining poverty, increased education, and other aspects of development clearly contributed greatly to the rapid improvements in longevity. East Asia's shift to low fertility was also dramatic. Development undoubtedly played an important role, but fertility levels are much more loosely connected to development than are mortality levels. The countries of East Asia that experienced rapid fertility declines also had strong policies and well-funded programs aimed at reducing childbearing (see Chapter 16).

Although differing in its timing, pace, and magnitude from both the demographic transitions experienced in the West and the transitions that are under way in today's developing regions, East Asia's transition has some elements in common with them. Several characteristics of the transition may have served as demographic underpinnings of the region's rapid economic growth; others may impede further growth. Six features of the transition stand out.

First, the countries of East Asia experienced an enormous increase in their populations. Between 1950 and 1995 every country but Japan saw its population double or triple in size. Today, Japan, South Korea, Singapore, Taiwan, and Java, home to most of Indonesia's population, are among the most densely populated places in the world.

Second, population growth is slowing. Japan's population will cease growing and will begin to decline within this decade. The other countries in the region will experience a substantial amount of additional population growth, but growth rates are declining, and the end of the era of high population growth is clearly within sight.

Third, the region has experienced large swings in child dependency, evident at both the aggregate level and the family level. With gains in child survival the percentage of the population consisting of children grew substantially. Likewise, women experienced a rise in the number of surviving children to unprecedented levels. The rise was followed by an even more precipitous decline in child dependency, because reduced rates of childbearing overwhelmed further gains in child survival.

Fourth, the productive potential of the populations of the region has increased enormously during the study period. In 1960 40–45% of the region's population fell within the working ages. By 1990 about 60% was concentrated into the 20–64-year age span in Japan, South Korea, Taiwan, and Singapore. In these countries the number of working-age persons increased by one-third because of changes in age structure.

Fifth, changes in marriage and family are increasingly apparent. Age at marriage has risen to unusually high levels, and some observers express concern that many young adults in Japan, South Korea, Taiwan, and Singapore may never marry. The elderly are increasingly likely to live independently of their children. In many respects, however, the traditional family has proven to be a resilient institution. Except in Japan, young adults rarely establish separate households until after they marry. Few children are born to single mothers. Rates of divorce are relatively low. Many elderly continue to live with their children.

The sixth change is population aging. A basic feature of human life—the length of life—has changed. In the past, reaching old age was the exception. Now it is the rule. In the past, a small portion of the population included the elderly. Now the elderly are the fastest growing segment of the population. In Japan the number of persons 65 and older exceeds the number under 15. The other countries of East Asia are following the same path as Japan.

The demographic transition in East Asia is far from complete. The population is younger than is consistent with the end of the transition. During the first half of the twenty-first century, the countries of East Asia other than Japan will experience substantial increases in their total populations. This growth will be concentrated at older ages and will produce a major shift toward an elderly population. This shift is similar to what the countries of the West are experiencing, but in East Asia it is occurring more rapidly.

4

Induced Innovation and Agricultural Development in East Asia

YUJIRO HAYAMI

OVER THE PERIOD 1960–90 East Asia has made remarkable progress in its industrialization and economic development. According to the classical thesis proposed by Ricardo in 1817 (Ricardo 1951), industrial development is bound to be constrained by limited natural resources, especially land for the production of food, which is the critical wage good for industrial workers. Ricardo argued that the shortage of food supplies for a growing industrial population would raise food prices and that the resulting rise in the cost of living would necessitate wage hikes, which would push up the cost of industrial production and lower the rate of returns to capital. This situation in turn would depress investment in the industrial sector. The economic stagnation resulting from the process is commonly called the Ricardian trap. Nearly a century and a half later Schultz (1953) observed that advanced industrial economies had escaped from this trap in their development process by applying modern science and technology to raise agricultural productivity. A major question today is whether low-income economies have the same capacity to overcome their resource constraints, given their much faster population growth than the high-income economies ever experienced.

Compared with other major regions of the world, both East and South Asia have poor endowments of land resources relative to the size of their populations and labor forces. Yet during the past several decades, the rates of increase in food output in the region have been significantly higher than those of more land-abundant economies, particularly in Africa and Latin America. The rise in food production has been especially rapid in East Asia and is an important part of the region's economic success, suggesting that East Asia has avoided the Ricardian trap in the process of its miraculous industrial development. Of major interest is whether East Asia's development experience can be replicated in the other parts of the Third World.

I examine this issue in this chapter. I begin by comparing land-resource constraints and food-output increases in East Asia and the other major regions. Next, drawing on historical records of rice yields, I trace the growth of food output in response to transfers of agricultural technology across areas with different natural environments. In the third section I postulate that this technological transfer was induced by changes in relative factor prices under the pressure of population growth on limited land resources. In the following section I consider the replicability of East Asia's agricultural development experience. In the concluding section I caution that Asian agriculture, which relied on relatively homogeneous peasant producers to achieve its productivity growth in the early stage of development, may become trapped by inefficient agricultural protectionism as its economies advance.[1] In this chapter I focus on East and South Asia and exclude West Asia (the Middle East) and the Pacific.

Resource Constraints and Productivity Growth

As is evident from the data summarized for 1994 in Table 4.1, Asia has much poorer endowments of land resources than do other developing regions. Its population density is high: The availability of total surface area and agricultural area per capita are only about one-seventh of those of Africa and Latin America. Asia's higher population density finds a parallel in much smaller endowments of land resources relative to the size of its labor force in agriculture.

The high population density and the unfavorable land-labor ratio in Asia induced more intensive land use, resulting in high percentages of land used for agricultural production, especially for annual arable cropping. The methods used to achieve a better land infrastructure included land leveling, terracing, and, above all, irrigation. The improved infrastructure prepared conditions for introducing modern land-saving technologies, such as high-yielding varieties and chemical fertilizers. As a result, Asia was able to achieve, during 1991–95, average grain yields as high as 2,115 kg per hectare of arable land, compared with 571 kg in Africa and 848 kg in Latin America. With this high land productivity Asia was able to produce 281 kg of grains per capita, slightly higher than Latin America's 261 kg and surpassing Africa's 155 kg by as much as 80%.

The ability of Asian agriculture to feed its population on its meager land resources grew remarkably from 1960 to 1990. Although rapid population growth resulted in about a 40% decline in the availability of arable land per

TABLE 4.1

Land-Resource Endowments and Agricultural Productivity: Six Major Regions, 1994

Endowment	Asia			Africa	Latin America	North America	Europe	World
	Total[a]	East Asia[b]	South Asia[c]					
Land per capita[d] (ha)								
Total area	0.61	0.76	0.39	4.18	4.26	6.34	0.94	2.32
Agricultural area	0.28	0.33	0.21	1.51	1.55	1.73	0.43	0.86
Arable area[e]	0.13	0.10	0.17	0.26	0.30	0.80	0.27	0.26
Agricultural land per worker[f] (ha)								
Agricultural area	0.9	0.9	0.8	5.9	16.6	127.0	9.9	3.8
Arable area[e]	0.4	0.3	0.7	1.0	3.2	59.2	6.2	1.1
Percentage of land areas								
Agricultural part of total area	46	43	55	36	36	27	45	37
Arable part of agricultural area	47	32	81	17	20	47	63	30
Irrigated part of arable area	34	35	34	7	12	9	12	17
Food grain output[g] (kg, 1991–95 avg.)								
Per capita	281	312	234	155	261	1,249	550	356
Per hectare of arable area[h]	2,115	2,982	1,327	571	848	1,536	2,032	1,360

SOURCE: UN FAO (1997).

[a] Excludes West Asia.
[b] Includes Southeast Asia, excluding Brunei, East Timor, Hong Kong, Macau, Mongolia, and Singapore.
[c] Excludes Maldives.
[d] Land area divided by total population.
[e] Includes area under permanent crops.
[f] Land area divided by population that is economically active in agriculture.
[g] Includes total cereals and pulses.
[h] 1994 data are used for 1995.

TABLE 4.2

*Indexes of Food Output per Capita, Arable Land Area per Capita,
and Food Output per Hectare of Arable Area:
Asia, Africa, and Latin America, 1963–93[a]*

Region	Index					Growth rate,[b] 1963–93 (%/year)
	1963	1965	1975	1985	1993	
Asia[c]						
Food output per capita	100	102	112	125	139	1.1 (100)
Arable area[d] per capita	100	96	78	66	59	−1.8 (−164)
Food output/ha	100	106	143	190	235	2.9 (264)
East Asia[e]						
Food output per capita	100	105	117	136	152	1.4 (100)
Arable area[d] per capita	100	96	76	67	61	−1.7 (−121)
Food output/ha	100	109	153	204	249	3.1 (221)
South Asia[f]						
Food output per capita	100	98	103	109	120	0.6 (100)
Arable area[d] per capita	100	97	79	64	56	−2.0 (−333)
Food output/ha	100	102	131	171	216	2.6 (433)
Africa						
Food output per capita	100	101	104	95	95	−0.2 (100)
Arable area[d] per capita	100	97	80	64	53	−2.1 (1,050)
Food output/ha	100	105	130	148	180	1.9 (−950)
Latin America						
Food output per capita	100	102	104	119	114	0.4 (100)
Arable area[d] per capita	100	97	88	80	69	−1.3 (−325)
Food output/ha	100	105	118	149	165	1.7 (425)
World						
Food output per capita	100	102	105	109	111	0.3 (100)
Arable area[d] per capita	100	97	82	71	63	−1.6 (−533)
Food output/ha	100	106	129	155	175	1.9 (633)

SOURCE: UN FAO (1997).

[a] Food output data are five-year averages centering on the years shown, and population and land area data are for the years shown.

[b] Values in parentheses are the percentage contributions of per capita area growth and per hectare output growth to per capita output growth.

[c] Excludes West Asia.

[d] Includes permanent crops.

[e] Includes Southeast Asia, excluding Brunei, East Timor, Hong Kong, Macau, Mongolia, and Singapore.

[f] Excludes Maldives.

capita between 1963 and 1993, the more than 130% increase in food output per hectare raised food output per capita by nearly 40% (Table 4.2). In contrast, a similar rate of decrease in the arable land per capita in Africa during the same period resulted in the reduction of food supply per capita by 5%. In Latin America the increase in land productivity was barely sufficient to compensate for the decline in arable land per capita, resulting in only a 14% increase in food output per capita.

The performance of Asian agriculture is more impressive in East Asia than in South Asia. From 1963 to 1993 food output per hectare rose at the average annual rate of 3.1% in East Asia, compared with 2.6% in South Asia. This gap in land-productivity growth rates was the major factor underlying the difference between East Asia's 50% increase in food output per capita and South Asia's 20% increase over the 1960–90 period (Table 4.2). In absolute terms East Asia was able to produce 312 kg of grain per capita in 1994 (1991–95 average), compared with South Asia's 234 kg, despite its smaller endowment of arable land (0.10 compared with 0.17 hectare per capita). It is easy to imagine that such remarkable growth of land productivity in agriculture underlay East Asia's escape from the Ricardian trap of economic stagnation, which otherwise might have emerged during the region's early stage of industrialization.

Growth of Land Productivity through Technology Transfer

The aggregative growth of Asian agriculture involved sequential spurts of growth in land productivity across the region. These spurts are thought to have emerged through technology transfers from the earlier to the later starters of modern agricultural development. We can observe this process by examining rice yields over time in selected Asian economies.

Modern agricultural development geared to raising land productivity began in Japan in the late nineteenth century to meet the needs of Japan's newly industrializing economy despite the constraint of severely limited land resources. Long before the Meiji restoration in 1868, Japanese agriculture had been under strong population pressure on land. This pressure induced efforts by local communities to develop irrigation and encouraged individual farmers to improve crop varieties and their cultivation practices to produce increased yields. By the end of the feudal Tokugawa period Japan had developed improved rice varieties and practices in several advanced areas where population density was high. It had also improved its irrigation infrastructure. These areas were located mainly in the western part of Japan.

With the removal of feudal barriers to communication and transportation and with the support of extension activities sponsored by the new Meiji government, these advanced indigenous technologies, previously isolated in narrow localities, began to diffuse, first within western Japan and later to eastern Japan. The diffusion involved not simply the new varieties and practices but also their adaptation to different environmental conditions and the transformation of those environments through investments in irrigation and drainage systems. Rice production was boosted in the early stage of Japan's industrialization, and the economy was able to avoid slipping into the Ricardian trap.

Nonetheless, there was a limit to growth based simply on technology transfer. As shown in Figure 4.1, the initial spurt in the growth of average rice yields in western Japan began to decelerate by the beginning of the twentieth century. The successful technology transfer from western to eastern Japan caused yields in the east to rise dramatically and for a while kept the national average yield growing with no sign of deceleration. During the next 20 years (1915–35), however, as the technology transfer closed the gap between the two regions, Japan's rice production entered into a stagnant phase.

The deceleration in rice production coincided with increases in the demand for food resulting from the economic boom associated with World War I. In 1918 rice shortages and high prices resulted in a major urban disruption known as the Rice Riot. This symptom of an emerging Ricardian trap led the government, after the war, to transfer Japan's rice technology to two new overseas colonies, Taiwan and Korea, through public investments in adaptive research and irrigation infrastructure. The success of this effort created a large export surplus from the colonies, which caused rice prices in the Japanese market to fall (Hayami and Ruttan 1971, chap. 10). Thus Japan solved its food problem in the 1920s by means of colonial exploitation along the lines of Ricardo's prescription.

During the first decade of the twentieth century, before rice production entered into the stagnant phase, Japanese agricultural experiment stations began research on modern crop breeding, but nearly 30 years passed before it produced major practical results. The experiment station system in its infancy contributed to yield increases by facilitating the diffusion of indigenous technologies. It did so mainly by conducting simple comparative yield tests among various varieties and practices rather than by creating new technological potential. The eventual stagnation in rice production during the interwar period resulted in part from the success of the extension system in improving and adapting indigenous technologies for wide diffusion. However, the system failed to use advanced scientific methods to strengthen its capacity for creating new technologies (Hayami and Yamada 1991, chap. 2).

The dramatic development and diffusion of modern rice and wheat varieties in tropical Asia since the late 1960s, popularly known as the Green Revolution, can be regarded as an extension of the technology transfer from Japan to Taiwan and Korea. Along with the technology transfer sequential spurts and decelerations in rice yields have been occurring across Asia since World War II.

Figure 4.2 shows that the growth rates of rice yields in South Korea and

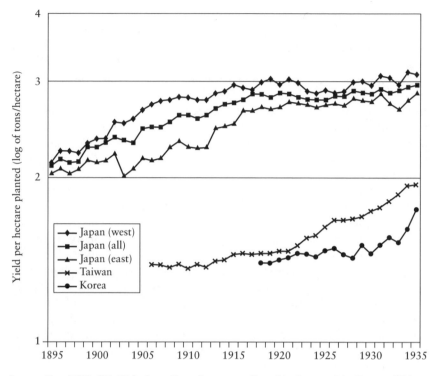

Sources: Kayo (1958: 607–52) for Japan; Korea Government-General (various years) for Korea, and Taiwan Government-General (various years) for Taiwan.

FIGURE 4.1. Rice Yields per Hectare Planted: Japan, Korea, and Taiwan, Five-year Moving Average, 1895–1935 (Semilogarithmic Scale).

Taiwan have begun to stagnate as those yields have approached the ceiling reached by Japan. Indonesia and the Philippines, two Southeast Asian economies whose technology transfers preceded those of South Asia, also show signs of having begun to reach a plateau in yields, whereas India and Bangladesh appear to be continuing their yield spurts. In South Korea and Taiwan the average annual growth rate of rice yield declined from 2.3% in the 1970s to 1.0% in the 1980s. It remained generally the same, 2.3%, in Southeast Asia, and it accelerated significantly, from 1.4% to 3.0%, in South Asia over that period.[2] These observations indicate that the Green Revolution in Asian rice culture has been an ongoing process of technology transfer, spreading from Northeast Asia first to Southeast Asia and then to South Asia.

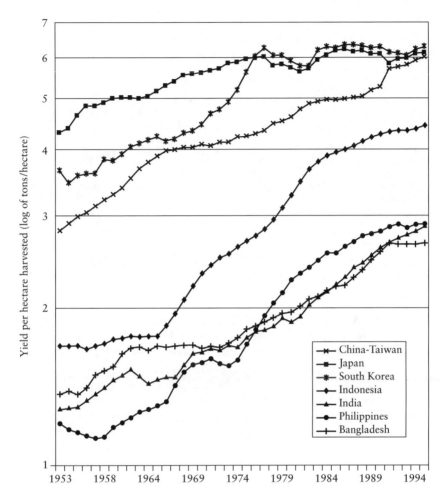

Source: IRRI (1997).

FIGURE 4.2. Rice Yields per Hectare Harvested: Selected Asian Countries, Five-year Moving Average, 1953–95 (semilogarithmic scale).

Induced Innovation Hypothesis

The process of technology transfer that resulted in the Green Revolution can be considered an innovation induced by changes in relative factor prices. The modern high-yielding varieties of rice and wheat that emerged in the tropics with the Green Revolution are similar in their strong responsiveness to fer-

TABLE 4.3

Yield Response to Nitrogen Input by Rice Varieties:
Bangladesh and Japan, Early 1960s

| | Yield (lb/acre) at the levels of nitrogen | | | | Marginal product of nitrogen $[(2) - (1)/55]$ | |
| | 95 lb/acre (1) | | 150 lb/acre (2) | | | |
Variety	Paddy	Straw	Paddy	Straw	Paddy	Straw
Habiganj[a]	4,785	7,948	4,372	10,478	−7.5	46.0
Batak[a]	5,445	9,488	5,875	11,743	7.8	41.0
Kamenoo[b]	5,417	5,500	6,077	7,617	12.0	38.5
Norin 1[c]	6,352	7,205	7,700	8,225	24.5	18.5
Norin 87[c]	5,118	6,352	6,517	7,892	25.4	28.0
Rikuu 232[c]	5,802	6,902	7,425	8,553	29.5	30.0

SOURCE: IAEA (1961, 14).
[a] Indigenous variety in Bangladesh.
[b] A variety selected by a veteran farmer, the use of which became prevalent in Japan from 1905 to 1925.
[c] A variety selected through hybridization by agricultural experiment stations in Japan after the nation-wide coordinated experiment system called "Assigned Experiment System" was established in 1926–27.

tilizer to the prototypical high-yielding varieties used in temperate zone agriculture. For the purpose of illustration Table 4.3 compares the yield response to nitrogen of indigenous rice varieties in Bangladesh with the response of some older improved varieties in Japan. The comparison shows that the indigenous varieties produce yields as high as those of the improved varieties at a low level of fertilization but respond negatively or only modestly to higher levels of fertilizer. For example, with the indigenous varieties a larger dose of fertilizer results in a larger output of straw but not of grain. On the other hand, the improved varieties fully realize their fertilizer-responsive capacity only when improved husbandry practices (for example, weed and insect control) are used to cultivate them and when there is adequate water control. Traditional varieties long survived with little fertilization under unfavorable conditions, including a precarious water supply and rampant weeds. Under such conditions the traditional varieties were an optimal technology (Jennings 1964).

The fertilizer-response curves for the traditional and the modern varieties are typically drawn as u_0 and u_1 (Figure 4.3). I assume the existence of a meta-production function U, which is the envelope of many such response curves, each representing a variety characterized by a different degree of fertilizer responsiveness. Within this function u_0 is an optimal (profit-maximizing) variety for the fertilizer-rice price ratio p_0, and u_1 is an optimum for p_1. Even if the fertilizer-rice price ratio declines from p_0 to p_1, individual farmers cannot move from A to C; they will be trapped at B unless u_1 becomes available. B is an equilibrium for a response curve u_0 that is actually available for farm-

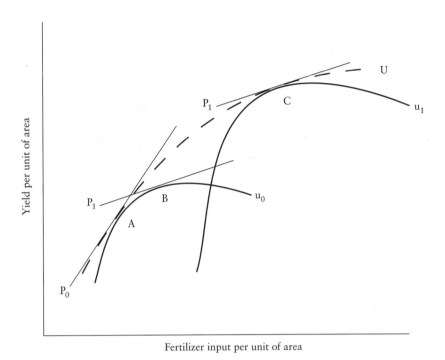

FIGURE 4.3. Shift in Fertilizer Response Curve along the Meta-Response Curve.

ers but a disequilibrium of potential alternatives described by the metaproduction function. I hypothesize that the development of a new variety u_1 will be undertaken when the benefit of adjustment from B to C exceeds the cost of developing u_1.

This hypothesis oversimplifies the situation. The location and shape of the fertilizer-response curve also depends on the conditions of water control and husbandry practices. If water supply and control are inadequate, the modern varieties will fail to show the response to fertilizer. It is possible, however, that in paddy fields with good irrigation and drainage facilities the modern varieties will produce higher yields than the traditional varieties, even at a zero level of inorganic fertilization. In such fields the efficient decomposition of organic materials and the nutrients carried by irrigation water supply significant amounts of plant nutrients. Yield response to fertilizer also depends on effective weed control because short-stalked modern varieties are more subject than traditional varieties to competition for sunlight. The competition results from the vigorous growth of weeds encouraged by the high level of fertilization. The application of herbicides and weed-preventing practices, such as check row planting, become critically important to the accurate measurement of the fertilizer-response relationships. In this formulation the fertilizer input per hectare should be regarded as an index representing the level of all inputs used with fertilizer to realize the yield potential of the modern varieties.

The choice of varieties (u_0 or u_1) depends not only on fertilizer and rice prices but also on cultural practices and the cost of water control. It is a reasonable assumption, however, that the rise in marginal productivity of fertilizer resulting from the development of the modern varieties (u_1) raises the marginal productivity of these complementary inputs. A decline in the price of fertilizer can thus play a leading role in improving the economic return on investment in developing the modern varieties, and the development of higher yielding varieties can sharply increase the return on investment in irrigation and plant protection.

Adjustments along the metaproduction function usually involve time and costs. The development of fertilizer-responsive modern varieties requires investment in research. Better husbandry practices must be developed and learned. Complementary investment in irrigation and drainage may be required to secure adequate control of water. It takes time to reorient the efforts of public agencies in response to price changes. It is particularly costly and time consuming to build adequate institutions and develop competent research staff.

These processes can be inferred from Table 4.4, which shows for Japan and four tropical Asian countries the price of fertilizers over time relative to the price of rice and the rice yield per unit of planted paddy area. The data indicate that (1) the higher rice yield in Japan than in the other four countries was associated with a considerably lower price of fertilizer than of rice; (2) in Japan an inverse association existed between the rice yield and the fertilizer-rice price ratio over time; (3) the substantial decline in the fertilizer-rice price ratios from 1955–57 to 1963–65 in the tropical Asian countries was associated with only small gains in rice yield; (4) the fertilizer-rice price ratios in those countries in 1963–65, the years immediately preceding the Green Revolution, were much more favorable than those that prevailed in Japan at the beginning of the twentieth century and earlier; and (5) significant gains in rice yield per hectare in the tropical Asian countries from 1963–65 to 1975–77 were not associated with further decreases in the fertilizer-rice price ratios.

Given the yield comparisons in Table 4.4, it seems reasonable to infer that the considerable differences in rice yields and the price ratio between Japan and the four tropical Asian countries can best be attributed to different fertilizer-response curves, as shown by u_0 and u_1 in Figure 4.3. Japan's consistent increase in rice yield accompanied by the consistent decline in the fertilizer-rice price ratio indicates a process of relatively continuous movement along the metaproduction function. The historical development of Japanese agricultural technology [including the deliberate efforts of veteran farmers to

TABLE 4.4

Fertilizer–Rice Price Ratio and Rice Yield per Hectare for Japan, 1883–1987, and for Four Tropical Asian Countries

Country and period	Currency/unit	Price of fertilizer per ton of nitrogen (1)	Price of rice per ton of milled rice[a] (2)	Fertilizer– rice price ratio (1)/(2)	Paddy yield[b] (tons/ha)
Japan					
1883–87	yen	450	42	10.7	2.6
1893–97	yen	670	69	9.7	2.6
1903–07	yen	815	106	7.7	3.1
1913–17	yen	803	125	6.4	3.5
1923–27	yen	1,021	277	3.7	3.6
1933–37	yen	566	208	2.7	3.8
1953–57	1,000 yen	113	75	1.5	4.3
1963–67	1,000 yen	100	85	1.2	5.1
1973–77	1,000 yen	125	305	0.4	5.8
1983–87	1,000 yen	179	471	0.4	6.2
Tropical Asia					
1955–57					
India	rupee	1,675	469	3.6	1.3
Indonesia	1,000 rupiah	u	u	u	1.7
Philippines	peso	962	363	2.7	1.1
Thailand	US$	393	78	5.0	1.4
1963–65					
India	rupee	1,360	708	1.9	1.5
Indonesia	1,000 rupiah	46	u	n.a	1.8
Philippines	peso	849	531	1.6	1.3
Thailand	US$	256	76	3.4	1.8
1975–77					
India	rupee	3,782	1,738	2.2	1.9
Indonesia	1,000 rupiah	162	114	1.4	2.7
Philippines	peso	2,692	1,894	1.4	1.9
Thailand	US$	523	187	2.8	1.8
1988–92					
India	rupee	5,589	3,904	1.4	2.6
Indonesia	1,000 rupiah	428	528	0.8	4.3
Philippines	peso	11,813	8,038	1.5	2.8
Thailand	US$	439	273	1.6	2.1

SOURCES: For South and Southeast countries, IRRI (1990, 1995). For Japan, Ohkawa, Shinohara, and Umemura (1966: 202–03), Kayo (1958: 514), Toyokeizaishimposha (1967: 80), IDE (1969: 136), and Japan MOAFF (various years).

u, data are unavailable.

n.a., not applicable.

[a] Wholesale price on a milled rice basis. Data for Japan are converted from a brown rice basis to a milled rice basis assuming 10% for processing cost.

[b] Data for Japan are converted from a brown rice basis to a paddy basis assuming a conversion factor of 0.8.

select and propagate superior varieties, the vigorous activities of experiment stations and other research institutions, and the remarkable shifts in rice varieties over time (Hayami and Yamada 1991)] is clearly inconsistent with an assumption of movement along a fixed production response curve, such as u_0.

When we examine the data for tropical Asia, some intriguing questions remain unanswered. Why did rice yields in the tropical Asian economies increase so slowly before the mid-1960s, despite the substantial decline in the fertilizer-rice price ratio? Why did rice yields in these countries remain at low levels despite fertilizer-rice price ratios that were more favorable than those in Japan at the beginning of the twentieth century? The answer must be sought in the time lag required to move along the metaproduction function. This time lag tends to be extremely long in situations characterized by a lack of adequate institutions and human capital needed to generate the flow of new techniques. Apparently, before 1960, even though the fertilizer-rice price ratio declined from p_0 to p_1, the countries in tropical Asia could not move from A to C in Figure 4.3 because they had not yet developed the agricultural research institutions needed to create a new technology (u_1). They seem to have been trapped at B. After agricultural research became institutionalized in the mid-1960s, their rice yields per hectare began to increase. This development is represented by the movement from B toward C in Figure 4.3.

The dramatic appearance of the modern varieties after 1965 can be interpreted in this light. The International Rice Research Institute, the University of the Philippines College of Agriculture, and the Bureau of Plant Industry in the Philippines; the Japanese plant breeders working in Malaysia under the Colombo Plan; the Indian Council of Agricultural Research; and various other national organizations and groups were working on developing modern varieties responsive to fertilizer. By the mid-1960s a number of varieties satisfying these requirements, including IR-8, C4–63, Masuri, and ADT-27, were becoming available to farmers. It now seems clear that these innovations were induced by a potentially high payoff of investment in crop-breeding research, one that would permit movement from B toward C. Indeed, even though the price of fertilizer relative to the price of rice did not decline further between 1963–65 and 1975–77, rice yields rose significantly as a result of developments in modern varieties that enabled the movement from inside to the frontier of the metaproduction function.

Because high-yielding varieties were already in existence in Japan and other temperate zone rice-producing countries before the Green Revolution began, it was possible to realize major advances in productivity with relatively modest investments in time and cost. A critical element was that the high payoff from investment in research depended on decisions by governments, international organizations, and other agencies, such as foundations and universities, to invest in research rather than on decisions made by individual firms. Except for the plantations that produce a few export commodities, the farms operated by Asian producers are too small to internalize the gains necessary to pay for research investments. It is only when public or semipublic agencies perceive this opportunity and allocate funds for such research that technological development or transfer becomes feasible.

The price of fertilizer declined relative to the price of rice during the 1950s and 1960s as a result of increased productivity in the fertilizer industries of the more developed economies. The lower cost was transmitted to less developed economies initially through international trade and later through the growth of domestic fertilizer production based on industrial technology transfer (Ghatak 1981). The modern varieties developed by crop-breeding research enabled farmers to substitute fertilizer, an increasingly abundant resource, for land, an increasingly scarce one. Had the real price of fertilizer not fallen, such research might not have been attempted. Even if it had been attempted, the results would have been incompatible with price relationships among factors and products, and the outcome would have been similar to that following earlier attempts to introduce mechanization in tropical rice production.

The increasing scarcity of land resulting from population pressure impelled the adaptive research to facilitate the transfer of agricultural technology. It is reasonable to assume that the same constraint stimulated improvements in land infrastructure. Such improvements, especially irrigation, are a precondition for successful adoption of the seed-fertilizer technology that makes sustained increases in land productivity possible. A close association between the limited supply of land and the development of land infrastructure can be seen clearly for Japan in Figure 4.4. and for the Philippines in Figure 4.5.

Although Japan was already densely populated at the beginning of its era of modern economic growth, the cultivated area could still be expanded, mainly in the northern regions of Hokkaido and Tohoku. But by around 1910, even this option had been exhausted. In a dramatic fashion the acceleration of improvement in land infrastructure coincided with the halt in the expansion of cultivated area and the land-labor ratio. The timing suggests that the Arable Land Replotment Law, passed in 1889 and revised in 1905 and 1909, prompted the acceleration in infrastructural improvement. The law required all farmers and landlords to participate in a land-improvement project if two-thirds of the landlords owning two-thirds of the land proposed for improvement agreed. This was an institutional innovation similar to the Enclosure Acts of England, which embodied the response of both the private and the public sector to the increasing scarcity of land in that country.

In the Philippines cultivated land of good quality expanded more rapidly than did the agricultural labor force in Mindanao, Visayan, and Luzon

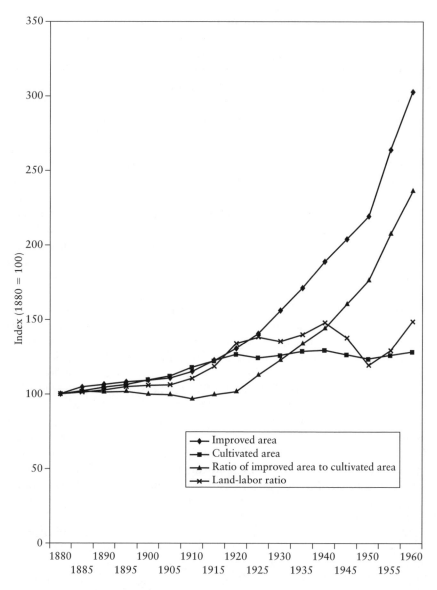

Source: Kikuchi and Hayami (1985: 77).

FIGURE 4.4. Trends in Irrigation Improvement, Cultivated Land Area, and Land-Labor Ratio: Japan, 1880–1960.

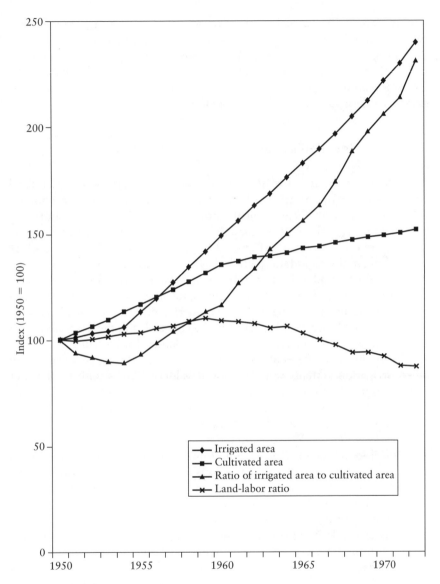

Source: Kikuchi and Hayami (1985: 77).

FIGURE 4.5. Trends in Irrigation Improvement, Cultivated Land Area, and Land-Labor Ratio: Philippines, 1950–72.

until the late 1950s. Since then, the growth rate of the cultivated area has decelerated and the land-labor ratio has declined. In contrast, irrigation development has accelerated. The process and the underlying mechanism appear to be the same in the Philippines as in Japan. During the early phase of the Green Revolution, this irrigation infrastructure facilitated the rapid diffusion of modern varieties in the Philippines.

How Replicable Is the East Asian Experience?

The innovations that led to the remarkable improvements in agricultural productivity in tropical Asia over the 1960–90 period were both technological and institutional. Technological innovations, such as the development of high-yielding varieties that adapt well to tropical environments, take time. Much more time, however, is required for institutional innovations, such as establishing national and international agricultural research systems needed to mount effective adaptive research. As we have seen, the Green Revolution did not begin in tropical Asia until some time after the relative price of fertilizers had declined, making the use of modern high-yielding varieties profitable. One would therefore expect to find a similar lag in the development of institutions for building irrigation and other land infrastructure.

Indeed, the Green Revolution progressed first in the areas of tropical Asia where irrigation systems were initially developed. Areas with poor water control, especially the floodplains of major rivers, were left behind. Recently, however, rice yields in those unfavorable areas have been catching up. This can be seen from a comparison of regions within the Indian subcontinent (Figures 4.6 and 4.7). With the rapid diffusion of modern varieties under relatively well-developed irrigation conditions, rice yields in North and South India rose sharply between the late 1960s and the 1970s. Meanwhile, eastern India and Bangladesh, lying in the Ganges delta, experienced little gain in rice yields until the late 1970s, when yields began to rise rapidly. Changes in cropping systems accelerated diffusion of modern varieties in these flood-prone areas. Modern rice varieties have also been adopted there, not so much in the traditional rice-growing season under monsoon rain but increasingly in the dry season with pump irrigation (Hossain 1993). This experience demonstrates the possibility of overcoming environmental constraints against improvements in land productivity by means of technological developments and adequate inputs that help farmers maximize their incomes from meager resources.

What is the prospect of extending this mechanism of induced technology transfer to other developing regions? Could this not be a solution to the worsening food shortages in sub-Saharan Africa? The major impediment to the exploitation of this possibility appears to be the social and institutional

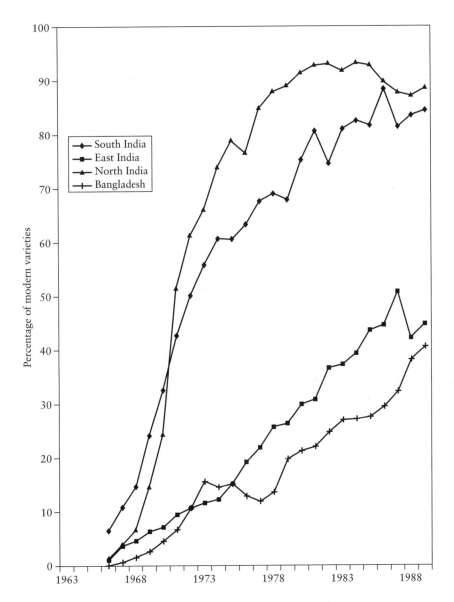

Source: IRRI (1995).

FIGURE 4.6. Percentages of Rice Areas Harvested in Modern Varieties: Bangladesh and Selected Regions of India, 1966–89 (Five-year Moving Average). North India includes Haryana and Punjab; South India includes Andhra Pradesh, Karnataka, and Tamil Nadu; East India includes Bihar, Orissa, and West Bengal.

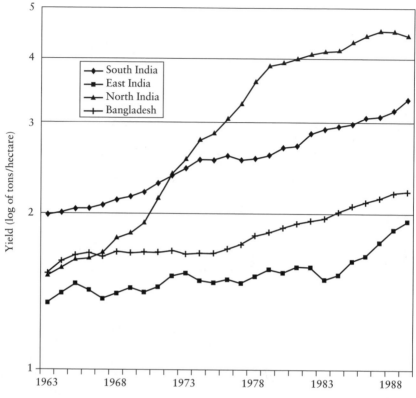

Source: IRRI (1995).

FIGURE 4.7. Average Rice Yields: Bangladesh and Selected Regions of India, 1963–89 (Five-year Moving Average). North India includes Haryana and Punjab; South India includes Andhra Pradesh, Karnataka, and Tamil Nadu; East India includes Bihar, Orissa, and West Bengal.

complex that was created under the land-abundant regime. In Africa, especially East Africa, population density has been traditionally much lower than in Asia, so that shifting cultivation and nomadic grazing have commonly been practiced. Much farmland has remained in the communal possession of tribes, and therefore the development of private property rights has been slow. Property rights facilitate long-term investments in land infrastructure.

The lag in the shift to settled agriculture in tropical Africa underlies the lag in the formation of overhead capital, such as roads and irrigation systems. According to a survey by Spencer (1994), in the 18 countries in the humid and subhumid tropics of Africa, only 2.5% of cropland was irrigated in 1987–89 (3.0% in Tanzania and Nigeria). This ratio was one-tenth of India's 25% in 1950, when India's population density was about the same as that in the surveyed areas of Africa today. Moreover, the extension of roads in most of these areas was 53 km per 100 km², less than 20% of India's 388 km per 100 km² in 1950. (In Tanzania it was 36% of India's 1950 extension, and in Nigeria it was 14%.)

Such underdeveloped infrastructure is hardly sufficient to support a Green Revolution of the Asian type, based as it was on irrigation and the supply of commercial inputs. Africa's handicap is especially pronounced because its economies, which traditionally depended on an abundance of natural resources, have suddenly become resource scarce, as in the economies of Asia. One hopeful sign is that individual peasants in Africa appear to be making efforts to shift to intensive agricultural production by investing in land infrastructure, such as terracing and the introduction of high-value commercial crops. Yet the governments of that region have not adequately supported the farmers' efforts with complementary investments (Tiffen and Mortimore 1994). The agricultural crisis in Africa, as reflected in the decrease in per capita food output between 1963 and 1993 (Table 4.2), stems from the intrinsic difficulty of creating, overnight, state and local institutions that can supply public goods. Those goods are needed to overcome the recent constraint of natural resources caused by explosive population growth (Platteau and Hayami 1996; Hayami 1997, ch. 9).

What makes this situation especially serious appears to be African governments' propensity to intervene in the markets of private goods rather than to make efforts to provide public goods that are in great social demand. Reacting to the private marketing system dominated by foreign middlemen that had prevailed before independence, many African states adopted the socialist mode of economic management, imposing strong regulations on markets. Policies frequently used to eliminate private traders from the marketing channels for agricultural commodities involved the creation of government-run monopolistic organizations called marketing boards or parastatal agencies.

These governmental intrusions into markets not only fostered inefficiency and corruption but also were a means of exploiting agriculture for the sake of promoting industrialization. The monopoly purchase of agricultural products and the monopoly sale of farm inputs by these governmental agencies exploited farmers by offering them lower product prices and charging them higher input prices than would prevail in an open market. This exploitation mechanism was augmented by policies offering protection to industries, such as overvalued exchange rates, tariffs and quotas on manufactured commodities, and export duties on agricultural commodities.

Exploiting agriculture for the sake of promoting industrialization was not unique to African states but rather a common strategy in developing countries, especially during the first 30 years after World War II (Anderson and Hayami 1986; Krueger, Schiff, and Valdes 1991). Even in Taiwan, known for its success in achieving the world's highest land productivity in agriculture as a basis of healthy industrial development, the government monopolized the supply of fertilizers and forced farmers to barter rice for fertilizers at unfavorable terms until the 1960s. It is also well known that Thailand used the export duty (called an export premium) on rice as an important source of government revenue. Nevertheless, although these Asian states exploited agriculture, they did not neglect to make necessary investments in irrigation and agricultural research to increase land productivity.

In contrast, there has been a tendency among politicians in Africa to compensate for agricultural exploitation by distributing subsidized credits and inputs to particular rural elites instead of providing public goods. According to Bates (1981, 1983), the selective distribution of such private goods ("divisible inputs" in Bates's terminology) to rural elites is more advantageous to politicians wanting to remain in office than is supplying public goods, which benefit large numbers of farmers indiscriminately. Such political behavior has led to serious underinvestments in public goods.

Why did Asian governments invest in public goods as a compensation for agricultural exploitation, whereas the dominant mode of compensation in Africa has been a selective distribution of private goods? A partial explanation may be that the rapid shift from land-abundant to land-scarce economies in Africa has not allowed rural communities enough time to develop traditions for building local infrastructure through their collective efforts or even to lobby for state provision of large-scale infrastructure. Moreover, the territorial boundaries of many African nations were determined by colonial powers with little regard for the social integrity of the indigenous populations. It is not surprising that, even after those nations gained independence, both politicians and citizens continued to identify more strongly with their own ethnic groups and communities than with their nations. What has prevailed there is a limited group morality, applicable to close acquaintances and relatives, rather than a generalized morality, applicable to the wider society (Platteau 1992, 1994a,b). Given such a social norm, politicians are more interested in maximizing the profits of the communities they belong to than in promoting the welfare of the whole nation.

The rice-growing societies of Asia seem to be different in this regard. Their densely populated, settled farm populations were traditionally the convenient base from which rulers expropriated taxes. Because peasants bore the major tax burden, an ideology of peasant fundamentalism developed that regarded them as the foundation of society. According to this view, it was legitimate for a ruler to tax away the surplus above peasants' subsistence, but in return he had to maintain their sustenance by providing such benefits as flood control and major irrigation and drainage systems (Wittfogel 1957). This tradition seems to underlie the development strategy of modern Asian states to provide public goods for agricultural development while exploiting farmers for the sake of industrial development. Examples of such exploitation are the rice-fertilizer barter system in Taiwan and the rice premium in Thailand.

This contrast between Africa and Asia is most clearly visible in a comparison of Indonesia and Nigeria as major oil exporters. Both economies experienced a major boom during the oil crises of 1973–75 and 1979–81. The strong Dutch disease effect (the negative effect of real exchange rate appreciation as a result of increased foreign exchange earnings from oil exports) nearly ruined Nigeria's agriculture. Indonesia avoided the disease by increasing its assistance to agriculture through public investment in irrigation and agricultural research. In fact, Indonesia, which had been the world's largest rice importer in the 1970s, was able to achieve rice self-sufficiency by the late 1980s by adopting modern high-yielding varieties.

This healthy development of agriculture, based on the traditional peasant fundamentalism, appears to have contributed to both economic efficiency and social stability in the early stage of East Asia's industrialization (Hayami and Ruttan 1985, ch. 13). How to create in African societies the social and political atmosphere for supporting agriculture in the absence of a peasant fundamentalist tradition is a question that must be resolved if the deteriorating trend of African economies is to be reversed (Platteau and Hayami 1996).

Beyond Early Industrial Development

A new problem faces the economies of East Asia. Now that they have passed through the stage of newly industrializing economies (NIEs), their peasant fundamentalism has become rural populism, prompting inefficient and costly agricultural protection policies.[3] Economic growth in the region has been accompanied by a rapid decline in the comparative advantage of agriculture. During the period of Japan's most rapid industrial growth, 1955–70, Japanese labor productivity in agriculture grew at a pace similar to that in North America and Western Europe, whereas Japan's labor productivity in manufacturing grew at more than twice the average rate of other industrial economies. A similar but even more extreme contrast occurred during the 1970s between South Korea and Taiwan on the one hand and North America and Western Europe on the other. The chief restraint on raising East Asia's labor productivity at a faster pace has been its small farm size. In Japan, South Korea, and Taiwan the average farm size is still only a little more than 1 hectare. This small size severely limits the scope of mechanization to substitute capital for labor.

Adjusting the agrarian structure to the new labor-saving and scale-biased technology in ways that are consistent with a high-wage economy seems to be the most serious problem of agricultural adjustment facing East Asia. A major impediment to this adjustment in Japan, South Korea, and Taiwan has been land tenure regulations that have been in effect since the postwar land reforms. Although the regulations have been relaxed gradually in recent years, they still strongly protect tenants' rights, making it almost impossible for landlords to evict tenants. In addition, land rent has been controlled at a low level, giving landowners little incentive to lease out their holdings. As a result, nonfarmers who inherit land tend to hold on to it and farm it on a part-time basis, even inefficiently, rather than lease it out. Ironically, it was these relatively egalitarian structures, now the major checks on structural adjustment, that facilitated the diffusion of the labor-intensive, land-saving, and scale-neutral technology in the earlier low-wage economies of the region.

Shifts of comparative advantage away from agriculture in Japan, South Korea, and Taiwan during their rapid industrial development required a major adjustment in intersectoral resource allocations. If this adjustment had been left to the market mechanism, its cost would have been shouldered mainly by the agricultural population in such forms as rural-urban income disparity and the depopulation of rural communities. Increases in the cost of adjustment led agricultural producers to demand agricultural trade protection and programs supporting farm prices and incomes. Concurrently, the resistance of the nonagricultural population to the policies protecting agriculture declined. Food costs as a share of urban household expenditure fell appreciably because of rises in wages and income per capita, thereby reducing the influence of food prices on the cost of living. The secular decline in agriculture's share of national income, employment, and consumption made it less burdensome for the nonagricultural population to support domestic agricultural producers through high food prices or direct subsidies.

The increasing demand for and the decreasing resistance to policies protecting agriculture have resulted in sharp increases in the level of agricultural protection in East Asia, as measured by the rates at which producer (domestic) prices exceed border (international) prices, shown in Table 4.5. The nominal rate of agricultural protection for Japan in 1955 was only 18%, which was considerably lower than the average for the countries that later formed the European Community (EC). It rose rapidly, reaching the EC level in 1960 and the Swiss level in 1965. (The Swiss level is exceptionally high for reasons of national security and environmental conservation protecting Alpine tourism.) Similar but even more dramatic changes occurred in South Korea and Taiwan between 1965 and 1980. In 1965 their nominal rates of agricultural protection were still negative, reflecting their policies of exploiting agriculture, which are typical of economies in the early stage of economic development. During the subsequent 15 years, their levels of agricultural protection rose sharply, surpassing the EC level and reaching a level broadly comparable with that of Japan after 1980.

Such high rates of protection result in significant losses in domestic welfare and create serious international friction. Japan has been under strong

TABLE 4.5

Nominal Rates of Agricultural Protection (%): 3 Northeast Asian Countries and 11 Other Developed Countries, 1955–90[a]

Region and country	1955	1960	1965	1970	1975	1980	1985	1990
Northeast Asia								
Japan	18	41	69	74	76	85	108	116
South Korea	−46	−15	−4	29	30	117	110	151
Taiwan	−17	−3	−1	2	20	52	31	55
European Community								
Denmark	5	3	5	17	19	25	34	44
France	33	26	30	47	29	30	37	54
Germany (West)	35	48	55	50	39	44	40	46
Italy	47	50	66	69	38	57	72	103
Netherlands	14	21	35	41	32	27	38	26
United Kingdom	40	37	20	27	6	35	39	44
Average[b]	35	37	45	52	29	38	43	54
Nonaligned Europe								
Sweden	34	44	50	65	43	59	65	79
Switzerland	60	64	73	96	96	126	181	218
Food exporters								
Australia	5	7	5	7	−5	−2	−7	−4
Canada	0	4	2	−5	−4	2	0	4
United States	2	1	9	11	4	0	11	3

SOURCE: Honma (1994: 62).

[a]The rate of agricultural protection is defined as the percentage by which the producer price exceeds the international (border) price. The estimates shown are the weighted averages for 12 commodities, with production valued at border prices as the weight. The 12 commodities are rice, wheat, barley, corn, oats, rye, beef, pork, chicken, eggs, milk, and sugar.

[b]Weighted average for all six countries shown for 1975, 1980, 1985, and 1990 but excluding Denmark and the United Kingdom for earlier years.

pressure to liberalize its agricultural trade. The pressure has come not only from major food exporters in North America and Australia but also from developing countries that produce silk, sugar, and other tropical products. Likewise, pressure has been mounting on South Korea and Taiwan as their importance in the world economy has continued to grow. That pressure is becoming more difficult to ignore, given the increasing integration of the world economy, as epitomized by the formation of the World Trade Organization.

An important final point is that the agricultural protection practiced by East Asian countries has risen to the highest level in the world not because they have a unique bias for preserving domestic agriculture but because their comparative advantage shifted from agriculture to industry so rapidly that they may not have been able to overcome the social and political obstacles to intersectoral resource adjustments without imposing protection (Anderson and Hayami 1986). East Asia's experience is likely to be duplicated in the densely populated, resource-poor developing economies of South and

Southeast Asia as they follow Northeast Asia in their economic development and overcome the overriding problem of poverty. If that happens, the diffusion of agricultural protectionism throughout Asia may become a major hindrance to international economic order. It is yet to be seen whether the Asia-Pacific Economic Cooperation agreement of 1994, intended to eliminate trade barriers within the region by 2020, will be able to counteract the rise of agricultural protectionism.

II. SAVING AND INVESTMENT

The Accumulation and Demography Connection in East Asia

JEFFREY G. WILLIAMSON AND MATTHEW HIGGINS

EVERY ANALYST KNOWS that the East Asian economic miracle has been accompanied by high and rising saving and investment rates. Indeed, Krugman (1994b) likened the past quarter-century in East Asia to Soviet-style development, wherein massive saving rates generate accumulation rates so rapid that diminishing returns are bound to set in soon. Oddly enough, few recent analysts have noted that the region has also undergone a demographic transition so dramatic that it may help to account for the accumulation miracle. This state of affairs seems even more peculiar given that Coale and Hoover (1958) predicted these events nearly 40 years ago.

The Coale-Hoover thesis is simple enough: High fertility combined with falling infant mortality creates economies full of households and governments burdened with high (child) dependency rates, which are therefore unable to save more than a small share of their household incomes or tax revenues. Symmetry suggests that low dependency rates ought to be associated with high savings. Although the hypothesis has had its empirical ups and downs since 1958, nobody seems to disagree that it has had its greatest success in Asia and that postwar experience in the region offers the greatest variance in the demographic variables that matter most to the hypothesis. In this chapter we use that experience to say something about accumulation during

We acknowledge with pleasure the research assistance of Ben Dennis, Taku Imagawa, and Suny Lay. In addition, we acknowledge helpful comments by David Bloom, Allen Kelley, Ron Lee, Peter Lindert, Andy Mason, Jonathan Morduch, Jeffrey Sachs, Alan Taylor, Peter Timmer, and participants at the Conference on Population and the East Asian Economic Miracle (East-West Center, Honolulu, January 7–10, 1997), where an earlier version of this chapter was presented.

the recent high performance of East Asian economies and about the region's future.

The literature on the dependency-rate hypothesis died out in the mid-1970s, but it underwent a revival in the mid-1980s. The newer, and better, literature still has three surprising limitations, however. First, typically the research stops after testing the hypothesis. Rarely does the researcher take the next step and ask how much of the changes in saving rates over time or of their differences across countries can be explained by changes or differences in dependency rates. Second, critics of the dependency-rate hypothesis use steady-state analysis to attack a thesis that was derived to confront a problem of transitional dynamics. Proponents fail to counter that steady-state analysis is not only irrelevant but also misleading. Third, and perhaps most important, this literature has focused almost exclusively on domestic savings. Rarely has anyone asked whether dependency rates (or other demographic variables correlated with them) might have a significant impact on domestic investment. Hardly ever has anyone explored the effect of these demographic events on excess investment demand and thus on net capital inflows. Indeed, as Taylor and Williamson (1994) argued when explaining the massive late-nineteenth-century capital flows out of demographically old Europe and into the demographically young New World, one may view the East Asian capital inflow between the 1950s and the 1970s as an intergenerational transfer from older foreigners to younger East Asians. One may also view the capital outflow from East Asia projected into the twenty-first century as an intergenerational transfer from older East Asians to younger South Asians and Africans.

In this chapter we seek answers to such questions as the following: How much of the impressive rise in East Asian saving rates during East Asia's economic transformation can be explained by the impressive decline in dependency burdens rather than by policy or by culture? Have changing dependency rates had a bigger impact on investment or on savings? How much of the decline in external capital dependency in East Asia since the 1970s can be explained by the same demographic forces? Will the young Southeast Asian tigers become net capital exporters by the year 2025 as they fill up with productive adults? What will happen to savings and investment when the old Northeast Asian tigers begin to fill up with retired adults?

We need to add two warnings about what this chapter will not do. The first warning is that it does not undertake a comprehensive survey. The literature already contains many surveys of Third World saving and investment, the most recent additions being those offered by Deaton (1989) and by the World Bank and Inter-American Bank team of Schmidt-Hebbel, Serven, and Solimano (1996). Asia gets the attention it deserves in those two publications, but there have been other surveys that have focused solely on Asian accumulation issues [for example, Fry (1984, 1991), Abbott (1985), and Dowling and Lahiri (1990)].

The second warning has to do with the distinction one needs to make between long-run fundamentals and short-run timing when accounting for capital flows. Capital flows to Asia and the rest of the Third World have moved in fits and starts since the early 1970s.[1] The boom in that decade preceded a debt crisis and a bust. The 1980s were slow to recover the big flows, but the first half of the 1990s recorded another impressive surge in capital flows. A recent survey by Calvo, Leiderman, and Reinhart (1996) explored the causes of the 1990–94 boom [see also Calvo, Leiderman, and Reinhart (1993, 1994a,b) and Sachs and Larrain (1993)]. Their list of causes (pp. 126–28) includes a sustained decline in world interest rates; a recession among the older industrialized nations belonging to the Organisation for Economic Co-operation and Development (OECD) that raised the relative attractiveness of investment opportunities in the Third World; a trend toward diversification in major financial markets; significant progress by heavily indebted countries toward improving relations with external creditors; the adoption of sound monetary and fiscal policies in many recipient countries, yielding sound real exchange rates; and the adoption of market-oriented reforms in many recipient countries, reforms that have included capital market liberalization. The last of these causes is important because it reinforces the gradual late-twentieth-century evolution toward policies that have allowed domestic capital markets to become more fully integrated with world capital markets. The other causes seem to deal with short-run factors, the business cycle, or proxies for more fundamental forces. Most items on the list seem to have little to do with underlying economic and demographic fundamentals. Our interest is with those long-run fundamentals.

In the next section we survey the evidence on the evolution of the dependency rate in East Asia and confirm that there was a demographic revolution somewhere around the 1950s. We show that the revolution has had a large exogenous component; that is, it was not driven by the region's economic success. We also assess the magnitude of the dependency-rate changes by comparing them with the experience of countries in other regions at comparable stages of development. In the third section we document the evolution of domestic savings, investment, and foreign capital flows as shares of gross domestic product (GDP). All three appear to have been at least crudely correlated with the evolution of dependency burdens over time and across regions in East Asia. In the fourth section we briefly review the theory relevant to the dependency-rate debate, and in the fifth section we report new research on the effects of dependency-rate changes on Asian savings, investment, and thus net capital flows. We then use these findings to identify the role of dependency rates in accounting for changes in East Asian savings, investment, and capital flows since the 1950s. In the final section we explore the likely role of dependency rates in shaping changes by the year 2025.

A Revolutionary Change in East Asian Dependency Rates

Coale and Hoover (1958) argued that the sharp decline in Asia's infant mortality rates implied a huge future increase in its youth dependency rate, especially if reinforced by the persistence of high birth rates. They were correct, of course. With only one precocious exception (Japan), East Asia's populations surged to peak youth dependency rates in the 1960s and 1970s (Table 5.1). The modal country peaked in the 1960s. As is well known, these dependency rates and cohort shares are highly correlated with other demographic variables, such as the population growth rate and the number of children per household. They are so closely correlated, in fact, that we concentrate on cohort shares in the discussion that follows and use poetic license by calling them dependency rates. We also define East Asia to include Southeast Asia, stretching southeastward from Thailand to Indonesia and up to South Korea. To help distinguish between leaders and followers in the region, we define Northeast Asia to include Japan, South Korea, Taiwan, Hong Kong, and Singapore (the last deserving that status by performance rather than by location). China is treated separately. The Southeast Asian countries considered here are Indonesia, Malaysia, the Philippines, and Thailand.

In none of these countries did the elderly dependency rate matter until recently. The future influence of this rate was only hinted at by the region's economic and demographic leader, Japan, when her share of the population age 65 and older began to rise noticeably in the 1970s. With this exception, increases in the elderly share have had a modest impact on Asia in the twentieth century, because that group is still small compared with the young and working-age populations. The elderly dependency rate, however, will assume paramount relevance to the older East Asian tigers as they enter the twenty-first century.

The youth dependency rates, or cohort shares, were much higher in developing East Asia than they were in the developed countries during their period of demographic transition. Although the industrialized countries' youth share averaged about 26% during the baby boom in the 1950s, the peak rates in East Asia were in most cases 15–20 percentage points higher. Three of the most extreme Northeast Asian examples are South Korea (42.8%), Taiwan (45.2%), and Singapore (43.5%). All four of the Southeast Asian countries in our sample appear at the top of these peak ranges (42–46%). The youth dependency burden was also far higher in East Asia at its late-twentieth-century peak than it was in Europe at its nineteenth-century peak (Taylor and Williamson 1994, Table A1). This period of high youth depen-

TABLE 5.1

Dependency Rates (%) in East Asia during the Second Half
of the Twentieth Century

Region and country	Period of peak youth dependency and recent period	Age group			Change to peak[a]	Change from peak
		Young (0–14)	Prime (25–59)	Old (65+)		
Northeast Asia						
Japan	1950–54	34.7	38.0	5.1	0	−16.7
	1990–92	18.0	48.9	12.4		
South Korea	1965–69	42.8	34.6	3.3	+2.0	−18.0
	1990–92	24.8	47.3	5.0		
Taiwan	1960–64	45.2	34.8	2.6	+0.9	−18.8
	1990–92	26.4	45.5	6.5		
Singapore	1960–64	43.5	35.0	2.4	+2.5	−20.2
	1990–92	23.3	51.8	5.9		
China	1965–69	40.0	35.5	4.4	+5.0	−13.6
	1990–92	26.4	43.6	6.0		
Hong Kong	1960–64	40.7	40.9	3.0	+8.3	−20.6
	1990–92	20.1	50.8	9.3		
Southeast Asia						
Thailand	1965–69	46.2	31.4	3.0	+3.6	−14.7
	1990–92	31.5	40.6	4.1		
Indonesia	1970–74	42.2	34.4	3.1	+3.1	−7.3
	1990–92	34.9	37.6	4.1		
Malaysia	1960–64	45.6	31.8	3.3	+4.1	−7.7
	1990–92	38.0	37.2	3.8		
Philippines	1965–69	45.2	30.7	2.8	+1.3	−5.6
	1990–92	39.6	35.3	3.4		

SOURCES: UN DESIPA (1991) and Higgins and Williamson (1996, Table 2).
[a] Percentage change between the earliest date, usually 1950–54, and the period of peak youth dependency.

dency during the 1950s and 1960s must have created an economic burden for East Asia because those youths did not save or work.

Table 5.1 also documents an enormous decline in East Asian youth dependency rates from peak to the present, a decline that was matched by a rise in the share of working adults. Some of these declines in youth dependency have been spectacular, creating a demographic gift in the form of working and saving adults. Perhaps the gift was large enough to help account for a good share of the ensuing economic growth, at least in Northeast Asia. The biggest percentage point declines have occurred in Southeast Asia. This decline in youth dependency was compressed into two or three decades, only half the time it took most late-nineteenth-century industrializing countries to record even less spectacular reductions (Taylor and Williamson 1994, Table A1). Even by historical standards, the changes in East Asian dependency rates in the late twentieth century have been revolutionary, consistent with the region's miraculous economic growth.

Another way of assessing the gift that these demographic events have given East Asia since the 1960s is to compare the growth rate of the dependent population (those who do not work or save) with the growth rate of the economically active population (those who work and save). The annual growth rates presented in Table 5.2 show how enormous the Northeast Asian advantage has been. Although it is true that every region but Africa had a favorable balance between the growth rates of the active and dependent populations, the difference between the favorable balance in Northeast Asia (2.14%) and the rest of the developing world was very large: It was almost double that of Southeast Asia, more than 3 times that of Latin America, and almost 4 times that of South Asia.

How did these unusually favorable demographic events contribute to East Asia's economic success after the 1960s? The answer depends on what forces were driving the demographic events. To the extent that they were driven by imported foreign health technologies, which lowered infant mortality rates dramatically in the early postwar period, the subsequent dependency-rate evolution can be treated as a favorable exogenous force that made an independent contribution to East Asia's economic transformation. Supporting this argument is the fact that most of the postwar decline in Asia's infant and child mortality rates occurred long before the economic transformation began to affect living standards. The argument that the demographic transition made an independent contribution to East Asia's economic transformation is strengthened when we add the evidence suggesting that strong government commitments to family planning programs were instrumental in lowering (over time) East Asian fertility (see Chapter 16). To the extent that the fertility decline was driven instead by improved labor market opportunities for mothers and their children as a result of the economic transformation, the independent contribution of these demographic events is lessened. Similarly, to the extent that the fall in infant mortality was driven by improvements in nutrition as a result of the region's phenomenal economic growth, these spectacular demographic events would have made a more modest indepen-

TABLE 5.2

Annual Population Growth Rates (%) by Region: 1965–90

Region	Active population	Dependent population	Difference
Northeast Asia	2.39	0.25	+2.14
Southeast Asia	2.90	1.66	+1.24
South Asia	2.51	1.95	+0.56
Africa	2.78	2.85	−0.07
Europe	0.68	0.15	+0.53
Latin America	2.64	1.77	+0.87

SOURCE: Bloom and Williamson (1997, Table 3.1).

dent contribution. In these last two cases the demographic events would be partially endogenous, generated by the economic growth itself. The evidence seems to support the thesis that the contributions made by health technology and family planning programs to the demographic transition were exogenous, and that fact inspires our confidence in the hypothesis that a significant part of the East Asian economic miracle was driven by favorable and independent demographic events. For a review of the evidence supporting this view, see Bloom and Williamson (1997).

How does East Asia look today? Column 1 of Table 5.3 reports the evidence for 1990–92. This time the figures are given for the prime age group (ages 25–59). The rich city-states of Hong Kong and Singapore are most favored, with slightly more than half of their populations in prime ages. Japan, South Korea, and Taiwan are close behind. Southeast Asia lags behind its more demographically advanced neighbors, with more than 16 percentage points separating Singapore and the Philippines.

Now let us consider the demographic future. The United Nations projections in Table 5.3 imply considerable demographic convergence up to 2025. The prime-age share will rise in Southeast Asia, by about 12 percentage points in Indonesia, Malaysia, and the Philippines. The prime-age share will fall in the richest parts of Asia, the canonical case being Japan, whose share will fall by 5.3 percentage points. Except for China, where the share in the prime ages will rise by 6.7 percentage points, the gap between rich Northeast Asia and

TABLE 5.3

Actual and Projected Prime-age Shares (%): East Asia, 1990–2025

Region and country	1990–92	2005	2025	Change, 1990–2025
Northeast Asia				
Japan	48.9	47.6	43.6	−5.3
South Korea	47.3	53.6	49.5	+2.2
Taiwan	45.3	51.6	46.2	+0.9
Singapore	51.8	53.4	45.0	−6.8
China	43.6	50.0	50.4	+6.7
Hong Kong	50.8	u	u	u
Southeast Asia				
Thailand	40.6	48.8	48.9	+8.3
Indonesia	37.6	44.1	49.5	+11.9
Malaysia	37.2	41.7	49.2	+12.0
Philippines	35.3	39.9	47.5	+12.2
Northeast–Southeast[a]	11.1	7.9	−2.7	−13.8

SOURCES: UN DESIPA (1991) for all countries except Taiwan; for Taiwan, the data come from Andrew Mason (personal communication, 1998).

u, data are unavailable.

[a]In the range reported for this row, Northeast excludes China, and the averages are unweighted [see Higgins and Williamson (1996, Table 3)].

poor but catching-up Southeast Asia will be completely erased. Most of that demographic catching-up will occur over the two decades from 2005 to 2025.

In the rest of this chapter we provide a quantitative assessment of how the revolutionary change in East Asian dependency rates has spilled over onto domestic saving rates, investment shares, accumulation responses, and foreign capital flows. We also assess the effects of the equally revolutionary demographic changes expected over the coming decades.

East Asian Savings, Investment, and Foreign Capital Dependency since the 1950s

Table 5.4 reports the GDP shares for domestic savings, investment, and net capital flows for Northeast and Southeast Asia. We use the current account balance (CAB) to measure capital flows, negative numbers implying net inflows and dependency on foreign capital.

The (unweighted) regional averages show that the investment rate has boomed almost everywhere in East Asia since the early 1950s, rising by an impressive 12.8 percentage points in Northeast Asia and by an even steamier 20.7 percentage points in Southeast Asia. Despite this enormous surge in investment rates, Northeast Asia has been outgrowing foreign capital dependence since the 1950s, with the CAB share falling from −4.9% in 1955–59 to 2.4% in 1990–92, for a total fall of 7.3 percentage points. Southeast Asia, however, has outgrown foreign capital dependence much more slowly and less markedly—a delayed weaning from foreign capital dependence, if you will, consistent with the more spectacular investment boom there.

It is worth noting that the countries that have been most successful in shaking off the foreign capital dependency habit since the early 1970s also seem to be the ones that have undergone the most dramatic decline in dependency rates. They are all in Northeast Asia: South Korea, Singapore, Taiwan, and even China [country-specific details are given by Higgins and Williamson (1996, Table 4)]. Japan achieved a rise in the CAB share, but it was more modest. Japan, however, has been unique in Asia to the extent that its rise in the share of elderly partly offset the fall in the youth share.

South Korea's recent history illustrates the classic correlation between dependency rates and dependency on foreign capital. In the early 1970s South Korea was concerned about its heavy dependence on Japanese financing and commissioned World Bank papers to explore why Korea saved so little (Williamson 1979). By the late 1980s South Korea had doubled its saving rate, and its CAB share had swung from −8% in 1970–74 to 3.2%. Over the same period the dependency rate fell by more than 12 percentage points, and at least one analyst (Kang 1994) argued persuasively that the correlation is not spurious.

TABLE 5.4

Savings, Investment, and Net Capital Flows as Percentage Shares of GDP: East Asia, 1950–92[a]

Region and period	Savings	Investment	Current account balance
Northeast Asia			
1950–54		18.0	
1955–59	13.9	18.8	−4.9
1960–64	18.3	23.5	−4.6
1965–69	24.0	25.1	−3.4
1970–74	29.0	28.5	−1.4
1975–79	29.6	30.0	−0.7
1980–84	28.6	29.1	+0.1
1985–89	34.0	28.3	+5.3
1990–92	35.0	30.8	+2.4
Southeast Asia			
1950–54	13.2	13.9	−2.0
1955–59	15.5	14.1	+1.4
1960–64	15.4	15.6	−0.3
1965–69	16.2	19.0	−2.8
1970–74	22.3	26.5	−4.2
1975–79	26.8	29.7	−2.9
1980–84	27.2	32.4	−5.3
1985–89	28.3	28.2	+0.1
1990–92	32.6	34.6	−2.0

[a]Unweighted country averages. For population-weighted averages, see Higgins and Williamson (1996, Table 5).

The Life-Cycle Model and the Debate over the Dependency Rate

Coale and Hoover (1958) based their dependency hypothesis on a simple but powerful intuition: that rapid population growth from falling infant mortality and stable fertility swells the ranks of dependent young and that this demographic event increases consumption requirements at the expense of savings. A decade later, Leff (1969) placed the youth dependency hypothesis on solid empirical footing. Later research by Goldberger (1973), Ram (1982), and others failed to confirm the dependency hypothesis and thus cast doubt on the validity of the empirical methods used in the earlier studies.

   Theoretical developments also seemed to shake the foundations of the dependency hypothesis. The life-cycle models developed in the 1960s held that the national saving rate should *increase* with faster population growth. The reason is simple, at least in those models: Faster population growth tilts the age distribution toward young saving households and away from older dissaving ones. The elaboration of the representative agent in Solow's neo-classical growth model pointed in the same direction, indicating that faster population growth raised saving rates in response to augmented investment demand (Solow 1956; Phelps 1968).

However, the growth models just mentioned failed to deal with the dynamics implied by the demographic transition studied by Coale and Hoover (1958). The age tilt in many steady-state models arises because they describe a world restricted to working adults and retired elderly dependents; a different tilt would result if they also acknowledged the existence of youth dependency. Similarly, the older neoclassical growth models assume fixed labor participation rates and, by implication, no change in the dependency rate. That is exactly what one would assume in a model of steady-state behavior, but it is completely inconsistent with the facts of demographic change. To obtain elegant solutions, the modelers sacrificed the rich population dynamics implicit in Coale and Hoover's predictions about the Asian demographic *transition*. This is too high a price to pay for elegance if, as a consequence, they give us the wrong answers.

In the 1980s Fry and Mason (1982) and Mason (1987b, 1988) addressed the tension between the dependency rate and the life-cycle model. These researchers developed what they called a variable rate-of-growth effect model to link youth dependency and national saving rates. Their new model rests on the premise that a decline in the youth dependency rate may induce changes in the *timing* of life-cycle consumption. If consumption is shifted from child rearing to later non-child-rearing stages of the life cycle, aggregate savings rise with a strength that depends directly on the growth rate of national income. As a result, the model argues that the saving rate depends on the *product* of the youth dependency ratio and the growth rate of national income (the growth-tilt effect) and on the dependency ratio itself (the level effect).

Under the aegis of this new model and supported by better data, the dependency hypothesis has enjoyed something of a renaissance. Drawing on a cross-section of about 50 countries, Mason (1988) isolated a negative relationship between youth dependency and saving rates after controlling for the interactive effect of dependency and income growth. Collins (1991) reported similar results using the variable rate-of-growth effect model to study saving rates for a smaller cross-section of developing countries. Taylor and Williamson (1994) applied it to a century of saving behavior in Canada, Australia, and Argentina, finding evidence pointing to demographic origins of these massive late-nineteenth-century capital flows. Kelley and Schmidt (1996) offered evidence supporting the strong effects of the dependency rate on savings in Asia. In Chapter 6 of this volume, Lee, Mason, and Miller provide further support for that thesis.

Older skepticism, illustrated by the reviews by Hammer (1986) and Kelley (1988a), is giving way to a more supportive position illustrated by the more recent studies cited here. Despite their empirical successes, however, we believe that the literature does not quite yet provide the comprehensive framework needed to understand the link between East Asian demographic change on the one hand and accumulation and foreign capital dependency on the other. The literature focuses exclusively on the link between dependency and savings, pretty much ignoring the determinants of investment. [An exception is the recent work of Auerbach and Kotlikoff (1992) and Higgins (1998), which shows that these demographic transition effects are important determinants of investment demand.] Domestic saving is independent of investment only under the unrealistic assumption of perfect international capital mobility, that is, for a small, open economy facing an exogenous world interest rate. Under any other assumption the observed saving rate depends on both domestic savings supply and investment demand [see, for example, Feldstein and Horioka (1980), Obstfeld (1986), Feldstein and Bacchetta (1991), and Frankel (1991)]. By abstracting from demographic influences on investment demand, the literature provides no guidance concerning the effects of demographic change on the residual, net capital flows.

To confront these issues, we sketch a simple neoclassical growth model, inhabited by a population with overlapping generations. The details can be found elsewhere (Higgins and Williamson 1996, 1997a). The model admits demographic effects on both savings supply and investment demand, and through the use of simulation we are able to study the evolution of these variables outside a steady state. Our model should be viewed as a generalization of the dependency-rate models that are increasingly dominating the literature. Indeed, we regard this model as describing an open-economy steady state of our own.

The Model in Brief

The model's demographic structure allows for three periods of life: youth, the prime of life, and old age. We assume that prime-age adults care about the welfare of their dependent offspring but that elderly adults have no bequest motive. Labor income is divided among current consumption, child support, and savings for old age.

The capital intensity of production depends on the extent to which an economy is linked to the international capital market. We consider the polar cases of perfect and zero international capital mobility as bounds. In the perfect capital mobility case domestic residents can borrow and lend in the international capital market as much as they wish at a given world interest rate. This condition fixes domestic capital intensity and, given the working-age population, the aggregate capital stock. Prime-age adults lend in the international capital market when their savings are greater than the value of the capital stock required for the next period, and they borrow when the opposite is the case. In contrast, if the economy is closed to capital flows, domestic savings supply and investment demand must be equal, with the marginal product of capital equated to the marginal rate of substitution in consumption between the two periods of adult life. In what follows we discuss the model's implications for the effects of demographic change under partial capital mobility, arguably the most relevant case for East Asia since the 1950s.

The Steady State

For an open economy, given constant fertility, savings will assume the following steady-state values as a share of GDP:

$$s(n^*) = \bar{s}(n^*)\frac{w(k^*)}{f(k^*)}\left(1 - \frac{1}{n^*g}\right), \tag{5.1}$$

where $\bar{s}(n^*)$ is saving as a share of labor income, n is the rate of population or labor force growth (population growth and labor force growth being the same in this steady state), k is the capital-labor ratio, and $(g - 1)$ is the exogenous rate of technical progress. Thus population growth affects the saving rate through two distinct channels. It boosts savings by increasing the population of prime-age adults relative to elderly dissaving adults; this effect is captured by the term $1 - (1/n^*g)$. At the same time, higher population growth lowers savings by increasing the youth dependency burden; this effect is captured by the term $\bar{s}(n^*)$, with $\bar{s}'(n^*) < 0$.[2]

The principal insight of the model's variable rate-of-growth effect is confirmed: Lower youth dependency may increase the saving rate but only for a rapidly growing economy. Moreover, the result sheds light on the effects of changes in both the youth and elderly dependency ratios. The condition is more likely to be satisfied for a country experiencing rapid population growth, with a decline in population growth raising savings by reducing the youth dependency burden. The condition is more likely to be violated for a country experiencing slow population growth, with a decline lowering the saving rate by increasing the elderly share.

The steady-state investment rate is given by

$$i(n^*) = (n^*g - 1)\frac{k^*}{f(k^*)}, \tag{5.2}$$

and faster population growth always leads to an increase in the investment rate. Thus, for a rapidly growing economy, higher steady-state fertility brings a lower saving rate but a higher investment rate, creating a tendency toward current account deficits. For a slow-growth economy both savings and investment increase. It can be shown, however, that the higher investment effect dominates (at least in the neighborhood of the steady state), so that higher fertility always reduces the CAB.

For the closed economy savings supply and investment demand must be equal. Under these extreme conditions, higher fertility brings an increase in the saving rate when

$$n^*g + (n^*g - 1)\lambda_L\varepsilon_{k,n} > 0, \tag{5.3}$$

where λ_L is labor's income share and $\varepsilon_{k,n}$ is the elasticity of steady-state capital intensity with respect to population growth. This elasticity is always negative so long as higher interest rates do not lower savings. The closed-economy model thus allows for the possibility that the saving (and investment) rate may fall with an increase in fertility, in effect generalizing the basic insight of the variable rate-of-growth effect model to a closed-economy setting.

Transitional Dynamics

Although the steady-state analysis is suggestive, it leaves a notable gap: the behavior of savings and investment outside the steady state. This gap is especially unfortunate, given our belief that the large swings in savings and investment observed in East Asia since the 1950s are due primarily to transitional dynamics. We rely on simulations to facilitate the dynamic analysis of empirically plausible patterns of demographic change. A simulated demographic transition, in which infant mortality falls for several generations before returning to a new lower steady-state level, provides an attractive experiment because such a pattern roughly describes the demographic history of all nations in East Asia. In Chapter 6 Lee, Mason, and Miller use an alternative approach to simulating saving that confirms the analysis provided here.

Suppose that the economy follows a steady-state growth path up to period $t - 1$ and then experiences rising fertility — or falling infant mortality (it makes no difference in the simulation)—over periods t and $t + 1$ (Figure 5.1). Fertility declines gradually during the subsequent periods, returning to its previous level by $t + 3$ and falling to a new and lower steady-state value by $t + 4$. As a result, the population's age distribution follows a cyclical pattern, reaching its new steady state at $t + 5$. The share of dependent young rises sharply during t and $t + 1$, declining gradually in the following periods. The share of prime-age adults falls at first but then rises for a time past its new, higher steady-state level. The share of elderly declines for the first three generations before rising for the following three generations. The time paths followed by savings and investment are simulated according to a set of plausible parameter values guided by the econometrics we present later.

For an open economy saving falls at the beginning of the transition in response to the increased dependency burden but follows the prime-age population upward during the two succeeding generations, declining gradually thereafter. Investment jumps during the initial generations of the transition

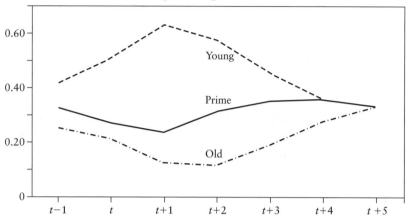

Population Age Distribution

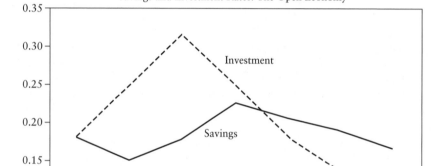

Savings and Investment Rates: The Open Economy

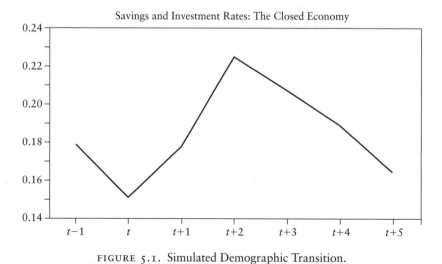

Savings and Investment Rates: The Closed Economy

FIGURE 5.1. Simulated Demographic Transition.

($t - 1$ to $t + 1$) in response to higher labor force growth; and it follows the downward path of fertility during the subsequent periods, reaching a new, lower steady state at $t + 4$. The CAB follows the path implied by the evolution of saving and investment, moving into deficit for t through $t + 2$ but swinging into surplus by $t + 3$. The surplus declines thereafter, but even so, the CAB remains positive in the new steady state, because investment falls more sharply than saving.

How would a closed economy respond to similar demographic shocks? Saving (and hence investment) falls in response to the initial fertility increase, but it rises over the next two generations in response to the increasing prime-age and declining elderly shares. After its initial rise, however, the saving rate declines over several generations to a new, lower steady-state level that reflects the diminished pace of labor force growth. Even so, rapid labor force growth during the middle generations of the transition ($t + 1$ and $t + 2$) causes a prolonged rise in the marginal product of capital and hence in interest rates; these variables attain lower values in the new steady state. It should be noted that demographic shocks in a closed economy may cause shifts in savings supply and investment demand that are at least partly offsetting, muting the amplitude of any change in the equilibrium quantity. Thus the quantitative swing in the saving rate is much smaller for the closed economy than for the open economy modeled in Figure 5.1. (Note that the graphs for the open and closed economies in Figure 5.1 have different values along the vertical axis.) This important result is consistent with the simultaneous appearance of openness and high saving rates in the East Asian economies, which has not been the case in South Asia, Latin America, or other parts of the Third World.[3]

These simulation results offer two principal lessons. First, simple patterns of demographic change may induce complex and even counterintuitive saving dynamics. After all, for both the open- and closed-economy models the saving rate rises between t and $t + 1$ even though the youth dependency ratio rises and prime-age share falls, a pattern made possible by the fact that the elderly share is falling even more quickly. This observation highlights the need to make use of all the information contained in the population age distribution, rather than focusing on the youth or the elderly dependency ratios by themselves, and draws attention to the importance of non-steady-state behavior in understanding the empirical links between demographic change and saving rates. Second, the demographic center of gravity for investment demand can be expected to be earlier in the age distribution than that for savings supply. Investment demand is more closely related to the youth share (through its connection with new labor force entrants and thus labor force growth), whereas saving is more closely related to the mature adult share (through its connection with retirement needs). Thus, in an open economy at least, a shift in the population age distribution toward younger ages should produce a tendency toward current account deficits and foreign capital dependency because saving rates decline more than investment rates do.

It is not immediately clear whether the open- or closed-economy model provides the better guide in exploring the impact of demographic dependency on foreign capital dependency. True, the two models seem to imply roughly similar saving dynamics, but what about foreign capital dependency? The fact that many Asian countries have relied, since the 1950s, so heavily on capital imports may appear to create a strong prima facie case against the closed-economy assumption. However, the real issue is whether investment has been constrained by domestic saving. If an economy faces a binding constraint on capital inflows, equilibrium in the domestic capital market will depend on both domestic saving and investment demand, and demographic dependency will alter the market outcome in a way that is qualitatively similar to the completely closed economy. For example, an increase in fertility under such conditions would lower the saving at a given interest rate, leading to an equal decline in saving and investment and leaving the volume of capital inflows unchanged. Under weaker restrictions on foreign mobility changes in the dependency rate will affect equilibrium in the domestic capital market in a way that will display features of both the closed- and open-economy models. Suppose, for example, that potential borrowers must pay a risk premium to attract foreign capital and that the premium rises with the desired inflow. A dependency-rate-induced fall in domestic saving at a given interest rate would then be only partly offset by increased capital inflows, forcing up the interest rate and causing a decline in investment. A positive link between youth dependency and capital dependency would be observed, but it would be weaker than the one generated under full capital mobility or under perfect world capital markets.

Estimating the Effects of Dependency Rates in East Asia

Recent econometric studies have estimated the links between youth and old-age dependency and national savings and investment rates for both Asia and the world economy in the late twentieth century (Higgins 1994, 1998; Higgins and Williamson 1996). The results point to substantial demographic effects, with increases in both youth and old-age dependency bringing about lower saving rates. The estimates indicate that the demographic swing in the saving rate has been quite large, exceeding 8 percentage points over the last 40 years for much of East Asia. The results also point to differential demographic effects on saving and investment. Higher youth dependency depresses saving more than investment, inducing capital imports, whereas higher elderly dependency depresses investment more than saving, inducing capital exports. The estimated effect of the demographic swing on changes in the CAB share in GDP exceeds 5 percentage points for much of East Asia, and it is likely to become larger still over the coming decades. But we are getting ahead of our story.

Econometric Specification

We follow the dependency literature in treating changes in national saving (and investment) rates as the result of changes in demographic variables, growth in national income, and interactions among these variables. We also add the relative price of investment goods to control for their possible effects on saving or investment (DeLong and Summers 1991). Thus the equations estimated are of the form of

$$s_{i,t} = \beta_{0,i} + \beta_1 s_{i,t-1} + \beta_2 Z_{i,t} + \beta_3 g_{i,t} + \beta_4 Z_{i,t} g_{i,t} + \beta_5 \text{RPI}_{i,t} + u_{i,t}, \quad (5.4)$$

where $s_{i,t}$ is the dependent variable in country i at time t, $Z_{i,t}$ is a vector of demographic variables, $g_{i,t}$ is the growth rate of national income, and $\text{RPI}_{i,t}$ is the relative price of investment goods.

We construct $Z_{i,t}$ by using a quadratic polynomial to represent 15 population age shares. This technique for incorporating demographic information into macroeconomic equations, introduced by Fair and Dominguez (1991), captures the information contained in the entire age distribution while maintaining a parsimonious parameterization. It is a significant improvement over the more conventional econometric assessment of dependency rate effects, which estimates age coefficients for one or at most two age shares.[4]

The models estimated are of the fixed-effects variety: The intercept term is allowed to vary across countries, but the slope coefficients are treated as common to all countries. This procedure in effect transforms the data into deviations from their country-specific means, so that the estimates are based on the time-series variation in the data. Such a specification is natural, given our focus on the evolution of national saving and investment rates over time. Moreover, this procedure has the advantage of controlling for persistent idiosyncratic factors that affect the average value of saving or investment in a particular country. Thus, except for these important demographic conditions, we have little to say about why else saving and investment rates have been high in Asia or why they have been higher in some parts of Asia than in others. We also specify a lagged dependent variable (LDV) to control for autocorrelation in the savings or investment rates.

Many previous studies do not address the issue of simultaneity bias despite the likelihood that some of the explanatory variables, particularly income growth and the relative price of investment goods, are themselves endogenous. In fact, standard specification tests suggest that ordinary least-squares analysis produces inconsistent estimates of the model parameters. As a result, we rely on instrumental variables techniques.

Estimation Results

Estimates reported elsewhere (Higgins and Williamson 1996, table 4), based on a database that includes South Asia, indicate that changing age distributions have had a statistically significant effect on Asian saving and investment rates. The results also confirm a link between demographic factors and foreign capital dependency.

Using the parameter estimates for the demographic variables, Figure 5.2 reveals the relationship between Asian age distributions and savings, investment, and CAB shares in GDP. The plotted coefficients are the change in each of the three shares associated with a unit increase in the natural logarithm of the age shares; that is, they assess the effect of changes in the age share, other things being equal. The figure shows clearly that youth and old-age dependency have a depressing effect on savings, the largest effect being for ages 0–10 and ages older than 64. Moreover, the coefficients appear to be consistent with the hump savings pattern predicted by the life-cycle hypothesis, attaining the highest values during mid-life. But they reach a peak rather early in Asia, at ages 35–39, declining sharply thereafter so as to become negative by ages 55–59.[5] Yet the rather young center of gravity found for the saving rate is what might have been expected if Asia had been only imperfectly integrated into the world capital market.

Saving and investment are identified separately in the empirical models we develop here only to the extent that countries can borrow and lend on the international capital market without constraint and at a given world interest rate. In the absence of perfect capital mobility the estimates for saving reflect a mixture of the separate demographic influences on both saving and investment—a lesson made clear by the simulation model. In this setting an increase in the share of young adults, who presumably save little, may lead to an increase in the equilibrium quantity of saving by causing an outward shift in the investment-demand schedule. Similarly, an increase in the share of middle-aged adults may actually reduce saving if any outward shift in saving is more than offset by an inward shift in investment.

The implicit age distribution coefficients for the CAB are plotted in the bottom half of Figure 5.2. The coefficients are clearly negative for the early portion of life (up to age 39), indicating that an increased investment demand induced by young adults (a demand transmitted by means of both employment and infrastructure needs) outweighs an increased saving induced by them. This implies that young nations pass through a relatively long period of foreign capital dependency that includes periods of child, adolescent, and young-adult gluts. The coefficients turn positive after age 40 as the induced decrease in investment moves way ahead of the induced decrease in saving.

Young nations are net capital importers, and old nations are net capital

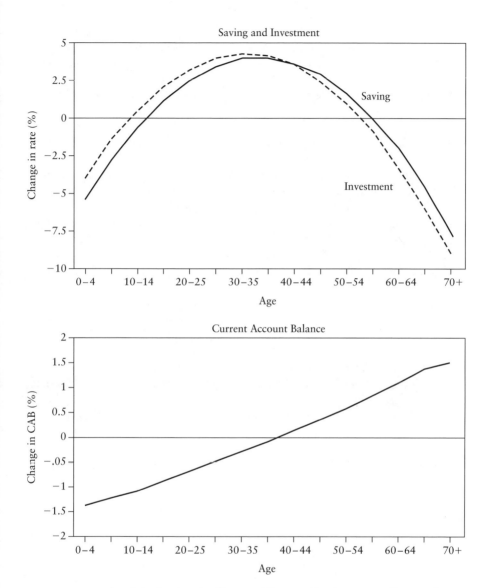

FIGURE 5.2. Age Distribution Coefficients. The age distribution coefficients show the change in the national saving rate, investment rate, and current account balance associated with a unit increase in the corresponding ln age shares. A unit increase means that the age share rises by the factor *e*.

exporters. If global capital markets let it happen, international capital in the late twentieth century tends to move between nations like an intergenerational transfer, moving from old countries to young. As we will see, this tendency also implies that the size of capital imports to East Asia will shrink as that region matures. Indeed, by 2025 East Asia is likely to become a major capital exporter.

Was East Asia Different?

Have the effects of East Asia's dependency rate been different from those in the rest of the world? That question has two parts: Were the demographic shocks there greater? And were there different coefficients in East Asia that translated those shocks into an economic impact on savings, investment, and the CAB? In the second section of this chapter we gave the answer to the first question: In no region of the world have dependency-rate changes associated with the demographic transition been greater than in East Asia since 1950. What about the second question?

To explore this issue, we performed a test by interacting an East Asian dummy variable with the demographic variables for a large sample of countries throughout the world (Higgins and Williamson 1997b). The coefficients on the demographic variables are everywhere statistically significant, indicating that the effect of age structure on domestic saving and investment is consistently larger for East Asia than for other regions. (However, the net effect of a given demographic shock on the CAB has been the same in East Asia as in the rest of the world.) In short, East Asia *was* different during the economic transformation that took place over the past quarter-century. Demographic changes there were more pronounced, and East Asia has been more sensitive to them.

Assessing the Impact of Demographic Change

We use these results to construct estimates of the effects of the changing dependency burden on East Asian savings, investment, and net capital dependency. The estimates refer to demographically induced deviations of, say, a country's saving rate from the country average for the full sample period. In particular, we calculate the demographic effect on the saving rate for country i at time t as

$$
\begin{aligned}
\text{Demographic Effect}_{i,t} = {} & \frac{\beta_{Z_1}}{1 - \beta_{\text{LDV}}}[(Z_1)_{i,t} - (\overline{Z}_1)_i] \\
& + \frac{\beta_{Z_2}}{1 - \beta_{\text{LDV}}}[(Z_2)_{i,t} - (\overline{Z}_2)_i],
\end{aligned} \tag{5.5}
$$

where β_{Z_1} and β_{Z_2} are the estimated coefficients for Z_1 and Z_2, $(\overline{Z}_1)_i$ and $(\overline{Z}_2)_i$ are the country i averages for these variables, and β_{LDV} is the estimated coefficient of the lagged dependent variable. Calculating demographic effects in this way flows naturally from our fixed-effects specification, which transforms the data into deviations from country-specific means. To capture the long-run effect of changes in the demographic variables, $1 - \beta_{LDV}$ appears in the denominator.

We next construct projections of the effects of expected changes in the dependency burden on savings, investment, and capital flows. We use United Nations projected population age shares for 2005, 2015, and 2025 to construct the implied values of Z_1 and Z_2. The effect of changes in country i's age structure on its saving rate between, say, 1990 and 2025 is then given by

$$\Delta_{NSAVE_i} = \frac{\beta_{Z_1}}{1 - \beta_{LDV}}[(Z_1)_{i,2025} - (Z_1)_{i,1990}]$$

$$+ \frac{B_{Z_2}}{1 - \beta_{LDV}}[(Z_2)_{i,2025} - (Z_2)_{i,1990}].$$

(5.6)

The same procedure, of course, is followed for investment and the CAB.

Did Dependency Rates Drive East Asian Savings, Investment, and Capital Flows in the Past?

We use the estimated model to assess the effect of dependency rates on savings, investment, and capital flows in two ways. First, we ask how much of the observed change in these variables between 1950 and 1992 can be explained by changes in the dependency burden. That is, we isolate the effect of the East Asian demographic transition on these three aspects of accumulation by applying observed demographic changes to the estimated β coefficients discussed in the previous section. Second, using the same decomposition procedure, we ask how much of East Asia's rapid accumulation performance, compared with that in other regions, has been due to more favorable demographic conditions. How would East Asia have performed, given the heavier dependency burdens of South Asia? How would East Asia have performed under the far less dramatic fall in dependency rates in the OECD nations or Latin America?

Effect of the Dependency Rate over Time

Following Equation (5.5), we calculate the effect of the demographic transition on accumulation performance over time relative to the mean values

TABLE 5.5

Impact of Dependency Rates on Savings, Investment,
and Net Capital Flows as Percentage Shares of GDP:
East Asia, 1950–92

Region and period	Savings	Investment	Current account balance
Northeast Asia			
1950–54	1.0	1.2	−0.2
1955–59	−2.1	−1.5	−0.6
1960–64	−3.4	−2.4	−1.0
1965–69	−4.9	−3.4	−1.4
1970–74	−5.2	−3.7	−1.5
1975–79	−2.5	−1.7	−0.8
1980–84	2.4	1.8	+0.6
1985–89	6.3	4.4	+2.0
1990–92	8.4	5.4	+3.0
Southeast Asia			
1950–54	−0.1	−0.5	+0.4
1955–59	−1.3	−1.0	−0.3
1960–64	−2.5	−1.7	−0.9
1965–69	−3.4	−2.3	−1.1
1970–74	−3.6	−2.4	−1.2
1975–79	−2.0	−1.3	−0.7
1980–84	0.9	0.6	+0.2
1985–89	4.3	3.0	+1.2
1990–92	7.9	5.5	+2.4

SOURCE: Higgins and Williamson (1996, table 8).

over the four decades between 1950 and 1992 (Table 5.5). Thus the values in the Savings column of Table 5.5 tell us the effect of changes in population age shares on the saving rate as it deviated around the 1950–92 mean. Another way of stating this is that saving rates would have been x percentage points higher or lower during a given period if the population age shares had remained constant at their 1950–92 means.

According to our estimates in Table 5.5, Northeast Asia's saving rate in 1970–74 was 5.2 percentage points below its 1950–92 average because of the heavy dependency rate burden (lower working-age adult share) at that time. Similarly, Northeast Asia's saving rate was 8.4 percentage points above its 1950–92 average in 1990–92 because of the transition to a much lighter dependency burden, or, if you prefer, to a much larger working-age adult share. The total demographically induced change in the saving rate amounted to an enormous 13.6 percentage points over these 20 years, accounting for *all* the rise in the saving rate in Northeast Asia between 1970–74 and 1990–92 (6.0 percentage points, 35.0 − 29.0, as shown in Table 5.4). The figures for Southeast Asia are similar but not quite so dramatic. Southeast Asia's saving rate was 3.6 percentage points lower in 1970–74 because of the heavier burden at that time, and Southeast Asia's 1990–92 saving rate was 7.9 percentage points higher than its 1950–92 average because of its lighter dependency burden late in the twentieth century. The total demographically induced change in the saving rate was 11.5 percentage points, accounting, once again, for *all* the rise in the saving rate in Southeast Asia after 1970 (10.3 percentage points, as shown in Table 5.4).[6]

Let us consider the upswing of the East Asian demographic transition, or at least that part of it we can observe. [Although rapid population growth started earlier than 1950, perhaps even as early as the 1930s, the national accounts are not good enough to measure its impact earlier than 1950 (Bloom and Williamson 1997)]. Between 1950–54 and 1970–74 the rising dependency rate served by itself to lower the saving rate in Northeast Asia by 6.1 percentage points and by 3.5 percentage points in Southeast Asia. Dependency rates thus had nothing to do with the rise in saving rates in Northeast Asia until the early 1970s. Indeed, had dependency rates not risen, saving rates would have risen by much more. East Asia underwent an impressive accumulation performance up to the early 1970s despite these demographic forces, not because of them. These demographic events actually served to postpone and suppress the East Asian economic transformation during the first two decades after the Korean War.

Although the literature rarely notes it, these demographic variables also had their impact on investment demand, and in the same direction: Dependents generate lower investment demand than do mature adults, who have to be equipped at work and transported to job sites. (A fall in the youth dependency rate implies a rise in labor force growth as those aging teenagers hit the labor market.) But the demographic impact on East Asian investment rates has been less dramatic in the recent past than the demographic impact on saving rates, as the previous section implied. To take just one example, the impressive 8.1 percentage point rise in Southeast Asian investment rates since 1970–74 (Table 5.4) was induced largely by demographic effects, but the demographically induced rise in the saving rate was greater (11.5 percentage points), contributing powerfully to a decline in Southeast Asia's dependency on foreign capital.

The net effect of the dependency rate would by itself have produced a long historic swing in foreign capital dependency in East Asia over the past half-century. During their periods of peak dependency burdens, both Northeast and Southeast Asia were net importers of foreign capital. But the demographic transition, when left to its own devices and when not offset by other forces, caused foreign capital dependency to wax and wane. In Northeast Asia the rising dependency rate served by itself to worsen the CAB share in GDP by 1.3 percentage points between 1950–54 and 1970–74 and then to improve it by 4.5 percentage points by 1990–92 (Table 5.5). Indeed, the declining dependency burden after 1970–74 served by itself to cause Northeast Asia to switch from a net capital-importing position (−1.5%) to a net capital-exporting position in 1990–92 (+3.0%). Similarly, changing demographic dependency in Southeast Asia would by itself have produced the same swing in foreign capital dependency after 1950, although not quite as dramatically as in Northeast Asia.

Certainly the dependency rate was not the only factor driving savings and investment in East Asia, nor was dependency on foreign capital. There may well have been offsetting forces at work, some of them related to changing policies toward foreign presence in local capital markets and others related to investment booms in countries where the pace of development had accelerated abruptly. No long-run model can expect to accommodate such short- and medium-term changes. Nevertheless, the proof of the pudding is in the eating: How much of the past performance can be explained by dependency-rate changes? Demographic events explain all the decline in foreign capital dependency in Southeast Asia after the early 1970s (a 3.6 percentage point change between 1970–74 and 1990–92 predicted from Table 5.5 of the actual 2.2 percentage point change shown in Table 5.4); and they explain all the decline in Northeast Asia (4.5 versus 3.8 percentage points).

Although not shown in any table here, individual Northeast Asian countries' experiences retell the aggregate regional story with remarkably little deviance. Some countries' dependency-rate effects, however, have been truly spectacular (Higgins and Williamson 1996, table 9). Recall that Northeast Asia as a whole experienced its peak dependency-rate impact in 1970–74 (although some countries within the region reached their peaks earlier) and that the decline in the dependency rate thereafter served to augment the saving rate by 13.6 percentage points. Although the decline from peak to 1990–92 served to raise the saving rate in Japan by "only" 12.2 percentage points, it raised it by almost 26 percentage points in both South Korea and Taiwan. The other Northeast Asian countries fell between these two extremes. The effect of dependency rates on investment rates was somewhat less than on saving rates everywhere in Northeast Asia, so that declining dependency rates implied declining dependency on foreign capital. For example, from the 1955–59 peak to 1985–89 this demographic effect by itself caused Taiwan's share of the CAB in GDP to switch from −4.8% to +4.8%, for a total swing of 9.6%. Another example is Singapore, where, in response to the dependency-rate decline alone, the share of the CAB in GDP would have switched from −1.7% in 1965–69 to +6.8% in 1990–92, for a total rise of 8.5 percentage points. Even the smallest effects in Northeast Asia were impressive. On the basis of the dependency-rate effects alone, South Korea would have evolved from a CAB share of −1.7% in 1955–59 to +5.4% in 1990–92 and China would have gone from a CAB share of −1.5% in 1970–74 to +2.9% in 1990–92.

Once again, other fundamentals were also at work driving the CAB share. To consider Taiwan once more, her actual CAB share rose by 22.3 percentage points between 1955–59 and 1985–89, so that the declining dependency rate accounted for more than four-tenths. It accounted for one-half in the case of Singapore.

What about Southeast Asia? Here, too, the effect of dependency-rate changes on savings outweighed their effect on investment, so that, when left to their own devices, declining dependency rates in Southeast Asia implied declining foreign capital dependency, just as in Northeast Asia. Although the effect was not as great in Southeast Asia, it was still impressive. In Indonesia, Malaysia, the Philippines, and Thailand the dependency-rate effects by themselves served to raise the CAB share by about 3–5 percentage points between 1970–74 and 1990–92, less than in Northeast Asia but substantial nonetheless. (Singapore is an even better example, but we have placed it in the Northeast Asian group.) In a sense, these four cases are the most interesting in Southeast Asia because the strong dependency-rate effects they experienced were completely swamped by other offsetting and even stronger forces. Falling dependency rates by themselves should have reduced foreign capital dependency among these new tigers. Yet all four *increased* their foreign capital dependency, and two (Malaysia and Thailand) did so dramatically. Rising foreign capital dependency was inconsistent with the moderating influences of the dependency rate. Other forces, such as a steamy investment boom, were pushing in the opposite direction, and they dominated.

Impact of Dependency Rates across Asia

The poor countries of South Asia carried bigger dependency burdens, implying bigger shortfalls in net domestic savings and greater dependency on foreign capital. The best way to illustrate this fact is to exploit the counterfactual situation. Suppose, for example, that the fast-transition countries of East Asia had carried the heavier demographic burdens of South Asia. Suppose they had carried the heavier burdens of Latin America. Or suppose they had carried the lighter burdens of the OECD. We examine these hypothetical situations in Table 5.6 for three points in time: early in East Asia's demographic transition (1955–59), the middle period (1975–79), and toward the end (1990–92). The group includes Japan, South Korea, Taiwan, Singapore, China, and Hong Kong. The table reports the share of the savings, investment, and CAB in GDP that was actually recorded (columns labeled "Actual"). Using Equation (5.6), we can also report the share that would have prevailed had the country carried the dependency burden characterizing the region being compared (the counterfactual share; columns labeled "CF"). The table also shows the difference (columns labeled "Difference") between the two. Even though national accounts data may make it impossible to

TABLE 5.6

How Different Were the Fast-transition East Asian Countries?
Actual Savings, Investment, and Current Account Balance as Percentages of GDP,
Counterfactual (CF) Shares, and the Difference between Actual and
Counterfactual Shares: East Asia, 1955–92 [a]

Country and period	Savings			Investment			Current account balance		
	Actual	CF	Difference	Actual	CF	Difference	Actual	CF	Difference
A. Fast-transition East Asian countries with South Asian demographic characteristics									
Japan									
1955–59	28.4	17.4	−11.0	28.1	22.0	−6.1	0.3	−4.6	−4.9
1975–79	32.4	10.5	−21.9	31.8	19.8	−12.0	0.7	−9.3	−9.9
1990–92	34.6	15.7	−18.8	32.1	26.4	−5.7	2.5	−10.6	−13.1
South Korea									
1955–59	3.4	7.8	4.4	12.1	15.3	3.2	−8.7	−7.4	1.3
1975–79	23.9	19.0	−4.9	29.3	24.8	−4.6	−5.4	−5.8	−0.4
1990–92			−18.9	38.0	24.0	−14.0			−4.9
Taiwan									
1955–59	10.0	18.9	8.8	16.2	20.9	4.7	−6.2	−2.0	4.1
1975–79	32.0	23.2	−8.8	30.0	22.9	−7.1	1.9	0.2	−1.7
1990–92			−16.3	22.3	12.1	−10.2			−6.1
Singapore									
1955–59			4.8			0.4			4.3
1975–79	32.7	22.3	−10.4	39.9	31.7	−8.2	−7.1	−9.4	−2.3
1990–92	49.2	29.3	−20.0	39.6	25.9	−13.7	9.6	3.3	−6.3
China									
1955–59			−4.3			−1.2			−3.1
1975–79	30.3	25.5	−4.8	30.2	27.5	−2.7	0.2	−2.0	−2.2
1990–92	35.5	21.3	−14.2	33.2	24.0	−9.2	2.3	−2.8	−5.1
Hong Kong									
1955–59			−3.1			−4.5			1.4
1975–79			−15.1	28.5	19.6	−8.9			−6.2
1990–92			−19.9	28.4	18.0	−10.4			−9.6
All six countries									
1955–59			0.6			−0.6			0.5
1975–79			−11.0			−7.2			−3.8
1990–92			−18.0			−10.5			−7.5
B. Fast-transition East Asian countries with Latin American demographic characteristics									
Japan									
1955–59	28.4	11.7	−16.7	28.1	17.9	−10.2	0.3	−6.2	−6.5
1975–79	32.4	6.8	−25.7	31.8	16.8	−14.9	0.7	−10.1	−10.7
1990–92	34.6	17.6	−17.0	32.1	27.6	−4.5	2.5	−10.1	−12.5
South Korea									
1955–59	3.4	2.1	−1.2	12.1	11.2	−0.9	−8.7	−9.1	−0.3
1975–79	23.9	15.2	−8.7	29.3	21.8	−7.5	−5.4	−6.6	−1.2
1990–92			−17.1	38.0	25.2	−12.8			−4.3
Taiwan									
1955–59	10.0	13.2	3.1	16.2	16.8	0.6	−6.2	−3.6	2.5
1975–79	32.0	19.41	−12.6	30.0	20.0	−10.0	1.9	−0.6	−2.5
1990–92			−14.4	22.3	13.4	−8.9			−5.5

TABLE 5.6

(continued)

Country and period	Savings			Investment			Current account balance		
	Actual	CF	Difference	Actual	CF	Difference	Actual	CF	Difference
Singapore									
1955–59			−0.9			−3.7			−2.7
1975–79	32.7	18.6	−14.2	39.9	28.8	−11.1	−7.1	−10.2	−3.1
1990–92	49.2	31.1	−18.1	39.6	27.2	−12.4	9.6	3.9	−5.7
China									
1955–59			−10.0			−5.3			−4.7
1975–79	30.3	21.7	−8.6	30.2	24.5	−5.6	0.2	−2.8	−3.0
1990–92	35.5	23.1	−12.4	33.2	25.3	−7.9	2.3	−2.2	−4.5
Hong Kong									
1955–59			−8.8			−8.6			−0.2
1975–79			−18.9	28.5	16.7	−11.8			−7.0
1990–92			−18.1	28.4	19.2	−9.1			−9.0
All six countries									
1955–59			−5.8			−4.7			−1.1
1975–79			−14.8			−10.2			−4.6
1990–92			−16.2			−9.3			−6.9

C. Fast-transition East Asian countries with OECD demographic characteristics

Country and period	Savings			Investment			Current account balance		
	Actual	CF	Difference	Actual	CF	Difference	Actual	CF	Difference
Japan									
1955–59	28.4	28.6	0.2	28.1	25.5	−2.6	0.3	3.1	2.8
1975–79	32.4	24.5	−8.0	31.8	24.7	−7.1	0.7	−0.2	−0.9
1990–92	34.6	29.6	−5.0	32.1	30.3	−1.8	2.5	−0.7	−3.2
South Korea									
1955–59	3.4	19.0	15.6	12.1	16.7	6.6	−8.7	0.3	9.0
1975–79	23.9	32.9	9.0	29.3	29.7	0.4	−5.4	3.3	8.7
1990–92			−5.0	38.0	27.9	−10.1			5.0
Taiwan									
1955–59	10.0	30.1	20.0	16.2	24.4	8.2	−6.2	5.7	11.9
1975–79	32.0	37.1	5.2	30.0	27.8	−2.2	1.9	9.3	7.3
1990–92			−2.4	22.3	16.0	−6.2			3.8
Singapore									
1955–59			16.0			3.9			12.0
1975–79	32.7	36.3	3.6	39.9	36.6	−3.2	−7.1	−0.3	6.8
1990–92	49.2	43.1	−6.1	39.6	29.9	−9.7	9.6	12.2	3.6
China									
1955–59			6.9			2.2			4.7
1975–79	30.3	39.4	9.1	30.2	32.4	2.2	0.2	7.0	6.9
1990–92	35.5	35.1	−0.4	33.2	28.0	−5.2	2.3	7.1	4.8
Hong Kong									
1955–59			8.1			−1.0			9.1
1975–79			−1.2	28.5	24.5	4.0			2.8
1990–92			−6.1	23.4	21.9	−6.4			0.4
All six countries									
1955–59			11.1			2.9			8.2
1975–79			3.0			−2.3			5.3
1990–92			−4.2			−6.6			2.4

[a]Periods left blank reflect the absence of national accounts data, but the calculated difference does not need those data. See text.

document the actual CAB for some periods and for some countries, the difference can always be calculated from the estimated within-sample β coefficients and the observed dependency burdens.

Part A in Table 5.6 shows how fast-transition East Asia would have behaved given South Asia's demographics. The figures are revealing. In 1990–92 the six fast-transition countries would have recorded saving rates 18 percentage points lower, investment rates almost 11 percentage points lower, and CAB shares about 7.5 percentage points lower. Furthermore, a significant portion of the savings and investment boom between the late 1970s and the early 1990s would have disappeared.

Part B of Table 5.6 reports how the six fast-transition countries would have behaved with Latin American demographics. The situation is much like that of the South Asian counterfactual situation: lower levels of savings and accumulation and higher dependence on foreign capital.

Part C of Table 5.6 presents a different scenario. It supposes that fast-transition East Asia had the demographic experience of the early-OECD member states, where the favorable demographic conditions were so much weaker. In that case a significant share of the boom in savings and investment rates would have disappeared. These results offer one reason why fast-transition East Asia has achieved such impressive savings and accumulation and had so little dependence on foreign capital. It is simply because the region underwent an unusual demographic experience.

Will Dependency Rates Drive East Asian Savings, Investment, and Capital Flows in the Future?

Many unpredictable factors may offset the predictable effects of demographic variables on savings, investment, and foreign capital dependency over the next 30 years. Global capital markets may retreat behind autarkic barriers, just as they did between 1914 and the early 1970s (Williamson 1996). China may open its doors wide to foreign capital or slam them shut. Capital scarcity in world markets may rise or fall (Barro 1992), and the recent sustained decline in world interest rates may or may not persist (Calvo, Leiderman, and Reinhart 1996: 126). The recent currency crisis in Southeast Asia may herald the end of the region's steamy investment boom—or the boom may quickly revive, penetrating further into South Asia. We have nothing to say about these important influences, but we have seen how in the recent past they have often muted the effects of demographic change in Southeast Asia.

What we intend to do is to project the impact of demographic events alone on savings, investment, and foreign capital dependency to 2025. After harvesting the benefits of an enormous past decline in the youth dependency rate, how will Japan and the old East Asian tigers respond to a future rise in the elderly dependency rate? What will happen to foreign capital dependency in Southeast Asia as Indonesia, Malaysia, the Philippines, and Thailand enjoy a further rise in their prime-age shares? Our guess for the future is based on the predictable demographic facts underlying Table 5.3 and the estimated demographic coefficients reported in the section titled "Estimating the Effects of Dependency Rates in East Asia." Nothing else enters into the calculations, and therefore our projections, presented in Table 5.7, address only the impact of future demographic events.

Aging, of course, will serve to lower the saving rate in Japan, a prediction that International Monetary Fund (IMF) economists have supported recently. We estimate that the saving rate will fall to less than one-half of its 1990–92 level by 2025, and the resulting 16% GDP share will look ordinary compared with that of the 1980s. Although we agree with the IMF economists on the saving impact, we do not agree with the inference they draw. Their recent simulations forecast that "countries where population aging is most pronounced . . . [will] tend to run current account deficits" (Masson 1990: 7). It appears that the IMF has made no effort to explore the impact of demographic forces on investment. For Japan those demographic forces also lower the investment rate, and by a bit more than savings. Thus, if demographic forces are permitted to have their way, Japan will not become a nation of old people unable or unwilling to find the resources to export capital to the poorer parts of Asia. Instead, we project that the CAB share will rise by about 2 percentage points. But what distinguishes aging Japan is that the rise there is so modest. In contrast, it will be much more dramatic in those countries of Asia that will be passing through more youthful stages of the demographic transition.

As Table 5.7 indicates, the CAB share will rise by about 9 percentage points in both China and Taiwan and by nearly 11 percentage points in South Korea. (The projected 25% CAB share for Taiwan in 2025 certainly seems implausibly large, exceeding even Britain's net foreign investment share of about 10% on the eve of World War I. Nevertheless, the official Taiwanese figure for 1885–89 was more than 16%.) All three countries pass through a hump-shaped transition consisting of first a rise in savings and investment rates followed by a fall to 2025. The savings peak is reached in 2015 for China and in 2005 for South Korea and Taiwan. Singapore replicates this transitional pattern almost exactly.

The movement toward net capital-export positions will be most dramatic in Southeast Asia, however. Between 1990–92 and 2025 the CAB share will rise by 10.4 percentage points in Indonesia, by 11.3 percentage points in Malaysia, by 10.5 percentage points in the Philippines, and by 11.7 percentage

TABLE 5.7

Actual and Projected Impact of Dependency Rates on Savings,
Investment, and Foreign Capital Dependency (%):
East Asia and South Asia, 1990–2025[a]

Region, country, and year	Savings	Investment	Current account balance
Northeast Asia			
Japan			
1990–92	34.6	32.1	+2.5
2005	25.3	20.9	+4.4
2015	20.1	15.3	+4.8
2025	16.3	11.8	+4.5
South Korea			
1985–89	33.4	30.2	+3.2[b]
2005	39.7	30.9	+8.8
2015	37.6	25.9	+11.7
2025	31.3	17.4	+13.9
Taiwan			
1985–89	36.8	20.7	+16.1
2005	42.4	21.8	+20.6
2015	40.2	16.5	+23.7
2025	33.4	8.0	+25.4
Singapore			
1990–92	49.2	39.6	+9.6
2005	52.5	37.6	+14.9
2015	48.0	29.9	+18.0
2025	38.9	19.7	+19.1
China			
1990–92	35.5	33.2	+2.3
2005	42.1	36.2	+5.9
2015	44.0	34.8	+9.2
2025	38.6	27.4	+11.2
Southeast Asia			
Indonesia			
1990–92	31.8	35.2	−3.4
2005	42.8	41.9	+0.9
2015	48.5	44.5	+4.0
2025	48.8	41.9	+7.0
Malaysia			
1990–92	27.9	34.1	−6.2
2005	42.1	43.8	−1.7
2015	49.0	46.8	+2.2
2025	49.1	44.0	+5.1
Philippines			
1990–92	20.5	22.8	−2.3
2005	33.0	31.7	+1.3
2015	40.5	35.9	+4.7
2025	45.2	37.0	+8.2
Thailand			
1990–92	33.5	41.1	−7.7
2005	46.2	48.5	−2.3
2015	49.0	47.9	+1.1
2025	46.9	42.8	+4.0

[a]The CAB share for Nepal is not available for 1985–89 and thus was excluded from this table. Hong Kong is not included in these projections.

[b]The CAB share for 1990–92 cannot be documented in our source; we therefore use the figure for 1985–89 instead.

points in Thailand. Furthermore, savings and investment rates will soar, some of them hovering above 45%. And, to repeat, saving rates will rise faster and farther than investment rates in this region, generating robust capital-export positions.

If demographic forces are allowed to have their way, capital flows over East Asian borders will be dramatically different in 2025. Furthermore, we won't have to wait until 2025 to see this switch from capital dependence to independence. The underlying fundamentals are at work right now.

Conclusion

The demographic transition has had a profound impact on East Asian savings, investment, and foreign capital dependency since 1950. Although the dependency-rate literature looks almost exclusively at domestic savings, in this chapter we have also examined investment and the CAB. Our attention to these variables has paid off, providing insight into East Asian foreign capital dependency in the past, present, and future. And we have done it with economic modeling that rejects steady-state analysis in favor of a dynamic approach, an approach that offers a compatible marriage between the demographic transition and the economics used to explore its impact.

We find that much of the impressive rise in East Asian saving and investment rates since the late 1960s can be explained by the equally impressive decline in youth dependency burdens. The demographically induced rise in savings has been greater than that of investment. Thus, where the region has kicked the habit of foreign capital dependency, the youth dependency burden has fallen and the working-age adult share has risen most dramatically. The aging of Japan's population will not diminish its capacity to export capital in the next century, but little of that capital will go to Southeast Asia, at least if dependency rates are allowed to have their way. Rather, Southeast Asia will become a capital exporter, kicking the foreign capital dependency habit.

We should stress that our estimate of the demographic transition's impact on East Asian accumulation performance is large. Other research supporting these qualitative findings may find somewhat smaller numbers. However, the numbers reported here are sufficiently large to absorb substantial downward revisions.

We have also made many assumptions that can be attacked by a critical reader: that more abundant world savings supplies will not alter capital's incentive to seek new Asian locations, that world capital markets will stay relatively open, and that the demographic transition is exogenous to accumulation performance. Our assumptions about the world capital market have been discussed at length already, but the assumption that the demographic transition has been largely independent of East Asia's stupendous economic growth needs to be stressed.

We have assumed that dependency rates are exogenous, as if the demographic transition were solely a response to the (exogenous) importation of foreign health technology in the 1940s and 1950s. According to that assumption, improvements in public health and nutrition produced by that technology sharply lowered infant mortality over a decade or two, ushering in a half-century of evolution in the age structure and dependency rates. Of course, that assumption is much too simple, especially as applied to Japan. It is even much too simple for less developed countries in Asia where fertility rates have also fallen, although with a greater lag. Fertility rates have fallen in response to, among other things, economic success (and their decline has been limited by economic failure). Economic success has also assured additional reductions in infant mortality through improvements in nutrition and health, just as economic failure has limited further mortality reductions. In this chapter we ignore these important connections, which may matter to our interpretation of the past and projections of the future. To the extent that economic success has driven these demographic events, we have exaggerated their independent influence; and to that extent they should be assigned to other fundamentals driving the East Asian economic transformation.

We have also projected the future in full knowledge that our assumptions about integrated world capital markets will be unrealistic if East Asia retreats to pre-1970 autarky. A policy decision by China in either direction could swamp the otherwise powerful demographic forces. Furthermore, we have ignored the possibility that changes in global capital supplies may have an important independent influence on future East Asian investment and net capital flows.

Subject to these important qualifications, the dependency-rate hypothesis is alive and well in East Asia. Dependency rates have played an important role in the region's economic success since the 1960s and probably will do so over the next quarter-century as the aging tigers undergo economic retardation. To the extent that the demographic transition has driven a significant portion of East Asia's economic transformation, it limits the economic policy lessons that can be transferred to areas of the world where a demographic transition of this magnitude is absent. But the East Asian experience does offer some unambiguous lessons for two important Third World regions that are about to pass through the favorable stages of their own demographic transitions: Africa and South Asia. If Africa and South Asia can harness their falling dependency and rising activity rates, they may well be able to achieve something of an economic miracle too. They may, of course, waste those advantages. Only time will tell.

6

Saving, Wealth, and the Demographic Transition in East Asia

RONALD D. LEE, ANDREW MASON, AND TIMOTHY MILLER

In 1958 Coale and Hoover published an influential analysis of population and economic development, arguing that growth in per capita income would be strongly accelerated by an earlier fertility decline in Third World countries and particularly in India, their case study. At the center of their analysis was the hypothesis that higher fertility and the resulting higher proportion of children in the population would depress aggregate saving rates and thereby slow the growth of capital. Controversial empirical work by Leff (1969) supported this hypothesis about savings, and the Coale-Hoover conclusions were widely accepted and had an important influence on public policy for two or three decades.

In the mid-1980s several revisionist syntheses of the research literature argued that there was no clear evidence that demographic factors influenced saving rates or that capital accumulation was the key factor in economic development [see, for example, World Bank (1984), US NRC (1986), and Kelley (1988b)]. According to Solow's (1956) growth model, wide variations in the population growth rate have no effect on the rate of per capita income

We are grateful to John Bauer and Matthew Higgins for their helpful comments on an earlier draft and to Frank Harrigan, Tsung Li-Hom, and Huang Fung-Mey for their help with data issues. We also acknowledge the assistance of Jeff Brown and Noreen Tanouye (Program on Population of the East-West Center) and Mike Clune (Demography, University of California, Berkeley). Ronald Lee and Timothy Miller's research for this chapter was funded by the National Institute on Aging (through grant AG11761). Support for the research also came from the United States Agency for International Development, the Rockefeller Foundation, the William and Flora Hewlett Foundation, and the Ministry of Foreign Affairs of Japan.

growth in the steady state and only a modest effect on the level of per capita income. Exercises in growth accounting typically accorded capital a small role in explaining differences in economic growth rates. Moreover, most of this revisionist literature assigned population growth and age distribution only minor roles in hampering or encouraging development.

More recently, a post-revisionist literature has begun to emerge. Many studies based on international cross-sections now report negative associations between population growth rates and per capita income growth rates, associations that were previously found to be negligible or insignificant. This literature finds larger effects of saving rates and population growth rates on income growth when models include human capital formation in addition to physical capital (Mankiw, Romer, and Weil 1992). Some analysts have found that the recent phenomenal economic growth rates in East Asia are due almost entirely to factor accumulation, with the accumulation of physical capital playing by far the dominant role. In his research on the life-cycle saving hypothesis Mason (1987b, 1988) explained why demographic variables have appeared to have ambiguous effects in the past and found an important role for them with an improved specification. Other empirical studies [for example, Kelley and Schmidt (1996)] support Mason's research. In Chapter 5 of this volume Williamson and Higgins argue that the early and rapid demographic transition in East Asia accounts for much of the high saving rates and negative foreign capital flows in recent decades and suggest that the same may occur throughout the Third World. In other words, they conclude that Coale and Hoover were right.

Although most proponents of this view invoke the life-cycle saving hypothesis to motivate empirical studies of the relationship between demographic change and saving rates, little research has actually been done to model that relationship under the life-cycle saving hypothesis. The early work of Tobin (1967) may still represent the leading effort to incorporate and simulate the effects of realistic demographic trends on individual and aggregate savings. Tobin's analysis, however, was a comparative static analysis and was based on the US population of the 1960s. Therefore it is of limited relevance to demographic transitions in developing countries.

In the classic transition declines in child mortality initially produce increases in the proportion of children in the population. Eventually, fertility also begins to decline, reversing the trend toward a large dependent child population. The proportion of the elderly begins to grow rapidly, however, in part because of increasing survival rates and in part because the elderly spring from large cohorts born during the high-fertility era. At the end of the demographic transition fertility remains at a low level and mortality continues to decline, so far without limit. Population aging continues, reaching levels not yet experienced at the national level.

The distinctive features of East Asia's demographic transition are described in Chapter 3. Other chapters present much of the relevant background for this chapter. Chapter 2 describes economic growth in East Asia, and Chapter 5 reviews the literature on population and saving. Our emphasis here is on a careful articulation of the connection between population and life-cycle saving under the unusually rapid demographic changes that have occurred in East Asia. We rely extensively on the experience of Taiwan. As a first approximation to assessing the economic implications of the demographic transition, we calculate the support ratio (Cutler et al. 1990). A refined version of the dependency ratio, the support ratio is an estimate of the number of producers per consumer in the population. The estimate of the number of producers incorporates age variation in productivity and the number of consumers incorporates age variation in consumption needs. We have calculated two variants, which represent extreme assumptions about the relative consumption of the young and the old. Details are provided in the appendix.

Between 1950 and 2000 Taiwan's support ratio rose by between 17% and 35%, depending on the weights used (Figure 6.1). This means that the average person could consume 17–35% more at each age in 2000 than in 1950, even if there were no economic growth, solely because the average working-age person is supporting fewer dependents. Alternatively, workers could maintain consumption and saving at 1950 levels and increase time spent in leisure activities. As a third alternative, workers could divert 17–35% of labor earnings to savings in 2000, with no reduction in consumption at each age relative to 1950.

Judging from the swing in the support ratio, we see that the demographic transition makes possible dramatic increases in saving and investment, but did the transition actually account for the increase in saving that occurred in Taiwan and elsewhere in East Asia? In Chapter 5 Williamson and Higgins rely on econometric evidence to answer this question with a resounding yes. Here, we take a different approach to the question by examining the impact of demographic change on saving through the lens of the life-cycle saving model. We use a new analytical model that incorporates detailed demographic information in a dynamic life-cycle framework. We extend the basic modeling strategy set out by Tobin (1967) and use it to examine the effects of various demographic regimes, drawn from Taiwan's experience. First, we compare several static scenarios. Then we carry out dynamic simulations, exploring the effects of Taiwan's demographic transition, assuming that interest rates and productivity growth rates are exogenous. We also attempt to take into account the familial system of old-age support in our comparative static analysis but not in our dynamic analysis.

Assuming life-cycle savings and using plausible values for the key parameters, we find that several important conclusions emerge. The first is that the changes in age structure emphasized in the literature account for only part

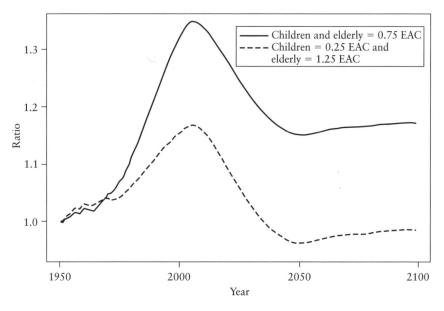

FIGURE 6.1. Economic Support Ratio: Taiwan, 1950–2100.

of the effect of demography on saving. Changes in life expectancy also lead to substantially higher rates of saving by working-age individuals who are anticipating a longer duration of retirement. The second conclusion is that the impact of demography on saving depends on the institutional setting, in particular, the nature and extent of support systems for the elderly. If the elderly are supported either by family-based or public-sector transfers, then the impact of demographic change on saving is attenuated. The erosion of the familial system of old-age support, however, would lead to substantially higher rates of saving. Finally, if the life-cycle model is correct, the demographic transition in Taiwan indeed explains a portion of the remarkable rise in saving rates and capital accumulation there since 1950. The effect is smaller than that estimated by Williamson and Higgins (Chapter 5) but still substantial.

Unresolved Issues in the Saving Literature

Several unresolved issues and empirical features of Asian households have an important bearing on aggregate saving rates. The first is the issue of dynamics. Most saving models are comparative static models. For example, the variable rate-of-growth model (Mason 1981, 1987b, 1988; Fry and Mason 1982) considers the implications for saving of high versus low fertility rates in a stable equilibrium. These two conditions would be approximated by a population that had not yet begun its demographic transition or had long since completed its transition. The countries of East Asia are, in contrast, in the midst of their transitions. Consequently, the current saving behavior of young households may be consistent with the saving behavior likely to be observed in a low-fertility regime. But in older households women have borne well more than two children on average. Even though older women have completed their child rearing, their saving behavior would be consistent with a higher fertility regime. In Chapter 5 Williamson and Higgins take an important step forward, exploring this issue by means of an overlapping-generations model.

A second unresolved issue bearing on aggregate saving rates is that the household conceptualized in the simple life-cycle model is essentially a nuclear household relying exclusively on the resources generated over the lifetime of an adult husband and wife. This is a substantial abstraction from the reality of family life in any society, including Western societies, but it is a particularly poor representation of Asian households. In East Asia the importance of the multigeneration extended household has poorly understood implications for aggregate saving.

According to the life-cycle saving model, people save largely to fund their consumption during retirement years. Two separate lines of research on saving in developed countries have augmented or challenged this theory by emphasizing the role of interage transfers. Kotlikoff and Summers (1981) argued that people save primarily because they wish to leave bequests to their children. Feldstein (1974) asserted that the life-cycle saving motive is undermined by the public provision of pay-as-you-go savings, another sort of intergenerational transfer. Given the importance attached to transfers as a key element for understanding saving behavior in the developed countries, it is odd that economists have paid so little attention to the role of intergenerational transfers in explaining saving behavior in developing countries. Yet it is widely realized that in traditional societies—and in many countries that are already highly developed—the principal means of support in old age is through transfers from the elderly person's adult children, often facilitated by co-residence. This central role of children has been confirmed by cross-cultural surveys on motivations for childbearing, by analyses of patterns of co-residence, by ethnographic studies, and by empirical studies of the life-cycle savings hypothesis in such settings and indeed in more modern settings during the transition to a market economy. In many East Asian countries, even those that are substantially or fully industrialized, such as Japan, familial support of the elderly continues to be important. Nonetheless, there is no question that various aspects of economic development and demographic transition have weakened the familial support system. For example, many adult offspring have moved away from the rural areas in which their elderly parents reside, and occupational and geographic mobility lessens the economic dependence of children on their parents. Another development is the availability of alternative instruments for saving and risk spreading. One implication of these changes is that models that assume that accumulated assets provide for all old-age consumption greatly overstate the life-cycle motive for saving. Another implication is that the transfer transition may itself provide a strong reason to expect saving rates to rise. Furthermore, the problems in moving from a family-based system of old-age support to life-cycle saving or a funded pension system parallel exactly the problems of moving from a public pay-as-you-go system of support to a fully funded system. In both cases there is a generation that must provide both for its parents' retirement and for its own.

Modeling of the bequest motive requires careful attention in the context of such rapid increases in productivity, which, if sustained, would mean that each generation would have income many times higher than the preceding generation. Under such circumstances one would expect the bequest motive to be greatly weakened and the direction of transfers perhaps even reversed.

A third issue, the increase in educational attainment and other costly investments in children, is largely ignored, although it may play an important causal or joint role in the decline in fertility; and it certainly has important implications for the study of saving behavior. On the one hand, the expenditure on children's human capital may be viewed as a kind of saving and investment. Indeed, such investment may be motivated in part by the desire to provide optimally for the parents' own old-age security. In their report on focus group studies, Knodel, Chamratrithirong, and Debavalya (1987a: 153) quoted a participant who, referring to old-age support as repayment, commented that "two children with education can repay better than ten [without]." Increasing expenditures on child quality may mean that the simple assumption made in most life-cycle savings models, that children have a fixed cost, misses the mark; it is conceivable that the total expenditure on children may not decline when fertility does because of rising expenditures per child.

A fourth issue is the relationship between economic growth and age-earnings profiles in the East Asian economies. That relationship appears to be inconsistent with standard assumptions of the life-cycle saving model. The life-cycle model typically assumes a fixed longitudinal income profile. Moreover, it assumes that economic growth shifts the profile uniformly upward, in percentage terms, cohort by cohort. However, the data from East Asia, especially those from Taiwan, are more consistent with a fixed cross-sectional profile and a longitudinal profile that rises with age and the rate of economic growth (Carroll and Summers 1991; Deaton and Paxson 1994). The implications of this alternative specification of the age-earnings profile have not been fully explored, but it is obvious that the average age of earning will rise with the productivity growth rate in this case.

Finally, some observers have challenged the models of saving behavior that imply long or infinite planning horizons, and there are aspects of consumer behavior that may be inconsistent with the standard assumptions used in life-cycle or permanent-income models. For example, the longitudinal age profile of consumption may be inconsistent with models that assume that households save primarily to smooth (that is, evenly distribute) their income over the life cycle. Given standard assumptions, one might expect young households in a rapidly growing economy to engage in major dissaving to maintain consumption levels consistent with an expected lifetime income that far exceeds their current income. In fact, we do not observe this phenomenon in East Asia. Rather, we find in longitudinal data that consumption increases rapidly with age, and it is by all appearances highly correlated with income [Deaton 1989; Carroll and Summers 1991; but see Attanasio et al. (1999) for a contrasting view].

Our Analytical Approach

We begin our own analysis with the observation that there is a strong age pattern to people's consumption and earning streams over the life cycle. In childhood individuals consume far more than they earn, as they also do in old age, whereas in the prime working years they produce more than they consume. This life-cycle pattern gives rise to a demand for wealth (positive or negative) at each stage of the life cycle. We might say that children have a demand for negative wealth, or debt, because they must begin their life cycle by consuming more than they earn and thereby in some general sense go into debt. Prime-age workers, and anyone older, have a demand for positive wealth, to be spent down in old age. Under various assumptions we could calculate the life-cycle pattern of the demand for wealth, $L(x)$ [see, for example, Tobin (1967, figure 2 or figure 6) and Lee (2000)]. The demand for wealth can be met by two very different kinds of assets: (1) capital, or physical wealth, $K(x)$; and (2) transfer wealth, $T(x)$. Transfer wealth at age x is defined as the difference between the present values of expected survival-weighted transfers to be received and the present values of those transfers to be made over the remainder of the life cycle. At each age x we have the identity

$$L(x) = K(x) + T(x). \qquad (6.1)$$

If we aggregate across people of all ages in the population, weighting by the number of people at each age, then we obtain the aggregate identity

$$L = K + T \qquad (6.2)$$

[see, for example, Kotlikoff and Summers (1981) and Lee (1994)].

Physical capital can be held in the form of household assets, such as farmland, structures, livestock, or consumer durables, or it can be held in the form of equity in other production enterprises. Household assets are dominant in preindustrial societies, whereas equity becomes increasingly important in industrial societies. Transfer wealth can be held in a familial form, for example, as the expectation of future support from one's children, or in the form arising from public-sector transfers, as in the expectation of a government pension, paid for by taxes. Familial transfer wealth is dominant in preindustrial societies, whereas public-sector transfer wealth becomes important mainly in the later stages of industrialization. (Some Latin American countries, however, have introduced extensive pension programs early on.)

From this perspective, we must ask the following questions:

- In what ways should changes in fertility and mortality alter the demand for wealth at each stage of the life cycle?
- How should the changes in the population age distribution to which they give rise alter the aggregate demand for wealth by shifting the population weights for different life-cycle stages?
- How should these changes alter the aggregate proportion of output that is saved?
- How do the results differ when transfers for old-age support change?
- How do the results differ when transfers to children (for example, for education) change?

In addition, we need to consider a range of assumptions about interest rates, productivity growth rates, rates of subjective time preference, and the elasticity of intertemporal substitution for consumption. To address these questions, we first use a comparative steady-state analysis and then do a dynamic analysis.

Our analysis builds on Tobin's (1967) life-cycle saving model. We incorporate actual East Asian demographic variables and explicit intergenerational transfers for old-age support, and we use a more general specification of the intertemporal utility function than Tobin's. In the first stage we adopt Tobin's steady-state assumption. In the second stage we perform a dynamic simulation in which fertility and mortality vary, and we take the trajectories of interest rates and productivity growth rates to be given exogenously by their historical values. The dynamic simulation model does not yet include familial transfers.

Life-Cycle Savings in Steady States

Our model and assumptions are described in detail in Appendix A. Here, we discuss them in general terms. The basic unit of analysis is the household, consisting of a single adult and this adult's children. The children are assumed to set up their own households when they reach age 21. Old-age support is achieved by transfers to the household of the elderly parent, not by incorporating the elderly parent into the adult child's household. Each adult knows the probabilities of survival for him- or herself and for the children, at all ages, and takes these into account in planning. Uncertainty about age at death is absorbed by institutions with which we do not concern ourselves. Each adult also knows the interest rate and the across-all-ages growth rate in earnings as well as the cross-sectional age-earnings profile for all ages. With this information the adult is able to calculate the present value of the survival-weighted earnings of all members of the household; for children only the years up to age 21 are counted. The adult calculates the expected survival-weighted number of equivalent adult consumers (EACs) in the household for each year of its existence and derives consumption utility from the product of this number of EACs in each year and some function of consumption per EAC in the household. The specification is chosen so that the marginal utility of total household consumption each year depends only on the consumption per EAC and not on the number of EACs in the household. The adult then plans a life-cycle trajectory of total household consumption to maximize an intertemporal utility function, one depending on a subjective rate of time preference and on the elasticity of intertemporal substitution.

From the trajectories of earnings and consumption and from the interest rate we can calculate the trajectory of household assets. Using this trajectory, we can calculate total household income, including income from both labor and assets. By subtracting consumption from this household income, we find household savings at each age.

We treat familial transfers for old-age support as follows. We define an index t that describes the size of the total transfer received by an elder at age 60 and older. This index measures the fraction of the gap between the current earnings of a 40-year-old male and the current earnings of the elder that is made up by the familial transfer. Thus for $t = 1$ the elder would have total income equal to the labor earnings of a 40-year-old. The cost of this transfer is borne equally by all the surviving children of the elder. Any given value of t defines a stream of transfers, called $\tau(x)$, made or received across all ages over the life cycle; $\tau(x)$ is simply added to the household labor earnings at each age. Bequests can be handled in a similar manner.

For the comparative steady-state analysis we define a baseline set of assumptions and examine the effects of deviations from this baseline. The baseline set of assumptions comprises a life expectancy of 54 years, a total fertility rate of 3.1 children per woman, a rate of interest of 5%, a rate of productivity growth of 3%, and a zero rate of time preference. There are no transfers from adult children to their elderly parents for old-age support, and there is no bequest motive. Children of ages 0–4, 5–9, 10–14, and 15–18 have EAC weights of 0.3, 0.4, 0.6, and 0.7, respectively, whereas all others have weights of 1.0. The intertemporal elasticity of substitution is a key parameter in our model of life-cycle consumption, as explained in Appendix A. For the United States there is a rough consensus on the range of 0.2–0.35 (Auerbach and Kotlikoff 1987). For developing countries and for Taiwan in particular we are fortunate to have a recent study (Ogaki, Ostry, and Reinhart 1996) that finds a value of 0.6 for Taiwan and for other countries in the same income class. We have used this value in both our steady-state and our dynamic simulations.

Our tables report the results of simulations in which one or two of these assumptions are varied while all others are kept at the baseline levels. From these simulations we learn the following about comparative steady states:

- Mortality decline strongly raises saving rates (from 0.00 to +0.08) and the wealth ratio K/Y (from 0.14 to 1.67) (see Table 6.1).
- Fertility decline has little effect on saving rates, but it strongly raises the wealth ratio (from 0.77 to 2.33) (see Table 6.2).
- When mortality and fertility decline together, saving rates rise (from 0.02 to 0.09) and the wealth ratio rises strongly (from 0.52 to 3.76) (see Table 6.3).
- When productivity rises by itself, saving rates decline sharply (from 0.03 to −0.51), as does the wealth ratio (from 3.76 to −7.27) (see Table 6.4).
- When interest rates rise while productivity is fixed, saving rates rise (from −0.06 to +0.08) and the wealth ratio also rises (from −1.90 to +2.82) (see Table 6.5).
- When productivity growth rates and interest rates rise together, saving rates decline strongly (from 0.03 to −0.11), as does the wealth ratio (from 3.04 to −1.57) (see Table 6.6).
- Old-age support through transfers strongly reduces savings and the wealth ratio (see Table 6.7).
- With fertility held constant, increased investment in children reduces saving and the wealth ratio, defined narrowly as physical capital (see Table 6.8).

Although some of these results depend sensitively on the elasticity of substitution, the effects of demographic differences appear to be fairly robust. Not one of these many steady states generates an aggregate saving rate as high as 10%. But demographic changes across the demographic transition generate an increase in the capital output ratio from 0.5 to 3.8, which is very large. Combined with the fact that per capita income was growing at around 5% or 6% per year in Taiwan, this implies a massive increase in capital per worker, by a factor of 90 or so: $90 = (3.8/0.5)[\exp(45)(0.055)]$. To achieve this massive increase in the capital stock over the course of 45 years, net saving rates would have had to be much higher than 10% during this transitional phase.

TABLE 6.1

Steady-state Effects of Different Mortality Regimes
with Other Variables Set at Baseline Values

e_0	s	K/Y_l	K/Y
29.00	0.00	0.14	0.14
44.00	0.02	0.65	0.63
54.00	0.03	0.73	0.71
69.00	0.06	1.43	1.33
75.00	0.08	1.83	1.67

e_0, life expectancy at birth.
s, saving rate.
K/Y_l, wealth/labor income.
K/Y, wealth/income.

TABLE 6.2

Steady-state Effects of Different Fertility Regimes
with Other Variables Set at Baseline Values

TFR	s	K/Y_l	K/Y
6.34	0.05	0.80	0.77
3.94	0.03	0.64	0.62
3.14	0.03	0.73	0.71
2.45	0.04	1.38	1.29
1.72	0.04	2.63	2.33

TFR, total fertility rate.
s, saving rate.
K/Y_l, wealth/labor income.
K/Y, wealth/income.

TABLE 6.3

Steady-state Effects of Fertility and Mortality Varying Together,
with Other Variables Set at Baseline Values

TFR	e_0	s	K/Y_l	K/Y
6.34	29.00	0.02	0.53	0.52
3.95	43.50	0.02	0.57	0.55
3.14	53.50	0.03	0.73	0.71
2.45	69.00	0.07	2.28	2.05
1.72	75.90	0.09	4.62	3.76

TFR, total fertility rate.
e_0, life expectancy at birth.
s, saving rate.
K/Y_l, wealth/labor income.
K/Y, wealth/income.

TABLE 6.4

*Steady-state Effects of Varying Productivity Growth
with Fixed Interest Rate (at 0.03) and Other
Variables Set at Baseline Values*

g	s	K/Y_l	K/Y
0.00	0.03	4.24	3.76
0.02	0.02	0.66	0.64
0.04	−0.13	−2.54	−2.75
0.06	−0.51	−5.97	−7.27

g, productivity growth.
s, saving rate.
K/Y_l, wealth/labor income.
K/Y, wealth/income.

TABLE 6.5

*Steady-state Effects of Varying Interest Rate
with Fixed Productivity Growth (at 0.02)
and Other Variables Set at Baseline Values*

r	s	K/Y_l	K/Y
0	−0.06	−0.90	−1.90
0.02	−0.01	−0.19	−0.19
0.04	0.04	1.52	1.44
0.06	0.08	3.40	2.82

r, interest rate.
s, saving rate.
K/Y_l, wealth/labor income.
K/Y, wealth/income.

TABLE 6.6

*Steady-state Effects of Interest Rates
and Productivity Growth Varying Together,
with Other Variables Set at Baseline Values*

r	g	s	K/Y_l	K/Y
0.02	0.00	0.03	3.23	3.04
0.04	0.02	0.04	1.52	1.44
0.06	0.04	0.00	−0.02	−0.02
0.08	0.06	−0.11	−1.40	−1.57

r, interest rate.
g, productivity growth.
s, saving rate.
K/Y_l, wealth/labor income.
K/Y, wealth/income.

TABLE 6.7

Steady-state Effects of Different Levels of Familial Transfers to Elderly, with Other Variables Set at Baseline Values

Level of transfers[a]	s	K/Y_l	K/Y
0.0	0.03	0.73	0.71
0.2	−0.01	−0.28	−0.28
0.4	−0.05	−1.29	−1.38

s, saving rate.
K/Y_l, wealth/labor income.
K/Y, wealth/income.
[a]Transfers received by elderly from their children divided by the gap between elderly persons' earnings and those of a 40-year-old.

TABLE 6.8

Steady-state Effects of Different Levels of Parental Investment in Children, with Other Variables Set at Baseline Values

Investment per child[a]	s	K/Y_l	K/Y
0.25	0.05	1.37	1.29
0.50	0.03	0.73	0.71
0.75	0.01	0.22	0.22

s, saving rate.
K/Y_l, wealth/labor income.
K/Y, wealth/income.
[a]Consumption by a child (averaged across ages) as a fraction of consumption by an adult, that is, the average equivalent adult consumption, or EAC weight, for a child.

In Chapter 5 of this volume Williamson and Higgins rightly stress that comparative steady-state analyses can be misleading and that we need studies of transitional dynamics. That fact has encouraged us to conduct dynamic simulations of savings and capital accumulation that take into account the changing age distribution of a population during the demographic transition. It is to these dynamic simulations that we now turn.

Life-Cycle Savings in Dynamic Simulations

Ultimately, we intend to perform simulations in which interest rates and productivity growth rates are determined endogenously along with saving rates and wealth, using a growth model fitted to Taiwan's experience. For the present, however, we restrict ourselves to a simpler task, in which interest rates and earnings growth rates are treated as exogenous and are taken from the historical record. The agents in our analysis do not make optimal decisions under uncertainty; rather, they always view their frequently revised expectations as completely accurate. In this sense our analysis is not fully dynamic, and there is no precautionary motive for savings.

Whereas in steady-state models it is appropriate to assume that all actors have full information about the future, the situation is more complicated in a dynamic simulation. Here, we simulate two scenarios. In the first scenario we assume that adults know the demographic conditions (life expectancy and fertility) of only the current period. In the second scenario we assume that all adults have full knowledge of their future fertility and of future cohort mortality, including that of their children. (It is arguable that it would make more sense to assume that adults are ignorant of future mortality while knowing future fertility.) Our hypothetical adults also know the shape of cross-sectional earnings profiles, averaged across males and females, and therefore they implicitly know future trends in the labor supply for both men and women. However, they do not know what future real interest rates will be, and they do not know how rapidly the level of the age-earnings profile will be rising. We make an ad hoc assumption about how these expectations are formed. We assume that adults form an estimate of the current underlying rates of interest and wage growth by averaging levels in the current and previous four years. But we also assume that they do not necessarily expect these average real interest rates and earnings growth rates to continue indefinitely into the future. Instead, they project a gradual exponential change from the current underlying rates to some given ultimate levels of the rates. In our base scenario these ultimate rates are set at 3.0% per year for the real interest rate and at 1.5% per year for the growth rate of earnings. Both these rates are well below the averages recorded over our period of observation, 1950–1990, during which they were 7.4% and 5.5%, respectively. Our rationale is that adults may look to the experience of the United States or other high-income countries to assess their own long-term future. Our experience with the simulations suggests that expectations should be even less responsive to current events than we have made them be.

Given this assumed knowledge about current or future demographic conditions and about future earnings and interest rates, each household solves the same optimization problem as that outlined earlier and in Appendix A for the static model. However, they must re-solve it each year as new information becomes available from current interest and earnings growth rates, factoring in their actual wealth holdings in the current year. Typically, they will find that the amount of wealth they actually hold does not correspond to their optimal amount under the new circumstances. Thus each year they revise their plans and consume, save, and invest accordingly. To form their optimal plans, they must look ahead to the end of their life, which we assume to occur at age 100.

Of course, few people survive into extreme old age, and adults take these survival probabilities into account when formulating their plans. Adults of

21 years in 1994 must project their future fertility and mortality all the way out to 2073. In practice, we have given them expectations corresponding to the official projections of the Taiwanese government. We have used these projections to consider saving rates through 2100, requiring projections through 2179. Obviously, projections so far into the future are extremely uncertain, but what matters most is not what actually happens but what people expect to happen. Our dynamic model is described in detail in Appendix B.

Real rates of interest and GDP growth per worker were fairly volatile between 1951 to 1989. The oil crisis of the 1970s produced a huge negative spike in the real rate of interest. When interest rates or earnings rates change dramatically, there will be dramatic effects on expectations about the future, which can lead to sharp changes in saving behavior. Preliminary simulations using these actual rates of interest and earnings growth per worker yielded an erratic pattern of saving rates and capital-output ratios. The interest rate of −33% in 1974 had a huge influence, because holders of capital stock lost one-third of it in one year—at the same time that the present value of their future earnings rose through the roof. Although such predictions of the model are of interest, they do not advance our understanding of the role that demographic change plays in people's economic planning, and so we performed simulations in which the interest rate was fixed at its average value of 7.4% and earnings growth at 5.5% for the period 1950–94. After 1994 the rates were assumed to drift slowly downward, closing 10% of the gap each year, toward a long-run interest rate of 3.0% and an earnings growth of 1.5%.

Figure 6.2 shows the results of the two simulations. In the first simulation (solid curve) the actors are ignorant of future demographic changes; and in the second simulation (dotted curve) the actors are assumed to know their future mortality and fertility. The saving rate in the first simulation begins at 8.5% in 1950 and declines a bit initially before beginning a sustained climb to 18.5% in 2010. It then declines gradually, stabilizing at 6.5%, slightly below initial levels. In the second simulation the saving rate begins at a higher level of 16.5% in 1950 and then declines to 7.6% in 1974 before beginning a sustained climb to 20.5% in 2006. The rate then declines gradually to a level of 6.5%. It is surprising to see the significant difference in saving behavior in the two models for the period 1950–60. We are currently investigating the source of this difference, which ultimately lies in our assumption that actors anticipate future changes in fertility and mortality. When dependency ratios fall during the period 1970–2005, we find that both simulations show significant increases in saving rates because of life-cycle saving. When dependency ratios rise in the post-2005 period, we again find close agreement between the simulations, showing declines in saving rates and eventual stabilization at 6.5%—in close agreement with the results from the static analysis.

It is also instructive to compare the timing of these changes in the two mod-

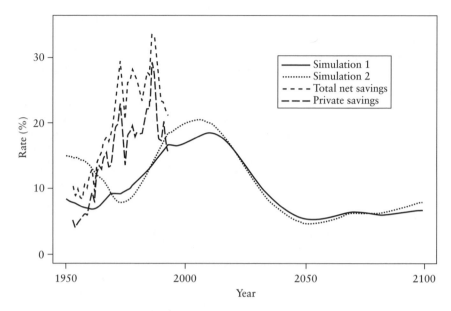

FIGURE 6.2. Simulated Saving Rates: Taiwan, 1950–2100.

els. In our two simulation models (Figure 6.2) both the historical demographic change experienced by a cohort and the anticipated future changes affect current saving behavior. Therefore the current age distribution (and the economic support ratio) may be a faulty guide to current saving behavior. This is one potentially serious problem for the many empirical studies that relate contemporaneous age distributions to saving behavior. Nevertheless, we generally find close agreement between the economic support ratio and the timing of saving changes, except in the initial years of the simulation.

We placed no constraints on indebtedness in these simulation models. Young households were able to borrow to finance current consumption in anticipation of higher future earnings. Anticipating that some analysts might question the realism of such borrowing behavior, we also ran a model in which we constrained net worth to be positive. It made little difference to the aggregate saving behavior predicted by the model. The large increase in savings associated with the demographic transition was still evident.

Figure 6.3 plots the changes in the capital-output ratio implied by the time path of saving rates. The ratio rises from a very low level (around 0.3) in 1950 to a plateau of about 5 in 2030.

These dynamic simulations tell a dramatically different story than do the steady-state simulations, confirming the point made by Higgins and William-

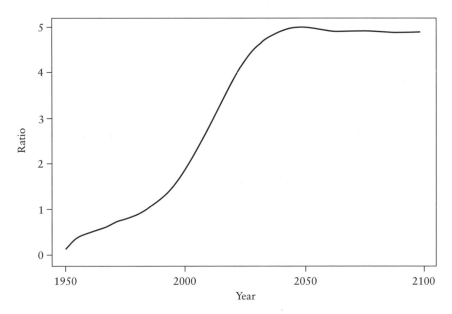

FIGURE 6.3. Simulated Capital-Output Ratio: Taiwan, 1950–2100.

son in Chapter 5. Whereas steady-state simulations closely match the dynamic simulations after population growth has been stabilized, they are obviously incapable of capturing the changes in saving rates during the demographic transition. To what extent does the demographic transition account for the increase in Taiwan? In our simulations we find large increases in saving over the period of the demographic transition, from 1970 to 1993. Saving increased by 7.5–9.8%—roughly one-half to two-thirds of the actual change in saving over the period.

We must bear in mind, however, that the principal means by which the elderly are supported in Taiwan and the rest of East Asia is not by drawing down on their earlier savings, as the life-cycle savings model assumes, but rather through transfers within the family. We have not yet incorporated this element into the dynamic simulation, although we do plan to do so in the future. As our steady-state analysis shows, old-age support through transfers has a dominating effect on saving and capital formation. At a minimum, we should reduce the size of the swing in saving rates that can be accounted for by the life-cycle saving hypothesis. By ignoring transfers to the elderly, our dynamic simulations probably overstate the effects of demographic change on capital accumulation. At the same time, the weakening of the familial old-age support system, which has accompanied economic development in East Asia, is itself an additional cause of the increase in saving rates.

Summary and Conclusion

Demographic transition in East Asia has been unusually rapid, and the swings in age structure have been dramatic. Child dependency first rose, then fell strongly. Old-age dependency is rising. Total dependency first rose, then fell steeply. In the future it will rise again, ending up roughly where it began. Evidently, a comparative stable-population analysis of the effect of the transition on the total dependency ratio would show little change, although the transitional dynamics are dramatic.

We used our data on Taiwan's population during the transition to calculate a refined dependency ratio, the economic support ratio, which gives for each year the number of equivalent adult producers in the population divided by the number of equivalent adult consumers. We saw that this ratio rose by 17–35% between 1950 and 2000, indicating that consumption at each age could rise by this amount even if there was no change in the productivity of labor. Alternatively, this additional demographic bonus could have been used to raise savings.

By assuming that consumption and saving behavior are governed by the desire to smooth consumption over life-cycle variations in expected household earnings—in effect, to provide for old-age retirement—we have explored how this demographic bonus would be used. Our first analysis assumed an essentially steady state, simply comparing the implications of the pre- and post-transitional age distributions. We found that lower mortality implied substantially higher saving rates and a substantially higher capital-output ratio. Lower fertility implied no change in saving rates coupled with a higher capital-output ratio. When fertility and mortality change together from high to low levels, as happens eventually across the transition, saving rates rise modestly, but the capital-output ratio rises considerably. Because we are examining net savings, it is possible to have either a high or a low capital-output ratio with the same saving rate. This tells us that we should not expect the demographic transition to lead to a large permanent change in the saving rate, even though longer life and lower fertility will lead to a substantial increase in the demand for wealth and in the amount of capital per worker and per unit of output. Dynamic analysis is necessary to see what transpires between these two steady states and how the economy moves from a low-wealth situation to a situation in which there is a high level of capital per worker.

Our dynamic analysis reveals that significant increases in saving occur over the period 1970–2005. This trend is followed by decreases in the saving rate over the first half of the twenty-first century, until rates stabilize at close to initial levels. Taking these results at face value, we would have to conclude that Taiwan's demographic transition significantly contributed to the increase in the saving rate there since 1970.

Although the simulated saving path mirrors the rise of savings experienced in Taiwan during the 1970s and 1980s, many important features of Taiwan's saving are not captured by the dynamic life-cycle model. Saving rates rise more substantially during the transition than do the simulated rates, they are much higher in most years than is consistent with saving motivated solely by life-cycle smoothing, they rose steadily throughout the 1950s and 1960s in contrast to our simulated rates, and they are subject to short-term influences that are not captured by the life-cycle model we have used.

Returning to the question posed at the outset—whether rapid demographic transition accounted for or at least contributed to East Asia's rapid economic progress—we note that between 1970 and 1993 the economic support ratio increased by 22–28% in Taiwan, providing a demographic bonus. Our simulations indicate that the saving rate rose by 8–10% over the same period. It appears, therefore, that between one-third and one-half of the entire demographic bonus would be saved under the life-cycle saving hypothesis.

Demographic aging will lead to declines in saving rates in the twenty-first century. By 2050 saving rates are forecast to decline to pretransitional levels, but the equilibrium capital-output ratio will have increased more than tenfold compared with that in 1950.

This discussion has taken our results at face value, ignoring the role of familial transfers in the provision of old-age support in East Asian populations and indeed throughout the Third World. In the 1950s and more generally in the period before fertility declined, it seems likely that the familial provision for old-age support was strong and pervasive throughout the region, with all generations expecting it to continue in the future. Under such circumstances the life-cycle saving motive would be extremely weak. Some of our comparative static simulations depicted this situation and showed that indeed strong familial transfers for old-age support would lead to low savings and correspondingly low capital-output ratios. There is abundant evidence, however, that attitudes about the familial old-age support system are changing radically and have been changing for several decades. Although elderly coresidence with adult children remains pervasive throughout the region, it is declining, and surveys show weakening expectations. Under these circumstances the working-age population is beginning to feel obliged to provide for its own old-age support through life-cycle savings. This generation is caught in a squeeze, for it must make transfers to elderly parents and at the same time provide for its own retirement through saving. This is precisely the situation of young workers in those OECD (Organisation for Economic

Co-operation and Development) countries that are instituting privatized or funded public pension programs. The transition from public or familial transfer-based old-age support to publicly or privately funded old-age support places a double burden on the transitional generation. Therefore saving and wealth should rise for two reasons: (1) because of the demographic transition and (2) because of the transition from familial transfers to funded provision for old-age support.

Details of the Static Model Underlying
the Life-Cycle Saving Simulations

Demographic Variables

The household consists of one adult and his or her dependent children. We assume that children leave home to form their own households at age z, an average for male and female children. We take $p(x)$ to refer to cohort survival probability to age x. The expectation that the household will reach age x from age z (the age at which all households are assumed to be formed) is expressed as $p(x)/p(z)$. The *expected* number of adults at each age x $(x > z)$ is therefore equal to

$$\frac{p(x)}{p(z)} = n(x, x). \tag{6.3}$$

Fertility at age x is given by

$$f(x) = \frac{m(x)}{2}, \tag{6.4}$$

which is half of female fertility at age x. Surviving parents or their siblings share the total number of surviving children produced by a parental cohort. (We assume that uncles and aunts who have the same age as a deceased parent adopt the orphans.) The number of children at exact age i for a parental age x (for all $i < x$) is given by

$$\frac{p(x - i)f(x - i)p(i)}{p(x)} = o(i, x). \tag{6.5}$$

This expression is used in what follows.

The *expected* number of dependent children at exact age i (for all $i < z$) evaluated by an individual at the age of household formation z for a future age x and future time t is given by

$$n(i, x) = \left(\frac{p(x)}{p(z)}\right)\left(\frac{p(x - i)f(x - i)p(i)}{p(x)}\right) = \frac{p(x - i)f(x - i)p(i)}{p(z)}. \tag{6.6}$$

For $i \geq z$ and $i \neq x$, $n(i, x) = 0$.

The expected (from age z) household size at age x of head is

$$\sum_{i=0}^{x} n(i, x) = \frac{p(x)}{p(z)} + \sum_{i=0}^{z-1} \frac{p(x - i)f(x - i)p(i)}{p(z)}. \tag{6.7}$$

Basic Household Model

The basic model for the household is a generalization of the one used by Tobin (1967). Our notations assume that interest rates and the growth in the level of the age-earnings profile are constant, but the generalization to varying rates is straightforward. We apply it in the section on dynamic simulations. Given the following notations

$$H(x) = \sum_{i=0}^{x} e(i)n(i, x), \tag{6.8}$$

$$Y_l(x) = we^{\lambda x} \sum_{i=0}^{x} l(i)n(i, x), \tag{6.9}$$

$$PV[Y_l] = \int_{z}^{w} e^{-rx} Y_l(x) \, dx, \tag{6.10}$$

$$PV[C] = \int_{z}^{w} e^{-rx} C(x) \, dx, \tag{6.11}$$

$$V = \int_{z}^{\omega} e^{-\rho x} u[C(x), H(x)] \, dx, \tag{6.12}$$

the optimization problem when the household is formed is to choose a trajectory of $C(x)$ so as to maximize V, subject to

$$PV[Y_l] = PV[C]. \tag{6.13}$$

Here, the notation is mostly transparent. $H(x)$ is the expected household size measured in EAC units, with $e(i)$ measuring the fractional value of consumption of an individual of age i relative to an adult. $Y_l(x)$ is the expected household labor income, with $l(i)$ measuring equivalent producer units (the geometric mean of labor income for both sexes combined over the period 1976 to 1992) and $we^{\lambda x}$ representing an across-all-ages shifter for labor productivity. $Y_l(x)$ depends on the level of the wage index when the household is age x. This, in turn, depends on how rapidly the wage index is rising. We assume a steady-state increase at rate λ and avoid introducing time subscripts by setting w equal to the level of the wage index at the time the household head was age 0. This device works so long as we do not try to compare households with heads of different ages. $C(x)$ represents total household consumption. In this specification the rate at which the planner derives utility from household consumption depends on household size, measured in EAC units in a way yet to be specified. We enrich this basic model later by including transfers from adult children to their elderly parents.

Life-Cycle Optimization

We define the instantaneous household utility function to be

$$u[H(x), C(x)] = \begin{cases} H(x)\left(\dfrac{\left\{ \left[\dfrac{C(x)}{H(x)}\right]^{1-\gamma} - 1\right\}}{1 - \gamma} \right) & \text{for } \gamma \neq 1, \\[20pt] H(x)\ln\left[\dfrac{C(x)}{H(x)}\right] & \text{for } \gamma = 1. \end{cases} \tag{6.14}$$

In this specification household utility is proportional to the number of EACs in the household, denoted as $H(x)$, multiplied by a standard constant relative risk-aversion utility function, with consumption per EAC as its argument. This is a natural generalization of Tobin's household utility function. Although this household utility function appears to be complex, its derivative is simple:

$$\frac{\partial u}{\partial C(x)} = \left[\frac{C(x)}{H(x)}\right]^{-\gamma} = \left[\frac{H(x)}{C(x)}\right]^{\gamma}. \tag{6.15}$$

Next, we derive the optimal household-consumption path over the life cycle, after forming the Lagrangian and differentiating it:

$$L = V - \lambda[PV(Y_l) - PV(C)], \tag{6.16}$$

$$\frac{\partial L}{\partial C(x)} = e^{-\rho x}\left[\frac{H(x)}{C(x)}\right]^{\lambda} - \lambda e^{-rx} = 0, \tag{6.17}$$

$$C(x) = H(x)e^{(r-\rho)x/\gamma}\lambda^{-1/\gamma}. \tag{6.18}$$

Substituting $C(x)$ into the budget constraint yields

$$\lambda^{-1/\gamma} = \frac{PV[Y_l]}{\displaystyle\int_z^\omega e^{-rx}H(x)e^{-(r-\rho)x/\gamma}\, dx}. \tag{6.19}$$

Substituting back for $\lambda^{-1/\gamma}$ yields

$$C(x) = \frac{PV[Y_l]H(x)e^{(r-\rho)x/\gamma}}{\displaystyle\int_z^\omega e^{-rx}H(x)e^{-(r-\rho)x/\gamma}\, dx}. \tag{6.20}$$

From this result we can observe the following:

• Consumption is proportional to the household size measured in EAC units, other things being equal.

- Consumption per EAC unit in the household rises over the life cycle at the rate of $(r - \rho)/\gamma$, which becomes slower as γ becomes larger.
- Although utility is undefined for $\gamma = 1$, its derivative with respect to $C(x)$ is defined and equals the derivative of the Tobin (1967) utility function, $H(x)\ln[C(x)/H(x)]$.
- The larger γ is, the lower the rate of intertemporal substitution and the less responsive consumption and saving are to variations in the interest rate.

Adding Intergenerational Transfers for Old-Age Support

Now let us suppose that there is an age schedule of net intergenerational transfers measured by $\tau(x)$, where positive $\tau(x)$ means that transfers received at age x exceed transfers made. We have already included the basic consumption costs of children by way of the $e(i)$ function, so we do not include them here in the transfer function; rather, the function mainly reflects transfers to the elderly from their children. The function also does not include bequests, which we treat separately. A person of age x has $o(i, x)$ children of age i. Suppose that each surviving child contributes an equal share to his or her elderly parent. We then have the following relationship:

$$\tau(x) = \sum_{i=0}^{x} o(i, x)\tau_{ch} = \tau_{ch}o(x), \qquad (6.21)$$

where $o(x)$ is the total number of surviving children (subscript "ch") of a surviving elderly person.

It is convenient to specify the size of the transfer to be received by an elder. For each person of age 60 and older, we set net transfers received at a fraction τ of the difference between the labor earnings of this elder at age 40, updated to his or her current age by productivity growth in the interim (equivalently, this is a fraction of the labor earnings of a current 40-year-old adult) and the elder's current earnings. Thus, if the fraction is 1.0, then the elder would have his or her income upgraded to the income of a current 40-year-old adult through familial transfers:

$$\tau(x) = \tau\{[e^{\lambda(x-40)}y_l(40)] - y_l(x)\} \qquad \text{for all } x \geq 60. \quad (6.22)$$

Then we can calculate the share to be paid by each surviving child, per surviving elder parent, by dividing this result by $o(x)$. This must be calculated so as to be consistent with the schedule of transfers received by the elderly. A surviving child at age a under the age of 60 will have a surviving parent at age x, over the age of 60, with the probability equal to $[2/\text{TFR}] \times [f(x - a)][p(x)/p(x - a)]$ for $x \geq 60$. (The factor of $2/\text{TFR}$ converts the fertility distribution into a probability distribution. TFR is the total fertility rate.) The cost of supporting each such parent of age x will be shared by all the surviving siblings, of whom there are $o(x)$. For such a surviving parent the child will make a transfer of $\tau(x)/o(x)$. The total expected value of transfers made by a child of age a in support of elderly parents is given by the sum over these ages x:

$$\tau(a) = \left(\frac{2}{\text{TFR}}\right) \sum_{x=60}^{\omega} \frac{\left[\frac{\tau(x)}{o(x)}\right] f(x - a) p(x)}{p(x - a)} \qquad \text{for } a < 60, \quad (6.23)$$

and by $\tau(x)$ for $x \geq 60$, as given in Equation (6.22).

When this transfer function is added to the optimization problem, the revised budget constraint will be as before, except that $\tau(a)$ is added to $Y_l(a)$. Life-cycle wealth is now given by $PV(\tau) + Y_l$. When $r > n + \lambda$, $PV(\tau) < 0$, because these are upward transfers.

Details of the Dynamic Models Underlying the Life-Cycle Saving Simulations

Demographic Variables

There are two dynamic models, which differ only in regard to the demographic foresight of actors. In the basic dynamic model actors are assumed to know future cohort demography. This dynamic model differs from the static model described in appendix A in that we use the actual time series of cohort fertility and mortality rates of Taiwan's demographic transition rather than fixed pre- and post-transition rates. In the second dynamic model actors are assumed to know only the current period demography. Their expectations about future household size and future survival are based on what they observe in the current period.

Basic Model

The basic model is the same as the static model, except that decisions are made at all ages $x \geq z$ rather than only at age $x = z$. Expressions are evaluated at age x looking forward a years ($a \geq 0$) into the future when the household head will be age $x + a$ in year $t + a$:

$$H(x, a, t) = \sum_{i=0}^{x+a} e(i)n(i, x + a, t + a), \tag{6.24}$$

$$Y_l(x, a, t) = w(t + a) \sum_{i=0}^{x+a} l(i)n(i, x + a, t + a), \tag{6.25}$$

$$PV[Y_l(x, a, t)] = \int_0^{w-x} e^{-ra}Y_l(x, a, t)\, da, \tag{6.26}$$

$$PV[C(x, a, t)] = \int_0^{w-x} e^{-ra}C(x, a, t)\, da, \tag{6.27}$$

$$V(x, t) = \int_0^{w-x} e^{-pa}u\left\{C(x, a, t), \left[\frac{p(z, t - x + z)}{p(x, t)}\right]H(x, a, t)\right\}\, da. \tag{6.28}$$

Maximize V subject to

$$W(x, t) + \frac{p(z, t - x + z)}{p(x, t)} PV[Y_l(x, a, t)] = PV[C(x, a, t)], \quad (6.29)$$

$$W(x, t) = \left(\frac{p(x - 1, t - 1)}{p(x, t)} \right)$$

$$\times \left[(e^r W(x - 1, t - 1)) + \left(e^{r/2} \left\{ \left[\frac{p(z, t - x + z - 1) Y_l(x - 1, 0, t - 1)}{p(x - 1, t - 1)} \right] \right. \right. \right.$$

$$\left. \left. \left. - C(x - 1, 0, t - 1) \right\} \right) \right]. \quad (6.30)$$

The expectations in expected household size (measured in EAC units) and expected household labor income must both be adjusted by $p(z, t - x + z)/p(x, t)$ to reflect survival to age x. $W(x, t)$ measures wealth and is defined so that cohort wealth is maintained. That is, there are lateral, not vertical, bequests—wealth saved by last year's households age $x - 1$ is shared among this year's surviving heads aged x.

Life-Cycle Optimization

We define the instantaneous household utility function to be

$$u \left\{ C(x, a, t), \left[\frac{p(z, t - x + z)}{p(x, t)} \right] H(x, a, t) \right\} = \left[\frac{p(z, t - x + z)}{p(x, t)} \right]$$

$$\times H(x, a, t) \left[\frac{\left(\left\{ \dfrac{C(x, a, t)}{\left[\dfrac{p(z, t - x + z)}{p(x, t)} \right] H(x, a, t)} \right\}^{1 - \gamma} - 1 \right)}{1 - \gamma} \right]. \quad (6.31)$$

Although this household utility function appears to be complex, its derivative is simple:

$$\frac{\partial u}{\partial C(x, a, t)} = \left[\frac{C(x, a, t)}{H(x, a, t)} \right]^{-\gamma} = \left[\frac{H(x, a, t)}{C(x, a, t)} \right]^{\gamma}. \quad (6.32)$$

We derive the optimal household consumption path over the life cycle as follows, after forming the Lagrangian and differentiating it:

$$L = V - \lambda \left\{ W(x, t) + \frac{p(z, t - x + z)}{p(x, t)} PV[Y_l(x, a, t)] - PV[C(x, a, t)] \right\}, \quad (6.33)$$

$$\frac{\partial L}{\partial C(x, a, t)} = e^{-pa}\left[\frac{H(x, a, t)}{C(x, a, t)}\right]^{\gamma} - \lambda e^{-ra} = 0, \qquad (6.34)$$

$$C(x, a, t) = H(x, a, t)e^{(r-\rho)a/\gamma}\lambda^{-1/\gamma}. \qquad (6.35)$$

Substituting $C(x, a, t)$ into the budget constraint yields

$$\lambda^{-1/\gamma} = \frac{W(x, t) + \left[\dfrac{p(z, t - x + z)}{p(x, t)}\right]PV[Y_I(x, a, t)]}{\displaystyle\int_0^{\omega-x} e^{-ra}H(x, a, t)e^{(r-\rho)a/\gamma}\, dx}. \qquad (6.36)$$

Substituting for $\lambda^{-1/\gamma}$ yields the expression for consumption a years in the future as assessed at current age x:

$$C(x, a, t) = \frac{\left\{W(x, t) + \left[\dfrac{p(z, t - x + z)}{p(x, t)}\right]PV[Y_I(x, a, t)]\right\}H(x, a, t)e^{(r-\rho)a/\gamma}}{\displaystyle\int_0^{\omega-x} e^{-ra}H(x, a, t)e^{(r-\rho)a/\gamma}\, da}.$$

$$(6.37)$$

Data and Calculation-Related
Details of the Simulations

Earnings

Earnings by age and sex are available for the period from 1976 to 1993. The data provide total labor earnings, including self-employment earnings, per member of the population in each age-sex group. These we averaged for the two sexes for each year. A standard age profile of earnings was calculated as the exponentiated average over time of the natural logarithms of earnings at each age. Evidently, this standard age schedule abstracts from changes over time in the earnings of children and in the labor force participation of men and women, but an examination of the data suggests that it does not present a major problem.

We then used the standard age profile formed in this way to calculate a measure of household labor supply for each age of household head, by using it to weight the average age composition of the household at each age of the head. We then found actual household earnings in any given year by multiplying this measure by the level of earnings in that year.

We constructed the earnings level variable by calculating the actual total labor earnings each year. We did this by combining the population age distribution with the actual age-earnings profile for each year and then by dividing this total by the standard labor supply measure, formed by combining the population age distribution with the standard age-earnings schedule. The resultant earnings-level measure reflects both productivity growth and changes in participation rates over time. Its growth rate slightly exceeds that of productivity over this period, as would be expected because of rising female labor force participation. For that reason this empirical implementation of $w(t)$ does not correspond exactly to the variable as we defined it earlier.

Households are assumed to calculate their expected future earnings by forming the measure of household labor supply for all future periods in the manner described earlier, based on the standard age schedule of earnings. They then multiply future household labor supply by the projected future level of earnings for each period to form their estimate of household earnings in future years, which they then discount back to the present at an appropriate rate.

Support Ratio

Calculating the support ratio requires weights to use for earnings and weights to use for consumption. For earnings we used the standard age schedule of earnings described earlier. For consumption the calculation of weights is much more complicated. We used household survey data on total expenditure and household composition. Within each household we used Deaton and Muellbauer's (1986) weights to allocate consumption to household members of each age. Then, for a given age we averaged consumption across all these allocated amounts. In this way the consumption weights reflect not only the Deaton-Muellbauer weights but also the expenditure level of households with the age of the head with whom they typically reside. For example, children will tend to reside with younger heads and therefore to have a share of lower consumption levels.

Expectation Formation

We assume that adults form an expectation of a current underlying rate of interest or of earnings growth by taking a five-year unweighted average of the most recent observations. However, the adults do not necessarily believe that the current underlying rates will persist over the long run. Instead, they project that current rates will slowly converge to an ultimate value, which may be chosen on the basis of the experience of other developed countries, for example. In each future year the gap between the projected level and the ultimate level is assumed to shrink by 10%. This assumption leads to the following specification for the future rates of change and future levels of interest or earnings. The expectation in year t of the underlying rate of interest is

$$r_e(t, 0) = \frac{\sum_{b=t-4}^{t} r(b)}{5}. \tag{6.38}$$

The expectation for $t + a$ years in the future (for all $a > 0$) converges to a long-run ultimate rate of r_e^*.

Savings, Capital Formation, and Economic Growth in Singapore

MUN HENG TOH

THE WORLD BANK'S (1993a) study on high-performing Asian economies has identified five major factors responsible for rapid growth: (1) a high saving and investment rate, (2) high and growing human capital formation, (3) rapid growth of exports, (4) prudent macroeconomic policies and management, and (5) institutions that foster cooperation between government and the private sector and the creation of a business-friendly environment. Of course, these are not the only factors, nor can any one of them claim the entire credit for growth creation. The allocation of resources between present consumption and future consumption (saving) is one of the most fundamental economic choices facing any economy. This choice affects not only the rate of economic growth of a country but also the standard of living for generations yet unborn.

In this chapter I consider how Singapore has mobilized its domestic and foreign resources to create the productive capacity needed to generate economic growth and development. I begin with an overview of Singapore's economic performance since the 1960s. The discussion focuses on Singapore's institutional structure and planning process, highlighting the philosophy of resource mobilization that has powered Singapore's industrialization program. Next, I briefly describe the types of savings and the salient features of savings in Singapore. Then, in the following section I assess the compulsory saving scheme, known as the Central Provident Fund (CPF), describing its role of fulfilling social and economic objectives. I also discuss the management of CPF savings and public sector surpluses. In the next three sections

I thank Andrew Mason for his constructive suggestions in the writing and revision of this chapter.

I examine in turn the role of foreign investment in financing domestic capital formation and the impact of Singapore's investments abroad, the management and use of various sources of savings within Singapore's macroeconomic policy framework, and how savings have affected growth. The last of these sections considers whether compulsory saving crowds out voluntary saving in the private sector. The chapter concludes with several policy recommendations for further liberalizing the use of the CPF by its members. Singapore's way of managing savings in fostering economic growth can serve as a model for other resource-poor nations.

Overview of Singapore's Performance

Between 1960 and 1995 the Singapore economy grew at an average annual rate of 9.1%, well above the average of 4.6% among the world's developing economies (ADB 1995). Singapore's real gross domestic product (GDP) per capita increased more than eightfold, from S$3,072 to S$26,400. In 1995 the economy provided jobs for 1.7 million people, including foreign workers, compared with 471,900 working adults recorded by the 1957 census.

In Chapter 2 of this volume Bauer describes and compares many features of Singapore's growth experience with the experiences of other East and Southeast Asian countries. In several important respects Singapore's experience is distinctive and worthy of attention. First, Singapore is a land-scarce economy. Agriculture and mining contributed only 3.4% to the GDP in the 1960s and still less, 0.2%, in 1995. The service sector dominates the economy, contributing close to two-thirds of GDP. The manufacturing sector grew in tandem with the economy between 1965 and 1995.

The stability in these broad sectors disguises the transformation of Singapore from an entrepôt economy in the early 1960s to a capital- and technology-driven economy in the 1990s. The role of foreign capital and expertise in this process cannot be underestimated. After Singapore's expulsion from the Malaysian union in 1963 and the collapse of an anticipated pan-Malaysian domestic market that would have supported Singapore's nascent industrialization program, Singapore embarked on an aggressive open-economy policy. It considers the world its hinterland, welcoming foreign companies that establish production bases within its borders and accelerating development by tapping into the international market network, technologies, and managerial skills of foreign enterprises. Singapore has rigorously pursued an export-oriented development strategy. It has also created the necessary infrastructure to make itself an international financial center and information and communication hub. It attained these targets by making use of domestic and international resources and expertise. By the end of the

1980s Singapore emerged as a capital-surplus economy, joining other new industrial economies of the region in investing in developing economies.

The ratio of total trade to GDP indicates the open nature of the Singapore economy. That ratio has been greater than 300% for most of the years between 1960 and 1995. Singapore's export-oriented development strategy has helped it to turn the current accounts in the balance of payments from deficits into surpluses since 1987. Moreover, the overall balance in the balance of payments has consistently shown a surplus, and, as a consequence, the country's official foreign reserve has been accumulating steadily, reaching S$97,300 million by 1995. Whereas foreign reserves steadily increased, external government debt, which is usually targeted for financing capital formation, had virtually vanished by 1995.

Price stability is a hallmark of the Singapore economy. The inflation rate, measured by changes in the consumer price index, is kept low by the orderly adjustment of wages negotiated through the National Wage Council and by the sustained strength of the Singapore dollar through exchange rate intervention by the Monetary Authority of Singapore. Regulation of the money supply is not a policy intervention in view of the free mobility of capital, and the money supply has expanded in line with money demand and economic growth, with little or no inflationary pressure.

National Savings in Perspective

The saving behavior of an economy reveals much about the nature of a society, because saving behavior reflects various values, institutions, and incentives. Above all, saving behavior reflects the relative values placed on the present and the future by citizens and political institutions (Boskin 1986). The concept of saving extends far beyond the purely personal decision to spend or not to spend. An important aggregate is national savings: the sum of public-sector or government saving (S_G), private domestic savings (S_P), and foreign savings (S_F).

Public-sector saving consists primarily of budgetary saving (S_{Gb}), which arises from any excess of government revenues over government consumption. In a few countries the savings of government-owned enterprises (S_{Ge}) also contribute to public-sector savings.

Private domestic savings arise from two sources: corporate saving (S_{Pc}) and household saving (S_{Ph}). Corporate saving is defined as the retained earnings of corporate enterprises. Household saving is simply that part of household disposable income not consumed. It includes saving from unincorporated enterprises (single proprietorships, partnerships, and other noncorporated forms of business enterprise).

Foreign saving also arises from two basic sources: official foreign saving (S_{Fo}), or foreign aid, and private foreign saving (S_{Fp}). Private foreign saving has three components: external commercial borrowing, or debt finance (S_{Fpd}); foreign direct investment (S_{Fdi}); and foreign portfolio investment (S_{Ppi}).

Thus the total available saving can be viewed as

$$S = S_P + S_G + S_F = (S_P + S_G) + (S_{Fo} + S_{Fp}). \qquad (7.1)$$

For purposes of understanding saving patterns and policies, one can disaggregate saving further into

$$S = [(S_{Pc} + S_{Pb}) + (S_{Gb} + S_{Gc})] + (S_{Fo} + S_{Fpd} + S_{Fdi} + S_{Fpi}). \qquad (7.2)$$

These different types of saving have independent characteristics and need not always move in unison.

Sources of saving differ greatly among developing nations, depending not only on such factors as the level of per capita income, natural resource endowments, and sectoral composition of the GDP but also on the governments' saving-mobilization policies and development strategies. Singapore has been able to finance its high investment-GDP ratios through intensified efforts to mobilize savings from various sources—domestic and foreign, public and private.

Salient Features of Saving in Singapore

Singapore is often described as a high-saving, high-investment economy. Indeed, it has one of the highest saving rates in the world, typically saving a higher portion of its GDP than the other high-saving economies of East and Southeast Asia. As Table 7.1 indicates, Singapore's saving rates were relatively low in the 1960s (column labeled "Gross national savings/GDP"), but they rose steadily over the next three decades. During the 1970s, Singapore's saving rates were already higher than in most countries. They reached record levels in the 1980s and 1990s.

In the 1960s and 1970s national saving was insufficient to finance investment, and Singapore relied heavily on net capital inflows. The peak dependence on foreign sources came in 1971, when net capital inflows represented more than one-half of gross capital formation (GCF). Singapore's transformation into a capital-surplus economy occurred in the late 1980s. In recent years its gross national saving has substantially exceeded its investment needs, with the result that Singapore has become a net capital exporter. In 1995 net capital outflows constituted essentially one-third of Singapore's gross national saving and more than 15% of its GDP.

An examination of the private and public saving components of gross national saving reveals distinctive features of saving in Singapore. The public

TABLE 7.1

Selected Indicators of Saving and Investment (%): Singapore, 1960–95

Period or year	GCF/GDP	Gross national savings/GDP	Net capital inflows/GDP	Gross national savings/GCF	Net capital inflows/GCF
Average,					
1960–95	34.2	29.4	4.8	80.0	20.0
1960–70	21.3	10.6	10.6	42.1	57.9
1971–80	41.2	29.0	12.2	70.7	29.3
1981–90	41.2	41.3	−0.1	102.3	−2.3
1991–95	34.6	47.3	−12.7	137.3	−37.3
1991	34.2	45.4	−11.2	132.8	−32.8
1992	35.9	47.2	−11.3	131.4	−31.4
1993	37.7	44.9	−7.2	119.1	−19.1
1994	32.7	48.6	−15.9	148.7	−48.7
1995	32.6	50.3	−17.7	154.4	−54.4

SOURCE: ROS DOS (1995).
GDP, gross domestic product.
GCF, gross capital formation.

sector has consistently played a major role in capital formation. It has done so directly through governmental and quasi-governmental enterprises and indirectly through mandated contributions to the CPF, a comprehensive and mandatory saving scheme administered by the state.

The public sector has been a consistent net saver. Public-sector saving accounted for more than 25% of national saving in the 1970s and hit a peak of 59% in 1986. Since then it has declined to a proportion closer to that in the 1970s (Table 7.2).

Data are not available for disaggregating private saving into savings by private corporations and savings by households. However, information is available on a major component of private individual savings: the compulsory savings deposited to the CPF. These involuntary private savings have contributed substantially to the increased saving rate in Singapore. The CPF increased its share of private savings from 38% in 1970 to well over 77% in 1985 (Table 7.2). The ratio of CPF saving to private saving then declined to approximately 30% by the end of 1995. In dollar terms involuntary private CPF savings achieved rapid positive growth rates until 1986, when Singapore was recovering from its first recession. It nevertheless continued its upward trend into the 1990s as more people joined the labor force. Voluntary private savings were more volatile and more likely to be affected by the economic performance of the economy.

Accompanying the rapid growth in both public and involuntary private savings has been the changing process of Singapore's capital formation. The public share of total GCF has been substantial, averaging 27% over the period 1960–95. In the 1970s and 1980s more than one-third of the GCF

TABLE 7.2

Sources and Uses of Gross Saving: Singapore, 1975–95

Source or use	1970	1975	1980	1985	1990	1993	1994	1995
	Singapore dollars (billions)							
Gross saving	2.2	5.4	11.6	16.6	24.3	35.5	35.4	39.3
Private saving	0.4	2.6	4.9	7.7	21.6	29.8	36.7	45.5
CPF saving	0.2	0.9	2.3	6.0	7.2	10.4	11.3	13.5
Public saving	0.7	1.4	3.4	8.8	8.3	12.5	16.0	15.3
Net capital inflow	1.1	1.4	3.3	0.0	−5.6	−6.8	−17.2	−21.4
Gross capital formation	2.2	5.4	11.6	16.6	24.3	35.5	35.4	39.3
Private sector	0.4	3.5	7.7	10.5	17.3	26.5	28.8	32.2
Public sector	1.8	1.9	3.9	6.1	7.0	9.1	6.6	7.1
	Percentage distribution							
Gross saving	100.0	100.0	100.0	100.0	100.0	100.0	100.0	100.0
Private saving	18.5	48.8	41.9	46.7	88.9	83.9	103.6	115.6
CPF saving[a]	37.6	33.8	47.1	77.5	33.1	35.0	30.8	29.8
Public saving	31.8	25.4	29.3	53.2	34.2	35.2	45.1	38.8
Net capital inflow	49.7	25.8	28.8	0.0	−23.1	−19.1	−48.7	−54.4
Gross capital formation	100.0	100.0	100.0	100.0	100.0	100.0	100.0	100.0
Private sector	18.5	65.1	66.3	63.4	71.2	74.5	81.3	82.0
Public sector	81.5	34.9	33.7	36.6	28.8	25.5	18.7	18.0

SOURCES: ROS EDB (1995); ROS MOTAI (various years), *Economic Survey of Singapore.*
CPF, Central Provident Fund.
[a] CPF saving as a percentage of private saving.

came from the public sector. With the completion of major infrastructural projects, the public sector's share in the GCF declined to 18% of total GCF in 1995.

In the next two sections I focus on two elements of saving that are peculiar to Singapore. The first is the CPF and its role in the government's public-sector capital formation and overall investment strategy. The second is the role of capital inflow and outflow in the use of savings.

The CPF and Funding of Government Investment

The CPF was set up in 1955 during the colonial period. Its original purpose was to provide for the retirement needs of Singapore's workers and their dependents. [For a history of the CPF scheme and related economic and social issues, see Lim et al. (1986). See also Asher (1985, 1989, 1996), Hoon (1991), Tay (1992), Sherraden et al. (1995), and Tyabji (1996).] The CPF is self-financed and does not rely on resources drawn from the state treasury. As of 1995 the CPF contribution rate was 40% of workers' wages, equally divided between employee and employer. Each worker's account includes the worker's contribution plus credited earnings. When members reach age 55, they can withdraw their CPF, tax free, after setting aside a minimum sum (S$40,000 in 1995). The minimum sum helps to ensure that members can support a modest standard of living during retirement.

As the CPF increased in size, the government introduced additional schemes that have liberalized the conditions under which CPF funds can be withdrawn before retirement. An early and important reform was the government's decision to allow CPF funds to be used to finance home ownership, beginning in 1968. Other reforms allow an individual's account to be used for medical costs and education. In the event of the account holder's death, the balance of funds in the account is distributed to the contributor's beneficiaries. Since the late 1970s additional schemes introduced under the CPF system have broadened the available benefits to members (Table 7.3).

TABLE 7.3
Schemes Introduced under the CPF, 1968–95

Type and scheme	Year introduced
Home ownership	
Approved Housing Scheme	1968
Approved Residential Property Scheme	1981
Investment	
Singapore Bus Services Ltd. Share	1978
Approved Investment Scheme	1986[a]
Approved Nonresidential Property Scheme	1986
Basic Investment Scheme	1993
Enhanced Investment Scheme	1993
CPF Investment Scheme	1997
Insurance	
Home Protection Insurance Scheme	1982
Dependents' Protection Insurance Scheme	1989
Medishield Scheme	1990
Medishield II Scheme	1994
Other	
Company Welfarism through Employers' Contribution Scheme	1984
Medisave Scheme	1984
Minimum Sum Scheme	1987
Topping-Up of Minimum Sum Scheme	1987
Financing of Tertiary Education in Singapore	1989
Edusave Scheme	1992
Share Ownership Top-Up Scheme	1995
Pre-Medisave Top-Up Scheme	1995

SOURCES: Adapted and updated from Asher (1996, table 4); ROS CPF Board (various years), *Annual Report* for 1995.

[a]Beginning in 1993, the Approved Investment Scheme was replaced by a Basic Investment Scheme and an Enhanced Investment Scheme. The two schemes were rationalized and combined in the CPF Investment Scheme in January 1997.

TABLE 7.4

Coverage of CPF Scheme, 1965–95

Population	1965	1970	1975	1980	1985	1990	1995
Number (in thousands)							
Total population	1,887	2,075	2,263	2,282	2,483	2,705	2,987
Employed	560	651	813	1,054	1,235	1,486	1,701
Members	418	639	1,104	1,519	1,892	2,195	2,684
Contributors	256	373	647	864	890	1,022	1,359
Members as percentage of total population	22.1	30.8	48.8	66.5	76.2	81.2	89.9
Contributors as percentage of							
Total population	13.6	18.0	28.6	37.8	35.8	37.8	45.5
Employed	45.7	57.2	79.6	81.9	72.1	68.8	79.9
Members	61.3	58.3	58.6	56.9	47.0	46.5	50.6

sources: ROS DOS (various years), *Singapore Yearbook of Statistics*; ROS CPF Board (various years), *Annual Report*.

Membership in the CPF has grown rapidly during the last few decades. In 1965 only one-fifth of the population was covered by the scheme. By 1975 one-half was covered, and by 1980 two-thirds were included (Table 7.4). As of 1995, 80% of Singapore's employed population contributed to the CPF and nearly 90% of the total population were members. Members include current contributors, those who have made contributions in the past, and Malaysian citizens who are or have been working in Singapore. (Foreign workers from peninsular Malaysia are subject to the same rules as those affecting Singapore citizens with respect to contributions to and withdrawals from the CPF.) Self-employed workers, contract workers, unpaid family workers, and certain categories of foreign workers are not required to contribute to the fund, nor are those who are unemployed or out of the labor force. Partial coverage has recently been increased through a scheme called Medisave for the self-employed.

As the program has matured, the proportion of members who are contributors has declined. In 1965 more than 60% of the members were contributors, but by 1985 fewer than 50% were. The recent extension of Medisave to include the self-employed has prevented a further decline in contributors, and the proportion has stabilized at about 50% of the membership.

Contribution rates to the CPF have risen substantially since the plan's inception (Figure 7.1). In 1955 workers and employers each contributed 5% of employees' annual earnings to the fund. By 1984 the contribution rate had reached 50%, again equally divided between the employees and the employers. In April 1986 the employer's contribution rate was sharply reduced to cut labor costs in response to Singapore's recession. Since then the em-

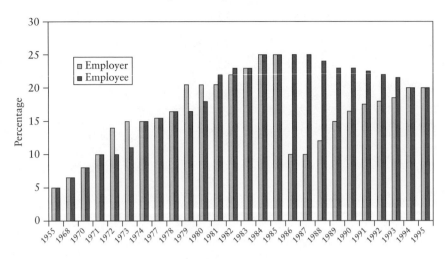

Source: ROS CPF Board (various years), *Annual Report* for 1995.

FIGURE 7.1. Rate of Contribution to the CPF as a Percentage of Wages.

ployee's contribution rate has declined gradually and the employer's rate has increased gradually. By 1995 both were at 20%.

Since the early 1980s the rising cost of health care has been a major concern of the government and Singaporeans at large. Population projections forecast a rapidly growing proportion of elderly over the next 40 years. The ratio of elderly (65 years and older) to the working-age population (15–64 years) is expected to rise from 0.11 in 1980 to 0.46 in 2030 (Chen and Jones 1989), creating a greatly increased demand for health care services.

In 1983 the Ministry of Health issued a National Health Plan that emphasized the crucial role of individuals in promoting and maintaining their own health. In accordance with the plan, in 1984 the government introduced a Medisave account within the CPF. Every CPF member was required to set aside 6% of his or her monthly wages, up to a total of S$15,000, in a separate Medisave account to meet future hospitalization expenses. The government closely monitors Medisave withdrawals and prevents unnecessary health care spending. However, Medisave is not an insurance scheme. Members can withdraw from their Medisave account only up to the limit of their balance. Any additional medical bills must be paid from other private sources. Since 1984 the scheme has been modified to allow members to use their Medisave accounts to pay for medical fees incurred by parents and siblings. In 1990 the government introduced an optional insurance health plan called Medishield. This insurance plan is based on neither income nor need.

Table 7.5 summarizes withdrawals from the CPF. In the early years withdrawals were substantially less than contributions. This is a characteristic of

TABLE 7.5

Withdrawals from the CPF by Type: 1968–95

Type	1968	1970	1975	1980	1985	1990	1995
Retirement and related							
S$ (millions)	21.7	21.6	80.5	252.7	693.0	1,013.8	1,112.1
%	71.9	47.9	37.1	32.1	20.6	25.4	15.3
Approved housing							
S$ (millions)	6.3	22.9	134.8	520.9	2,566.4	2,259.1	4,590.9
%	20.9	50.8	62.2	66.9	76.4	56.6	63.3
Medisave Scheme							
S$ (millions)	0.0	0.0	0.0	0.0	43.9	207.8	295.9
%	0.0	0.0	0.0	0.0	1.3	5.2	4.1
Other							
S$ (millions)	2.2	0.6	1.6	5.5	56.4	514.0	1,254.0
%	7.2	1.3	0.7	0.7	1.7	12.9	17.3
Total withdrawal							
S$ (millions)	30.2	45.1	216.9	779.1	3,359.7	3,994.7	7,252.9
%	100.0	100.0	100.0	100.0	100.0	100.0	100.0
Total withdrawal as percentage of total contribution	45.1	29.2	24.5	33.9	56.1	55.7	53.6

SOURCE: ROS DOS (various years), *Singapore Yearbook of Statistics.*

any immature funded pension scheme, because the number of retiring workers is relatively small. Because the system has matured, withdrawals for retirement purposes have increased substantially, but they are still smaller than contributions. Withdrawals for retirement have also decreased as a proportion of total withdrawals because many members drew down their accounts to purchase housing. Withdrawals for the financing of property reached a peak in 1985, although this trend began to rise again in the early 1990s. Withdrawals for medical services and other purposes have grown significantly. This trend is expected to continue.

The CPF has created a large resource base that has important uses for the society. Because the government is both the trustee and the administrator of the CPF, it has been primarily responsible for investment decisions. It has used the fund to finance domestic capital formation, especially basic infrastructure and housing, and to build up the national reserves by investing portions of the fund abroad. The government has also used the CPF as an important macroeconomic instrument for curbing inflationary pressure and for nonfiscal intervention to mitigate recessions, for example, by reducing the contribution rate of employers, as was done in 1986.

A particularly successful use of CPF funds has been in the construction and provision of public housing. In 1960 the government created the first statutory board, the Housing Development Board (HDB), which was charged with relieving an acute housing shortage. Some 580,000 people were living within the city center area of only about 10 km^2. The area was characterized by overcrowded slums, poor maintenance, and the absence of basic services (Wong and Yeh 1985: 40). With strong support from the government the HDB exceeded its own target of building 51,000 dwelling units within the first 5 years. By the early 1970s the HDB had solved the housing problem in an ingenious way. Initially, the public housing units were rented to citizens. In 1964 the government promoted the Home Ownership for the People Scheme. Singaporeans who qualified were able to purchase a 99-year lease on a flat at a standardized price. At the end of the 99 years they (actually their heirs) would have free and clear title to the flat. The scheme received a great boost in 1968 when the government began allowing CPF members to use their account balances to pay for the flats purchased under the Approved Housing Scheme. From 1981 onward the government permitted CPF account balances to be used for the purchase of private property under the Approved Residential Property Scheme. In 1995 alone more than S$4,500 billion was withdrawn from the CPF for housing acquisitions. As of 1995 the public housing program had provided homes for 86% of the population. About 90% of the households living in public housing own their dwellings. Because of these policies, the share of public residential construction in the GCF of the economy has been quite large, averaging 9.3% for the period 1960–95.

The CPF reforms have gradually increased members' control over their own retirement portfolios, with the result that Singapore has become one of the largest share-owning nations in the world. Initially, CPF members were allowed to invest their funds in certain government enterprises. The enactment of the Approved Investment Scheme in 1986 gave them latitude to invest their funds in approved private companies. Since 1995 members have had the option of investing in approved CPF unit trusts, made up of foreign shares and bonds traded on the Singapore Stock Exchange. Since 1997 members have been able to invest up to 80% of their CPF monies, after setting aside the required minimum sum. They can include in their portfolios bank fixed deposits, endowment insurance policies, and shares and unit trusts traded on the Singapore Stock Exchange and in regional economies. As of 1999 they can incorporate shares traded on a number of stock markets outside Asia. An individual member can invest up to 40% of his or her CPF in foreign shares and bonds. All these liberalization measures will likely boost the financial sector and promote Singapore as an international financial center.

Foreign Investments

Capital inflow in the form of direct investment has been a crucial factor in promoting capital formation and economic growth of the Singapore economy. Foreign direct investment (FDI) is the acquisition by foreigners of pro-

TABLE 7.6

Net Capital Inflow, Foreign Direct Investment,
and Portfolio Investment in Singapore: 1983–93

Year	Net capital inflow (S$ millions)	FDI inflow (S$ millions)	Percentage of total FDI stock in		Foreign portfolio investment inflow (S$ millions)
			Mfg.	Fin.	
1983	1,290	1,746	44	25	18
1985	8	710	51	27	−8
1987	332	5,244	49	33	712
1989	−5,700	5,264	43	33	489
1991	−8,437	4,732	38	32	242
1993	−6,795	6,106	36	37	u

SOURCE: ROS DOS [various years (1995)], *Singapore Yearbook of Statistics.*
u, data unavailable.
FDI, foreign direct investment.
Mfg., manufacturing.
Fin., financial services.

ductive assets, such as factories, plants, and machinery. Foreign capital is considered to have flowed in when foreign investors pay for the purchase of such productive assets. Portfolio investment is the purchase by foreign investors of a country's financial assets, such as bonds and shares. Table 7.6 shows trends in net capital inflow and the inflow of direct investment and portfolio investment made by foreign investors in Singapore between 1983 and 1993.

The flow of capital into the Singapore economy has been predominantly in the form of FDI. Starting from a low level of S$1,700 billion in 1970, the stock of FDI grew by 21% per annum on average in the 1970s and by 16% per annum in the 1980s, reaching nearly S$61,000 billion in 1993. The distribution of the stock of FDI has changed markedly over the years. Before 1986 the manufacturing sector accounted for more than one-half of the stock. Since then, foreign investment in manufacturing has declined while investment in services, particularly financial services, has increased. By the end of 1993 the share of financial services was slightly larger than the share of manufacturing (37% and 36%, respectively).

Foreign investment in Singapore originates mainly from the United States, Japan, and Europe. In 1993 those three sources accounted for 90% of cumulative investment in manufacturing, and their investments were nearly equally divided. Japan is a relative newcomer to the Singapore market. In 1970 Japanese firms were responsible for only 7% of foreign investments in the manufacturing sector. Their investments rose rapidly during the 1970s and 1980s. A similar pattern is evident in the service sector. There the United States has played the most important role, followed by Japan and then Europe.

What is important to understand is the dominance of FDI over local investments in the manufacturing sector. A large share of exports, value added, and other key attributes in the manufacturing sector can be traced to foreign-owned companies. Given Singapore's wealth and high saving rates, FDI is not required for funding purposes. In such key industries as electronics, petroleum, transportation, and telecommunications the role of FDI is not just capital infusion. The value of foreign investment lies in technology transfer, the acquisition of technical and management skills, the creation of employment, and access to world markets.

The positive net flow of capital into the Singapore economy in the latter part of the 1980s made Singapore a net exporter of capital by the 1990s. Concurrent with this new development has been the growing importance of Singapore investments abroad. The government has encouraged such investments because the economy has reached a stage in which the Singapore's limited space and labor shortages constrain further economic expansion at home. A drive to develop an external, regional economy is aimed at promoting further economic growth and prosperity.

Regionalization is not a wholly new strategy. History, proximity, and supply and demand factors have all propelled Singaporeans to make investments in Malaysia and Indonesia. Those investments predate the growth triangle with the islands of Johore and the Riau archipelago that was formalized in 1991. The economic committee that was formed in 1986 to tackle the 1985 recession recommended casting a wider net in identifying new directions for future growth. It proposed the promotion of offshore activities as an investment strategy (ROS MOTAI 1986: 17).

The Economic Development Board, Singapore's primary agency for promoting investment, stated in May 1993 that Singapore's external economy was still in its infancy, noting that only 6.3% of the 36,573 active companies in 1990 had invested abroad. The stock of Singapore-owned private direct investments abroad constituted about 8% of the gross national product (GNP), and the income derived from them contributed only 10.5% to GNP. Both figures were about one-quarter of those of Switzerland. If that rate had been sustained, it would have taken Singapore five to seven years to reach one-half the Swiss level of overseas investments [ROS EDB 1993b; see also ROS EDB (1993a) and ROS MOF (1993)]. Equally small was the number of Singaporeans working abroad: only 14,631, or barely 1% of the labor force of 1.516 million, according to the 1990 census. This figure might have been an underestimate because it did not include the many Singaporeans who were stationed in Singapore but frequently traveled abroad (Low and Toh 1992).

The Department of Statistics estimates that overseas operations' contribution to the value added to the Singapore economy amounted to 12% in 1994 (ROS MOTAI 1995: 14). By the end of 1994 the number of companies with overseas operations had grown to 4,128, nearly twice the number operating abroad in 1990. Total direct investment had more than doubled during the same period, reaching S$35 billion in 1994.

Singapore companies exhibit a preference for direct investment in Asia, especially in Malaysia and Hong Kong, followed by Indonesia, China, and Thailand. At the end of 1993, 54% of their direct equity investment abroad was invested in Asia. According to the Department of Statistics, an increasing number of Singaporean investors were venturing into other parts of Asia, such as China, Myanmar, and Vietnam, and into member countries of the Association of Southeast Asian Nations (ASEAN). The United States, Europe, and New Zealand each shared 7–8% of Singapore's direct foreign investment.

Savings and Macroeconomic Policies

The economic growth process requires an economy to raise savings and engage in capital formation. This can be done either by the domestic (private or public) sector or by capital inflows from abroad. The ability to save may not coincide with the desire to invest, however, and sector-specific imbalances are possible between saving and investment. Nevertheless, it is important that savings are mobilized effectively to fund investments. For Singapore two types of resource flow can be identified: domestic resource mobilization across sectors and external resource mobilization between Singapore and the rest of the world.

As I indicated earlier, the distinctive features of Singapore's saving mobilization are continuous public-sector saving leading to a surplus, compulsory saving through the CPF, and, since 1987, increasing export of capital. To understand the outcome of this saving strategy in Singapore, one must understand the development goals pursued by Singapore—economic growth, full employment, price stability, a competitive yet equitable society—and its macroeconomic policies for achieving those goals, given the constraints faced by the economy.

Initially faced with a small domestic market and a lack of domestic entrepreneurship, Singapore early adopted an export-oriented, foreign-investment-led development strategy. To attract foreign investors, the government realized it must have a conducive environment, including a good infrastructure (utilities, communications, and transportation), a disciplined work force, an efficient administration, and, above all, minimum uncertainties with respect to the repatriation of profits, foreign exchange risk, business legislation, and political conditions. The government therefore adopted a market-friendly, pro-business stance from the beginning. Shortly after gaining independence in 1965, Singapore began removing trade barriers; by 1970 the trade barriers were practically nonexistent. The flow of capital in and out of the country is completely free. Singapore has no exchange control, and more than 100 foreign banks have operations with branches or subsidiaries in the financial sector. Aspiring to become an international financial center, in 1968 Singapore established the Asian Dollar Market, an equivalent of the European Dollar Market, to tap into the offshore financial market.

In issuing currency, Singapore adheres to the currency board system inherited from the British colonial government. The Singapore dollar is therefore fully backed by foreign reserves and gold. This large foreign reserve assists the government in ensuring a market-oriented target exchange rate for promoting domestic price stability. It has provided confidence to foreign investors wishing to avoid exchange risk and hoping to procure inputs from the cheapest sources. The absence of barriers to international capital flow has left little room for independent monetary policy in Singapore. In fact, the money supply is determined by domestic money demand.

Foreign Reserves and National Wealth

Singapore's large foreign reserves constitute a significant part of its national wealth. The reserves back the currency and provide confidence to investors. In place of natural resources, which Singapore lacks, the stream of permanent income emanating from the accumulated national wealth ensures the long-term survival and sustainability of the Singapore economy. The reserves and national wealth need to grow in tandem with the flow of economic output and the stock of foreign investments in the country. A sufficient amount of reserves also performs the role of a countervailing force, which the government can invoke when there is a risk of an exodus by footloose multinational companies. In recent years Singapore has experienced a concurrent rise in foreign reserves and foreign investments, with foreign reserves exceeding foreign investments in 1993 (Table 7.7).

Thus the government has invested abroad much of Singapore's national savings, both public savings and involuntary CPF savings, rather than using them to contribute to domestic capital formation. (It should be emphasized,

TABLE 7.7

Stock of Foreign Direct Investments (FDI)
and Official Foreign Reserves (OFR): Singapore, 1982–93

FDI or OFR	1982	1986	1990	1993	1995
FDI (S$ billions)	20.4	28.6	57.9	73.3	99.2
OFR (S$ billions)	17.9	28.2	48.5	77.9	97.3
As percentage of FDI	87.7	98.6	83.8	106.3	98.1

SOURCE: ROS DOS (various years), *Singapore Yearbook of Statistics.*

however, that the government has been a prime mover in the building of basic infrastructure necessary for economic production and expansion.) The government invests the surplus funds abroad with the help of the Government of Singapore Investment Corporation, which is under the charge of the Ministry of Finance and the Prime Minister's Office. Gross inflows of foreign savings, mostly in the form of FDI by multinational companies, have financed a major portion of Singapore's domestic capital formation. It is not surprising, therefore, that the CPF contributions and Post Office saving deposits have been invested in the purchase of government securities, which the government in turn has used to acquire foreign assets. The income from those investments will add to the national wealth.

The government has yet another reason for channeling public-sector surpluses and accumulated CPF savings into foreign investments. If such sizable funds were deposited with the domestic private banking system, they could overwhelm the domestic economy with excessive liquidity and produce inflation. A withdrawal of liquidity is deemed to be useful in curbing inflationary pressure arising from higher wages. The building up of foreign reserves is therefore consistent with the government's goal of price stability.

The government achieved its disproportionately high share of total saving by the public sector by pursuing conservative budgetary policies and by having the statutory boards (run mostly on a competitive, cost-plus basis) accumulate surpluses. Public-sector surpluses are only partially transformed into domestic capital formation. The public sector's GCF averaged only 27% of total GCF over the period 1960–95. Most of the GCF was undertaken by the private sector, and this implies that the private sector faced a resource gap. The government's investment of both CPF funds and public savings abroad resulted in a massive outflow of national savings. But the private sector, with insufficient voluntary savings to finance its capital formation, was attracting large amounts of foreign savings to fill the resource gap. Clearly, the net capital inflow figure shown in Table 7.6 indicates a tremendous movement of resources within the economy and across the border.

In the Ministry of Finance's 1995 budget statement, Finance Minister Richard Hu defended the government's policy of generating healthy surpluses in its budget as one way to attract foreign investments. He noted that, because of its huge foreign reserves, Singapore is considered a low-risk investment environment. In 1995 alone the budget surplus of the Singapore government amounted to S$9,200 million, which represented more than 7.5% of the GDP. By the end of 1995 the official foreign reserves had reached S$97,300 million, representing 82.6% of the GDP and almost seven months' worth of merchandise imports for that year. Thus foreign investors do not have to fear a sudden increase in their tax burden in the near future. Healthy budgets also guarantee that the government will continue to invest in modern infrastructure to facilitate business operations in Singapore.

Public Investment and Government Involvement in Business

The government respects the basic freedom of private enterprises to conduct business in Singapore. Consistent with this philosophy, the only restriction it places on foreign investments is to close to private enterprises certain industries deemed essential to the country's maintenance. Those industries include utilities, telecommunications, public housing, education, weapons and ammunition production, and the legal system. The government also has extensive ownership in such key industries as banking, shipbuilding, tourism, and trade.

The government has several rationales for its strong participation in business activities, besides wishing to regulate certain industries (such as firearms and tobacco products) for the sake of public safety and environmental concerns. One is that the private sector was initially unable or unwilling to invest in projects the government considered necessary for economic development. The government determined that local entrepreneurs were lacking the information, external linkages, know-how, financial and management resources, and experience required for them to compete effectively with transnational corporations from developed countries. Therefore the government decided to counter these market failures by setting up government-linked companies.

To stimulate investments in Singapore, the government created joint-venture companies with private local and foreign investors. Government officials believed that through such public investments the government would remove bottlenecks to the expansion of private industry and thus encourage private investment. Most of these partnerships were in the Jurong Industrial Estate. Examples were the National Iron and Steel Mills, the Jurong Shipyard, the National Grain Elevator, and the Sugar Industries of Singapore. Subsequently, in larger projects that many viewed as higher-risk activities, the government took the lead in such industries as petroleum, chemicals, biotechnology, and aerospace. The government's goal was to help companies overcome initial entrepreneurial difficulties, strengthen the confidence of private investors, and spearhead new ventures. Public investment was intended to complement private investment, not to compete with it.

The recession in 1985 prodded the government to explore ways to divest government-owned enterprises in nonsensitive industries. The Public Sector Divestment Committee, set up in 1986, identified 41 of the 608 government-linked companies for privatization. By the end of 1993, 39 of those firms had been privatized. As of early 1999 another eight were being prepared for privatization.

The other way in which the government participates in industry is through statutory boards. A statutory board is created through special legislation and is empowered to perform specific functions. The state is its sole owner, and its activities are financed by government budget allocation, government loans, or other sources with guarantees from the government. Its board of directors has representation from government ministries, the private sector, professional organizations, and other groups. The boards were created to meet specific needs and to accelerate economic growth. The rationale for establishing these mostly monopolistic institutions was to provide the necessary infrastructure for the government's ambitious industrialization program and to supply low-priced public and merit goods and services.

In 1991 there were 41 statutory boards. The number has dwindled slightly over the last few years because of the government's initiative to privatize some business activities. Among those privatized were the Public Utilities Board, the Telecommunication Authority of Singapore, and the Port Authority of Singapore. The telecommunication sector in particular has undergone liberalization. The privatized Singapore Telecom is expected to face more competition as foreign companies enter the lucrative telecommunication industry.

Determinants of Saving in Singapore

Most empirical analyses of saving are based on some variant of the life-cycle or permanent-income hypothesis, which specifies that households save out of current income to maintain a smooth path of consumption. They do so in recognition that their earnings can fluctuate, as can conditions of the economy at large (Kotlikoff 1984; Shoven 1984). If a saver's time horizon is multigenerational, so that the saver reckons that his or her happiness also depends on the inheritance received by his or her heirs, the bequest motive may affect the amount that the saver wishes to save out of current income. The overlapping-generations model pioneered by Samuelson (1958) is the most popular for analyzing saving behavior [for a succinct exposition of the life-cycle overlapping-generations model, see also Modigliani (1988)]. Once the saver's time horizon extends to a lifetime or beyond, demographics and the existence of a national pension scheme become potentially important determinants of aggregate savings. The impact of demographics on saving is discussed in Chapters 5 and 6 of this volume. In short, because the aggregate saving rate is a weighted average of saving rates among all age groups, it will rise when the population is concentrated in high-saving ages and fall when the population is concentrated in low-saving ages.

The situation in Singapore is unusual because life-cycle saving has been institutionalized through the CPF. As the system matures and as Singapore's population ages, withdrawals will rise in relation to contributions. CPF saving as a fraction of national income will decline, and the CPF will grow more slowly [see Toh (1996) for a simulation exercise]. At equilibrium the fund will grow at the same rate as national income, just as life-cycle wealth grows at the same rate as national income in Lee, Mason, and Miller's model (Chapter 6).

The impact of demographic changes on national saving in Singapore is uncertain. At issue is the response of voluntary saving to mandatory saving under the CPF. If life-cycle concerns do not govern household saving motives and if households vary their saving to offset the effects of the CPF, then demographic changes need not have any of the effects on national (or private) saving hypothesized in the life-cycle saving literature. Alternatively, if life-cycle concerns govern household saving behavior, demographic changes will have the hypothesized effect on saving, but the CPF will be irrelevant. Funds accumulated in the CPF will merely have been accumulated by private households.

Hoon (1991) used an overlapping-generations model to investigate the long-run general equilibrium consequences of choosing the CPF contribution rate in Singapore. He showed that (1) in the presence of a perfect capital market the choice of the employee's CPF contribution rate has no effect on steady-state capital stock per worker; (2) with an inelastic labor supply the choice of the employer's CPF contribution rate has no effect on steady-state capital stock per worker; (3) in a world of completely free international labor mobility a higher employer's CPF contribution rate reduces the share of foreign workers in the total work force and raises total domestic savings;[1] and (4) in a world of completely free international capital mobility (with an inelastic labor supply) the current account balance does not vary with the choice of CPF contribution rates.

Analyses of aggregate data [for example, Leimer and Lesnoy (1982)] have yielded mixed evidence about the impact of pension plans on household saving, but microeconomic (cross-sectional) evidence has generally been favorable to the proposition that increasing social security reduces household saving. Estimates of how much it does so vary substantially. Hubbard (1984) showed that a fully funded social security system reduces individual saving by more than the tax paid. Hubbard (1986) reported that increases in anticipated social security benefits and private pension benefits do reduce individual nonpension wealth but, on average, on a less than a dollar-for-dollar basis implied by some earlier empirical evidence. Offsets for individuals with high levels of nonpension net worth are projected to be greater than dollar for dollar.

Effects of Compulsory Saving on Voluntary Saving

As Datta and Shome (1981) demonstrated, it is possible to distinguish three effects of compulsory saving on noncompulsory saving. The first effect is a substitution effect, which is expected to be negative: The introduction of compulsory saving is likely to lead to reduced voluntary saving, other things remaining equal. The second effect is an education effect, consisting in the savers becoming familiar with the idea of long-term financial management. This effect may be positive or negative. The third effect is a forced-saving effect, which is the positive effect of introducing a compulsory saving scheme that covers both nonsavers and marginal savers. The overall effect on total saving depends on the relative magnitudes of these three effects. For Singapore, which has the highest contribution rates in the world, the forced-saving effect is expected to predominate.

A specification used by Datta and Shome (1981) and by Wong (1986) to determine the effect of compulsory saving on noncompulsory saving takes the form of

$$NCS = \alpha + \phi YD + \beta CPFS + u, \tag{7.3}$$

where NCS is noncompulsory saving, YD is disposable income (proxied by the GDP less the CPF contribution and tax on income), CPFS is CPF saving, u is the standard stochastic term used in econometric modeling, and α, ϕ, and β are parameters to be estimated. Using Singapore data from 1970 to 1995, I estimated Equation (7.3) and obtained the following results:[2]

$$NCS = -7,245 + 0.698 YD - 0.547 CPFS - 4,000 DUM86 \tag{7.4}$$

$$t \text{ statistics:} (-16.5) \quad (22.0) \quad (-3.78) \quad (-6.58)$$

$$\text{Adjusted } R^2 = 0.994, \text{ DW} = 1.77, F \text{ statistic} = 1427.2.$$

The results are similar to those obtained by Wong (1986), although a structural break is discernible in the form of a different intercept for observations after 1985. For that reason I introduced into the equation a dummy variable, DUM86, which takes the value of 0 for the years before 1986 and the value of 1 for 1986 and subsequent years. In simple terms compulsory saving has partially crowded out voluntary saving. As compulsory saving increases, an individual's ability, willingness, and need to save in a voluntary capacity decline. The results indicate that every extra dollar of compulsory saving will reduce voluntary saving by about 55 cents, all else remaining constant.

Effects of Population Aging on Household Saving

A population ages as an inevitable consequence of declining fertility and mortality (see Chapter 3). Aging affects financial disbursements for health care, retraining, and employment of the aged. In short, it has effects on the overall dynamism of an economy. To some extent, these effects apply most directly to the population in the 45 and older cohorts. In Singapore those cohorts have benefited less than younger cohorts from the rapid growth of the economy and wages and the higher rates of CPF contributions. The reason is that, in general, their level of educational attainment is lower.

Population aging also affects saving. Using regression analysis, I analyzed changes in saving rates for Singapore between 1970 and 1995. I formulated the function for the saving propensity as

$$\frac{S}{YD} = f(YD, \text{DEM}, \text{FDREG}, \text{RATE}), \qquad (7.5)$$

where f denotes functional dependence; DEM is the demographic dependency ratio, measured by the sum of the proportions of persons younger than 15 and those older than 55 in the total population; FDREG is the financial deregulation variable, proxied by the ratio of bank loans to professionals and individuals to total bank loans in each year; and RATE is the real interest rate, proxied by the interbank minimum lending rate minus the inflation rate (the relative rate of change in the consumer price index).

One would expect disposable income YD to have a positive effect on the saving propensity and the demographic dependency ratio to have a negative effect, in accordance with the usual life-cycle hypothesis of saving. Higher interest rates are considered to stimulate saving in two ways: They discourage consumption and provide an incentive for saving. However, higher interest rates may also mean that less saving is needed now for planned consumption in the future. The effect of financial deregulation on saving can also be ambiguous (Bayoumi 1993). A well-planned and well-executed deregulation will lubricate and liberalize the financial sector of an economy. The cumulative effect is to strengthen investors' confidence in the economy and provide a more organized channel for drawing local and foreign savings into financial institutions. Deregulation can thus bring about higher savings and investment in the economy. On the other hand, deregulation enables people to obtain credit more easily, thus reducing their need to save for precautionary purposes. The ultimate effect of financial deregulation depends on the relative strength of these two effects.

In my regression exercise for Singapore, I considered two versions of the dependent variable: the ratio of gross domestic saving to disposable income (GDSRAT) and the ratio of noncompulsory saving to disposable income (NCSRAT). For NCSRAT I added to the regression equation the ratio of compulsory saving to disposable income as an explanatory variable.

The estimated equations are as follows:

$$\text{GDSRAT} = 1.222 + 0.258YD^* - 2.242\text{DEM} + 0.273\text{FDREG}$$

t statistics: $\quad(13.42)\quad\;(1.994)\qquad\;(-10.27)\qquad\quad(0.837)$

$$-\;0.0017\text{RATE} - 0.128\text{DUM86} \qquad\qquad (7.6)$$

$$(-1.358)\qquad\quad(-4.777)$$

Adjusted $R^2 = 0.9537$, DW $= 1.5085$.

$$\text{NCSRAT} = 0.918 + 0.364YD^* - 1.601\text{DEM} - 0.0042\text{FDREG}$$

t statistics: (4.021)   (2.496)   (−3.254)   (−0.111)

$$- 0.0019\text{RATE} - 0.583\text{CPFRAT} - 0.098\text{DUM86}. \quad (7.7)$$

(−1.532)   (−2.022)   (−2.940)

Adjusted $R^2 = 0.9004$, DW $= 1.5166$

where YD^* is the variable YD divided by 10^7.

The results indicate an unmistakable negative effect of aging on the propensity to save. The two variables FDREG and RATE are statistically nonsignificant in both equations. In Equation (7.6), where NCSRAT is the dependent variable, the ratio of compulsory CPF saving to the disposable income has a negative effect on the noncompulsory saving propensity. This concurs with the result of Equation (7.4).

There is general agreement, however, that Singapore's customary retirement age of 55 is an anachronism, given the country's improved health standards and longer life expectancy. The public sector has taken the lead in raising the retirement age to 60. That age, however, is not mandatory for the private sector. There is even talk of eventually raising the retirement age to 65. These would be positive moves for maintaining Singaporeans' high living standard during retirement and lessening the depressive effect of aging on saving.

Conclusion

Economic growth requires capital formation. Obtaining the necessary resources to finance capital formation is a key problem in development economics. Analysts have advanced various strategies for mobilizing savings or extracting surpluses from production to provide the domestic resources needed for investment. In recent years the alternative of relying on foreign capital to finance development has been recognized as offering many benefits.

As many economists have observed, capital accumulation, although an important factor, is not the only factor that determines the pace of economic development. The rate of development also depends on such factors as natural resources, the size and composition of the population, economic and social institutions, political conditions, and the efficiency of the economy's management. But capital accumulation may well be regarded as the core process that makes all other aspects of growth possible. Similarly, hard work and the habit of saving do not, by themselves, ensure economic growth. Peasants in many societies are hard working indeed. As Tangri and Gray (1967) pointed out, the crucial difference between growing and stagnant economies lies more in the *use* than in the *volume* of savings.

Singapore has relied successfully on both national saving and foreign capital to finance its growth over the last four decades. Two ways in which it has generated savings merit attention. The first is its prudent budgetary and fiscal policies; the second is the CPF. The government's operations have created a surplus that is used to finance public-sector capital formation. In addition, statutory boards that are in charge of basic social and infrastructural services add to the public-sector surplus when they are run along corporate lines and are sensitive to overall economic demand for competitiveness. Compulsory saving, through the CPF, has contributed significantly to private saving and hence to national saving.[3] The many ingenious schemes that the Singapore government has introduced over the years to liberalize the use of CPF funds by individual account holders have reduced the compulsory aspect of the CPF. They have also had the secondary but important effect of promoting financial liberalization and developing Singapore's financial sector.

The provision of public housing, which has contributed to Singapore's capital formation, can play a significant role in focusing and stimulating saving by individuals. Home ownership engenders a stake in the society and promotes social order. In turn, these have positive effects in the form of a motivated labor force and the public's willingness to endure a high rate of compulsory saving, especially when accumulated savings can be used to pay off mortgages and make investments. An asset-owning work force is reckoned to be more productive and committed than one without assets.

Good infrastructure, social and political stability, and a liberal economic environment that allows free capital mobility and free trade have attracted a steady inflow of foreign capital to boost Singapore's domestic capital formation. These conditions could well be a prelude to a reverse situation in which savings are used to finance investment abroad. Increased Singaporean investment abroad will pass wealth on to future generations, and in that regard it may be beneficial. Furthermore, increased capital outflows will likely be associated with improvements in the competitiveness of Singapore's domestic firms on world markets (Summers 1986).

The impact of changing population size and aging on savings needs to be recognized early in the process of saving and development. The likelihood of living beyond retirement from work is a powerful incentive to save and continue working. Because individuals are expected to assume more responsibility for providing for their own needs during their retirement years, a case can be made for the state to encourage saving through the demonstration effect of a mandatory saving scheme. There is also a need to protect the purchasing power of the social security funds. The diversion of individuals' saving into the acquisition of housing and investment shares is one way to achieve this end. Annuity markets in Singapore have been slow to develop reverse-annuity mortgages, whereby households use their housing equity to support an annuity, with the seller of the annuity receiving the house in payment upon the death of the purchaser. Certainly, population aging will have important implications for saving behavior, especially when it begins to assert downward pressure on saving propensities. When that happens, the relative importance of various sources of saving will change.

The accumulation of foreign reserves does more than simply back the Singapore currency. It has become a policy measure for sustaining the confidence of foreign investors, adding to the national wealth, and thereby creating permanent income. It also serves to compensate for Singapore's handicap of being without natural resources and its high dependency on foreign investments.

It is theoretically possible to derive an optimal saving rate for an economy using Modigliani's optimal growth model or the standard Phelps-Solow model (Modigliani 1980; Boskin 1986; Cutler et al. 1990). In practice, however, economic and political factors determine the national saving rate. The mandatory CPF scheme is a political choice, and it has been a main instrument for fostering asset ownership by citizens. Furthermore, Singapore's policymakers believe that lower rates of public and compulsory saving would reduce the potency of saving as an anti-cyclical measure.

Empirical studies have shown that mandatory CPF saving does discourage voluntary saving, but on a less than dollar-for-dollar basis. The net effect is that it raises the national saving rate. The apparent preference of Singaporeans for as high a saving rate as possible seems to be guided by long-term economic objectives, such as having a nest egg for retirement and bequests and as a hedge against uncertainty. So long as the accumulated savings are profitably invested and so long as individuals are allowed a reasonable degree of freedom in using their CPF savings for investments and entrepreneurial activities, excessive compulsory saving or too high a saving rate is unlikely to be an economic or political issue. In the current CPF scheme individuals have many options for using their CPF savings for investments if they have already set aside the minimum sum required for retirement needs. There is still room, however, for refining existing procedures to enable CPF members to make more effective use of their savings. For instance, members who wish to exercise their entrepreneurial talent would like to use their available CPF savings to start businesses. Doing that is currently prohibited unless a member is already 55 years of age. Another refinement would allow members to use their CPF savings to enroll in courses designed to upgrade their working skills.

Domestic saving need not be the only means of achieving long-run capital formation in an open economy. Imported capital and foreign direct investment in Singapore are viewed as equally important to its continued economic growth. The economic marginalist's principle, that the discounted benefit for every extra dollar of saving must be greater than the discounted cost of that extra dollar of saving, still needs to be heeded.

Population, Capital, and Labor

ANDREW MASON

IN THINKING ABOUT the relationship between population and economic growth, economists have been greatly influenced by the neoclassical growth model developed by Solow (1956). In that model a decline in the population growth rate leads to a permanent increase in per capita income and an increase in economic growth only during a period of transition. At equilibrium economic growth is not influenced by the rate of population growth.

The chapters in this volume and other recently published studies identify potentially important features of East Asia that are not captured by the simple neoclassical model. First, the model emphasizes equilibrium outcomes rather than dynamic relationships. Second, the model abstracts from differences in the rates of population and labor force growth, neglecting the impact of changes in the economic support ratio on per capita income. Third, the model assumes that saving rates are not influenced by demographic change. Fourth, the model makes no allowance for international capital flows, immigration, or trade.

My purpose in this chapter is to reassess the effect of population change on economic growth in light of the evidence presented elsewhere in this volume that East Asia's demographic situation is extraordinarily dynamic, that the region has experienced large swings in the support ratio, that demographic changes have influenced rates of saving and investment, and that economies have allowed international capital flows to varying degrees.

I undertake this reassessment not by abandoning the neoclassical growth model but rather through some simple extensions. In the first part of this chapter I consider an economy that is closed to international capital flows and examine the effect on per capita income of changes in the support ratio and demographically induced changes in the saving rate. In the final section I consider the implications of population change for economic growth and international capital flows in open economies.

Economic Support Ratio

One of the most important features of East Asia identified in this volume is the rapid growth of the labor force relative to the population. As summarized in Chapter 1, labor force growth exceeded population growth by 0.8% per year between 1960 and 1990 in the study countries. The gap between labor force growth and population growth was substantially smaller in Latin America, Europe, and North America. In South Asia and Africa the labor force grew more slowly than the population. As a consequence, the economic support ratio—the ratio of workers to consumers—increased substantially in East Asia.

A simple decomposition procedure suggested by Cutler et al. (1990) and Bloom and Williamson (1998) provides a useful starting point for assessing the implications of changes in the support ratio. With per capita income represented by $y = Y/N$, the economic support ratio by L/N,[1] and output per worker by $y^l = Y/L$, where l is the rate of growth of the labor force, we can write

$$y = y^l \times \left(\frac{L}{N} \right).$$ (8.1)

Introducing n, the rate of growth of the population and $\dot{x}$, the change per unit of time of other variables, we can express the rate of growth of per capita income as

$$\frac{\dot{y}}{y} = \frac{\dot{y}^l}{y^l} + l - n.$$ (8.2)

By holding growth in output per worker constant, an increase in the growth of the support ratio [the gap between the labor force and population growth rates $(l - n)$] yields a one-for-one increase in growth of output per capita.[2]

Over a sufficiently long period of time large divergences in growth rates between the population and the labor force cannot occur. But during the demographic transition, the labor force growth rate diverges from the population growth rate in a systematic fashion. Comparing the average population and labor force growth rates for 1960–90 in East Asia and the world demonstrates this to be so (Figure 8.1).[3] Among the countries with the most rapid population growth rates labor forces grew at about the same rate or slightly more slowly than the population. Countries with population growth below roughly 2% experienced labor force growth rates in excess of their population growth rates. The gap between labor force growth and population growth (the rate of growth in the support ratio) in the global pattern ranged as high as 0.5% per year for the 1960–90 period.

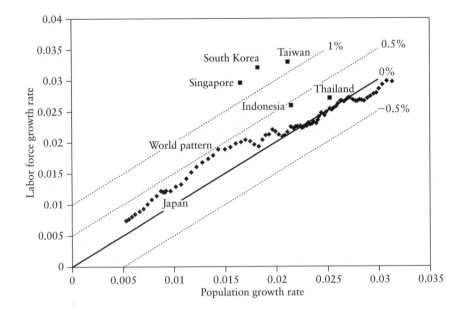

Source: Summers and Heston (1991).

FIGURE 8.1. Labor Force Growth and Population Growth, 1960–90: World and Six East Asian Countries. Diagonal Lines Represent Growth Rates of the Support Ratio.

South Korea, Taiwan, and Singapore are most distinctive, achieving growth in their support ratios that substantially exceeded the international norm. These three economies experienced particularly large swings in the working-age population during this period (see Chapter 3, Table 3.5) and substantial increases in female labor force participation (see Chapter 12, Table 12.2; and Chapter 14). In addition, Singapore experienced substantial labor force growth from immigration (see Chapter 13, Table 13.1). Changes in age structure were smaller in the other three countries. Japan experienced a substantial increase in the support ratio before 1960. The increase in Thailand and Indonesia did not begin until well after 1960. Moreover, in Thailand female participation rates were so high beginning in 1960 that the support ratio has not been greatly influenced by increased participation.

Taking the six East Asian countries as a group, we find that the rise in the support ratio by 0.8% per year between 1960 and 1990 led to growth in per capita income of 0.8% per year beyond growth in output per worker. Thus the upward swing in the support ratio produced a per capita income that was about 25% higher in 1990 than would otherwise have been the case. In the three newly industrializing economies (NIEs), Singapore, South Korea, and Taiwan, the swing in the support ratio produced a per capita income higher by as much as 50%. Changes in age structure accounted for roughly three-quarters of this increase, and changes in labor force participation accounted for the remainder.

Output per Worker, Labor Force
Growth, and Capital Deepening

Although income per capita is widely used to measure the material standard of living, output per worker more directly measures the performance of an economy. Analyses of economic performance, many of which are summarized in Chapter 2, distinguish two broad explanations for growth in output per worker. The first is the accumulation of factors, namely, human and physical capital. The second is the increase in factor productivity. Demographic variables bear directly on factor accumulation, and how they do so is the focus of the other chapters in Part II of this volume. Considerably less is known about the effects of population variables on factor productivity, although the issues are discussed in Chapter 2. Studies of East Asia uniformly point to the importance of factor accumulation, especially the increase in physical capital per worker, or capital deepening.

Capital deepening is driven by two factors. Either a decline in the rate of growth of the labor force or a rise in saving and investment rates produces more rapid growth in capital per worker. By abstracting from international capital flows, introduced later, one can represent the rate of capital deepening by

$$\frac{\dot{k}}{k} = s\left(\frac{Y}{K}\right) - l, \tag{8.3}$$

where $\dot{k}/k$ is the rate of growth of the capital-labor ratio, s is the fraction of output saved and invested, Y/K is the ratio of output to capital, and l is the rate of growth of the labor force (Solow 1956). Solow showed, however, that a change in the labor force growth rate or in the saving rate leads to capital deepening only for a transitory period. Eventually an economy with a constant saving rate and a constant rate of labor force growth will reach an equilibrium state in which the capital-labor ratio is constant ($\dot{k}/k = 0$). This equilibrium is reached through adjustments in the output-capital ratio and is achieved when $Y/K = l/s$.[4]

A plot of the rate of capital deepening against the rate of labor force growth for 1965–90 provides an empirical context for the theoretical rela-

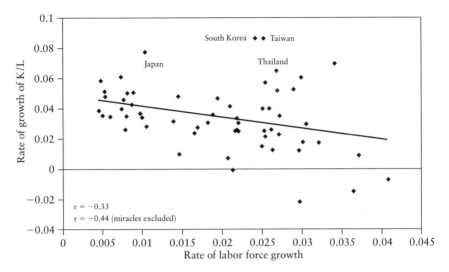

Source: Summers and Heston (1991).

FIGURE 8.2. Capital Deepening and Labor Force Growth: International Cross-Section, 1965–90.

tionships of Solow's neoclassical growth model (Figure 8.2).[5] Several important features of capital deepening in East Asia are apparent in Figure 8.2. First, countries with more slowly growing labor forces have somewhat higher rates of capital deepening than other countries. The least-squares regression line is intended only to be suggestive, but the slope is approximately −0.65, less than the initial effect of a change in labor force growth derived from the simple neoclassical model (−1) but considerably more than the steady-state effect of 0. Second, rates of capital deepening in East Asia are rivaled only by a few other countries. Japan is clearly an outlier with respect to countries that experienced low rates of labor force growth, as are South Korea, Taiwan, and Thailand with respect to countries that experienced rapid labor force growth. Third, rapid capital deepening of the kind found in East Asia cannot be explained by rapid changes in labor force growth. Saving and investment rates are the source of the rapid capital deepening that has characterized East Asia.

By 1960 saving rates in Japan had already increased to high levels, but the other study countries had low saving rates. Singapore had a negative saving rate. In South Korea gross domestic saving was only 1% of GDP (see Chapter 2, Table 2.2). Between 1960 and 1990, however, saving and investment rates rose enormously. Figure 8.3 compares East Asia's investment record with the rest of world's. Among the 104 countries for which data are available Japan's investment rate ranked eighteenth in 1960, but none of the other

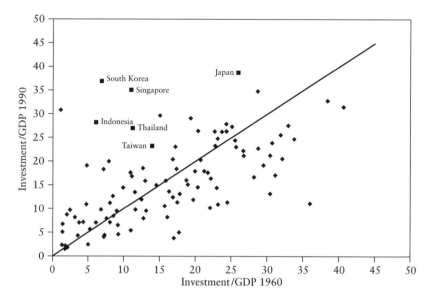

Source: Summers and Heston (1991).

FIGURE 8.3. Investment as a Percentage of Gross Domestic Product: 104 Countries, 1960 and 1990.

East Asian countries ranked in the top half at that time. South Korea and Indonesia had investment rates near the bottom, eighty-fourth and eighty-sixth, respectively. Both the high rates of investment in 1990 and, more important, the change between 1960 and 1990 (the height above the 45-degree line) are evident in Figure 8.3. In increased rate of investment, South Korea, Singapore, Indonesia, and Thailand all ranked among the top five, Japan ranked eighth, and Taiwan ranked twelfth. Japan was one of the few high-investment countries in 1960 that experienced an increase rather than a substantial decline in investment.

The other three chapters in Part II of this volume investigate the extent to which demographic factors contributed to the large increases in saving and investment experienced by the East Asian economies. The analyses presented in this volume and recent studies by Kelley and Schmidt (1996) and Deaton and Paxson (2000) find that demographic factors exert an upward influence on saving rates. The estimated impact varies widely, as is evident in the comparison of these studies that I presented in Chapter 1, Table 1.3. Any assessment of the contribution of demographic factors to capital deepening and to economic growth depends on which saving study we use. The approach I follow here is to use results drawn from Chapter 6 because they are middle-of-the-road results.

TABLE 8.1

Accounting for Growth in Output per Capita: Four Asian Countries, 1965–90 [a]

Factor	Japan	Taiwan	South Korea	Thailand	Taiwan with saving effects
Growth of output per worker	4.5	5.7	6.6	4.3	5.7
Contribution of specified factor					
Productivity	1.5	2.5	4.5	1.9	2.5
Investment	2.6	2.8	1.8	2.3	1.8
Investment (demographic)					0.9
Labor force growth	0.1	0.1	0.1	0.1	0.1
Interaction	0.3	0.3	0.3	0.1	0.3
Contribution of demographics	0.1	0.1	0.1	0.1	1.0
Percentage contribution of specified factor to growth in output per worker					
Productivity	33.8	44.4	67.4	43.1	44.4
Investment (nondemographic)	58.0	48.5	26.6	52.6	31.4
Combined demographic effects	2.2	2.5	1.3	1.3	18.2
Interaction	6.1	4.7	4.7	3.1	4.7
Growth of output per capita	4.7	6.9	7.7	4.8	6.3
Contribution of specified factor					
Output per worker	4.5	5.7	6.6	4.3	5.7
Support ratio	0.2	1.2	1.1	0.5	1.2
Contribution of demographics	0.3	1.3	1.2	0.5	1.8
Percentage contribution to growth in output per capita					
Productivity	32.1	36.8	58.0	38.8	39.8
Investment (nondemographic)	55.0	40.2	22.8	47.3	28.6
Combined demographic effects	7.1	19.2	15.1	11.2	27.7
Interaction	5.8	3.9	4.1	2.8	3.8

[a] Values are based on an elasticity of output with respect to capital of 0.4. The contribution of demographics includes the combined impact of changes in labor force growth and changes in saving and investment induced by demographics in Taiwan. The interaction is not included.

Using techniques described in more detail in the appendix to this chapter, I computed the factors that contribute to growth in output per worker between 1965 and 1990 for four East Asian countries for which suitable data are available. For Japan, South Korea, and Thailand I computed only the effect of slower labor force growth on output per worker. For Taiwan I also computed the effect of demographics on output per worker, using results from the saving analysis. I then computed the contribution of demographics to the growth in output per capita, incorporating the effect of the support ratio.

Growth in output per worker between 1965 and 1990 varied from 4.3% per year in Thailand to 6.6% per year in South Korea. Slower growth in the labor force had a negligible effect on economic growth. Output per worker grew more rapidly by only 0.1% per year in each of the 4 countries as a result of slower labor force growth (Table 8.1). The effects were so small because the decline in labor force growth was small.

The last column in Table 8.1 incorporates the effect of demographics on saving and investment. The effect can be readily incorporated into the growth-accounting analysis by calculating the rate of growth in output per worker while holding all variables except the rate of investment at their low-level equilibrium values. If the rate of investment followed the path estimated by Lee, Mason, and Miller in Chapter 6, output per worker would have grown by 0.9% per year between 1965 and 1990.[6] The combined effect of demographic factors was to raise growth in output per worker by 1.0 percentage points, thus accounting for 18% of Taiwan's growth in output per worker.

When we turn our attention to the growth in output per capita rather than output per worker, the role of demographics increases. The increase in the support ratio contributed 0.3% and 0.5% annually to per capita income growth in Japan and Thailand, respectively, and 1.1% and 1.2% in Taiwan and South Korea, respectively. Demographic factors excluding saving effects accounted for between 7% and 19% of the growth in per capita output between 1965 and 1990. Including saving effects, demographics accounted for 28% of Taiwan's growth in per capita output. (Demographics, as defined here, includes all the factors that led to the increase in labor force participation. As explained, about three-fourths of the increase can be attributed to changes in age structure and the remainder to greater participation by women, of which only some part is due to demographic factors.)

The results presented in Table 8.1 should be taken as indicative, not definitive, given the wide range of saving-effect estimates. If the econometric results presented by Williamson and Higgins (Chapter 5) and Toh (Chapter 7) or similar results by Kelley and Schmidt (1996) are accurate, the contribution of demographic factors to economic growth are substantially greater than represented in Table 8.1. If the effects are more in line with Deaton and Paxson's (2000) recent estimates, then the contribution of demographic factors to economic growth are overstated by Table 8.1.

Population and Development in Open Economies

Most analyses of economic growth have relied on a closed-economy model, in which rates of saving determine investment, immigration is ruled out, and all goods and services are consumed domestically. As discussed by Bauer (Chapter 2) and by Williamson and Higgins (Chapter 5), these assumptions are unrealistic with regard to East Asia. Both trade and international capital flows have been central features of the East Asian development experience, whereas immigration has been relatively modest except for Singapore.

Two issues arise once the simplifying assumption of a closed economy is abandoned. The first issue is how slower population growth and other demographic forces influence trade, immigration, and international capital flows.

The second issue is the impact of demographics on standards of living in an open, as opposed to a closed, economy.

Current theories of international economics maintain that trade and the flow of factors (capital and labor) across international borders arise because of differences in factor endowments. A central feature of the analysis presented in this volume is that the demographic transition in East Asia has led to two changes in factor endowments: an increase in capital relative to labor and an increase in skilled labor relative to unskilled labor. The change in factor endowments can set in motion three distinct responses. First, production and net exports by the economies of East Asia may shift toward more capital-intensive goods and services and away from labor-intensive goods and services. Second, the relative decline in the supply of home-grown labor may lead to an increased demand for foreign workers. As the demographic transition proceeds, countries that previously were labor exporters may become labor importers. Third, the demographic transition may lead to a reversal in the flows of international capital. Countries that previously imported capital should become capital exporters (Deardorff 1987).

These responses are all in evidence to greater or lesser degrees in East Asia, but the relative importance of the responses has depended on a variety of factors, including the culture, the geography, and the legal setting. Among the countries of East Asia Singapore stands out in its reliance on trade, immigration, and international capital flows. It has erected relatively few barriers to trade, encouraged international capital flows, including direct foreign investment, and actively sought workers from abroad who possessed special skills or who were willing to undertake "3D" (dirty, difficult, or dangerous) jobs. More than 30% of Singapore's labor force consists of immigrants (see Chapter 13, Table 13.1).

Most other countries in East Asia have been much more selective about the manner in which they have opened their economies. During the 1970s and early 1980s, South Korea and Thailand exported substantial numbers of workers to the Middle East. Indonesia continues to actively promote the export of their workers. In the early 1990s the number of Indonesians finding work abroad equaled 150,000 or about 6% of the number of new workers entering the labor force each year (see Chapter 13). East Asian countries have been much more restrictive about opening their countries to immigration, despite the emergence of labor shortages in the late 1980s and early 1990s in Northeast Asia, particularly in Japan. In Japan and South Korea foreign workers constitute less than 1% of the domestic work force. In Taiwan only 4% of all workers are foreign nationals (see Table 13.1). For the most part the governments of Northeast Asia have also discouraged direct foreign investment. Instead, the economies have responded to changing factors by adjusting both their industrial structure and their export mix (see Chapter 2). In Japan, Taiwan, and Singapore the accumulation of wealth has led to heavy investment abroad (see Chapter 5). The responses to capital deepening were different in the United States and Europe, which have been much more open to immigration.

The remainder of this section explores the open-economy setting in more detail, focusing on international capital flows. Here, I use the neoclassical model to compare a closed economy with a small open economy. For the small open economy I consider, first, how standards of living are influenced by demographic transition when accumulated wealth is not necessarily invested in the domestic economy. Second, I consider the implications of demographic change for international capital flows in a manner consistent in spirit with the analysis and empirical evidence presented by Williamson and Higgins in Chapter 5.

I begin by recasting and extending Solow's (1956) neoclassical growth model to incorporate Tobin's (1967) extension and the analysis presented by Lee, Mason, and Miller (Chapter 6). Tobin (1967) incorporated the life-cycle saving model into the neoclassical growth model, exploring how demographic factors influence saving rates and the demand for wealth (relative to income), W/Y. He showed that a change in the population growth rate will produce a steady-state equilibrium. The saving rate will be constant at the new equilibrium, but the new saving rate will differ from the old equilibrium value. The equilibrium level of income will change by more or less than in the Solow model, depending on the impact of demographics on saving or the demand for wealth (see Chapter 6 for a more complete discussion).

In a closed-economy version of the combined neoclassical and life-cycle saving model two relationships determine equilibrium: (1) the demand for wealth or capital, as determined by demographics, interest rates, tastes, and other factors; and (2) the aggregate production function, which in the simple formulation presented here is determined by capital and labor.[7] Figure 8.4 depicts the determination of equilibrium wealth and income and the impact of changing demographics on those equilibrium values. The low-level equilibrium shown in the figure occurs when the demand for wealth, represented by the line with a slope of $1/(w/y)_0$, and the production function intersect (w and y are wealth and income per worker). At this point wealth and capital per worker are equal to w_0, and output per worker is equal to y_0. The figure is drawn to be consistent with our simulation results in Chapter 6: a pretransition demand for wealth of 1.6 times annual income.

The high-level equilibrium is produced by a shift in the demand for wealth to $(w/y)_1$. Wealth and capital per worker increase to $w_1 = k_1$. Output per worker rises but by less in percentage terms than capital per worker because of diminishing returns to capital. Again, the shift in the demand for wealth is drawn to correspond to our simulations in Chapter 6: a post-transition demand for wealth of 5.4 times annual income.[8]

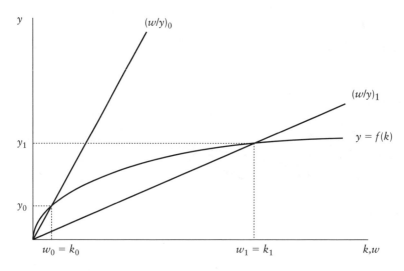

FIGURE 8.4. Closed-Economy Equilibria.

The impact on equilibrium output per worker of an increase in the demand for wealth is readily calculated if the production function is known. In the simplest case, the Cobb-Douglas production function, output per worker is equal to $(w/y)\exp[\beta/(1 - \beta)]$ where β is the elasticity of output per worker with respect to capital per worker. Given an elasticity of 0.4, used in the growth-accounting analysis presented earlier, an increase in the demand for wealth from 1.6 to 5.4 would produce an increase in output per worker, at equilibrium, of 2.25.

In a situation of free international capital mobility, an economy's capital stock and the wealth of its citizenry are independent. Wealth is determined by the life-cycle model, but capital adjusts until the returns available in the domestic economy are equal to the returns available elsewhere. To be more specific, at equilibrium the marginal product of capital equals the real rate of interest plus the rate of depreciation, $f'(k) = r + \delta$. Figure 8.5 shows the equilibrium capital-labor ratio (k) and the gross domestic product per worker (y_d). In Figure 8.5 the capital stock and domestic product per worker are independent of the demand for wealth (or saving rates) so long as the economy in question is sufficiently small that changes in the domestic demand for wealth do not affect international returns to capital.

Income per worker is given by y, the sum of domestic product and net foreign income.[9] Equilibrium income per worker and wealth per worker are determined by their intersection, as shown in Figure 8.5. The low-level equilibrium yields national income per worker of y_0 and wealth per worker of

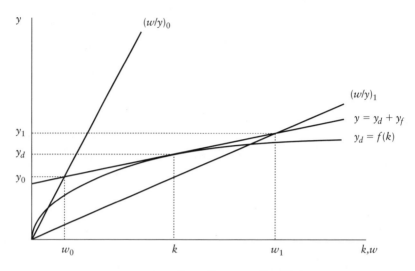

FIGURE 8.5. Open-Economy Equilibria.

w_0. The difference between y_0 and y_d is remitted to foreign investors. The difference between k and w_0 is foreign assets per domestic worker.

A shift to the high-level equilibrium has no influence on the equilibrium capital per worker or on output per worker if the economy in question is small in relation to global markets. Figure 8.5 is drawn so that the rise in wealth per worker to w_1 is sufficiently great that the country shifts from being a net debtor to being a net creditor. At equilibrium the country holds net foreign assets per worker equal to $w_1 - k$ and receives net foreign income per worker of $y_1 - y_d$.

The key question is how demographic transition influences income in an economy that is open to international capital flows, as opposed to one that is not, the case analyzed earlier. One cannot establish on a priori grounds whether income will rise by more or by less in the open economy. As is clear from an inspection of Figure 8.5, income is higher in the open economy so long as the equilibrium wealth per worker differs from the equilibrium capital per worker. Two factors account for this.

First, wealth is not subject to diminishing returns, and the equilibrium wealth per worker is higher in the open economy than in the closed economy. Whether the change in equilibrium income is greater or smaller in the open economy depends on the shape of the production function and the global rate of interest. The production function in Figure 8.5 is drawn so that the force of diminishing returns to the right of k is not much different from that to the left of k. However, if diminishing returns were relatively unimportant to the left of k (in which case the production function would be relatively linear) but set in with considerable force to the right of k, then income would increase by substantially more in the open economy than in the closed economy when the demand for wealth increased.

The second consideration is the global rate of interest. Suppose that the global rate of interest was considerably higher so that the equilibrium k was close to w_0. Under these circumstances income would rise much more substantially as wealth increased and the demographic transition would have a much greater impact on income than would otherwise be the case. Conversely, if interest rates were low and the equilibrium k was close to w_1, the rise in income would be much more modest in the open economy compared with the closed economy.

This simple model implies another potentially important result: Other things being equal, the economic gains from reduced population growth are greater for countries that proceed through the transition earliest. If the world consisted of many small, identical economies at the low-level equilibrium, the equilibrium k would be equal to w_0 in every country and the global returns to capital would be high. The first country to proceed through the demographic transition would achieve the largest possible gains in income. As additional countries completed the transition, global interest rates would decline, reducing the economic gains from the demographic transition. The last country to complete the transition would gain the least.

Although the economic impact of slowing population growth may be substantially less in an open economy than in a closed economy, this seems unlikely to be the case in East Asia. High rates of return to capital were maintained throughout the high-growth era (see Chapter 2). This was accomplished in one of two ways, or both: by avoiding diminishing returns to investment at home and by investing abroad. Either way, by helping to sustain high rates of investment, we find that the contribution of slower population growth to economic growth was as great as and possibly greater than that suggested by the simple growth-accounting analysis based on the closed-economy neoclassical model.

The empirical evidence on international capital flows presented by Williamson and Higgins (Chapter 5) is consistent with the simple theoretical predictions of the open-economy neoclassical model. Williamson and Higgins find that demographic transition has been accompanied by a transition from capital importer to capital exporter among the countries of East Asia. Those countries in the earliest stages of their demographic transitions, Thailand and Indonesia, continue to experience rapid growth in their labor forces, a high demand for capital, and large capital inflows through 1990 and later. Those countries further along in their demographic transitions, particularly Japan, were not only experiencing slower labor force growth and a lower demand for domestic investment but also had become major exporters of capital by the late 1980s and early 1990s.

In a world characterized by some measure of economic integration, the economic impact of demographic change is no longer confined to the country experiencing that change. If the increased demand for wealth is sufficiently large so as to reduce the global rate of interest, all capital-importing countries benefit. The result is easily demonstrated in Figure 8.5. The equilibrium capital-labor ratio shifts to the right as a result of the decline in interest rates. Both gross domestic product per worker (y_d) and income per worker (y_0) increase. Of course, the capital-exporting countries experience a decline in their foreign income because of the reduced rates of return on capital. Thus the shift in the demand for wealth shown in Figure 8.5 yields a smaller increase in income per worker if the economy experiencing the demographic transition is relatively large.

The theoretical model suggests a diffused effect on the global economy, but in reality Japan's foreign investment was geographically concentrated and had a major impact on several other Asian economies. In 1990 44% of Thailand's direct foreign investment and 57% of Indonesia's direct foreign investment originated in Japan (Chaiwoot 1994; ROI CBS 1992). Thus investment and economic growth in Thailand and Indonesia were influenced by their own demographics and by changing demographic conditions in Japan as well.

Growth-Accounting Analysis

The methods used here differ from traditional growth-accounting analysis in two ways. First, the objects of interest are growth in output per capita and output per worker instead of total output. Second, the emphasis is on isolating the major channels through which demographic factors operate. The approach, based on the neoclassical growth model, calculates two components of growth in output per capita: (1) growth in the labor force relative to the population (the support ratio) and (2) growth in output per worker. Growth in the support ratio arises because of the gap between labor force and population growth rates. Growth in output per worker depends on three factors: (1) the rate of labor-augmenting technological change, (2) an investment rate that differs from the steady-state equilibrium, and (3) labor force growth that differs from the steady-state equilibrium.

The analysis begins with a simple decomposition of per capita income ($y = Y/N$) into two components: output per worker ($y_l = Y/L$) and the support ratio (L/N):

$$\frac{Y}{N} = \frac{Y}{L}\frac{L}{N}. \tag{8.4}$$

A dynamic representation is used to analyze the sources of economic growth. Taking the natural logarithm of both sides and differentiating with respect to time yields

$$\frac{\dot{y}_t}{y_t} = \frac{\dot{y}_t^l}{y_t^l} + l_t - n_t, \tag{8.5}$$

where $\dot{x}_t$ is the derivative of a variable with respect to time and l and n are the rates of growth of the labor force and of the population, respectively. Bloom and Williamson (1998) used a similar decomposition in an econometric framework.

For the four countries for which detailed analysis is reported, the magnitudes of key variables are reported in Table 8.2. Between 1965 and 1990 growth in the support ratio varied from an average of 0.2% per year in Japan to an average of 1.2% per year in Taiwan. Growth in output per capita differed from output per worker by identical amounts.

The analysis of output per worker uses the neoclassical growth model. Following Solow (1956), capital (K_t), labor (L_t), and labor-augmenting technology (H_t) determine output. The production function is

$$Y_t = K_t^\beta (H_t L_t)^{1-\beta}. \tag{8.6}$$

TABLE 8.2
Growth Rates of Selected Variables: Four East Asian Countries, 1965–90

| | Average annual growth rate (%) | | | |
Variable	Japan	Taiwan	South Korea	Thailand
Output per capita	4.7	6.9	7.7	4.8
Output per worker	4.5	5.7	6.6	4.3
Support ratio	0.2	1.2	1.1	0.5
Capital–labor ratio	7.7	8.6	8.6	6.4
Population	0.9	1.9	1.6	2.4
Labor force	1.1	3.1	2.7	2.9
Investment rate	10.1	13.4	11.6	6.4

SOURCES: Summers and Heston (1991), UN DESIPA (1995b), and World Bank (1999).

Taking the natural logarithm of both sides, differentiating with respect to t, and rearranging terms yields one representation of growth in output per worker as depending on capital deepening (an increase in the capital-labor ratio k) and the rate of growth of technology (λ):

$$\frac{\dot{y}_t^l}{y_t^l} = \frac{\beta \dot{k}_t}{k_t} + (1 - \beta)\lambda_t. \tag{8.7}$$

The rate of capital deepening $\dot{k}/k$, is equal to $i_t Y_t / K_t - l_t$, where i_t is the investment rate net of depreciation. Substituting into Equation (8.3) yields

$$\frac{\dot{y}_t^l}{y_t^l} = \beta \left[\frac{i_t Y_t}{K_t - l_t} \right] + (1 - \beta)\lambda_t. \tag{8.8}$$

Combining Equations (8.8) and (8.5) and rearranging terms yields the growth components for per capita income:

$$\frac{\dot{y}_t}{y_t} = \frac{\beta i_t Y_t}{K_t} + (1 - \beta)\lambda_t - \beta l_t + (l_t - n_t). \tag{8.9}$$

Output per capita is determined by four additive terms that capture the impact of investment, technology, capital-deepening effects of labor force growth, and growth in the participation rate. The first three additive terms on the right-hand side determine growth in output per worker.

The results of the analysis depend on the counterfactual situation used because there is no unique set of right-hand-side variables that yields a growth rate of output per capita of zero. The objectives of this study and the East Asian experience suggest an obvious counterfactual situation. Suppose that the economies to be analyzed were moving along a neoclassical, steady-state growth path with high and equal rates of labor force and population growth, an equilibrium rate of investment (lK_t/Y_t), and no technological innovation. Under such conditions output per worker and output per capita would not have grown between 1965 and 1990. The growth that did occur was a result of technological change, investment rates above the steady-state equilibrium, labor force growth rates below the steady-state equilibrium, and the gap between labor force and population growth rates.

I calculated the values of the variables for the counterfactual simulation in the following manner. The rate of labor-augmenting technological change and the rate of growth of the support ratio $(l - n)$ were set at zero. The investment rate was set at the steady-state equilibrium value consistent with the actual 1965 capital-output ratio and the counterfactual rate of labor force growth. The labor force and the population growth rates were set at the maximum rate of population growth during any five-year period after 1950. For Taiwan I used the population growth rate for 1955–60 because the 1950–55 growth rate reflected large rates of immigration from the Chinese mainland. The counterfactual values are compared with the actual values in Table 8.3.

The contribution of higher rates of investment to economic growth is the average calculated rate of economic growth for 1965–90 obtained by using the actual investment rate and holding all other variables at their counterfactual level. The effect of each of the other growth factors is assessed in a similar fashion. A simulation analysis is used because the ratio of output to capital on the right-hand side of Equation (8.9) is itself determined by the growth components.

Data are available to analyze four East Asian countries: Japan, Taiwan, South Korea, and Thailand. Output per worker and capital are drawn

TABLE 8.3

Comparison of Steady-State and Actual Growth Variables:
Four East Asian Countries, 1965–90[a]

	Average annual growth rate (%)			
Variable	Japan	Taiwan	South Korea	Thailand
Technological growth				
Counterfactual	0.0	0.0	0.0	0.0
Actual	2.4	3.8	5.8	2.9
Investment rate				
Counterfactual	1.0	2.4	2.1	1.3
Actual	10.1	13.4	11.6	6.4
Labor force growth				
Counterfactual	1.4	3.5	3.1	3.1
Actual	1.1	3.1	2.7	2.9
Support ratio				
Counterfactual	0.0	0.0	0.0	0.0
Actual	0.2	1.2	1.1	0.5

[a]Values are based on an elasticity of output with respect to capital of 0.4.

from the Penn World Table (Summers and Heston 1991). The capital and output series are used to calculate the investment-rate series using $i_t = (K_{t+1} - K_t)/Y_t$.[10] Population data are drawn from the same sources as those used by Feeney and me in Chapter 3. Labor force data are drawn from the World Bank (1999). The rate of labor-augmenting technological change is calculated as a residual based on Equation (8.7). Technology, as used here, is a broad, all-encompassing variable that captures many variables that contribute to economic growth, including investment in human capital, structural changes in the economy, the more efficient use of resources, and innovation. Consequently, the contribution of technology, as measured here, is greater than that obtained in more detailed growth-accounting studies that separately identify many of these factors. The contribution of growth factors varies according to the elasticity of output with respect to capital β, assumed to be 0.4 in the main results presented. The elasticity is somewhat higher than estimates for the United States and many other countries because analysis of East Asian data suggests a relatively high capital elasticity (Chapter 2; Kim and Lau 1994; Harberger 1996). The implications of using alternative values are discussed later.

Estimates of the contributions of technology, investment, and labor force variables to growth in output per worker and output per capita are presented in Table 8.4. In Japan, Taiwan, and Thailand a high investment rate was the most important growth factor, accounting for between 40% of growth in output per capita in Taiwan and 55% in Japan. In South Korea technology was the most important growth factor, responsible for 58% of the growth in per capita output. The combined demographic effects were smaller but far from inconsequential, contributing as little as 7% (in Japan) and as much as 19% (in Taiwan) of the growth in output per capita. The contribution of demographic variables rises to 27.7% when investment effects are incorporated into the calculations for Taiwan, as shown in the last column of Table 8.4.

As shown in Table 8.3, in every country the rate of labor force growth was lower than the counterfactual growth rate, but by small amounts. Thus the slowdown in labor force growth contributed little to capital deepening or growth in output per worker. The annual contribution to output per worker was only 0.1% per year between 1965 and 1990 (Table 8.4). Because labor force growth rates slowed so modestly, the gap between labor force growth and population growth was correspondingly large. Thus the contribution of demographics to growth in output per capita was as high as 1.3% per year in Taiwan, nearly one-fifth of the actual growth.

Table 8.4 also incorporates for Taiwan the effects of demographics on saving and investment. The method used for constructing these estimates and a discussion of the results were presented in the main body of this chapter.

TABLE 8.4

Accounting for Growth in Output per Capita: Four Asian Countries, 1965–90[a]

Variable	Japan	Taiwan	South Korea	Thailand	Taiwan with saving effects
Growth of output per worker (%)	4.5	5.7	6.6	4.3	5.7
Contribution of specified factor					
Technology	1.5	2.5	4.5	1.9	2.5
Investment	2.6	2.8	1.8	2.3	1.8
Investment (demographic)					0.9
Labor force growth	0.1	0.1	0.1	0.1	0.1
Interaction	0.3	0.3	0.3	0.1	0.3
Contribution of demographics	0.1	0.1	0.1	0.1	1.0
Percentage contribution to growth in output per worker					
Technology	33.8	44.4	67.4	43.1	44.4
Investment (nondemographic)	58.0	48.5	26.6	52.6	31.4
Combined demographic effects	2.2	2.5	1.3	1.3	18.2
Interaction	6.1	4.7	4.7	3.1	4.7
Growth of output per capita (%)	4.7	6.9	7.7	4.8	6.3
Contribution of specified factor					
Output per worker	4.5	5.7	6.6	4.3	5.7
Support ratio	0.2	1.2	1.1	0.5	1.2
Contribution of demographics	0.3	1.3	1.2	0.5	1.8
Percentage contribution to growth in output per capita					
Technology	32.1	36.8	58.0	38.8	39.8
Investment (nondemographic)	55.0	40.2	22.8	47.3	28.6
Combined demographic effects	7.1	19.2	15.1	11.2	27.7
Interaction	5.8	3.9	4.1	2.8	3.8

[a]Values are based on elasticity of output with respect to capital of 0.4. The contribution of demographics includes the combined impact of changes in labor force growth and changes in saving and investment induced by demographics in Taiwan. Interaction is not included.

Estimates of the respective contribution of technology, investment, and labor force changes are sensitive to the elasticity of output with respect to capital. On the one hand, if the returns to capital are higher than assumed, then the values in Table 8.4 understate the contribution of investment and the capital-deepening effect associated with slower labor force growth and overstate the contribution of technology. The contribution of increases in the labor force participation rate are independent of the returns to capital. On the other hand, if returns to capital are lower, the contribution of technology is greater than calculated and the contributions of investment and the capital-deepening effects of slower labor force growth are lower than reported in Table 8.4. The sensitivity of the results can be assessed by repli-

TABLE 8.5

Accounting for Growth, with Sensitivity to Capital Elasticity:
Four East Asian Countries, 1965–90

Variable	Japan	Taiwan	South Korea	Thailand
Percentage contribution to growth, $\beta = 0.5$				
Technology	14.6	22.4	34.3	23.2
Investment	73.9	54.9	44.6	64.1
Combined labor effects	7.7	19.7	15.9	11.5
Interaction	3.8	3.0	5.1	1.3
Percentage contribution to growth, $\beta = 0.3$				
Technology	48.9	50.1	58.0	53.3
Investment	38.7	27.8	22.8	32.9
Combined labor effects	6.6	18.6	15.1	10.9
Interaction	5.8	3.5	4.1	2.9

cating the analysis using elasticities of 0.5 and 0.3. The results are summarized in Table 8.5. The relative importance of technology versus investment is sensitive to the assumed elasticity. The combined impact of labor force effects is relatively insensitive to the exact parameterization of the production function.

III. HUMAN RESOURCE ISSUES

Education and the East Asian Miracle

DENNIS A. AHLBURG AND ERIC R. JENSEN

THE EAST ASIAN MIRACLE has not been a purely economic phenomenon. Dramatic demographic and social changes have also occurred in East Asian countries. The average age at marriage and age at first birth have risen, completed fertility has declined, and rates of population growth have slowed throughout the region. School enrollment has increased significantly, and educational attainment has risen rapidly.

In this chapter we investigate the relationship between lower fertility and improvements in education, focusing on the six countries that are the subject of this volume. Rapidly growing human capital and private domestic investment have been identified as "the principal engines of growth" (World Bank 1993a: 5). If fertility reduction has led to increasing human capital formation, then it has also contributed to the economic transformation of East Asia. We begin by examining changes in expenditures on education and present data on other educational inputs and outputs. We then discuss both macroeconomic and microeconomic research on the link between demographic change and education.

Changes in Education Inputs and Outcomes

We use enrollment rates to measure the quantity of education provided. Following convention, we estimate quality by means of student-teacher ratios.

We have benefited greatly from discussions with Andrew Mason and Allen Kelley and from comments from Jeffrey Williamson, Karen Mason, Gerald Russo, Paul Shaw, and Matthew Higgins. We also acknowledge the research assistance of Aichia Chuang, Steven Hibbs, and Jeff Brown.

We also consider data on expenditure per student. One must take care in using these data, particularly when making comparisons across countries. Making comparisons over time within a country can also be problematic. Starting ages differ among countries and over time within a country. Similarly, the duration of schooling varies.

Education data are usually expressed as gross or net enrollment rates. A gross enrollment rate is the ratio of children enrolled to the number of children of an age considered appropriate for that educational level. A net enrollment rate is the percentage of children of the appropriate age who are enrolled in school. For example, the gross tertiary enrollment rate is the number of pupils enrolled in all post-secondary schools and universities, divided by the population that is 20–24 years of age. The net primary enrollment rate is the percentage of children 6–11 years old who are enrolled in school. Issues of comparability are more troublesome with gross enrollment rates than with net enrollment rates.

Literacy data are in some ways more appealing as a measure of educational output, but they too have problems of comparability because definitions of literacy differ. More important, real data on literacy are scarce and much of these data are outdated. Literacy is probably a good measure of educational stock only for lower-income countries.

Comparing educational expenditures among countries entails the usual problems of comparing financial data, although it is helpful to convert such expenditures to purchasing-power parity dollars. (Similar patterns are observed when expenditures are converted to US dollars rather than to purchasing-power parity dollars.) Although different levels of government in various countries have varying levels of responsibility for educational expenditures, published data are usually available only for the national government. Completed years of schooling are an appealing measure of education but are based on a limited number of censuses and surveys and are therefore not widely available.[1] Behrman and Rosenzweig (1994) discussed all these issues and showed that regression equations that explore the effects or the determinants of education are sensitive to measurement problems. Nevertheless, it seems that analysts have largely ignored these issues in the regressions that have become part of the new growth economics, including many macroeconomic regressions on the economic success of East Asia. It is important to know how sensitive the results of these studies are to the measurement of the education variables.

Enrollment Rates

According to the World Bank (1993b: 295), on average about 90% of children in upper-middle-income countries attend primary school. Enrollment rates in the six countries of interest here are nearly 100%, having risen sub-

TABLE 9.1

School Enrollment Rates: Six East Asian Countries, 1970–90

Level and rate	Japan	South Korea	Taiwan	Singapore	Thailand	Indonesia
Primary net enrollment rate						
1970	99	94	u	95	u	u
1975	u	99	u	100	u	70
1980	100	100	98	99	u	88
1985	100	94	96	u	u	98
1990	100	100	98	100	u	98
Secondary net enrollment rate						
1970	85	38	u	44	u	u
1975	u	85	u	49	u	17
1980	93	69	71	u	u	u
1985	95	84	78	u	u	u
1990	u	84	85	u	u	38
Tertiary gross enrollment rate						
1970	17.0	7.9	u	6.8	2.7	2.8
1975	24.6	9.6	u	9.2	3.4	2.3
1980	30.5	15.8	u	7.9	13.1	u
1985	28.7	34.2	u	u	u	u
1990	31.5	38.7	u	u	16.3	8.7

SOURCES: For Japan, South Korea, Singapore, Thailand, and Indonesia, UNESCO (various years), *Statistical Yearbook* for 1968, 1969, 1983, and 1994. For Taiwan, ROC DGBAS (various years), *Statistical Yearbook of the Republic of China* for 1995, table 47.

u, data are unavailable.

stantially since 1970. The largest increase took place in Indonesia, which in 1970 had a primary enrollment rate below the average for upper-middle-income countries. What has been most dramatic is the increase in enrollment at the secondary and tertiary levels. For all six countries except Indonesia, the secondary enrollment rates in 1990 exceeded the average (slightly more than 50%) for all upper-middle-income countries. The net secondary enrollment rate more than doubled in Indonesia and South Korea. In 1970 South Korea and Singapore had enrollments close to the average for all countries, whereas the rate in Indonesia was much lower. Gross enrollment rates at the tertiary level for all upper-middle-income countries averaged 17% in 1990. Those in Japan and South Korea far exceeded the average (Table 9.1).

Total enrollments have risen for all six countries since 1960, more than doubling except in Japan and Singapore, but the distribution of enrollments by level of education has changed (Table 9.2). Only in Indonesia and Thailand have there been large increases in primary enrollment. Secondary enrollment has expanded substantially in almost all the countries, as has tertiary enrollment.

In 1960 the East Asian countries did not have large inequities in primary enrollment between male and female students, and those differences that existed were quite small by 1990 (Table 9.3). Fairly significant differences by

TABLE 9.2

Total Primary, Secondary, and Tertiary Enrollments (in thousands):
Six East Asian Countries, 1960–90

Level and year	Japan	South Korea	Taiwan	Singapore	Thailand	Indonesia
Primary level						
1960	12,591	3,621	1,889	285	3,936	8,955
1965	9,927	4,941	2,258	357	4,640	11,687
1970	9,558	5,749	2,445	364	5,635	14,870
1975	10,281	5,599	2,365	328	6,686	17,777
1980	11,827	5,658	2,234	292	7,393	25,537
1985	11,095	4,857	2,322	278	7,150	29,897
1990	9,373	4,759	2,354	258	6,465	29,934
Secondary level						
1960	7,781	693	355	58	239	553
1965	1,172	1,201	664	116	380	1,454
1970	8,667	1,907	1,155	149	695	2,460
1975	8,796	3,112	1,506	183	1,194	3,570
1980	9,558	4,286	1,606	171	1,920	5,722
1985	11,058	4,935	1,679	190	2,109	9,479
1990	11,026	4,560	1,818	191	2,397	11,243
Tertiary level						
1960	699	99	35	9	14	45
1965	1,182	142	85	14	36	140
1970	1,819	201	203	14	55	248
1975	2,249	297	289	23	131	278
1980	2,412	648	343	u	u	u
1985	2,347	1,456	429	u	1,027	980
1990	2,899	1,691	577	u	u	1,516
All levels						
1960	21,071	4,413	2,279	u	4,189	9,553
1965	22,282	6,284	3,007	487	5,056	13,281
1970	20,044	7,858	3,804	526	6,385	17,578
1975	21,325	9,008	4,160	534	8,011	23,777
1980	23,796	10,591	4,182	u	u	u
1985	24,500	11,247	4,429	u	10,286	40,356
1990	23,298	11,010	4,749	u	u	43,142

SOURCES: For Japan, South Korea, Singapore, Thailand, and Indonesia, UNESCO (various years), *Statistical Yearbook* for 1968, 1969, 1983, and 1994. For Taiwan, ROC DGBAS (various years), *Statistical Yearbook of the Republic of China* for 1995, table 47.
u, data are unavailable.

sex at the secondary and tertiary levels did exist, however. By 1990 the differences had virtually disappeared at the secondary level. Although substantial improvement was made at the tertiary level, significantly fewer females than males continued to be enrolled in tertiary institutions in Indonesia, South Korea, and Japan.

The effect of these changes in enrollment on years of education attained by males and females is illustrated by data from Taiwan. Parish and Willis (1993) reported for Taiwan the mean number of years of education by sex for each decade starting in 1940. For the 1940s females averaged 3.8 years

TABLE 9.3

Percentage of Females in Enrollments, by Level:
Six East Asian Countries, 1960–90

Level and year	Japan	South Korea	Taiwan	Singapore	Thailand	Indonesia
Primary level						
1960	49	45	47	44	47	43
1965	49	48	48	46	47	45
1970	49	48	48	47	47	46
1975	49	48	49	47	47	46
1980	49	49	49	48	48	46
1985	49	49	49	47[a]	u	48
1990	49	49	48	47	49	48
Secondary level						
1960[a]	49	27	34	30	38	33
1965	49	39	38	47	42	33
1970	49	38	41	48	42	34
1975	50	41	45	49	44	38
1980	49	45	48	50	46[a]	u
1985	49	47	49	51[a]	u	u
1990	49	48	50	50	48	45
Tertiary level						
1960	20	17	23	23	30	u
1965	25	25	31	36	34	25
1970	28	24	36	30	42	25
1975	32	27	37	40	40	u
1980	33	u	41	u	u	u
1985	35	30	43	u	u	32
1990	40	32	46	u	53	14

SOURCES: For Japan, South Korea, Singapore, Thailand, and Indonesia, UNESCO (various years), *Statistical Yearbook* for 1968, 1969, 1983, and 1994. For Taiwan, ROC DGBAS (various years), *Statistical Yearbook of the Republic of China* for 1995, table 47.
u, data are unavailable.
[a]Percentages represent general secondary-level enrollment, not including teacher or vocational training (both relatively small numbers).

of schooling, compared with 6.0 years for males. For the 1950s females averaged 5.5 years of schooling, compared with 7.8 years for males. For the 1960s females averaged 8.6 years of schooling, males 9.7 years. For the 1970s the average for females was 11.0 years, for males 11.4 years; and between 1980 and 1985 the average for females was 10.9 years, compared with 11.1 years for males.

The rapid closing of the gap between the educational level of males and females in some countries has been interpreted as a reduction in parental preference for sons. Greenhalgh (1985) offered a convincing counterexplanation, arguing that rapid economic growth and the increased skill intensity of the demand for labor has made it rational for parents to invest in daughters, so long as the parents can recoup their investment before a daughter marries and leaves home. The rising age at marriage suggests that this condition is met.

Expenditures on Education

Improvements in expenditure per pupil have also occurred in East Asia. Real total expenditure per pupil (in purchasing-power parity dollars) has increased dramatically (Table 9.4). Taiwan, South Korea, and Thailand have made particularly rapid increases in public funding of primary education. Moreover, although all five countries for which data are available increased per pupil funding at the secondary level, the increases for South Korea and

TABLE 9.4

Public Expenditure on Education per Pupil, by Level (expressed in US dollars):
Six East Asian Countries, 1960–90

Level and year	Japan	South Korea	Taiwan	Singapore	Thailand	Indonesia
Primary level						
1960	u	u	264	u	u	u
1965	694	100	246	300	455	u
1970	1,280	234	367	437	536	u
1975	2,182	148	368	612	340	u
1980	2,470	338	632	1,080	u	u
1985	2,076	745	424	u	387	u
1990	u	959	793	u	629	u
Secondary level						
1960	u	u	264	u	u	u
1965	694	100	246	300	455	u
1970	1,280	234	367	436	536	u
1975	2,182	148	368	612	340	u
1980	2,470	338	632	1,080	u	u
1985	2,076	576	830	u	u	u
1990	u	770	1,360	u	654	u
Tertiary level						
1960	u	u	1,089	u	u	u
1965	1,818	428	1,079	1,420	2,703	u
1970	2,076	796	1,353	2,072	4,762	u
1975	2,340	740	1,052	2,545	2,142	u
1980	3,139	586	1,635	u	u	u
1985	u	580	2,188	u	638	u
1990	u	451	3,251	u	u	u
All levels						
1960	673	u	131	u	u	44
1965	877	86	167	296	214	u
1970	1,483	245	295	369	299	134
1975	2,420	200	366	612	313	159
1980	2,867	412	683	u	u	u
1985	2,901	688	971	u	u	u
1990	u	935	1,659	u	u	u

SOURCES: For Japan, South Korea, Singapore, Thailand, and Indonesia, UNESCO (various years), *Statistical Yearbook* for 1968, 1969, 1983, and 1994. For Taiwan, ROC DGBAS (various years), *Statistical Yearbook of the Republic of China* for 1995, table 47.
  u, data are unavailable.

Taiwan were particularly large. Japan, Singapore, and Taiwan also significantly increased expenditure per pupil at the tertiary level.

Although expenditures per pupil rose at all levels in most countries, the differing rates of increase by level resulted in changes in the allocation of public funds to education. Shares of public expenditure on education per pupil by level of education are shown in Table 9.5. In Japan, Taiwan, and Singapore the percentage of funds going to primary education fell, whereas the share going to tertiary education increased considerably. In South Korea and Thailand the share of expenditure allocated to primary education rose until the mid-1970s and then declined. In these countries and in Indonesia the share going to secondary education increased strongly. The percentage of public funds allocated to tertiary institutions more than doubled in Indone-

TABLE 9.5

Percentages of Current Public Expenditure on Education, by Level:
Six East Asian Countries, 1960–90[a]

Level and year	Japan	South Korea	Taiwan[b]	Singapore	Thailand	Indonesia
Primary level						
1960	36	44	39	66	60	u
1965	39	66	36	58	61	u
1970	38	64	27	44	54	48
1975	39	62	29	38	63	u
1980	38	50	28	36	55	u
1985	28	47	23	29	56	u
1990	26	44	24	u	56	u
Secondary level						
1960	37	16	32	19	14	u
1965	40	22	32	24	16	u
1970	38	23	38	34	20	33
1975	37	26	36	34	16	u
1980	35	33	36	41	28	u
1985	32	37	32	37	21	u
1990	32	34	31	u	22	52
Tertiary level						
1960	15	14	13	14	10	u
1965	11	11	18	14	9	u
1970	13	8	25	15	14	8
1975	10	12	20	18	11	u
1980	11	9	20	17	13	u
1985	21	11	22	31	13	u
1990	23	7	24	u	15	20

SOURCES: For Japan, South Korea, Singapore, Thailand, and Indonesia, UNESCO (various years), *Statistical Yearbook* for 1968, 1969, 1983, and 1994. For Taiwan, ROC DGBAS (various years), *Statistical Yearbook of the Republic of China* for 1995, table 47.

u, data are unavailable.

[a]Education categories not included in this table are instruction preceding the first level and special education. Hence percentages do not add to 100.

[b]Percentages for Taiwan are percentages of total expenditure rather than current expenditure.

TABLE 9.6

Total Educational Expenditure as a Percentage of GNP:
Six East Asian Countries, 1960–90

Year	Japan	South Korea	Taiwan	Singapore	Thailand	Indonesia
1960	4.1	3.2[a]	2.2	u	2.5[b]	0.7
1965	4.4	1.8	2.4	4.1	3.1	u
1970	3.9	3.6	3.5	3.1	3.5	2.8
1975	5.5	2.2	3.1	3.0	3.6	3.0
1980	5.8	3.7	3.6	2.8	3.4	1.7
1985	5.0	4.5	4.1	4.4	3.8	u
1990	4.7	3.6	4.8	3.4	3.6	1.0

SOURCES: For Japan, South Korea, Singapore, Thailand, and Indonesia, UNESCO (various years), *Statistical Yearbook* for 1968, 1969, 1983, and 1994. For Taiwan, ROC DGBAS (various years), *Statistical Yearbook of the Republic of China* for 1995, table 47.
   [a]Value in 1961.
   [b]Value in 1959.

sia, whereas in Thailand it increased by about 50% and in South Korea it fluctuated around 10%.

Expenditure on education and enrollment are related. Jones (1975) found that enrollment rates for all primary students in Thailand grew slowly during the 1960s, from around 66% in 1960 to 70% in 1970. This was due not to a lack of desire to enroll children but rather to an insufficient number of schools and teachers to meet demand.

Many economists have argued that population growth has an adverse effect on economic growth by crowding-out other areas of investment. They offer as evidence of such an effect an increase in the ratio of educational expenditures to gross national product (GNP). If this effect is symmetric, we would observe that the share of education in GNP declines as the rate of population growth slows. The data reported in Table 9.6 indicate no clear trend in public expenditures on education as a percentage of GNP, except in Taiwan and Thailand, where the shares rose rather than fell as fertility rates declined. In their study of education in Asia Tan and Mingat (1992: 15) concluded that "in general the education sector's claim on government spending neither expands nor diminishes dramatically as a result of intersectoral competition for public resources within each country." This lack of a simple relationship again underscores the fact that public allocations to education are the product of policy decisions, not of demographic determinism.

Pupil-Teacher Ratios

Earlier we noted the increase in expenditure per pupil at the primary-school level in all six East Asian countries. Table 9.7 suggests that at least part of the increase in expenditure was used to decrease the pupil-teacher ratio. Japan, South Korea, Taiwan, and Indonesia decreased this ratio by about

TABLE 9.7

Primary Pupil–Teacher Ratios: Six East Asian Countries, 1960–90

Year	Japan	South Korea	Taiwan	Singapore	Thailand	Indonesia
1960	35	58	46	33	36	39
1965	28	62	42	29	35	41
1970	26	57	41	30	35	29
1975	26	52	38	30	28	29
1980	25	48	32	31	23	32
1985	24	38	32	27	19	25
1990	21	36	29	26	18	23

SOURCES: For Japan, South Korea, Singapore, Thailand, and Indonesia, UNESCO (various years), *Statistical Yearbook* for 1968, 1969, 1983, and 1994. For Taiwan, ROC DGBAS (various years), *Statistical Yearbook of the Republic of China* for 1995, table 47.

40%, whereas Singapore reduced it by 21% and Thailand reduced it by 50%. For Taiwan, Singapore, and Indonesia this performance was similar to that of all upper-income countries, but the reduction in Thailand far exceeded the average for wealthier countries. Although South Korea and Taiwan had higher pupil-teacher ratios than average for upper-income countries in 1990, the absolute reduction in their ratios far exceeded that for upper-income countries as a group.

According to Kelley (1996: 84), a major determinant of expenditures per pupil is the salary rate of teachers. Kelley acknowledged, however, that the relationship between teacher salaries and teacher quality is complex. Therefore, even if we had consistent data on teacher salaries across countries and over time, the interpretation to be placed on such data would be open to debate.

It is clear that no simple single pattern of association exists between fertility decline and investment in education in East Asia. For instance, Indonesian fertility declined by about 8% from the late 1960s to the early 1970s, but primary-school enrollment rates increased 26% in the late 1970s. Fertility declined a further 8% in the late 1970s, but enrollment 5–10 years later grew by only 11%. From the early to the late 1960s Korean fertility declined by 16%, whereas primary-school enrollment rates rose by 5% and expenditure per pupil doubled. In the early 1980s secondary-school enrollment rates rose by 22%, but expenditure by pupil rose by 70%. Thus the direction of change was similar across countries, but the rates of change and their division differed between enrollment change and expenditure change and among primary, secondary, and tertiary levels.

The lack of a simple relationship between demographic change and education is further illustrated by comparing the experiences of Asia and Africa. Although fertility rates dropped dramatically in Asia, by and large they have not done so in Africa. Nevertheless, in both continents gross enrollment rates at the primary level increased by 30 percentage points between 1970 and 1990 (Kelley 1996: 74).

Educational Attainment

Have the increases in educational inputs in East Asia led to increases in direct educational outputs, such as test scores, years of school completed, or literacy? Data on educational outputs are difficult to find. Tan and Mingat (1992: 182) reported data on the percentages of adults who are literate in several of the countries under study. In Indonesia literacy rose from 54% of adults in 1970 to 74% of adults in 1985. The respective figures were 88% and 92% for South Korea, 69% and 86% for Singapore, and 79% and 91% for Thailand. By 1990 these figures had increased to 77% for Indonesia, 93% for Thailand, and 96% for South Korea (World Bank 1993b: 239–40).

Tan and Mingat (1992) reported that completion rates have also improved. For example, in Thailand those entering primary school now have completion rates of 100%, 89.0%, 88.1%, 86.3%, 84.6%, and 80% for grades 1 to 6, respectively; 32.2%, 30.5%, and 29.3% for secondary grades 7 to 9, respectively; and 15.0%, 13.2%, and 13.0% for secondary grades 10 to 12, respectively.

Educational attainment has also increased over time. Barro and Lee [cited by Kelley (1996: 77)] reported data by region for 1960 through 1985. In Asia years of education completed rose from 1.92 years to 3.91 years per adult, 25 years old and older. The gain for East Asian countries was much higher.

Another measure of attainment is performance on tests of cognitive skills standardized across economies. In the relatively few available comparisons East Asian children tend to perform better than children in other developing countries and have recently outscored children in high-income countries (World Bank 1993a: 45).

Linkages between Demographic Change, Education, and Economic Growth

The stylized facts of East Asia's rapid economic growth are that the governments' export-oriented, labor-demanding development strategy increased employment opportunities and wages and that access to high-quality basic education and health services increased. The corresponding facts of the demographic transition were an increase in the median age at marriage and a significant decline in fertility. The elements of the extended Solow (1956) growth model accord well with the economic facts. In Solow's model growth of gross domestic product (GDP) is a positive function of physical and human capital and a negative function of population growth. Human capital accumulation, in turn, is a positive function of the fraction of resources invested in it and a negative function of population growth (Mankiw, Romer, and Weil 1992). Cross-country regression studies by Barro (1991), Mankiw, Romer, and Weil (1992), and the World Bank (1993a) reported that, as predicted by the new growth theory, economic growth or income per capita are positively related to education.[2] The World Bank study (1993a: 52) concluded that primary education is the largest single contributor to economic growth, explaining between 58% of predicted growth in Japan and 87% of predicted growth in Thailand. Secondary education, in contrast, makes a significant contribution to growth (41%) only in Japan. These studies found investment in human capital to be so important that "poor countries tend to catch up with rich countries if the poor countries have high human capital per person (in relation to their level of per capita GDP), but not otherwise" (Barro 1991: 437).

Such a strong statement leads one to expect that the relationship between education and growth uncovered by these studies is robust, but that is not the case. The education measures in the World Bank (1993a) and Barro (1991) studies are the primary enrollment rate and the secondary enrollment rate, but only the primary rate is statistically significant. In most of the countries under consideration primary enrollment rates were already high by 1970, and the rapid increases in education came at the secondary and tertiary levels. What happened at the primary level was an increase in real expenditure and a fall in the pupil-teacher ratio, that is, an improvement in educational quality, not necessarily in enrollment rates. Investigation of alternative education measures produced mixed results. A measure based on years of education completed by adults was not statistically significant, but Barro (1991: 421) did find that the higher the student-teacher ratio, the lower the rate of economic growth. Moreover, if the literacy rate was used as the measure of education, the same significant relationship was obtained. Mankiw, Romer, and Weil (1992: 419) used as their measure an approximation of the percentage of the working-age population enrolled in secondary school, but they ignored primary and tertiary enrollment.

Recent examinations of the robustness of these important studies reach different conclusions. Levine and Renelt (1992) concluded that few, if any, of the educational variables are robust, whereas Sala-I-Martin (1997: 182) concluded that "a substantial number of variables can be found to be strongly related to growth." In ongoing research a number of analysts have found fragile relationships between education and growth. In some cases the number of years of education is significant; in others cases it is not. In some studies only male secondary enrollment is positive and significant (and only for males older than 25 years of age, but not for those older than 15 years of age), whereas female education hurts economic growth (A. C. Kelley, personal communication, 1997). The fragility of these results is to some extent a function of the quality of the data, which Kelley has criticized, and of variations in model specification. Thus, as of the time of this writing, there is no solid evidence from the new growth theory regressions of a robust relationship between education and economic growth.

Demographic Impact on Education

The new growth theory accepts the view that the rate of population growth affects the accumulation of human capital. Because this view is far from universally accepted, it is appropriate to discuss the theoretical and empirical evidence for such a link. Research on the link between demographic change and education has been done at both the macroeconomic level and the microeconomic level. We discuss each in turn.

Macroeconomic-Level Story

Why should a decline in fertility affect education? In most instances education is seen as something that enhances the quality of an individual, and therefore parents or the government usually expends funds on it. When the number of children increases, the amount to be spent has to be shared among a larger number of claimants; thus the amount each child receives declines. A decline in fertility should therefore be associated with an increase in the amount of education that each child receives.

This potential can be seen easily in a calculation of the demographic bonus, that is, the extra consumption or income that is freed-up by a reduction in births. The private bonus is $(N_1 - N_0)(C_k/N_0)$ and the public bonus is $(N_1 - N_0)(G_k/N_0)$, where N_1 and N_0 are the number of children without and with a decline in fertility, respectively, and C_k and G_k are private and public consumption by children, respectively. The derivation, by Andrew Mason, of the bonus in terms of equivalent consumer units is shown in the appendix.

Parents and governments can spend the demographic bonus in a number of ways. They can increase school enrollment so that more children are educated, they can deepen human capital by spending more per child, or they can use the bonus for some purpose other than education. The point here is that the demographic bonus represents a financial *potential* for improving human capital, but the decisions of parents and policymakers determine how the bonus will be spent. In East Asia the bonus appears to have been spent in at least two ways that have benefited education: The percentage of children enrolled in school has increased, and expenditures per child have increased.

Macroeconometric evidence of the demography-education link comes from four main studies. In the first study, Schultz (1987) found that, for a sample of 89 developed and developing countries over the period 1969–1980, demographic change was relatively unimportant in explaining variations in enrollment rates or the share of GNP spent on education but that expenditures per pupil were inversely related to the size of the school-age cohort. The second study, by Tan and Mingat (1992), measured the effect of demographic, economic, and other measures on educational outcomes rather than on inputs. Conducting a cross-country regression of 82 developing countries in the mid-1980s, Tan and Mingat found that an increase in the ratio of the population age 5–14 to the population age 15–64 was associated with a decrease in grade attainment. The dependent variable was the proportion of a cohort exiting the educational system; primary, secondary, and higher education were weighted by the length of schooling at each level.

In the third study, Kelley (1996) estimated the effects of demographic measures (population growth and the percentage of the population in the primary schooling ages) on education measures (the share of GDP spent on public education, and student-teacher ratios), controlling for the level of economic development and other factors. He used data from 30 developing countries that furnished consolidated data to the International Monetary Fund, arguing that those data were superior to the data from UNESCO, which are more commonly used (including here). He also reestimated his regressions using the UNESCO data, obtaining the same results. Kelley found that neither demographic measure had a statistically significant effect on the share of GDP spent on public education.

In the fourth study, Schultz (1996) investigated the effects of demographic change, income growth, and the relative cost of teachers on expenditure per student. His study included 60 countries observed at 5-year intervals from 1960 to 1980. He also decomposed the effects of the independent variables into effects on the enrollment ratio, the teacher-student ratio, current expenditures per teacher, and the physical capital intensity of the educational system. Schultz found that the relative size of the school-age population, which was highly correlated with recent levels of population growth, was negatively related to public education expenditures per school-age child. These effects were substantial, especially for primary education. A standard deviation increase of 20% in the proportion of the population of primary-school age was associated with a decrease of 23% in primary-school expenditure per child, and a similar increase in the population of secondary-school age was associated with a 7% decline in secondary-school expenditure per child, although only the primary-school effect was statistically significant. A decline in cohort size affected expenditures on primary education principally through increasing the teacher-student ratio (a measure of increased quality), but it may have increased expenditure per teacher. At the secondary level decreasing cohort size increased the teacher-student ratio but decreased the enrollment ratio.

The study by Tan and Mingat (1992) points out that there is no single East Asian model for the provision of education. This point is well illustrated by a comparison of South Korea and Thailand, both of which spent 3.6% of their GDP on education in 1990. South Korea spent more per pupil at both the primary and secondary levels and had higher-quality teachers (as measured by relative salaries) than did Thailand. South Korea also paid attention to all three levels of education. In contrast, in Thailand the main focus was on primary education; expenditure per pupil was high, and class size was low. Tan and Mingat (1992: 6) concluded that "outcomes are determined as much by the efficiency with which resources are used as by the aggregate amount of resources available." Among the lessons of their study are the following: Demographic pressures remain an important impediment to improving educational performance; although large increases in expenditure can produce appreciable results, such increases are nearly always difficult to achieve; and choosing the right policies can make a substantial difference because increased resources cannot overcome the effects of inappropriate policies, particularly those affecting the efficiency with which services are provided and financed (Tan and Mingat 1992: 8).

Thus the cross-country macroeconometric studies do not support the notion that demographic variables have a consistent effect on enrollment rates, student-teacher ratios, or the share of GNP spent on education, but they do suggest that higher fertility is associated with lower expenditure per student and with lower educational attainment. These cross-country regressions combine countries with sound economic policies and efficient education sectors and those without these features. The composition of the samples probably explains the results. Kelley (1996: 93) observed that "in those countries in which government economic policies are relatively sound and the education sector is quite efficient, incremental expenditures on education enabled by reduced population growth rates will enjoy relatively high rates of return." However, if countries use the gains from the demographic bonus resulting from declining fertility to "expand but replicate inefficient budgetary allocations, [they] could have disappointing impacts on educational outcomes" (Kelley 1996: 94). On the whole, the East Asian countries appear to have managed their demographic bonus better than most developing countries.

Microeconomic-Level Story

Theories of parental investment in children along the lines of Becker and Tomes (1976) suggest that, under assumed conditions of altruism and a perfect capital market, optimal investment is independent of the number and sex of children and of the degree of parental altruism and wealth. The only reason for the investment in education to vary is that rates of return to education vary. Such variations in rates of return may occur because of variations in children's characteristics (for example, their abilities) or the family's characteristics (for example, common genetic or environmental factors).

They may also occur because of external factors, such as shifts in the pattern of labor demand, changes in the cost or availability of education, or labor market discrimination (Lillard and Willis 1994: 1,129). Thus in a strict Becker-Tomes world the scope for lower fertility to affect education appears rather limited.

One avenue is through wages. Evenson (1988) showed that reduced population growth will result in higher equilibrium wages and incomes, even after allowance is made for population-induced structural change (or Boserup effects) on equilibrium prices and quantities. He also showed that policy interventions to reduce fertility (for example, by increasing education or subsidizing contraception, both of which occurred in East Asia) increase real wages and incomes. These increases, in turn, further reduce fertility so long as they are not biased against women. As we have seen, in East Asia they were not so biased.

When the assumption of a perfect capital market is relaxed, the scope for demographic effects on household investments in education expands. Financial constraints force parents to choose among children when allocating resources, and the allocation depends on the degree to which parents care about different children and their willingness to substitute among them (Behrman, Pollak, and Taubman 1991). For example, in a study of educational attainment in Taiwan Parish and Willis (1993) found that the number and sex of children mattered and had a larger effect on educational attainment in earlier birth cohorts and among the poor than in later cohorts or among the wealthy. These differences suggest differences in financial constraints.

Kelley (1996: 96–7) discussed more refinements to the model that make the effect of number of children on education theoretically indeterminate. In large families there may be economies of scale in education: Older siblings help younger siblings in their studies, and there may be some sharing of supplies. In addition, because the share of total resources potentially available for education decreases with family size and because contributions from child labor increase with family size, large family size may be a disadvantage only for middle children.

State interventions can also place a wedge between the number of children and education. For example, Malaysia's New Economic Policy, introduced in 1970, was biased strongly in favor of Malays, making it possible for them to educate their children and be assured of their successful employment at little private cost. Consequently, Malay fertility failed to decline at a time when the fertility of other groups in Malaysia was declining significantly (Jones 1990).

Lloyd (1994) pointed out that in addition to government policies, other factors (cultural practices, the stage of a society's development, and the phase of the demographic transition) can nullify any effect of the number of children on their educational attainment. Thus empirical studies of the relationship between family size and educational attainment must account for the effect of these variables on education.

The analysis of a trade-off between the number and quality of children assumes that parents can choose the number of children they will have. Montgomery, Kouame, and Oliver (1995) suggested that a lack of access to family planning services may undermine this assumption, particularly in rural areas. A notable feature of the demographic transition in East Asia was increased access to and use of contraception, which allowed parents to manage the quantity-quality trade-off more precisely.

For all these reasons we agree with Kelley (1996: 97) that the effect of fertility on education is an empirical matter. Testing the effect empirically, however, faces a host of problems. Principal among these is the likelihood that parents choose both the number and quality of their children; that is, the number of children that parents have is related to their investments in education, contrary to what most empirical studies assume. Another problem is that most studies that include two or more children from the same family do not allow for the correlation of educational outcomes of family members. A third problem is that parents' education may be endogenous to children's education, not exogenous, as is commonly assumed.[3] A fourth problem is that the timing of demographic events incorporated into empirical models may not match the timing of the education events under study. Finally, many studies assume that the effect of the number of children is linear, whereas it may not be [see Kelley (1996: 99–101) for further discussion of this last issue].

Both Lloyd (1994) and Kelley (1996) surveyed the literature on the effect of the number of children in a family on the amount of education each child receives. Lloyd (1994: 185) concluded that "the [negative] link between high fertility and lower levels of child investments, while generally in evidence, does not appear to be universally true or quantitatively important except in certain circumstances or for certain groups." She argued that negative effects are more likely to arise in urban settings than in rural settings and in the more developed countries of Southeast Asia and Latin America than in South Asia or sub-Saharan Africa. Her finding suggests that much remains unknown about what generates the trade-off in particular countries. For example, in East Asia the level of development probably increases the trade-off between family size and investments in children, but the importance of the extended family and the flow of resources across generations likely decreases it. But it is not clear how important each contributing factor is.

Kelley (1996: 102) concluded from his review of 30 studies that "the overall impact of family size on schooling enrollments and years attained is mixed, although when statistically significant, a small negative impact is the most representative result." By a small impact Kelley means that a 1-birth reduction is associated with less than a 2.5% change in the education-outcome variable. Some support is found for a possible break in the effect of family size at around four to five children, with relatively little effect for between one and four children and for five or more children (Kelley 1996: 107). Kelley also concluded that the negative relationship is most likely to appear at later rather than earlier stages of economic and demographic development.

Most of these studies measure only monetary expenditures on children. However, reducing population growth can improve education by increasing expenditures of either money or time. Mason (1993) projected that in Thailand the number of adults per child will increase from 1.3 to 2.2 between 1980 and 2000 and will increase to 2.7 in 2015, largely as a result of declining fertility. Similar increases are likely for other Asian countries. To the extent that parental time increases educational outputs, reducing population growth may contribute to increasing education through increasing monetary inputs and increasing the amount of time parents spend with each child.

Although the effects of the number of siblings on the amount of education they receive may be small, it does not necessarily follow that the effects on their productivity and earnings are also small. Behrman and Taubman (1986) found that 1 extra sibling had only a small negative effect on the number of years of education but decreased earnings by 3% for males and females, although the effect was not statistically significant for females. In addition, the effects of education are cumulative across generations; that is, parents' educational attainment increases the educational attainment of their children. A number of studies have found that parents' education predominantly influences children of the same sex. This finding underscores the importance of educating women to reduce their fertility in subsequent generations (Lillard and Willis 1994: 1,158–9).

In Table 9.8 we reproduce Kelley's summary of the studies on South Korea, Taiwan, Thailand, and Indonesia. Côte d'Ivoire is included in the table for comparison. The results for East Asia are more consistent than those from surveys of all countries. In most cases the more siblings a child has, particularly younger siblings, the less education he or she receives. The size of the effect increases over time (with economic development and the demographic transition), although the absolute size of the effects is small in Kelley's terms.

Some studies report asymmetries by sex of the child. For example, Greenhalgh (1985) found that in Taiwan having an older sister increased the investment in the education of boys, and Parish and Willis (1993) found that it increased the investment in the education of all younger siblings. For Malaysia Lillard and Willis (1994: 1,160) found that a boy's education would be increased if he had one more older sister or one less older brother but that a girl's education would be slightly reduced in these circumstances.

It is possible that not all births have the same effect on parent's investments in the human capital of their children. It may be that only children beyond a certain number—that is, children who are unwanted—are disadvantaged in parental resource allocations. Montgomery and Lloyd (1996) and Montgomery et al. (1997) explored the consequences of unintended fertility

TABLE 9.8

Results of Econometric Studies on the Effect of Sibset Size on Educational Outcomes: Four East Asian Countries and Côte d'Ivoire

Country, source, data, and statistical technique	Independent variables	Dependent variables	Results
South Korea and Thailand (Mason 1993); 1993 Income and Expenditure Survey (South Korea) and 1981 Socio-economic Survey (Thailand); logit and ordinary least-squares (OLS) regressions	Age and sex of children, household disposable income	Enrollment, family expenditures on children	Mixed effect on South Korean and Thai enrollments. In Thailand, older children help (larger quantitative effect and more likely statistically significant); younger children hurt. Overall effects generally offsetting, likely negative on average. Approximately the same pattern for South Korea. There, older girls have a positive effect on enrollments; older boys do not. Expenditures per child on education are negatively affected.
Taiwan (Hermalin, Seltzer, and Lin 1982); urban and rural married women, age 20–39 in 1973; OLS regressions	Sibset size, sex, father's education and work status, mother's age	Attainment	No overall effect. Negative effect emerges with younger women, but quantitative size is small (a reduction by 1 sibling increases average attainment by 2.2%).
Taiwan (Parish and Willis 1993); 1989 survey of women, age 25–60, in 2,897 households; OLS regressions	Siblings by sex and birth order; parents' education, occupation, and income	Attainment	Small mixed effects, positive and negative, varying by sex and over time. For 32 comparisons, 20 are statistically insignificant; 8 show a negative and 4 show a positive effect. A change by 1 sibling increases or decreases average attainment by about 2.5%. Over all negative effect reduces this net effect to 0.6% of average attainment. The negative effect of sibset size increases over time as family size declines and income rises, a puzzling result. Same-sex siblings hurt, older sisters always help, and cross-sex siblings are neutral to educational attainment.
Thailand (Cochrane and Jamison 1982); 400 rural households, 3 generations; OLS regressions	Younger siblings, age, parents' education and aspirations, land ownership, innate ability, distance from school, water availability	Attainment, work force participation, literacy, numeracy	Younger siblings have little effect on attainment or participation of most children. No effect on attainment of children age 5–13; sizable negative effect on young adults (14–25); i.e., a reduction by 1 sibling increases attainment by 0.35 year, or 6% of average attainment. Similar pattern for participation.

Indonesia (Chernichovsky and Meesook 1985); 1978 National Socioeconomic Survey (6,000 households); OLS regressions	Household size, household expenditure, child's age and sex, parents' education, school location	Enrollment, attainment by child's age	Effects mixed: some positive, others negative, all very small. No effect on attendance of children age 13–15; positive effect on persons age 16–26. Negative effect on schooling completed for ages 10–15; no effect for ages 16–18; positive effect for ages 19–25. A change in household size by 1 child leads to 0.05 year's change in schooling completed (sample averages not presented). Boys advantaged in attendance. No sex effect on schooling completed for children age 10–15; boys age 16+ advantaged.
Indonesia, Pakistan, and Philippines (King et al. 1986); Asian Marriage Surveys, 1979-80, two adult generations, middle-class urban, urban poor, rural (4,787 respondents in Indonesia, 4,352 in Pakistan, 6,224 in Philippines); maximum likelihood, variance components model with sibset size endogenous	Cohort, age, sibset size (predictor), parents' education and occupation, land ownership, mother's age at marriage	Attainment (years completed)	Small positive effects. Most estimates (12 of 18) not statistically significant. Where significant, effect is always positive, a result occurring in all three country samples. Positive effects are more likely in female samples (4 of 6 estimates).
Côte d'Ivoire (Montgomery and Kouame 1993); 1985–87 Living Standards Survey covering 4,310 women and 8,175 children; OLS regressions, probit ordered probit	Fertility, mother's education, consumption per adult, residence, ethnicity, age, school location and amenities	Cumulative schooling, enrollment projected, completed schooling	Effect is positive in rural areas, negative in urban areas.

SOURCE: Adapted and revised slightly from Kelley (1996, table A). Reprinted with permission.

(unwanted at the time of conception or mistimed) and excess fertility (in excess of ideal family size) for children's educational attainment. They found that in the Dominican Republic, the Philippines, and Thailand unintended and excess births were associated with clear reductions in children's years of schooling and the likelihood of their attaining at least one year of secondary school, but that in Egypt and Kenya these effects did not occur. The effects tended to be small (less than 1 year of education completed and a 5–10 percentage point lower probability of attending at least 1 year of high school) except in families where 2 or more unwanted births had occurred within 5 years or where ideal family size had been exceeded by 2 or more births.

Myhrman et al. (1995) found that Finnish children who were unwanted by their mother during pregnancy were less likely than wanted children to have gone beyond the basic nine years of education by age 24. The educational attainment of children whose births were mistimed rather than unwanted was greater than for unwanted children but less than that of wanted children. Educational differentials by the wanted status of children were larger for females than for males. Rosenzweig and Wolpin (1980) and Rosenzweig and Schultz (1987) also found that unplanned or unexpected births had negative effects on child investments. We have found that an unwanted birth generally results in less investment in a child's health in developing countries (Jensen and Ahlburg 1998).

Declines in unwanted births may have contributed to the rise in education observed in Asia. Bongaarts (1997) argued that unwantedness declines toward the end of the demographic transition. For countries that had demographic surveys in the late 1970s or early 1980s and again in the late 1980s or early 1990s, this appears to have been the case. For example, in Thailand, as the total fertility rate fell from 4.3 to 2.2 children per woman, the number of unwanted children fell from 1.1 per woman to 0.4 per woman.

The microeconometric studies suggest that the financial demographic bonus resulting from declining fertility is not limited to governments but also benefits individual households. Such a bonus appears to have been more common in contemporary East Asia than in most other regions. Even if declining fertility does not bring such a bonus, education and health investments per child are likely to rise if the percentage of unwanted children declines with declining fertility. In addition to the financial bonus, declining fertility provides parents with a bonus in the form of time that may be used to increase the human capital development of their children.

Educational Inputs, Educational Outputs, and Economic Growth

Although some of the cross-country regression analyses display an association between education and economic growth, they tell us little about how this actually occurs. If a demographic bonus occurs and expenditure on education increases, do educational outputs increase? That is, does increased investment in education produce better students, ones who will be more productive as adults?

A substantial literature on educational production functions in the United States does not reveal a consistent positive relationship between expenditures on schooling and student performance on tests of cognitive skill (Hanushek 1986, 1991). James, King, and Suryadi (1996) assumed that this is because school managers either do not know what constitutes the educational production function or do not have the incentive or decision-making power to operate efficiently. Few studies have examined the relationship between educational expenditures per se and outcomes in developing countries (Kelley 1996: 78), but the presumption is that there is at best a weak relationship between expenditure and outcomes. James, King, and Suryadi (1996) found that Indonesia is an exception to this generalization. Tan and Mingat (1992) found that South Korea and Taiwan have similarly efficient educational systems. A number of studies have examined the effect of school characteristics on student achievement. Fuller [1986, cited by Glewwe and Jacoby (1994: 859)] surveyed 72 studies and reported that most of them found that textbooks, desks, and libraries enhanced achievement. In addition, half the studies found positive effects of teachers' experience or education. Thus it appears that it is not necessarily the amount of expenditure on education that improves outcomes but how the funds are spent.

Recent research has shown that students educated by better-paid teachers and in environments with lower student-teacher ratios obtain higher earnings in the labor market and thus are presumably more productive (Card and Krueger 1992a,b). A direct link between education and productivity is often imputed from such studies of earnings, but Black and Lynch (1996) directly estimated the relationship in a US study. They found that a 10% increase in the average education of an establishment's work force increased productivity by between 8.5% and 12.7% (p. 264).

Rosenzweig (1995) found that schooling enhanced the ability of a group of farmers to learn from observations about optimal input use but was not associated with advantageous access to external sources of information. He also found that education did not automatically increase productivity. It did so where new technologies increased the scope for learning or input misuse and where changes in markets and political regimes were occurring. Such changes have been a feature of East Asian experience.

In short, the mechanism by which increased spending on education enhances productivity is not clear. If more spending does not increase cognitive skills, better schools may nevertheless give students better information about their own abilities and thus enable them to make better job matches. Such schools may also teach them useful problem-solving skills, as suggested by Rosenzweig's findings, or better work habits, neither of which are captured in standardized cognitive ability tests (Ehrenberg and Smith 1994: 312). Improved education may increase productivity because education and further training are complements. Altonji and Spletzer (1991) showed that on-the-job training is positively correlated with both education and ability. Workers with more training earn more than other workers, presumably because they are more productive.

Conclusion

In the standard economic growth model higher population growth reduces income because capital must be shared among a larger number of workers. In the new growth theory model human capital must also be spread more thinly. Thus a slowing in population growth, as has occurred in East Asia, allows for the deepening of both physical and human capital. As Barro (1991: 422) put it, "In effect, people shift from saving in the form of children to saving in the form of physical and human capital."

The data examined in this chapter show that both human capital widening and deepening appear to have occurred in East Asia. School enrollment rates, expenditure per student, and educational attainment have risen. At the same time, fertility rates have fallen. Cross-country regression studies have shown that these increases in education play a central role in explaining the rapid economic growth in East Asian countries.

The literature we have reviewed links demographic changes to educational changes and educational inputs to outputs. The new growth theory posits a link between education and economic growth. Understanding these linkages among demographic change, educational change, and economic growth is important for policy formulation. Macroeconometric studies do not provide much support for a link between fertility decline and school enrollments or education's share of GDP. They do, however, provide some support for a link between fertility decline and educational expenditure per pupil and educational attainment. There is little microeconometric evidence of a general negative effect of high fertility on household allocations to education per child. This result is perhaps not too surprising given that the quantity-quality trade-off is affected by, among other things, the level of a society's development, government policies, and local customs. The microeconometric studies conducted in East Asia seem to find more evidence of a negative effect of high fertility than do studies in developing countries of other regions, although they are subject to the methodological problems raised by Kelley. The other group of studies finds that macroeconometric associations between education and economic growth are not robust to different definitions of education.

There is a debate in the education literature about whether increases in expenditures on education are translated into improvements in the quality of education. It appears that the educational systems of at least some of the East Asian countries, by being efficiently organized and well run, were able to convert increases in expenditures into improved outcomes. On balance, therefore, it appears that the fertility declines in East Asia provided a demographic bonus to parents and governments. It seems that at the household level conditions were such that parents traded off large numbers of children for fewer children of higher quality. At the governmental level policy decisions were favorable to the educational sector, and the sector itself was sufficiently efficient to convert increased expenditures into higher levels of educational attainment.

No single path was chosen, however. The countries of East Asia differed in the ways they used the demographic bonus to modify their educational systems. Some reduced class size, whereas others chose to improve the quality of teachers and increase other expenditures per child. They also differed in the degree to which they were able to increase educational attainment. In the end, education policy, more than any other factor, has determined Asia's diverse patterns of providing education. The role of demography has been to widen the options of policy. In some countries the bonus was wisely spent; in other countries the choices were more problematic.

The Demographic Bonus

We define terms in the following way: N_0 and N_1 are the number of children in the base and alternative scenarios, respectively; A_0 and A_1 are the number of adults in the base and alternative scenarios, respectively; DR_i is the dependency ratio for scenario i; C and G are the private consumption and the government consumption base scenarios, respectively; P_K, P_A, and P are the prices of a child, an adult, and a child relative to an adult P_K/P_A; W_c and W_g are children's share of private and government consumption, respectively; and C_K and G_K are private and government consumption by children, respectively.

Let N_0 be the number of children in the base scenario, for example, in the absence of a fertility decline. Given a fertility decline, the number of children is N_1. The private bonus is given by

$$\text{BONUS}_c = (N_1 - N_0)\left(\frac{C_k}{N_0}\right). \tag{9.1}$$

The public bonus is given by

$$\text{BONUS}_g = (N_1 - N_0)\left(\frac{G_K}{N_0}\right). \tag{9.2}$$

The bonus is the total amount of income that can be reallocated under the alternative scenario without reducing expenditure per child.

The relationship between the bonus and the equivalent adult consumer unit is easily derived.

Children's consumption is given by

$$C_k = \left[\frac{P_k N_0}{(P_K N_0 + P_A A_0)}\right] C. \tag{9.3}$$

Dividing the numerator and denominator of the right-hand side by P_A and A_0 yields

$$C_k = \left\{\frac{P(DR_0)}{[P(DR_0) + 1]}\right\} C. \tag{9.4}$$

Substituting Equation (9.4) for C_k yields

$$\text{BONUS}_c = \left(\left[\frac{(N_1 - N_0)}{N_0}\right]\left\{\frac{P(DR_0)}{[P(DR_0) + 1]}\right\}\right) C. \tag{9.5}$$

A similar expression can be derived for the government sector. Presumably the relative prices of children in the public and private sectors are different. Suggested by Andrew Mason.

Child Health and Health Care in Indonesia and the Philippines

ERIC R. JENSEN AND DENNIS A. AHLBURG

OUR AIM IN THIS chapter is to examine, at the family level, the allocation of resources to children for evidence of responses to fertility or family size. Specifically, we investigate the impact of wanted and unwanted fertility on child health. Our premise is that family resources are finite and therefore that allocative choices must be made. These choices, or their consequences, may be observable in survey data on child health. To examine this contention, we inspect five outcome measures and two measures of resource availability and parental willingness to commit resources to a given child. The outcomes are diarrheal and respiratory disease incidence in children, curative care provision to children for either illness, and preventive care (in the form of vaccinations) provided to children. Assuming that family resources are spread more thinly with increases in numbers of children, we examine the impact of numbers of siblings on outcome variables for reference children. If fertility is imperfectly controlled, unwanted births are likely to occur, and family resources are stretched more thinly than is desired by the parents. Therefore many choices requiring resource commitments by parents, including our measures of child health, will be affected by the occurrence of unwanted births. We view the occurrence of an unwanted birth as a largely exogenous shock occurring outside the parents' decision-making calculus. However, because the proportion of unwanted births is low (16% or less in the countries we study), we view sibset (sibling set) size as largely reflective of deliberate choice by parents.

We thank Minja Kim Choe for her generosity and patience in providing data, translation, and guidance; Ron Lee, Andy Mason, Jerry Russo, Amy Tsui, and seminar participants at the East-West Center, College of William and Mary, and World Bank for additional helpful comments; and Jeff Brown, Shi-Jen He, and Lixia Xu for capable research assistance.

We examine data from two Asian countries: Indonesia and the Philippines. We focus on (1) the observable impact of resource constraints on the incidence of diarrhea and respiratory disease morbidity in children and (2) the provision of simple care, in terms of curative health care for these conditions, or vaccinations. We expect that as incomes increase the relative costs of basic nutrition and child health care decline, quality of care rises, and institutions, such as health insurance, evolve to spread the burden of child health care beyond the family. The allocative mechanisms with which we are concerned are ones that we expect to see operating with some degree of force in a relatively poor country, such as Indonesia or the Philippines.

Methods

Inferring Resources Devoted to Child Health

Child health is interesting as an indication of parents' willingness and ability to commit resources to children, at a point in time near birth. If the underlying family-level allocative mechanism is one based on scarcity, then the family resources being doled out, whether for child nutrition, health care of children, or their education, reflect the same process. Examining relationships between fertility or sibset size and child health is an appealing way to get at underlying resource allocation decisions, because observable consequences of these decisions may begin to appear almost immediately after a child is born. The presumption underlying our analysis of child morbidity is that the relative frequency of illness decreases with increases in resources committed to children. Other indirect measures of child welfare (such as weight-for-height measures) are available but are equally imperfect. Just as with health outcomes, the tie between inputs, in the form of nutrition and so forth, and anthropometric outcomes depends on a range of unobserved factors, including genetic, metabolic, and other factors.[1]

An additional confounding factor is theoretical in nature and leads to statistical problems of identification. Parents are making choices regarding a host of factors simultaneously. In the broadest of terms they are making decisions regarding number of children, resource commitment per child, and non-child-related expenditures. Some parents may choose relatively more children, with relatively less commitment per child, than other parents. As Montgomery and Lloyd (1996b) pointed out, the simple finding of an inverse relationship between fertility and child well-being therefore does not, of itself, constitute justification for policy. It is completely consistent with standard economic models of family formation [for example, Becker and Lewis (1973)] that parents with a taste for lower quality per child choose to have more children, because the price per child is lower compared to children of higher quality. Independent effects are inherently difficult to tease out, rendering statistical identification of structural quantity and quality equations difficult.

In considering parents' decision-making process, we have thus far spent little time on discussing how their decisions translate into actual fertility. Conception carries with it a substantial element of randomness and therefore so does contraception imperfectly used.[2] Desired births may not happen, undesired births may occur, or births may come earlier or later than desired. The occurrence of an unwanted birth is the exogenous impact of fertility. Unless one makes the heroic assumption that parents anticipate (perfectly) not only the likelihood but also the actual occurrence of contraceptive failure, the unplanned nature of an unwanted birth implies that the event is independent of the parents' decision-making calculus. Therefore a pure causal impact of unwanted births on measures of child quality may be estimable. The child may feel the impact in question, or the impact may be distributed over a larger group of children. For instance, in Thailand Frenzen and Hogan [1982, cited by Montgomery and Lloyd (1996c)] found that children wanted by both parents have a significantly higher probability of surviving their first year than do children wanted by only one or neither parent.

In considering within-family resource allocation, a more fully developed strand in the literature examines differential allocations of family resources on the basis of an indirect measure of wantedness: the child's sex. In a sense this strand is a logical extension of the research by Rosenzweig and Wolpin (1993), in that the birth of a girl is outside parents' preconception decision-making calculus. Studies by Chen, Huq, and D'Souza (1981), Simmons et al. (1982), and Dasgupta (1987) have shown that South Asian girls receive less food than their male siblings and are less likely to survive their childhood. The Simmons et al. (1982) study is noteworthy in demonstrating the strengthening effect of sibling competition for resources on the impact of an unwanted daughter's birth. Rosenzweig and Schultz (1982) tied this to unfavorable labor market outcomes for some Indian girls.

Mothers participating in Demographic and Health Surveys are asked specifically about wantedness at the time of conception for each live birth in a period of 3 to 5 years preceding the survey. Because they are asked retrospectively, responses to these questions are often thought to be subject to post hoc rationalization. The direction of such rationalization is not clear, however. For example, Knodel and Prachuabmoh (1973) believed that their Thai data on unwantedness understates the degree of unwantedness, because mothers are reluctant to say that a given child was in fact unwanted. On the other hand, Rosenzweig and Wolpin (1993) claimed that their United States data show the opposite. On the basis of an undesirable outcome, such as an unhealthy baby, Rosenzweig and Wolpin claimed that some women (perhaps nearly one-fourth) who, before conceiving, said that they wanted a

birth changed their postpartum response to "unwanted." It seems prudent
to take both arguments into account by allowing wantedness (potentially) to
be endogenous, that is, dependent on characteristics of the mother, siblings,
and the reference child, and we do so in our empirical work.

The Model

We model three measures of child well-being as functions of child, family,
and community characteristics: (1) probability of illness with either diarrhea,
or fever or cough, (2) use of curative care for these conditions, and (3) use of
preventive care (in the form of vaccinations). Pragmatic concerns dictate this
strategy, because diarrhea and respiratory infections are the two illnesses
most readily observed in survey data. However, they are also of policy interest, because these two disease categories account for roughly one-third of
infant and child mortality in the developing world. We construct a model
based on the concept of a child-specific index of child value, or parents' willingness to commit resources to a particular child. This index is posited to be
a function of exogenous individual, household, and community variables.
Household resource commitments are measured directly by use of health
care, with associated monetary, time, and other costs, and indirectly by the
incidence of morbidity.

Define Z as the index value for a given child:

$$Z = f(X, w, s), \qquad (10.1)$$

where X is a vector of family- and child-specific values, such as age, educational attainment, and wealth holding, w is a scalar index of wantedness,
and s is a scalar count of sibset size.

Define A as a vector of variables measuring family access to health care,
and define R as a vector measuring risks of illness. Then the following conditions characterize the incidence of illness, curative care, and preventive
care for living children:

$$\text{Illness observed: } I = 1 \text{ if } Z_1^* \geq Z|X, w, s, R, \qquad (10.2)$$

$$\text{Treatment observed: } T = 1 \text{ if } Z_2^* \leq Z|X, w, s, A, I = 1, \quad (10.3)$$

$$\text{Preventive care observed: } V = 1 \text{ if } Z_3^* \leq Z|X, w, s, A, \qquad (10.4)$$

where the Z^* are unobserved threshold variables. Illness occurs if the index
of child value, conditioned on child- and family-specific covariates and risks
of illness, falls below an unobserved threshold value; curative treatment occurs if child value, conditioned on access, covariates, and illness, exceeds a
minimum (unobserved) threshold. Preventive care is much like curative care,
although not conditioned on illness. The presumption is that, all else being

constant, wantedness is associated with decreased probability of illness and increased probability of curative and preventive treatment, whereas sibset size is assumed to work in the opposite direction. Family-level covariates associated with increased wealth, income, or socioeconomic status are expected to exert a similar effect on wantedness, and increases in accessibility and risk are presumed to increase the probability of treatment and illness, respectively.[3]

Wantedness responses, because they are given after the birth has occurred, may be subject to the sort of post hoc rationalizations we have discussed previously, and we therefore model wantedness as a function of family characteristics and sibset size. Finally, sibset size is a reflection of past values of child value indexes. These values are likely to be highly correlated with current values. Therefore, to complete the model, we have

$$w = g(X_w, s), \tag{10.5}$$

$$s = h(Z_{-T}), \tag{10.6}$$

where X_w is a vector of variables measuring family-specific considerations, including characteristics of the child, such as sex, birth weight, and nonsingleton status. Sibset size is a function of Z_{-T}, notational shorthand for the set of past values of the satisfaction index Z. It is feasible to allow for endogeneity of sibset size[4] and to test statistically for such a possibility. Comparable caveats to testing for endogenous wantedness apply, because the test specifically regards the impact of illness in the immediate presurvey period (or treatment for this illness) on sibset size and not the impact of some more general measure of child endowments on sibset size.

The within-family mechanism through which unwantedness operates could be one in which per capita resource decreases are spread more or less evenly over household members or, as seems more likely, given models of within-household allocation (Simmons et al. 1982; Rosenzweig and Schultz 1982), unequally according to preferences or past investments. Children who are older or otherwise relatively favored are less likely to feel the consequences of the birth of an unwanted younger sibling, therefore concentrating the observable response on younger children, particularly the unwanted child itself. If the resource pressures accompanying an unwanted birth are spread evenly over all children and if one were to examine the consequences only on the child of his or her unwantedness, the apparent effect of unwantedness would be understated because the impact on only one child is included in the analysis. So long as the response of parents to an unwanted birth is not to concentrate resources on unwanted births, the impact of unwanted status on the most recent birth can be taken as a lower bound to the total intrahousehold allocative response to unwantedness.[5]

Data and Country Settings

The Philippines data come from the 1993 Philippines National Demographic Survey (Philippines National Statistics Office and Macro International 1994). This is a nationally representative survey in the Demographic and Health Surveys series, in which 15,029 women were interviewed. Of these women 8,961 were married at the time of the survey. There were 8,803 births to respondents in the 5 years preceding the survey, and the estimated total fertility rate for women age 15 to 44 years was 4.05.

The Indonesian data come from the last two Demographic and Health Surveys, administered in 1991 and 1994 (Indonesia CBS et al. 1992, 1995). The 1991 survey uses interviews with 22,909 ever-married women, of whom 21,109 were married at the time of the survey, and reports births of 14,393 children in the 5 years preceding the interview date. The 1994 survey interviewed 28,168 ever-married women, of whom 26,220 were married at the time of the survey. There were 16,831 births reported in the 5 years preceding the survey. Estimated total fertility rates for 15–44-year-olds in 1991 and 1994 were 2.99 and 2.83, respectively.[6]

For births in the five years preceding the sample, detailed information on immunization and health were collected. Mothers were asked whether their children had experienced diarrhea or a cough or fever in the two weeks preceding the survey and what treatment the children were given. Treatments can consist of commodities, advice, or some combination of both. As in many developing countries, there are active traditional sectors providing health care in both Indonesia and the Philippines. We are unable to differentiate among various folk cures in many instances. For example, "herbs" as a treatment for an illness is difficult to assess in terms of effectiveness. We have therefore focused on treatment supplied by the modern sector. The presumption is that effectiveness differentials are known to some reasonable approximation by mothers and that modern methods cost at least as much as traditional methods and are less accessible. Therefore use of modern treatments reflects greater willingness on the part of parents to seek out effective care and commit resources.

The Demographic and Health Survey question on wantedness comes in a section of the questionnaire extracting detailed information on recent births. The mother is asked whether she wanted the current birth at the time she became pregnant, whether she wanted the birth but would have preferred that it had come later, or whether she would have preferred that the birth had not occurred at all. In our regression analyses we classify a birth as wanted if it was wanted either at the time of conception or later. Roughly 84% of births occurring in the retrospective calendar interval are classified as wanted at the time of pregnancy or at some future date in the Philippines, and 95% and

93% of births were classified in this way in the 1991 and 1994 Indonesia surveys. There were a minimum of 720 unwanted births in Indonesia (1991) and a maximum of 1,485 unwanted births in the Philippines.

Results

Philippines

Brief definitions, means, and standard errors for variables used in the subsequent analysis appear in Table 10.1. Many variables are familiar, but some bear further explanation. The first is our measure of permanent income or wealth. Demographic and Health Surveys do not collect direct data on income or wealth. Instead, they use a collection of questions about asset ownership (vehicles and appliances), housing quality (roof and floor materials and plumbing) and access to fresh water. We have combined the responses to many of these questions, using factor analysis, into two factors. This makes the subsequent regression results less cluttered and allows us to control for variations in a fairly large number of asset variables. Ownership of a television or a refrigerator and the housing attributes nondirt floor and in-house electricity load on the first factor; ownership of an automobile or a stove and number of rooms for sleeping load on the second factor. Taken together, these variables capture asset ownership and, as such, are proxies for permanent income. There are three variables constructed as provincial-level means: the mean incidence of fever or cough, the mean incidence of diarrhea, and the mean travel time to health facilities. These are constructed using responses for children of every eligible respondent in the province *except* the reference birth and therefore indicate the community-level conditions faced by the reference birth. The sewer variable is another community-level factor in the analysis, whereas the variables for water and type of toilet are household specific. Because we are examining care given to living children, the sample is restricted to currently living children.[7]

Two sets of results are discussed here. The first set reflects the impacts of area-, family-, and individual-level determinants, including wantedness and sibset size, on child morbidity. The second set reflects the impacts of a similar set of determinants on curative and preventive child health care. The results are based on model specifications that use actual values of wantedness and sibset size rather than their instruments. We generated instruments for wantedness and sibset size using reduced-form equations.[8] We then used the residuals from these equations to construct Hausman tests for endogeneity of wantedness and sibset size in each of the morbidity and health care equations. In only one case, for sibset size in the diarrhea illness equation, were we able to reject the null hypothesis of exogeneity for either wantedness or

TABLE 10.1

Description of Variables Used in the Analysis: Philippines[a]

Variable	Definition	Mean	Standard deviation
Vaccination	Number of vaccinations received	5.92	2.88
Fever/cough	Child ill with fever or cough in the last two weeks	0.41	0.49
Fever care	Seek modern advice or give modern treatment for the fever/cough	0.64	0.48
Diarrhea	Child ill with diarrhea in the last two weeks	0.10	0.31
Diarrhea care	Seek modern advice or give modern treatment for the diarrhea	0.45	0.50
Wanted birth	Dummy for wantedness of reference birth; 1 if the birth was wanted, either then or later	0.84	0.37
Siblings alive	Number of siblings alive at the time of birth	2.26	2.22
Male	Dummy for male; 1 if the birth is male	0.52	0.50
Child's age	Child's age in years	2.45	1.41
Mother's age	Mother's age in years	30.16	6.48
Mother's education	Mother's education in years	8.41	4.72
Husband's education	Education of mother's current husband, in years	7.55	3.69
Assets 1	Factor score based on television, refrigerator, floor, and electricity[b]	0.073	0.974
Assets 2	Factor score based on automobile, range and rooms for sleeping[b]	0.086	0.925
Water	Dummy for access to piped or well water for drinking; 1 if yes	0.11	0.31
Type of toilet	Dummy for flush or pit toilet access; 1 if yes	0.69	0.46
Sewer	Dummy for community access to sewers; 1 if *barangay* has sewer system	0.16	0.36
Prenatal care	Equals 1 if mother sought prenatal care during the pregnancy	0.36	0.48
Travel time	*Barangay* mean time to family planning service-provision point in minutes	39.41	61.16

[a]Mean levels of treatment are conditioned on illness. Thus, in the Philippines, for example, roughly 41% of sampled children had a fever or cough in the 2 weeks preceding the survey, and of these, 64% received some sort of modern treatment. Statistics in descriptive tables are otherwise based on a full sample. Not presented in this table are descriptive statistics for birth weights (four categories on a subjective scale ranging from "much smaller than average" to "much larger than average," with "average" the omitted category). Birth weights are assumed to be part of the set of predetermined variables in the structural equation for wantedness and are used only in generating reduced-form instruments for wantedness and sibset size.

[b]See the text for a more complete description of the constructed variables.

sibset size.[9] In other words, we have virtually no evidence that illness in the last two weeks or health care provision to children affects either wantedness or sibset size. Therefore the results we present do not use instrumental variables for wantedness or sibset size.

An additional question of model specification is the manner in which sibset size might influence allocations to children. Kelley (1996) claimed that failure to include potential nonlinearities in studies of the effect of sibset size on educational attainment of children is an error leading to overstatement of the impact of sibset size on resources allocated per child. We find no evidence for such scale effects on the incidence of morbidity or allocation of health care. To test the proposition, we specified a variable that equaled 1 for large families and 0 otherwise, where a large family was defined as sibset sizes of 5 or more living children.[10] We used this large-family dummy variable, interacted with the full set of covariates, to perform Wald tests on jointly restricting the coefficients across values of the large-family dummy and were unable to reject the null hypothesis that they did not differ. Individually, the signs and rough magnitudes of sibset size coefficients and their associated statistical significance levels were the same. Therefore we present estimates that include the impact of sibset size (alone and untransformed) on illness and treatment.[11]

Ideally, one would estimate the parameters of the illness and treatment sequence jointly. That is, if the underlying issue is one of the resource commitment of parents, then the susceptibility of children to illness and their subsequent use of care, conditional on illness, are two manifestations of an unobserved resource allocation decision. Given the binary outcomes of the two measures, a bivariate probit model of sample selection is most efficient. However, the process is sufficiently noisy that the bivariate likelihood function would not converge.[12] We therefore estimated the determinants of treatment in two ways. We estimated a univariate probit for the probability of receiving treatment, ignoring that the child must first be sick before receiving treatment. As an alternative, we estimated the treatment equation as a linear probability with a two-stage Heckman sample selectivity correction.[13] When transformed to derivatives evaluated at sample means, the simple probit gave results virtually identical to the Heckman estimates, and subsequent discussion of the estimates applies to either formulation. In either instance we estimated a univariate probit transformation of the determinants of morbidity.

Child Morbidity in the Philippines

Table 10.2 shows that for both diarrhea and cough and fever, there are four statistically and practically significant elements accounting for either sort of morbidity: family assets, wantedness, child age, and areal disease prevalence. Wantedness decreases the probability of occurrence of diarrhea by roughly 22%.[14] The probability of contracting diarrhea initially increases with age but begins to decrease after age 14 months. This pattern may reflect infants being fed increasing quantities of foods other than breast milk with the initiation of weaning. Asset availability, or roughly speaking, wealth, accounts for some variation in diarrhea incidence. A one standard deviation increase in the first assets factor generates a decrease of roughly 10% in the probability of contracting diarrhea.

TABLE 10.2
Coefficients of Probit Models of Child Morbidity: Philippines

	Probit partial derivative (p value)	
Variable	Diarrhea	Fever/cough
Wanted birth	−0.0220 (0.03)	−0.0575 (0.00)
Sibset size	−0.0002 (0.96)	0.0006 (0.86)
Male	0.003 (0.59)	−0.004 (0.75)
Child's age	0.0220 (0.02)	0.0721 (0.00)
Child's age squared	−0.0101 (0.00)	−0.0237 (0.00)
Mother's education	−0.0012 (0.22)	−0.0050 (0.01)
Husband's education	−0.0006 (0.62)	0.0031 (0.18)
Assets 1	−0.0103 (0.02)	−0.0189 (0.01)
Assets 2	−0.0050 (0.21)	−0.0151 (0.03)
Water	0.0109 (0.31)	0.0568 (0.01)
Type of toilet	0.0118 (0.14)	−0.0050 (0.70)
Areal mean prevalence	0.5753 (0.00)	0.6279 (0.00)

For fever or cough the pattern is similar. If a child was wanted at birth, his or her probability of being sick with a fever or cough is about 15% less than for an unwanted child, expressed in terms of the sample mean probability of respiratory illness. As was the case with diarrhea, the probability of illness first rises and then falls with age. For fever or cough morbidity the estimated age of maximum risk is 18 months, which seems close enough to the value for diarrhea to be consistent with the loss of mother's antibodies as a result of weaning. The presence of family assets in any form leads to lower probability of fever or cough appearing. A unit increase of both factors together would generate an estimated decline in the probability of fever or cough of roughly 8%.

Two additional variables are statistically significant determinants of fever or cough incidence: water quality and mother's education. Children of more educated mothers are less likely to be sick than other children are. The marginal impact of a mother's completion of secondary school, versus completion of primary school, is to decrease the incidence of fevers and coughs in her children by 7%. Also, the availability of good water (in the form of piped or well water) is associated with statistically significant increases in fever and cough morbidity of roughly 14%. We speculate that this may be an artifact of population density accompanying the water supply infrastructure.

For both diarrhea and respiratory infections the direction of the effect of areal prevalence seems intuitively clear. We do not find any impact of the child's sex on either fever or respiratory infections. Although males are slightly more likely to get diarrhea and females are slightly more likely to get respiratory disease, in neither case are the associated Z values greater than 1.

Akin, Guilkey, and Popkin (1991) presented similar findings for Cebu; they found that girls are slightly less likely than boys to get either respiratory disease or diarrhea.[15]

Curative Health Care in the Philippines

The structural covariates accounting for treatment differentials contain substantial overlap with the morbidity set, including wantedness status, sibset size, measures of family resources, mother's education, and the child's age and sex. Added to the list of covariates are measures of access to health care facilities, and deleted are measures of environmental exposure to illness.

Roughly 40% of the children age 0–4 years in the sample had experienced a cough or fever in the 2 weeks preceding the survey. Of these, 64% received some sort of modern treatment (either a visit to a modern provider, treatment with a modern cure, or both). The incidence of diarrhea in the same period was lower, 10%, and of these children 45% received modern treatment. The simplest and best treatment for diarrhea is administration of oral rehydration therapy (ORT). Paper packets of salts are widely available at low cost. It is surprising that modern treatment is not sought more often, given the ease with which diarrhea can be treated. In a detailed analysis of the Philippine ORT data Costello and Lleno (1995) pointed out that treatment with an antibiotic regime seems much more common than it should be under accepted treatment protocols. We discuss possible consequences of this finding later.

The determinants of use of curative care are somewhat similar for both types of illness (Table 10.3). Sibset size is statistically significant and of the expected sign. On the margin, each additional sibling decreases treatment probability by about 5% for diarrhea and 3.5% for fever. Comparing an only child to a child in a family at the current total fertility rate, the impact of sibset size is to decrease treatment probability by about 15% for diarrhea and 11% for fever.[16] If, as we have argued, sibset size reflects the impact of resource constraints, it is unexpected that diarrhea treatment, which ideally is cheap and easy, is affected more by sibset size than is respiratory illness treatment.[17] One possible explanation, as just discussed, is that actual treatments differ from suggested standard (ORT) protocol. Parents therefore wrongly perceive modern diarrhea treatment to be expensive, with corresponding effects on utilization. A second possibility is that respiratory disease is more contagious than diarrhea. Therefore the benefits that accrue to preventing illness in other family members by treating a sick child are larger for respiratory disease. As sibset size increases, so does this external benefit, which partially offsets the resource-diluting impact of sibset size.

The impact of wantedness on treatment is statistically insignificant at typical confidence levels. For fever and cough wantedness implies a *decrease* (al-

TABLE 10.3

Coefficients of the Models of Treatment for Child Morbidity: Philippines[a]

Variable	Treatment for diarrhea		Treatment for fever/cough	
	Heckman coefficient (p value)	Probit partial derivative (p value)	Heckman coefficient (p value)	Probit partial derivative (p value)
Wanted birth	0.0837 (0.07)	0.0868 (0.07)	−0.0426 (0.11)	−0.0414 (0.07)
Sibset size	−0.0223 (0.03)	−0.0229 (0.03)	−0.0112 (0.03)	−0.0119 (0.02)
Male	0.0131 (0.70)	0.0135 (0.70)	0.0168 (0.30)	0.0187 (0.27)
Child's age	0.1209 (0.03)	0.1256 (0.03)	0.0186 (0.49)	0.0241 (0.35)
Child's age squared	−0.0190 (0.09)	−0.0197 (0.09)	−0.0022 (0.71)	−0.0029 (−0.57)
Mother's age	0.0065 (0.06)	0.0067 (0.06)	0.0027 (0.11)	0.0030 (0.08)
Mother's education	−0.0050 (0.35)	−0.0050 (0.37)	0.0038 (0.12)	0.0048 (0.08)
Husband's education	0.0072 (0.27)	0.0075 (0.26)	0.0069 (0.03)	0.0070 (0.03)
Assets 1	0.0753 (0.01)	0.0770 (0.00)	0.0532 (0.00)	0.0589 (0.00)
Assets 2	0.0084 (0.69)	0.0088 (0.69)	0.0100 (0.34)	0.0151 (0.19)
Prenatal care	0.0241 (0.56)	0.0237 (0.54)	0.0528 (0.01)	0.0546 (0.01)
Travel time	-1.5×10^{-5} (0.97)	-1.5×10^{-5} (0.71)	1.6×10^{-6} (0.96)	7.3×10^{-6} (0.97)
Constant	0.0433 (0.74)	−0.4715 (0.00)	0.4898 (0.00)	−0.0115 (0.02)
Selection coefficient (λ)	0.0009 (0.00)		0.0065 (0.93)	

[a]In this and the following tables that present treatment results, the Heckman regressions represent a linear probability model, and therefore in estimating them, we have used the square root of the predicted odds ratio to remove this source of heteroskedasticity. The selection equation is the appropriate probit equation (by illness) presented in Table 10.2.

though also statistically insignificant at the 5% level) in treatment probability of roughly 10%.[18]

Males do not enjoy a treatment advantage for either disease; the probability of treatment for diarrhea first increases and then decreases with child's age, with a peak at age 3 years. Older mothers are more likely to seek treatment for their children for either disease, although the effect is statistically significant only at the 6% level for diarrhea and at greater than the 10% level for fever or cough. Education of parents, especially the father, increases the probability of fever or cough treatment, and the first factor score for asset ownership has a marked positive effect on either sort of treatment. A one standard deviation increase in this proxy for wealth accounts for a roughly 15% increase in treatment probability for either type of illness. Mothers who made prenatal visits are more likely to take their own children in for treatment of fever or cough. However, a seemingly more direct measure of access, *barangay* ("community") mean travel time to a family planning facility,[19] is unimportant in accounting for treatment of either illness. It seems likely that travel time is a relatively pure measure of accessibility, whereas mother's own use of prenatal care reveals an element of her preferences for health care and, as such, serves partially as a control for heterogeneity in health care preferences of mothers. The consistent findings for treatment of both respiratory and diarrheal disease are (1) that children from families with more resources (assets factor 1) are more likely to be treated and (2) that competitors for these resources (siblings) decrease the probability of receiving treatment.

Preventive Care in the Philippines

As the results presented in Table 10.4 show, there are several systematic influences on the number of vaccinations received. Table 10.4 presents ordinary least-squares, Tobit, and Poisson regression estimates. The results are completely robust across these specifications, and so no distinction by estimation method is made in discussing the results. By the nature of the vaccination protocol, child's age plays a dominant role. Of more policy interest are other covariates. As was the case for curative care, wantedness is not important in accounting for number of vaccinations received. Sibset size works in the expected direction but is statistically significant at the 5% level only

TABLE 10.4

Coefficients of Ordinary Least-Squares (OLS), Tobit, and Poisson Regressions for Vaccinations: Philippines

Variable	OLS coefficient (*p* value)	Tobit coefficient (*p* value)	Poisson incidence rate ratio (*p* value)
Wanted birth	0.0573 (0.48)	0.0594 (0.50)	1.011 (0.41)
Sibset size	−0.0301 (0.06)	−0.0330 (0.07)	0.9951 (0.07)
Male	−0.0996 (0.07)	−0.1153 (0.06)	0.9839 (0.07)
Child's age	2.203 (0.00)	2.409 (0.00)	1.463 (0.00)
Child's age squared	−0.3974 (0.00)	−0.4350 (0.00)	0.9340 (0.00)
Mother's age	−0.0071 (0.20)	−0.0083 (0.18)	0.9987 (0.16)
Mother's education	0.0660 (0.00)	0.0740 (0.00)	1.010 (0.00)
Husband's education	0.0515 (0.00)	0.0602 (0.00)	1.009 (0.00)
Assets 1	0.0937 (0.02)	0.1020 (0.02)	1.014 (0.02)
Assets 2	−0.1151 (0.00)	−0.1296 (0.00)	0.9808 (0.00)
Prenatal care	0.4814 (0.00)	0.5041 (0.00)	1.079 (0.00)
Travel time	−0.0039 (0.00)	−0.0045 (0.00)	0.9992 (0.00)
Constant	2.56 (0.00)	2.150 (0.00)	

against a one-tailed alternative hypothesis and is sufficiently small that a child with a sibset size of 10 would receive only about one-third of a vaccination fewer (a 5% reduction from the mean number of 6.1) than an only child.

Education plays a statistically important role. The marginal impact of completion of secondary school by both mother and father, compared to their completion only of primary school, is to increase the predicted number of vaccinations received by the child by about two-thirds of a vaccination. Measures of health care preferences and access play a role in accounting for vaccination, with women who used clinics for prenatal care likely to get 0.5 more vaccinations for their children. Travel time plays a statistically significant role, but a doubling of mean travel time (to 79 minutes) would account for only a tiny fraction of a vaccination.

Indonesia, 1991

As we did in our discussion of the results from the Philippines, we first discuss the impacts of area-, family-, and individual-level determinants, including wantedness and sibset size, on child morbidity. We then examine the impact of a similar set of determinants on curative and preventive care. In our discussion of the Philippines results, several modeling issues were examined. These points need not be revisited in detail in the Indonesian context; however, we address issues of model specification that rely on specific statistical tests. The questions in the two Demographic and Health Surveys are similar, but there are a few differences between the Philippines and Indonesia surveys. Measures of access to modern plumbing are slightly different, for example, with access to a *private* flush toilet required in Indonesia but access to *any* flush toilet required in the Philippines. There are similarly minor differences in the definitions of modern treatments for fever or cough and in the specific assets tabulated (Indonesians are asked about radios, whereas Filipinos are asked about refrigerators), but most of the survey questions of interest are identical in the two surveys.

As in the Philippines, we use a linear specification for sibset size in the equations for morbidity and treatment. We use the same two-stage Heckman model for selection into treatment, conditional on illness. We test for the potential endogeneity of wantedness and sibset size on both morbidity and treatment equations, again based on residuals from reduced-form equations on wantedness and sibset size. Table 10.5 presents descriptive statistics.

Child Morbidity in Indonesia, 1991

Table 10.6 shows that wantedness at birth plays the same role in reducing morbidity in Indonesia as in the Philippines. The impact of wantedness is to decrease the chance of contracting diarrhea by 50% compared to the

TABLE 10.5
Description of Variables Used in the Analysis: Indonesia, 1991 [a]

Variable	Definition	Mean	Standard deviation
Vaccination	Number of vaccines received	2.38	2.63
Fever/cough	Child ill with fever or cough in the last two weeks	0.35	0.48
Fever care	Seek modern advice or give modern care for fever/cough	0.83	0.38
Diarrhea	Child with diarrhea in the last two weeks	0.10	0.30
Diarrhea care	Seek modern advice or give modern care for diarrhea	0.78	0.42
Wanted birth	Dummy for birth wantedness; 1 if the birth was wanted, then or later	0.95	0.22
Siblings alive	Number of siblings alive at time of birth	1.58	1.70
Male	Dummy for male; 1 if birth is male	0.52	0.50
Child's age	Child's age in months	29.24	16.92
Mother's age	Age of mother at child's birth in years	29.09	6.15
Mother's education	Mother's education in years	6.22	5.29
Husband's education	Education of mother's current husband in years	7.40	5.47
Assets 1	Factor score based on asset ownership [b]	−0.07	0.98
Assets 2	Factor score based on asset ownership [b]	−0.08	0.98
Water	Dummy for access to piped or well water for drinking; 1 if yes	0.09	0.29
Type of toilet	Dummy for flush or pit toilet access; 1 if yes	0.18	0.39
Travel time	Mean travel time to family planning service provision point in minutes	32.16	7.41

[a] Mean levels of treatment are conditioned on illness. Thus, in Indonesia, for example, roughly 35% of sampled children had a fever or cough in the 2 weeks preceding the survey, and of these, 83% received some sort of modern treatment. Statistics in descriptive tables are otherwise based on a full sample. Not presented in this table are descriptive statistics for birth weights (four from a subjective scale ranging from "much smaller than average" to "much larger than average," with "average" the omitted category). Birth weights are assumed to be part of the set of predetermined variables in the structural equation for wantedness and are used only in generating reduced-form instruments for wantedness and sibset size.

[b] See text for a more complete description of the constructed variables.

overall prevalence level of diarrhea, a very large and statistically significant effect and one that is somewhat greater than the comparable impact in the Philippines. Diarrhea incidence peaks at age 1 year, somewhat younger than in the Philippines. In contrast to the Philippines, asset availability, as measured by the constructed factors, shows no impact on diarrhea incidence. On the other hand, mother's education, access to flush toilets, and the mean areal prevalence are statistically significant in Indonesia, and all operate in expected fashion: Children of more educated mothers, children with access to flush toilets, and children living in areas where diarrhea prevalence is lower experience less diarrheal disease, all else being constant. Unexpectedly, increasing number of siblings is associated with a small but statistically

TABLE 10.6

Coefficients of Probit Models of Child Morbidity: Indonesia, 1991

Variable	Probit partial derivative (p value)	
	Diarrhea	Fever/cough
Wanted birth	−0.047 (0.00)	−0.083 (0.00)
Sibset size	−0.004 (0.01)	−0.011 (0.00)
Male	0.009 (0.08)	0.018 (0.05)
Child's age	0.012 (0.10)	0.022 (0.08)
Child's age squared	−0.008 (0.00)	−0.103 (0.00)
Mother's education	−0.002 (0.00)	−0.000 (0.94)
Husband's education	0.001 (0.03)	0.001 (0.15)
Assets 1	0.006 (0.14)	0.019 (0.01)
Assets 2	−0.002 (0.41)	0.001 (0.81)
Urban	0.001 (0.94)	−0.019 (0.17)
Water	0.011 (0.25)	0.027 (0.10)
Toilet	−0.016 (0.06)	−0.038 (0.01)
Areal mean prevalence	0.754 (0.00)	1.02 (0.00)

significant *decrease* in the probability that a child will contract diarrhea. The estimated decline in diarrheal morbidity probability is approximately 4% per sibling.

The pattern for respiratory infections is much the same. According to the single-stage estimates, wanted children are 24% less likely to contract respiratory infections than are unwanted children. Asset ownership is statistically significant but of little importance, with a one standard deviation increase in wealth yielding an increase of 5% in acute respiratory infection (ARI) morbidity. As was the case with diarrheal disease, the probability of illness peaks at a young age, and respiratory illness is more likely in areas where its prevalence is high. Access to a private flush toilet decreases the probability of contracting a respiratory illness. It is doubtful that this represents as direct a link in disease reduction as for diarrheal disease, so perhaps this variable is acting as some sort of proxy for housing quality. Boys are (barely) statistically more likely to contract respiratory illnesses, although only by 5%. As was the case for diarrhea, children with many living siblings are *less* likely to contract respiratory disease than are those from smaller families. Once again, the magnitude is small, with each additional sibling accounting for a drop of 3% in the probability of illness. The apparent beneficial impact of siblings is swamped if that child is unwanted.

The impact of sibset size on disease incidence, although small, is statistically significant and of the opposite sign predicted by a model of household resource allocation. This stands in contrast to the results for the Philippines, which showed no significant impact of sibset size on disease incidence. One possible explanation draws on the well-known claim of Bongaarts (1987a) that family planning programs, when successful, increase mean infant and child mortality rates. This occurs because, as fertility falls, the proportion of births that are first births increases, and for physiological reasons first births are at higher risk of mortality. In fact, the Indonesian sample contains markedly more first births than does the Philippines sample. In the 1993 Philippines sample the median sibset size was 2 and the mean sibset size was 2.25. In the 1991 Indonesia sample median sibset size was 1 and mean sibset size was 1.58. Of the Indonesian children in the 1991 sample 33% were first births and 59% had either no siblings or 1 sibling. In contrast, just less than 25% of children in the Philippines sample were first births, and only 46% had either no siblings or 1 sibling. If Bongaarts's notion of first birth frailty carries force, then the data are consistent with a morbidity pattern dominated by the differentials between first and subsequent births in Indonesia, but, in either country, sibset size is not an especially useful measure of the impact of family resource allocation on subsequent morbidity.[20]

The negative impact of unwantedness on child health is robust to an instrumental variable specification of unwantedness and sibset size, although the estimated magnitude of the impact of unwantedness is much greater for the instrumental variables estimates. ARI incidence falls by 95%, compared to mean prevalence, for wanted births, and a prediction of no diarrheal disease at all for wanted births is within the 95% confidence interval.

Curative Health Care in Indonesia, 1991

Of ill children 76% of those with diarrhea and 81% of those with ARI received modern treatment. Both values are significantly higher than the corresponding figures of 45% for diarrhea and 64% for ARI in the Philippines. There is some evidence in Indonesia of the preference for (typically incorrect) antibiotic-based treatment regimens for diarrhea, which Costello and Lleno (1995) found in the Philippines, with only about 20% of children ill with diarrhea receiving oral rehydration salts. It therefore seems unlikely that the higher treatment rates in Indonesia are attributable to adherence to oral rehydration salts protocol. Another explanation of the higher treatment levels in Indonesia is that there is a difference, compared to the Philippines, in access to health care facilities. One measure of accessibility is average travel time to a treatment facility. By this measure, treatment was only slightly less accessible in the Philippines, where mean travel time was 40 minutes, than in Indonesia, where travel time averaged 32 minutes. On the other hand, the standard deviation of travel time was over 1 hour in the Philippines, compared to only 7 minutes for Indonesia, which may say that access differentials within the Philippines are relatively pronounced.

For a child with ARI Table 10.7 shows that family wealth, education of the husband and of the wife, and the mother's use of prenatal care all in-

TABLE 10.7
Coefficients of Models of Treatment for Child Morbidity: Indonesia, 1991

Variable	Treatment for diarrhea		Treatment for fever/cough	
	Heckman coefficient (p value)	Probit partial derivative (p value)	Heckman coefficient (p value)	Probit partial derivative
Wanted birth	0.127	0.137	0.218	−1.49
	(0.05)	(0.04)	(0.60)	(0.01)
Siblings alive	−0.002	−0.005	0.018	−0.063
	(0.83)	(0.66)	(0.37)	(0.01)
Male	0.001	0.014	0.011	0.008
	(0.97)	(0.65)	(0.31)	(0.53)
Child's age	0.108	0.135	0.089	0.091
	(0.03)	(0.01)	(0.00)	(0.00)
Age squared	−0.016	−0.026	−0.010	−0.014
	(0.16)	(0.01)	(0.01)	(0.00)
Mother's age	0.001	0.001	−0.003	−0.002
	(0.68)	(0.68)	(0.07)	(0.19)
Mother's education	0.003	−0.001	0.002	0.004
	(0.48)	(0.78)	(0.12)	(0.01)
Husband's education	0.004	0.005	0.002	0.003
	(0.20)	(0.16)	(0.03)	(0.05)
Assets 1	0.030	0.046	0.037	0.060
	(0.15)	(0.06)	(0.00)	(0.00)
Assets 2	0.047	0.055	0.029	0.292
	(0.01)	(0.00)	(0.00)	(0.00)
Prenatal care	0.054	0.046	0.053	0.079
	(0.10)	(0.18)	(0.00)	(0.00)
Travel time	−0.005	0.009	−0.000	−0.001
	(0.01)	(0.01)	(0.93)	(0.192)
Urban	−0.011	0.009	0.053	0.025
	(0.80)	(0.85)	(0.00)	(0.208)
Outer islands	−0.057	−0.052	0.013	0.003
	(0.13)	(0.19)	(0.27)	(0.83)
Java/Bali	0.031	0.066	0.046	−0.085
	(0.45)	(0.14)	(0.18)	(0.07)
Constant	0.840		0.682	
	(0.00)		(0.14)	
Selection coefficient	−0.137		−0.279	
	(0.12)		(0.00)	

creased the probability that the child will be treated. The probability of ARI treatment peaked at age 4.5 years. Neither wantedness nor sibset size played a role in accounting for ARI treatment in the instrumental-variables Heckman specification,[21] with the largest premium for residence on Java or Bali, but the only statistically significant residence variable was urban domicile. By far the largest impact among the group of statistically significant covariates is mother's use of prenatal care, which increased ARI treatment probability by 13%. Both asset ownership factors had positive, statistically significant coefficients, with a simultaneous one standard deviation change accounting for an increase of 8% in treatment probability. None of the other covariates could account for a deviation of more than 1% from mean treatment probability.

For children with diarrhea the list of determinants of treatment is somewhat different. Increases in one of the family assets factors still were associated with increases in treatment probability, and probability of treatment peaked at age 4 years. However, wanted births were 17% more likely to receive treatment than were unwanted births, and increases in travel times were associated with decreases in treatment probability, with an additional 30 minutes of travel time (half a standard deviation) decreasing treatment probability by about 20%. Wantedness was statistically significant, accounting for an increase of 16% in treatment probability.

Wantedness and access played a much more important role for diarrhea treatment than for ARI treatment. This is somewhat of a puzzle, because diarrhea treatment is, at least in theory, somewhat cheaper and easier. Possibly, parents take ARI more seriously than diarrhea (so that costs play a less important role in assessing treatment choices), but the clear differentials in mean treatment levels for these conditions that might support such a contention in the Philippines are not in evidence in Indonesia. On the other hand, whatever is driving these results appears to be acting in a similar fashion in both countries. In the Philippines wantedness was statistically significant at the 6.5% level,[22] with a coefficient of magnitude comparable to that estimated for Indonesia, but, as in Indonesia, wantedness was unimportant in explaining variation in ARI treatment.

The bottom line is that, at least for treatment of diarrheal disease, a set of results consistent with the predictions of a within-family model of resource allocation again emerges. In the Philippines sibset size, family assets, and mother's use of prenatal care played prominent roles in accounting for differentials in use of curative care for diarrhea or ARI. In Indonesia family assets also play a role. The variables that account for substantial differences in use of curative care are unwantedness and the time cost of care for diarrheal disease and mother's use of prenatal care for ARI. The evidence shows that unwanted births are less likely to receive treatment for diarrhea in Indonesia. There is no support for the notion that sibset size matters in accounting for variations in curative care.

Preventive Care in Indonesia, 1991

In the Demographic and Health Surveys for both the Philippines and Indonesia, mothers were asked about vaccinations in the following sequential fashion. First, they were asked to show vaccination cards. Each child's vaccinations are recorded on the cards, and, if the mother was able to show the

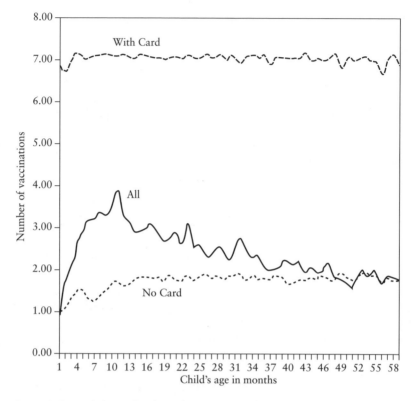

Source: Authors' calculations, based on Indonesia CBS et al. (1992).

FIGURE 10.1. Vaccinations by Child's Age and Whether Mother Produced Vacci-nation Card: Indonesia, 1991 Demographic and Health Survey.

card, the information was simply transcribed from it. If she could not show the card, she was asked which vaccinations her child had received. In the Philippines most mothers have the cards for their children, and much of the vaccination information comes from the vaccination cards. On the other hand, in Indonesia most mothers do not have the cards, and those who do are far more likely to have them for young children than for four- or five-year-olds. When vaccinations are calculated as the reported number from the card (if the mother has it) or as the recalled number on probing (if she does not), number of vaccinations (which could be as large as 8 in Indone-sia) peaks at age 12 months, at just under 4 vaccinations, and then declines. However, number of vaccinations is consistently around seven for children with cards, and below two for children without cards. Therefore the ap-parently declining number of vaccinations as children age represents an in-creasing number of lost cards. Our results for Indonesia rely only on those children who had vaccination cards (about 21% of all children with some vaccination information). Even these responses probably should be viewed with some suspicion, because they show high mean numbers of vaccinations at young ages, even though some vaccinations are not normally given until later in life. Figure 10.1 illustrates the age pattern of vaccination data in the 1991 Indonesia Demographic and Health Survey.

As was the case in the Philippines, Table 10.8 shows that the impacts of most covariates on number of vaccinations are small. In the Poisson specification no covariates are significant. This is sensible, given that the count of vaccinations rarely varies from the mean of seven. For the Tobit and ordinary least-squares regressions, only child age, mother's use of prenatal care, and sibset size have statistically significant effects on the number of vaccinations. However, all these effects are small. The impact of child age is initially positive, but aging eventually decreases the number of vaccinations. Because vaccinations cumulate and because there has been no programmatic change that could account for higher vaccination rates at younger ages, this seems to be a questionable result. The impacts of both prior usage of antenatal care and sibset size are statistically significant but small, together accounting for at most one-tenth of a vaccination, at a sibset size of three. The bottom line, unfortunately, is that we can say very little about systematic impacts of covariates on preventive health care.

TABLE 10.8

Coefficients of Ordinary Least-Squares (OLS), Tobit, and Poisson Regressions for Vaccinations: Indonesia, 1991 [a]

Variable	OLS coefficient (p value)	Tobit coefficient (p value)	Poisson incidence rate ratio (p value)
Wanted birth	−0.023 (0.58)	−0.023 (0.58)	0.997 (0.92)
Live siblings	0.029 (0.00)	0.029 (0.00)	1.004 (0.50)
Male	−0.016 (0.39)	−0.016 (0.34)	0.998 (0.87)
Child's age	0.103 (0.00)	0.103 (0.00)	1.015 (0.50)
Child's age squared	−0.024 (0.00)	−0.024 (0.00)	0.997 (0.45)
Mother's age	−0.002 (0.26)	−0.002 (0.23)	1.000 (0.84)
Mother's education	0.003 (0.19)	0.003 (0.08)	1.000 (0.81)
Husband's education	0.002 (0.24)	0.003 (0.18)	1.000 (0.83)
Assets 1	0.008 (0.56)	0.008 (0.43)	1.001 (0.92)
Assets 2	0.014 (0.13)	0.014 (0.11)	1.002 (0.71)
Prenatal care	0.049 (0.04)	0.049 (0.01)	1.007 (0.71)
Travel time	0.000 (0.82)	0.000 (0.77)	1.000 (0.97)
Urban	0.009 (0.72)	0.009 (0.71)	1.001 (0.95)
Java/Bali	−0.019 (0.47)	−0.019 (0.38)	0.997 (0.90)
Outer islands	0.011 (0.65)	0.011 (0.57)	1.002 (0.93)
Constant	6.956 (0.00)	6.956 (0.00)	

[a] Includes only those children whose mothers could present vaccination cards to the interviewer.

Indonesia, 1994

Although the sample is somewhat larger, the structure of the 1994 Indonesia Demographic and Health Survey was, for our purposes, virtually identical to the 1991 Indonesia survey. One clear difference between the two surveys is the declining proportion of ill children who received treatment. The proportion of ill children receiving treatment fell by roughly half for both diseases by 1994. This period coincides with a move toward fees for service for primary health care in Indonesia, and the decline in treatment probability that we observe may be tied to increasing treatment prices in Indonesia.

Rather than a full discussion of the results for 1994, we highlight differences between these results and those of 1991. Diarrheal disease incidence was unaffected by wantedness or sibset size in the 1994 Indonesian data, even though wantedness played a significant role in the 1991 data. One conjecture that would account for this fact is that the rapid pace of change, both economic and demographic, in Indonesia has led to greater family resources on average and fewer competitors for these resources. Per capita income growth averaged near double-digit levels for much of the period preceding the 1994 survey, and fertility was at low levels (the estimated total fertility rate was 2.83 in 1994), which together would decrease competition for resources within families on average, compared to the 1991 data. Although incomes are reasonably evenly distributed in Indonesia, the pace of change is most rapid on the core islands of Java and Bali. Therefore a cross-section of Indonesia that excludes observations from Java and Bali might give an approximation of the core islands' situation in the recent past. In other regressions that excluded observations from Java and Bali (data not presented here) we found that the impact of unwantedness is large, of the expected sign, and statistically significant, at least in the instrumental-variables specification.

On the other hand, the evidence for respiratory infection provides another unambiguous example of the impact of wantedness on health. Wanted children were 18% less likely to contract ARI and children with toilet facilities in their homes were 6% less likely. Each additional sibling *reduced* predicted ARI incidence by 2.5%, which, like the results from the 1991 survey, runs counter to our expectations but which, also like the results from the 1991 survey, is a fairly small effect.[23]

Each additional sibling decreased ARI treatment probability by 5%. As in Indonesia in 1991, the impact of unwantedness on ARI treatment was statistically insignificant. In contrast to the earlier data, the impact of sibset size was statistically significant in 1994. To put the magnitude of the effect in perspective, our estimates show that three siblings roughly cancel out the impact of easy clinic access. This finding has significant policy implications, because it implies that clinic use may be constrained by demand for families with relatively large numbers of children.

As was the case in 1991, there were only a few significant determinants of diarrhea treatment differentials in Indonesia in 1994. These were mother's education, child's age and sex, and mother's use of prenatal care.

We find that vaccination probability varied in predictable ways. Most interesting for matters at hand, wanted children received about one-fourth of a vaccination more than unwanted children (although this result is not robust to a Poisson specification), and each additional sibling decreased the number of vaccinations by one-tenth. These are fairly small values but still significant. Because of the discrete nature of vaccinations, the results are best interpreted in the following way: One in 4 unwanted children got 1 fewer vaccination than average, and, choosing 4 siblings as an arbitrary family size, 40% of children in these large families got 1 fewer vaccination, on average, than only children.

Discussion

Our aim in this chapter has been to demonstrate the impact of within-family resource pressures on allocations to children. We use one measure of such pressures, namely, sibset size, which is potentially endogenous to the overall decision-making process of the family. Our second measure, unwantedness at conception, is more a reflection of exogenous shocks outside the decision-making calculus of the parents. We focus on the impacts on measures of child health because human capital improvements appear to account for a large share of the output increases that have occurred in many societies. Such human capital increases come from a willingness to commit resources to children.

In the Philippines modern contraceptive prevalence is very low (25% in the survey data), and the health care infrastructure is not well developed. Although contraceptive prevalence is higher in Indonesia, incomes are lower there than in the Philippines and reported travel time to health care facilities is roughly equal in both countries. Compared to the remaining five Asian miracle economies (Japan, South Korea, Taiwan, Singapore, and Thailand), incomes are low in both Indonesia and the Philippines, and low incomes imply harsher trade-offs between number and quality of children, in that quality reductions translate into reductions in calories, protein, or other measures of nutrition. These are expected to generate observable implications for child morbidity, and indeed we find that unwantedness leads to increases in morbidity in most of the cases we examined. The morbidity implications are large from a policy context. In the Philippines a child whose mother said that the child was wanted at conception is roughly 15% less likely to contract a fever or cough and 19% less likely to contract diarrhea than an unwanted child. The diseases associated with these symptoms account for one-third of the under-five child mortality in the Philippines. Therefore reducing un-wantedness should be a powerful policy lever in reducing under-five child mortality. We also find that sibset size plays a role, somewhat less clearly defined, in subsequent use of curative care, with children from larger families less likely to receive care.

11

Education, Earning, and Fertility in Taiwan

FUNG-MEY HUANG

DURING PERIODS OF sustained rapid economic growth and educational expansion, the younger generation of a society acquires more human capital (education and training) than the older generation. A question of interest to economists is whether, given the same educational level, the younger generation also has higher labor productivity. If one assumes that the labor market is perfectly competitive, individuals' wage rates are determined by their labor's marginal productivity. In that case, given the same education level, it is of interest to know whether the younger generation has a higher wage rate than the older generation.

It is generally true that, on average, individuals with more education earn higher wages than those with less education. Hundreds of studies from many countries confirm that average wage rates are higher for higher-educated workers [see, for example, Psacharopoulos (1985)]. Moreover, much micro-econometric-level evidence indicates that a good family background, intelligence, and school quality are positively correlated with education and wages (Griliches 1979; Altonji and Dunn 1995). Children who grow up in economically well-off and emotionally supportive families are more likely to have higher education and higher wages than children from poor family backgrounds.

I have benefited from comments by Eric Jensen, Andrew Mason, Ronald Lee, Jeff Williamson, Amy Tsui, Haidy Pasay, Dennis Ahlburg, Matthew Higgins, Toh Mun Heng, and other participants at the Conference on Population and the Asian Economic Miracle, East-West Center, Honolulu, HI, January 7–10, 1997. Special thanks are due to Paul K. C. Liu for estimating total fertility rates in Taiwan before World War II. Thanks are also due to Paul Liu, Fung-Yea Huang, and Feng-Fuh Jiang for helpful discussions and to Chia-Chang Tsay and Jen-Wei Chyn for their excellent research assistance.

Another interesting question is whether, when an economy is growing and the stock of human capital is increasing, parents transmit their human capital to their children. That is, on average, does a generation with a higher stock of human capital (education) raise more-capable children than a generation with a lower stock of human capital, thus making its children more productive? If so, each generation is likely to be more productive than the previous generation and the rate of return to education increases from one generation to the next.

In the standard neoclassical growth model diminishing returns play an essential role in determining the relationship between increases in labor, capital, and other inputs and economic production. The rapid accumulation of economic factors (for example, physical or human capital) may lead to rapid growth in output per worker for a while, but as workers acquire more physical or human capital, each additional increment raises output by a smaller amount. Eventually, high rates of investment in either physical or human capital are insufficient to sustain rapid economic growth. If the neoclassical approach is correct, economic growth in newly industrialized economies will slow to levels no greater than those found in advanced economies irrespective of rates of investment in human or physical capital.

In recent years some economists have developed a class of models, called endogenous growth models, in which the long-term rate of economic growth is not determined exogenously, as in the neoclassical model, but by factors endogenous to the model, such as investment in education or spending on research. A number of endogenous growth models (Lucas 1988; Romer 1986, 1990; King and Rebelo 1993; Becker, Murphy, and Tamura 1990; Rosenzweig 1990) and some cross-country empirical studies [for example, Barro (1991)] have identified human capital accumulation as an important catalyst for growth, either increasing labor productivity or fostering technological innovation. Among those studies Lucas (1988) and Becker, Murphy, and Tamura (1990) stressed that investment in human capital produces spillover benefits that can lead to higher sustained rates of economic growth.

Becker, Murphy, and Tamura (1990) hypothesized that over some range rates of return to investments in human capital actually rise rather than decline as the stock of human capital increases. The reason is that the sectors of the economy that produce human capital require more-educated workers than sectors that produce consumer goods and physical capital. Lucas (1988) stressed that the rate of return to some kinds of ability, such as talent in the field of communications, is higher if other people are also more capable. In this setting increases in education levels lead to higher rates of return to investment in human and physical capital and hence to higher per capita income growth. A supporting force is that more human capital per person reduces fertility rates because human capital is more productive in producing goods and additional human capital than in producing children.

Between 1950 and 1995 Taiwan experienced sustained, rapid economic growth and expansion of its education system. The real gross domestic product (GDP) grew by an average of 8.1% annually. National income per capita grew from US$186 in 1952 to US$11,315 by 1995 [ROC DGBAS, various years (1996), *Statistical Yearbook of the Republic of China*]. Meanwhile, the total fertility rate declined sharply, from 6 births per woman in 1950 to 1.6 in 1995, and the crude birth rate declined sharply from 50 births per 1,000 persons in 1952 to 16 births per 1,000 persons in 1995. With a nearly 61-fold increase in national income per capita the education sector expanded dramatically. The elementary enrollment rate (ages 6–11) rose from 85% in 1951 to nearly 100% by 1975. Between 1976 and 1995 enrollment rates increased from 76% to 94% for junior high school (ages 12–14), from 43% to 78% for senior high school (ages 15–17), and from 9% to 28% for college level and above.

Consequently, the education level of the labor force rose rapidly during that period. In 1956, 85% of the labor force had only a primary school education or less, 12% had completed secondary school, and only 2.6% had a college or higher-level education. By 1990 only 36% had a primary school education or less, 48% had a secondary school education, and nearly 16% had completed college or gone beyond a bachelor's degree. For the male labor force 79% had only a primary education or less in 1956, whereas by 1990 only 31% were in this category. Over the same period the percentage of the male labor force with a college education rose from 4.5% to 19%. Within the female labor force the educational advance was even more dramatic.

In this chapter I first examine the spillover effects of human capital formation by generation. Using survey data, I attempt to answer the question of whether the rate of return to investment in human capital in Taiwan increased rather than decreased as the stock of human capital rose during the 45-year period between 1950 and 1995. Next, I examine the relationships among economic growth, educational expansion, and fertility in Taiwan. Becker, Murphy, and Tamura's (1990) endogenous growth model provides the structural framework for the empirical analysis. To study intergenerational transmission, I have constructed pseudo-longitudinal cohort data from the annual Manpower Utilization Survey in Taiwan for the years 1978–95. I also analyze real earnings over that period in relation to the education of the male birth cohort born between 1926 and 1970.

In the following section I describe the data in greater detail and compare changes among birth cohorts in education and in earnings at various education levels, providing a background for the empirical analysis that follows. In the next two sections I focus on Becker, Murphy, and Tamura's (1990) growth model of education and fertility decisions and then describe the measurement of the structural variables. I follow this up by estimating results and, finally, drawing conclusions.

Intercohort Changes in Education
and Life-Cycle Earning Patterns

The data for the analysis are from the Manpower Utilization Survey, Taiwan Area, for 1978–95, conducted by the Directorate-General of Budget, Accounting, and Statistics (DGBAS), Executive Yuan. Approximately 40,000 to 60,000 civilians age 15 and older are selected anew and interviewed for the survey in May of each year. The collected information includes data on respondents' age, education, marital status, labor force status, occupation and industry of current job and of previous job, monthly earnings, reservation wage, and job-seeking process. The survey has the advantage of size and of being statistically representative of Taiwan's labor market.[1]

Currently there is no panel data set containing mainly labor market information about Taiwan. To study intergenerational transmission of human capital, therefore, I constructed a pseudo-birth-cohort panel data set using the Manpower Utilization Survey's cross-sectional data. Deaton (1985) demonstrated that sample cohort means obtained from cross-sectional surveys are consistent estimates of unobservable cohort population means. To construct my pseudo-cohort panel data set, I first computed the year of birth (cohort year) for each individual in each survey year and then calculated the sample means of variables relevant to each pseudo-cohort in each survey year, connecting those variables over the 18 years from 1978 to 1995. This made it possible to analyze a series of variables for each cohort. For example, the life-cycle earnings from age 33 to age 50 for males born in 1945 were derived from the sample mean of earnings among men of age 33 in 1978, age 34 in 1979, . . . and age 50 in 1995. To focus on the relationship between education and earning and to avoid the problem of determining causality between female labor market participation and fertility, I analyzed data only for males born between 1926 and 1970 who were between the ages of 25 and 65 over the survey period and who worked 40 or more hours per week. I deflated or inflated their monthly earnings according to the 1991 consumer price index. Altogether, I obtained 657 observations.

In addition, I merged two other variables with the pseudo-cohort panel data. Per capita gross national product (GNP per capita) from 1952 to 1995 was used to calculate the earnings of cohorts' parents and the earning ratios between the current generation and the previous generation. Because GNPs per capita before 1952 were not available and because the level of GNP per capita in 1952 was as low as US$196, I set GNP per capita in the years before 1952 to equal that in 1952. I obtained total fertility rates for 1910 to 1943 from Paul Liu and for 1950 to 1970 from the *Taiwan-Fukien Demographic Fact Book* (ROC MOI 1994).[2] I give detailed definitions of the variables used in the empirical model later.

Intercohort Changes in Educational Attainment

During periods of dramatic educational expansion, the educational patterns of older cohorts are totally different from those of younger cohorts. Table 11.1, which illustrates intercohort changes in completed education of both males and females, indicates, for example, that 13–16% of males born before 1941 were illiterate or self-educated but that among males born after 1955 less than 1% fell into that category. Among females the decline in the percentage of illiterate or self-educated was even sharper, from 37–56% among those born before 1941 to 1% or less among those born after 1955. The percentages of males and females with only an elementary school education also decreased rapidly from one cohort to the next. Forty-nine percent of males born between 1926 and 1930 were in this category, compared with 2.4% among males born between 1966 and 1970. The corresponding percentages among females were 33% and 6.4%. After compulsory education was extended from six years of elementary school to nine years of elementary and junior high school in 1968, the proportions of both male and female junior high school graduates rose sharply between cohorts born before 1956 and those born afterward. Among males 9–16% of the pre-1956 birth cohort completed junior high school, compared with 27–32% of those born later. Among females the corresponding percentages were 5–11% and 22–27%. The percentages of senior high school graduates increased moderately from the earlier cohorts to the later ones, roughly 4–11% among males and 2–11% among females.

The intercohort changes in the percentages of vocational school and college graduates had almost the same magnitudes as the changes among those attaining only an elementary school education, but in the opposite direction. For males the percentages of vocational school graduates rose from 8% or 9% among those born before 1936 to 48% among those born after 1965. For females the corresponding increase was from less than 2% to nearly 49%. For college graduates the percentages steadily increased. Because larger and larger proportions of male college graduates and postgraduates have served in the military for 2 years after reaching age 25 and because those populations are not interviewed in the Manpower Utilization Survey, the percentages of male college graduates are slightly underestimated for later cohorts.

It is clear from Table 11.1 that the average number of years of schooling for males and females was rising from one cohort to the next. For males who reached school age during or before War World II the period of schooling was stable at between 6.7 years and 6.9 years, slightly above the elementary level. However, among those reaching school age after War World II the period of education increased dramatically from one cohort to the next. For male cohorts born between 1941 and 1970 the number of years of education

TABLE 11.1

Distribution (%) of Birth Cohorts by Sex and Education Level: Taiwan, 1926–70

Educational level	Birth cohort									
	1926–30	1931–35	1936–40	1941–45	1946–50	1951–55	1956–60	1961–65	1966–70
Males									
Illiterate and self-educated	16.4	13.4	13.4	5.9	1.5	0.6	0.2	0.2	0.2
Elementary school	49.3	58.6	58.9	55.2	47.1	39.0	17.7	6.9	2.4
Junior middle school	13.3	10.8	8.9	12.9	15.3	15.6	27.5	32.4	28.0
Senior high school	6.9	5.2	3.9	5.8	7.9	9.5	10.6	9.5	9.6
Vocational school	9.4	8.4	10.4	13.7	18.9	26.8	35.3	40.5	48.0
College and above	4.6	3.6	4.4	6.5	9.2	8.5	8.7	10.6	11.8
Average years of schooling	7.0	6.8	6.8	7.9	9.0	9.7	10.7	11.3	11.9
Number of observations	3,257	3,269	3,352	3,425	3,807	5,562	4,511	2,958	1,056
Females									
Illiterate and self-educated	56.2	41.3	37.4	26.9	10.6	4.3	1.4	0.2	0.1
Elementary school	33.4	47.7	50.9	53.9	58.3	54.2	33.4	16.0	6.4
Junior middle school	5.0	6.3	6.0	8.7	10.9	10.7	21.6	27.1	23.7
Senior high school	3.2	2.5	2.1	3.4	4.3	5.7	7.6	9.5	10.7
Vocational school	1.6	1.7	2.9	5.6	12.4	20.5	30.2	39.9	48.7
College and above	0.6	0.4	0.6	1.4	3.6	4.6	5.9	7.3	10.4
Average years of schooling	3.2	4.0	4.3	5.4	7.1	8.2	9.6	10.7	11.6
Number of observations	2,470	2,919	3,368	3,383	3,739	5,321	4,341	2,726	949

SOURCE: Calculated from information in ROC DGBAS (n.d.).

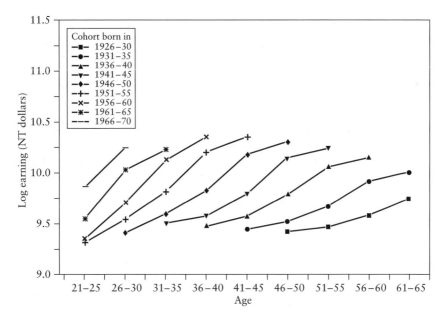

FIGURE 11.1. Age Profiles of Monthly Earnings for Birth Cohorts of Male Elementary School Graduates.

increased markedly, from 6.9 years to 11.9 years. For females the number of years more than doubled, from 5.4 years to 11.6 years.

Although women had a large initial disadvantage, their educational levels improved more quickly than those of men. Female educational attainment was clearly rising, even among cohorts who entered school before World War II, and during the surveyed period, the gender gap in education disappeared.

Intercohort Changes in the Life-Cycle Earning Profile

By using the pseudo-cohort panel data, I can illustrate 18-year longitudinal patterns of monthly ln earnings for successive male cohorts born between 1926–30 and 1966–70 by education level. Figures 11.1 through 11.5 illustrate long-term ln earning profiles for elementary school graduates, junior high school graduates, senior high school graduates, vocational school graduates, and college graduates, respectively. The figures depict changes in long-term monthly ln earnings at different stages of the life cycle for each cohort.

For elementary school graduates (Figure 11.1), three observations stand out. First, there has been a sharp rise in monthly ln earnings from one cohort to the next at all stages of the life cycle. That is, the real earnings at a given education level and age are greater for later-born cohorts than for earlier-

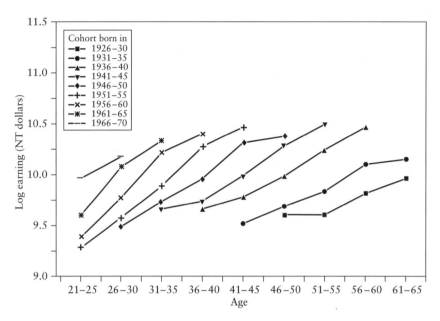

FIGURE 11.2. Age Profiles of Monthly Earnings for Birth Cohorts of Male Junior High School Graduates.

born cohorts (the real earnings profiles are higher for later cohorts). Second, for each cohort average real earnings increase throughout their working years. Because information for only 18 years at most can be used for each cohort, the entire earning history of no single cohort is available; but no cohort experienced a decline in average earnings before age 65 during the period of observation (that is, all the earnings profiles are upward sloping). Third, the rate at which real earnings are rising varies systematically from cohort to cohort. Later-born cohorts have experienced faster earnings growth than earlier-born cohorts (the slopes of the earnings profiles for later-born cohorts are steeper than the earnings profiles for earlier-born cohorts over the same age span).

Two similar patterns of lifetime earnings are also evident for all other education levels: Earnings are higher for later-born cohorts than for earlier-born cohorts at all ages, and all cohorts have experienced rising earnings throughout the period of life that can be documented. However, only among elementary and junior high school graduates have real earnings clearly risen more slowly for earlier-born cohorts than for later-born cohorts. Among higher-education graduates earnings have risen as rapidly for older cohorts as for younger cohorts.

A comparison of earnings shown in Figures 11.1–11.5 reveals that earnings are consistently higher for workers with higher educational attainment.

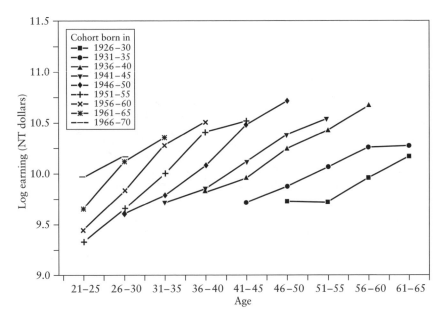

FIGURE 11.3. Age Profiles of Monthly Earnings for Birth Cohorts of Male Senior High School Graduates.

As shown in Figures 11.1 and 11.2, for example, the lifetime ln earning profiles are higher for junior high school graduates than for elementary school graduates. Similarly, the lifetime ln earning profiles are higher for senior high school graduates than for junior high school graduates at all stages of the life cycle (Figures 11.2 and 11.3). A comparison of the cohorts in Figures 11.3 and 11.4 makes it clear that the lifetime earning profiles of cohorts born between 1946 and 1965 are almost the same for senior high school graduates and vocational school graduates. For the earlier birth cohorts, however, the ln earning profiles of vocational school graduates are higher than those of senior high school graduates. By comparing the cohorts in Figures 11.4 and 11.5 (or Figure 11.3), one sees that the lifetime earning profiles are much higher for college graduates than for vocational school graduates (or senior high school graduates). These results are consistent with the predictions of human capital theory and with other empirical evidence.

In summary, during Taiwan's period of rapid and sustained economic growth, educational attainment increased dramatically from one cohort to the next. For cohorts born before World War II more than one-half of the population had only an elementary school education or less. Within 30 years after War World II more than one-half of the population had at least a senior high school or vocational school education. Meanwhile, the payoff for any given education level increased from one cohort to the next.

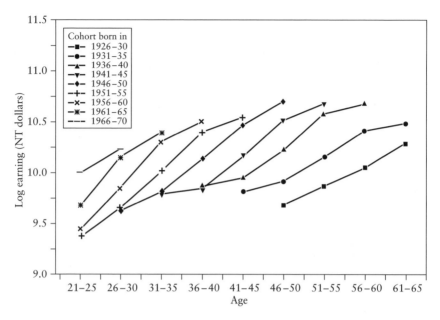

FIGURE 11.4. Age Profiles of Monthly Earnings for Birth Cohorts of Male Vocational School Graduates.

In the following sections I examine the relationships between cohorts' earnings and the education investment and fertility decisions that their parents made, and I calculate the rate of return to education investment for each cohort.

Structural Model of Education Investment, Fertility, and Earning

I derive my empirical model of parents' decision on educational investment and fertility, and their children's earnings from Becker, Murphy, and Tamura's (1990) endogenous growth model. Details of the derivation are given by Huang (1997).

The main assumption about human capital investment in Becker, Murphy, and Tamura's (1990) model is that rates of return to investment in human capital do not monotonically decline as the stock of human capital increases. The reason is that the production of human capital is human capital intensive and uses relatively more human capital per unit of output than the consumption, child-rearing, and physical capital sectors do. Rates of return are low when there is little human capital, and they grow at least for a while

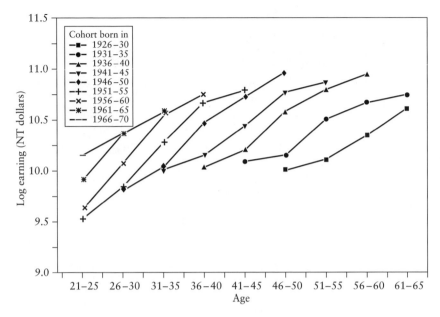

FIGURE 11.5. Age Profiles of Monthly Earnings for Birth Cohorts of Male College Graduates.

as human capital increases. Eventually, they may begin to decline because it becomes increasingly difficult to absorb more knowledge.

Let $t + 1$ denote the children's generation, and let t denote the parents' generation. The optimum level of investment in children's human capital stock is at the level at which the marginal rate of return $\partial Y_{t+1}/\partial H_{t+1}$, equals the marginal utility forgone to invest one more unit of human capital in the children. The marginal utility forgone depends on the marginal rates of substitution between current consumption and future consumption, the relative productivity of the consumption sector with regard to human capital, and the comparative advantage of using human capital in the human capital sector instead of in the consumption sector in the parents' generation. Because the rate of return measures the effect, on children's future consumption, of increasing children's human capital stock, H_{t+1}, the rate of return depends on the productivity of the consumption sector and the time devoted to the labor market when the children grow up. The rate of return also depends on the comparative advantage gained from using human capital in the human capital sector instead of in the consumption sector. When the human capital sector relies on skilled and trained labor more than the consumption sector does, then the comparative advantage of using human capital in the human capital sector rather than in the consumption sector is higher. When the education sector uses educated and other skilled inputs to produce human capital more intensively than the consumption sector does, the rate of return on investment in human capital is higher. When the rate of return on investment in human capital is higher, parents are more willing to give up current consumption to invest in their children's human capital.

From this discussion it is clear that the stock of children's human capital depends on the rate of return on investment in human capital $\partial Y_{t+1}/\partial H_{t+1}$, the comparative advantage gained from using human capital in the human capital sector instead of in the consumption sector in the parents' generation, and the marginal utility of substitution between current consumption and future consumption.

Assume that the comparative advantage of using human capital in the human capital sector instead of in the consumption sector in the parents' generation is a function of parents' human capital stock, H_t. Assume, for a full-time male worker, that the relation among working hours (l), number of children (n), and the time spent on children's education (h) is fairly constant from one generation to another. The rate of return on investment in human capital depends on the comparative advantage of using human capital in the human capital sector instead of in the consumption sector in the children's generation, which is a function of H_{t+1}. Assume further that the marginal utility of substitution between current consumption and discounted future consumption depends on the discount rate, which is a function of the number of children (n_t) and the ratio of future consumption and current consumption. In a situation of stable economic growth the ratio of future consumption and current consumption equals the ratio of future income to current income, Y_{t+1}/Y_t. If one takes Taylor's expansion on variables Ht_{+1}, H_t, n_t, and Y_{t+1}/Y_t, the empirical equation for the determinant for children's human capital is

$$H_{t+1} = \gamma_0 + \gamma_1 \frac{Y_{t+1}}{Y_t} + \gamma_2 H_t + \gamma_3 n_t + \varepsilon_2. \qquad (11.1)$$

The main assumption about fertility is that the discount rate applied by the present generation to the per capita consumption of subsequent generations depends inversely on the fertility of the present generation. Diminishing marginal utility implies that the discount rate applied to the utility of each child declines as the number of children in a family increases. The higher fertility of a given generation increases the discount on per capita future consumption in the intertemporal utility functions. Therefore higher fertility discourages investments in human capital. Conversely, the demand for children is raised by higher stocks of human capital because they raise the cost of the time spent on child care. The discount rate between generations is determined by the degree of parental altruism toward each child.

Accordingly, the equilibrium condition for the number of children that parents will choose is the point at which the discounted marginal utility from an additional child equals the sum of the costs, in time and goods, of producing and rearing that child. The change in the discount rate between generations is a function of n_t. The marginal utility of parents' consumption is a function of parents' income Y_t. The time and goods costs of producing and rearing a child are a function of parents' human capital H_t. The higher the parents' human capital, the higher the cost of the time required to produce and rear a child; thus the parents' fertility will be lower. Taking Taylor's expansion on variables H_t, n_t, and Y_t changes the empirical equation on the determinant of children's human capital to

$$n_t = \beta_0 + \beta_1 H_t + \beta_2 Y_t + \beta_3 PV + \varepsilon_3, \qquad (11.2)$$

where PV is the population policy variable, which examines the effect of a family planning program on fertility rates. The family planning program has played an active role in Taiwan since 1964 (Liu 2001).

The rate of return on investment in human capital is a function of H_{t+1}, which represents the spillover benefits described by Lucas (1988) and the comparative advantage of using human capital in the human capital sector instead of in the consumption sector, as described by Becker, Murphy, and Tamura (1990). By integrating $\partial Y_{t+1}/\partial H_{t+1}$ with respect to H_{t+1}, one can express the empirical earnings equation as follows:

$$Y_{t+1,j} = \alpha_0 + (\alpha_1 + \alpha_2 H_{t+1})H_{t+1} + \alpha_3 wkexp + \alpha_4 wkexp^2 + \varepsilon_1. \quad (11.3)$$

Because ε_1, ε_2, and ε_3 are correlated with one another, the consistent estimates of sets of α, β, and γ can be obtained by running simultaneous equation models (11.1), (11.2), and (11.3). The first step is to run an ordinary least-squares (OLS) analysis on the fertility equation (11.2). The second step is to run an OLS analysis on the education-investment equation (11.1) by substituting n_t with its predicted value $\hat{n}_t$, which is calculated from Equation (11.2). The final step is to run an OLS analysis on the ln earnings equation (11.3) by substituting the cohorts' education with their predicted values.

Measurement of the Structural Variables

Before presenting the estimation results, it is necessary to describe the measurement of the structural variables identified previously. The pseudo-cohort panel data set constructed from Manpower Utilization Survey data for 1978–95 and merged with total fertility rates from 1926–91 and GNP per capita is the basis for the following discussion.

According to empirical model Equation (11.1), parents choose the average human capital of each birth cohort on the basis of three variables: (1) the income they expect their children to earn relative to their own, (2) their own human capital, and (3) the number of children they bear, which is endogenous. To operationalize the model, I take the generation length to be 25 years. The average number of years of completed schooling of the cohort born in year j is measured as the human capital stock H_{t+1}. The human capital of the parents H_t is approximated as the average number of years of completed schooling by the cohort born in year $j - 25$. Two variables are measured as the human capital stock of parents: (1) the average number of years of schooling for a male cohort born 25 years earlier (father's education) and (2) the average number of years of schooling for a female cohort born 25 years earlier (mother's education). The parents' income is measured as GNP per capita in the year in which members of the cohort were born (GNP_t), and the expected income of members of the cohort is measured as GNP per capita 25 years later (GNP_{t+1}). The number of children is approximated as the total fertility rate for the year in which the cohort was born (TFR_t). Average years of schooling are for males only. The human capital equation is estimated with the values for 46 cohorts born between 1925 and 1970. Parents' education is approximated by educational attainment for cohorts born between 1900 and 1945.

The number of children that parents choose [Equation (11.2)] is governed by three variables: (1) the human capital stock of parents, (2) parents' income, and (3) a population policy variable, which captures the effect of family planning. As in the human capital equation, the number of children is approximated by the total fertility rate in year j, human capital by the average number of years of completed schooling attained by males born in year j, and income by GNP per capita in year j. The effect of population policy is the number of women who are currently using contraceptive methods distributed by public family planning programs. Because Taiwan's family planning program became active in 1964, a dummy variable, D64, is interacted with the population variable. The fertility model is estimated with data available for 61 years, 1925–43 and 1950–91. Total fertility rates are not available for 1944–49 because of the disruption caused by World War II.

The natural logarithm of average annual earnings for 1978–95 by males born in year j is determined by the human capital of the cohort and the cohort's work experience. Because of the discontinuity in the relationship between education and earnings, in the earnings equation the human capital of the cohort is measured by means of a set of dummy variables corresponding to five educational levels (primary, junior high school, high school, vocational school, and college). The human capital variable is interacted with a measure of education to capture hypothesized spillovers. If these spillovers exist, the effect of education on earnings will be greater when the level of education is higher. Work experience is approximated in conventional fashion on the assumption that males enter school at age 6, complete their schooling, serve two years in the Armed Forces as required in Taiwan, and then en-

TABLE 11.2

Definition of Variables

Variable	Definition
t	Parent's generation
$t + 1$	Child's generation
H_t	Parent's human capital stock, measured as the average number of years of completed schooling for males born in year $j - 25$
H_{t+1}	Child's human capital stock, measured as the average number of years of completed schooling for males born in year j
GNP_t	Parent's income (Y_t), measured as GNP per capita in year j
GNP_{t+1}	Child's future income (Y_{t+1}), measured as GNP per capita in year $j + 25$
TFR_t	Total fertility rate, or number of births per woman of childbearing age (15–49), in year j
PV_t	Number of women of childbearing age (15–49) using contraception
D64	D64 = 1 if year $j \geq 1964$; D64 = 0 otherwise
Y_{t+1}	Mean of the natural logarithm of monthly real earnings for cohorts born in year j (18 years, 1978–95, of real earnings are available for each cohort born between 1926 and 1970)
Prmdum	Dummy variable equal to 1 if cohort completed primary school
Middum	Dummy variable equal to 1 if cohort completed junior middle school
Highdum	Dummy variable equal to 1 if cohort completed high school
Vocadum	Dummy variable equal to 1 if cohort completed vocation school
Coldum	Dummy variable equal to 1 if cohort completed college
Wkexp	Work experience

ter the work force. Hence their work experience is given by age, less number of years of schooling, less 8.

The earnings equation is estimated for 18 years (1978–95) for 46 cohorts born between 1925 and 1970 who attained each of the 5 educational levels. Eighteen years of earnings data are not available for some cohorts. Hence the total number of observations is 3,804 rather than 4,140 (18 × 46 × 5). The variables used are summarized in Table 11.2.

The Estimation Results

Table 11.3 presents the estimates of the coefficients (t ratio) of the structural model described earlier. Column 1 reports the coefficient estimates for the education equation (11.1). These results reveal why education has increased so rapidly in Taiwan, especially for male cohorts who reached school age after World War II.

Columns 1 and 2 of Table 11.3 reveal three noteworthy relationships. First, there is a clear trade-off between the quantity and quality of children. The total fertility rate is significantly and negatively associated with investment in children's education. Children who belonged to high-fertility cohorts

TABLE 11.3
Coefficient Estimates (t ratio) of Structural Model: Taiwan[a]

Variable name	Education (H_{t+1})		TFR (n_t)		ln earnings (Y_{t+1})	
	Coefficient	t ratio	Coefficient	t ratio	Coefficient	t ratio
Constant	6.611[b]	14.74	6.013[b]	22.10	8.599[b]	252.24
Prmdum (= 1 if primary school completed)					-0.104[b]	-2.90
Middum (= 1 if middle school completed)					0.139[b]	3.82
Highdum (= 1 if high school completed)					0.306[b]	8.23
Vocadum (= 1 if vocational school completed)					0.444[b]	11.84
Coldum (= 1 if college completed)					0.710[b]	18.58
Education (H_{t+1}) × Prmdum					0.038[b]	6.87
Education (H_{t+1}) × Middum					0.025[b]	4.25
Education (H_{t+1}) × Highdum					0.023[b]	3.67
Education (H_{t+1}) × Vocadum					0.014[c]	2.23
Education (H_{t+1}) × Coldum					0.019[b]	2.92
Work experience					0.047[b]	26.83
Work experience squared					-0.0008[b]	-38.13
TFR (n_t)	-0.003[b]	-2.48				
Father's education (H_f)	-1.244[b]	-5.29	0.317[b]	3.34		
Father's education squared (H_f^2)	0.131[b]	5.63				
Mother's education (H_t)	1.951[b]	8.21	-0.665[b]	-6.33		
Mother education squared (H_t^2)	-0.187[b]	-7.46				
GNP_{t+1}/GNP_t	0.044[b]	4.65				
GNP_t			0.0002[b]	3.52		
PV × D64			-0.0014[b]	-3.66		
R^2	0.989		0.963		0.867	
Observations	47		61		3,804	

[a]The coefficient estimates of year dummies in ln earnings equation (11.3) are 0.092 (D79), 0.102 (D80), 0.113 (D81), 0.201 (D82), 0.250 (D83), 0.260 (D84), 0.280 (D85), 0.352 (D86), 0.398 (D87), 0.472 (D88), 0.531 (D89), 0.612 (D90), 0.688 (D91), 0.740 (D92), 0.806 (D93), 0.835 (D94), and 0.797 (D95).
[b]Significant at the 1% level, two-tailed test.
[c]Significant at the 5% level, two-tailed test.

had lower educational attainment than children who belonged to low-fertility cohorts. Second, parents' education has a strong influence on children's education. Father's education has either a negative or a positive effect on the children's education, depending on his educational level. The effect is positive if he has completed at least 4.7 years of schooling. Likewise, mother's education has a negative or positive effect on the children's education, becoming negative if she has completed at least 5.2 years of schooling. Third, Taiwan's rapid economic growth, which lessened financial constraints on families, also played a substantial role in raising children's education. The ratios of GNP per capita at age 25 to GNP per capita at age 0 (approximating the ratio of future versus current consumption) are positively and significantly associated with investment in children's education. In other words, the high growth rate of GNP per capita that Taiwan experienced over the period of analysis encouraged investment in children's human capital.

The data show that the average number of years of completed schooling rose by 4.7 years for cohorts born between 1939 and 1970. Over the same periods the total fertility rate in Taiwan dropped from 6.6 to 4.0 children per woman; the average number of years of completed schooling of fathers and mothers rose from 4.8 to 8.4 and from 1.5 to 6.2, respectively; and the ratio of future versus current incomes increased from 1.3 to 27.5. If we multiply these discrepancies by their corresponding coefficient given in column 1 of Table 11.3, we see that the decline in total fertility rate between 1939 and 1970 induced an increase in children's years of schooling by only 0.008 year. Among the cohorts born between 1939 and 1970 the increase in father's average education by 3.6 years raised child's schooling by 1.7 years, whereas the average increase in mother's education by 4.67 years raised child's schooling by 2.2 years. The ratio of future versus current incomes increased from 1.3 to 27.5, substantially raising children's education by an average of 1.2 years. To sum up, the decline in fertility, increases in fathers' education, increases in mothers' education, and economic growth contributed 0.2%, 34%, 43%, and 23% of the increase in children's education, respectively.

Columns 3 and 4 of Table 11.3 report the coefficient estimates of the fertility equation (11.2), which is run with 61 observations for the years 1925–43 and 1950–91. Three factors are examined: parents' education, parents' income, and parents' current contraceptive use. The total fertility rate in Taiwan was roughly 6.5–7.0 children per woman before 1957 (except in 1941–43, when fertility was lower) and then fell rapidly, reaching 1.7 children per women by 1991. The regression results explain why Taiwan's fertility decline was particularly rapid during 1957–91.

First, mother's education has a large negative effect on childbearing. A one-year increase in that variable leads to an average fertility decline of nearly 1 (0.67) birth. Not only is this twice the size of the coefficient of father's education, but also education has increased much more rapidly for women than for men in Taiwan. Over the period examined, the average number of years of schooling for women rose by 7.0 years, leading to a drop in childbearing by 4.7 births per woman. The higher a woman's education, the greater the probability of her participating in the labor market and the higher the time cost of producing and raising a child, thus the lower her fertility.

In contrast, an increase in income leads to modestly higher fertility. Two variables are included to capture the effect of income on fertility: father's education and GNP per capita. Both show a significant and positive value. A one-year increase in father's education leads to an additional 0.3 birth, and an increase in GNP per capita by US$1,000 leads to an additional 0.2 birth. Over the period analyzed, father's education increased by 4 years and GNP per capita increased by US$8,000, leading to an additional 1.2 and 1.6 births on average, respectively. Clearly, the main cause of the drop in fertility rates in Taiwan during the period of rapid economic growth was not the increase in GNP per capita itself but the increase in women's education. The growth in GNP per capita has had the indirect effect of lowering fertility by improving female education.

In addition, the family planning program in Taiwan has played an important role in reducing fertility. For each 1,000 women in the childbearing age span (15–49) currently using contraceptive methods provided by the family planning program there is a decline of 0.0014 birth per woman. During the 34 years between 1957 and 1991, the number of childbearing-age women using contraceptives obtained through the family planning program increased by 1.6 million, causing total fertility to a drop by 2.3 births per woman.

The last two columns of Table 11.3 represent the estimates for the earning equation (11.3). The three factors examined here are education level, work experience, and year dummies (year dummies, which capture the year-specific effects on individuals' earnings, are not shown in the table itself, but their coefficients are significant, positive, and higher each year). The natural logarithm of cohorts' monthly real earnings rises with their years of schooling at an increasing rate. That is, a cohort with greater human capital will have a higher payoff on the investment made in its human capital, a result that robustly confirms the evidence observed in Figures 11.1 through 11.5. The younger cohorts who accumulated more education have higher earnings than older cohorts who had less education, given equal work experience and economic situations. Because the rate of return of a given educational level for each cohort equals the average years of schooling multiplied by the corresponding coefficient for that educational level in Table 11.3, the average duration of schooling increased from 6.79 years for men born in 1926 to 12.0 for those born in 1970. Thus the average rate of return for each year of elementary education rises rapidly from 1.09% per year for the cohort born in 1926 to 7.67% per year for the cohort born in 1970. Similar but much slower increases in the rate of return are seen for other educational groups.

The average rate of return for each year of vocational education rises from 6.00 for the cohort born in 1926 to 6.47 for the cohort born in 1970. The average rate of return for each year of college education rises from 9.50 for the cohort born in 1926 to 11.23 for the cohort born in 1970. A final point is that the natural logarithm of the cohorts' monthly real earnings increases with their work experience at a decreasing rate. The turning point occurs at 30 years of work experience.

Conclusion

As a result of the dramatic expansion in education in Taiwan, the average number of years of schooling for males born between 1941 and 1970 increased nearly twofold, from 6.9 years to 12.0 years. The regression results show that at any given level of work experience a cohort's monthly real earnings rose at an increasing rate as its members' years of schooling increased. Therefore younger cohorts with more education had higher labor productivity than older cohorts at the same education level. The evidence examined here supports the hypothesis of Becker, Murphy, and Tamura (1990) that the rates of return on human capital rise monotonically rather than decline monotonically as the stock of human capital increases; it also supports the hypothesis of Lucas (1988) that education has spillover benefits. Thus educating a populace at higher levels promotes economic growth. Likewise, higher growth rates of GNP per capita encourage investment in children's education. Fathers' education has a substantially positive effect on the children's education and a mildly positive effect on the fertility rate. Mothers' education has a substantial positive effect on the children's education and a strong negative effect on the fertility rate. The main cause of Taiwan's dramatic fertility decline during the recent period of rapid economic growth was not the increase in GNP per capita itself but rather the dramatic increase in female education. The growth in GNP per capita has had the direct income effect of raising fertility and the indirect effect of lowering fertility by improving female education.

The younger generation has not only higher education than the previous generation but also higher labor productivity than its predecessor, given the same education level and work experience. This finding implies that a work force consisting of the two generations produces heterogeneity in labor productivity. The nature of this heterogeneity changes systematically over time, but cross-sectional analysis alone cannot provide a full understanding of the change.

The Education System in Taiwan

Taiwan has had a formal education system governed by written regulations since the Manchu emperor Kuanghshu promulgated a school law for China in 1902. Since then, a number of modifications have been made. The Constitution of the Republic of China established six years of compulsory primary education in 1944. Compulsory education was extended to nine years beginning in 1968. After 1968 all junior vocational schools ceased to admit

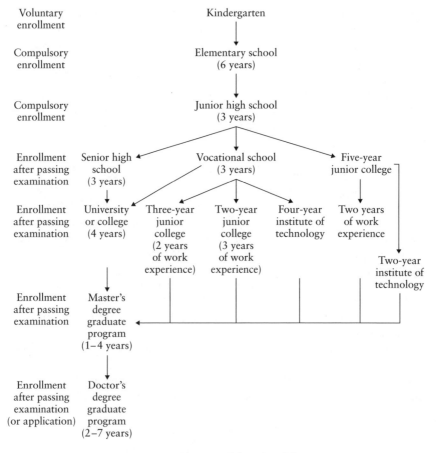

FIGURE 11.6. Taiwan's Educational System.

new students and were eventually phased out. The current education system consists of the elements given in Figure 11.6.

Enrollment in kindergarten is voluntary. Six years of elementary school (ages 6–11) and three years of junior high school (ages 12–14) are compulsory. Candidates who pass an entrance examination may enroll in a three-year senior high school, a three-year vocational school, or a five-year junior college. Likewise, high school or vocational school graduates who pass an entrance examination may enroll in a four-year college or university. Vocational school graduates may also enroll in a two-year or three-year junior college or a four-year institute of technology upon passing an entrance examination. Besides passage of an entrance examination, the qualifications for entering a master's degree program (one to four years) are (1) a college or university bachelor's degree, (2) a degree from a three-year junior college plus two years of work experience, (3) a degree from a two-year junior college plus three years of work experience, (4) a degree from a four-year technological institute, (5) a degree from a five-year junior college plus two years of work experience, or (6) degrees from a five-year junior college and a two-year technological institute. Enrollment in a doctoral program (two to seven years) requires completion of a master's degree and passage of an entrance examination.

Changing Labor Forces and Labor Markets in Asia's Miracle Economies

YOSHIO OKUNISHI

AS IS WELL KNOWN, the pace of demographic transition from high to low mortality and fertility determines the size and age structure of a country's population, provided that the volume of international migration is negligible. For example, high fertility will produce a large influx into the labor market about 15 to 20 years later (Bloom and Freeman 1986). Population size and structure combined with labor force participation rates determine the size and structure of the labor force.

A rapid increase in a country's labor force, however, is not a sufficient condition to ensure a high rate of economic growth. It may not be even a necessary condition. As the World Bank's (1993a) report on the East Asian miracle emphasized, qualitative aspects of the labor force and its efficient allocation are also important. Investment in human capital through higher education, rural to urban migration, a shift in the work force from agriculture to manufacturing, and flexible wage determination are all factors that contribute to an improved labor force. The experiences of Japan and the Asian newly industrialized economies (NIEs) suggest that two other factors are also important, namely, human capital accumulation *after* school education and efficient work force allocation in a dynamic rather than a static sense.

Rapid and sustained economic growth causes wages to rise sharply, thereby changing a country's comparative advantage. Such a country can no

Thanks are due to John Bauer, Andrew Mason, and Kazuo Koike for their invaluable comments on an earlier draft of this chapter. I also gratefully acknowledge help from Jeff Brown, Ping-Lung Hsin, and Young-Soo Shin, who provided me with some of the data reported here.

longer depend on cheap labor-intensive products but must begin to produce high-quality products. Each of the countries considered here has faced this necessity.

In this chapter I examine these labor force developments in the six countries, focusing mainly on their common features rather than on unique national characteristics. For that purpose I have drawn on surveys on the labor force, employment, wages, and labor turnover in each country. To the extent permitted by the data, the discussion includes cross-country and intertemporal comparisons.

In the following three sections I describe quantitative aspects of the labor force in each country, including the total labor force growth rate, factors contributing to it, changes in labor force participation rates, and changes in the sex and age structure. Next, I examine such qualitative issues as changes in educational attainment and industry composition of the work force. After describing changes in wage levels, I propose a simple hypothesis about the relationship between economic development and labor markets. The hypothesis posits that a country that has had sustained and rapid growth must transform its economy, introducing technological advancements and upgrading workers' skills. The transformation entails structural changes in work organization, wage structures, and labor turnover. For example, production workers may upgrade their skills and share some traits of white-collar workers. This white collarization—a term coined by Koike (1988)—will reduce the wage gap between them. In-house skill formation may cause longer job tenures and lower job turnover rates. The survey evidence from the six countries is broadly consistent with this hypothesis, although other interpretations are possible.

Labor Force Growth Rates

Economic growth has three sources: (1) an increased quantity of production factors, (2) quality improvement of those factors, and (3) a more efficient use of those factors, called total factor productivity. Recent studies of East Asia's successful economies emphasize increased quantity (and quality) of production factors (see, for example, chapter).

The average per annum total labor force growth rates over the past 20 or 25 years were 1.0% for Japan (1970–95), 2.9% for South Korea (1970–95), 2.5% for Taiwan (1975–95), 3.6% for Singapore (1970–95), 3.1% for Thailand (1971–95), and 3.4% for Indonesia (1971–94). Rates fluctuated, however, over this period. Japan's growth rate was relatively high in the late 1960s and late 1980s, in part because of an influx of baby boomers (those born in 1947–49) and their children. South Korea experienced upward surges in the early 1970s and the late 1980s. The early 1970s surge was population driven, whereas an increase in the female labor force participation rate played a significant role in the late 1980s. Taiwan's labor force growth rate is on a downward trend, largely as a result of declining population growth. In fact, for the past 20 or 30 years Japan, South Korea, and Taiwan have all experienced decreased contributions of population growth to their labor force growth. Singapore has maintained a high rate of labor force growth despite its rapid and early completion of the demographic transition. A large influx of foreign workers, who represent about 20% of the total work force, is thought to be responsible.[1] The labor force growth rate of Thailand was high in the late 1970s and early 1980s, but it has been dwindling since then. The pattern for Indonesia looks somewhat similar to that of Thailand.

The sources of labor force growth are quantified by means of a decomposition analysis, reported in Table 12.1. Each five-year interval is described by three rows. The first row gives the change in the labor force as a percentage of the total labor force. The values are reported separately for males and females. For example, for Japan the labor force increased by 6.1% between 1960 and 1965. Of that increase, 4.7% was due to the rise in male workers and 1.4% was due to the rise in female workers. The increase for the male and female workers is further broken down into three broad age groups. The second row in each five-year interval gives the percentage increase in population for both the total group and each subgroup. Given constant labor force participation rates, the percentage increase in the labor force would match the percentage increase in the population. The differences between the values in the first and second rows, reported in the third row, are an estimate of the effect of changes in participation rates (see note a in Table 12.1 for the equation used in this analysis).

Table 12.1 indicates that the contribution of population changes to labor force growth rates tends to dominate the contribution of population changes to the participation rate. If we focus on the total (that is, both sexes and all ages), this is true for all countries and all periods covered in the table. If we decompose the size of the contribution further by sex and age, then participation rates may have a larger effect in some cases, for example, in young age groups, whose population growth rates are small.

Another interesting feature of Table 12.1 is the contribution made by each sex. In all six countries during the 1980s, the female contribution to the total labor force was comparable to or exceeded the male contribution. Because population change is roughly the same between men and women (except in Singapore, where until recently more female than male immigrants of working age were admitted to the country), this change came from differences in participation rate changes. Japan, South Korea, Taiwan, Thailand, and Indonesia are similar in this regard. In Singapore the female contribution has been consistently high, except in the early 1990s.

TABLE 12.1

Labor Force Change Rate, the Contribution of Population,
and the Contribution of Participation Rate Change by Sex and Age (%):
Six East Asian Countries, Recent Decades

Country and period[a]	Total age (15+)	Male age				Female age			
		15+	15–29	30–49	50+	15+	15–29	30–49	50+
Japan									
1960–65	6.1	4.7	1.8	2.4	0.4	1.4	0.1	1.0	0.4
	11.8	5.8	3.7	1.7	0.4	6.0	2.8	1.7	1.5
	−5.6	−1.1	−1.9	0.8	0.0	−4.5	−2.7	−0.7	−1.1
1970–75	3.3	4.0	−1.2	3.9	1.3	−0.7	−2.4	0.7	1.0
	7.1	3.5	−0.7	2.6	1.6	3.6	−0.8	1.9	2.6
	−3.8	0.5	−0.5	1.3	−0.3	−4.3	−1.5	−1.2	−1.5
1980–85	5.5	2.3	−0.7	0.7	2.4	3.2	0.0	1.6	1.6
	6.0	2.9	−0.1	0.5	2.5	3.0	−0.2	0.5	2.8
	−0.4	−0.6	−0.6	0.2	−0.1	0.2	0.2	1.1	−1.2
1990–95	4.4	2.7	1.1	−0.8	2.4	1.7	0.9	−0.7	1.4
	4.2	2.0	0.2	−0.6	2.3	2.2	0.2	−0.6	2.7
	0.2	0.8	0.9	−0.2	0.1	−0.5	0.7	0.0	−1.3
South Korea									
1970–75[b]	21.0	13.4	5.5	4.8	3.2	7.6	2.7	2.6	2.3
	19.6	10.4	5.9	2.6	1.8	9.2	5.2	1.7	2.3
	1.4	3.0	−0.5	2.2	1.3	−1.7	−2.6	0.9	0.0
1980–85[b]	7.6	3.9	−0.1	2.6	1.4	3.7	0.3	1.9	1.5
	12.5	6.0	2.9	1.8	1.4	6.5	2.7	1.7	2.2
	−4.9	−2.1	−2.9	0.8	0.0	−2.8	−2.4	0.3	−0.7
1990–95	12.5	7.7	0.2	5.5	1.9	4.8	0.7	2.8	1.3
	9.0	4.4	−0.5	3.4	1.5	4.6	−0.2	2.8	2.0
	3.5	3.3	0.7	2.2	0.4	0.2	0.9	0.0	−0.7
Taiwan									
1980–85	15.4	6.8	−0.1	5.7	1.2	8.6	1.5	5.6	1.4
	13.0	6.4	0.8	3.5	2.1	6.6	0.8	3.8	2.0
	2.4	0.5	−0.8	2.2	−0.9	1.9	0.7	1.8	−0.6
1990–95	9.3	4.7	−0.9	5.4	0.3	4.6	−0.9	4.9	0.7
	10.3	5.2	0.5	3.4	1.3	5.1	−0.1	3.5	1.8
	−1.0	−0.5	−1.4	1.9	−1.0	0.5	−0.8	1.4	−1.1
Singapore									
1970–75[c]	20.1	9.6	6.9	1.9	0.8	10.5	7.0	3.2	0.3
	15.6	7.3	5.3	1.1	0.9	8.3	5.3	1.8	1.3
	4.5	2.3	1.6	0.8	−0.1	2.2	1.8	1.4	−1.0
1980–85	16.8	9.4	−0.7	9.2	1.0	7.4	0.8	5.9	0.7
	17.7	8.0	0.5	5.8	1.7	9.7	1.4	6.2	2.1
	−0.9	1.4	−1.2	3.4	−0.7	−2.3	−0.6	−0.3	−1.4
1990–95	17.1	10.8	0.4	9.5	0.9	6.3	0.8	5.0	0.5
	14.8	8.6	1.1	6.4	1.2	6.2	0.5	4.7	1.0
	2.3	2.2	−0.7	3.1	−0.3	0.1	0.3	0.2	−0.5
Thailand									
1971–75	10.3	6.2	2.0	3.5	0.6	4.1	1.9	1.9	0.3
	16.7	8.1	3.8	3.1	1.2	8.6	4.2	3.1	1.3
	−6.4	−1.9	−1.8	0.5	−0.6	−4.5	−2.3	−1.2	−1.0
1980–85	20.0	11.6	7.4	3.2	1.0	8.4	5.1	2.4	0.8
	22.5	11.5	7.2	2.8	1.5	11.0	6.0	2.8	2.1
	−2.5	0.1	0.2	0.4	−0.5	−2.6	−0.9	−0.4	−1.3

TABLE 12.1 *(Continued)*

Country and period[a]	Total age (15+)	Male age				Female age			
		15+	15–29	30–49	50+	15+	15–29	30–49	50+
1990–95	6.0	4.5	−2.7	5.1	2.2	1.5	−3.4	4.0	1.0
	14.1	6.9	−0.5	4.2	3.1	7.1	−0.5	4.3	3.3
	−8.1	−2.4	−2.3	0.8	−1.0	−5.6	−3.0	−0.3	−2.3
Indonesia									
1971–76	18.9	11.1	4.3	4.2	2.6	7.8	2.5	4.2	1.1
	10.3	5.2	1.9	1.7	1.6	5.1	1.6	2.3	1.2
	8.6	5.9	2.4	2.5	1.0	2.7	1.0	1.9	−0.2
1980–86	33.8	14.1	3.5	7.5	3.1	19.7	7.9	8.5	3.3
	17.1	8.5	2.7	3.9	1.9	8.6	3.5	3.2	1.8
	16.7	5.6	0.8	3.6	1.2	11.2	4.3	5.4	1.5
1991–94	9.8	5.4	1.4	3.0	1.0	4.4	1.4	2.3	0.8
	8.4	3.9	1.0	2.0	0.9	4.5	1.2	2.4	1.0
	1.4	1.5	0.4	1.0	0.1	−0.1	0.2	−0.1	−0.2

SOURCES: For Japan, Japan SB (various years), Annual Report on the Labor Force Survey. For South Korea, ROK NSO (selected years), Annual Report on the Economically Active Population Survey for 1975, 1985, and 1995. For Taiwan, ROC DGBAS (various years), Yearbook of Manpower Survey Statistics for 1995, and ROC DGBAS (various years), Statistical Yearbook for 1975. For Singapore, ROS DOS (1996); ROS MOL (various years), Singapore Yearbook of Labour Statistics for 1976 and 1980; ROS MOL (1995); and ILO (various years), Year Book of Labour Statistics for 1982. For Thailand, Thailand NSO (various years), Report of the Labor Force Survey, for July–September 1971 (round 2), July–September 1975 (round 2), July–September 1980, August 1985 (round 3), August 1990 (round 3), and August 1995 (round 3). For Indonesia, Indonesia CBS [various years (1976, 1986, 1991, and 1994)] and ILO (various years).

[a] Each cell (five-year interval) shows the contribution to the total labor force change rate, that is, the upper leftmost number in the first row of values. The decomposition is based on the identity $(\Delta L/L = \Delta P/P + \Delta l/(L/(P+\Delta P)))$ where L is the labor force, P is the population, and l is the labor force participation rate. In each cell the contribution of population to change rates is shown in the second row of values and the contribution of participation rate change is shown in the third row of values. The third row in each cell was calculated by subtracting the second row from the first row. This number largely reflects the changes in the labor force participation rates.

[b] 14+ years old.

[c] 10+ years old.

Labor Force Participation Rates

Although we have just seen that population growth was more important than changes in labor force participation rates in determining rates of labor force growth in the six countries, participation rates in East Asia have changed over time and have varied among countries. Those changes and the variation are thought to be related to demographic characteristics, economic development, and labor market conditions. More specifically, although the participation rates of prime-age males are close to 100% and stable in most of the economies, the participation rates of youth, females, and the elderly vary across economies and over time. The participation rates of these groups are affected by the value of alternative activities, for example, schooling for youth, child rearing and household chores for women, and retirement for the elderly.

If parents deem education to be more beneficial for their children or the family than the children's participation in the labor force, the resulting higher rate of school enrollment will lower the rate of labor force participation among school-age youth and delay their entry into and retirement from the labor market. Health improvements, which are closely related to declines in morbidity and mortality, may delay the retirement of the elderly as well. But more income support to the elderly, for example, through government social security programs, will encourage earlier retirement. Female labor force participation rates will increase if lower fertility means that women can spend less time rearing children. Conversely, increased labor force participation by women may reduce fertility further. Higher education and more favorable opportunities in the labor market will also raise women's labor force participation rates.

Table 12.2 shows labor force participation rates of males and females over the past several decades in the six countries under study. It reveals several salient trends.

First, participation rates of teenagers have decreased as the proportion of young people pursuing higher education has risen. In 1995 the rate was lowest in South Korea, followed by Japan, Taiwan, and Singapore. Decreasing trends were not prominent in Thailand and Indonesia until recently, but between 1990 and 1995 Thailand's trend dropped about 20 percentage points.

Second, the labor force participation rates of men of prime age (late 20s to early 50s) have remained stable and around 90% or higher in all countries. The trends among elderly men, however, vary among countries. The rate among those in their 60s and older has declined in Japan and Singapore, although in Japan this group had a small upswing in the early 1990s. The rate has risen in South Korea but has been roughly stable in Taiwan, Thailand, and Indonesia. The latest (1994 or 1995) rate is highest in Indonesia (65.4%), followed by South Korea (54.2%), Japan (49.5%), Thailand (47.6%), Singapore (28.8%), and Taiwan (27.9%) (not all these percentages are shown in Table 12.3). This variation seems to be due to several factors, such as the importance of the agrarian sector and familial and governmental support systems for the elderly.

Third, the age pattern of female labor force participation rates varies among the countries. In 1955 it was M-shaped (that is, high in the 20s and 40s and low in the 30s) in Japan and South Korea, but there is no such obvious trough in the other countries. For example, in Taiwan and Singapore the rate is highest in the late 20s, then gradually decreases. In Thailand and Indonesia the rate is highest in the 30s or 40s. Perhaps causal factors include the relative importance of the agrarian sector, the timing of marriage and childbearing, and the methods and intensity of investments in child rearing.

Fourth, most of these countries have experienced large increases in the labor force participation rates of women in some age groups: women in their

TABLE 12.2

Labor Force Participation Rates by Sex and Age (%): Six East Asian Countries, Recent Decades

Country, sex, and year	All adults (15+)	Age										
		15–19	20–24	25–29	30–34	35–39	40–44	45–49	50–54	55–59	60–64	65+
Japan, male												
1965	81.7	36.3	85.8	96.8	97.0	97.1	97.0	96.8	95.0	90.0	82.8	56.3
1975	81.4	20.5	76.5	97.2	98.1	98.1	97.6	96.7	96.2	92.2	79.4	44.4
1985	78.1	17.3	70.1	95.7	97.2	97.6	97.2	96.8	95.4	90.3	72.5	37.0
1995	77.6	17.9	74.0	96.4	97.8	98.0	97.8	97.7	97.3	94.1	74.9	37.3
Japan, female												
1965	50.6	35.8	70.2	49.0	51.1	59.6	63.2	60.9	55.8	49.8	39.8	21.6
1975	45.7	21.7	66.2	42.6	43.9	54.0	59.9	61.5	57.8	48.8	38.0	15.3
1985	48.7	16.6	71.9	54.1	50.6	60.0	67.9	68.1	61.0	51.0	38.5	15.5
1995	50.0	16.0	74.1	66.4	53.7	60.5	69.5	71.3	67.1	57.0	39.7	15.6
South Korea, male												
1975	74.6[a]	33.7[b]	78.5	95.1	97.3	96.7	95.6	92.9	90.5	83.4	63.4	32.6
1985	72.3	14.5	63.3	90.8	96.4	96.4	94.9	93.2	88.0	77.4	44.3[c]	
1995	76.5	9.3	58.0	89.6	97.1	96.9	96.6	95.3	91.3	83.9	54.2[c]	
South Korea, female												
1975	39.6[a]	36.4[b]	47.3	29.5	37.0	48.0	51.6	50.9	50.8	44.8	28.1	11.5
1985	41.9	21.1	55.0	35.8	43.6	52.8	58.3	59.3	52.4	47.2	19.2[c]	
1995	48.3	14.6	66.1	47.8	47.5	59.2	66.0	61.1	58.3	54.2	28.9[c]	
Taiwan, male												
1975	78.0	46.6	80.0	96.6	98.9	99.1	98.0	96.2	90.7	79.3	57.0	11.2
1985	75.5	32.6	74.2	94.9	97.9	98.0	97.6	96.0	90.4	79.1	58.2	15.8
1995	72.0	20.4	64.8	92.7	96.8	97.2	96.7	95.3	90.1	80.8	59.2	14.3
Taiwan, female												
1975	38.1	49.5	53.7	34.5	37.1	39.9	40.5	37.0	30.2	21.7	5.5	1.4
1985	43.5	35.4	62.3	50.4	49.1	52.1	51.7	46.0	38.4	28.0	17.2	3.3
1995	45.3	18.5	61.5	65.2	58.3	59.0	58.7	52.0	41.2	31.0	21.1	4.3

Singapore, male												
1975	66.9[d]	45.6	92.1	97.1	97.3	97.2	96.8	94.6	87.8	73.6	54.2	31.7
1985	79.9	32.6	88.8	97.3	98.3	98.7	98.4	96.8	88.5	69.5	52.3	25.9
1995	78.4	20.4	76.3	94.6	97.0	97.6	97.5	96.3	90.6	73.7	46.4	19.2
Singapore, female												
1975	29.6[d]	39.2	64.5	43.3	32.9	28.1	25.4	20.1	18.3	14.2	14.0	6.4
1985	44.9	33.8	78.9	66.5	48.8	44.7	39.6	36.3	25.9	18.4	11.9	5.9
1995	50.1	19.3	77.4	78.9	63.7	57.7	53.8	50.8	37.1	25.2	11.6	4.2
Thailand, male												
1975	85.6	64.3	88.3	96.2	98.2	98.0	97.8[e]		92.9[f]		55.2[g]	
1985	86.9	69.3	89.4	97.2	98.2	98.9	97.5[e]		92.7[f]		51.5[g]	
1995	83.5	48.5	86.5	96.3	98.2	98.2	97.9[e]		92.5[f]		47.6[g]	
Thailand, female												
1975	68.5	65.2	76.4	75.0	74.5	77.3	77.1[e]		67.7[f]		27.5[g]	
1985	74.1	69.3	78.7	82.3	83.3	85.8	85.4[e]		73.4[f]		25.4[g]	
1995	68.9	46.8	74.7	80.3	84.3	86.6	83.0[e]		70.5[f]		25.0[g]	
Indonesia, male												
1976	86.5	58.8	87.1	96.9	98.7	98.8	98.2	97.1	93.2	88.2	81.6	60.9
1986	82.8	46.6	79.9	95.5	98.3	98.8	98.4	97.4	95.2	87.2	77.3	55.3
1994	83.6	47.8	81.5	94.6	97.8	98.3	98.3	97.5	94.0	88.3	78.8	55.4
Indonesia, female												
1976	41.7	34.2	37.5	40.1	44.4	48.3	51.6	51.6	49.1	43.2	37.1	20.0
1986	50.9	36.3	49.7	53.5	57.1	60.1	63.2	63.4	58.7	53.7	43.8	22.9
1994	50.8	37.1	51.2	53.1	56.7	60.0	60.3	60.5	57.6	53.9	42.7	24.5

SOURCES: Same as in Table 12.1.

[a] 14+.
[b] 14–19.
[c] 60+.
[d] 10+.
[e] 40–49.
[f] 50–59.
[g] 60+.

late 20s, 40s, and 50s in Japan and women in most age groups in South Korea, Taiwan, Singapore, and Indonesia. For these last four countries the increases are quite conspicuous for all ages: 10–20 percentage points in just 20 years. The rise probably has something to do with the rapid fertility decline there, but that is not the full story because Japan, which also underwent a rapid fertility decline, did not experience a drastic increase in labor force participation rates among women in their 30s.

Finally, the labor force participation rate of elderly women is much lower than that of elderly men in all countries. The reason may be that when women in this age bracket were younger, it was much less common for them to remain in the labor force than it is now.

Age Structure of the Labor Force

Changes in a population's structure and labor force participation rates by age affect the age structure of the labor force. Table 12.3, which shows the composition of the labor force in the six countries by six sex-age groups, reveals that the proportion of young males (ages 15–29) has been decreasing in Japan, South Korea, Taiwan, and Singapore for the past 20 or 30 years. In Thailand and Indonesia, however, young males still make up about one-fifth of the labor force. Not only the relative size of this group but also the proportion of the other sex-age groups has remained rather stable in these two countries. In South Korea, Taiwan, and Singapore about one-third of the work force consists of prime-age males (ages 30–49). That ratio is lower in Japan because of the larger share of working elderly and in Thailand and Indonesia because of the larger share of working youth. These differences reflect the timing of demographic transition in each country.

The proportion of working elderly is highest in Japan and is rising there. A similar aging process seems to have just started in South Korea, yet Taiwan and Singapore have not experienced an increase in the proportion of older workers, despite having undergone their demographic transitions at about the same time as South Korea. Instead, the proportion of middle-aged working women has risen significantly in these two countries, especially in Singapore. Between 1975 and 1995 the proportion of females in the work force increased by about 5 percentage points in South Korea and Taiwan and by 8.5 percentage points in Singapore as a consequence of the participation rate increase. The proportion of females in the work force has remained stable in Japan and Thailand.

Changes in the age structure of the labor force affect labor markets and the economy as a whole. For example, they may affect labor mobility, wage profiles, productivity, consumption, savings, and fiscal balance (Clark and Spengler 1980; Mitchell 1993). Later in this chapter I discuss some of the is-

TABLE 12.3

Composition of Labor Force by Sex and Age (%):
Six East Asian Countries, Recent Decades

Country and year	Total age (15+)	Male age				Female age			
		15+	15–29	30–49	50+	15+	15–29	30–49	50+
Japan									
1965	100.0	60.2	20.8	25.5	14.0	39.8	15.0	16.6	8.1
1975	100.0	62.7	17.9	30.4	14.3	37.3	11.5	17.0	8.9
1985	100.0	60.3	12.6	30.3	17.4	39.7	9.6	19.1	11.0
1995	100.0	59.5	13.3	26.1	20.1	40.5	10.7	17.0	12.8
South Korea									
1975[a]	100.0	63.9	22.2	30.5	11.2	36.1	15.1	14.7	6.3
1985	100.0	61.6	18.9	31.5	11.3	38.4	13.8	16.9	7.6
1995	100.0	59.8	13.7	32.7	13.4	40.2	12.5	18.3	9.4
Taiwan									
1975	100.0	67.5	24.2	32.0	11.4	32.5	18.6	11.5	2.3
1985	100.0	63.5	21.3	29.1	13.1	36.5	18.3	14.4	3.7
1995	100.0	61.4	15.9	34.1	11.5	38.6	14.2	19.9	4.4
Singapore									
1975[b]	100.0	69.8	32.9	26.8	10.1	30.2	20.7	7.3	2.2
1985	100.0	63.6	25.3	29.3	9.1	36.4	20.5	13.4	2.5
1995	100.0	61.3	16.8	35.3	9.2	38.7	15.6	20.0	3.0
Thailand									
1975	100.0	54.6	23.4	22.7	8.4	45.4	21.6	17.9	5.9
1985	100.0	53.8	25.6	20.7	7.5	46.2	22.6	17.8	5.8
1995	100.0	54.4	20.2	24.5	9.7	45.6	17.1	21.2	7.2
Indonesia									
1976	100.0	65.9	24.0	30.2	11.7	34.1	12.9	15.8	5.4
1986	100.0	60.8	22.6	26.6	11.6	39.2	16.1	16.3	6.8
1994	100.0	61.1	21.4	27.7	12.0	38.9	15.2	16.8	6.9

SOURCES: Same as in Table 12.1.
[a] 14+ years old.
[b] 10+ years old.

sues concerning the relationship between work force composition and labor markets. Here, I focus briefly on the problems of the elderly work force in Japan.

As is well known, the labor force participation rate of the elderly in Japan is conspicuously high among industrialized countries (Clark 1993: 74). Even so, the rising fiscal burden of social security programs for the elderly is a subject of fierce public debate. The state pension program for retired employees in private businesses started in the early 1940s. The program was redesigned after World War II, and the benefit level was raised several times in the late 1960s and the 1970s, a period of high economic growth. That was possible because the ratio of beneficiaries to contributors was still small and the program was basically pay as you go. The benefit schedule then was based on the assumptions that rapid economic growth and high interest rates would continue and that the population would not age as rapidly as it has. Since the 1985 reform, however, the government has acknowledged the need to reduce the ratio of benefits to contributions, and some reforms have been implemented.

The government's pension program for retired employees currently has an eligibility age of 60 years. That age is scheduled to be raised to age 65 by fiscal year 2013, according to the 1994 reform. Additional measures to reduce the fiscal burden, such as a cut in benefits and a further extension of the eligibility age, are under consideration. Such measures may raise the already high unemployment rate of the elderly, especially of those aged 60–64.[2] Employment opportunities for the elderly are rather limited, and the supply of elderly workers is expected to increase.

Most large and medium-size Japanese firms have mandatory retirement. The modal age at retirement used to be 55; but during the 1980s, partly in response to new legislation, most firms extended it to age 60. Extending the mandatory retirement age further to age 65, an option now being considered, could have unintended side effects. When the mandatory retirement age was raised from 55 to 60, firms cut reemployment or employment-extension programs and introduced or intensified early-retirement programs, causing the actual average age at retirement to go up by just one year instead of five (Okunishi 1993). Firms also reduced average wages for the elderly, and they probably increased the variance in wages for middle-aged and older workers.

Flexible wage adjustments and job placement assistance by the career job employers are thought to have positive effects on employment (Rebick 1993). Given a slowdown in the growth of Japan's work force or an actual decrease, firms may shift their demand toward older workers, and employment opportunities for the elderly may well be maintained unless the economy stagnates severely. Nevertheless, the likely cut in public pensions may cause income distribution among the elderly to become less equal.

Quality and Allocation of the Labor Force

The qualitative aspects of human resources and their allocation are as important as the size and age-sex structure of the labor force. The quality of workers can be enhanced by human capital investments, such as school education and vocational training, both off the job and on the job. Human capital investment increases the output per worker even when the level of physical capital is fixed. How much is invested in human capital depends on the costs incurred and how labor markets reward and promote such investments, for example, through higher wages for better-trained workers and through firms' incentive structures.

The World Bank's (1993a) report on the East Asian miracle economies emphasizes both human capital accumulation and flexible labor markets, the latter promoting efficient allocation of human capital. Both factors are important. As for human capital accumulation, however, the report's main concern is schooling. I would argue that the role of on-the-job training and proper incentive systems at firms should be emphasized as well.

On the basis of their fieldwork, Koike and Inoki (1990) reported that a cement plant in Japan was three times or more productive than similar plants in Thailand and Malaysia, even though the technology of the Thai and Malaysian plants was slightly more advanced and even though workers in Thailand and Malaysia worked as hard as their Japanese counterparts. They explained that the difference in productivity was due to the Japanese workers' superior skills, especially their ability to cope with nonroutine tasks, such as detecting and handling defects, which Koike and Inoki called intellectual skill. They argued that intellectual skill is acquired mainly through on-the-job training, not in schools, and that it is fostered by long-term employment offering appropriate incentives, such as higher wages and promotion. An important point that their study makes is that the provision of incentives and the encouragement of cooperation among workers may be critical to the achievement of efficiency within a firm. But researchers sometimes neglect such mechanisms of the internal labor market because they tend to rely on readily available data, such as the number of school years attained by workers and the amount of a firm's tangible assets.

Of course, this criticism does not negate the importance of formal education [for a detailed description of the education and formal training systems in South Korea, Thailand, and Indonesia, see ADB (1990)]. Kiyokawa (1988) convincingly argued that female supervisors who had graduated from technical schools played a key role in the success of Japan's prewar silk industry. Japanese silk manufacturers were able to adapt quickly to the demand for higher-quality products in the international market because a new type of supervisor, educated at technical schools, transformed the industry's production and management systems.

Of interest in this context is how the composition of the work force by education has changed over the past 20 or 30 years in the six Asian countries considered here. Table 12.4 indicates that in all six countries the work force has been growing more highly educated. In Japan, South Korea, Taiwan, and Singapore the proportion of the employed with a junior college or higher education was about 20% or more in 1995. But even in these countries the proportion of college graduates was small during the early stages of rapid economic growth. Although economic growth has been impressive in Thailand and Indonesia, most workers still have at most a primary education.

One may be tempted to think that higher education is a result, not a cause, of economic growth. Several studies have explored this issue. Hayami (1995:

TABLE 12.4

Percentages of Employed Persons by Educational Attainment:
Six East Asian Countries, Two Recent Decades[a]

Country and year	Total	Less than primary	Primary	Junior high	Senior high	Junior college	College+
Japan							
1960	100.0	0.9	69.2		23.1	3.2	3.5
1990	100.0	0.0	25.8		47.9	9.4	15.6
South Korea							
1980	100.0	51.5		20.1	21.7	6.7	
1995	100.0	21.4		16.3	43.5	18.8	
Taiwan							
1967	100.0	22.2	53.8	11.8	8.4	3.9	
1995	100.0	3.3	22.8	20.1	33.2	11.8	8.8
Singapore							
1975	100.0	34.8	31.8	23.9	6.8		2.3
1995	100.0	11.4	24.8	30.4	20.1		13.4
Thailand							
1971	100.0	14.4	80.7	3.3	0.4		0.5
1995	100.0	4.2	73.8	8.9	6.1		5.1
Indonesia							
1976	100.0	67.1	24.2	4.6	3.5	0.4	0.2
1994	100.0	35.3	37.5	11.4	13.2	1.5	1.2

SOURCES: For Japan, Japan SB (various years), *Population Census of Japan* for 1960 and 1990. For South Korea, ROK NSO (selected years), *Annual Report on the Economically Active Population Survey* for 1985 and 1995. For Taiwan, ROC DGBAS (various years), *Yearbook of Manpower Survey Statistics.* For Singapore, ROS MOL (various years), *Singapore Yearbook of Labour Statistics* for 1976, and ROS MOL (1997). For Thailand, Thailand NSO (various years), *Report of the Labor Force Survey* for July–September 1971 (round 2) and August 1995 (round 3). For Indonesia, Indonesia CBS (1976 and 1994).

[a]Percentages in cells that straddle two levels of educational attainment represent the percentages of persons employed in those two levels combined. For example, in Japan in 1960, 69.2% of employed persons had completed primary or junior high school.

49) suggested that the positive correlation between education and income levels observed across countries is due to mutual causation. Barro (1997: 19), who obtained regression results from a panel study of about 100 countries observed from 1960 to 1990, reported "a significantly positive effect on growth" from secondary and higher levels of schooling for males age 25 and older. Male primary schooling and female education, however, were not significantly related to subsequent growth, at least in a direct way. More study is needed on this complex issue.

Human resources are allocated to various jobs through labor markets, including internal (within-firm) ones. If an allocation is efficient, an economy can enjoy maximum outputs, even given fixed amounts of inputs and technology. In addition to the quality of human resources, the World Bank (1993a) emphasized the flexibility of labor markets to achieve efficient allocation. This is a broad topic, ranging from an economy-wide level to a microeconomic (firm or shop-floor) level and from wage determination within a spot market (which the World Bank and other researchers have emphasized) to more dynamic, institutional changes. In a survey of a wide range of labor market studies in Asia, for example, Manning and Pang (1990: 71) stated that "in contrast to patterns in several African and Latin American countries, labor markets in the [East Asian] region appear to be fairly free of labour market distortions."

Two points should be added here. The first point is about the significance of the work force's age structure. An abundant supply of young workers probably made the industrial transformation of the successful Asian economies easier. For example, Kim and Topel (1995: 241) observed in a study on South Korea that "almost all intersectoral mobility occurs among young workers and new entrants to the labor force. . . . They account for virtually all the growth in manufacturing employment, and it appears that their numbers are large enough to arbitrage intersectoral wage differences." Japan's experience is similar. The second point concerns the changes that occur within the urban industrial sector. As wages in that sector rise, industrial firms must adapt to the new situation. That is the topic of the next three sections.

Changes in Comparative Advantage and the Need for Structural Change

As labor productivity continues to increase, wages must eventually rise. Krugman (1994a: 116) observed that "economic history offers no example of a country that experienced long-term productivity growth without a roughly equal rise in real wages." East Asia is no exception. Figure 12.1 shows upward trends in hourly wages within the manufacturing sectors of the United States and five East Asian economies. Here, the exchange rates used to convert to US dollars are market rates, not purchasing-power parity rates, because the focus is on the production costs of firms, not the living standards of consumers. Although the definitions of wages and work hours and the survey coverage vary somewhat among these countries, the trend and level for each country are clear.

Since the 1960s Japan has experienced a much faster increase in its manufacturing wages than the United States; and probably the Japanese wage level surpassed the US level in the early 1990s. Two periods of especially rapid wage increases in Japan were the early 1970s and the late 1980s. The immediate cause was a drastic appreciation of the yen, but over the long run the rise reflects an increase in the productivity of the Japanese export-manufacturing industries. South Korea, Taiwan, and Singapore, all NIEs, have similar trends and levels of wages. Their manufacturing wages rose especially rapidly in the

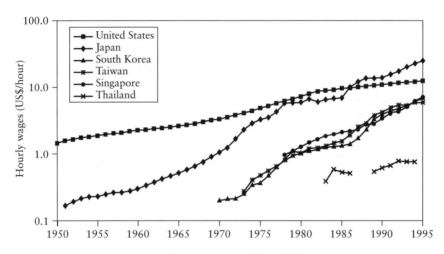

Sources and notes: For Japan, Japan MOL (1988, 1994, 1997); establishments with at least 30 employees are covered. For South Korea, ROK MOL (various years), *Yearbook of Labor Statistics* for 1986–95; and ROK NSO (selected years), *Major Statistics of Korean Economy* for 1977 and 1993; establishments with at least 10 employees are covered. For Taiwan, ROC DGBAS (various years), *Yearbook of Earnings and Productivity Statistics* for 1973–95; no lower limit on the establishment size covered, and exchange rates used in converting Taiwanese currency to US dollars are annual averages of market exchange rates and were taken from ROC DGBAS (various years), *Statistical Yearbook of the Republic of China* for 1996. For Singapore, ROS DOS (various years), *Yearbook of Statistics, Singapore* for 1988, 1994, and 1995; earnings are Central Provident Fund Board data from August of each year and include bonuses but exclude employer's CPF contributions; hours are in August for 1978–85, in June for 1986–87, and in September for 1988–95; those covered are private and public firms with at least 10 employees for 1978–87 and private firms with at least 25 employees for 1988–95. For Thailand, ILO (various years), *Year Book of Labour Statistics* for 1988 and 1996; earnings are average wage rates for normal or usual hours of work in March; the 1994 figure excludes public enterprises; hours for 1983–86 are based on labor force sample surveys, and hours for 1989–94, which exclude overtime, were calculated from weekly hours in March; exchange rates used in converting Thai currency to US dollars are annual averages of market exchange rates (official rates for Thailand) and were taken from IMF (selected years), *International Financial Statistics Yearbook* for 1996. For the United States, US DOL (1994) and US BOC (1996); only production workers are covered, and hours are paid hours.

FIGURE 12.1. Hourly Wages in Manufacturing: Five East Asian Countries and the United States, Recent Decades.

1970s and again beginning in the late 1980s. The wage gaps have narrowed substantially with those of the United States and somewhat with those of Japan. Thailand's wage increase rate is rather modest compared with the rates of the three NIEs. It is modest, too, in comparison with Thailand's economic growth rate. Although a shortage of skilled workers is a matter of concern in Thailand, the large agricultural work force, a source of the large influx to the modern manufacturing sector, may contribute to a overall wage increase.

Figure 12.2 compares working hours in the manufacturing sector of the five Asian economies and the United States. These trends are more diverse than those of wages. Japan and Taiwan show a decline over the long term, whereas no such obvious long-term trends are observed in the United States

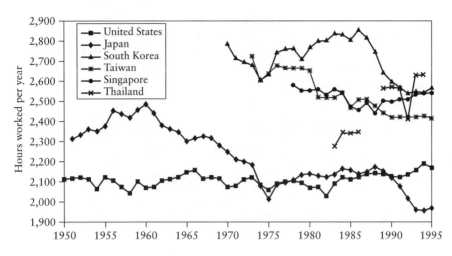

Sources and notes: Same as in Figure 12.1.

FIGURE 12.2. Yearly Hours Worked in Manufacturing: Five East Asian Countries and the United States, Recent Decades.

or Singapore. Korean working hours declined dramatically in the late 1980s but leveled off in the early 1990s. Like wage increases, the shortening of working hours can be seen as a dividend of higher productivity. Diversity in working hours indicates the various ways in which a productivity increase can be divided. The differences may stem from such factors as income levels, workers' preferences, the nature of production processes, and government regulations.

The fact that wages are rising rapidly or that working hours are becoming shorter in the Asian economies considered here does not necessarily mean that those economies are losing a competitive edge. If labor productivity rises in tandem with or more rapidly than the wage increase, labor costs will not increase. An increase in productivity can take various forms: more investment in physical capital (higher technology), the development of high-tech or niche products, improvements in human capital, organizational innovation in production and distribution systems, etc. If production factors such as capital and labor cannot be moved from one country to another, domestic production factors should be reallocated from labor-intensive sectors to capital-intensive or high-tech sectors. In a more realistic scenario in which capital and some managerial resources can be moved across borders there will be flows of direct investments from a high-wage country to a low-wage country. To ease domestic labor shortages, some countries may dare to introduce foreign workers, as in Singapore. All these developments have attracted researchers' attention to the issue of restructuring, that is, achieving the transformation from a labor-surplus economy to a labor-scarce economy [see, for example, Bauer (1992, 1995); Clark and Kim (1995) examined various ways that economies cope with restructuring and actual responses taken by firms in Asia's NIEs)].

Relationships among Population, Development, and Labor Markets

With these trends in mind I propose a simple hypothesis about the relationships among population, economic development, and labor markets. The hypothesis is summarized by the three stages, or regimes, modeled in Table 12.5.

TABLE 12.5

Relationships among Population, Development, and Labor Markets[a]

Characteristic of economy	Regime 1	Regime 2	Regime 3
Leading products or services	Cheap products	High-quality products	High-tech or "creative" products or services
Demographic structure	Abundant youth	Large middle-aged population	Large old-aged population
Work force structure	Many unskilled, cheap workers; few elite managers	Many motivated workers with higher skills	Few talented workers—and the rest?
Work organization	Demarcation; simple and strict hierarchy; mid-career hire (← rapid growth and general skills)	Less demarcation (← "intellectual" skills); hierarchical but participatory; internal promotion (← skill formation through on-the-job training)	Network or flexible organization?; mid-career hire (← general and rapidly changing skills?)
Wage level and structure	Generally low wages; high wages for a few; short-term incentives (e.g., piece-rate)	Generally high wages; equalization; long-term incentives (e.g., salary and periodic pay raise)	Generally high wages; toward inequality?; short-term incentives (e.g., performance-based pay)?
Labor turnover	High (← young work force and general skills)	Low (← older work force, specific skills, and development of long-term employment)	Increasing (← rapidly changing economic environment and general skills)?

[a] The left-pointing arrows signify the direction of causality.

Before and early in the demographic transition an economy has an expansive population pyramid. In such a population a high child-dependency ratio may be an obstacle to economic development. As fertility declines, that negative effect will be mitigated, and for a while the economy can enjoy an abundant supply of young workers (regime 1). This may make it possible for industries relying on cheap, unskilled labor to develop. The key concern of policymakers at this stage is labor absorption: How can a labor-abundant economy effectively utilize its human resources? The answer, in theory, is to develop labor-intensive industries. In practice, however, developing economies have had varied experiences with urban unemployment, rural underemployment, and underemployment in the urban informal sector. Japan, South Korea, Taiwan, and Singapore somehow succeeded in sustaining economic growth by relying initially on labor-intensive industries.

As an economy continues to grow rapidly, wages rise. This causes the economy to begin losing the competitive edge it has enjoyed by relying on its cheap work force (regime 2). To produce quality products that can be sold at higher prices, industries must enhance workers' skills. Doing that requires transforming work organizations and incentive systems. The key policy issue at this stage is restructuring.

Maintaining a clear demarcation between supervisors and shop-floor rank-and-file workers may be efficient under regime 1, but it is not efficient under regime 2. Even production workers must acquire high skill levels, and firms must provide enough incentives (for example, employment security, higher wages, and more chances of promotion) to keep their employees. Thus wage differentials by educational level and between white-collar and blue-collar workers should shrink as an economy moves from regime 1 to regime 2. Blue-collar workers are now expected to share some features of white-collar workers, such as higher motivation for advancement and the ability to perform more flexible job tasks (Koike's white collarization). Moreover, women, who are used as a source of cheap labor in many developing economies during regime 1, can command more equitable wages when the economies advance to regime 2.

Labor turnover rates will also change as the regime changes. Under regime 1 the skills of both production workers and elite managerial workers are not firm specific, and therefore workers face no impediments in moving from one company to another. Under regime 2, however, internal labor markets develop that are characterized by long-term employment and internal promotion. These developments tend to lower labor turnover rates. Aging of the work force will accelerate this tendency, because older workers are generally less mobile than young workers.

Regime 3 is an even more highly specialized labor market, modeled after the labor market found in the computer industry of Silicon Valley in California. It is characterized by high-tech products and services and by a flexible work force and loosely structured organizations. The key players in this regime are creative entrepreneurs and talented experts who support them. They will be young, although the economy as a whole may consist of a large elderly population.

Regimes 1 and 2 mirror the historical evolution of the Japanese labor market, which appears to have had two major transformations, the first around 1920 and the second around 1960. Before 1920 the labor market was characterized by regime 1. After 1920 some traits of regime 2 began to be evident, but they did not prevail until about 1960. Since the 1960s, regime 2 traits have become more and more evident. It is premature at the moment to judge whether Japan is experiencing regime 3.

Early in the 20th century, when Japan's modern industries were still new, one of the main tasks of personnel managers was to reduce labor turnover among production workers. By 1920 various measures had gradually come into effect in the large heavy industries. Those measures included plant-level consultation committees, in-house training, tenure-based bonuses, internal promotion, a periodic pay raise system in accordance with promotion, severance pay differentiated by tenure and reasons for separation, and mandatory retirement (Hyodo 1971: 404–46). Until the end of World War II, however, sharp distinctions were made between blue-collar and white-collar workers. According to Hyodo (1971: 471–9) and Odaka (1984: 110), 1920 also marked the emergence of a dual structure by firm size, that is, wage differentials of comparable workers between large and small industrial firms.

After World War II unions burgeoned, and in many cases blue-collar and white-collar workers joined forces to organize them (Nimura 1994). Various policies that had discriminated against blue-collar workers were abolished. It was not until the 1960s, however, that the change in payment method for blue-collar workers, from a piece rate or hourly wage to a fixed compensation, or salary, was completed. According to Nimura (1994: 69), the reasons for this change were union demands and the fact that high school graduates, who had earlier been predominantly white-collar workers, were now being hired as production workers. Two other changes affecting workers that began in the late 1950s were job rotation on the shop floor of large steel plants and multi-machine operation at large machinery plants (Koike 1997: 99). These new practices offered production workers broad on-the-job training. By the 1970s they prevailed at most workshops in large firms and at some small firms (Koike 1997: 108).

Two caveats about the model that I have proposed are in order. First, each of the three regimes described by the model focuses on the key sector of an economy. Obviously, at any time in its evolution an economy has various sectors and many different kinds of industries and firms; and even in highly developed economies, some sector will depend on cheap, unskilled labor. Second, the model is not intended to describe every industrializing economy.

As I have indicated, my characterization of regimes 1 and 2 is based on Japan's experience. Labor markets, even in developed economies, vary widely in their characteristics and historical evolution (Piore and Sabel 1984; Saito 1997, ch. 5). Indeed, recently some observers have argued that Japan's current employment system, described by regime 2, is no longer effective and should be transformed into something more like regime 3. I would not presume to suggest that regime 3 is a model that Japan should adopt, nor am I suggesting that other developing economies should follow Japan's example. My point is that it may be instructive to examine whether the patterns of labor market evolution in Asia's other successful economies are similar to the pattern that evolved in Japan.

Wage Structures

Most comparative studies of wage structures in Asian countries have focused on cross-country differences at a single point in time.[3] It is instructive, however, to add a dynamic aspect to the research agenda. My own discussion of this topic concentrates on Japan, South Korea, Taiwan, and, only peripherally, Singapore.

Figure 12.3 shows wage differentials between male blue-collar and white-collar workers in manufacturing over time in Japan, South Korea, and Taiwan. In Japan the wage differential shrank appreciably in the 1950s and 1960s. Since then it has been rather stable, although recently blue-collar wages have shown a slight downward trend. There are no corresponding data for the period before World War II, but it has often been noted that wage differentials between blue-collar and white-collar workers were much larger before the postwar era. For example, in 1936 at Hitachi's factory blue-collar wages were 48% of white-collar wages (that is, of white-collar workers who had graduated from vocational secondary schools) at ages 20–24, 46% at ages 30–34, and 29% at ages 40–44 (Sugayama 1989, table 5).

The most striking trends shown in Figure 12.3, however, are the sharp reductions in wage differentials in South Korea and Taiwan. In South Korea blue-collar wages were just 51% of white-collar wages in 1978 but rose to 77% by 1990. The narrowing of the wage gap in Taiwan probably started in the late 1970s, and it continued until recently. By 1995 blue-collar workers were being paid 73% of white-collar workers' wages, close to Japan's blue-collar level of 79%.

As Figure 12.4 shows, the proportion of blue-collar workers among male manufacturing workers declined over the past several decades in Japan, South Korea, and Taiwan. This trend suggests both that the labor productivity of blue-collar workers increased more rapidly than that of white-collar workers and that manufacturing products have become more dependent on a

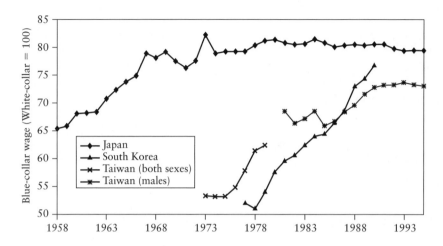

Sources and notes: For Japan, Japan MOL (various years), *Wage Structure Survey* for each year. For South Korea, ROK MOL (various years), *Yearbook of Labor Statistics* for each year, but the original source is the ROK MOL *Wage Structure Survey* (previously *Occupational Wage Survey*); white-collar is the sum of the occupational categories of professional, administrative, clerical, sales, and services, and blue-collar is production workers. For Taiwan, ROC DGBAS (various years), *Yearbook of Earnings and Productivity Statistics* for each year; white-collar is *zhiyuan*, and blue-collar is *gongren*.

FIGURE 12.3. Index of Monthly Wage Differentials Between Blue-collar and White-collar Male Workers Employed in Manufacturing: Japan, South Korea, and Taiwan, Recent Decades (White-collar = 100).

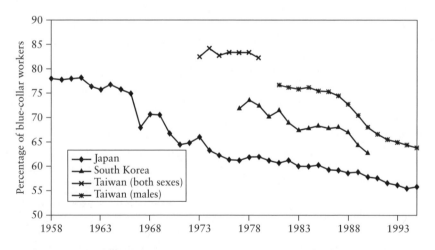

Sources and notes: Same as in Figure 12.3.

FIGURE 12.4. Percentage of Blue-collar Workers among (Male) Manufacturing Workers: Japan, South Korea, and Taiwan, Recent Decades.

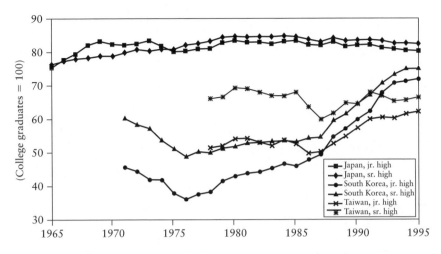

Sources: For Japan, Japan MOL (various years), *Wage Structure Survey*. For South Korea, ROK MOL (various years), *Yearbook of Labor Statistics*, but original source is the ROK MOL *Wage Structure Survey* (previously *Occupational Wage Survey*). For Taiwan, ROC DGBAS (various years), *Report on the Manpower Utilization Survey*.

FIGURE 12.5. Index of Monthly Wage Differentials by Education for Males in All Industries: Japan, South Korea, and Taiwan, Recent Decades (College Graduates = 100).

nonproduction work force. The proportion of blue-collar workers is lowest in Japan (55.8% in 1995) followed by South Korea (62.7% in 1990) and Taiwan (63.8% in 1995).

Wage differentials by education for male workers in all industries have remained small and fairly stable in Japan since the 1960s (Figure 12.5). The wages of senior high school graduates were 76.3% of those of college graduates in 1965, but by 1995 they had risen slightly, to 82.4%. As was the case with wage differentials by occupation, wage differentials by education have also shrunk in South Korea and Taiwan. In South Korea the wage index of senior high school graduates was 48.7 (against 100 for college graduates) in 1976. Then it started to increase, reaching 75.2 in 1995. The sharpest increase occurred in the late 1980s. The narrowing process can be observed not only between senior high school graduates and college graduates but also between junior high school graduates and senior high school graduates. Taiwan's process has been a bit uneven. During the early 1980s, the gap between college and high school graduates actually widened somewhat, but since 1987 it has narrowed and so has the gap between senior and junior high school graduates.

As Figure 12.6 indicates, wage differentials between males and females have narrowed in recent years in Japan, South Korea, Taiwan, and Singa-

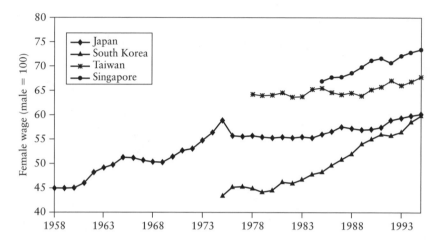

Sources: For Japan, Japan MOL (various years), *Wage Structure Survey*. For South Korea, ROK MOL (various years), *Yearbook of Labor Statistics*, but original source is the ROK MOL *Wage Structure Survey* (previously *Occupational Wage Survey*). For Taiwan, ROC DGBAS (various years), *Report on the Manpower Utilization Survey*. For Singapore, ROS MOL (1996).

FIGURE 12.6. Index of Monthly Wage Differentials by Sex for All Industries: Japan, South Korea, Taiwan, and Singapore, Recent Decades (Males = 100).

pore. All four countries show a narrowing trend, but the speed and the most recent gap levels differ. The trend was particularly rapid in Singapore and South Korea. By 1995 the wage gap was smallest in Singapore, with female wages being 73.5% of male wages, followed by Taiwan (67.8%), Japan (60.2%), and South Korea (59.9%). In fact, by 1995 the wage gap levels in Singapore and Taiwan were no lower than in many Western countries (Blau and Kahn 1995, figure 3.1). The relatively small wage gaps in Singapore and Taiwan may have something to do with their patterns of labor force participation rates, which show no trough (see Table 12.3). The rapid narrowing process in Singapore and South Korea may be related to a large increase in the middle-aged female work force of both countries (see Table 12.4). Of course, in both cases the causality can run in either direction.

In Table 12.6, which shows male wage differentials by age in Japan and South Korea, we see that wages rise with age, especially among college graduates. The wages of college graduates in the 50–59-year age group are more than twice those of workers age 20–29. Japanese high school graduates also have an upward-sloping wage profile by age, although it is flatter than that of college graduates. Korean high school graduates had an upward-sloping profile in the 1980s, but their profile assumed a moderate inverted U shape in the 1990s.

Indeed, among the striking features of Table 12.6 are the trends in wage differentials by age. Among Korean high school graduates wage differentials

TABLE 12.6

Male Wage Differentials by Age (20–29 Wage = 100) and Percentage of Workers by Age (in Parentheses): High School and College Graduates, Japan and South Korea, Recent Decades[a]

Country, educational level, and year	Age					
	<20	20–29	30–39	40–49	50–59	60+
Japan, high school graduates						
1980	71.0	100.0	141.0	164.2	158.8	110.8
	(4.5)	(30.8)	(34.8)	(20.2)	(7.7)	(1.9)
1985	75.7	100.0	142.8	174.1	167.2	114.7
	(4.0)	(26.3)	(32.7)	(24.2)	(10.9)	(1.9)
1990	74.3	100.0	136.8	166.5	166.0	108.5
	(3.8)	(24.9)	(25.8)	(27.9)	(14.9)	(2.6)
1995	75.4	100.0	132.3	160.4	170.1	114.5
	(2.8)	(24.6)	(22.9)	(27.3)	(18.8)	(3.5)
Japan, college graduates						
1980	–	100.0	153.0	212.5	236.8	174.6
		(35.3)	(39.6)	(18.6)	(5.2)	(1.3)
1985	–	100.0	149.8	204.2	232.3	184.8
		(32.1)	(39.5)	(20.0)	(7.2)	(1.3)
1990	–	100.0	141.9	192.0	221.7	172.6
		(29.2)	(35.2)	(24.4)	(9.5)	(1.7)
1995	–	100.0	141.7	185.4	217.1	174.2
		(26.3)	(34.2)	(25.8)	(11.4)	(2.2)
South Korea, high school graduates						
1980	68.4	100.0	143.6	166.2	195.0	214.0
	(3.9)	(46.7)	(33.8)	(12.2)	(2.9)	(0.5)
1985	63.4	100.0	143.0	168.2	176.6	216.3
	(2.7)	(43.9)	(35.9)	(13.5)	(3.4)	(0.6)
1990	71.7	100.0	132.2	151.2	144.2	134.9
	(2.5)	(38.2)	(32.2)	(15.0)	(4.8)	(0.5)
1995	77.6	100.0	131.5	147.9	137.0	112.7
	(1.6)	(32.3)	(38.5)	(18.5)	(7.5)	(1.4)
South Korea, college graduates						
1980	–	100.0	145.1	191.4	226.3	238.0
	–	(24.1)	(46.7)	(22.0)	(6.3)	(1.0)
1985	–	100.0	152.5	204.7	224.7	226.0
	–	(23.6)	(44.6)	(22.4)	(7.9)	(1.4)
1990	–	100.0	144.2	206.3	224.9	231.3
	–	(30.1)	(44.3)	(17.2)	(7.1)	(1.3)
1995	–	100.0	141.4	200.1	234.3	228.6
	–	(25.1)	(49.3)	(17.0)	(6.9)	(1.7)

SOURCES: For Japan, Japan MOL (various years), *Wage Structure Survey*. For South Korea, ROK MOL (various years), *Wage Structure Survey* for 1995, and ROK MOL (various years), *Occupational Wage Survey* for 1980, 1985, and 1990.

[a]Wages are monthly wages, including overtime pay but not bonuses. Numbers in parentheses are the percentages of workers in each age group in each year.

by age have shrunk substantially since 1985, whereas among Korean college graduates they have been relatively stable. This difference combined with the fact that Korean wage differentials by education shrank appreciably in the late 1980s suggests that younger high school graduates (those in their 20s and 30s) gained most in relative wages. Although the proportion of younger high school graduates declined somewhat between 1985 and 1990, it is doubtful that a change in labor force size alone can explain such a large change in relative wages. Japanese college graduates and to some extent high school graduates have also experienced a flattening of the wage profile. Changes in work force size by age may be at least partially responsible.

Discussion

The analysis indicates that wage differentials by occupation, education, sex, and age generally narrowed between the mid-1970s and the mid-1990s in Japan, South Korea, and Taiwan. Particularly striking has been the narrowing of wage gaps between blue-collar and white-collar workers and between college and high school graduates in South Korea and Taiwan. In contrast, as other observers have noted, wage gaps within these two groups *widened* in the United States during the 1980s (Freeman and Katz 1995: 6–9). South Korea and Taiwan, therefore, seem to present a mirror image of the US wage profile.

The narrowing of wage gaps between blue-collar and white-collar workers and between high school and college graduates in South Korea and Taiwan seems consistent with the conceptual framework presented in Table 12.6. As an economy becomes more dependent on more expensive, higher-quality products and less dependent on inexpensive, lower-quality products, production workers must upgrade their skills, probably through on-the-job training. If they do so more rapidly than white-collar workers, it is not surprising that their wages rise more quickly. If on-the-job training has a more important role than formal schooling in upgrading their skills, wage differentials by education will also shrink. Smaller wage gaps in turn may induce cooperative and participatory work attitudes, but one must observe several caveats and consider other explanations for the shrinking wage gap before jumping to that conclusion.

The first consideration is the question of data reliability. Although the Taiwanese data I have used on wage differentials by education and sex come from household surveys, other data are available from surveys of firms; in those surveys wages are reported from wage rosters. The wage data taken from wage rosters probably contain fewer reporting errors than the data reported by individuals, but the definitions of wages are basically consistent between the two types of surveys. Furthermore, the Japanese and Korean governments' surveys of wage structures use large sample sizes and similar questionnaire designs. I believe, therefore, that the data I have used are reliable.

Second, it may be argued that the wage differentials discussed in the previous section do not control for enough covariates. For example, white-collar workers and college graduates tend to be younger because younger cohorts are increasingly so; that is, observed occupational wage gaps may well include age effects. Given an upward-sloping age-wage profile, the wage gaps probably underestimate the gaps that are measured by controlling for age. To cope with this problem, my colleague Young-Soo Shin and I estimated simple wage equations by using firm-level data from Wage Structure Surveys conducted in Japan in 1980 and 1993 (Japan MOL, various years) and in South Korea in 1983 and 1993 (ROK MOL, various years). Our results indicate that in South Korea the gap between blue-collar and white-collar wages shrank in large and middle-size firms even after we controlled for such factors as education, age, duration of job tenure, and rank, whereas in Japan the gap widened. In large Korean firms (those with 1,000 or more employees), for example, male blue-collar wages were 21% lower than male white-collar wages in 1983, with education, age, job tenure, and rank controlled, but this gap was reduced to 16% by 1993. Wage gaps by education also shrank, especially among younger Korean workers. By controlling for job tenure and rank, for example, Shin and I found that in large Korean firms the hourly wage difference between college graduates and high school graduates narrowed between 1983 and 1993: from 68% to 39% at age 30, from 99% to 75% at age 40, and from 139% to 120% at age 50. We found similar trends for other firm sizes [details of the summary statistics and ordinary least-squares estimation results can be found in Okunishi (1997, appendix tables)].

A third caveat is that unobservable traits, such as innate ability, may have important effects on labor productivity and wages. If higher education has no effect on a worker's productive ability, as posited by the screening hypothesis (which posits that education does not enhance productivity but merely sorts out able workers), and if the distribution of innate ability is the same over generations, then rising college enrollment rates imply a degradation of the average ability of college graduates. To explore this idea, Table 12.7 illustrates the wage premiums and the proportion of college graduates in South Korea's total work force. Looking at the numbers diagonally from the lower left to the upper right, we see a variation between cohorts at the same career stage over time. Looking at the numbers horizontally, we see a variation in the same cohort over time, and looking at the numbers vertically, we see a cross-sectional variation between cohorts in the same year.

By observing the diagonal variation, we find that those entering the labor market in their 20s and 30s are increasingly likely to be college graduates and to receive smaller wage premiums as the years pass. This finding is at

TABLE 12.7

Wage Premiums and Worker Ratios (in Parentheses) of Male College Graduates, by Age Cohort: South Korea, 1980–95[a]

Age in 1980	1980	1985	1990	1995
5–9	–	–	–	1.085
				(0.037)
10–14	–	–	1.280	1.029
			(0.033)	(0.304)
15–19	–	1.497	1.152	1.084
		(0.021)	(0.242)	(0.343)
20–24	1.723	1.357	1.241	1.205
	(0.015)	(0.134)	(0.233)	(0.254)
25–29	1.417	1.431	1.434	1.348
	(0.140)	(0.186)	(0.195)	(0.210)
30–34	1.440	1.592	1.576	1.499
	(0.196)	(0.193)	(0.186)	(0.188)
35–39	1.641	1.702	1.700	1.726
	(0.203)	(0.192)	(0.170)	(0.154)
40–44	1.727	1.804	1.829	1.875
	(0.201)	(0.196)	(0.172)	(0.164)
45–49	1.805	1.770	1.865	2.016
	(0.199)	(0.225)	(0.207)	(0.176)
50–54	1.863	1.889	1.906	–
	(0.203)	(0.231)	(0.236)	
55–59	1.913	1.716	–	–
	(0.205)	(0.245)		
60+	1.775	–	–	–
	(0.206)			

SOURCES: ROK MOL (various years) *Wage Structure Survey* for 1995; ROK MOL (various years) *Occupational Wage Survey* for 1980, 1985, and 1990.

[a] Wage premiums are the wage ratios of college graduates to the total of all education categories in each corresponding cell. Wages are monthly wages, including overtime pay but not bonuses. Numbers in parentheses are the proportions of college graduates to the total number of workers in each corresponding cell.

least consistent with the hypothesis of college graduate degradation. Another way of testing the hypothesis is to observe the horizontal variation. If college graduates represent the upper part of a time-invariant ability distribution and if wages are determined mainly by ability, then the wage premiums of college graduates should be constant in the same cohort over time.[4] This pattern holds roughly in several cohorts, particularly in the 35–39 and 40–44 age cohorts in 1980. But college graduates in some younger cohorts experienced a decline in wage premiums, especially from 1990 to 1995. Therefore other factors are probably at work.

A fourth caveat is that the observed phenomenon of narrowing wage gaps by occupation and education may be explained by simple demand-supply theories that do not assume quality changes among workers. For example, the supply of white-collar workers and college graduates may have increased more than the demand for them. An excess demand for blue-collar workers and those with less schooling may have arisen as a result of an economy's greater specialization in labor-intensive products, which the theory of factor-price equalization in trade suggests (Krugman and Obstfeld 1994, ch. 4). Furthermore, because workers increasingly shun blue-collar jobs, higher wages may need to be paid to attract them to such jobs. Among these possible explanations, that of factor-price equalization is implausible because the proportion of blue-collar workers and those with lower schooling has been declining, and it is counterfactual in that the Korean and Taiwanese economies are becoming more dependent on unskilled labor.[5] In their econometric study of Korean wage structures, Kim and Topel (1995) reached a conclusion consistent with this view. They stated that the change in relative wages "comes from the supply side—changing the stock of human capital via education—rather than from industry shifts that could change the relative demand for skills" (p. 255).

Finally, an egalitarian ideology pushed by unions may have contributed to the narrowing of the wage gap between different classes of workers. A widely shared view in Japan is that the union movement after World War II played a key role in reducing the wage differentials between blue-collar and white-collar workers (Nimura 1994). Similarly, in South Korea the Democratization Declaration of June 1987 (Park and Lee 1995) and in Taiwan the lifting of martial law in 1987 (Lee 1995) caused union activities to burgeon. Such big bang explanations may seem at first glance to have validity, but they do not explain why the pressures for freer union activities became stronger before those reforms or what the source was of union bargaining power, or why the changes have been rather continuous and sustained (see Figures 12.3 and 12.5). If equal compensation were assured regardless of skill level or work performance, there would be no incentive for workers to improve their skills or performance. This explanation thus seems at odds with the spectacular performance of the East Asian economies.

Labor Turnover Rates

When discussing Table 12.5, I conjectured that labor turnover rates would be high when an economy was characterized by cheap products and a young labor force but that turnover rates would decline as the importance of high-quality products increased and the labor force matured. Figure 12.7 illustrates this progression, depicting the trends of labor turnover rates in Japan, South Korea, Taiwan, and Singapore. All the rates are based on similar surveys of establishments, although the sizes of the establishments covered differ somewhat among the four countries. The rates are averages of accession and separation rates per year. The reason for taking an average of the two rates is graphical simplicity. Accession and separation rates have similar lev-

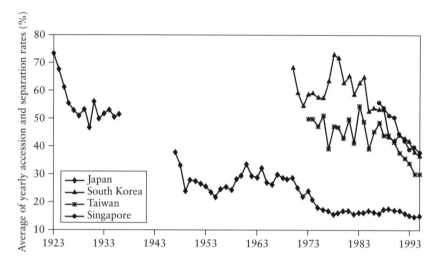

Sources and notes: For Japan, for 1923–36, Japan CLMHR (1959); for 1947–95, Japan MOL (various years), *Monthly Labor Survey*; establishments with at least 30 employees are covered. For South Korea, ROK MOL (various years), *Yearbook of Labor Statistics* for 1996 and previous issues based on ROK MOL's monthly labor survey; establishments with at least 10 employees are covered. For Taiwan, ROC DGBAS (various years), *Yearbook of Earnings and Productivity Statistics* for 1995 and previous issues; no lower limit on the establishment size covered. For Singapore, ROS MOL (various years), *Singapore Yearbook of Labour Statistics* for 1995; private-sector establishments with at least 25 employees are covered; separation ("resignation" in the original source) is limited to termination of employment initiated by an employee.

FIGURE 12.7. Labor Turnover Rates in Manufacturing: Japan, South Korea, Taiwan, and Singapore, Recent Decades. Turnover rates are the average of yearly accession and separation rates. Yearly rates are calculated as the average monthly rates multiplied by 12.

els and trends, although the accession rate exceeds the separation rate when employment is rising.

Figure 12.7 has at least two striking features. First, in South Korea, Taiwan, and Singapore labor turnover rates have been decreasing since the late 1980s. Second, the levels are similar among the three countries, although the rate in Taiwan is lower than in South Korea or Singapore. Their rates in 1995 were only slightly higher than Japan's rate in the 1960s. This is rather surprising because the economies and labor markets of the four countries are often characterized quite differently. For example, South Korea, Taiwan, and Singapore have not provided lifetime employment, as has Japan; the Korean economy is dominated by conglomerates (*chaebol*); in Taiwan small and medium-size firms have had an active role; and in Singapore a large share of the economy is controlled by multinational corporations [see, for example, Clark and Kim (1995)].

As for reasons for the decreasing labor turnover, one possibility is that it is due to the slowdown of economic growth. That is not the case in Singapore. In South Korea and Taiwan the growth rates did decline in the early 1990s, but they were still as high as those in the early 1980s. Therefore economic growth rates alone cannot explain this change. Some structural change must have occurred.

The turnover rates based on establishment surveys tend to be higher than those based on surveys of individual workers or households, which ask merely whether a person changed jobs during a particular year or not. In an establishment survey a worker who moved from company A to company B and then from company B to company C in the same year will be counted four times (separation from companies A and B and accession to companies B and C). Table 12.8 illustrates labor turnover rates by age and occupation, based on household surveys in Japan and Singapore. In Japan the turnover rate in 1982 was among the lowest recorded in the series of Japanese Employment Status Surveys begun in 1956. In 1997, the most recent year for which figures are available, it was one of the highest.

As expected, the turnover rates shown in Table 12.8 are lower than those plotted in Figure 12.7 for both Japan and Singapore. Furthermore, the tendency for younger workers to be more mobile than older workers is common to both countries, but there are at least two major differences between Japan and Singapore. First, the turnover rates of prime-age workers are higher in Singapore than in Japan, and, second, the turnover rates of white-collar workers are higher in Singapore. The turnover rates of blue-collar workers were higher in Singapore than in Japan in 1982 but identical in the two countries in the early 1990s.

Conclusion

The high rates of economic growth experienced by the six East Asian countries during the two to three decades before the late 1990s were due in part to rapid labor force growth, especially during the earlier part of that period. Population growth rather than changes in labor force participation rates contributed most to total labor force growth. Nonetheless, large increases in the female participation rate, particularly in South Korea, Taiwan, and Singapore, caused the proportion of women in the work force to rise. Furthermore, the sex wage gaps in the three countries narrowed substantially.

Although international migration and changes in the participation rate can affect the age composition of the work force, population composition has had the greatest effect on the labor force in each of the countries considered here. Japan is ahead of other Asian countries in the aging of its population and labor force. It already faces serious challenges associated with

TABLE 12.8

Labor Turnover Rates (%) and Percentages of Workers (in Parentheses)
by Age and Occupation: Japan, 1982 and 1997, and Singapore, 1995

Category	Japan[a]		Singapore,[b] 1995
	1982	1997	
All categories	2.6	4.3	6.2
	(100.0)	(100.0)	(100.0)
By age			
15–24	5.6	9.8	7.7
	(12.2)	(12.2)	(16.0)
25–34	3.6	6.6	8.3
	(24.1)	(20.4)	(32.5)
35–44	2.0	3.9	5.3
	(24.8)	(19.5)	(29.0)
45–54	1.4	2.5	3.7
	(21.3)	(24.4)	(15.7)
55+	1.5	1.9	2.7
	(17.1)	(23.5)	(6.8)
By occupation			
Professional and technical	1.9	3.1	7.8
	(9.2)	(12.8)	(23.1)
Managerial	1.4	2.1	5.0
	(4.3)	(3.4)	(12.8)
Clerical	2.7	4.4	9.0
	(17.7)	(20.3)	(12.9)
Sales and service	3.2	5.7	6.4
	(22.3)	(23.6)	(12.3)
Agriculture, fishery, forestry	1.0	0.8	3.3
	(9.8)	(5.4)	(0.1)
Production, construction, transport, communications	3.0	4.5	5.1
	(36.5)	(33.7)	(34.6)
Not classifiable	3.5	9.0	1.7
	(0.2)	(0.8)	(4.2)

SOURCE: For Japan, Japan SB (selected years), *Employment Status Survey* for 1982 and 1997. For Singapore, ROS DOS (1996).

[a]The number of those who changed jobs during the previous year divided by the number of those currently working. Numbers in parentheses are the percentages of workers currently working.

[b]The number of those who changed jobs during the previous two years divided by the number of those currently working, then divided further by two. Numbers in parentheses are the percentages of workers currently working.

aging, such as maintaining the fiscal balance of its social security programs and resolving issues of employment, wages, and productivity of older workers, especially in large firms.

In all six countries the work force has become more and more highly educated, although it is not easy to judge whether higher education caused economic growth or the other way around. Urbanward migration and changes in the industrial composition of the work force from agriculture to manufacturing and services have also been widely observed. Probably an abundant supply of young workers made the industrial transformation easier in the earlier period of economic growth.

As the rapid growth continued, Japan and the Asian NIEs, particularly South Korea and Taiwan, experienced substantial wage increases, which caused them to lose the competitive edge they had when producing cheap products. They have had to upgrade the skills of their work force, especially those of production workers, so that high-quality, value-added products could be produced. The consequence of this transformation has been a narrowing of wage differentials between blue-collar and white-collar workers (white collarization), narrower wage differentials by education, and lower labor turnover rates. Of course, other explanations of the narrowing wage differentials besides white collarization are possible, such as simple supply and demand or an institutional explanation. Probing their causes is the key to a deeper understanding of the rapid economic development achieved by the six countries during the period considered here.

The Role Played by Labor Migration in the Asian Economic Miracle

PHILIP L. MARTIN

The Mediterranean is the ocean of the past; the Atlantic, the ocean of the present; the Pacific, the ocean of the future.
—John Hay, Secretary of State, 1898–1905 [quoted by Feinstein (1996)]

INTERNATIONAL LABOR MIGRATION has played a minor role in the economic growth and population changes of East and Southeast Asia since 1970. In 1995 there were 3.7 million foreign workers in the 138 million–strong labor forces of the 7 major East and Southeast Asian immigration destinations—Japan, South Korea, Taiwan, Hong Kong, Singapore, Malaysia, and Thailand. Foreigners thus constituted 2.7% of these countries' labor forces.

Most rich Asian nations have proportionately fewer foreign workers than do industrial democracies in North America and Western Europe, where 5–12% of the work force and population are typically foreigners or are foreign born. No East Asian nation is generally open to immigration. Migration for employment is likely to increase in the region if rapid economic growth resumes, and this migration will continue to be largely of the type not legally recognized as consisting of foreign workers. Fears of uncontrolled mass migration from sending countries, which are generally more populous than the receiving countries, and the prospect of a migration hump if migration channels are opened wider as economic integration proceeds are likely to keep most foreign workers in the categories of students, trainees, and unauthorized workers.

Decisions made in destination countries will largely shape the migration patterns of East Asia. The strategy of such nations as Japan, South Korea, and Taiwan seems to be to avoid the mistakes of Western Europe during the guest worker period of the 1960s, when foreign workers settled with their families. If East Asian nations opened their doors to guest workers to sustain rapid economic growth, the number of guest workers could rise quickly, and that could retard wage inflation and generate pension contributions for retirees. Faced with much larger numbers of guest workers, East Asia would probably pioneer such economic instruments as employer or worker taxes or levies to ensure that the guest workers remained temporary additions to the labor force and not permanent residents.

This chapter has three parts. In the first part I review global and regional migration patterns in East and Southeast Asia. In the second part I review migration policies and issues in the six countries that are the focus of this volume. In the third section I focus on the relationships among economic growth, economic integration, and migration in the region. I emphasize that front-door migration for employment is more likely to be the exception than the rule in Asia. The migration discussion focuses on how to manage the migration hump as economic growth continues and integration proceeds. Guest workers promise the benefits of additional workers without the cost of additional residents, and so in the final section I consider how Asian guest worker programs are likely to evolve.

Global and Regional Migration Patterns

Migration is as old as humankind wandering in search of food, but international migration for temporary employment abroad is a recent development. The system of nation-states, passports, border controls, and visas was developed fully only after World War I, and it was not until after World War II that countries in Western Europe and North America began large-scale programs to admit temporary foreign workers.

In 1990 there were 120 million foreigners and foreign-born residents in 214 countries and territories for which the United Nations collects data. (The UN statistics on foreign populations summarize data provided by governments on persons born outside a territory—that is, the foreign-born—and persons born in the territory who are considered foreigners.) This means that 2.3% of the world's population consists of international migrants residing in another country for 12 months or more. The number of international migrants has kept pace with worldwide population growth. According to the United Nations [published data tables for 1994, cited by Martin and Widgren (1996)], there were 76 million migrants in 1965, 84 million in 1975, 106 million in 1985, and 120 million in 1990.

The UN data distinguish between developed and developing countries. Developed countries are defined as including those in Europe, the countries of the former Soviet Union, the United States and Canada, and Japan, Australia, and New Zealand. Most of the growth in foreign populations between 1965 and 1990 occurred in developed countries, where the total foreign population almost doubled, from 30 million to 54 million. In contrast, the foreign population of East and Southeast Asia declined from 7.9 million to 7.6 million over the same period. In 1990 East and Southeast Asia had about 6% of the world's migrants. Within the region only Hong Kong (with 2.3 million migrants) and Taiwan (with 1.5 million) had 1 million or more migrants. Together, these two destinations accounted for half the region's 7.6 million foreign-born persons in 1990. Most of the migrants included in the UN data for Hong Kong and Taiwan arrived from the Chinese mainland in the late 1940s; migrant workers who arrived in the 1990s are not included.

No estimate is available of the global stock or flow of migrant workers. On the basis of government and press reports, in 1997 the International Labour Office estimated that in 1995 there were 36–42 million nonnationals in 200 countries worldwide, including 11–13 million in Europe (9 million in Western Europe), 8 million in North America (there are 13 million foreign-born workers in the United States, but many of them are naturalized US citizens and thus are not counted as migrant workers), 6–7 million in Africa, 6 million in the Arab states, 3–5 million in Central and South America, and 2–3 million in South and East Asia (*Migration News*, June 1997). The worldwide labor force in 1995 numbered 2,600 million, of whom foreigners accounted for roughly 1.5%.

Table 13.1, based on government and press reports, summarizes estimates of the number of migrant workers in the seven major labor-importing countries in East and Southeast Asia in 1995–96. The table shows that among the 137 million workers in Japan, South Korea, Taiwan, Hong Kong, Singapore, Malaysia, and Thailand, 3.8 million (2.7%) were foreign workers. Another estimate (Silverman 1996: 61) gave a migrant worker population in 1996 of 500,000 foreign workers in Japan, 78,000 in South Korea, 311,000 in Hong Kong, 240,000 in Taiwan, 600,000 in Thailand, 1.1 million in Malaysia, and 200,000 in Singapore.

Table 13.1 indicates that the percentage of migrants in the labor force varies from 1% in South Korea and Japan to 13% in Malaysia and 29% in Singapore. Except in Singapore, there are typically more foreign students and trainees and illegal foreigners than legally recognized foreign workers. Moreover, the number of migrant workers has increased since 1990.

Most migrants in the seven major labor-importing countries come from nearby Asian nations (Battistella 1993). The region's major labor exporter is the Philippines, which deploys 500,000 to 700,000 workers overseas each year and has, by some estimates, more than 4 million migrants abroad. Indonesia has more than 1 million workers abroad, followed by Thailand (500,000), China (500,000), and Malaysia (250,000). Indonesia, China, and Vietnam announced plans in the mid-1990s to increase their labor exports.

TABLE 13.1

Recognized Legal Immigrants and Total Migrants: Major Asian Labor Importers and Exporters, 1997–99

Importers/exporters, country, and year	Foreign population (thousands)	Workers abroad (thousands)	Total labor force (thousands)	Legal migrant workers (thousands)[a]	Total migrants (thousands)[b]	Migrant portion of total labor force (%)	Legal migrant worker portion of migrant labor force (%)
Labor importers							
Japan, 1998	1,500		63,000	190	529	1	36
South Korea, 1998	300		20,326	53	160	1	33
Taiwan, 1998	270		9,081	256	345	4	74
Singapore, 1997	633		1,800	507	525	29	96
Hong Kong, 1997	400		2,970	170	300	10	57
Subtotal	3,103		97,177	1,176	1,859	2	63
Labor exporters and importers							
Thailand, 1998	u	500	32,845	200	900	3	22
Malaysia, 1999	u	250	7,846	714	1,000	13	71
Subtotal	u	750	40,691	914	1,900	3	56
Labor exporters							
China, 1997		500	750,000				
Indonesia, 1998		1,500	94,000				
Philippines, 1998		4,000[c]	30,000				
Bangladesh, 1997		1,600[d]	63,000				
Vietnam, 1997		300	39,000				
Subtotal		7,900	976,000				

SOURCES: Government data and estimates summarized in *Migration News* (various issues).
u, data are unavailable.
[a]Foreign workers (1) with work permits and (2) considered workers under labor law.
[b]Includes foreign workers, students and trainees, and unauthorized workers.
[c]In 1998, 756,000 workers were deployed abroad.
[d]In 1997, 231,000 workers were deployed abroad.

Remittances are that portion of the monies earned by migrants abroad that are returned to the country of origin. Remittances include three types of unrequited transfers (payments that are not offset by explicit exports of goods or services): worker remittances, employee compensation, and migrant transfers. Worker remittances [International Monetary Fund (IMF) code 2391] are the wages and salaries of resident foreign workers, that is, workers employed in the responding country for 12 or more months. Employee compensation (IMF code 2310), previously called labor income, is the gross earnings of foreigners residing in a country for less than 12 months; it includes the value of in-kind benefits, such as housing and payroll taxes. Migrant transfers (IMF code 2431) are the net worth of migrants who move from one country to another and take their assets with them. According to data files prepared by the IMF, in 1995 the Philippines received $5,300 million in total remittances, followed by South Korea and Indonesia, with $630 million each, and China, with $350 million. The IMF database does not contain remittance information for Thailand or Malaysia.

Migration is a result of differences—in resources and employment opportunities, in demographic trajectories, and in security and human rights. These differences between nations are widening, thus increasing the potential for international migration. For example, according to World Bank calculations, the gap between average incomes in the richest and poorest countries was about 11 to 1 in 1870, 38 to 1 in 1960, and 52 to 1 in 1985 (World Bank 1995: 9). In the nineteenth and early twentieth centuries North and South America and Australia accepted practically all migrants who arrived; today, there is no such open destination for migrants.

Given these large and growing differences that should prompt more migration, it may seem surprising that only 2%, rather than 20%, of the world's residents live outside their country of citizenship. There are several reasons for this relatively small amount of international migration, that is, reasons that make migration the exceptional response to differences, not the usual one. First, the expansion of trade has enabled trade to act as a substitute for migration. Labor-abundant countries can and do export labor-intensive goods rather than workers; and economically motivated migration tends to fall sharply after per capita income differences are reduced to 4 or 5 to 1 and when income growth in the sending country exceeds income growth in the receiving country (Straubhaar 1988). Second, most people want to remain near friends and family in familiar cultural and language settings. Third, policy matters. The countries that migrants seek to enter are spending large and growing sums on immigration control. The Organisation for Economic Cooperation and Development (OECD) has noted "an overall trend towards a leveling off of migration flows [due primarily to] measures taken in host countries to better control the flows" (OECD SOPEMI 1995: 11). For example, since 1990 the United States has tripled its spending on immigration control to almost $4 billion per year, equivalent to half its annual expenditure on foreign aid.

There are as many reasons for migration as there are migrants. However, for most individuals who cross national borders for employment or settlement, the reasons are broadly economic or noneconomic. Individuals who migrate are motivated and sustained by three major types of influences: demand or pull, supply or push, and network and other factors. These factors can be arrayed in a 2 × 3 matrix summarizing why people migrate and what sustains particular migration flows (Table 13.2). Each cell contains specific kinds of migrants, and individual migrants may fit into more than one cell. For example, economic migrants may require all three influences before deciding to move across borders for employment: a supply-push reason for seeking employment elsewhere, a network that provides information about job availability and perhaps the means to finance migration to a foreign job, and demand-pull confidence that once the migrant is abroad, a job is waiting. Individual migrants may shift from category to category. Pull, push, and network factors rarely have equal weights in any particular migration. Moreover, the weight of each factor in a particular migration stream tends to change over time.

In East and Southeast Asia labor migration began in the mid-1970s with recruitment for jobs in the Middle East. When the demand for labor in the Middle East shrank after 1985, the migrant infrastructure that was established to move workers outside the region was reoriented to move workers within the region. In the latter half of the 1990s supply-push and network factors seemed to play more important roles in promoting intra-Asian migration than demand-pull factors, construed to mean government-approved labor recruitment.

TABLE 13.2

Factors Influencing the Decision to Migrate

Type of migrant	Demand-pull	Supply-push	Network or other
Economic migrant	Labor recruitment, e.g., of guest workers	Unemployment or underemployment; low wages, e.g., farmers whose crops fail	Job and wage information; sons following fathers; family unification
Noneconomic migrant	Family unification, e.g., family members join established spouse in destination country	War or persecution, e.g., displaced persons and refugees or asylum seekers	Communication; transportation; assistance organizations; desire for new experience or adventure

Labor Migration in Asia

Three types of migration predominate in Asia: emigration to other regions, humanitarian migration within and from the region, and labor migration from and within the region (Fields 1994). Each year more than 500,000 Asians emigrate from the Philippines, Vietnam, China, India, and South Korea to destinations outside Asia, primarily to North America and Australia. For example, between 1991 and 1994 the Philippines was the second leading exporter of immigrants to the United States, sending 241,610 immigrants; Vietnam was third, sending 234,001; China was fifth, sending 191,495; India was seventh, sending 156,861; and South Korea was eleventh, sending 79,914 immigrants (US INS 1997). Humanitarian migrations within and from the region have also been substantial. According to the United Nations High Commissioner for Refugees, in 1995 2.6 million Afghan refugees were in Iran and Pakistan, 300,000 Vietnamese were in China, and more than 200,000 Burmese resided in Thailand and Bangladesh (UNHCR 1995). The most visible refugee migration from the region occurred after 1975, when more than 1 million Vietnamese and Cambodians moved to the United States and Canada. The export of workers to Middle Eastern oil-rich countries during the 1970s was also substantial. According to one estimate (Huguet 1992: 251), the number of Asian workers leaving Asia for the Middle East rose from 10,000 in 1971 to 1 million in 1981. Between 1975 and 1990 12 million Asian workers are believed to have worked in another nation, two-thirds of them leaving the region for employment. The stock of legal Asian workers in the Middle East and Asia is estimated to have exceeded 4 million in 1992.

Asian Migrants in the Middle East

Until oil prices shot up in 1973 and again in 1979 the mostly desert kingdoms of the Middle East played host to a handful of foreign oil experts, most of them from the United States and Europe, and to foreign teachers, doctors, and administrators, mostly Palestinians or nationals of Egypt, Sudan, and Pakistan. Today, the region's oil-exporting countries have some of the highest ratios of foreigners to natives in the world. In many Middle Eastern countries foreigners outnumber natives.

After 1973 the Middle Eastern governments used their oil wealth to build airports, roads, and housing. The construction boom brought millions of unskilled foreign workers into the region. When foreigners began to outnumber natives in Middle Eastern work forces and populations, many Arabian Gulf nations announced plans to reduce their reliance on foreign workers. Saudi Arabia's 1995–2000 economic plan, for example, calls for the creation of 650,000 jobs for Saudis, with 300,000 of those jobs being created by having Saudis replace foreigners. The Saudi government tried to increase the demand for Saudi workers in 1996 through a variety of measures, including prohibiting the admission of foreign secretaries, and it tried to make Saudi workers more attractive to employers by teaching them how to be better workers.

In the United Arab Emirates, where foreigners constitute 75% of the 2.4 million residents, illegal migrants from India, Bangladesh, the Philippines, Sri Lanka, Pakistan, Afghanistan, and Iran were expelled in large numbers in the fall of 1996, causing water and power demand to fall by 10–15%. Tough new penalties for illegal aliens went into effect in November 1996, including fines of up to 30,000 dirhams (US$8,200) and 3 years in prison. Boat owners bringing illegal aliens into the country face up to 15 years in prison and fines ranging from 15,000 dirhams to 100,000 dirhams (US$4,100-$27,000). Even though many are doubtful that Middle Eastern nations will quickly substitute natives for foreign workers, most observers do not expect the number of jobs available for Asian migrants to increase in the Middle East (Kim 1996).

Israel may have the world's highest rate of immigration. It welcomes Jews from around the world, and *aliyah*, or the law of return, is considered by many to be the *raison d'être* of Israel. After conquering territory from neighboring Egypt, Jordan, and Syria in 1967 and 1973, Israel permitted Arab residents from the West Bank and Gaza to work as foreign workers in Israel. The number of Arab workers employed in Israel peaked in 1987 at 110,000. Israel began to restrict the entry of Arab workers in reaction to terrorist incidents in the 1990s, first with temporary closures of its borders and later by substituting Thai, Romanian, and other foreign workers for Arab migrants. Today, about 40,000 Palestinians are authorized to work in Israel, down from a peak of 180,000 in 1989.

In 1996 Israel had 100,000 legal guest workers from other countries, including 17,500 Thai farm workers. An estimated 50,000–150,000 foreigners are working in Israel with expired tourist permits. Most of the Thai workers live in mobile homes, and in 1995 Israeli farmers transferred at least $700 million directly to their Thai workers' accounts at the Bank of Bangkok (*Migration News*, August 1997).

Factors Likely To Increase Asian Labor Migration

Asia includes some of the world's fastest growing and most rapidly aging industrial economies (for example, Japan) and the world's second leading country of emigration (the Philippines), setting the stage for an apparent match between labor demand and supply that many expect to lead to increased migration for employment regardless of migration policies. Widening wage and income differentials within the region are contributing to migration pressures. The richest Asian nations, with per capita incomes that are 10–50 times higher than their neighbors', have seen their populations and labor forces peak at current fertility rates. To maintain or increase the population and labor force of Japan or South Korea, immigration will be necessary (ILO 1990; Skeldon 1992).

Another factor likely to increase Asian labor migration is economic shifts within the region. Asia's major labor-importing nations are transforming themselves from manufacturing economies to service economies, creating jobs for migrant workers in declining small and medium-size manufacturing firms and in service occupations that range from entertainment to domestic service (Fields 1994). The employment elasticity (the number of jobs created by each $1,000 million increase in gross domestic product) seems to be rising in the richer service-dominated economies, increasing the number of jobs to be filled at a time when there are fewer new labor force entrants.

Yet a third factor is cultural shifts (Matsunaga 1993; Meissner et al. 1993; Massey et al. 1993). Better-educated youth are increasingly shunning so-called 3D jobs—jobs that are dirty, dangerous, and difficult—but the employers who create the jobs, the businesses that depend on their output, and the governments are not willing to close the door firmly to migrant workers in order to speed up adjustments that might eliminate such work. Instead, migrants arrive, and Say's law operates: Migrants make a place for themselves in the host economy.[1]

A fourth and final factor is migration infrastructure. Migration networks that were established to move large numbers of migrant workers to Middle Eastern nations are redirecting migrants within Asia. Those networks consist of labor brokers, policies to promote employment abroad, and support systems to finance international migration for employment. Some of the Asian nations that earlier exported managers and professionals and that are now attracting them home as their economies grow include the Philippines, Taiwan, China, India, South Korea, and Malaysia.

Migrant workers in East Asian countries range from people with doctorates to workers who did not complete elementary school. A one-to-one relationship does not necessarily exist between a migrant's skills and the skill level of his foreign job. Many Asian migrants accept jobs abroad that do not use their education. An example is college-educated Filipino women who work in Hong Kong or Japan as maids or entertainers.

Asian nations began permitting or tolerating the entry of foreign workers after labor shortages cropped up in particular sectors of their economies and after domestic reservoirs of flexible labor were exhausted. This relaxation of restrictions on foreign workers has led Abella (1995: 125), for example, to argue that "labor migration is a normal part of economic development." In many countries opening the door to foreign workers was accomplished not through guest worker programs, as in the United States and Western Europe, but by admitting students and trainees or tolerating illegal immigrants. Some Asian nations, such as Malaysia and Thailand, both import and export unskilled labor.

Of course, there could be alternatives to migration, including more investment designed to take work to workers. Other proposals include establishing retirement communities for Asians from more affluent countries in other countries of the region, mostly to stretch the retirees' fixed incomes, but one effect might be to reduce the need for immigrant nurses and orderlies in their countries of origin.

Issues for Labor Importers

Japan, South Korea, Taiwan, and Singapore are major labor importers. Each has its own migration concerns and has developed policies designed to address them. The following discussion of these labor importers draws principally on articles in *Migration News* and two recent collections by Martin, Mason, and Tsay (1995) and Martin, Mason, and Nagayama (1996).

Japan

Japan experienced an economic boom in the late 1980s and early 1990s, and the number of foreign workers rose in lockstep with economic growth. In 1996 most of the 529,000 foreign workers (excluding resident Koreans) were not legally recognized foreign workers; they represented less than 1% of Japan's 63 million workers. Labor shortages, the internationalization of Japan's economy and society, and changes in Japanese immigration law were predicted in the early 1990s to produce in Japan by the mid-1990s a foreign work force comparable to the 5–10% of foreigners living there (Shimada 1994). This has not happened, and in December 1995 the Japanese government announced that it would continue to ban the admission of unskilled foreign workers. In May 1997 Japan revised its Immigration Control and Refugee Recognition Law to deal with illegal Chinese immigration. An average of 250 illegal Chinese per month were apprehended in Japan in 1997, compared with 30 per month in 1996.

Foreign workers in Japan fall into six major categories: permanent resident Korean workers (316,000 in 1993), legal temporary professionals (95,000), trainees (17,000), working students (63,000), ethnic Japanese from South America (152,000 in 1992), and illegal workers (about 300,000). As the last figure indicates, the volume of illegal immigration is considerable. More than 60,000 foreigners were apprehended in Japan in 1995, despite the high unemployment rate, and another 288,000 did not leave when their tourist visas expired. About 70% of the apprehended foreigners in 1995 had been in Japan for at least 1 year, compared with only 30% in 1990. One reason may be that labor brokers are becoming more sophisticated. A Japanese firm needing 10 extra workers for 1 day reportedly can pay a broker about 13,000 yen (US$120) for each worker, and the broker pays the illegal foreign worker 8,000 yen (about $75).

Since 1954 the Japanese government has permitted young foreign Asians to enter the country for training (JAI 1991; Kuptsch and Oishi 1995). The training is provided in work-and-learn programs. In 1994 Japan had 40,000 trainees, 40% of them from China. Most of the trainees, 83%, were employed in manufacturing, usually by small and medium-size firms. Trainees are paid the equivalent of US$400–$800 per month, one-fourth to one-half as much as Japanese workers, with the quality and content of the training left up to the Japanese employers. Trainees may remain in Japan for one year, but employers are pushing for a two-year limit so that they can recoup some of the costs of the training.

Several special categories of foreign workers exist in Japan (Okunishi 1996). The first is *nisei*, second-generation Japanese from Brazil and Peru. Since October 1994 Brazilian Japanese have been able to use a branch of the Japanese Employment Service in São Paulo to find jobs in Japan. The second category is women migrants. About one-third of the illegal immigrants detained in Japan in 1995 were women, many of whom were forced into prostitution after being recruited in Thailand and then "sold" to Japanese nightclubs for US$25,000–$30,000. A third category is Chinese who are smuggled into Japan by other Chinese, called snake heads. Depending on the complexity of arrangements for the trip, the smugglers charge fees ranging from US$20,000 to US$40,000. They require a down payment before a smuggling operation begins and collect the remainder when the illegal immigrant arrives in Japan. If an immigrant refuses to pay the balance, the smuggler may threaten the physical well-being of the migrant, his family members who remain in China, or both.

By 2000, 1% of Japan's workers were foreigners. Most are young men who are in Japan without their families. The number of illegal foreign workers, which peaked at 300,000 in 1993, was estimated to be 250,000 in 2000, and several commissions recommended that Japan reconsider its ban on the admission of temporary unskilled workers. However, polls suggest that most Japanese continue to oppose immigration and guest workers; many commentators point to the difficulty Japan has with integrating long-term Korean residents to argue that Japan should remain largely closed to foreigners. There are about 600,000 ethnic Koreans in Japan, and 8,000–10,000 a year naturalize; naturalization requires the adoption of a Japanese name. Koreans living in Japan have been demanding more rights, including the right to vote in local elections without naturalizing.

South Korea

South Korea has experienced one of the world's fastest migration transitions. About 200,000 Koreans emigrated to other countries in 1982, and a decade later approximately 100,000 legal and illegal foreign workers were residing in South Korea (Park 1990). At the end of 1996 about 210,000 foreign workers and trainees were living in South Korea, representing 2% of that country's 12 million–strong work force. According to the Korean government, the foreign workers included 81,000 legal workers (of whom 68,000 had trainee visas and 13,000 had work visas) and another 130,000 illegal workers. The unauthorized workers, who predominate among foreigners in South Korea's labor force, fall into three major groups: trainees who abandon their assigned workplaces to earn more money, people who violate the terms of their tourist visas by going to work, and people who slip into South Korea without authorization and go to work. About 40% of these foreign workers are Chinese Koreans, the descendants of Chossun-Zok who emigrated from the Korean Peninsula to China between 1910 and 1945 when Korea was a colony of Japan (Kang 1996).

South Korea prohibits unskilled worker immigration. Only unskilled trainees are admitted, and in 1996 they earned US$300–$350 per month. Trainees must sign contracts stipulating that their stay will be limited to three years with a designated employer. The prospect of earning higher wages as unskilled illegal workers, for example, in construction, however, encourages about 30% of them to abandon their employers each year. Some question whether this policy of prohibiting unskilled guest workers but permitting the entry of trainees is sustainable, especially when illegal workers can earn US$400 to US$700 per month. For example, in small manufacturing firms with fewer than 30 workers, typically less than 10% are foreigners; but two-thirds of these foreigners are trainees. This suggests that small businesses are relying on poorly paid trainees to remain competitive (Kang 1996).

The Korean trainee program was begun under the auspices of private businesses with unpublished rules governing the rights and obligations of trainees and their employers. As the rules evolved, the firms laid out what seemed to be a coherent program. Employers must offer the trainees housing, limit the number of trainees to a small proportion (usually 10%) of the work force, and develop a plan for phasing out their dependence on trainees (Kang 1996). Nepalese trainees protested these rules in January 1995, and in response the government promised to review the trainee program.

Korean employers who currently employ foreign trainees believe that Korean women, part-time workers, and older and handicapped workers cannot replace the foreign workers. The reason, they usually assert, is that the work is too hard, not that the wages are too low. Smaller firms prefer foreign trainees to automation because investing in machinery is expensive and risky, whereas the foreigners can be laid off if demand slackens. In 2000 the major issue in Korea was whether foreign trainees should become guest workers, with the same rights to minimum wages as Korean workers.

Taiwan

Taiwan began to import foreign workers for public construction projects in 1989 (Lee and Wang 1996). In 1991 Taiwan permitted private-sector employers to hire foreign workers, and a year later the government established a legislative framework for foreign worker employment. In 1995 employers in 74 economic sectors were permitted to have up to one-third of their employees be foreign workers; but the government, worried about rising unemployment among Taiwanese, froze new entries.

As of mid-1996 about 300,000 permits had been issued to employers to admit foreign workers, and about 190,000 foreign workers were living in Taiwan. Foreign workers are admitted for one year and can have their work permits renewed for another year. After two years they are required to leave and not to return again as foreign workers. Two-thirds of the foreign workers are Thais, and two-thirds are employed in manufacturing.

Under the unskilled foreign worker program employers request permission from the Council on Labor Affairs to import foreign workers after trying to recruit local workers by offering at least the minimum wage, NT$14,880 per month in 1996. Taiwanese employers pay foreign workers this minimum wage plus NT$2,100 into a training fund and NT$867 into a workers' compensation fund. In most cases labor brokers offer to recruit and bring foreign workers to Taiwan for a one-time service fee of about NT$25,000 (about US$1,000), which is paid by the Taiwanese employer but is often recouped from the migrant worker.

Foreign workers compete for the right to work in Taiwan, and some brokers charge migrants the equivalent of two to six months' salary for a Taiwanese work permit. Many foreign workers therefore enter Taiwan in debt. Because they receive minimum rather than higher market wages, many foreign workers abandon their contracts and work illegally. In 1995 legal foreign workers earned about US$700 for an average of 240 hours each month, or almost US$3 per hour. Most are housed and fed by the employer at no cost to the worker.

The number of illegal workers appears to be equal to the 10% or more of the work force that is foreign and legally employed, and the proportion of illegal workers is rising. In 1996 the government established an NT$1 million fund that pays policemen and residents about NT$600 for each illegal worker they report to authorities. The reward and deportation program proved ineffective because employers were permitted to hire a replacement worker for each runaway deported. Some brokers were accused of encouraging runaways so that they could collect more fees from replacement foreign workers (Lee and Wang 1996).

Singapore

Singapore is a country of immigrants. About 1 in 5 of Singapore's workers is a foreigner. Some 50,000 foreigners are supervisors, managers, and professionals; and another 300,000 work in factories, construction sites, and shipyards. Singapore averaged 9% economic growth between 1965 and 1995, and the Singapore government uses foreign workers as a macroeconomic stabilizer and a source of revenue (Pang 1992). Unemployed foreigners must depart, and employers must pay monthly levies for each foreign worker, for example, S$440 per month for each foreign construction worker. These levies effectively lower the wages of foreign workers. (Singapore has no minimum-wage laws.)

Singapore welcomes professionals who have at least a secondary school education and earn S$1,500 or more per month, and it allows them to become permanent residents, work in the government, and live in public housing. Guest or permit workers, on the other hand, are foreigners who earn less than S$1,500 per month. They are permitted to stay in Singapore up to four years, may not bring their dependents to Singapore, and find it almost impossible to become permanent residents. Guest workers are seen as an economic buffer, imported when needed and exported when laid off. Because the two major countries of origin of the guest workers, Malaysia and Thailand, have the same business cycle as Singapore, Singapore's guest worker policies can aggravate their business cycles, increasing labor shortages in boom times and surpluses during recessions.

However, it is the social aspects of guest workers that have recently raised the most concern in Singapore and the sending countries. Singapore uses caning as punishment for certain offenses. The government has offered amnesty to some illegal Thai workers to avoid caning them, but many Thais left the country after several Thai workers reportedly died in their sleep at their work site. In 1995 Singapore hanged a Filipino maid convicted of murder, and this led to a Philippine ban on sending maids to Singapore.

Employers of illegal alien workers in Singapore can be fined for up to 24 months of the levy due on them. With levies running S$300–$450 per month, fines can range from S$7,200 (US$4,900) to S$9,600 per illegal worker. Employers of illegal aliens can also be jailed for six months to two years and, if they hired more than five illegal workers at the same time, caned. In 1993, 415 employers were fined a combined S$4.3 million. Between January and September 1994 Singapore courts levied fines totaling S$4.1 million on 278 employers of illegal foreign workers. A law went into effect in March 1996 that makes a general contractor responsible for all violations of immigration laws at construction sites. Late in 1996 a South Korean joint-venture firm was fined a record S$1.56 million for employing illegal foreign workers. Despite these tough controls, illegal immigration is rising.

Most observers expect Singapore to continue to fine-tune rather than radically change its immigration and guest worker policies. In November 1992 the construction sector was allowed to use 5 foreign workers for each local worker, up from the previous 3 to 1 ratio. When construction productivity did not improve, the levy on unskilled construction workers went up by 10% (in April 1995), from S$400 (US$275) to S$440 per month, whereas the levy on skilled workers went down by 20%, from S$250 to S$200.

Issues for Labor Exporters

Thailand and Indonesia are two East Asian countries that export labor and have taken similar approaches to the issue. Indonesia is trying to increase its exports of skilled workers. Until the 1997 financial crisis struck, Thailand was simultaneously exporting and importing labor.

Thailand

About 500,000 Thai workers were employed abroad in 1996—200,000 legally, including 25% each in Saudi Arabia and Singapore. There were also about 500,000 foreign workers in Thailand: 200,000 professional expatriates and 300,000 unskilled farm and construction workers from poorer neighboring countries.

Thailand's impressive macroeconomic performance obscured the imbalances that promoted internal migration, emigration, and immigration. Medium-technology manufacturing growth was concentrated in the Bangkok region. The wage gap between Bangkok and the rest of the country widened in the 1980s, encouraging internal migration. According to one estimate, in 1995 Bangkok generated 56% of Thailand's gross domestic product but accounted for only 17% of the population (*Forbes*, July 15, 1996). As the Thai economy has become integrated into the world economy, shortages of highly skilled workers have enabled the best educated one-fourth of the Thai work force to earn higher wages quickly, whereas wages for less educated workers have risen slowly, encouraging some Thais to emigrate. Skilled Thais are actively recruited to work abroad. Saudi Arabia announced plans in December 1993 to recruit 70,000 skilled Thai workers (*Straits Times*, December 8, 1993).

In 1996 Thailand offered amnesty to illegal workers in the country by allowing their employers in agriculture, construction, fishing, and water transportation to pay a 5,000 baht (US$200) fee and register them with the Immigration Police. The legalized migrants received two-year work permits. As of October 1996 only 27,000 of the estimated 700,000 illegal alien workers in Thailand had been legalized.

Indonesia

As the most populous country in Southeast Asia, Indonesia in the mid-1990s planned to increase its exports of skilled workers to relieve unemployment pressures and to generate remittances. Some 2.4 million school leavers joined the work force in 1996, and many looked abroad for jobs. Indonesians have long migrated to nearby Malaysia, but most officially recorded temporary labor emigration during the 1980s involved women moving to the Middle East to work as maids. In the early 1990s the number of migrant workers going abroad was officially put at 150,000 per year, half of them going to Asian destinations. In an effort to protect Indonesian workers from exploitation and to collect exit taxes, the government established a 10-step procedure that requires most migrant workers to use middlemen to go abroad. The complexity of the system and the fees involved encouraged many Indonesians to emigrate illegally.

The largest concentration of illegal Indonesian workers is in nearby Malaysia, where the men are employed on plantations and construction sites and the women are employed in factories and as maids. Three-fourths of the illegal aliens apprehended in Malaysia are Indonesians.

In 1996 Indonesia announced a goal of sending more than 250,000 migrants abroad per year and having them remit at least US$1,700 billion annually. The government hoped to gain more remittances and to reduce worker exploitation by sending abroad mostly skilled workers who could command US$600 or more per month (per capita income was about US$1,100 per year, or US$92 a month in 1996). The government also expressed concerns about the number of foreign professionals employed in Indonesia (about 57,000 in 1995). Most are professionals and managers.

Growth, Integration, and Migration in Asia

Until the mid-1980s international migration played a minor role in Asian economic growth. Instead of importing labor from abroad, governments kept the number of migrant workers low by drawing on women entrants to the labor force and domestic migrants from rural areas and by automating at home and investing abroad. Appreciating currencies encouraged investments abroad, especially after 1985.

Trade and investment rather than migration have been the driving force for economic integration in Asia. Between 1979 and 1992 intraregional exports in East and Southeast Asia grew at an annual rate of 12%. If trade continues to expand faster than economic growth, economic theory predicts an increase in economically motivated migration pressures because freer trade accelerates economic and job growth in a region and trade in goods substitutes for migration. Economic theory also suggests that migration should wither away, but most migration specialists and governments expect more rather than less employment-motivated migration over the next decade. If that is so, migration could be a potential third pillar of Asian economic integration, leading, in the view of some, to a European Union–style freedom-of-movement regime, in which migration is encouraged as a means of improving labor market efficiency and helping bind member countries closer together. The alternative extreme would be for fears of uncontrolled migration to slow economic integration, as occurred between the European Union and Turkey.

Governments' immigration decisions will largely shape migration patterns in Asia, and currently those decisions are influenced by fears that opening the door to immigrants or guest workers could quickly lead to mass migration. Only in Asia are sending countries far more populous than receiving countries (compare the United States and Mexico or Germany and Turkey with Japan and China or Malaysia and Indonesia). Bolstering the receiving countries' fears of being overrun by immigrants from more populous nations are rapid labor force growth, high unemployment, low wages, and urban-ward migration in such sending countries as the Philippines and China and an ever more sophisticated migration infrastructure for moving migrants across borders regardless of migration policies. There is another demographic twist to the fears that migration could get out of control: The disproportionate number of boys born in China may contribute to emigration pressure there, because young men are the most likely group to migrate.

Should East Asian societies that open themselves to immigrants fear massive or uncontrolled migration? Will the migration that is occurring promote or retard the economic integration that contributed to East Asia's rapid economic growth? One way to answer these questions is first to consider the use of guest worker programs to manage the migration that is occurring, emphasizing the choices open to destination countries, and then to examine the prospects for a migration hump, or temporary increase in migration as a result of closer economic integration.

Guest Workers

In thinking about the future of international migration in East and Southeast Asia, it is useful to distinguish immigration from temporary migration for employment. Within the region only Singapore is a declared country of immigration, in the sense that foreign professionals can obtain forms and apply to immigrate. Few of the other countries of the region are open to immigrants. Instead, most of them have immigration laws that are analogous to those in Japan, which allow the indefinite renewal of residence and work permits for some types of foreigners but do not have clear paths to naturalization for resident foreigners and their children.

When foreigners are needed but not wanted, many countries admit them as nonimmigrant guest workers. Guest or foreign worker programs aim to add workers to the labor force without adding permanent residents to the population. Guest worker programs have two major variations, and they have distinctly different implications for migration control. Most of the European guest worker programs of the 1960s were actually probationary immigration systems, in the sense that newly arrived guest workers received temporary but renewable work and residence permits and, after two to five years of legal work and residence, could obtain permanent resident status. Resident status in turn permitted workers to unify their families and to remain in the host country, collecting unemployment benefits if they lost their jobs (Martin 1997). The alternative to European-style probationary immigrant guest worker systems are US- and Canadian-style nonimmigrant temporary worker programs. Regardless of how many times *braceros* (laborers) or H-visa workers return to the United States to fill vacant jobs, they gain no priority for entry as immigrants. In other words, the immigrant and nonimmigrant systems are entirely separate. In fact, many nonimmigrant foreigners in the United States, especially students and professionals, are able to become immigrants by having a US employer sponsor them as a needed worker, and many of the unskilled nonimmigrant workers gain enough US work experience to return as unauthorized workers.

Asian nations want to avoid both the planned transition from temporary to permanent resident status implicit in the European guest worker model and the de facto conversion to immigrant or unauthorized worker that often occurs in the North American model. But many Asian governments are attempting to keep foreign workers as nonimmigrants without having explicit policies on returns. They too may learn that, as most studies of guest workers conclude, there is nothing more permanent than temporary workers [see, for example, Miller and Martin (1982: 110)].

All guest worker programs have two major problems: distortion and dependence. Distortion occurs because economies and labor markets are flexible and hence can adjust to the availability of foreign workers. Eventually foreign workers are seen to be needed, and employers, investors, and local workers begin to make decisions that assume that unskilled foreign workers will continue to be available. Economies and labor markets in both the sending and the receiving countries evolve in ways that create and reinforce international labor markets. Immigration-country governments then find it difficult to manage migration. An example of distortion can be found in southwestern US agriculture.

Dependence, the other problem associated with guest workers, is the reliance on remittances in the sending country from guest workers in the receiving country. Some young immigrants who plan to stay abroad for only one or two years find their plans changing as they form or unite their families abroad and as their employers petition governments for them to remain. In sending areas young people who are impatient to get ahead soon learn that, with wages abroad 10 or 20 times higher than those at home and with labor brokers available to move them across borders, they can more quickly achieve their goals by emigrating. The sending country can then become dependent on an external labor market.

Governments of destination countries have tried to prevent distortion and dependence by imposing administrative rules, by limiting work and residence permits to one year, by enforcing returns after a period of foreign study or training, and by stepping up immigration and labor law enforcement. But as the experience of Western Europe and North America has demonstrated, so long as there are incentives for migration, employers and migrants will get around those rules.

Asian governments worried about settlement may pioneer the use of economic instruments to manage economically motivated labor migration. For example, several countries have taxes and levies that aim to prevent distortion in the labor markets that employ foreign workers. Singapore and Malaysia charge employers a monthly levy for the right to hire foreign workers, which enables those two countries to redirect some of the private economic gains from migration to the training and retraining of native workers.

There may be room to introduce a levy system to promote returns because of the high fees that brokers currently charge workers—often 25% of what a migrant will earn in his or her first year abroad. If sending and receiving countries could cooperate to reduce illegal immigration by charging a levy for legal entry that was equivalent to 25% of the typical US$2,000 to US$6,000 per year earned by unskilled foreign workers in East Asia, they could generate significant funds for return bonuses. For example, a 25% levy on a US$3,000 annual wage would generate US$750 per worker per year, a significant return bonus.

Creating legal opportunities for migrants to enter and work abroad, charging their employers for the privilege of their foreign employment, and offering return bonuses could dampen smuggling and give receiving-country governments an economic instrument for influencing employers' investment and technology choices. Simultaneously, with smugglers and brokers already charging high fees to migrants, there may be room for government levies to lower migration costs while increasing control over migration.

The Migration Hump

Rich, labor-short Asian nations have invested in nearby labor-surplus nations rather than bringing workers to their available capital. According to Bloom and Noor (1995: 112), the $50 billion invested abroad by Japan, Hong Kong, Singapore, South Korea, and Taiwan between the mid-1980s and the mid-1990s created 6 million jobs for potential migrants, but would have created 500,000 jobs if it had been invested at home at $100,000 per job. However, these foreign investments in fact created 6 million jobs from China to Indonesia, thereby lowering the demand for migrant workers in Japan and the four Asian tigers and decreasing emigration pressures in China and elsewhere (Bloom and Noor 1995).

In the long run the predictions of economic theory are usually borne out: Trade and migration are long-term substitutes. This was the major conclusion of the US Commission for the Study of International Migration and Cooperative Economic Development, which concluded in 1990 that free trade and investment were the best mutually beneficial policies to accelerate economic and job growth and thus reduce emigration pressures. But there can be contrary short-term results, both in theory and in reality. The US Commission acknowledged these, asserting that "the economic development process itself tends in the short to medium term to stimulate migration" (US CSIMCED 1990: xiv).

Figure 13.1 illustrates the migration hump, the temporary increase in immigration that is followed by declining migration (Martin 1993). The important point about the figure is that the same economic policies that increase emigration pressures in the short run reduce them in the longer run.

Economic integration and migration can be short-run complements for several reasons (Martin and Taylor 1996). Under the Stolper-Samuelson and the Heckscher-Ohlin theorems trade liberalization permits capital- and labor-rich countries to specialize in producing the goods in which each has a comparative advantage and to satisfy their demand for other goods through trade (Mundell 1957).

However, by relaxing some of trade theory's standard assumptions, free trade can be shown to produce a migration hump. One of these assumptions is that both countries share the same technologies (production functions), so that differences in the labor and capital intensities of production between the two countries are due solely to differences in their factor endowments, not to the unavailability of technology to the poorer country. If instead the basis for trade is a difference in technologies across borders, migration and trade may be complementary.

Another reason that trade and migration may be short-term complements is that differences in factor productivity, the basis for trade, may be due to the better availability of complementary public inputs in destination coun-

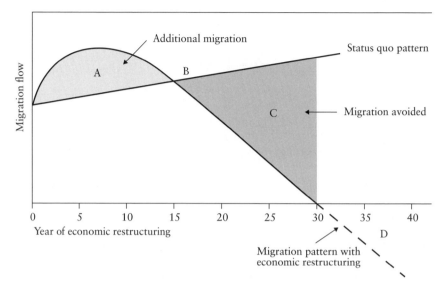

Source: Martin (1993, figure 9).

FIGURE 13.1. The Migration Hump.

tries, such as public services, transportation, communication, and legal and education systems that sending countries cannot develop quickly. The availability of complementary public inputs thus causes factors of production to be more productive in immigration than in emigration areas.

A third reason that trade and migration may increase together is that adjustments in both immigration and emigration areas may be slow. The demand for immigrant labor may thus persist even with freer trade, and workers displaced by freer trade in the emigration country may find it difficult to find new jobs quickly in expanding sectors.

Slow adjustments to freer trade can produce a migration hump. Closer economic integration can generate demand-pull, supply-push, and network factors that temporarily increase migration. There are several reasons for this. First, if the destination country uses foreign workers to produce goods for the sending country, then lowering trade barriers may temporarily increase the demand for foreign workers in the destination country. Second, supply-push pressures to emigrate from the sending country can increase as a result of closer economic integration as some industries and sectors in emigration areas prove to be noncompetitive. Examples are state-owned enterprises and agriculture. In many cases economic integration adds jobs in areas far removed from where workers are displaced, encouraging internal migration that brings jobless workers into contact with labor brokers who can take them abroad. Third, economic integration can strengthen the networks that move people across borders. These networks encompass everything that enables people to move across borders and earn money in another country, from expanded tourism to training programs to easier entry procedures for business visitors. One observer (Sassen 1993) described the strengthening of networks as the creation and strengthening of objective and subjective bridges between countries.

East Asia may be facing the world's largest migration hump. Kim (1996: 309) suggested that the region has not yet reached the peak of its migration hump. He predicted that the peak of Asian labor migration will not arrive for three or four decades. Furthermore, Kim speculated that for some Asian countries, notably India and China, economic integration and migration may be long-term complements because of those countries' massive populations.

Crisis and Migration

In July 1997 Thailand devalued its currency, setting in motion a chain of devaluations that led to recession, higher unemployment, and political unrest in East and Southeast Asia. What are the consequences of the economic crisis for labor migration? In many migrant destinations migrant employment has not fallen sharply as unemployment has increased, suggesting that the demand for migrant workers is structural.

The hypothesis of a structural demand for migrants is tentative for several reasons. First, in most destination countries half or more of the migrants are not defined as legal foreign workers and thus are not included in employment and unemployment data; therefore it is hard to chart trends in migrant and native employment with precision. Second, the economic crisis was only months old at the end of 1998, making it hard to predict what native workers would do if unemployment remained high. Third, many Asian nations are adding to their social safety nets, and this development is likely to affect the supply of native workers for lower-level jobs and the demand for migrants.

The evidence so far, however, suggests that migrants will not easily be replaced by unemployed natives. In Thailand and Malaysia, for example, governments anticipated higher unemployment and announced aggressive campaigns to remove legal foreign workers and expel illegal foreigners in order to make jobs available for natives who had lost jobs. Both governments later relaxed these expulsion policies, because employers protested and unemployed natives did not protest the presence of migrants.

Thai authorities announced severe penalties for illegal foreign workers apprehended after July 15, 1998. As the deadline approached, 600 of 1,000 Thai rice mills closed because, the owners claimed, the government would not permit them to employ foreign workers and because unemployed Thai workers refused to replace workers who were forced to return to Burma. In mid-1998 an estimated 20,000 rice mill workers, mostly Burmese, earned the minimum wage of US$4 a day, or US$122 a month, to carry bags of rice that weighed up to 100 kg (220 lb). The Thai government proposed that the mills raise wages and reduce the weight of the bags to 120 lb to attract Thai workers. After the strike by mill owners threatened a leading export, however, the government relented and agreed that 95,000 Burmese, Laotian, and Cambodian workers, most employed in agriculture and fishing, could remain until July 15, 1999. The Thai government continued to postpone the ban on foreign workers after 1999.

Malaysia had a similar reversal of policy. In the fall of 1997, when an estimated 2 million foreign workers were in the country, including 800,000 legal workers, the government announced a ban on the entry of additional unskilled foreign workers. It also declared that after August 15, 1998, foreign workers would be permitted to remain in the country only under exceptional circumstances. As the deadline approached, employers protested that Malaysians refused to fill jobs vacated by foreigners and that without migrants production and exports would fall at a time when Malaysia needed to earn foreign currency.

As the deadline approached, exceptions proliferated, first for plantation workers to maintain agricultural exports and then for workers in export-oriented manufacturing. Finally, in July 1998 the Malaysian Special Cabinet Committee on Foreign Workers agreed to permit 96,000 foreign workers who held "jobs shunned by Malaysians" to remain until 2005 and then agreed that employers could have work permits renewed for foreigners employed in restaurants, gas stations, cemeteries, golf courses, vegetable gardens, food manufacturing, orphanages and senior homes, laundries, janitorial jobs, male barber shops, and tailor shops. The committee refused work permit renewals for foreigners employed as golf caddies or supermarket helpers or as workers in medical centers or private clinics, beauty salons, karaoke lounges, or courier services.

South Korea was the third hard-hit migrant destination, and it too learned that it was not easy to substitute unemployed Koreans for migrants. Despite a record unemployment rate of 8% in the fall of 1998, the government estimated that almost 100,000 illegal foreign workers still remained in the country, down about 25% from 136,000 a year earlier. Governmental efforts to reduce the number of foreign trainees in small and medium-size manufacturing firms brought protests from firms whose owners argued that they could not remain competitive without the trainees.

Japan provides some of the strongest evidence of structural dependence. The government's estimate of the number of illegal foreign workers has been stable at about 300,000 throughout the 1990s. The number of foreign trainees and Brazilians of Japanese ancestry (*nikkeijin*), has also remained stable despite the recession, and the number of Chinese apprehended in Japan reached record levels in 1997–98. In May 1998 Prime Minister Ryutaro Hashimoto called on the G-8 nations to examine ways to reduce "illegal trafficking of human beings."

The lesson for labor migration from the economic crisis is clear: Migration not reduced by recession is poised to increase with recovery. Thus labor migration is not likely to fade away as an issue in East and Southeast Asia.

Conclusion

Most of the East Asian nations that experienced rapid fertility declines and fast economic growth did not experience labor shortages until the 1990s because, until then, foreign investment and trade combined with rapid labor force growth at home made international migration for employment unnecessary. Beginning in the late 1980s and accelerating in the 1990s, however, most of the richest East Asian nations became significant labor importers, with foreign workers in the mid-1990s accounting for 1–15% of their labor forces. Most predictions are that the foreign share of Asian labor forces will increase, implying that demographic and economic differences between East Asian nations will be balanced in part by migration. But most of the receiving countries that hold the key to the volume and character of labor flows have proceeded cautiously, either shutting the door to unskilled foreign workers, as in Japan, or admitting only trainees and students and tolerating illegal immigrants, as elsewhere.

Policies toward foreigners are in a state of flux in East Asia. If countries keep the door to foreigners open, they may pioneer a new approach to managing migration: the use of economic instruments to minimize the distortion and dependence that often accompany guest workers. This may become especially important as closer economic integration produces a migration hump resulting from the short-term complementarity of trade and migration.

IV. INEQUALITY AND THE ECONOMIC ROLE OF WOMEN

Demographic Change, Development, and the Economic Status of Women in East Asia

JOHN BAUER

DEVELOPMENT AND DEMOGRAPHIC CHANGE have interacted to advance the economic status of women in East Asia, at least to the extent that increases in educational attainment and formal employment reflect improved status. Although the labor market outcomes for men and women still differ, changes associated with the demographic transition should continue to improve the opportunities available to women in the region.

Increases in age at marriage, dramatic declines in fertility, and fewer years spent rearing children have reduced the conflicts between home and career that women face. These demographic changes also have had indirect effects on female employment. The other chapters in this volume suggest that fertility declines promote rapid economic growth. This growth in turn increases the demand for female employment and education. Fertility reduction also results, after a lag of 15–20 years, in slower labor force growth. This change in turn contributes to rising wage levels in East Asia, and rising wages have acted to draw more women into the labor market.

In this chapter I first describe trends in female labor force participation, employment, and educational attainment in East Asia. I then focus on the contributions made by women to the industrialization drives in the region. Finally, I examine the effects of demographic changes on women's educational attainment and employment.

Trends in Female Labor Force Participation, Employment, and Education

Female labor force participation has increased dramatically since the 1960s in East Asia. Not only has rapid economic development in the region caused more women to enter the labor market, but it has also changed substantially the nature of female employment. Although the incidence of agricultural and unpaid family work among women has declined, the number of women working in clerical and labor jobs has risen sharply.

Labor Force Participation

Labor force statistics have been criticized for underreporting work by women (Anker 1983; Dixon-Mueller and Anker 1988). Differences in the reporting of unpaid family work can make it difficult to compare participation rates across countries. In some cases it can even be difficult to examine trends within a country because of changes in definitions and enumeration practices.

Despite these problems, it is clear that labor force participation among women in East Asia has increased dramatically in recent decades. Table 14.1, which outlines trends in aggregate female participation rates for six successful East Asian economies, shows that the largest gains have been made by women in the newly industrialized economies (NIEs): South Korea and especially Singapore and Taiwan. In Indonesia women's participation rates also increased during the 1980s. However, at least some of the increase in Indonesia appears to have been due to a change in the classification of unpaid family workers from one census to another.

The female participation rate in Singapore rose from about 22% in 1957 to 53% by 1990. Women's share of the total labor force there grew from 26% in 1970 to 40% in 1990 (see Table 14.6). Singapore's rapid industrialization generated increased labor demand, drawing women into the market, and the lack of any rural labor surplus made women an especially important labor pool. In Taiwan the female participation rate rose from 24.5% in 1966 to 44.5% by 1990.

Aggregate participation rates in Japan and Thailand did not change substantially during the periods examined. However, as we will see, important changes occurred in the nature of female employment in both countries. The participation rate in Japan has been stable since the 1950s, in part because increases in the incidence of paid employment have been offset by declines in unpaid family work among women. Female participation in Thailand has always been high because of the importance of women in agriculture. Their participation in urban areas, however, has grown substantially, rising from 39% in 1971 to nearly 61% by 1991 (Phananiramai 1995).

TABLE 14.1

*Labor Force Participation Rates for Women Age 15
and Older: Six Asian Countries, Recent Decades*

Country and year	Percentage
Japan	
1950	50.2
1960	50.9
1970	50.9
1980	46.9
1990	48.3
South Korea	
1963	36.3
1970	38.5
1980	41.6
1990	47.0
Taiwan	
1966	24.5
1970	31.0
1980	39.2
1990	44.5
Singapore	
1957	21.6
1970	29.5
1980	44.3
1990	53.0
Thailand	
1971	73.4
1980	76.6
1990	76.3
Indonesia	
1961	31.2
1971	37.0
1980	37.1
1990	44.2

SOURCES: For Japan, Singapore, and Indonesia, census data ILO (various years), *Year Book of Labour Statistics*, and 1990 census reports for Singapore and Indonesia. For South Korea, ROK NSO (selected years), *Annual report on the economically active population survey*. For Taiwan, ROC CLA (various years) for 1977 and 1995. For Thailand, Thailand NSO (various years).

Educational Attainment and School Enrollment

Educational attainment has risen among East Asian women, both in absolute terms and relative to men (Mason 1995). Primary schooling has been nearly universal in the successful East Asian economies for quite some time, and therefore I focus here on secondary and tertiary enrollments.

Female secondary enrollment ratios have increased sharply in each of the selected countries (Table 14.2). The most dramatic increases have been in the

TABLE 14.2

*Percentages of Secondary School-Age Girls Enrolled for Secondary Education:
Six Asian Countries, 1965–90*

Country	1965	1970	1975	1980	1990[a]
Japan	83	86	92	94	98
South Korea	25	32	48	74	87
Taiwan	29	45	60	70	87
Singapore	45	45	53	59	71
Thailand	9	15	23	28	32
Indonesia	u	10	15	23	41

SOURCES: UNESCO (various years). Taiwan: ROC DGBAS (various years), *Statistical Yearbook of the Republic of China*.
u, data are unavailable.
[a] Indonesia and Singapore values are for 1989.

TABLE 14.3

*Ratio of Female to Male Secondary School Students:
Six Asian Countries, 1960–90*

Country	1960	1970	1975	1980	1990[a]
Japan	0.96	0.96	1.00	0.96	0.96
South Korea	0.37	0.61	0.69	0.82	0.92
Taiwan	0.52	0.69	0.82	0.92	1.00
Singapore	0.43	0.92	0.96	1.00	1.00
Thailand	0.61	0.72	0.79	0.85	0.92
Indonesia	0.49	0.52	0.61	u	0.82

SOURCES: UNESCO (various years). For Taiwan, ROC DGBAS (various years), *Statistical Yearbook of the Republic of China*.
u, data are unavailable.
[a] Indonesia and Singapore values are for 1989.

NIEs. In South Korea and Taiwan only 25% and 29%, respectively, of girls in the secondary-school age group were enrolled in the mid-1960s. These enrollment ratios reached 87% by 1990 in both countries. Enrollment ratios are lower in the more populous countries of the region, but they have been rising rapidly. In Indonesia, for example, the ratio jumped from 10% in 1970 to 41% by 1989.

Table 14.3, which shows the ratio of female to male secondary students, suggests that the gender gap in secondary enrollments has largely disappeared. A value of 1 indicates gender equality, and this has been achieved or is rapidly being approached in each of these countries.

TABLE 14.4
Ratio of Female to Male Tertiary School Students:
Six Asian Countries, 1960–90

Country	1960	1970	1975	1985	1990
Japan	0.25	0.39	0.47	0.54	0.67[a]
South Korea	0.20	0.32	0.37	0.43	0.52
Taiwan	0.30	0.56	0.59	0.75	0.85
Singapore	0.30[b]	0.43	0.67	u	u
Thailand	0.43	0.72	0.67	u	1.13
Indonesia	u	0.33	u	0.47[c]	u

SOURCES: UNESCO (various years). For Taiwan: ROC DGBAS (various years), *Statistical Yearbook of the Republic of China*.
u, data are unavailable.
[a] Value is for 1991.
[b] Value is for 1961.
[c] Value is for 1984.

Increasing numbers of East Asian women have been attending university, closing the gender gap in tertiary schooling (Table 14.4). Nevertheless, women remain at a disadvantage in five of the six countries, Thailand being the exception. In South Korea, for example, women are only half as likely as men to enter a university. There are also sex differences in fields of study within higher education. Mason (1995) concluded that this segregation has been easing in recent years and that differences in fields of study between men and women have shrunk.

Occupational Distribution of Female Employment

Economic development has changed the occupational composition of female employment. Table 14.5 examines trends in Japan, South Korea, Singapore, and Thailand since 1960. The most dramatic changes have been the declines in agricultural employment and the increases in clerical jobs. For example, in Japan the share of working women engaged in agriculture (the "Farm" category in Table 14.5) fell from 43% in 1960 to only 8% by 1990. The share of working women employed in clerical work rose from about 10% to almost 30% during that period. In South Korea there has also been a decrease in agriculture's share of female employment and an increase in clerical work. The labor share also rose dramatically, from 7% to 21%, during the industrialization drive that took place between 1960 and 1980. In Singapore agricultural employment was much less important in 1960 than in the other East Asian countries. Service employment among Singaporean

TABLE 14.5

Percentage Distribution of Working Women by Occupation:
Four Asian Countries, 1960–90[a]

Country and occupation	1960[b]	1970	1980	1990
Japan				
Prof./tech.	4.5	6.2	10.1	12.1
Admin.	0.2	0.5	0.9	1.0
Clerical	9.7	17.8	23.7	29.7
Sales	11.5	13.0	15.0	13.2
Service	9.9	11.2	12.0	11.6
Farm	42.9	26.1	13.6	8.0
Labor	21.3	25.3	24.7	24.4
South Korea				
Prof./tech.	1.5	2.1	3.5	8.3
Admin.	0.8	0.1	0.0	0.2
Clerical	0.5	2.8	8.6	15.5
Sales	9.7	9.6	11.6	14.6
Service	9.7	10.8	9.9	13.3
Farm	70.5	59.8	46.4	27.0
Labor	7.2	14.8	19.9	21.0
Singapore				
Prof./tech.	9.8	14.2	10.1	u
Admin.	0.4	0.4	2.2	u
Clerical	5.9	17.0	27.7	u
Sales	10.3	10.7	10.3	u
Service	35.8	23.4	13.6	u
Farm	12.0	3.2	1.0	u
Labor	25.8	31.0	35.0	u
Thailand				
Prof./tech.	0.9	1.5	3.1	4.8
Admin.	0.0	0.2	0.4	0.5
Clerical	0.3	0.8	1.5	2.6
Sales	6.2	5.9	8.4	9.8
Service	1.8	2.9	3.1	3.3
Farm	86.6	83.6	75.3	69.4
Labor	4.2	5.1	8.1	9.6

SOURCE: Census data.

u, data are unavailable.

[a]Unclassified workers and the unemployed are excluded. Occupational classifications are as follows: Prof./tech., professional, technical, and related; Admin., administrative and managerial; Clerical, clerical and related; Sales, sales workers; Service, service workers; Farm, agriculture, husbandry, forestry; Labor, Production workers, transport equipment, laborers.

[b]Some of the classifications for 1960 may not conform exactly to later years.

women declined dramatically between 1957 and 1980, whereas clerical and labor employment rose substantially. (Table 14.5 excludes 1990 data for Singapore because the occupational categories reported in the 1990 census were different from those used in earlier censuses.) In Thailand the share of women engaged in farming declined more gradually than in the NIEs, and by 1990 most Thai women were still working in agriculture. Jobs in sales and labor increased, however, reaching nearly 10% in each category.

The share of working women who are unpaid family workers has also declined in East Asia. Such employment gives women less control over resources than does independent paid employment. Mason (1995) argued that the shift away from unpaid family work has enhanced women's status in the region.

Women's Contribution to Economic Development

Women entered East Asia's labor markets in greater and greater numbers, and the resulting increases in labor supply contributed substantially to economic growth. Working women helped to sustain the labor-intensive, export-led industrialization drives in the region.

Labor Supply and GDP Growth

Growth-accounting studies suggest that increases in labor supply have been a major source of economic growth in the NIEs. For example, Kim and Lau (1994) attributed 15–32% of the NIEs' growth in real gross domestic product (GDP) between 1960 and 1990 to increases in labor supply. Young (1992) estimated that about one-fourth of GDP growth in Singapore was due to labor force growth.

Rising participation among women accounts for much of the increase in labor supply in the region. In the NIEs the number of working women has tended to grow much more rapidly than the number of working men, and women have accounted for substantial percentages of total labor force growth since 1960 (Table 14.6).

Increases in age-specific female participation rates accounted for 35% of South Korea's total labor force growth during the 1960s, 33% of Singapore's labor force growth during the 1970s and 29% of its growth during the 1980s, and nearly 31% of Taiwan's growth from 1966 to 1976 (Table 14.7). I derived these estimates by predicting what the size of the labor force would have been had female age-specific participation rates not changed over a decade. A comparison of the predicted and actual labor force sizes yielded the estimated effect of changing participation behavior.

Labor force growth in Japan was already slow by the early 1960s. During the 1960s and 1970s changes in age-specific female participation rates did not add to total labor force growth. In fact, during the 1970s declines in female participation, largely among young women for whom school enrollments increased, moderated labor force growth. However, rising female participation during the 1980s did contribute to increases in labor supply, accounting for about 24% of total labor force growth (Table 14.7).

TABLE 14.6

Women as a Percentage of the Total Labor Force:
Four East Asian Countries, 1960–90

Country	1960	1970	1980	1990
Japan	39.1	39.1	37.7	39.4
South Korea	28.4	34.7	36.5	([a])
Taiwan	u	19.8[b]	29.2[c]	33.6
Singapore	u	25.6	34.5	40.2

SOURCE: Calculated from census data.
u, data are unavailable.
[a] 1990 census data were not used because of changes in the classification of female employment.
[b] Value is for 1966.
[c] Value is for 1976.

TABLE 14.7

Women and Labor Force Growth: Four East Asian Countries, Recent Decades

Country and period	Average annual growth rate of labor force (%)			Percentage of labor force growth due to changes in age-specific female participation rates
	Total	Male	Female	
Japan				
1960–70	1.8	1.8	1.8	0.5
1970–80	0.7	0.9	0.3	−31.4
1980–90	1.1	0.8	1.5	23.8
South Korea				
1960–70	3.2	2.3	5.2	34.7
1970–80	2.8	2.5	3.3	6.6
Taiwan				
1966–76	3.4	2.2	7.3	30.6
1976–90	1.8	1.3	2.8	14.0
Singapore				
1970–80	4.4	3.1	7.4	32.9
1980–90	3.4	2.5	4.9	29.0

SOURCE: Calculated from census data.

Many observers believe that openness to trade and rapid export growth were the most important factors underlying the region's rapid economic development [for example, Balassa (1991), Hughes (1992), and Krueger (1993, 1995)]. Women played an important role in East Asia's labor-intensive, export-led industrialization drives. It is difficult to imagine those drives occurring without the efforts of female workers, whose labor fueled the growth in manufacturing and helped to moderate wage growth.

Women and Labor-Intensive, Export-Led Growth

The importance of women in the manufacturing sectors of East Asia grew substantially during the 1960s and 1970s. Lim (1993) observed that female employment in the Pacific Rim countries increased rapidly during the 1960s and early 1970s in the export-oriented, labor-intensive manufacturing industries that were the engines of growth. The female share of low-wage employment rose in countries that set up export processing zones: Singapore, Hong Kong, South Korea, Taiwan, Malaysia, the Philippines, and Thailand. In some cases the share of women in employment in industrial export zones exceeded 80% (Lim 1993: 176).

The female shares of total manufacturing employment rose in South Korea from 27% in 1960 to 36% by 1980, in Taiwan from 24% in 1966 to 42% by 1981, and in Singapore from 34% in 1970 to 46% by 1980 (Table 14.8). Rising employment among women accounted for 56% of the total growth in manufacturing employment in Singapore during the 1970s.

Women have been especially important in labor-intensive manufacturing (Joekes 1987; Lim 1993; Bai and Cho 1995). Surveys by the International Labour Organization (ILO) in Seoul, Kuala Lumpur, and Bangkok, for example, found that women employed in manufacturing are heavily concentrated in labor-intensive, low-wage, export-oriented industries such as textiles, clothing, and electronics (Bai and Cho 1995). In Thailand roughly three-quarters of manufacturing employment for women is in textiles, footwear, and apparel (Phananiramai 1993).

According to Schultz (1989), the rapid growth of labor-intensive manufacturing is the main cause for the rapid growth of female employment in developing countries. Another perspective, however, is that labor-intensive industrialization drives would not have been possible without women. Some have argued that East Asian industrialization is as much female led as export led (Joekes 1987; Lim 1993). Lim, for example, asserted (p. 179):

What is significant, . . . is not that rapid economic growth based on dynamic export-oriented industrialization led to large increases in female participation, but rather how female participation contributed to the successful industrialization and growth efforts. It was the ready and seemingly endless supply of young, malleable, and cheap female labour that was (and still is) the cornerstone of industrial success and the magnet for foreign investments.

Sex discrimination by employers has affected employment patterns. Folbre (1996: 142) argued that in some countries, such as South Korea, sex discrimination has been used as a tool for improving export competitiveness. Anker

TABLE 14.8

Percentage of Women in Manufacturing Employment:
Six Asian Countries, Recent Decades

Country and year	Percentage
Japan	
1950	28.7
1960	32.7
1970	35.9
1980	36.3
South Korea	
1960	26.7
1970	35.9
1980	36.2
Taiwan	
1966	24.1
1971	33.6
1981	41.9
Singapore	
1957	18.4
1970	33.6
1980	46.3
1990	46.8
Thailand	
1960	37.6
1970	42.7
1980	46.6
1990	49.1
Indonesia	
1961	37.6
1971	42.6
1980	44.8
1990	44.7

SOURCES: ILO (various years). For Taiwan, ROC CLA (various years) for 1979 and 1983. For Indonesia, 1990 census report.

and Hein (1985) made the assertion, based on ILO surveys in developing countries, that employers consider women more suitable for certain jobs because they are willing to work for lower wages, are perceived to be more docile than men, and are less likely to join unions or demand wage increases.

Demographic Changes, Educational Attainment, and Women's Labor Force Participation

To what extent have demographic changes in East Asia contributed to the rising educational attainment of women and facilitated their increased participation in the labor market? In Chapter 3 Feeney and Mason identify two critical demographic trends: the rise in age at marriage among women (Table 3.6) and the decline in total fertility rates (Table 3.3).

Age at marriage was already high and fertility already low in Japan by the early 1960s. Since then, in the NIEs and ASEAN countries fertility has declined dramatically and age at marriage has increased substantially. The total fertility rate was about six children per woman in the NIEs during the late 1950s and early 1960s. It had dropped to below two children per woman by the late 1980s. Between 1960 and 1990 the average age at marriage for women rose by almost seven years in Singapore, by five years in Taiwan, and by three years in South Korea. The populous ASEAN countries also experienced substantial demographic changes. The total fertility rate declined from 5.4 to 2.9 children per woman in Indonesia and from 6.4 to 2.1 children per woman in Thailand.

Effects of Demographic Changes on Educational Attainment

As we have already seen, women in East Asia have enjoyed substantial improvement in educational attainment in recent decades. The gender gap in secondary enrollment has largely disappeared, and the gap in tertiary enrollment has narrowed substantially. Delayed marriage and lower fertility may have contributed to these advances through a number of channels, but the strength of these effects is by no means clear.

Scholars have searched for beneficial effects of fertility decline by adopting both macroeconomic and household perspectives. As viewed from a macroeconomic perspective, falling total fertility rates cause the size of student cohorts to shrink. Government educational expenditures are therefore spread over fewer students. Expenditures per student rise, and the quality of schooling may improve. This should benefit girls as well as boys, and some observers have argued this to be the case in East Asia [see, for example, Williamson (1993) and Chapter 11 in this volume]. Viewed from a household perspective, declines in fertility result in smaller families. Smaller families are thought to promote increased school enrollments for offspring and larger expenditures per child within the family, and some analysts have argued that smaller household size has especially benefited girls. One argument is that when daughters have fewer siblings to help care for, the value of their time spent in household work declines, reducing the opportunity cost of their schooling. Another argument is that in smaller households there is less competition within the family for resources.

Unfortunately, there is little evidence for these household-level effects. Greenhalgh (1985) contended that Taiwanese parents favor investing in their sons and that increases in sons' schooling have come at the expense of daughters. Analyzing a sample of 80 families, Greenhalgh found that a larger number of sons in a family was associated with lower education for daughters.

However, Chang and Weinstein (1992), using a 1986 survey of 4,312 Taiwanese women, did not find the number of brothers to have an effect on sisters' education.

In a recent review of the literature, Ahlburg, Kelley, and Mason (1996: 6) concluded that the evidence is mixed regarding the effect of declining household size on educational outcomes. They found no convincingly consistent or strong negative effect of large household size. Moreover, they reported that the evidence of the effect of family size on educational outcomes by sex was inconclusive.

Rising age at marriage gives girls more time to complete higher levels of education, and this may have contributed to the increase in female enrollments. Lower fertility and gains in female life expectancy also may have increased the returns to female education by expanding the potential amount of time spent by women in the labor market. Human capital theory, as formulated by Becker (1962), suggests that an increase in the span of time over which the gains from education can accrue should increase investments in it.

Of course, there is the question of who actually makes decisions about education—daughters or their parents. Because education occurs early in life, it may make sense to model it as a parental decision. Moreover, the traditional family systems in East Asia were ones in which daughters married into their husbands' families. A girl's own parents had claim to her earnings only before her marriage. However, to the extent that parents could continue to rely on transfers from their daughters or that the parents acted altruistically, greater benefits from female schooling should have induced them to invest more in their daughters' education.

Effects of Demographic Changes on Labor Force Participation

How have demographic changes facilitated the rise in female labor force participation in East Asia? There are several channels. Rising age at marriage promotes participation among young women. Moreover, participation before marriage also increases the probability that women work after marriage. Lower fertility and reduced child-rearing responsibilities promote participation among married women. Labor-supply studies usually find that the presence of children constrains female participation.

My colleagues and I have found this to be the case in South Korea, Thailand, and Indonesia. We found fairly large effects for the presence of children under age 7 in South Korea, even after controlling for a long list of variables (Bauer and Shin 1987).[1] For example, the predicted probability that women in their late 20s to early 30s participate in the labor market declines from 0.54 when no children are present to 0.40 with 1 child present and to 0.28

with 2 children present. In Indonesia we found substantial effects for the presence of infants (Bauer, Sinuraya, and Iryanti 1991).[2] The predicted participation rate for women age 25–39 declines from 0.38 for those with no children to 0.29 for those with 1 infant. The negative effect of preschoolers is more modest. For example, the predicted participation rate for a woman with 2 preschoolers is 0.32. In Thailand we found the effects to be large only in urban areas (Bauer et al. 1992).[3] Among urban married women between the ages of 19 and 39 the predicted participation rate declines from 0.71 for women with no children to 0.65 for women with a child 3–6 years old and to 0.55 for women with an infant.

This literature, of course, raises the question of causality. Did the reduction in childbearing cause the increase in participation, or did the rise in female employment cause the decline in fertility? It is reasonable to infer, however, that declining fertility should reduce conflicts for women between home and the market, thereby promoting their labor force participation.

One reason that the presence of young children is a constraint in East Asia is that few childcare facilities exist in the region. Surveys conducted in Seoul, Kuala Lumpur, and Bangkok during 1991 indicate that the use of childcare is low. In Seoul only 8% of working women with children under age 10 used childcare facilities. Thirty-nine percent of those women relied on their parents or other relatives for childcare, and another 39% left their children at home alone. In Kuala Lumpur only 5% of women used childcare facilities, and in Bangkok fewer than 3% used them (Bai and Cho 1995: 312–8).

The use of childcare facilities is also limited in Taiwan and Japan. In 1993, 75% of Taiwanese women with children under age 3 took care of the children themselves, 19% relied on relatives, and only about 6% used babysitters or nurseries (ROC DGBAS 1994b, table 5). Most nurseries in Taiwan are at babysitters' homes. According to a 1983 survey, in Japan women cited the lack of childcare facilities as a major barrier to long-term employment (NIEVR 1988).

Declining fertility can also reduce demand-side constraints on female employment by lessening the reluctance of employers to hire married women. Employer discrimination against married women has been great in East Asia. For example, in South Korea women were often forced to quit jobs after marriage (Perkins 1990).

Anker and Hein (1985) discussed the higher costs that employers typically associate with employing women. Those perceived costs act to limit the demand for female workers. Pregnancy and childbirth can force employers to replace female workers during their maternity leave and can create costs arising from the discontinuity in work. Employer interviews in developing countries suggest that this is a particular concern when women are in management-level positions because their absence can disrupt work programs. Payment of maternity leave benefits and the possibility that women may not return after childbirth are also concerns. Absenteeism is the most common complaint made by employers about women in ILO case studies from developing countries. Because absenteeism is often linked to women's childcare responsibilities, declines in fertility and childcare responsibilities should reduce this concern among employers.

Lower fertility may have had a substantial indirect effect on female employment by contributing to labor scarcity and rising wages in the region. Fertility declines in the early 1960s resulted in slower labor force growth beginning in the early 1980s. This has exacerbated the problem of labor scarcity and put upward pressure on wages, which have helped to draw women into the labor market. The effect is potentially large. Gregory and Lal (1977) reported that a 1% decrease in the labor force growth rate results in a 1% increase in real wage growth across countries. Moreover, female labor supply is fairly elastic. A typical estimate for the wage elasticity of female labor supply is about 1. That is, a 1% increase in wage rates tends to be associated with a 1% increase in female labor supply.

Female Employment and the Economic Status of Women

Many argue that increases in formal employment among women have improved women's economic status. Market work provides women with a role outside the home and may give them greater control over resources. I believe this to be generally true, but there are several aspects of the formal employment of women that raise concerns.

An obvious problem is that women now face the dual burden of market and household work. This burden is great in East Asia, where working women have little time for leisure or rest. Japanese and Korean men do little to reduce this burden. A 1990 South Korean survey found that married women on average spent 5 hours and 10 minutes per day on household chores and childcare, compared with an average of 37 minutes spent by men. A 1986 Japanese survey found that married men spent 0.11 hour per day on household duties, whereas married women spent 3.28 hours per day. Married women with jobs spent 2.44 hours, and women without jobs spent 4.16 hours (Tsuya and Choe 1991). The situation has apparently not changed much since then. Atoh (1994) claimed that the time spent by Japanese men doing household chores has not increased over time, and it has remained relatively fixed for women. In Taiwan, too, working women's dual burden is great. In 1993 married women who were employed spent an average of 5.2 hours per day doing household work, only slightly less than the 7.5 hours per day spent by married women who were not in the labor force (ROC DGBAS 1994b, table 31).

Lim (1993) reported that foreign domestic workers in Singapore, Hong Kong, and Malaysia have helped to free local women for other types of employment. The luxury of relying on domestic workers, however, does not appear to be widespread in the region. Bai and Cho (1995) found that 92% of married working women in Seoul and 81% of those in Kuala Lumpur performed household work without the help of maids. Phananiramai (1993) found that in 1989 employed women in Thailand worked an average of 52 hours per week in the labor market and were still responsible for most of the household chores.

A second concern is that job security for women is less than that for men. Lim (1993), for example, noted that women bore the brunt of layoffs in East Asian and ASEAN countries during the first oil shock in the mid-1970s and during the global recession of the early 1980s.

I found that women in the NIEs also suffered disproportionately from losses in manufacturing jobs during the industrial restructuring of the 1980s. Currency appreciation and rising labor costs eroded competitiveness in labor-intensive manufacturing. The NIEs have had to restructure their economies by moving into higher value-added, more skill- and capital-intensive manufacturing and business services. Some labor-intensive manufacturing was moved overseas by means of foreign direct investment (Bauer 1992).

Women, who tended to dominate the work forces in the labor-intensive industries, suffered heavy job losses during this restructuring. For example, in Hong Kong total employment in manufacturing declined by roughly 72,000 jobs between 1987 and 1989. For every 10 men who lost their jobs during this period, there were 16 displaced women. Almost 90% of the decline in manufacturing employment can be accounted for by job losses in the apparel, plastic products, and electronics industries, in which female employment was heavily concentrated. A similar trend was observed from 1987 to 1990 in Taiwan, where more than 360,000 manufacturing jobs disappeared. Declines in female employment accounted for almost 60% of all job losses. Again, the cause was the heavy job loss in labor-intensive industries such as textiles, apparel, and electronics (Bauer 1992).

A third concern is the large wage differentials between men and women. The average earnings of women in manufacturing were only 42% of men's in Japan during 1989, 50% in South Korea, 58% in Singapore, and 73% in Hong Kong. Survey data for 1991 indicate that women earned about 70% as much as men in Kuala Lumpur and roughly 75% as much in Bangkok (Bai and Cho 1995: 190).

The wage gap may be closing in some countries, but trends vary. Data on wages for all nonagricultural activities suggest, for example, that sex differences in earnings are declining in South Korea and Singapore (ILO, *Year Book of Labour Statistics*, various years). The ratio of female to male earnings in South Korea increased from 0.48 in 1985 to 0.59 in 1993. The ratio rose in Singapore form 0.63 in 1980 to 0.73 in 1994. The wage gap in Japan, however, has been more persistent. The ratio of female to male earnings there was 0.52 in 1985 and 0.51 in 1991. Ogawa and Matsukura (1995) noted that the sex-wage differential among full-time workers in Japan has been narrowing because of the closing gap in education. However, the overall wage gap is still large because of sex differences in levels of experience and the high incidence of part-time work among women.

Occupational segregation contributes to the wage differentials in the region. As noted, female employment in manufacturing has been heavily concentrated in low-wage, labor-intensive industries. Moreover, within these industries women have been segregated into the lower-paying jobs. Recently women have been moving into other sectors, but they still tend to be confined to lower-rank occupations (Lim 1993).

Mason (1995) argued that development in Asia has tended to exacerbate occupational segregation by sex: "Although development draws women into paid and relatively clean forms of work in the white-collar sector, it also segregates them out of the better-paid jobs in the manufacturing sector, thereby perpetuating gender inequality in the labor force" (p. 14).

Table 14.9 summarizes trends in occupational segregation by sex in Japan, South Korea, Singapore, and Thailand. The values are the ratios of each occupation's share of total female employment to its share of total male employment. A value greater than 1 indicates that women are more heavily concentrated in that occupation.

The extent of segregation varies across countries and over time. In Japan and Singapore the most striking trend has been the increasing concentration of women in clerical work. As of 1990, women in these two countries were more than twice as likely as men to be clerical workers. In South Korea and Thailand the importance of clerical work for women has also been growing rapidly. In the 1960s relatively few women were employed in clerical jobs. By 1990, however, women and men where equally likely to have such jobs.

In each of the four countries in Table 14.9 women have been consistently underrepresented in administrative and managerial positions. Women are much more likely than men to be in services in Japan and South Korea. This is true to a lesser extent in Singapore, where the fraction of women employed in services declined substantially between 1957 and 1980. In Thailand women are much more likely to be in sales than are men.

Fertility and the Continuity of Female Employment

The fact that many women leave the labor market upon marrying or having children contributes to their employment problems. Bai and Cho (1995) ar-

TABLE 14.9

Occupational Segregation by Sex (Percentage of Women in Occupation/Percentage of Men in Occupation): Four Asian Countries, 1960–90

Country and occupation	1960[a]	1970	1980	1990
Japan				
Prof./tech.	0.8	0.9	1.3	1.0
Admin.	0.1	0.1	0.1	0.1
Clerical	0.9	1.5	2.0	2.3
Sales	1.1	1.1	1.1	0.9
Service	2.2	2.0	2.0	1.7
Farm	1.6	1.8	1.5	1.2
Labor	0.5	0.6	0.6	0.6
South Korea				
Prof./tech.	0.5	0.5	0.7	1.2
Admin.	0.6	0.1	0.0	0.1
Clerical	0.1	0.4	0.9	1.0
Sales	1.3	0.9	0.9	1.1
Service	2.2	2.4	1.8	2.1
Farm	1.1	1.3	1.4	1.5
Labor	0.5	0.6	0.6	0.6
Singapore[b]				
Prof./tech.	2.6	2.0	1.1	u
Admin.	0.2	0.2	0.3	u
Clerical	0.5	1.4	2.7	u
Sales	0.5	0.6	0.7	u
Service	3.2	2.1	1.4	u
Farm	1.7	0.7	0.4	u
Labor	0.6	0.7	0.7	u
Thailand				
Prof./tech.	0.5	0.8	1.1	1.2
Admin.	0.1	0.1	0.1	0.1
Clerical	0.2	0.5	0.8	1.1
Sales	1.3	1.4	1.5	1.7
Service	0.8	1.1	1.2	1.3
Farm	1.1	1.1	1.1	1.1
Labor	0.4	0.5	0.6	0.6

SOURCE: Calculated from census data.

u, data are unavailable.

[a]Some of the classifications for 1960 may not conform exactly to later years.

[b]Data in first column are for 1957. Some of the classifications for 1957 may not conform exactly to later years.

gued that women's departure from the labor market upon marriage is a major cause of the wage gap in South Korea, given that country's strong seniority wage system. In Japan companies are reluctant to invest in training women because of the perception that they are temporary workers who leave service upon marriage and childbearing. As a result, many companies give preference to men in recruitment and training, and women have few opportunities for promotion (NIEVR 1988). The number and spacing of children affect women's commitment to and continuity of market work. This in turn affects how women choose to invest in human capital (education and occupational choice) and how employers treat them.

Demographics and the Life-Cycle Phases of Women

Demographic events define three critical phases in a woman's life. The first phase is the period after leaving school and before marriage. Labor market participation is typically high in this "single" phase. The second is the period from marriage to the entry of the youngest child into school. Participation is lower during this "child-rearing" phase because many women leave the market. The third, "post-child-rearing" phase begins when that youngest child enters school. Household responsibilities decline, and labor force participation is typically greater. Moreover, participation becomes more continuous in this phase.

Not only do women forgo earnings during child rearing, but they also forgo gains in experience and returns to tenure. In fact, a woman's earnings upon reentry into the market may actually be lower than when she left, because of the depreciation of her skills. Labor economists have used this observation to explain human capital investment and occupational choices among women in the United States (Mincer and Polachek 1974; Polachek 1981; Mincer and Ofek 1982).

One argument is that women tend to choose occupations in which the penalties associated with leaving the market temporarily are low, hence the heavy concentration of women in clerical and sales positions. A related argument is that women's disproportionate share of household duties affects their occupational choice (O'Neill 1985; Fuchs 1989). Again, this burden should be heaviest during the child-rearing phase.

The lengths of these three phases could have strong effects on the position of women in the labor market. A longer child-rearing phase would clearly be detrimental. Shortening this phase should contribute to the continuity of female participation and reduce employer discrimination, which is based on the presumption that women are less committed to the labor market than are men.

This discussion ignores the burden of caring for elderly parents, which Feeney and Mason, in Chapter 3 of this volume, suggest will become greater over the next few decades. Ogawa and Matsukura (1995) argued that given the relatively low level of institutional care for the elderly in Japan, the rapid aging that is taking place there will constrain female employment in the future. Women will be forced to spend more time caring for elderly parents and parents-in-law.

Demographic Changes and the Life-Cycle Phases

Three important demographic factors affect the length of the life-cycle phases. One is fertility reduction. Obviously, fewer births and shorter spacing would reduce the length of the child-rearing phase. The declines in total fertility rates suggest that the child-rearing phases of women throughout East Asia have become much shorter since the early 1960s. A second factor is the increased age at marriage. Delayed marriage lengthens the phase of singlehood and promotes participation by young women. For example, Domingo (1995) argued that delayed marriage in ASEAN countries improved women's opportunities for education and work. The third factor is lower mortality.

Increased years of schooling can counter the rising age at marriage, so that the single phase (the period between leaving school and marriage) is actually shortened. In South Korea the mean age at marriage for women rose from 22.6 years in 1960 to 25.4 years by 1990. According to census data, however, the average number of years of schooling among women 21–29 years old increased by about 6 years. The single phase, therefore, declined from 11.2 years to 8.5 years over this period. Estimates presented in the next section suggest that this has also occurred in Japan.

In addition to promoting the labor force participation of young women, delayed marriage can improve their status in other ways. Mason (1995) asserted that early marriage can undermine women's power for at least three reasons. First, it is associated with the bride's residence in an extended-family household, where she is likely to fall under the control of elders. Second, women who marry earlier are likely to have fewer material and psychological resources at their command. Third, young brides tend to marry men who are much older than themselves, and this may put them at a disadvantage. "Insofar as a higher age at marriage gives women greater resources and power after marrying, the trend toward delayed marriage in Asia suggests that the status of women is improving" (Mason 1995: 15).

Lower infant and child mortality reduces the need for child replacement and may therefore shorten the child-rearing phase. Longer female life expectancy lengthens the post-child-rearing phase, and this can increase the working life of women. There have been dramatic increases in life expectancy for women across East Asia. The average number of years that a female infant at birth was expected to live rose from 70.2 to 82.2 between 1960 and 1992 in Japan, from 53.7 to 75 between the late 1950s and 1989 in South Korea, from 67.6 to 78.3 between the early 1960s and 1992 in Singapore, and from 58.2 to 73 between 1956 and the early 1990s in Malaysia (UN DIESA 1979, table 8; UN DESIPA 1995a, table 25).

In sum, higher ages at marriage and declines in fertility have reduced the length of the child-rearing phase, and longer life expectancy has dramatically prolonged the post-child-rearing phase. Together, these changes should broaden women's career options and alter their perspectives on the trade-off between home responsibilities and outside work.

Estimates of Life-Cycle Changes in East Asia

The extent to which these demographic changes have affected the three life-cycle phases of women in East Asia varies from country to country. Estimates of the effects have been made for Japan, South Korea, and Taiwan and suggest that the collective impact has been significant.

Table 14.10 summarizes estimates for Japan made by the National Institute of Employment and Vocational Research (NIEVR 1988). Two birth cohorts are compared: (1) the 1927 cohort, consisting of women who would have married around 1950, and (2) the 1959 cohort, comprising women who would have married around 1984.

Although the average age at marriage rose between the two cohorts, the single phase (from leaving school to marriage) became shorter because a large increase also occurred in the average number of years of schooling. A change in fertility behavior between the two cohorts caused the child-rearing phase (from marriage to last child in school) to decline from an average of 14 years to 11 years. The NIEVR (1988) study also provided estimates of the life-cycle phases for the 1905 birth cohort (not shown in Table 14.10). The women in

TABLE 14.10

Women's Life-Cycle Phases: Japan, 1927 and 1959 Birth Cohorts

Measure	1927 cohort	1959 cohort
Age at event		
Leaving school	15	19
Marriage	23	25
First birth	24	27
Last birth	31	29
Last child in school	37	36
Death	70	81
Length of phase (years)		
Single[a]	8	6
Child rearing[b]	14	11
Post-child rearing[c]	33	45

SOURCE: NIEVR (1988).
[a]Period between leaving school and marriage.
[b]Period between marriage and last child in school.
[c]Period between last child in school and death of the woman.

that cohort, who tended to marry around the year 1928, had an average child-rearing phase lasting 22 years.

The most substantial difference between the 1927 and 1959 birth cohorts was caused by the dramatic increase in female life expectancy. This along with the shorter duration of child rearing caused the projected post-child-rearing phase (from last child in school to death of the women) to increase from 33 years to 45 years. The report concluded that these changes altered women's perspectives on careers. Given that the child-rearing period had become a relatively short part of an 80-year life span, women began to place greater emphasis on their careers (NIEVR 1988: 25).

In South Korea fertility declines since the late 1950s have been more substantial than in Japan, and so there has been a greater potential for recent life-cycle phase changes in that country. This is what we observe in the estimates by Kong et al. (1987), which are summarized in Table 14.11. These estimates, which are based on period fertility rates, compare those marrying during 1955–64 and 1975–85. (The estimates for ages at leaving school are my own and are based on census data for 1960 and 1980.)

The duration of the single phase declined across the two marriage groups, from 11 years to 8 years. Once again, increases in the age at marriage were more than offset by increases in years of schooling. Lower fertility among the more recent marriage group generated a substantial compression in the child-

TABLE 14.11

Women's Life-Cycle Phases: South Korea,
1955–64 and 1975–85 Rates[a]

Measure	1955–64	1975–85
Age at event		
Leaving school	11	16
Marriage	22	24
First birth	24	25
Last birth	33	27
Last child in school	39	33
Death	68	76
Length of phase (years)		
Single[b]	11	8
Child rearing[c]	17	9
Post-child rearing[d]	29	42

SOURCES: For age at leaving school, estimates calculated from census data on average number of years of schooling for women of age 20–29 in 1960 and 1980. For other measures, Kong et al. (1987, chart 5.5).

[a]Kong et al. (1987) based their estimates on rates observed in the given time periods. Marriage ages are singulate mean ages at marriage for 1960 and 1980.

[b]Period between leaving school and marriage.

[c]Period between marriage and last child in school.

[d]Period between last child in school and death of the woman.

rearing phase, reducing it from 17 years to 9 years. The post-child-rearing phase increased, as it did in Japan, because of the shorter duration of child rearing and the dramatic increase in female life expectancy.

Chang, Chung, and Kang (1991) also provided estimates of the life-cycle phases for two cohorts of South Korean women. They compared the experience of women who married during 1935–44 with the projected experience of those who married during 1975–85. Their estimates suggest that the child-rearing phase declined from 25.6 years to 9.4 years between these 2 marriage cohorts.

I am not aware of published estimates of the life-cycle phases for Taiwan, but it is clear that substantial changes have occurred there as well. Consider the following rough estimate. The total fertility rate declined from 6.5 children per woman in the late 1950s to 1.9 by the late 1980s. The average birth interval in Taiwan during the mid-1980s was 21 months (ROC DGBAS 1986, table 10). If we ignore changes in birth intervals across parities (that is, numbers of children borne) and over time, women who bore 6 children would have had a child-rearing phase of roughly 17 years, whereas women who bore 2 children would have had a child-rearing phase of only 9 years.

Life-Cycle Changes and Labor Force
Participation across Cohorts

How have these changes affected women's attachment to the labor market? It is obviously difficult to answer this question. Many things have changed among these cohorts, and it is probably impossible to disentangle the causal relationships. Nevertheless, I examined changes in participation behavior across several cohorts in Japan, Taiwan, and Singapore using census data from 1960 to 1990. (I also used labor force survey data for Singapore.) The changes I observed are at least consistent with the view that shorter child-rearing phases have allowed married women to participate in the labor force for longer periods. Fewer women now leave the labor market, and their departures are apparently shorter in duration.

Figure 14.1 illustrates the participation histories for five-year birth cohorts of Japanese women. The oldest cohort, born between 1936 and 1940, would have entered the labor market in the early to mid-1950s. The youngest cohort, born between 1961 and 1965, would have entered the market in the early 1980s.

Age-specific participation rates generally increased from the oldest to the youngest cohorts. The rates for women of age 25–29 began to rise dramatically after the 1946–50 birth cohort. The participation rate among that age group in the 1946–50 cohort was about 43% (this would have been in 1971). Participation for the same age group in the 1961–65 cohort was above

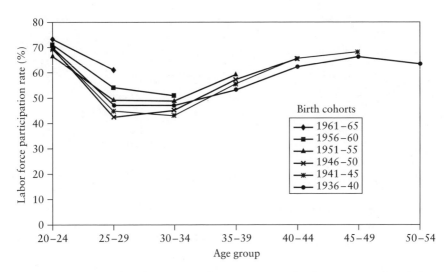

FIGURE 14.1. Female Labor Force Participation Rates by Age Group and Birth Cohort: Japan, 1936–40 to 1961–65 Cohorts.

60% (in 1986). The participation of women age 30–34 also increased across these cohorts.

Although some women still withdraw from the labor market after marriage, fewer of them do so. Female participation has become more continuous, and the M-shaped pattern has moderated a bit. Atoh (1994) asserted that the higher participation rates for the 25–34-year age group since the mid-1970s reflect both delayed marriage and a reduced tendency to withdraw from the market upon marriage and childbirth. Employment-trend surveys conducted by the Japanese Ministry of Labor have found that the proportion of women who reported leaving their jobs because of marriage or childbirth declined from 25% in 1975 to 14% in 1991. According to the NIEVR (1988, table II-1), the share of female workers leaving jobs because of marriage or pregnancy declined by 20% from 1970 to 1985, and the share of female workers with 10 or more years of continuous service increased from 12% to 20% over this period.

Demand-side changes have also been important in promoting the participation of married women. Increases in part-time work opportunities have played a critical role. The number of female part-time workers (those working fewer than 35 hours per week) rose by 2.03 million from 1970 to 1985. With labor becoming increasingly scarce, firms turned to middle-aged women as a labor pool. To draw housewives into the market, they needed to devise working arrangements that were more compatible with household responsi-

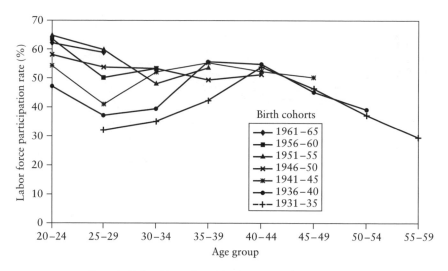

FIGURE 14.2. Female Labor Force Participation Rates by Age Group and Birth Cohort: Taiwan, 1931–35 to 1961–65 Cohorts.

bilities. The establishment of part-time jobs facilitated the reentry of married women into the market (NIEVR 1988).

In Taiwan the participation of women between the ages of 20 and 39 has increased across cohorts (Figure 14.2). The declines in participation observed after age 24 have moderated over time, participation by married women has become more continuous, and the M-shaped pattern has largely disappeared. The percentage of married women who never quit their jobs is increasing. Among all married women in the economically active age group (15–64 years) in 1979, only 22% had never quit working after marriage. By 1993 this figure had risen to 30% (ROC DGBAS 1994b, table 6).

A comparison of the behavior of married women in Taiwan and South Korea suggests that the effects of demographic changes on female employment can be tempered by other factors, such as general labor market conditions. Age at marriage rose and fertility declined substantially in both economies, but the M-shaped pattern of female participation has disappeared more completely in Taiwan than in South Korea. In Taiwan the participation of women age 25–34 has increased more substantially.

Lee, Brinton, and Parish (1992) argued that during the late 1970s and the 1980s the marriage bar softened to a much greater extent in Taiwan than in South Korea. Taiwanese employers were more willing to hire married women because of the tighter labor market. South Korea's labor market was less tight because of government policies that promoted greater capital intensity and large conglomerates. South Korea's focus on heavy industry provided

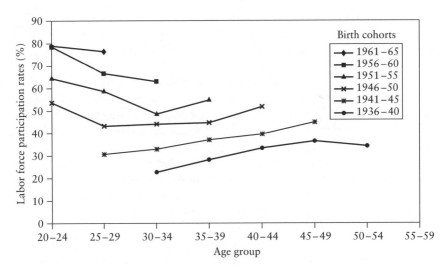

FIGURE 14.3. Female Labor Force Participation Rates by Age Group and Birth Cohort: Singapore, 1936–40 to 1961–65 Cohorts.

fewer jobs that favored women. Moreover, an oversupply of educated men in South Korea meant that there were fewer opportunities for educated women.

The participation across birth cohorts of Singaporean women has increased at all ages (Figure 14.3). Although participation still declines from ages 20–24 to 30–34, the declines seem to be moderating. The percentage of women of childbearing age who work has risen dramatically. For example, among women born between 1941 and 1945 only about 30% were working at ages 25–29 (during 1970). Among women born between 1961 and 1965 about 77% were working at those ages (during 1990).

Conclusion

The lives of women in East Asia have changed dramatically since the early 1960s. They now marry much later and have fewer children. They are much better educated and have been entering the labor market in greater and greater numbers. The types of work they are engaged in have changed. In particular, the incidence of agricultural and unpaid family work has been declining.

Women have made major contributions to economic growth in the region. Rising female labor force participation rates have generated large increases in labor supply, and these increases have contributed substantially to GDP growth in East Asia. Women have played an especially important role in labor-intensive, export-led industrialization. Some observers have argued that the region's industrialization was as much female led as export led. The increasing number of women entering the labor market has caused aggregate labor force participation rates to rise, allowing GDP per capita to grow faster than GDP per worker.

Rising ages at marriage and lower fertility rates have facilitated the increase in female labor force participation. These demographic trends have reduced the conflicts for women between household responsibilities and work in the market. They may have also reduced the reluctance among employers to hire married women.

Nevertheless, women continue to be at a distinct disadvantage in East Asian labor markets. They face the dual burden of market and household work, have less job security than men, are paid less than their male counterparts, and are heavily segregated into certain occupations.

These problems are exacerbated by the fact that women have tended to leave the labor market upon marriage or childbirth. But change is under way. Later marriage, fewer children, and longer life expectancies have radically altered the life-cycle phases of East Asian women. The child-rearing phase has been compressed and the post-child-rearing phase extended. These changes have acted to increase the continuity of female participation and to alter women's perspectives on their own human capital investment and occupational choice. Changes in participation behavior across cohorts in the region are consistent with this view.

15

Population and Inequality
in East Asia

HARRY OSHIMA AND ANDREW MASON

ONE OF THE MOST IMPORTANT LESSONS of the East Asian development experience is that growth with equity is an achievable objective. In a recent study, *The East Asian Miracle*, the World Bank noted that the successful Asian economies are "unique in that they combine . . . rapid, sustained growth with highly equal income distributions" (World Bank 1993a: 8). Their experience thus appears to repudiate the view that the region's development policy overemphasized economic growth at the expense of broader social welfare concerns. Moreover, their experience establishes the existence of a development path that is much preferred to the well-known Kuznets curve, which posits an initial rise in income inequality that is followed by a decline (Kuznets, Moore, and Spengler 1955).

In this chapter we examine trends and differences in income inequality in the high-performing countries of East Asia and identify important factors that influenced inequality. We begin with a brief discussion of the practical difficulties encountered in measuring income inequality. We then turn to a closer examination of the East Asian experience. As a group, the countries of East Asia have lower income inequality than the countries of Latin America or Africa. Within the region, however, there is wide variation. In Northeast Asia income inequality is low, whereas in Southeast Asia the level is similar to that found in Latin America and Africa. Moreover, the trends in income inequality differ greatly from one country to another. Even the most cursory inspection of the data suggests that income inequality is governed by exceedingly complex forces that differ greatly from country to country. Simple generalizations about the connection between income inequality and eco-

We thank Jeff Brown for his assistance on this chapter.

nomic growth or income inequality and the demographic transition are elusive. Development policies, economic structure, politics, culture, and agricultural conditions all play a role.

Some Pitfalls in Measuring Income Inequality

Studies of income distribution must deal with many practical and conceptual difficulties. A pervasive problem is the limited availability and poor quality of income data. Compared with most developing areas, Asian survey data are plentiful and high in quality. Most East Asian countries conduct income surveys every few years, and several conduct annual surveys. The high level of literacy in the region contributes to the quality of the collected data. Despite these advantages, data problems are still substantial. Income data have been available only since the 1960s, and collection efforts were much more sporadic in the 1960s and early 1970s than recently. Literacy was a more serious problem in early surveys. Illiterate families are unable to record their incomes and expenditures; interviewers must therefore rely on recall methods that are subject to serious errors. Adequately measuring income is particularly difficult when substantial sectors of the economy are nonmonetized, as would have been the case in the 1960s and, in some countries, the 1970s. Modern surveys have their own difficulties. Conducting a representative survey has become increasingly difficult in some countries because many high-income individuals decline to be interviewed or understate their income. The poorest members of a society are often underrepresented in surveys. Because of these problems, income inequality is probably underestimated in all surveys and more so in some countries (for example, Indonesia) than in other countries.

The data used in this chapter to summarize the trends in income inequality are drawn from several sources. We rely on country studies written by specialists for a volume on income distribution in 14 Asian countries (see the sources cited in Table 15.4). Although these data have some of the problems just mentioned, we believe that they provide the best available estimates. For some purposes we rely on the international database described by Deininger and Squire (1996).

These studies and most others rely on the Gini ratio to summarize the degree of income inequality. The Gini ratio varies between 0, the extreme case in which all members of the population have the same income, and 1, the case in which all income is earned by only one individual. In practice, countries with relatively equal income distributions have Gini ratios near 0.3, whereas those with unequal distributions have Gini ratios of 0.5 or somewhat higher.

Other measures are also used to summarize income inequality. The variance in the natural logarithm of income is often used in analyses of the sources of income inequality because changes in the variance can be decomposed into constituent parts. We make use of this property in our discussion of the relationship between demographic factors and income inequality.

Most studies use household income rather than individual income to measure income inequality, but for several important reasons household income may be a poor way to compare welfare or living standards among individuals or households. The use of the household as the unit of analysis is necessitated by practical and conceptual considerations. Although wages and salaries can be assigned to individuals, property income, interest income, and proprietor's income cannot, except in a relatively arbitrary fashion. Given the importance of family enterprises in many developing countries, inequality measures based on the incomes of individuals may be seriously flawed. Consequently, economists typically use the household as the unit of analysis. Although doing so circumvents the practical problems of measuring income, it also ignores consideration of the distribution of income within households. If the strong sex stratification and primogeniture characteristic of East Asia, especially Northeast Asia, produce income inequality within households, standard approaches may understate East Asian income inequality more so than in other regions.

A second important issue is how to compare incomes among households with different compositions. The standard approach, suggested by Kuznets (1976), is to use per capita household income rather than household income. A simple refinement of Kuznets's method, which recognizes that consumption needs vary systematically depending on the characteristics of family members, uses income per equivalent adult. Either approach requires data that are not usually published. Consequently, trends in inequality based on per capita income measures are infrequently available. Given the great changes in household composition in East Asia, this is a serious drawback for any assessment of the impact of population change on income inequality.

The choice of income measure does have an important effect on the trend in inequality in the one economy for which comparisons are available. In Taiwan the ln variance of household income increased substantially between 1980 and 1995. During the same period, however, the ln variance of income per adult was essentially flat and the ln variance of income per capita declined modestly (Schultz 1997).

A third issue is the use of current income to compare households. Current income may be a poor measure of welfare because it neglects the capacity of families to smooth consumption over the life cycle by accumulating and spending wealth. Thus the income of the young or, especially, retirees may greatly understate their living standards compared with that of prime-age workers. This issue has particular relevance to analyses of the effect of changes in age composition on income inequality and has led some [for example, Lam (1997b)] to argue that changes in income inequality that result from changes in the age composition of the population have no welfare implications. The use of lifetime income as a measure of inequality would also naturally incorporate considerations of the length of life into income inequality measures. This is a topic that is usually ignored but one that we discuss briefly later.

A fourth, pervasive issue is that of choice. Household income often reflects decisions made by household members that involve trade-offs between income and unmeasured sources of welfare. A simple example is the trade-off between leisure and labor. Individuals with a strong taste for leisure choose to work fewer hours and earn less income than their counterparts, but in no meaningful sense can we say that they have lower welfare than those who choose to work more hours and earn higher incomes. Other decisions have potentially important implications for income distribution, including the labor force participation decisions by women, fertility decision making, and living arrangements.

All these difficulties should be kept in mind as we examine income inequality in East Asia and assess the effects of demographic factors on it.

Overview of East Asian Income Inequality

"Growth with equity" is a label often used to characterize East Asia's economic record between 1960 and 1990. As with any generalization, however, broad characterizations of East Asian income inequality can be misleading. The East Asian economies as a group had a more equal income distribution circa 1990 than the developing countries of Latin America or Africa (Table 15.1). However, income inequality was greater in East Asia (Taiwan excluded) than in South Asia or the industrialized countries.

The level of income inequality in individual East Asian countries is quite varied. In Northeast Asia, Japan, Taiwan, and South Korea had levels of income inequality comparable to those of OECD (Organisation for Economic Co-operation and Development) countries. The extent of income inequality in South Korea is a subject of some dispute, as we discuss momentarily. The Southeast Asian countries of Hong Kong, Malaysia, and Thailand had Gini ratios that were much closer to those found in Africa or Latin America. Indonesia's Gini ratio was also low, but the calculations for Indonesia are based on expenditure rather than income and consequently understate the degree of income inequality.

The clear demarcation between Northeast and Southeast Asia has been a persistent phenomenon. Figure 15.1, which shows the trends in income

TABLE 15.1

Income Inequality: Regions of the World and Eight East Asian Countries, Recent Years[a]

Region or country	Number of countries	Gini ratio
Region		
Africa	22	0.43
High-performing Asia	8	0.37
South Asia	5	0.31
Latin America	17	0.50
Industrialized	19	0.32
East Asian countries		
Japan		0.37
South Korea		0.39
Taiwan		0.32
Singapore		0.39
Hong Kong		0.48
Thailand		0.49
Indonesia		0.34
Malaysia		0.46

SOURCES: Compiled from Deininger and Squire (1996). Data for individual East Asian countries drawn from Table 15.4.

[a]Data are for the latest available year (after 1980). Only high-quality data are included. For regions, the values are medians.

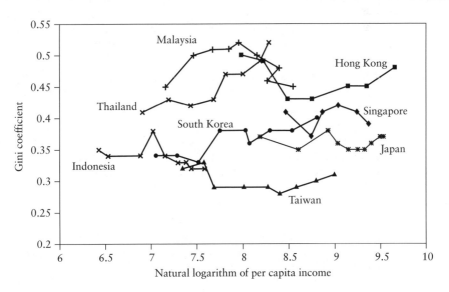

FIGURE 15.1. Inequality and Development in East Asia.

inequality for the eight high-performing economies of East Asia, plots the Gini ratio against the natural logarithm of per capita income.[1] Gini ratios in the Southeast Asian countries of Hong Kong, Malaysia, and Thailand were greater in all the years charted, irrespective of the level of income, than were the Gini ratios among the countries of Northeast Asia. Singapore generally falls between the two groups. Thus it is the countries of Northeast Asia that have been especially successful at achieving rapid economic growth while maintaining a low degree of income inequality.

Figure 15.1 provides scant evidence of a Kuznets curve. Indeed, there appears to be no relationship at all between income inequality and the level of development. Inequality does not seem to be increasing with income at low income levels, nor does it seem to be declining with income at higher income levels. Only in Thailand does there appear to be any strong correlation between income inequality and development.

We can suggest several reasons why the simple relationship between income inequality and development postulated by Kuznets may not be apparent in the East Asian experience. The Kuznets curve is intended as a long-term characterization, whereas Figure 15.1 covers only 20–30 years. Limited information on income inequality is available earlier for Japan and Taiwan, but individual countries cannot be followed over the entire development process. However, the eight countries cover such a wide development range that, taken as a group, we might reasonably expect them to capture a portion of the development experience sufficient to reveal the Kuznets curve. Japan's income in the last year observed exceeds Indonesia's first observation by more than twenty-fold. Differences in economic structure and other idiosyncratic features of individual countries may have masked the long-term relationship. Some of the important changes in income distribution are clearly the consequence of short-run phenomena: random, episodic events such oil shocks, weather variations, exchange rate movements, and commodity price fluctuations. Income inequality reflects the influences of demographic change and other long-run trends, the timing of which has varied from country to country. Countries have used different development strategies and adopted different income distribution policies that clearly had important effects on inequality. Finally, some unknown portion of the differences and changes shown in Figure 15.1 reflect differences in data collection procedures and measurement error.

Both the interregional differences and the intercountry differences in income inequality reflect differences in culture, history, and economic structure. Huge haciendas dominate the plains of many Latin American countries, generating large incomes for the owners while employing large numbers of low-paid laborers. In the hills indigenous peasants live at near-subsistence levels, tilling small patches of land. Latin American countries have relatively large urban sectors dominated by large-scale, capital-intensive enterprise. The situation is quite different in densely populated monsoon Asia. Most farms there are small, averaging about 2 hectares, compared with 200 hectares in Latin America. Numerous small and medium-size industries and services are prevalent throughout most of monsoon Asia.

A variety of factors account for the different patterns of development. In the densely packed lowlands of Asia villages were large groupings of farm families that could support small workshops and stores. Off-farm jobs in the factories, shops, and stores of nearby towns were sources of wages to supplement the incomes earned on the farms, thus reducing income inequality between the rural and urban sectors. In Latin America farmers could travel on horses to faraway towns to market their wares and purchase supplies, but in land-scarce Asia horses were too expensive to raise (Oshima 1993).

Important structural, historical, and cultural differences also account for differences between Northeast and Southeast Asia. Japan, Taiwan, and South Korea are characterized by a large middle class and an agricultural sector dominated by small-scale holdings, in large part because of land reform in the aftermath of World War II. Their populations tend to be homogeneous, in large part because these countries have been relatively closed to immigration (see Chapter 10). Ethnic and racial income differentials therefore have had little bearing on the overall degree of income inequality. Likewise, regional disparities are relatively unimportant in these countries. Compared with most of Latin America, they are small and compact, and their excellent transportation and communication infrastructures have facilitated economic integration.

The city-states of Hong Kong and Singapore have higher levels of income inequality, in part because they do not have any sizable agricultural sectors, which tend to be homogeneous under Asian monsoon conditions. The diversities between and within the branches of the industrial and service sectors tend to generate higher levels of income inequality than exist in agriculture. Incomes in the services are much lower in retail, restaurants, and personal services than in banking, real estate, and insurance. Within industries the disparity in incomes is high between laborers on the one hand and executives, managers, and professionals on the other. Moreover, the nonagricultural sector contains a large number of proprietors whose incomes vary more than those of farmers and tenant farmers. They range from wealthy entrepreneurs in manufacturing, real estate, commerce, and finance to poor street vendors, stall-keeper hawkers, and family craft shops.

The high degrees of income inequality in Malaysia and Thailand are due in part to greater heterogeneity of agriculture there than in Northeast Asia. Malaysian agriculture is dominated, on the one hand, by huge rubber and palm-oil plantations that employ large groups of low-paid laborers and small groups of highly paid managers and other white-collar staff and, on the other hand, by small (2-hectare) rice farms that are found in the northern and coastal regions. In between are holders of modest-size farms that grow rubber and palm oil. In Thailand income inequality reflects important regional differences in the pace of development during recent years. In the southern region are plantations, in the northern regions are poor peasants, and in the irrigated central region are large, prosperous rice farms.

Urban income inequality in Malaysia and Thailand is as pronounced as in the city-states and for a similar reason—the heterogeneity of industry and services—but traditional types of industry and service enterprises are of much greater importance there than in the city-states. There is a greater range of income between rich industrial and mercantile proprietors and small handicraft proprietors, stall keepers, sidewalk vendors, and so on. Incomes within the modern industries and commerce of Bangkok are much higher than in other Thai cities and towns, where crafts and small shops predominate. In urban Malaysia the income differences between ethnic groups are wide, with the Chinese at the top, the Indians in the middle, and the Malays at the bottom.

A comparison of South Korea with Taiwan illustrates the importance of development strategy. Income inequality was at similar levels in South Korea and Taiwan in the 1960s. The two countries diverged sharply in the early 1970s, when per capita income passed the US$2,000 mark. The Gini ratio rose substantially in South Korea and dropped in Taiwan.[2] Neither the level of per capita income nor demographic trends account for this difference. Taiwan and South Korea have similar demographic features, particularly their trends in age structure, fertility, mortality, family size, and the number of workers per household. If demographic factors had had an influence on income inequality, they would have affected both countries in the same way.

The divergence between South Korea and Taiwan can be explained by differences in their development policies. In the 1970s and 1980s South Korea veered away from agricultural development and labor-intensive industries in favor of heavy and chemical industries. Its import-substitution policies favored capital-intensive industries and large conglomerates, which received liberal government credit, subsidies, and tariff protection. Agriculture was neglected and grew slowly, with average incomes lagging behind nonagricultural incomes (Choo 1975). Between 1975 and 1985 the index of production for capital-intensive basic metals (for example, steel and machinery) increased 5.5 times, compared with a 3.5-fold increase in all industrial production. Light industry and agriculture were squeezed in several ways, including the use of favorable credit terms for 50 or so large *chaebols*, or conglomerates (Jones and Sakong 1980).

On the other hand, in Taiwan development did not favor large-scale, capital-intensive industry over agriculture and small-scale, labor-intensive light industry. With the rapid growth of industries the cities became fully employed and firms were forced to seek labor in rural areas. Nonagricultural employment and wages rose rapidly in the countryside, and productivity increased in all sectors of the economy. These changes favored income equality. The importance of nonagricultural income rose rapidly for farm families, in contrast to the situation in South Korea (Mizoguchi and Terasaki 1992). Smaller farms, with their surplus labor, benefited most from nonagricultural work, which reduced income inequality within farm families and lessened the gap between average farm-family and nonfarm-family incomes (Oshima 1993, footnote 27).

The rise in income inequality that has accompanied economic growth in Thailand can be traced to some of the important forces that Kuznets identified in his characterization of development and inequality. Regional variation in income is greater in Thailand than in any other country of East Asia. In 1990 gross regional product per capita in Bangkok was almost 10 times that of northeast Thailand. In part, regional income disparities in Thailand reflect historical factors. Thailand was never occupied by foreign powers who might have developed transportation systems. Residents of the north and central regions can reach Bangkok only by way of the Chao Phraya River and its tributaries. Only the transport system near Bangkok is well developed. Foreign investment has been heavily concentrated in Bangkok and neighboring areas, causing income to grow much more rapidly there than in the north or northeast.

Several other aspects of Thai development have contributed to the rise of income inequality. Foreign investment in the 1990s was concentrated in industries with relatively high technology, such as electrical appliances, computer parts, and automobiles. When superimposed on existing low-paying textile, food, shoe, toy, and garment industries, a dualistic industrial structure characterized by large wage differentials resulted (ADB 1995, footnote 52). Compared with workers in other East Asian countries, Thailand's work force has low educational attainment. Shortages of well-educated workers and plentiful supplies of less-educated workers have contributed to rising wage differentials.

Population and Income Inequality

The demographic transition is characterized by declining rates of mortality and childbearing that affect population growth, age structure, living arrangements, and the roles of women. In Chapter 3 Feeney and Mason provide a detailed accounting of those changes in the six successful Asian economies that are the focus of this volume. Those changes in turn have influenced income inequality in various ways. The most important changes have been the mortality decline, reduced levels of childbearing, lower rates of population growth, and shifts in economic activity among women. Other demographic changes have been more modest and have probably not had a great influence on income inequality. Several key points bear on our assessment of the connection between trends in income inequality and demographic change.

First, average household size dropped precipitously in East Asia as a consequence of reduced rates of childbearing. In every country but Indonesia the average household in 1990 had at least one less member in 1990 than in the 1960s (Table 15.2). In Singapore, Thailand, and Indonesia a drop in the number of children age 0–14 accounted for virtually the entire decline in household size. In Japan, South Korea, and Taiwan the number of working-age adults (age 15–64) also dropped, primarily because of reduced numbers in the 15–24-year age group.

Second, the change in the number of elderly persons per household and the proportion of elderly in the population varied considerably from country to country. In three countries (Japan, South Korea, and Taiwan) the elderly population increased substantially as a proportion of the adult population. In Japan, where population aging is most advanced, the proportion of the adult population age 65 and older grew from less than 10% in 1960 to about 17% in 1990. In contrast, the number of elderly persons *per household* and the number of elderly *as a percentage of adults* changed little in Singapore, Thailand, and Indonesia.

TABLE 15.2

Household Size and Composition: Six East Asian Countries, circa 1960–90

Family members and period[a]	Japan	South Korea	Taiwan	Singapore	Thailand	Indonesia
All members						
1960–70	4.5	5.7	5.7	5.6	5.7	4.9
1990	3.0	3.8	4.0	4.2	4.4	4.5
Children (age 0–14)						
1960–70	1.4	2.3	2.3	2.3	2.5	2.1
1990	0.6	1.0	1.1	0.9	1.3	1.7
Elderly (age 65+)						
1960–70	0.3	0.2	0.1	0.2	0.2	0.1
1990	0.4	0.2	0.3	0.2	0.2	0.2
Working-age adults (age 15–64)						
1960–70	2.8	3.2	3.3	3.1	3.1	2.6
1990	2.0	2.7	2.6	3.0	2.9	2.7
Workers						
1960–70	2.2	1.7	1.8	2.2	3.0	2.2
1990	1.6	1.8	1.9	2.6	2.6	2.0

SOURCES: Population data compiled from population censuses for each country. Labor force data, except for Taiwan, from ILO (various years). Taiwan labor force data from ROC DGBAS (various years), *Statistical Yearbook of the Republic of China* for 1996 (table 21).

[a] First observation is from 1960, except for Taiwan (1966), Singapore (1970), and Indonesia (1971).

Third, the average number of workers per household declined significantly in only two countries, Japan and Thailand (Table 15.2). In Japan a decline in the working-age population pushed the number of workers per household down by about one-quarter. In Thailand increased school enrollments led to reduced labor force participation by young Thais. In the other East Asian countries the average number of workers per household was stable or increased. Rising female labor force participation offset the decline in the number of working-age adults in Korean and Taiwanese households and led to a substantial increase in the number of workers per household in Singapore (see Chapters 9 and 14 for a more extensive discussion of these changes).

Fourth, changes in living arrangements, described in more detail in Chapter 3, were relatively modest. The greatest changes occurred in Japan. By 1990, young Japanese adults were much more likely to live independently from their parents and elderly parents were much more likely to live independently from their adult children than had been true in 1960. Nonetheless, extended living arrangements are still much more the norm in Japan than in the West. Changes in other East Asian countries, where they have occurred, have been considerably more modest and quite recent.

Finally, mortality conditions have improved substantially in all the successful East Asian countries. In the more advanced countries life expectancy equals or exceeds levels reached in the Western industrialized countries. In Indonesia, where life expectancy is lower than in the other five countries, it nevertheless rose by a remarkable 25 years between the end of World War II and 1990–95.

Recent studies of the influence of population on income inequality examine three broad sets of issues. The first issue is the composition of the population or households. Changes in family size, living arrangements, and age structure that accompany the demographic transition may lead to important changes in income inequality. The number of workers per household also changes because of the rise of female labor force participation that accompanies reduced childbearing. The second line of research emphasizes the influence of population on the factor distribution of income and hence income inequality. A third line of research considers the intergenerational transmission of income inequality [for example, Lam (1997b)]. Research in this area is not yet sufficiently advanced to support firm conclusions about East Asia's experience.

Our examination of demographic factors is based on the variance of the natural logarithm of per capita income, $Var(\ln Y/N)$, a convenient alternative to the Gini ratio. A principal advantage of this measure is that it can be decomposed into additive components that distinguish inequality in income per adult and income per capita. The decomposition also allows us to isolate the effect of some of the important demographic changes. $Var(\ln Y/N)$ can be represented as

$$\mathrm{Var}\left(\ln \frac{Y}{N}\right) = \mathrm{Var}\left(\ln \frac{Y}{A}\right) + \mathrm{Var}\left(\ln \frac{N}{A}\right) - 2\,\mathrm{Cov}\left(\ln \frac{Y}{A}, \ln \frac{N}{A}\right),$$

(15.1)

where N is the number of household members, Y is income, and A is the number of adults in the household. The first term, Var(ln Y/A) (inequality in income per adult), is influenced by three distinct demographic effects: the effect of population growth on factor prices, the effect of changes in the age structure of the adult population, and changes in female labor force participation that accompany declining fertility. We discuss each of these effects in what follows.

The effect of changes in child dependency is captured by the last two terms of Equation (15.1): Var(ln N/A) and 2 Cov(ln Y/A, ln N/A). Var(ln N/A) measures the variability of child dependency within the population; 2 Cov(ln Y/A, ln N/A), the covariance between income and child dependency, measures whether low-income adults support more household members than high-income adults. If low-income adults support more children and if the variance in the dependency ratio is greater in high-fertility populations, then a decline in childbearing leads to lower income inequality.

Child Dependency

Variation in child dependency over the entire demographic transition is not well documented. One might suppose that the variance in child dependency follows a pattern that is similar to and reinforces the Kuznets curve. In the 1960s and 1970s, when child dependency was at a peak in East Asia, family size could have been uniformly high and variance in household members per adult low. If fertility began to decline first among those who were educated, living in urban areas, and earning high incomes, the effect would have been to increase the heterogeneity in child dependency within a society, thus increasing inequality in per capita income. If low rates of childbearing were subsequently adopted by broader segments of the society, the resulting decline in heterogeneity in child dependency would have led to a decline in income inequality.

The available evidence shows that the variance in the number of children is high when completed family size is high and that the variance declines substantially as the fertility transition is completed. We find no evidence that the early stages of the transition are marked by a rise in the variance in the number of children per woman. Early in the demographic transition, the number of children is influenced by variation in fecundity, age at marriage, and infant and child mortality that lead to a wide rather than a narrow dispersion in the number of surviving children.

Our first piece of evidence relies on regional variation in the number of children per woman in contemporary India. Reliable state estimates of fertility and surviving number of children are available from the National Family Health Survey conducted in the early 1990s. The total fertility rate varied from 4.75 births per woman in Uttar Pradesh to 1.89 births per woman in Goa. In the eight states with the highest numbers of children ever born, we calculate that the variance in the number of children per woman is higher than in other states, and there is no evidence that the variance increases or declines with the number of births. Among the lower-fertility states, however, we calculate a substantial decline in the variance in the number of children per woman.

The second piece of evidence is drawn from South Korean census data on the number of surviving children by mother's age in 1970, 1980, and 1990 (ROK EPB and NBS, various years). We used these data to calculate the mean and variance in the number of surviving children per mother by mother's age. For the 14 cohorts of women with the highest number of surviving children, between 4.0 and 4.6, the average variance in the number of surviving children was 3.9. For the 12 cohorts of women who averaged 3 or more surviving children but fewer than 4, the average variance was 3.1; and for the 3 cohorts of women who had between 2 and 3 surviving children, the average variance was only 1.2. The shift to smaller families in South Korea has been accompanied by a decline in the variation in family size within cohorts of women.

The effect of declining childbearing on the variance in household size per adult also depends on the variation in the number of children across cohorts. Because fertility declined so rapidly in South Korea and other East Asian countries, differences among cohorts may be substantial for a short period of time during the demographic transition. At least in South Korea, the net effect of fertility decline was to reduce the variation in the number of children. For women age 25 and older the variance declined from 4.0 in 1970 to 3.8 in 1980 and to 3.2 in 1990. Unless higher-income parents had more children, fertility decline would have had an equalizing effect on the distribution of per capita income in South Korea.

The numerous studies of the socioeconomic determinants of fertility decision making provide a strong empirical basis for determining whether or not higher-income adults have more or fewer children than low-income adults [see Mueller and Short (1983) for an extensive review of the evidence]. Most studies show that the father's income is not highly correlated with the number of births. However, the mother's wage or income has a strong negative correlation with births in societies that have not reached low fertility levels. Thus the relationship between household income and the number of children depends on whether the contributions to household income by children are more important than the inverse relationship between the mother's earnings and the number of children.

The relationship between household size and household income is one of the key issues addressed by Kuznets (1976). In the five countries he investigated (West Germany, Israel, Taiwan, the Philippines, and the United States), larger households had greater household income but lower household income per person or per equivalent adult. (Kuznets counted a child as equivalent to one-half an adult.) Schultz (1982) found that the covariance between fertility and total household income is negative in both India and Colombia, supporting the view that high fertility leads to increased inequality in per capita household income. Analysis of data from South Korea and Thailand indicates that the number of young children in the household either depressed or had no effect on household income in the 1980s (Mason 1993). Teenagers of either sex in Thailand and female teens in South Korea had a modest positive effect on household income. However, the effect was not so large that greater variance in the number of teens in a household would reduce the variance in per capita household income. The available evidence indicates, then, that the covariance between per capita income and child dependency is typically negative. The decline in the number of surviving children over the demographic transition should have an equalizing effect on per capita household income.

In one instance, Taiwan, it is possible to calculate directly the effect of the decline in the heterogeneity of child dependency on income inequality. Schultz (1997, figure 6) provided annual estimates of Var(ln Y/N) and Var(ln Y/A) from 1976 to 1995. The difference between the two values gives the effect of declining heterogeneity in child dependency, that is, the last two terms in Equation (15.1). Between 1987 and 1995 the variance in the natural logarithm of per capita income declined by approximately 10% in Taiwan because of the changes in child dependency.

Some instances have been documented in which higher income leads to higher rates of childbearing and greater family size. For the most part, these instances have occurred in traditional settings at low income levels where the impact of income on fecundity and infant and child mortality is likely to be greatest (Bongaarts and Menken 1983).

Income per Adult

Next, we examine inequality in income per adult and three channels through which population may have an important influence. We begin by considering changes in the age structure of the adult population. Next, we examine the rise in female labor force participation. Finally, we address the effect of demographic transition on changing factor prices and hence on income inequality.

Age Structure

In a recent survey, Lam (1997b) provided a careful discussion of the effects of changes in adult age structure on income inequality. First, the average income of some age groups may differ substantially from the average income of the population as a whole. A rise in the proportion with either very high or very low income has a disequalizing affect. Second, some age groups have substantially more within-group income inequality than other age groups. An increase in the subpopulation in these age groups is disequalizing. The net effect of changes in age structure will depend on whether the within-age-group and between-age-group effects are reinforcing or offsetting and on their respective strengths.

Empirical studies have examined the effects of age structure on three income measures: individual earnings, household income, and household income per adult. In the United States the earnings of teens and young adults have a lower mean and higher variances than those of other age groups. Consequently, a decline in the percentage of teens and young adults, such as has occurred recently in some East Asian countries, is equalizing. In Brazil young age groups have low means but also low variances in earnings. Consequently, a shift to an older age structure does not have an equalizing effect on earnings. Earnings inequality is essentially unaffected by shifts in age structure in Brazil (Lam 1997b; Lam and Levison 1992).

The analysis of inequality in household income has several advantages over the analysis of individuals' earnings. Household income includes additional sources of income (for example, rents and profit) that may also be closely associated with age. Moreover, household income incorporates the important redistributive role of the family. The earnings of teens and young adults may be low and highly variable, but most teens and young adults do not live independently from their parents in Asia. Deaton and Paxson's (1997) analysis examined how changes in the structure of households by the age of the head influence household income. In the four countries they analyzed (the United States, Great Britain, Taiwan, and Thailand) they found that within-age-group income inequality increases substantially with the household head's age. They assessed the overall effect on income inequality of population aging produced by slower population growth in Taiwan and concluded that the net effect will depend on whether or not Taiwan achieves high rates of economic growth. If per capita income growth continues at 6% per year, a decline in the population growth rate will produce a rise in income inequality equivalent to an increase in the Gini coefficient from 0.31 to 0.42. However, if per capita income growth slows to low levels, population aging will lead to a decline in income inequality. Deaton and Paxson (1997) did not provide estimates of how historical changes in Taiwan's adult age structure have influenced income inequality.

Schultz's (1997) analysis of the effect of age structure on inequality in income per adult bears most directly on the decomposition approach taken here. Schultz (1997) estimated the effect of changing age structure in Taiwan between 1976 and 1995, holding the inequality age patterns constant. Given the 1976 age pattern of income inequality, changes in the adult age structure would have produced an increase in the ln variance of income per adult from 0.249 to 0.254. Given the 1995 age pattern of income inequality, changes in the adult age structure would have produced an increase from 0.257 to 0.263. Either approach yields a modest increase in the ln variance. Given that the rise in the elderly population has been more rapid in Taiwan than in any other East Asian country except Japan, it seems unlikely that changes in the age structure of the adult population have had an important influence on income inequality in other East Asian countries.

Economic Role of Women

Changes in the economic roles of women are a central feature of East Asian economic development, with potentially important implications for income distribution. The proportion of women who are in the labor force has risen relative to that of men. The educational gap between men and women has declined. In some countries there have been modest declines in the wage gap. As a consequence, the share of household income contributed by women is rising (see Chapter 14). This trend is not confined to East Asia, of course, because similar changes have occurred in many countries throughout the world.

How have changes in the economic roles of women influenced income inequality? This question has been addressed in a number of studies using a simple accounting approach. A counterfactual scenario is posed. Suppose women had no income; what would happen to income inequality? The question is answered by comparing the inequality of total household income to the inequality of income earned only by males (or husbands). With rare exceptions the analysis indicates that women reduce inequality in household income (Lam 1997a).

That income inequality declines with the addition of female workers is due largely to a pooling effect. An increase in the number of earners of any type within the household will typically lead to lower income inequality because in many households higher income by one earner will be balanced by lower income by a second earner. Under some circumstances the pooling effect is insufficient to produce a reduction in income inequality. If women's income is characterized by high inequality and if women with high income tend to be married to men with high income, then women's income can increase income inequality. This has been found to be the case for African Americans in the United States but is quite atypical (Lehrer and Nerlove 1981).

The few studies of East Asian economies support the conclusion that women's income has an equalizing effect. Pong (1991) reached that conclusion in an analysis of family income in Hong Kong in 1976 and 1981. Liu and Chang (1987) reached similar conclusions for Taiwan, as did Ogawa and Bauer (1996) in a more recent study of family income in Japan.

These analyses demonstrate the effect of two extremes on income inequality: the observed earnings by women versus no earnings by women. They do not tell us, however, how the rise in earnings by women has influenced income inequality. To examine this issue, we make use of data from the Survey of Personal Income Distribution in Taiwan, conducted from 1976 to 1993, to replicate standard analyses (ROC DGBAS, various years, *Report on the Survey of Personal Income Distribution*). We use the income data to calculate one measure of inequality, the coefficient of variation, for the income of males, females, and their combined income. Estimates for the years 1976, 1982, 1988, and 1993 are presented in Table 15.3.

The results have several noteworthy features. First, the contribution of women to household income increased substantially during this 17-year period (1976–93). In 1976 women earned only 16% of household income. By 1993 their contribution had grown to 24%. Second, the coefficient of variation in women's income is substantially greater than for men's income, but the coefficient declined substantially during the period analyzed. Third, the correlation between the incomes of males and females was negative throughout the period but less so at the end of the period. In fact, in 1988 and 1993 the correlation between the incomes of men and women was quite small.

As other studies of East Asian economies have shown, women's income has had a consistently equalizing effect on household income. The coefficient of variation of household income is five points lower than the coefficient of variation of male income in 1976, that is, 0.64 compared with 0.69. The ef-

TABLE 15.3

Income Inequality among Males, Females, and Households: Taiwan, 1976–93

Measure	1976	1982	1988	1993
Mean income (NT$)				
Males	105,845	244,736	365,006	652,032
Females	19,417	59,498	102,137	205,841
Income share (%)				
Males	84.5	80.4	78.1	76.0
Females	15.5	19.6	21.9	24.0
Simple correlation	−0.073	−0.082	−0.020	−0.027
Coefficient of variation				
Males' income	0.691	0.697	0.702	0.678
Females' income	1.860	1.531	1.524	1.330
Total income	0.641	0.631	0.658	0.630
Males (total)	0.050	0.066	0.044	0.048

SOURCES: Calculated from ROC DGBAS (various years), *Report on the Survey of Personal Income Distribution*.

fect in 1993 is essentially identical, a five-point reduction. Results for the intervening years are similar.

In contrast, the effect of women's income on inequality has not increased as their contribution to household income has grown. The effect of their income on inequality was just as great in 1976, when women contributed only 15% of household income, as in 1993, when they contributed 24% of household income. Looking at each year individually, one may conclude that an increase in the incomes of women relative to the incomes of men has an equalizing effect. Looking at the trend, however, one may conclude that it does not. The only interpretation that can be made is that an increase in women's share of household income from 0% to 15% reduced inequality in household income, but a further increase to 25% has had no further effect.

At least in Taiwan, therefore, the increased integration of women into the work force during the last two decades has not had an important effect on income inequality. Can we generalize to other countries? The studies needed to answer this question for other East Asian countries are not available. Lam (1997a) reported estimates for the United States from 1973 to 1987. During that time, women's share of household income rose from 15% to 25%, an increase remarkably similar to that in Taiwan. At the end of the period, women's income reduced the coefficient of variation by 8 points, compared with 6 points at the beginning of the period. Hence the only study available for another economy points to a different conclusion than that for Taiwan.

This analysis ignores a potentially important issue. The rise in the contribution of household income by women may have an effect on the distribution of income within households that is far more important than the effect on the distribution of income between households. However, we have no information on which to base an assessment.

Capital Deepening, Factor Prices, and Income Inequality

In the neoclassical growth model population growth has an unambiguous effect on the factor distribution of income. A decline in population growth leads to a rise in the capital-labor ratio and, consequently, to a decline in interest rates relative to wages. The effect on the size distribution of income is uncertain, depending on how economic factors, capital, and labor, are distributed within the population. If wealth is more heavily concentrated than labor, then slower population growth leads to a reduction in income inequality. Empirical studies generally support this view, but their results have been questioned on several econometric grounds (Lam 1997a).

A closer look at the East Asian experience shows that slower population growth has led to a rise in the capital-labor ratio, but the mechanism by which this has occurred is different from that envisioned in the simple neoclassical model. Slower population growth has not produced slower labor force growth except in Japan. The decline in population growth, however, has led to higher rates of saving and investment. Hence the rise in the capital-labor ratio and its effect on the distribution of income can be traced to demographic forces, but not for the reasons predicted in standard economic growth models.

As the end of the demographic transition approaches and population growth continues to slow, labor force growth unquestionably will decline, as anticipated by the neoclassical model. But, as described more fully in Chapter 3, the initial slowdown in population growth is a result of slower growth in the number of children, not in the number of working-age adults. Moreover, delayed marriage and reduced childbearing has facilitated a rapid increase in the number of working women. Consequently, the immediate effect of slower population growth has been to increase, not to reduce, labor force growth.

The divergence between population growth and labor force growth in East Asian is discussed in some detail in Chapter 1 of this volume. Between 1960 and 1990 the labor forces of the three countries earliest in their demographic transitions (Malaysia, Thailand, and Indonesia) grew at rates varying from 2.7% to 3.4% per year. During the same period, four of the five remaining countries that are further in their transitions (Taiwan, Hong Kong, South Korea, and Singapore) experienced labor force growth that varied between 2.8% and 3.5% per year. Slower population growth there did not translate into slower labor force growth. The sole exception is Japan, where the demographic transition is sufficiently advanced and the growth of the working-age population has subsided (see Chapter 1, Table 1.2).

Although one might suspect that labor force growth slowed toward the end of the 1960–90 period, this was not the case. Labor force growth was more rapid during the 1980s than in the two preceding decades in every economy but Hong Kong. Barring a reversal in birth rates, labor force growth will eventually begin to slow in East Asia. The working-age population will peak and begin to decline. Female participation rates will stabilize at higher levels. As this happens, labor markets will tighten, creating upward pressure on wages, and inequality in the size distribution of income may well be reduced. But only in Japan have demographically induced changes in the supply of labor begun to have this effect.

Despite the continuation of rapid labor force growth, the capital-labor ratio has increased rapidly in the countries of East Asia (see Chapter 2, Figure 2.4). The change is a consequence of the substantial rise in saving and investment rates that have occurred throughout the region. Analyses presented in Chapters 5, 6, and 7 document the importance of demographic factors, specifically, changes in life expectancy, childbearing, and age structure, to the rise in saving and investment. Hence demographic forces depressed interest rates relative to wages, but for reasons different from those described in the textbook model. The change occurred because slower population growth led to more rapid capital accumulation, not to slower labor force growth.

We are aware of no analysis that has fully explored the implications of higher rates of saving and investment for income inequality. By depressing interest rates, capital deepening may have had an equalizing effect on income, but some low-income groups (widows) may be heavily dependent on interest income. The distribution of wealth has surely changed as rates of saving have reached such high levels. It may be that wealth has become more equally distributed over time, producing an equalizing effect on income distribution, but this may not be the case.

Inequality in Years of Life

Our discussion to this point has been limited to the relationship of demographic change to inequality in current income. A richer analysis would consider inequality in lifetime income. This is not attempted here, but it is practical to consider an important aspect of this issue, inequality in years lived. In Chapter 3 Feeney and Mason provide a detailed discussion of changes in mortality, both in general and in East Asia. Figure 3.2 graphs the extremes of human survivorship, showing that age at death or years lived varies widely in a high-mortality population. By contrast, in a low-mortality population deaths are heavily concentrated at older ages.

We assess the implications of mortality for inequality using data from model life tables to calculate a Gini ratio for years of life lived.[3] The Gini ratio is calculated in the same fashion as for any other variable. For each level of life expectancy the population is classified by age at death in years (<1, $1-4$, $5-9$, ..., $100+$). For each group the total number of years lived is calculated. The values are then cumulated to construct a Lorenz curve. The curve provides the proportion of total years lived by the "unluckiest" proportion of the population. Given a life expectancy of 40, for example, the Lorenz curve tells us that the half of the population that dies first lives only 14% of the total years lived by the entire population.

First, the results charted in Figure 15.2 show that high mortality rates are a direct source of enormous inequality within a population. The Gini ratio of 0.43 for years lived for a life expectancy of 40 exceeds the cross-sectional inequality in income reported for many East Asian countries. Largely neglected, variation in years lived is a source of inequality in a high-mortality population that is as great or greater than varying economic circumstances. Second, the decline in the Gini coefficient over the mortality transition is strikingly large and far greater than what is ever observed for standard measures of income inequality. For a population with a life expectancy of 80, the vast majority are living to an old age and inequality in years lived is largely eliminated, the Gini ratio being 0.08.

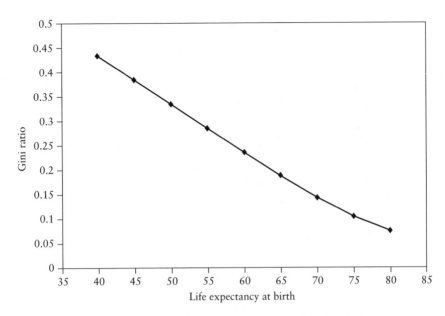

FIGURE 15.2. Inequality in Years Lived, Model Life Tables.

Life expectancy increased rapidly in East Asia during the post–World War II era, but no country experienced an increase as great as the 40-year span presented in Figure 15.2. Life expectancy rose the most in Indonesia, by 25 years. In Taiwan it rose by only 12 years between 1950–55 and 1990–95 (Chapter 3, Table 3.2). Over the entire twentieth century even more dramatic changes have occurred. In Taiwan life expectancy grew from 28 years in 1906 to 74 years in 1990–95. Even in Japan life expectancy did not exceed 45 years until the mid-1930s (Japan Statistical Association 1987, table 2-38). Mortality represented an enormous risk throughout much of the twentieth century, and success at increasing life expectancy greatly reduced inequality in welfare resulting from differences in the length of life.

Conclusions

There is tremendous variety in the level and trends in economic inequality in East Asia. It is accurate to say that income inequality did not generally rise to high levels in East Asia as a consequence of rapid economic growth, justifying the growth with equity label. In Northeast Asian countries income inequality remained at low levels throughout the 1960s, 1970s, and 1980s. South Korea probably experienced a rise in income inequality but to levels that are still well below those found in many Latin American and African countries.

The successful countries of Southeast Asia typically have levels of income inequality that are similar to those found in Latin America and Africa and higher than those in Northeast Asia or South Asia. In some countries income inequality has declined modestly in recent years. In Thailand, however, income inequality increased substantially as economic growth rates reached high levels.

Simple models do not capture the enormous complexity that is characteristic of East Asia. The differences and the trends in income inequality reflect a variety of historical, cultural, political, and geographic forces that have influenced agricultural systems, economic structure, technological innovation, social heterogeneity and cohesion, and the distributions of land, human capital, and other forms of wealth. All these factors have influenced the extent of income inequality in the region.

The extent to which changing demographic conditions have influenced income inequality cannot be easily assessed. Widely available measures of income inequality are not appropriate for examining the effect of demographic variables, such as household composition, on income inequality. Nevertheless, demographic factors influence income inequality in clear, identifiable ways. Empirical studies of East Asian and other countries provide strong indications of the likely role of population variables.

One of the most important demographic changes in the region has been the decline in child dependency, or the number of children per household. The available evidence shows that the decline in child dependency has been accompanied by a decline in the variation in child dependency. This has, in turn, led to a decline in income inequality, as measured by the ln variance of per capita household income. Experts disagree over the welfare implications of this change because per capita income does not incorporate the value that parents attach to their children.

Population aging frequently attracts attention in analyses of income inequality. Several studies have shown that an increase in the elderly proportion of a population causes income inequality because the elderly have incomes that are lower than average or, as is more often the case, because income varies more among the elderly than among other age groups in the population. A population heavily concentrated at young-adult ages may also produce income inequality for the same reasons, although the evidence is less conclusive in this instance. Changes in the age structure of the adult population have been sufficiently small during the post–World War II era that any effect on income inequality has probably been modest. Perhaps the increase in the elderly population in Japan has had a significant effect on income inequality, but probably not elsewhere.

Slower population growth in East Asia has not yet influenced income inequality, except in Japan, by slowing labor force growth rates and depressing interest rates relative to wages. As is typical of early stages of the demographic transition, the working-age population has grown much more rapidly than the total population. Growth of the female labor force has been particularly rapid because women have increased their participation rates.

The capital stock has grown much more rapidly than the labor force in East Asia because of the region's substantial increase in saving and investment rates. Evidence presented elsewhere in this volume concludes that saving rates were pushed higher in large part because of changes in fertility, mortality, and age structure. The rise in the capital-labor ratio has depressed interest rates relative to wage, and this change has potentially important implications for income inequality. Thus the demographic transition influenced the distribution of factor income in important ways that are different from the ways envisioned in standard textbook growth models. The implication for income inequality requires further study.

Finally, the transition to low mortality in East Asia has led to an enormous decline in inequality in length of life. The shift to uniformly long life, not captured in typical studies of income inequality, dwarfs the changes in current income inequality that have occurred in East Asia and elsewhere.

The changes in demographic inequality that occur over the demographic transition appear to differ considerably from the changes in income inequality that Kuznets hypothesized with respect to development. Traditional societies were subject to enormous risks that influenced both fertility and mortality. The early part of the demographic transition is characterized by great diversity in family size, child dependency, and length of life. It appears more plausible, although not conclusive, that improvements in health and contraceptive technology have led to a monotonic decline in income inequality.

Table 15.4 provides the Gini ratios and sources for the data on income distribution in 14 Asian countries.

TABLE 15.4

Income and Expenditure Inequality in Postwar Asia: Gini Ratios for 14 Asian Countries by Subregion and Period

Northeast Asia

Country	Gini ratio	Country	Gini ratio	Country	Gini ratio	Country	Gini ratio	Country	Gini ratio
Japan		South Korea[a]		Taiwan		Hong Kong		China[b]	
1962	0.37	1965–67	0.34	1964	0.32	1957	0.48	1960s	0.20
1967	0.35	1968–70	0.34	1968	0.33	1963/64	0.50	1970s	0.25
1971	0.38	1971–73	0.33	1970	0.29	1966	0.49	1980s	0.28
1974	0.36	1974–76	0.38	1974	0.29	1971	0.43	Early 1990s	0.45
1978	0.35	1977–79	0.38	1978	0.29	1976	0.43	Average	0.33
1981	0.35	1980–82	0.36	1980	0.38	1981	0.45		
1984	0.35	1983–85	0.35	1984	0.29	1986	0.45		
1986	0.36	1986–88	0.38	1987	0.30	1991	0.48		
1988	0.37	1989–91	0.40	1990	0.31	Average	0.46		
1989	0.37	1992–94	0.39	1993	0.32				
Average	0.33	Average	0.37	Average	0.31				

Southeast Asia

Country	Gini ratio	Country	Gini ratio	Country	Gini ratio	Country	Gini ratio	Country	Gini ratio
Singapore		Thailand		Indonesia[c]		Malaysia		Philippines	
1973	0.41	1962	0.41	1964/65	0.35	1957	0.45	1961	0.50
1978	0.37	1968/69	0.43	1969/70	0.34	1967	0.50	1965	0.51
1980	0.41	1975/76	0.42	1976	0.34	1970	0.51	1971	0.49
1983	0.42	1980/81	0.43	1978	0.38	1973	0.51	1985	0.45
1988	0.41	1985/86	0.47	1980	0.34	1976	0.52	1991	0.48
1989	0.39	1988	0.47	1981	0.33	1979	0.50	Average	0.48
Average	0.40	1990	0.49	1984	0.33	1984	0.48		
		1992	0.52	1987	0.32	1987	0.46		
		Average	0.46	1990	0.32	1990	0.45		
				1993	0.34	1995	0.46		
				Average	0.34	Average	0.48		

continued

TABLE 15.4
(continued)

Country	Gini ratio	Country	Gini ratio	Country	Gini ratio	Country	Gini ratio
South Asia		Pakistan		Sri Lanka		Bangladesh	
India[a]		1963/64	0.39	1963	0.45	1963/64	0.36
1952/53	0.37	1966/67	0.36	1973	0.35	1966/67	0.34
1957/58	0.35	1969/70	0.34	1978/79	0.44	1968/69	0.29
1963/64	0.32	1971/72	0.35	1981/82	0.45	1973/74	0.36
1967/68	0.31	1979	0.37	1986/87	0.46	1977/78	0.45
1972/73	0.32	1984/85	0.37	Average	0.44	1981/82	0.39
1983	0.34	1986/87	0.35			1983/84	0.35
1986/87	0.33	1990/91	0.41			1988	0.39
1989/90	0.34	Average	0.36			Average	0.37
Average	0.34						

SOURCES: For Japan, Mizoguchi and Terasaki (1992). For South Korea, Ahn (1997). For Taiwan, Chu (1995). For Singapore, Deininger and Squire (1996). For Hong Kong, Chau (n.d.). For China, Oshima and Estudillo (n.d.). For Thailand, Ikemoto and Santisart (n.d.). For Indonesia, Hill (1996). For Malaysia, Ikemoto (n.d.). For the Philippines, Estudillo (1997). For India, Oshima and Estudillo (1997). For Pakistan, Hill (1995). For Sri Lanka, Karunatilake (n.d.). For Bangladesh, Osmani and Rahman (n.d.).

[a] Average of three years.
[b] Per capita household income.
[c] Consumption expenditure.
[d] Per capita expenditure.

V. POPULATION POLICY AND PROGRAMS

16

Population Policies and Family Planning Programs in Asia's Rapidly Developing Economies

AMY ONG TSUI

SIX ASIAN MIRACLE COUNTRIES (Indonesia, Japan, Singapore, South Korea, Taiwan, and Thailand), representing 454.7 million people, have the distinction of commanding some of the fastest growing market economies in the modern world. Japan's well-known strong economic performance is reflected in its rising per capita gross national product (GNP): in 1995 dollars, from $556 in 1962 to $34,630 in 1995. Over the same period Indonesia, demographically the largest of the group with 201.4 million inhabitants, saw its per capita GNP rise tenfold, from $85 to $880. Taiwan and Singapore likewise have demonstrated phenomenal gains in per capita GNP, with their 1962 levels of $154 and $584, respectively, climbing to $12,439 and $23,360, respectively, in 1994. During the same period of 1962–94, per capita income levels rose nearly 100-fold in South Korea, from $83 to $8,220, and nearly 20-fold in Thailand, from $100 to $2,210. Although their economic performance in the late 1990s has faltered somewhat, there are signs of recovery, suggesting optimism for continued growth over the long term.

Not only have the economic trends been remarkable in these populations, but also their fertility transitions have been among the fastest documented. Over a brief 30 years total fertility rates in Thailand, Singapore, South Korea, and Taiwan declined from more than 6.0 children per woman to the replacement level of 2.1 children or less by 1995. In Japan, where fertility lev-

Thanks are due to Zhang Feng Yu, who compiled the database used in my analysis of family planning effort while he was a visiting scholar at the Carolina Population Center. I am also grateful to W. Parker Mauldin and John Ross for giving me access to the family planning effort scores for 1972–94.

els were already near 2.1 in the 1960s, the government's concern about population quality led to early support for fertility regulation (Muramatsu 1966). Expanded access to contraception and induced abortion kept fertility rates low, and by 1995 the total fertility rate was 1.5.

Delayed marriage has contributed to the fertility decline. Median age at first marriage for women has risen by two years or more for all six Asian populations during the period from 1960 to 1990 (see Chapter 14). Singapore has experienced the greatest increase, 6.7 years (from age 20.3 to age 27.0); but impressive gains also have been posted in Taiwan, South Korea, Indonesia, and Thailand. Increases in the age at first birth have likewise been significant. Hirschman (1985) reported that the mean age at first birth of 21.4 years for South Korean women and 21.8 years for women in Taiwan born between 1930 and 1934 rose to 23.1 years and 22.0 years, respectively, for women born just 10 years later. Moreover, in the span of one generation, average completed family size (the mean number of children ever born) has fallen by more than one-half. The average mother today in most of the six East Asian countries may have two or three children, whereas her mother would have had five or six children. For national populations to exercise such a significant change in fertility behavior in such a short period of time is unprecedented in the demographic history of the West.

The demographic drama in the six East Asian populations has unfolded over a series of episodes, in most cases scripted clearly in national development plans that contain focused population policies. The historical setting is the period beginning in the 1950s, when national governments were being tested for their ability to provide for the basic needs of their citizens and secure political stability in the region. Peace, food security, infectious disease control, and economic reconstruction and development topped the list of needs of most Asian governments emerging from the devastation of World War II. Chandrasekhar (1967, p. 33) wrote:

All the Asian countries—free and Communist—are dedicated to the task of liquidating poverty, raising the general standard of living and evolving ultimately some kind of welfare state. Almost every country, particularly those which regained their political freedom after the Second World War, has drawn up plans—Five-, Six-, Seven- or Ten-Year Plans—for overall economic and social development. They have taken an inventory of available resources—natural, human, monetary, managerial and technological—have set up targets on the basis of priorities of the countries' pressing needs, and are doing their best to achieve their objectives.

In the 1950s India and China were the first two Asian nations to articulate, draft, and adopt national policies for managing their population growth (Chandrasekhar 1967; Tsui 1996). In India the first five-year plan contained the objective of stabilizing population growth to achieve national development goals. Moreover, India included support for family planning as a nationwide movement, with the reduction of population growth as a major desideratum. In China 1954 was a watershed year for official approval of birth control. Until then this Marxism-embracing nation had rejected birth control as a Malthusian notion. After major debates took place within the government in the mid-1950s, the momentum of acceptance for family planning increased considerably. In 1956 Premier Chou En-Lai directed the Ministry of Health to intensify national birth control measures to protect the health of mothers and children.

Other countries in the region emulated the actions of India and China in the 1960s. National population policies were inextricably linked to expectations that, unless rapid population growth was brought under control, any economic gains would be obviated by the increased resource consumption required to support the growing number of people. The assumption that the economic consequences of rapid population growth were negative and developmentally self-defeating prevailed among senior government officials and national planners. The paradigm linking economic development with reduced population growth, although perhaps simplistic, became a fundamental component of population policies in nearly all Asian countries, particularly among the six so-called Asian miracle economies.

In this chapter I compare the population policies and programs of the six East Asian countries and review the role of those policies and programs in addressing national development. In particular, I show how similar those population policies were with respect to their economic rationale and their focus on family planning in their population programs. I also examine how the six countries implemented their population and family planning programs and how the family planning programs were distinctively successful in influencing the pace of fertility change. I do not purport to test the validity of the economic development paradigm for population policy, a task that would require analyzing time-series data on the demographic and economic experiences of other countries besides the six of interest here. My analysis does, however, suggest that the economic rationale for the adopted population policies was consistent not only with the six governments' emerging welfare initiatives at the time but also with the use of quantitative demographic targets for population growth. Numerical goals for population growth coexisted with those for economic development. The symbolic power of numerical targets simplified program definition and implementation for many governments, and the fact that population size represented both demographic and economic capital reinforced the utility of the development paradigm for population policy.

In the following two sections I review demographic changes in the six populations and describe the governments' population policies. Next, I trace the evolution of the population programs, including trends in public funding for family planning services as an indicator of national commitment toward population growth management. Then I compare trends in contraceptive prevalence, the foremost proximate determinant of fertility behavior, and profile the methods used. In the final section I present an empirical analysis of the relationship between trends in fertility and development on the one hand and population policy indicators on the other over a 20-year period.

Actual and Projected Demographic Changes between 1950 and 2025

In 1950 the combined population of Indonesia, Japan, Singapore, South Korea, Taiwan, and Thailand was 212.1 million. By 1995 it had more than doubled, rising to 454.7 million. The six populations account for roughly one-quarter of the total population of East and Southeast Asia, or roughly three-fifths if China is excluded. Asia as a whole, including East, South, Southeast, and West Asia, had nearly 1,403 million inhabitants in 1950 and 3,186 million by 1990 (Table 16.1). It is by far the most populous continent. East and Southeast Asia are either well into or beyond their fertility transition. Annual population growth rates, which were 1.75% for East Asia and 1.92% for Southeast Asia in 1950 reached high levels of 2.43% and 2.52%, respectively, by 1965–70. By 1985–90 they had declined to 1.42% and 1.97%, respectively; and by 2000–2005 they are projected to decline even further, to 0.76% and 1.52%, respectively, according to United Nations assumptions made in 1995. In another 25 years the expected growth rates will be below 1%, at 0.32% and 0.94% per year for East and Southeast Asia, respectively. Population momentum, however, will maintain growth rates in South and West Asia at a high level (Bongaarts and Amin 1996).

Levels of population growth in the six countries with rapidly expanding market economies are in general somewhat lower than regional averages, with Japan evidencing the least growth among them. In the 1950s Japan's annual growth rate was 1.43%, and by 1985–90 the rate had dropped to 0.44%. The other five countries experienced rapid population growth throughout the 1960s and 1970s; but in the 1980s and 1990s, as their fertility declined, their growth rates fell significantly, in many cases by one-half. Fastest growing during the early part of this transition period (1950–55) was Singapore, with 4.90% per year, followed by Taiwan, at 3.42%. South Korea's growth rate of 1.02% in 1950–55 was depressed by wartime circumstances but rose to 3.09% by 1955–60.

By 2025 annual growth rates are projected to be less than 1% in all 6 populations, less than 0.5% in all but Thailand and Indonesia, and negative in Japan (at −0.41%). Although many of these populations will have doubled

TABLE 16.1

Actual and Projected Population Size and Growth Rates: Six Asian Countries, Regions of Asia, and the Developing World, 1950–2030ᵃ

Country or region	Population (thousands)				Annual rate of change (%)				
	1950	1990	2000	2025	1950–55	1965–70	1985–90	2000–05	2025–30
Japan	83,625	123,537	126,472	121,481	1.43	1.07	0.44	0.22	-0.41
South Korea	20,357	42,869	47,149	54,357	1.02ᵇ	2.25	0.99	0.93	0.39
Taiwan	7,554	20,353	u	u	3.42	3.19	1.13	u	u
Singapore	1,022	2,705	2,967	3,340	4.90	1.97	1.12	0.82	0.27
Thailand	20,010	55,583	61,909	73,773	2.58	3.08	1.67	1.03	0.62
Indonesia	79,538	182,812	239,601	275,469	1.69	2.33	1.77	1.48	0.83
East Asia	671,391	1,351,710	1,493,284	1,745,813	1.75	2.43	1.42	0.76	0.32
South Asia	498,845	1,243,314	1,525,812	2,196,267	2.03	2.39	2.21	1.83	1.00
Southeast Asia	182,035	442,312	527,103	713,350	1.92	2.52	1.97	1.52	0.94
West Asia	50,453	149,110	189,646	304,558	2.59	2.65	2.65	2.19	1.38
Asia	1,402,725	3,186,446	3,735,846	4,959,987	1.90	2.43	1.86	1.38	0.78
Developing world	1,711,210	4,141,474	4,972,515	7,055,935	2.05	2.52	2.06	1.63	1.05

SOURCES: UN DESIPA (1995b, tables A.1 and A.2). For Taiwan for 1950–70, ROC DGBAS [various years (1980)], *Statistical Yearbook of the Republic of China*; for 1971 and later years, ROC MOI [various years (1995)]].

u, data are unavailable.

ᵃData for 1995 onward are based on the medium variant projection. Projected population figures (size) for the six countries for 2025 are interpolated from projections for 2020 and 2030. Projected growth rates for the six countries are for 1995–2000 and 2020–30, whereas projected regional rates are for 2000–05 and 2025–30.

ᵇSouth Korea's annual rate of change was 3.09% in 1955–60. The much lower rate of 1.02% recorded for 1950–55 occurred during the Korean War.

or tripled in size since 1950, the transition from high to low fertility rates will have been completed in the 75 years between 1950 and 2025, a period considerably shorter than the 150–300 years over which European transitions occurred.

Why was the demographic transition accelerated for these six populations? Were the challenges of economic development more easily addressed after World War II in Asia, as well as in Latin America, than during the era of industrialization in nineteenth-century Europe? Several similarities—and dissimilarities—in the social, political, and economic conditions of the two regions and eras can be identified. On the one hand, health conditions were equally poor in pretransition Europe and Asia, with the result that life expectancy at birth did not exceed 45 years in either region. On the other hand, literacy and education levels were probably higher in the six Asian populations and the rest of Asia and may have become a mass phenomenon more quickly than in Europe.

One possible reason for the faster-paced fertility transitions in Asia is that the governments of that region framed population policies and programs to support economic development. In the six rapidly developing countries in particular, those policies and programs had clear development-oriented objectives. They also shared four other important features: (1) a family planning and health-related focus on initiatives designed to manage population growth, (2) strong political support and the absence of religious opposition, (3) significant and sustained public funding, and (4) an active partnership between government and the private sector in implementing family planning programs. Moreover, because all these features tended to be present in the population policies pursued by the five higher-fertility populations, the fertility declines they experienced tended to be more rapid and permanent than those occurring in other countries of Asia, such as the Philippines or India, or elsewhere in the world, such as in Kenya.

Government Positions on Population Growth and Family Planning

The governments of five of the six economically successful countries adopted policies for managing their population growth levels early in the 1960s. As seen in Table 16.2, South Korea was the first of the five countries, in 1961, to assume an official position to reduce its population growth rate. Singapore followed in 1965, Indonesia and Taiwan in 1968, and Thailand in 1970. Nortman and Hofstatter (1978: 30) classified the positions of all five governments as proactive, that is, having an "official policy to reduce the population growth rate." They noted that, "in addition to supporting family planning to implement this policy, countries in this category also support family planning for reasons of health and as a human right." Table 16.2 includes similar descriptions from Nortman (1970, table 6) of government positions in the Philippines and Malaysia, two other Asian market economies, for comparison purposes. As a sign of the times, both governments adopted proactive population policies at around the same time as the five other countries, Malaysia in 1966 and the Philippines in 1970.

The positions of these seven countries, as described in Table 16.2, have several important similarities. First, all except the Philippines targeted a reduction in either the population growth rate or the birth rate. In most cases the targeted reduction was numerically specific. For example, the government's goal was to reduce the growth rate to 2% per year in South Korea by the end of 1971; in Taiwan, to 1.9% by 1975; in Thailand, to 2.4% by 1980; and in Malaysia, to 2% by 1985. In Singapore the goal was a crude birth rate of less than 20 births per 1,000 persons by 1970; in Taiwan it was 25.1 births per 1,000 persons by 1975. Indonesia's National Family Planning Coordinating Board, established in 1970, adopted as its goal a 50% reduction in the fertility level between 1975 and 2000. Not only are the terms of the targeted achievements strikingly substantial, but also, as population policy objectives, they are remarkably uniform in their demographic intent.

Nowhere was this intent clearer than in the governments' actions taken to achieve the objectives, that is, to reduce fertility rates, which were seen as the major cause of rapid population growth. The perceived means for regulating fertility was contraceptives, which in the 1960s were limited to the newly developed but far from refined technologies of oral contraceptive pills, intrauterine devices (IUDs), and condoms. The family planning orientation of fertility reduction efforts in these populations and in most developing countries is perhaps as fundamental to modern population history as the economic development paradigm.

A second unifying theme among the six Asian countries, including Japan, I would argue then, is the evolution of their national family planning programs. Government policies to reduce fertility or limit population growth might have included more Draconian measures, such as criminalizing early marriage, compelling abortions, enforcing separate living arrangements for the sexes, heavily taxing the third or later child, or legislating mandatory sexual abstinence before age 25 or after age 30. Instead, the policies judiciously relied on voluntary and nonpunitive means of fertility regulation for married couples and expanded the couples' access to family planning information and services. What most observers regard in retrospect as patently sensible national policy and sound economic investment—the public funding of family planning programs—was at the time a rather serendipitous, naturalistic connection drawn by policymakers among limited economic resources, rapid population growth, and human reproduction.

TABLE 16.2

Government Position on Population Growth and Family Planning:
Seven Asian Countries, Circa 1970

Country	Position category[a]	Year adopted	Comment on position
South Korea	A	1961	"The national policy target is a 2 percent population growth rate by December 1971. An intensive national IUD program operates under the Ministry of Health. Since August 1969 oral contraceptives, previously given only to women who discontinued use of the IUD, have been available to all women after medical screening. Many agencies are cooperating in the program, e.g., Planned Parenthood Federation and universities. President Chung Hee Park signed the Statement on Population."
Taiwan	A	1968	"The national policy target is to reduce the crude birth rate to 25.1 per 1,000 and the rate of natural increase to 1.9 percent per year by 1975. The official government policy favoring program implementation was adopted in May 1968, but the major national program dates from 1964. Under the province-wide IUD program, oral contraceptives, which had been given only to women who discontinued use of the IUD, are now offered to all women under age 30. In December 1968, the Family Planning Institute, incorporating the former Population Studies Center, was created. Vice President C. Yen signed the Statement on Population."
Singapore	A	1965	"The national policy goal is to reduce the crude birth rate from 32 per 1,000 in 1964 to below 20 per 1,000 in the Five-Year National Family Planning Program Plan, 1966–1970. Implementation of the plan rests with the Family Planning and Population Board, a corporate body created by an act of the Legislature in 1965. Prime Minister Lee Kuan Yew signed the Statement on Population."
Thailand	A	1970	"On the basis of a proposal by the National Economic Development Board, the Thai Cabinet approved a policy in March 1970. The specific objective of the program is to reduce the rate of natural increase from the present (1970) level of 3.3 percent per year to 2.4 percent in ten years (1980). IUDs and oral contraceptives are available in government hospitals and first class health centers. Prime Minister Thanom Kittikachorn signed the Statement on Population."

TABLE 16.2

(continued)

Country	Position category[a]	Year adopted	Comment on position
Indonesia	A	1968	"The goal of the national policy is to inform people about family planning, provide services, and decrease the birth rate. The current Five-Year Plan sets a target of 3 million acceptors (100,000 in 1969). The National Family Planning Institute, established in 1968, is responsible to the State Minister of People's Welfare. The national program utilizes health centers, doctors, and midwives as well as the private Family Planning Association. In his Independence Day address to Parliament on August 10, 1969, President Suharto made a strong appeal for increased activity in the field of family planning, emphasizing that the program should be started now lest the gains in production be cancelled out by the greater increase in population. President Suharto signed the Statement on Population."
Malaysia	A	1966	"The goal of the national policy is to achieve a 2 percent population growth rate by 1985. An Act of Parliament created the National Family Planning Board on the Ministerial level. According to the *First Malaysian Plan, 1966–1970*, 'to prevent any increase in income from being nullified by rapid population growth, a large program of family planning will be implemented.' Malaysia has long had an active private Family Planning Association which continues to play an important role in the government program. Prime Minister Tunku Abdul Rahman signed the Statement on Population."
Philippines	A	1970	"President F.E. Marcos issued Executive Order 233 on May 15, 1970, creating the Commission of Population and calling on all agencies to cooperate in making family planning efforts effective. In 1969, the Department of Justice legalized the importation of contraceptives. President Marcos signed the Statement on Population."

SOURCES: For the position categories, Nortman and Hofstatter (1978, table 6). For comments on position, Nortman (1970, table 6).

[a]Position category A is an official policy to reduce the population growth rate. In addition to supporting family planning to implement this policy, countries in this category support family planning for reasons of health and as a human right.

To what extent did Japan's population policies depart from those of the other five countries? Many analysts ignore Japan when discussing Asian family planning programs because of its early industrialized status or presumed lack of national interest in family planning resulting from its low birth rate. In fact, it appears that Japanese officials occasionally shared the concerns of their counterparts elsewhere in Asia about the deleterious effects of rapid population growth on development. However, the Japanese demographic transition had begun earlier, around 1920, and the baby boom that followed World War II merely interrupted a progressive fertility decline that by 1940 had produced a crude birth rate of only about 30 births per 1,000 inhabitants (Yasukawa 1977).

The Japanese became aware of their country's rapid demographic growth in the late 1940s, about 15 years earlier than such awareness developed in the other 5 countries. In 1948 Japan's population was estimated to be 80 million, and its crude birth rate was 33.5 births per 1,000 inhabitants, implying 2.7 million births annually. According to Muramatsu (1966: 7), "concern over the country's overpopulation and its inevitable relation to the nation's economic future came to the fore, and awareness of the need for birth limitation rose spontaneously among the people." The postwar repatriation of soldiers had led to a marriage boom and subsequently to the baby boom, which, coupled with a war-devastated economy, prompted the government to liberalize access to induced abortion in the early 1950s (Inoue 2001). In 1952 the government amended the Eugenic Protection Law, first formulated in 1940, to eliminate the requirement that a physician group review a client's request for an induced abortion. The amendment gave greater latitude to individual physicians and expanded women's access to the procedure.

In the early 1950s a number of private birth control organizations were established in Japan, and the government created a Population Problems Council. In 1952 the Ministry of Health and Welfare adopted guidelines for the promotion of birth control and, through its Bureau of Health, introduced the first government effort to promote family planning through various clinical, community education, counseling, and training programs. Between 1952 and 1964 the Ministry budgeted annual appropriations for family planning activities. Although the amounts were nominal, they increased from $59,000 to $184,000 over that period and were augmented by local community and prefectural budgets (Muramatsu 1966).

The subsequent diffusion of contraception in Japan was rapid and, combined with rising numbers of induced abortions, allowed the prewar fertility decline to resume and complete its course by 1960. The government's policies for managing population growth therefore may have reduced the need for extensive, long-term subsidization of contraceptive services.

A third common element among the population policies and programs of the six countries was the high level of government support and commitment extended through various types of resources—political, organizational, and financial. Heads of state—from Presidents Suharto of Indonesia, Chung Hee Park of South Korea, and Ferdinand Marcos of the Philippines to Vice President C. Yen of Taiwan and Prime Ministers Lee Kuan Yew of Singapore, Thanom Kittikachorn of Thailand, and Tunku Abdul Rahman of Malaysia—openly supported population growth management in public speeches and as signatories of the 1967 Statement on Population. As Nortman (1970: 37) explained,

the Statement on Population was issued by UN Secretary-General U Thant on Human Rights Day, December 10, 1966, and signed by the heads of state of twelve countries. During 1967 the Statement was signed by eighteen additional heads of state and was re-issued on December 11, 1967, by the Secretary-General. It affirms the belief of the thirty signatories that "the population problem must be recognized as a principal element in long-range national planning if governments are to achieve their economic goals and fulfill the aspirations of their people; . . . that the opportunity to decide the number and spacing of children is a basic human right; . . . that lasting and meaningful peace will depend to a considerable measure upon how the challenge of population growth is met."

The government positions described in Table 16.2 annotate other political actions, including the formation of ministerial-level or dedicated units to coordinate population or family planning activities. Indonesia's National Family Planning Coordinating Board, the Korean Institute for Family Planning, the Malaysian National Family Planning Board, the Singapore Family Planning and Population Board, the Taiwan Provincial Institute for Family Planning, Thailand's National Family Planning Program, the Philippines Commission on Population, China's State Family Planning Commission, and Vietnam's National Committee on Population and Family Planning exemplify current or past efforts of East and Southeast Asian governments to respond institutionally to concerns about rapid population growth and high fertility. Each of these institutions has become an icon in its nation's social and economic development history. Collectively they represent a massive public effort to introduce sustained change in childbearing behavior among relatively impoverished and rural populations.

These governments also had the ability to mobilize organizational resources outside the public domain on behalf of their population policies and programs. One such action is what Lee et al. (n.d.) referred to as coalition building, constructing a strategic partnership among key groups pursuing a common mission. Given their population policies, governments in the six countries were likely to be proactive in or actively receptive to recruiting private, nonprofit, and commercial groups to expand the national coverage of family planning information, education, and service delivery. Several governments, in particular, those in South Korea and Taiwan, recognized their inability to finance indefinitely family planning services for all users. They instituted coupon-based systems both to involve private physicians in service delivery and to acclimate users to nominal service fees. The Taiwan program, for example, is described as being

designed from the outset without expectation of much foreign assistance or local allocations for a separate free-standing system. The health care infrastructure and personnel were used for family planning. . . . User fees, albeit small ones, were charged from the beginning, so clients were familiar with the idea and providers had experience in implementing sliding-scale fees. . . . [A] considerable effort was made in program experimentation, leading to such changes as a coupon system for contraceptive supplies and involvement of private physicians. (US NRC, Committee on Population 1995: 20)

The early involvement of private family planning associations, physicians, midwives, and pharmacies in Indonesia, South Korea, Taiwan, and Thailand laid the foundation for a service capacity that offered clients a broad choice of service providers, reduced their dependency on the public health infrastructure, and developed permanence in service provision. In Japan, too, a series of pilot family planning projects in the 1950s supplemented the government's efforts. Muramatsu (1966: 14) described what must be one of the first employer- and community-based family planning initiatives:

Family planning education has gradually become an integral part of the health and welfare services offered by large industrial establishments to their employees. At first a few establishments instituted the programs experimentally. They hired a small number of family planning instructors who, through frequent home visits, soon established a favorable rapport with their clients. Elaborate teaching in the techniques of contraception was conducted. Contraceptive materials were provided at a reduced price. The programs were accepted by the employees and the rate of family planning practice picked up sharply.

In this manner the national programs in these and other countries were able to define themselves as both public and private in service composition and to encourage various organizations and service agents to focus their resources (personnel, clinical, and financial) on national population policy and programmatic concerns.

Table 16.3, based on published data, compares the financial resources committed to population and family planning programs in five of the six economically successful Asian countries. It shows average annual per capita funding for family planning from government sources and from all sources for two five-year periods, 1972–77 and 1987–92. It also shows the percentage of all funding that came from the government. Figures 16.1 through 16.5 graph annual trends in per capita support for family planning from governmental and other sources between 1972 and 1992. Two notes of caution are warranted regarding the reliability of the available financial data.

TABLE 16.3

Average Annual per capita Funding (in US cents) for Family Planning by Source:
Five Asian Countries, Circa 1972–92

Period and source	South Korea	Taiwan	Singapore	Indonesia	Thailand
1972–77					
Government	18	11	31	11	2
All sources	24	13	32	18	8
Percentage government	75	85	97	61	25
1987–92					
Government	58	75	32	51	31
All sources	61	75	32	66	32
Percentage government	95	100	100	77	97
Estimated number of contraceptive users (in thousands), 1990	5,831	3,576	587	16,070	6,278

SOURCES: Data for 1972–76 from Nortman and Hofstatter (1978, table 10). Data for 1977–83 from Nortman (1985, table 9). Data for 1984 onward from Ross, Mauldin, and Miller (1993, table 22).

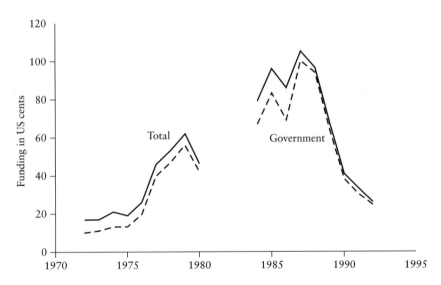

Sources: Data for 1972–76 from Nortman and Hofstatter (1978, table 10). Data for 1977–83 from Nortman (1985, table 9). Data for 1984 onward from Ross, Mauldin, and Miller (1993, table 22).

FIGURE 16.1. Annual per Capita Funding for Family Planning by Source: South Korea, 1972–92.

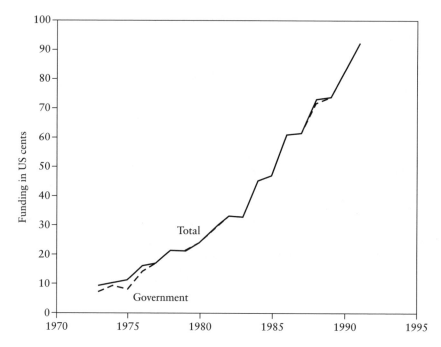

Sources: Same as in Figure 16.1.

FIGURE 16.2. Annual per Capita Funding for Family Planning by Source: Taiwan, 1973–91.

The first is that financial reports not only tend to be biased by errors of omission or commission but also are unstandardized, being based alternatively on allocated, obligated, or expended funds and variously defined budget items. However, wherever a long series of trend data on family planning allocations is available, it is likely to be more accurate and internally consistent than reports from countries where data are more sporadic. The second caveat is that the treatment of shared infrastructural costs, such as personnel, buildings, and equipment, is not standardized, particularly where family planning and maternal and child health services are heavily integrated.

Taking the per capita allocations at face value, we see that government funding for family planning ranged from US$0.02 per capita in Thailand to US$0.31 in Singapore in the early period and from US$0.31 in Thailand to US$0.75 in Taiwan in the later period. In all five countries per capita funding for family planning increased between the two time periods. The increase was negligible in Singapore but almost sevenfold in Taiwan. (Singapore achieved replacement-level fertility in 1975 and began to reduce its funding for family planning in 1983. See Figure 16.3.)

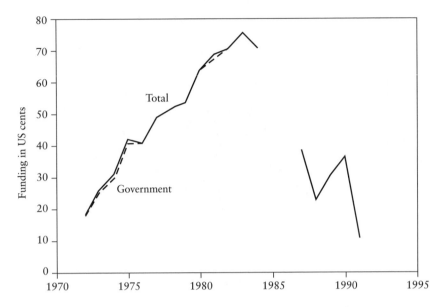

Sources: Same as in Figure 16.1.

FIGURE 16.3. Annual per Capita Funding for Family Planning by Source: Singapore, 1972–91.

Family planning funding from nongovernmental sources provided a significant additional margin early on in Thailand (6 cents more per capita) and a moderate additional margin in Indonesia (an added 7 cents). Overall, though, in the 1972–77 period a high proportion of family planning funding—three-quarters or more in South Korea, Taiwan, and Singapore—came from government revenues. The financial sustainability of the programs in these populations can be seen in the increased proportions of per capita funding from government sources in the latter period. By 1987–92 the governments of four of the five countries (South Korea, Taiwan, Singapore, and Thailand) supplied all or nearly all the revenues for their local family planning allocations, and in Indonesia the government supplied more than three-quarters. Figures 16.1 through 16.5 illustrate the trend by showing a common pattern of simultaneous growth in funding commitments to family planning and declining shares derived from nongovernmental sources.

The programmatic caseloads, as measured by the number of contraceptive users in each country around 1990, were substantial in most cases (last column of Table 16.3). Although significant shares of contraceptive users in Indonesia, South Korea, and Thailand obtained their supplies privately, in all three of those countries, where the number of contraceptive users ranged

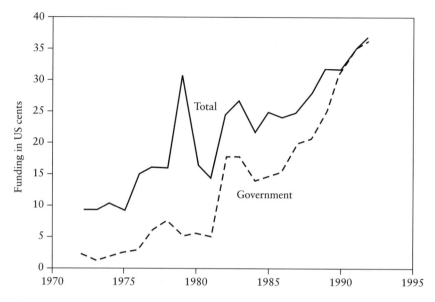

Sources: Same as in Figure 16.1.

FIGURE 16.4. Annual per Capita Funding for Family Planning by Source: Thailand, 1972–92.

from 5.8 million to 16.1 million, most received their supplies from the national program.

Although the total government resources invested in family planning were substantial, they were only a small percentage of each country's total health budget and an even smaller share of the national budget (Tsui 1996). Nevertheless, given the increasing size of populations at risk and the rising demand for contraception over the period examined here, the five governments' sustained financial commitment to family planning programs reflects the great importance they have accorded to population growth management in their development plans. Pasay and Wongkaren (2001) reported that the proportion of Indonesia's national budget devoted to family planning has improved from 0.33% to 0.60% over the fiscal year periods beginning in 1975 and ending in 1997. As Gullaprawit (2001) reported, the Thai government's family planning program expenditures accounted for 0.22% of total government expenditures in 1970, rose to a high of 0.38% in 1977, and declined more recently to 0.15% by 1994. In dollar terms, however, annual government expenditures on family planning in Thailand have risen steadily, from US$1.4 million in 1970 to US$2.1 million in 1994. Total spending in Taiwan has paralleled Thailand's course, rising from NT$35 million

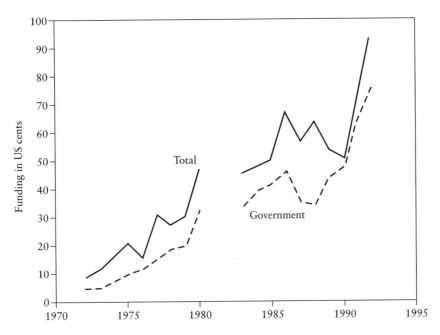

Sources: Same as in Figure 16.1.

FIGURE 16.5. Annual per Capita Funding for Family Planning by Source: Indonesia, 1972–92.

in 1964 (measured in 1986 constant dollars) to NT$113 million in 1974, NT$307 million in 1984, and NT$390 million in 1990 (Liu 2001). In both absolute and relative terms, therefore, these governments have exhibited a long-term commitment to their national family planning programs through the continuous allocation of sizable amounts of resources.

As the chapters on the five populations and other writings on Japan [for example, Muramatsu (1966) and Kono (1996)] suggest, the rationale for targeting population growth reduction was influenced by what was probably a simplistic view of the relationship between population dynamics and economic development. It was reasonable for government and civic leaders to support the management of population growth for its perceived development consequences. The prevailing belief and fear that rapid population growth has negative consequences for development resonate repeatedly in the population policy writings about this region and in the documentation of the programmatic achievements over the 1960–85 period. To illustrate, I again quote Chandrasekhar (1967: 31):

Now Asia is politically free. But political freedom without economic advancement and social progress is largely meaningless. Therefore almost all Asian countries have embarked today upon planned economic development. And they are finding that the greatest single obstacle to rapid economic betterment is runaway population growth. The net annual addition of millions of mouths to the existing large population base nullifies much of the national efforts towards a higher level of living. Thus the basic economic and social problem in Asia is really demographic.

Trends in Contraceptive Prevalence
and Method Composition

As is well known, between 1960 and 1990 modern contraceptive practice became widespread in most of Asia, as it did globally. In this section I focus on the rapid increase in the use of modern contraceptives because the use reflects (1) the intended outcome of population policy aimed at reducing fertility levels through concerted family planning efforts, (2) the principal proximate determinant of fertility and hence population growth, and (3) massive behavioral change through the adoption of artificial means of family limitation. By examining trends in the use of specific methods, it is also possible to assess the achievements of family planning programs in providing ready access to modern contraceptives.

Table 16.4 documents trends in contraceptive prevalence among married (or in union) women of childbearing ages in the six Asian populations. Figure 16.6 shows trends in modern contraceptive prevalence alone, and Figures 16.7 and 16.8 show trends in method composition for two of the countries, Indonesia and South Korea. Table 16.4 and its sources warrant a comment on the remarkable availability of prevalence estimates, based on national surveys, for contraceptive use, fertility, and other kinds of demographic behavior. Although time-series data are common in the natural and economic sciences, a leading indicator of human behavior is rarely available. With this informational resource, however, we can easily see the dramatic rise in contraceptive practice across the six populations in the course of four decades.

The earliest of the group is Japan, where contraceptive use was recorded at 33.6% in 1955, climbed to 64.3% in 1986, and declined slightly to 58.0% in 1990. Use of supply methods (specifically, condoms) predominates in Japan. Use of traditional methods (primarily periodic abstinence and withdrawal) has been moderate over time, although after dropping to a low in 1975, it appears to be on the increase.

In Indonesia between 1973 and 1994 contraceptive use exhibited the slowest rise among the six populations but still a substantial one. It climbed from 8.6% to 54.7%, with only nominal reliance on traditional methods and predominant reliance on supply methods (pills, IUDs, and more recently injectables) (Figure 16.7). The notably minimal use of permanent methods

TABLE 16.4

Trends in the Percentage of Women of Reproductive Age and in Unions using Contraception, by Method Type: Six Asian Countries, Recent Decades[a]

Country and year	Age of females	All methods	Modern methods		Traditional methods
			Permanent	Supply	
Japan					
1955	15–49[b]	33.6	1.5	23.3	8.8
1965	15–49	55.5	3.2	42.3	10.0
1975	15–49	60.5	2.8	56.4	1.3
1986	15–49	64.3	9.9	49.8	4.6
1990	15–49	58.0	5.7	46.2	6.1
South Korea					
1966	15–44	20.0	2.0	13.0	5.0
1976	15–44	44.2	8.3	24.6	11.3
1985	15–44	70.4	40.5	18.9	11.0
1994	15–49	77.4	40.2	23.4	10.6
Taiwan					
1965	22–39	23.0	0.0	13.0	10.0
1976	22–39	63.0	11.0	39.0	13.0
1985	22–39	78.0	26.0	38.0	14.0
1992	20–44	82.0	28.7	45.0	8.3
Singapore					
1973	15–44	60.1	10.8	42.0	7.3
1982	15–44	74.2	22.9	50.1	1.2
1987	15–44	67.4	21.8	31.2	14.4
1992	15–44	64.8	15.3	36.2	13.3
Thailand					
1969–70	15–44	14.4	7.1	6.4	0.9
1980	15–49	44.5	13.5	31.0	1.2
1987	15–49	65.5	28.5	35.1	1.9
1995	15–44	73.9	22.6	49.1	2.2
Indonesia					
1973	15–49	8.6	u	7.2	1.4
1980	10–49	26.8	u	21.9	4.9
1985	10–49	38.5	1.6	35.3	1.6
1994	15–49	54.7	3.8	48.3	2.7

SOURCES: Singapore, 1987–92 data, from Yap (1997, table 5). Data for other countries from an unpublished contraceptive prevalence database, Population Council, New York.

u, data are unavailable.

[a] Percentages are of couples currently using contraception at the time of the survey interviews.

[b] Includes wives and husbands.

distinguishes Indonesia from the other countries, including Japan, where more use of sterilization exists even without national promotion.

South Korea, Taiwan, and Thailand experienced similar rapid increases, reaching between 74% and 82%, in the latest year for which data are available, for the use of both permanent and supply methods. The use of sterilization (female and male) has outweighed supply method use (pills, IUDs, and

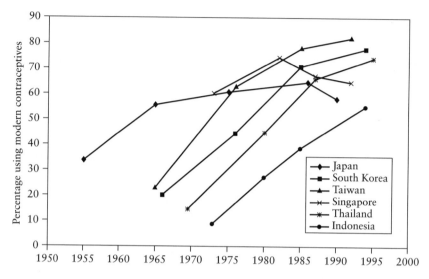

Source: Table 16.4.

FIGURE 16.6. Trends in Modern Contraceptive Prevalence among Reproductive-age Women in Unions: Six Rapidly Developing Asian Countries, 1955–95.

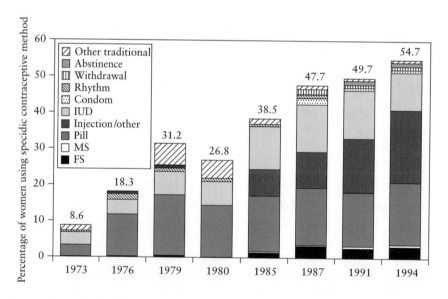

Sources: Same as in Figure 16.1.

FIGURE 16.7. Percentage of Women in Unions Using Various Contraceptive Methods: Indonesia, 1973–94. MS, male sterilization; FS, female sterilization.

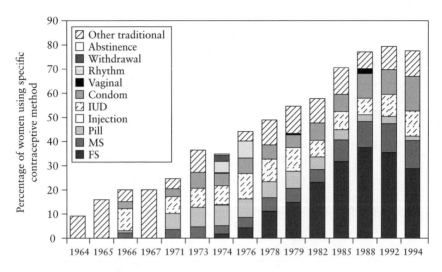

Sources: Same as in Table 16.1.

FIGURE 16.8. Percentage of Women in Unions Using Various Contraceptive Methods: South Korea, 1964–94. MS, male sterilization; FS, female sterilization.

condoms) in South Korea by a factor of almost 2; traditional method use has been steady at 11% over the past 20 years (Table 16.4 and Figure 16.8). In Taiwan traditional methods have declined somewhat, but supply methods (IUD and condoms primarily) are favored over permanent methods (Table 16.4). The same holds true in Thailand, where prominent use of pills and injectables and negligible use of traditional methods has been the pattern.

Judged by modern contraceptive prevalence alone, Figure 16.6 shows that Singapore's levels are nearly constant between 1973 and 1992 and that Japan's levels decline from 60% to 52% between 1986 and 1990. It is conceivable that in a postindustrial state, where marriage and family formation patterns can be dramatically altered, contraceptive use becomes more episodic and traditional methods are practiced with greater efficacy. Whatever the reason for the lower prevalence of modern methods in Japan and Singapore, it is apparent that contraceptive behavior has risen to maximal levels in all six populations except Indonesia. Indonesia, however, currently has a contraceptive profile remarkably similar to Japan's. Prevalence of supply methods are as high in Indonesia (48%) as in the other five populations (for example, 46% in Japan, 45% in Taiwan, and 49% in Thailand). Indonesia's overall level of modern contraceptive prevalence appears to be limited only by the absence of much use of permanent methods.

Given the region-wide objective of increasing contraceptive practice, the achievements of the six countries over the past 30–40 years attest to tremendous success. The levels of achievement likely exceeded the expectations of even the early advocates. There is little doubt that the widespread adoption of modern contraceptives produced the dramatic fertility declines seen in much of the region. Equally important, those adoption levels have risen independently, not as a substitution for traditional fertility regulation. Some analysts question, though, whether the organized family planning efforts deserve credit for much, or any, of the fertility decline.

Contribution of Family Planning
Efforts to the Fertility Decline

To gauge the contribution of family planning activities to the fertility decline in the six countries, I have undertaken a cross-national time-series analysis of components generally hypothesized to influence trends in family planning efforts and in fertility during the period 1972–94. This 22-year period, delimited by the availability of national data, is approximately a decade short of the period of major demographic and socioeconomic change (1960–90) in the six countries under review here. However, it brackets two decades of dynamic programmatic and fertility change in most of the rest of the developing world. The database used in the analysis includes information from four time points (1972, 1982, 1989, and 1994) on social and economic development indicators, family planning effort components, international funding for population assistance, and demographic rates for 80 developing countries. The data were compiled by my colleague Zhang Feng Yu, using estimates published by the United Nations, the World Bank, the United Nations Economic, Social, and Cultural Organization (UNESCO), the International Labour Office (ILO), the World Health Organization (WHO), and the Population Council.

The first step of the analysis was to assess the degree to which programmatic effort in family planning might be a policy response of national governments to perceived needs in nutritional welfare, infant and child mortality, population size, and opportunity for international donor funding. I hypothesized that the first three factors would be integral components of development plans, reflecting governments' recognition of the need for population policies, particularly in Asia, after World War II. Feeding the populace and reducing mortality risks are seen by public officials as basic needs; and population size is a measure of the challenge of meeting those needs. These variables, I reasoned, should influence the evolution of family planning effort in a given country. The fourth hypothesized influence, availability of international donor funding, I proxied in the analysis by using annual per capita funding for population program assistance from the US government.

In the second part of the analysis I examined the influence of family planning effort and other national welfare indicators on the natural logarithm of the total fertility rate (ln TFR) over the 22-year period. For this analysis I used an instrumental variable construction, which allowed me to control statistically for the potential endogeneity of family planning effort as an outgrowth of other developmental changes. The other national welfare indicators included a measure of non–human capital stocks [for example, the net export of mineral fuels as a share of GDP (Schultz 1994), the average number of years of education for males and females over the age of 15, the degree of urbanization, and the agricultural composition of the labor force]. I expected all the variables to influence fertility over time but was particularly interested in the influence of family planning programs. For both analyses I included a dummy factor for the rapidly developing Asian countries to enable me to observe the additive effect of their economies on programmatic effort. I was not able to include Japan or Taiwan in this group for lack of data. I did, however, add Malaysia and Hong Kong to the other four countries (South Korea, Singapore, Thailand, and Indonesia) as proxies for Japan and Taiwan.

Table 16.5 presents the means and standard deviations of the variables used in both analyses, stratified by whether the country was in the rapidly developing group or not. The downward course of the TFR between 1972 and 1994 across developing countries, from 5.79 to 4.40 children per woman, is clearly evident and is stronger in the rapidly developing countries (4.27 to 2.19) than elsewhere (5.92 to 4.58). The ratio of fuel exports to GDP exhibits an irregular trend between 1972 and 1994 in the developing countries, declining from 0.014 in 1972 to −0.001 in 1982, and then rising to 0.011 in 1989 and to 0.017 in 1994. The same trend line is found for the rapidly developing countries. Family planning effort (FPE) scores, as a percentage of the maximum, have risen from 21.3 to 50.6 across the developing countries but begin at 64.5 for the rapidly developing countries and remain at relatively strong levels between 1972 and 1994, reaching a high in 1989 of 74.0 before dropping back to 67.8 by 1994.

Nutritional intake, measured in daily calories, has similarly increased for all countries, with an average of 2,905 cal in 1994 for rapidly developing countries, compared with 2,487 cal for the other group of developing countries. Variation in population size was substantial during this period, as was the downward trend in infant mortality rates, shifting from 101 to 59 deaths per 1,000 births in the developing countries over the study period. In the rapidly developing countries the decline was more moderate (from 49 to 20 deaths per 1,000 births) than in the other developing countries (from 105 to 62 deaths per 1,000 births). Annual per capita funding for population from the US government was nil in 1972 but rose to US$0.18 by 1994 in the

TABLE 16.5

Averages and Standard Deviations (SDs) for Development Indicators and Family Planning Effort (FPE) Scores: Six Rapidly Developing Asian Countries and Other Developing Countries, 1972–94

Region and indicator	1972 Mean	1972 SD	1982 Mean	1982 SD	1989 Mean	1989 SD	1994 Mean	1994 SD
80 developing countries								
Total fertility rate	5.79	1.34	5.20	1.68	4.71	1.68	4.40	1.66
Export-import/GDP	0.014	0.089	−0.001	0.110	0.011	0.103	0.017	0.104
FPE score (% of maximum)	21.3	26.5	31.8	22.9	46.8	21.1	50.6	16.1
Calories/day	2,294	326	2,455	409	2,472	413	2,518	415
Population (in millions)	32.3	113.6	40.4	137.8	45.9	151.6	51.4	167.4
Infant mortality rate	101	44	79	41	65	37	59	36
Annual US funding per capita ($)	0	0	0.05	0.10	0.08	0.11	0.18	0.20
Percentage of population urban	35	22	40	22	44	23	45	22
Percentage of labor force in agriculture	56.9	24.6	51.0	24.9	46.8	25.6	43.7	25.3
Years of female schooling	2.4	1.8	3.4	2.1	4.2	2.4	4.8	2.6
Years of male schooling	4.0	2.2	5.2	2.3	6.0	2.4	6.6	2.5
6 rapidly developing Asian countries[a]								
Total fertility rate	4.27	1.11	2.95	1.13	2.39	0.91	2.19	0.72
Export-import/GDP	0.009	0.035	−0.034	0.139	0.023	0.065	0.011	0.052
FPE score (% of maximum)	64.5	20.0	69.0	11.2	74.0	8.7	67.8	10.9

Calories/day	2,471	349	2,674	275	2,719	236	2,905	120
Population (in millions)	35.9	46.5	44.2	57.2	49.6	65.0	55.0	73.2
Infant mortality rate	49	36	36	32	25	26	20	21
Annual US funding per capita ($)	0	0	0.01	0.02	0.02	0.03	0.08	0.18
Percentage of population urban	52	37	55	35	60	33	54	26
Percentage of labor force in agriculture	58.3	23.6	33.6	28.2	28.3	27.1	27.6	27.9
Years of female schooling	4.4	0.9	5.4	1.0	6.7	1.4	7.4	1.6
Years of male schooling	6.8	2.1	7.4	1.9	7.8	1.8	8.2	1.7
74 other developing countries								
Total fertility rate	5.92	1.29	5.38	1.58	4.90	1.59	4.58	1.59
Export-import/GDP	0.015	0.092	0.002	0.108	0.010	0.106	0.017	0.108
FPE score (% of maximum)	17.8	23.8	28.6	20.8	44.8	20.4	49.0	15.6
Calories/day	2,280	323	2,437	414	2,452	419	2,487	414
Population (in millions)	31.9	117.5	40.1	142.6	45.6	156.8	51.1	173.1
Infant mortality rate	105	43	82	40	69	36	62	35
Annual US funding per capita ($)	0	0	0.05	0.10	0.09	0.11	0.18	0.20
Percentage of population urban	34	20	39	21	43	21	44	21
Percentage of labor force in agriculture	58.3	23.6	52.4	24.3	48.3	25.1	44.9	24.9
Years of female schooling	2.3	1.7	3.3	2.1	4.0	2.3	4.5	2.5
Years of male schooling	3.8	2.1	5.0	2.3	5.8	2.4	6.5	2.6

SOURCE: See text. Details are available from the author.

[a] South Korea, Singapore, Hong Kong, Thailand, Indonesia, and Malaysia. Data for Japan and Taiwan are not available.

developing countries. Among the populous rapidly developing countries the per capita aid levels were small, with the highest level of US$0.08 per capita being reached in 1994.

The degree of urbanization, measured as the percentage of the population in living urban areas, was relatively stable in the rapidly developing group, whereas it increased moderately among the 74 other developing countries (from 34% to 44%). However, the share of the labor force engaged in agriculture declined by half among the six rapidly developing countries, from 58% to 28%, but declined only moderately in the other developing countries, from 58% to 45%. The average number of years of schooling received by females and males rose substantially over the study period for all countries, with the rapidly developing countries having higher levels than the other countries at the start of the period. The average number of years increased by 3.0 for females and by 1.4 for males in the rapidly developing group, whereas it increased by 2.2 years for females and 2.7 years for males in the other countries. These indicators suggest robust changes in this period of time, particularly for fertility and economic growth in the rapidly developing populations.

Using a fixed-effects regression estimator[1] to analyze this cross-national time series, I found that nutritional welfare, infant mortality, and population size did influence the strength of FPE in expected directions over this period, although caloric intake did not have a statistically significant effect (Table 16.6). The lower the caloric intake of a population and the lower its infant mortality rate, the greater the FPE expended. Ln population size, on the other hand, increased family planning effort by 6 points for every 100,000 persons. This model accounts for the fixed effect of being in the rapidly developing group but does not tell us whether being in that group enhances the FPE score. Secular changes over time, observed in the coefficients associated with the year dummies, show a rising trend in program effort, part of which may be due to unobserved influences. The model fits moderately well, and it fits even better for any one time point than across time points. The results indicate that FPE operates as a programmatic response to nationally perceived needs for improving population health and welfare and managing the consequences of demographic growth. Because of this, I have constructed the FPE score as an instrumental variable, obtaining predicted values of FPE for each unit of analysis, and I use this variable in my regression analysis of fertility change. Another reason for adopting this approach was to avoid measurement error thought to be associated with the subjective scoring of the FPE index.

Table 16.7 provides the results from the second time-series cross-national regression with fertility (ln TFR) as the outcome and FPE as an instrumental variable along with the other development indicators. The regression reveals a positive but insignificant effect from the FPE instrumental variable and

TABLE 16.6

Results from Fixed-Effects Time-Series Regression for Family Planning Effort (FPE) Score: 80 Developing Countries, Recent Years[a]

FPE score	Coefficient	SE	t	P > |t|	95% confidence interval
Calories	−6.206386	4.165501	−1.490	0.138	−14.41705, 2.004279
Infant mortality rate	−0.1812338	0.0710264	−2.552	0.011	−0.3212348, −0.0412329
Population (ln)	23.19165	9.216246	2.516	0.013	5.025407, 41.3579
AID dollars per capita	15.46112	7.649938	2.021	0.045	0.3822445, 30.54
Year = 1982	−0.0498023	3.258907	−0.015	0.988	−6.473471, 6.373866
Year = 1989	9.64587	4.722778	2.042	0.042	0.3367492, 18.95499
Year = 1994	6.108397	5.837311	1.046	0.297	−5.397592, 17.61439
Constant	−153.0969	84.28128	−1.816	0.071	−319.2247, 13.03085

SE, standard error.

$F(7, 214) = 46.54, p < 0.000$.

$R^2 = 0.231$ (overall), 0.504 (within), 0.184 (between).

Lagrange multiplier Breusch-Pagan test for random effects χ^2 (d.f. = 1) = 78.51, $p = 0.000$.

Hausman specification test (null hypothesis of nonsystematic differences with fixed-effects estimates) χ^2 (d.f. = 7) = 12.52, $p = 0.085$.

[a]See Table 16.5 for characteristics of variables. Model includes a dummy variable for the six rapidly developing Asian countries (South Korea, Singapore, Hong Kong, Thailand, Indonesia, and Malaysia). Year dummies are for 1982, 1989, and 1994, with 1972 as the reference year.

TABLE 16.7

Results from Fixed-Effects Time-Series Regression for Change in the Natural Logarithm
of the Total Fertility Rate: 73 Developing Countries, Recent Years[a]

	Coefficient	SE	t	$P > |t|$	95% confidence interval
FPE score (instrument)	0.0032136	0.0024771	1.297	0.196	-0.0016732, 0.0081005
Export-import to GDP	0.7313557	0.1718973	4.255	0.000	0.3922367, 1.070475
Female years of schooling	-0.0982074	0.0188812	-5.201	0.000	-0.1354563, -0.0609585
Male years of schooling	0.033351	0.0176895	1.885	0.061	-0.0015468, 0.0682488
Percentage urban	0.0002259	0.00155	0.146	0.884	-0.002832, 0.0032837
Percentage of labor force in agriculture	0.0097654	0.0021121	4.624	0.000	0.0055986, 0.0139321
ASIA×FPE	-0.0098195	0.0029914	-3.283	0.001	-0.015721, -0.0039179
Year = 1982	-0.0446015	0.0380489	-1.172	0.243	-0.1196643, 0.0304613
Year = 1992	-0.1177607	0.0769712	-1.530	0.128	-0.2696096, 0.0340881
Year = 1994	-0.1563579	0.0873814	-1.789	0.075	-0.3287439, 0.016028
Constant	1.231942	0.1520129	8.104	0.000	0.9320504, 1.531833

$F(10, 186) = 45.78, p < 0.000$.
$R^2 = 0.608$ (overall), 0.711 (within), 0.634 (between).
Lagrange multiplier Breusch-Pagan test for random effects χ^2 (d.f. = 1) = 122.03, $p = 0.000$.
Hausman specification test (null hypothesis of nonsystematic differences with fixed-effects estimates) χ^2 (d.f. = 6) = 20.68, $p = 0.024$.
[a] FPE score instrument is based on the model in Table 16.6. Model includes dummy variable for six rapidly developing Asian countries (South Korea, Singapore, Hong Kong, Thailand, Indonesia, and Malaysia). Year dummies are for 1982, 1989, and 1994, with 1972 as the reference year. ASIA × FPE is an interaction between rapid-development status and predicted FPE score values for various years.

significant positive effects from the net fuel-export variable, male schooling, and the percentage of the labor force in agriculture. Female schooling exerts a strong negative effect on ln TFR. One additional year of female schooling over the period, on average, can produce the equivalent of a 0.9 child decline in the TFR. In contrast, a ratio of net fuel export to GDP of 2% can raise the TFR by nearly three-quarters of a child. There is a secular trend toward lower fertility, as observed in the negative, although predominantly insignificant, effects of the year dummies. The few Asian countries with rapidly developing economies, though, experience an added advantage from their pursuit of family planning programs in this demographic equation. For example, membership in this group coupled with the 1994 strength of their FPE can reduce the TFR by one-half of a birth $(\exp(-0.01 \times 67.8) = -0.51)$.

These findings support the hypothesis that government efforts to slow rapid population growth and improve the human condition affected the strength of the FPE. In turn, trends in that effort, particularly in the rapidly developing populations, along with other development gains produced a downward course in fertility. To illustrate further the magnitude of the rapidly developing populations' achievements based on development-oriented family planning policies, I simulated fertility change with two scenarios. The first scenario assumed that all the rapidly developing populations possessed the FPE-related values (that is, both the predicted FPE scores and the ASIA × FPE interaction term) of other developing countries. The second scenario assumed the reverse, that is, that all countries not in the rapidly developing group had the FPE values of rapidly developing countries. Table 16.8 shows the outcome of these two scenarios.

The simulated fertility levels show that a less proactive FPE in the six rapidly developing populations would have kept their average TFR as much as one additional birth higher from 1982 onward. For example, in 1994 the rate would have been 3.17 children per woman rather than the actual level of 2.19. In contrast, if the 74 other developing countries had behaved as the 6 rapidly developing ones did over the 20 years, their fertility might have been lower by an average of at least 2 children, reaching a TFR of 2.50 in 1994 compared with the observed rate of 4.58. These hypothetical scenar-

TABLE 16.8

Simulated Total Fertility Rates: 6 Rapidly Developing Asian Countries and 74 Other Developing Countries, Recent Years

Total fertility rate	6 rapidly developing Asian countries				74 other developing countries			
	1972	1982	1989	1994	1972	1982	1989	1994
Observed	4.27	2.95	2.39	2.19	5.92	5.38	4.90	4.58
Simulated	4.65	3.91	3.43	3.17	3.84	3.18	2.66	2.50
Difference	−0.38	−0.96	−1.04	−0.98	2.08	2.20	2.24	2.08

ios serve to illustrate the magnitude of the effect of the family planning policies pursued by the six rapidly developing countries in the context of their national concern for population development relationships. It is improbable, however, that the rest of the developing world, with its heterogeneous social, economic, political, and cultural characteristics, would—or could—have acted as homogeneously as these rapidly developing countries did.

Conclusion

The six populations examined here have achieved phenomenal economic gains and reduced their fertility levels in an unprecedented and compressed period of time. Japan reached replacement-level fertility by 1960. The city-state of Singapore achieved this status by 1975, South Korea and Taiwan by 1985, and Thailand by 1990. At its present rate of fertility decline, Indonesia is likely to reach a TFR of 2.0–2.1 by 2000. Such rapid fertility declines have far-reaching implications for family and household living arrangements, the age composition of the populations, and their future social, economic, and health status. Substantial fertility declines in other countries with market economies in the region (for example, Hong Kong, Malaysia, India, and Bangladesh) and in several countries with centralized economies (for example, China and Vietnam) will soon close a chapter of historic international concern about high fertility and rapid population growth. For the six countries that have experienced phenomenal levels of economic growth and development over the past 25 years, it is easy to attribute that growth post hoc to their early adoption of policies for managing population growth and their investment in fertility-regulating programs. The tone of most retrospective accounts is one of confidence secured by 20/20 hindsight, but it is important to recall that uncertainty characterized early writings on the potential benefits of those policies and programs.

A combination of qualitative and quantitative methods of analysis provides valuable insights into the role that population policies and programs have played in the rapidly developing Asian countries. A full understanding of this historic episode in the region's development experience will not be possible, however, without an examination of local archives that document population dialogue and action at subnational levels. This task remains for others. Meanwhile, recent analytical and methodological insights [for example, by Ahlburg and Diamond (1996) and Bollen, Guilkey, and Mroz (1996)] have strengthened scholars' ability to isolate the influence of population policy on demographic and economic change, and the passage of time has contributed more data points from which to establish trends more clearly. With these advances it is hoped that future debate over the effectiveness of interventionist public policy, regardless of sector, can be informed by good data and science so as to avoid becoming mired in outmoded boundaries of discipline and philosophy.

I have attempted to explain how concerns about the consequences of rapid population growth for economic welfare in the six Asian countries evolved into a fairly uniform movement focusing on and sustaining support for public subsidization of contraceptive information and services. It appears to have been a strategy that paid off in accelerated fertility transitions, at least for these six populations. Lee et al. (n.d.) arrived at a similar conclusion in a study of four pairs of countries (Bangladesh and Pakistan, Zimbabwe and Zambia, Thailand and the Philippines, and Tunisia and Algeria). They contended that government policies can influence the timing of fertility decline and that once family planning has been put on the policy agenda, policy elites must sustain the momentum through broad coalition building. I would argue further that the economic rationale for family planning programs and their incorporation into national development plans have been central to the success of those programs in the six countries examined here. The belief that fertility reduction was necessary to promote economic development and was the correct national policy may have enabled family planning services to establish their presence and meet growing contraceptive demand. Undoubtedly this belief was bolstered in some places by international assistance.

Twenty-five years ago, Sam Keeny, observing Asia's experience, remarked that population growth rates could be brought down if family planning services were made convenient to the people. "The big question is whether the governments, and donor countries, have the staying power to do the job, which will take at least to the year 2000" [quoted by Watson (1977: 9)]. Clearly, the governments of the six successful Asian countries did. The question now is whether the same concern about economic development will—or should—continue to inform population policies and programs in developing countries of other regions.

Notes

CHAPTER 1

1. Throughout this book we use the term "East Asia" to refer to countries in both Northeast and Southeast Asia.

2. These calculations are drawn from Lee, Mason, and Miller (2000) and are described in more detail therein. The Kelley and Schmidt (1996) estimates are based on their preferred model, the variable rate-of-growth model. The Deaton and Paxson (2000) estimates use those authors' medium-productivity growth model.

CHAPTER 2

1. Using regression analysis, Barro and Sala-I-Martin (1995) estimated the effects of the following factors on the growth rate of real GDP per capita: the natural logarithm of initial GDP, male secondary education, female secondary education, male higher education, female higher education, life expectancy, the interaction of GDP and human capital, government spending on education as a fraction of GDP, the investment rate, government consumption as a share of GDP, the black market premium on foreign exchange, a political instability variable, and the growth rate of terms of trade.

2. These figures are from Kim and Lau's (1994) unconstrained estimates, in which they do not impose zero TFP growth for the NIEs. Kim and Lau actually tested the hypothesis of no technical progress (or TFP growth), demonstrating that it can be rejected for the G-5 countries (including Japan) but not for the Asian NIEs. In other words, technical progress is statistically insignificant in the NIEs.

CHAPTER 3

1. Population data in this chapter not otherwise referenced are from the digital version of UN DESIPA (1995b). There are occasional insignificant differences, probably resulting from rounding errors, between the digital data set and the published volume.

2. Not all traditional societies are demographically identical, of course, and all experience fluctuations in levels of fertility and mortality. The same is true for modern

societies. Nevertheless, the differences between traditional and modern demographic regimes are far larger than the variations within them, and the distinction stands easily in the face of empirical variability. For example, the level of fertility in traditional societies almost never falls below four births per woman, and the level of fertility in modern societies almost never rises above three births per woman. In traditional demographic regimes 20% or more of all children born typically die before reaching their first birthday, and this figure would rarely fall below 15%. In modern demographic regimes the same figure would almost never be as high as 5%.

3. "Stabilization" is a considerable, if justifiable, simplification. In the centuries-long perspective of the demographic transition, levels of fertility and mortality in developed countries have stabilized. Changes that appear small in this context, however, may loom large when the focus is on the current situation in developed countries. Mortality risks continue to decline, and there is the possibility that the length of life may be considerably extended. Fertility levels in developed countries fluctuate substantially, if at much lower levels than in the more distant past. The level of fertility in many developed countries falls short of population replacement, giving rise to concerns of population decline and excessive population aging.

4. Stylized depictions of the demographic transition appear prominently in the demographic literature, but the increasing death rates that occur during roughly the last third of the transition have generally been ignored or stylized out of the picture. See, for example, Coale (1974: 23), Thomlinson (1976), Keyfitz (1977: 24), McNamara (1982: 146), Nam and Philliber (1984: 43), Stockwell and Groat (1984: 37), Weeks (1989: 74), and Cleland (1994: 232).

5. Several countries with populations of more than 2 million in 1960 (for example, Cuba, Lebanon, and North Korea) have been excluded from this analysis because no income data were available for them in the Penn World Tables (Summers and Heston 1991).

6. Were income data available for Cuba, it might be included on the list of high-fertility countries that had achieved replacement fertility by the early 1990s. Whether Cuba should be included as a high-fertility country is moot. In 1960–64 Cuba's TFR was above the 4.5 births per woman that divides high- and low-fertility countries in 1960–64. In the 1950s, however, Cuba's TFR was well below this value.

7. Using the estimates prepared by the UN DESIPA (1995b), we plotted TFRs for the 5-year periods from 1950–54 through 1990–94 for 113 countries. TFRs for Taiwan, included in the UN estimates as part of China, were developed separately with data from the Taiwan demographic fact books (ROC MOI, various years). Forty-two countries experienced pronounced fertility declines for at least the three five-year periods before 1990, which we considered the minimum period needed to compute a reliable rate of decline. We set the cutoff date at 1990 rather than at 1995 because the limited data available for the 1990–94 period at the time the estimates were produced indicate that the 1990–94 estimates were substantially extrapolations from earlier data. For each of the 42 countries we determined the period of fertility decline judgmentally from the plots and from a straight line fitted to the relevant points by using a least-squares regression. The rate of decline is minus the slope of this line, expressed in units of children per woman per decade. The initial level is taken to be the average of the points from 1950–54 to the beginning of the decline or the 1950–54 point if the decline began in this period or earlier. We estimated the time at which fertility began to decline as the time at which the fitted decline line was at the initial level.

8. To calculate the year in which the fertility transition is completed, we used UN estimates and projections of the TFR (UN DESIPA 1995b). We estimated the exact year using linear interpolation based on rates reported for five-year intervals. We then calculated the duration of the fertility transition as the difference between the year in which replacement fertility is achieved and the year in which fertility decline began.

9. Systematic comparison with Western experience is problematic on account of limited data and scattered sources. Much of the research in historical demography of the West, including the well-known Princeton Fertility Study (Coale and Watkins 1986), provides little or no data on TFRs. The compilation by Mitchell (1975) includes crude birth and death rates and infant mortality rates, but not TFRs. We have used Keyfitz and Flieger's (1968) study for France and Sweden, Brunborg's (1988) study for Norway, Coale and Zelnick's (1963) study for the United States, and Lutz's (1987) study for Finland.

10. US estimates are available for the 1930s through the 1960s, a period during which family size was comparable to that in East Asia between 1960 and 1990. For each cohort of children the average family size (size of the sibling set, to be more precise) increased by about 20% between the preschool years and the teen years (Hernandez 1993: 43, Table 2.4).

11. We calculated these values using the age distribution of the adult population and the values reported in Figure 3.11 to produce a weighted average.

12. This projection is based on estimates of the number of surviving children for women who are middle-aged or older. No account is taken of the effect of adult mortality on the number of surviving children. See the earlier discussion of Figure 3.10 in the text.

13. Estimates for Asian economies presented in this section are based on published census reports and special tabulations. Details are available from Andrew Mason upon request.

CHAPTER 4

1. The second and third sections of the chapter draw on the studies by Hayami and Otsuka (1994), Hayami and Ruttan (1985, ch. 9), and Kikuchi and Hayami (1985). The fourth section draws on Hayami's (1997, ch. 4) book.

2. The growth rate for the 1970s cited here refers to the average compound rate in average yield per hectare of harvested area from 1968–72 to 1978–82, and the growth rate for the 1980s is calculated from the 1978–82 and 1988–92 averages. The growth rates for more recent years (1985–89 to 1990–94) declined to 1.4% in Southeast Asia and to 2.5% in South Asia (IRRI 1997).

3. This rural, or peasant, populism is a sharp contrast to the urban populism in Latin America, typically practiced in Argentina under Juan Peron's administration. Urban populism led to industrialization aimed at substituting local goods for imported goods. Industrialization of that sort favors organized urban labor.

CHAPTER 5

1. World capital flows have shown great instability at least over the last two centuries. Diaz-Alejandro (1983) and Eichengreen (1991) have provided historical perspectives on the issue of instability.

2. It can be shown that a steady-state increase in population growth will reduce the savings rate for $(n^*g - 1)\bar{\varepsilon}_{s,n} > 1$, where $\bar{\varepsilon}_{s,n}$ represents the elasticity of savings as a share of labor income with respect to the fertility rate. Plausible parameter values yield an elasticity of less than one-third, even given high fertility.

3. The dynamic patterns described here are surprisingly insensitive to parameter choice. For both the open economy and the closed economy any plausible set of values yields an initial decline in the saving rate (the dependency effect dominates), followed by a subsequent rise (the growth-tilt effect dominates) and later decline (the growth-tilt effect dominates but works in the opposite direction).

4. However, it does not allow for the independent exploration of aging effects very well—demographic trends that will matter for Northeast Asia's future. The time series from Asia simply does not offer enough observations to estimate with much confidence the independent influence of age in the recent past.

5. Park and Rhee (1996, figure 4) found much the same in Korean household survey data. In the cross-sectional profile saving rates peak at ages 30–34. In age profiles those who were 15–20 years old in 1970 also have peak saving rates at ages 30–34. Those who were 25 or 30 years old in 1970 have saving peaks at ages 35–39 and 40–44. These are all very young peaks compared with OECD findings.

6. These figures for Northeast Asia (13.6 percentage points) and Southeast Asia (11.5 percentage points) may seem very big, even by the standards of those reported by Webb and Zia (1990). Using simulation, they argued (p. 12) that "the decline of net reproductive rates could cause aggregate savings to rise by about 5 percent of GDP" in the future. Yet their figures apply to much more slowly growing countries (Nigeria and Brazil) or to countries where room for future reduction in net reproduction rates was far smaller than that observed after the 1960s in East Asia (South Korea).

CHAPTER 7

1. Nonprofessional foreign workers, except those from Peninsular Malaysia, are not required to contribute to the CPF, but domestic firms pay a levy for each foreign worker hired.

2. Equation (7.3) was estimated by the two-stage least-squares method to avoid the simultaneity bias that occurs when the ordinary least-squares method is used.

3. Recent studies of the social security system in the United States have recommended instituting a completely funded system over a suitable period of time to increase national saving [for example, Friend (1986)]. In a model simulation exercise involving 12 countries in Europe and North America, Gonnot (1995) found that with the exception of the Netherlands, the mixed-system (pay-as-you-go plus a complementary capital-funded scheme) performs much better than a pure pay-as-you-go system. Because a mixed system is less attractive for people with low work records, it could provide a strong incentive for people to join or stay in the labor force.

CHAPTER 8

1. L/N does not incorporate the effects of age on either productivity or consumption needs, but these factors can be readily incorporated into the analysis following Cutler et al. (1990).

2. A full accounting of the effects of the labor force, provided later in this chapter, incorporates the effects of changes in the labor force growth rate on output per worker.

3. The worldwide pattern was constructed from data for 103 countries, available from the International Labour Office (ILO Bureau of Statistics 1997). For each country the average labor force growth and population growth were calculated for 1960–90. The data were smoothed to produce the worldwide pattern. Smoothing was accomplished by ordering the countries from highest to lowest on the basis of their population growth rates. A moving average for 19 adjacent countries was then calculated and plotted.

4. Incorporating the role of technology into the neoclassical model introduces some complications, but the key ideas explained here hold.

5. Figure 8.2 includes 59 countries, including 4 of the study countries, for which data are available from the Penn World Table (Summers and Heston 1991).

6. The saving rate simulations of Lee, Mason, and Miller (Chapter 6) cannot be used directly because they represent a broad measure of saving, whereas the growth-accounting analyses are based on investment in fixed capital. Using the simulated saving rates would have produced a substantially greater effect on economic growth. To deal with this problem, I assumed that the ratio of the investment rate to the low-level equilibrium value in the growth-accounting analysis is equal to the ratio of the saving rate to the pretransition rate in Taiwan (the value in 1900) from the Lee, Mason, and Miller (Chapter 6) simulation. Hence the effect on saving includes the effect of all demographic changes after 1900 that influenced saving between 1965 and 1990.

7. Labor-augmenting technological progress is easily incorporated into the model, as in Solow's (1956) original formulation of the neoclassical model.

8. The upward shift in the demand for wealth incorporates the capital-deepening effects of both slower labor force growth and higher saving rates attributable to changing demographic conditions.

9. In this exposition it is assumed that all workers are nationals—that is, that there is no international immigration.

10. The obtained investment rates are substantially smaller than those typically reported for several reasons: They are net of depreciation; they exclude investment in residences; and they are adjusted for international differences in the price of capital goods.

CHAPTER 9

1. The World Bank is developing new measures of educational attainment.

2. In the World Bank (1993a) and Barro (1991) studies the dependent variable is average real per capita income growth over the period 1960–1985. Other independent variables in addition to education are investment, population growth, and GDP relative to US GDP. In the study by Mankiw, Romer, and Weil (1992) the dependent variables are ln GDP per working-age person in 1985 and growth in this variable over the period from 1960 to 1985. In addition to education, the other independent variables are investment, initial GDP per capita, and growth in labor and technology.

3. Lillard and Willis (1994: 1,139–40) posited that unobserved residual components of the child's education equation may be correlated with the mother's and fa-

ther's unobserved residual components, leading to endogeneity of the parents' education in the child's education investment equation. Such correlations can arise from intergenerational correlations of environments or genes. In their study of Malaysia, Lillard and Willis (1994) found that such correlations are significant and that the coefficients on parents' education are biased upward by about 30%.

CHAPTER 10

1. Not all Demographic and Health Surveys (and none of those we use) include anthropometric data, so an additional reason to focus on health outcomes is pragmatic.

2. Trussell and Kost (1987) provided estimates of annual failure rates, largely for the United States, that are typically an order of magnitude greater than their theoretical minima.

3. The model is one of resource allocation to living children. Clearly, prior mortality is relevant in selecting the sample of children for whom the allocation decisions are being made, and nonrandom prior mortality has the potential to bias empirical results based on this model. However, in our initial empirical work, we found no evidence of mortality selectivity. In related research Pitt (1997) found only small impacts of a failure to include the self-selectivity of fertility in models of child mortality. Therefore we treat survival to selection in our sample as exogenously determined.

4. One reason that this might be desirable is because past fertility contributes to current sibset size, and the past and current determinants of fertility, especially in survey data, may be difficult to separate.

5. It would be desirable to incorporate some sort of family-level effects in this model. However, data constraints make such effects impossible to estimate using Demographic and Health Survey–style data sets, because there are few multiple-birth households reporting the data we require.

6. We focus in this chapter on the 1991 results for Indonesia. More detailed 1994 results can be found in the study by Jensen and Ahlburg (1999).

7. If morbidity is a reflection of choice, then mortality might be a reflection of the same phenomenon. Therefore, in an analysis not reported here, we examined the possibility of selectivity bias induced by excluding dead children. Using a two-stage Heckman approach in models of morbidity, we were consistently and robustly far from being able to reject the null hypothesis of random mortality. In other words, had the children who died in fact survived, we would not predict the incidence of disease to be any greater among them than among the actual survivors.

8. Reduced forms for these variables are estimated and used to generate instruments for subsequent Hausman tests. All predetermined variables from the structural equations for illness and treatment as well as for years since first marriage, whether parents expected financial support or to live with their children in retirement, birth weight categories, and whether the reference birth was one of a multiple birth are used in estimating the reduced-form equations.

9. However, in this, structural coefficients of neither the raw variable nor the instrument were statistically significant at conventional levels (see Table 10.2).

10. This value was picked because it is slightly larger than the current total fertility rate. The findings are robust to a variable defined on family sizes of two and seven children, which we chose to represent low and high extremes of fertility.

11. It is often hypothesized that sibset size especially disadvantages girls. Research in the Philippines has shown that sons and daughters are treated differently but that daughters are compensated for smaller land bequests with more education than their brothers receive (Quisumbing 1994), and in fact we find that Filipino boys are at a slight (but statistically insignificant) disadvantage. Our interaction of large sibset size with child's sex shows no such effect for either morbidity or treatment.

12. Pitt (1997) reported similar difficulties in a model of fertility and mortality.

13. The linear probability model is consistent, even with the Heckman λ as a covariate. It is inefficient and heteroskedastic (but in a known fashion) and can yield predictions outside the unit interval. See, for example, van de Ven and van Pragg (1981).

For each illness, we first estimate the structural equation for morbidity and then use the estimated parameters in constructing the inverse Mills ratio term for the treatment equation.

14. The mean prevalence of diarrhea is 10% (Table 10.1) and the partial derivative of wantedness in the diarrhea incidence equation is -0.022 (Table 10.2), yielding a 22% reduction in diarrhea for wanted births, compared to the mean level of wantedness. This metric is used consistently in our discussions of regression results.

15. The result comes from a simulation, so no confidence interval is presented.

16. Mean sibset size is 2.2. The estimated total fertility rate is substantially larger, 4.1. A prediction this far from the sample mean should be viewed as a rough illustration.

17. The difference between the coefficients of sibset size in the diarrhea and fever equations is roughly the size of the standard error of the diarrhea coefficient and so is statistically negligible. However, ORT is *so* cheap and easy that even an effect of equal magnitude is unexpected.

18. Failure of the bivariate probit likelihood to converge and the combination of an extremely small Mills ratio term together with a wrong-signed (but insignificant) coefficient for wantedness in the Heckman regression for fever and cough are probably symptoms of a single underlying problem. It is difficult to determine who will receive treatment and therefore difficult to estimate the parameters describing this choice. An important unobservable variable is severity of illness. If wanted children have less severe respiratory illnesses or if the model does a poor job of controlling for the impact of wantedness through the morbidity equation, then odd findings such as the negative coefficient for wantedness are possible.

19. Travel time to health care provision points per se is not available in the Demographic and Health Survey data. Travel time to family planning provision points is known, and roughly 85% of family planning provision points were hospitals, clinics, *barangay* ("community") health stations or other joint health and family planning facilities. Still, this variable is an imperfect proxy for travel time to health care facility.

20. To test this contention, we reestimated the model using only those cases where sibset size was greater than 2. The coefficient of sibset size becomes statistically insignificant, with an asymptotic t ratio less than 1 in absolute value. The coefficient and statistical significance of wantedness was unchanged.

A second possibility is that ownership of assets is a bad measure of family income and that number of children is a normal good. In this case (unobserved) high incomes are associated with larger numbers of children, and the children of higher income families are better nourished, generating a spurious positive relationship between sibset size and the probability of illness. More widespread fertility control, as in Indonesia, would accentuate this problem.

21. These results are based on the instrumental variables specification, which in turn is the result of rejecting a Hausman test of exogeneity of wantedness and sibset size to ARI treatment. Although a case can be made for the causal impact of disease *incidence* on wantedness, it seems unlikely that there is true simultaneity in the wantedness-*treatment* relationship. The Hausman test is based on a symptom of misspecified endogeneity that is shared by other specification errors, and the instrumental-variables cure works on a wide range of such problems (including errors in variables, a likely candidate for wantedness). The results we describe are robust to a noninstrumental variables specification, except that Java or Bali residence is associated with a statistically significant increase in treatment probability of 5%.

22. Versus a two-tailed alternative hypothesis.

23. Economic growth and the trend toward small families continued in Indonesia in the years between 1991 and 1994. Both the Bongaarts first-birth frailty and the incomplete income-measurement arguments are therefore likely to be more important in 1994 than in 1991 in accounting for the seemingly beneficial impact of sibset size on morbidity.

CHAPTER 11

1. The survey uses a two-stage sampling process to sample households. Sample units drawn in the first stage of sampling are *tsun* (villages) or *li* (neighborhoods); those drawn in the second stage are households. Before the results of the first stage of sampling can be used, one must sort out the household registration data in the *tsun* or *li* and then stratify the data according to the degree of urbanization and the type of industry. In each stage a systematic sampling method is used. Approximately 515 *tsun* and *li* are drawn in the first stage of sampling, and about 19,600 households are then sampled in the second stage. From within these households come the 40,000 to 60,000 individuals who are interviewed.

2. The total fertility rates before World War II in Taiwan were constructed by Paul Liu. I would like to thank Professor Liu for providing this important information for this study.

CHAPTER 12

1. The Singapore government has not recently published the number of legal foreign workers, but estimates of the number of foreign workers in 1995 range from 350,000 (Guat 1996: 88) to 400,000 (Hui 1997: 1), of whom 50,000 were professionals or skilled workers employed under the employment pass scheme, with the rest being employed under the work permit scheme. Because the number of total employed was 1,702,100 in 1995 (ROS DOS 1996), the percentage of foreign workers among the total employed was 20.6% (based on Guat's estimate) or 23.5% (based on Hui's estimate).

2. In 1996 the overall unemployment rate in Japan was 3.4%, whereas that of

males age 60–64 was 8.5% (Japan SB 1997, *Annual Report on the Labor Force Survey, 1996*). The unemployment rate among males age 60–64 was not uniformly high, however; there was a big spike at age 60.

3. For example, analysts have often cited the large wage gap between blue-collar and white-collar workers in South Korea and Taiwan and attributed it to the Confucian social order. See, for example, Park and Lee (1995: 51) for South Korea and Lee (1995: 111–13) for Taiwan.

4. Usually the investment in school education is concentrated in the young age groups. The proportion of college graduates in the same age cohort should therefore be stabilized after, say, the late 20s. But this is not necessarily the case in Table 12.7. I have not investigated whether this result is due mainly to sampling errors or instead reflects either real variation resulting from schooling in the middle years or different entry rates into or exit rates from the civilian private sector by education.

5. Krugman (1994a: 120) doubted that factor-price equalization explains the relative wage decline of unskilled labor in the United States.

CHAPTER 13

1. Say's law, named after French economist J. B. Say, asserts that supply creates its own demand and that there can be no overproduction, as in Keynesian economics (Baumol and Blinder 1997: 832–33).

CHAPTER 14

1. Bauer and Shin (1987) examined the effect of a predicted number of children on female participation using a logit analysis and controlling for women's education, experience, household composition, residence, and the income of the household head. The data came from the 1983–84 *Annual Report on the Economically Active Population Survey* [ROK NSO, various years (1984, 1985)].

2. Bauer, Sinuraya, and Iryanti (1991) estimated participation logits using data from the 1985 Survei Perduduk Antar Sensus, or Intercensal Population Survey, commonly known as SUPAS. They controlled for age, education, urban versus rural residence, region, household composition, and the education of the household head.

3. Using data from the 1988 Socio-Economic Survey, Bauer et al. (1992) controlled for household composition, age, education, and net household income.

CHAPTER 15

1. Per capita income data are based on the Penn World Table (Summers and Heston 1991). Table 15.4 reports detailed Gini ratios and sources.

2. The trend in income inequality in the 1980s is the subject of disagreement. The estimates reported here are based on the work of Ahn (1997), who reported increasing income inequality during the 1980s. The estimates included in Deininger and Squire's (1996) study, which are based on government estimates and on work by Choo (1982), indicate declining income inequality during the 1980s. Using either set of estimates, however, we find that South Korean income inequality remains above that of Taiwan.

3. Model life tables have been constructed based on the mortality experience of many countries. The calculations presented here are based on the West pattern of mortality for females constructed by Coale and Demeny (1983).

CHAPTER 16

1. The equation for both the FPE and TFR models is as follows: $(y_{it} - y_i) = (x_{it} - x_i)\beta + (\varepsilon_{it} - \varepsilon_i)$, where I estimate parameters β to obtain the coefficients for the x covariates and the error term ε. In the TFR model I include FPE as an instrumental variable; that is, its predicted value for each unit is determined from the first model.

Bibliography

Abbott, G. 1985. "A Survey of Savings and Financial Development in Asian Developing Countries." *Savings and Development* 9: 395–419.

Abella, M. 1994. "Structural Change and Labour Migration within the Asian Region." In W. Goonerate, P. L. Martin, and H. Sazanami, eds., *Regional Development Impacts of Labour in Asia*, pp. 25–44. UNCRD Research Report Series, no. 2. Nagoya, Japan: United Nations Centre for Regional Development.

Abella, M. I. 1995. "Asian Labour Migration: Past, Present, and Future." *ASEAN Economic Bulletin* 12(2): 125–38.

Abimanyu, A. 1995. "The Indonesian Economy and Total Factor Productivity." *The Singapore Economic Review* 40(1): 25–40.

ADB [Asian Development Bank]. 1990. *Human Resource Policy and Economic Development: Selected Country Studies*. Manila: Asian Development Bank.

———. 1994. *Asian Development Outlook 1994*. Hong Kong: Oxford University Press for the Asian Development Bank.

———. 1995. *Asian Development Outlook, 1995 and 1996*. Hong Kong: Oxford University Press for the Asian Development Bank.

———. 1997. *Emerging Asia: Changes and Challenges*. Manila: Asian Development Bank.

Ahlburg, D. A. 1987. "The Impact of Population Growth on Economic Growth in Developing Nations: The Evidence from Macroeconomic-Demographic Models." In D. G. Johnson and R. D. Lee, eds., *Population Growth and Economic Development: Issues and Evidence*, pp. 479–522. Madison, WI: University of Wisconsin Press.

Ahlburg, D. A., and I. Diamond. 1996. "Evaluating the Impact of Family Planning Programs." In D. A. Alhburg, A. C. Kelly, and K. O. Mason, eds., *The Impact of Population Growth on Well-Being in Developing Countries*, pp. 299–335. Berlin: Springer-Verlag.

Ahlburg, D. A., A. C. Kelley, and K. O. Mason, eds. 1996. *The Impact of Population Growth on Well-Being in Developing Countries*. Berlin: Springer-Verlag.

Ahn, K. 1997. "Trends in and Determinants of Income Distribution in Korea." *Journal of Economic Development* 22(2): 27–56.

Akin, J. S., D. K. Guilkey, and B. M. Popkin. 1991. "The Production of Infant Health: Input Demand and Health Status Differentials Related to Gender of the Infant." *Research in Population Economics* 7: 267–89.

Altonji, J. G., and T. A. Dunn. 1995. *The Effects of School and Family Characteristics on the Return to Education.* Working Paper 5072. Washington, DC: National Bureau of Economic Research.

Altonji, J. G., and J. R. Spletzer. 1991. "Worker Characteristics, Job Characteristics, and the Receipt of On-the-Job Training." *Industrial and Labor Relations Review* 45(1): 58–71.

Amsden, A. 1989. *Asia's Next Giant: South Korea and Late Industrialization.* New York: Oxford University Press.

Anderson, K., and Y. Hayami. 1986. *The Political Economy of Agricultural Protection: East Asia in International Perspective.* London: Allen and Unwin.

Anker, R. 1983. "Female Labor Force Participation in Developing Countries: A Critique of Current Definitions and Data Collection Methods." *International Labour Review* 122(6): 709–23.

Anker, R., and C. Hein. 1985. "Why Third World Urban Employers Usually Prefer Men." *International Labour Review* 124(1): 73–90.

Asher, M. G. 1985. *Forced Saving to Finance Merit Goods: An Economic Analysis of the Central Provident Fund of Singapore.* Occasional Paper 36. Canberra: Centre for Research on Federal Financial Relations, Australian National University.

———. 1989. "Fiscal System and Practices in Singapore." In M. G. Asher, ed., *Fiscal Systems and Practices in ASEAN*, pp. 131–83. Singapore: Institute of Southeast Asian Studies.

———. 1996. "Financing Old Age in Southeast Asia: An Overview." In D. Singh and L. T. Kiat, eds., *Southeast Asian Affairs, 1996*, pp. 72–98. Singapore: Institute of Southeast Asian Studies.

Atoh, M. 1994. "The Recent Fertility Decline in Japan: Changes in Women's Role and Status and Their Policy Implications." In Population Problems Research Council, ed., *The Population and Society of Postwar Japan*, pp. 49–72. Tokyo: Mainichi Newspapers.

Attanasio, O. P., J. Banks, C. Meghir, and G. Weber. 1999. "Humps and Bumps in Lifetime Consumption." *Journal of Business and Economic Statistics* 17(1): 22–35.

Auerbach, A., and L. Kotlikoff. 1987. *Dynamic Fiscal Policy.* Cambridge: Cambridge University Press.

———. 1992. "The Impact of the Demographic Transition on Capital Formation." In E. Koskela and J. Paunio, eds., *Savings Behavior: Theory, International Evidence, and Policy Implications*, pp. 281–95. Scandinavian Journal of Economics Series. Cambridge and Oxford: Blackwell.

Azizah, K. 1994. "Foreign Labour in Malaysia." In W. Goonerate, P. L. Martin, and H. Sazanami, eds., *Regional Development Impacts of Labour Migration in Asia*, pp. 95–114. UNCRD Research Report Series, no. 2. Nagoya, Japan: United Nations Centre for Regional Development.

Bai, M. K., and W. H. Cho. 1995. *Women's Wages and Employment in Korea.* Seoul: Seoul National University Press.

Balassa, B. 1991. *Economic Policies in the Pacific Area Developing Countries.* New York: New York University Press.

Barro, R. 1991. "Economic Growth in a Cross Section of Countries." *Quarterly Journal of Economics* 106(2): 407–99.

———. 1992. "World Interest Rates and Investment." In E. Koskela and J. Paunio, eds., *Savings Behavior: Theory, International Evidence, and Policy Implications*, pp. 169–88. Scandinavian Journal of Economics Series. Cambridge and Oxford: Blackwell.

———. 1997. *Determinants of Economic Growth: A Cross-Country Empirical Study*. Cambridge, MA: MIT Press.

Barro, R., and G. Becker 1989. "Fertility Choice in a Model of Economic Growth." *Econometrica* 57(2): 481–502.

———. 1991. "Economic Growth in a Cross-Section of Countries." *Quarterly Journal of Economics* 106(2): 407–44.

Barro, R., and J.-W. Lee. 1993. *International Comparisons of Educational Attainment*. NBER Working Paper 4349. Boston: National Bureau of Economic Research.

Barro, R., and X. Sala-I-Martin. 1995. *Economic Growth*. New York: McGraw-Hill.

Bates, R. H. 1981. *Markets and States in Tropical Africa*. Berkeley and Los Angeles: University of California Press.

———. 1983. *Essays on the Political Economy of Rural Africa*. Cambridge: Cambridge University Press.

Battistella, G. 1993. "Working in the Promised Land: Migrant Labor in Asia." *Asia Currents* (August): 47.

Bauer, J. 1990. "Demographic Change and Asian Labor Markets in the 1990s." *Population and Development Review* 16(4): 615–46.

———. 1992. "Industrial Restructuring in the NIEs: Prospects and Challenges." *Asian Survey* 32(11): 1012–25.

———. 1995. *How Japan and the Newly Industrialized Economies of Asia Are Responding to Labor Scarcity*. Asia-Pacific Population Research Reports, no. 3. Honolulu: East-West Center.

Bauer, J., and Y.-S. Shin. 1987. "Female Labor Force Participation and Wages in the Republic of Korea." Paper presented at the Annual Meeting of the Population Association of America, Chicago, April.

Bauer, J., D. Sinuraya, and R. Iryanti. 1991. *HOMES Research Report: The Labor Sector*. Report prepared for the Asian Development Bank and the Government of Indonesia. Honolulu: Program on Population, East-West Center.

Bauer, J., S. Hutaserani, S. Kuandachakupt, A. Mason, M. Phananiramai, and P. Phapormyont. 1992. "Labor Supply of Women and Youth in Thailand." In J. Bauer and A. Mason, eds., *Family Size and Family Welfare in Thailand*, chap. 5. Report prepared for the Asian Development Bank. Honolulu: Program on Population, East-West Center.

Baumol, W., and A. Blinder. 1997. *Economics: Principles and Policy*. New York: Harcourt Brace.

Bayoumi, T. 1993. "Financial Deregulation and Household Saving." *Economic Journal* 103(3): 1432–43.

Becker, G. S. 1962. "Investment in Human Capital: A Theoretical Analysis." *Journal of Political Economy* 70(5, part 2, October supplement): 9–49.

———. 1993. *Human Capital: A Theoretical and Empirical Analysis with Special Reference to Education*. Chicago: University of Chicago Press.

Becker, G. S., and H. G. Lewis. 1973. "Interaction between Quantity and Quality of Children." In T. W. Schultz, ed., *Economics of the Family: Marriage, Children, and Human Capital*. Chicago: University of Chicago Press, 1974.

Becker, G. S., K. M. Murphy, and R. Tamura. 1990. "Human Capital, Fertility, and Economic Growth." *Journal of Political Economy* 98(5): S12–S37.

Becker, G. S., and N. Tomes. 1976. "Child Endowments and the Quantity and Quality of Children." *Journal of Political Economy* 84(4, part 2): S143–S162.

Behrman, J., R. Pollak, and P. Taubman. 1991. "The Wealth Model: Efficiency in Education and Distribution in the Family." Mimeograph, Department of Economics, University of Pennsylvania, Philadelphia.

Behrman, J., and M. R. Rosenzweig. 1994. "Caveat Emptor: Cross-Country Data on Education and Labor Force." *Journal of Development Economics* 44(1–2): 147–71.

Behrman, J., and P. Taubman. 1986. "Birth Order, Schooling, and Earnings." *Journal of Labor Economics* 4: S121–S154.

Black, S. E., and L. M. Lynch. 1996. "Human Capital Investments and Productivity." *American Economic Review* 86(2): 263–67.

Blau, F. D., and L. M. Kahn. 1995. "The Gender Earnings Gap: Some International Evidence." In R. B. Freeman and L. F. Katz, eds., *Differences and Changes in Wage Structures*, pp. 105–43. Chicago: University of Chicago Press.

Blomstrom, M., R. Lipsey, and M. Zejan. 1993. *Is Fixed Investment the Key to Economic Growth?* NBER Working Paper 4436. Cambridge, MA: National Bureau of Economic Research.

Bloom, D. E., and R. B. Freeman. 1986. "The Effects of Rapid Population Growth on Labor Supply and Employment in Developing Countries." *Population and Development Review* 12(3): 381–414.

Bloom, D. E., and W. Noor. 1995. "Overview of Labour Market Interdependence: Changes in the Regional Division of Labour." Paper no. 1, Forum on Labour in a Changing Economy, organized by the Institute of Labour Studies, Singapore, 23–26 January.

Bloom, D. E., and J. G. Williamson. 1997. "Demographic Transitions, Human Resource Development, and Economic Miracles in Emerging Asia." In Jeffrey Sachs and David Bloom, eds., *Emerging Asia*, ch. 3. Manila: Asian Development Bank.

———. 1998. "Demographic Transitions and Economic Miracles in Emerging Asia." *World Bank Economic Review* 12(3): 419–56.

Bollen, K., D. Guilkey, and T. Mroz. 1996. "Binary Outcomes and Endogenous Explanatory Variables: Tests and Solutions with an Application to the Demand for Contraceptive Use in Tunisia." *Demography* 32(1): 111–31.

Boltho, A. 1985. "Was Japan's Industrial Policy Successful?" *Cambridge Journal of Economics* 9(2): 187–201.

Bongaarts, J. 1987a. "Does Family Planning Reduce Infant Mortality Rates?" *Population and Development Review* 13(2): 323–34.

———. 1987b. "The Projection of Family Composition over the Life Course with Family Status Life Tables." In J. Bongaarts, T. Burch, and K. Wachter, eds., *Family Demography*, pp. 189–212. Oxford: Clarendon Press.

———. 1997. *Trends in Unwanted Childbearing in the Developing World.* Policy Research Division Working Paper 98. New York: Population Council.

Bongaarts, J., and S. Amin. 1996. "Prospects for Fertility Decline and Implications for Population Growth in South Asia." Paper presented at the International Union for the Scientific Study of Population Seminar on Comparative Perspectives on Fertility Transition in South Asia, Islamabad, December.

Bongaarts, J., and J. Menken. 1983. "The Supply of Children: A Critical Essay." In R. A. Bulatao and R. D. Lee, eds., *Determinants of Fertility in Developing Countries*, pp. 27–60. New York: Academic Press.

Boserup, E. 1965. *The Conditions of Agricultural Growth*. Chicago: Aldine.

———. 1981. *Population and Technological Change: A Study of Long-Term Trends*. Chicago: University of Chicago Press.

Boskin, M. J. 1986. "Theoretical and Empirical Issues in the Measurement, Evaluation, and Interpretation of Postwar U.S. Saving." In G. Adam and S. Wachter, eds., *Savings and Capital Formation*, pp. 11–44. Lexington, MA: D. C. Heath.

Boskin, M. J., and L. J. Lau. 1992. "Capital, Technology, and Economic Growth." In N. Rosenberg, R. Landau, and D. Mowery, eds., *Technology and Wealth of Nations*, pp. 17–55. Stanford, CA: Stanford University Press.

Brown, L. R. 1974. *In the Human Interest: A Strategy to Stabilize World Population*. New York: W. W. Norton for the Overseas Development Council, Aspen Institute for Humanistic Studies.

Brunborg, H. 1988. *Cohort and Period Fertility for Norway: 1845–1985*. Rapporter Fra Statistisk Sentralbyrå 88/4. Oslo: Central Bureau of Statistics of Norway.

Calvo, G., L. Leiderman, and C. Reinhart. 1993. "Capital Inflows to Latin America: The Role of External Factors." *IMF Staff Papers* 40:108–51. Washington, DC: International Monetary Fund.

———. 1994a. "The Capital Inflows Problem: Concepts and Issues." *Contemporary Economic Policy* 12: 54–66.

———. 1994b. "Capital Inflows to Latin America: The 1970s and 1980s." In E. Bacha, ed., *Economics in a Changing World*, v. 4, *Development, Trade, and the Environment*, pp. 123–48. London: Macmillan.

———. 1996. "Inflows of Capital to Developing Countries in the 1990s." *Journal of Economic Perspectives* 10: 123–39.

Card, D. 1994. *Earning, Schooling, and Ability Revised*. NBER Working Paper 4832. Washington, DC: National Bureau of Economic Research.

Card, D., and A. Krueger. 1992a. "Does School Quality Matter? Returns to Education and the Character of Public Schools in the United States." *Journal of Political Economy* 100(1): 1–40.

———. 1992b. "School Quality and Black-White Relative Earnings: A Direct Assessment." *Quarterly Journal of Economics* 107(1): 151–200.

Carliner, G. 1995. Comment on Anne Krueger, "East Asian Experience and Endogenous Growth Theory." In T. Ito and A. Krueger, eds., *Growth Theories in Light of the East Asian Experience*, pp. 30–33. NBER [National Bureau of Economic Research] East Asia Seminar on Economics, v. 4. Chicago: University of Chicago Press.

Carroll, C. D., and L. H. Summers. 1991. "Consumption Growth Parallels Income Growth: Some New Evidence." In B. D. Bernheim and J. B. Shoven, eds., *National Saving and Economic Performance: A National Bureau of Economic Research Project Report*, pp. 305–43. Chicago: University of Chicago Press.

Cassen, R., and Contributors. 1994. *Population and Development: Old Debates,*

New Conclusions. U.S.–Third World Policy Perspectives, no. 19. New Brunswick, NJ, and Oxford: Transaction Publishers for the Overseas Development Council.

Chaiwoot, C. 1994. *Foreign Direct Investment in Thailand from Japan and NIEs: A Local Perspective*. International Economic Conflict Discussion Paper. Nagoya: Economic Research Center, Faculty of Economics, Nagoya University.

Chandrasekhar, S. 1967. *Asia's Population Problems*. New York: Frederick A. Praeger.

Chang, C. H. 1992. "Public Finance." In G. Ranis, ed., *Taiwan from Developing to Mature Economy*. Boulder, CO: Westview Press.

Chang, M.-C., and M. Weinstein. 1992. "Have Declines in Fertility Affected the Status of Women in Taiwan?" Paper presented at the Annual Meeting of the Population Association of America, Denver, May.

Chang, S.-J., S.-Y. Chung, and S.-H. Kang. 1991. *Status of Women in Korea*. KWDI Reference Report on Women 400–15. Seoul: Korean Women's Development Institute.

Chau, L. n.d. "Economic Growth and Income Distribution of Hong Kong since the Early 1950s." Unpublished paper, Hitotsubashi Institute of Economic Research, Tokyo.

Chen, A. J., and G. W. Jones. 1989. *Aging in ASEAN: Its Socio-Economic Consequences*. Singapore: Institute of Southeast Asian Studies.

Chen, L. C., E. Huq, and S. D'Souza. 1981. "Sex Bias in the Family Allocation of Food and Health Care in Rural Bangladesh." *Population and Development Review* 7(1): 55–70.

Chernichovsky, D., and O. A. Meesook. 1985. *School Enrollment in Indonesia*. World Bank Staff Working Paper 746. Washington, DC: World Bank.

Cho, L.-J., and M. Yada, eds. 1994. *Tradition and Change in the Asian Family*. Honolulu: East-West Center.

Choo, H. 1975. "Some Sources of Relative Equity in Korean Income Distribution: A Historical Perspective." In H. T. Oshima and S. Ishikawa, eds., *Income Distribution, Employment, and Economic Development in Southeast and East Asia*, v. 1, pp. 48–79. Tokyo and Manila: Economic Research Center (Tokyo) and the Council for Asian Manpower Studies (Manila).

———. 1982. *Estimation of Size Distribution of Income and Its Sources of Changes on Korea*. Working Paper 8515. Seoul: Korea Development Institute.

Chowdhury, A., and I. Islam. 1993. *The Newly Industrializing Economies of East Asia*. New York: Routledge.

Chu, Y.-P. 1995. "Taiwan's Inequality in the Postwar Era." Unpublished paper, Sun Yat-Sen Institute for Social Sciences and Philosophy, Academia Sinica, Taiwan.

Clark, G. L., and W. B. Kim, eds. 1995. *Asian NIEs and the Global Economy: Industrial Restructuring and Corporate Strategy in the 1990s*. Baltimore: Johns Hopkins University Press.

Clark, R. L. 1993. "Population Aging and Work Rates of Older Persons: An International Comparison." In O. S. Mitchell, ed., *As the Workforce Ages: Costs, Benefits, and Policy Challenges*, pp. 57–77. Ithaca, NY: ILR Press, Cornell University.

Clark, R. L., and J. J. Spengler. 1980. *The Economics of Individual and Population Aging*. Cambridge: Cambridge University Press.

Cleland, J. 1994. "Different Pathways to Demographic Transition." In F. Graham-Smith, ed., *Population: The Complex Reality—A Report of the Population Summit of the World's Scientific Academies.* Cambridge: Cambridge University Press.

Coale, A. J. 1974. "The History of World Population." In *The Human Population: A Scientific American Book,* pp. 15–25. San Francisco: W. H. Freeman.

Coale, A. J., and P. Demeny. 1983. *Regional Model Life Tables and Stable Populations,* 2d ed. New York: Academic Press.

Coale, A. J., and E. Hoover. 1958. *Population Growth and Economic Development in Low-Income Countries: A Case Study of India.* Princeton, NJ: Princeton University Press.

Coale, A. J., and S. Watkins, eds. 1986. *The Decline of Fertility in Europe.* Princeton, NJ: Princeton University Press.

Coale, A. J., and M. Zelnick. 1963. *New Estimates of Fertility and Population in the United States.* Princeton, NJ: Princeton University Press.

Cochrane, S. H., and D. T. Jamison. 1982. "Educational Attainment and Achievement in Rural Thailand." In A. A. Summers, ed., *Productivity Assessment in Education,* pp. 43–59. San Francisco: Jossey-Bass.

Cohen, J. E. 1995. *How Many People Can the Earth Support?* New York: W. W. Norton.

Collins, S. 1991. "Saving Behavior in Ten Developing Countries." In D. Bernheim and J. Shoven, eds., *National Saving and Economic Performance,* pp. 349–75. Chicago: University of Chicago Press.

Cornelius, W. 1994. "Controlling Illegal Immigration: The Case of Japan." In W. Cornelius, P. L. Martin, and J. Hollifield, eds., *Controlling Illegal Immigration: A Global Perspective,* pp. 375–410. Stanford, CA: Stanford University Press.

Costello, M. A. 1988. "Infant and Childhood Mortality Research in the Philippines: Review and Agenda." *Journal of Philippine Development* 15(2): 257–74.

Costello, M. A., and L. C. Lleno. 1995. "Social and Economic Differentials in Treatment Patterns for Infant and Childhood Diseases: Philippines, 1993." Photocopy, Research Institute for Mindanao Culture, Cagayan De Oro City, the Philippines.

Cutler, D. M., J. M. Poterba, L. M. Sheiner, and L. H. Summers. 1990. "An Aging Society: Opportunity or Challenge?" *Brookings Papers on Economic Activity,* v. 1, pp. 1–73. Washington, DC: Brookings Institution.

Dasgupta, M. 1987. "Selective Discrimination against Female Children in Rural Punjab, India." *Population and Development Review* 13(1): 77–100.

Datta, G., and P. Shome. 1981. "Social Security and Household Savings: Asian Experience." *The Developing Economies* 19(1): 143–60.

David, P. A. 1975. *Technical Choice, Innovation, and Economic Growth.* Cambridge: Cambridge University Press.

Deardorff, A. V. 1987. "Trade and Capital Mobility in a World of Diverging Populations." In D. G. Johnson and R. D. Lee, eds., *Population Growth and Economic Development: Issues and Evidence,* pp. 561–88. Madison, WI: University of Wisconsin Press.

Deaton, A. 1985. "Panel Data from Time Series of Cross-Sections." *Journal of Econometrics* 30(1,2): 109–26.

———. 1989. "Savings in Developing Countries: Theory and Review." In *Proceed-

ings of the World Bank Annual Conference on Development Economics, Supplement to the World Bank Economic Review and the World Bank Research Observer, pp. 61–96. Washington, D.C.: World Bank.

Deaton, A., and J. Muellbauer. 1986. "On Measuring Child Costs: With Applications to Poor Countries." *Journal of Political Economy* 94(4): 720–44.

Deaton, A., and C. Paxson. 1994. "Saving, Growth, and Aging in Taiwan." In D. Wise, ed., *Studies in the Economics of Aging*, pp. 331–64. Chicago: University of Chicago Press.

———. 1997. "The Effects of Economic and Population Growth on National Saving and Inequality." *Demography* 34(1): 97–114.

———. 2000. "Growth, Demographic Structure, and National Saving in Taiwan." *Population and Development Review* 26(suppl.): 141–73.

Deininger, K., and L. Squire. 1996. "A New Data Set Measuring Income Inequality." *World Bank Economic Review* 10(3): 565–91.

Delong, J. B., and L. Summers. 1991. "Equipment Investment and Economic Growth." *Quarterly Journal of Economics* 106: 445–502.

Desai, S. 1995. "When Are Children from Large Families Disadvantaged? Evidence from Cross-National Analyses." *Population Studies* 49: 195–210.

Dessus, S., J.-D. Shea, and M.-S. Shi. 1995. *Total Factor Productivity and Growth in Taiwan Area, 1950–1990*. Discussion Paper 9504. Taipei: Institute of Economics, Academia Sinica.

———. 1996. *Chinese Taipei: The Origins of the Economic Miracle*. Economic Studies Series, no. 18. Taipei: Institute of Economics, Academia Sinica.

Diaz-Alejandro, C. 1983. "Stories of the 1930s for the 1980s." In A. Armella, R. Dornbusch, and M. Obstfeld, eds., *Financial Policies and the World Capital Market: The Problem of Latin American Countries*, pp. 5–40. Chicago: University of Chicago Press.

Divine, W. D., Jr. 1982. "From Shafts to Wires: Historical Perspectives on Electrification." *Journal of Economic History* 43(2): 347–72.

Dixon-Mueller, R., and R. Anker. 1988. *Assessing Women's Economic Contributions to Development*. World Employment Programme: Background Papers for Training in Population, Human Resources, and Development Planning, no. 6, Geneva: International Labour Organization.

Domingo, L. 1995. "Women, Work, and Family in Southeast Asia." In Asian Population and Development Association, *Women's Labor Participation and Economic Development in Asia*, pp. 81–104. Tokyo: Asian Population and Development Association.

Dowling, J., and A. Lahiri. 1990. "Growth Structural Transformation and Consumption Behavior: Evidence from Asia." *The Developing Economies* 28: 123–51.

Dowrick, S. 1994. Review of *The East Asian Miracle: Economic Growth and Public Policy*. *The Economic Record* 70(208): 469–70.

Doyle, C., and M. Weale. 1994. "Education, Externalities, Fertility, and Economic Growth." *Education Economics* 2(2): 129–67.

Edwards, S. 1993. "Openness, Trade Liberalization, and Growth in Developing Countries." *Journal of Economic Literature* 31(3): 1358–93.

Ehrenberg, R. G., and R. S. Smith. 1994. *Modern Labor Economics*, 5th ed. New York: Harper Collins.

Ehrlich, P. R. 1968. *The Population Bomb.* New York: Ballantine Books.

Eichengreen, B. 1991. "Trends and Cycles in Foreign Lending." In H. Siebert, ed., *Capital Flows in the World Economy*, pp. 3–28. Tubingen, Germany: Mohr.

Estudillo, J. 1997. "Income Inequality in the Philippines, 1961–91." *Developing Economics* 35(1): 68–95.

Evenson, R. E. 1988. "Population Growth, Infrastructure, and Real Income in North India." In R. D. Lee, W. B. Arthur, A. C. Kelley, G. Rodgers, and T. S. Srinivasan, eds., *Population, Food, and Rural Development*, pp. 118–39. Oxford: Clarendon Press.

Fair, R., and K. Dominguez. 1991. "Effects of the Changing U.S. Age Distribution on Macroeconomic Equations." *American Economic Review* 81: 1276–94.

Feeney, G., and A. Mason. 1998. *Population in East Asia.* East-West Center Working Papers, Population Series 88–2. Honolulu: East-West Center.

Fei, J. C. H., and G. Ranis. 1975. "A Model of Growth and Employment in the Open Dualistic Economy: The Case of Korea and Taiwan." *Journal of Development Studies* 11(1): 32–63.

Feinstein, D. 1996. "The Pacific Ocean: Wave of the Future." *Roll Call*, July 29.

Feldstein, M. S. 1974. "Social Security, Induced Retirement, and Aggregate Capital Formation." *Journal of Political Economy* 82(5): 905–27.

Feldstein, M. S., and P. Bacchetta. 1991. "National Saving and International Investment." In D. Bernheim and J. Shoven, eds., *National Saving and Economic Performance*, pp. 201–20. Chicago: University of Chicago Press.

Feldstein, M. S., and C. Horioka. 1980. "Domestic Saving and International Capital Flows." *Economic Journal* 90(358): 314–29.

Fields, G. S. 1992. "Changing Labor Market Conditions and Economic Development in Hong Kong, Korea, Singapore, and Taiwan, China." Background paper for the volume *The East Asian Miracle.* Cornell University, Ithaca, NY.

———. 1994. "The Migration Transition in Asia." *Asian and Pacific Migration Journal* 3(1): 7–30.

Fischer, S. 1993. "The Role of Macroeconomic Factors in Growth." *Journal of Monetary Economics* 32(3): 485–512.

Folbre, N. 1996. "Engendering Economics: New Perspectives on Women, Work, and Demographic Change." In M. Bruno and B. Pleskovic, eds., *Annual World Bank Conference on Development Economics*, pp. 127–53. Washington, DC: World Bank.

Frankel, J. 1991. "Quantifying International Capital Mobility in the 1980s." In D. Bernheim and J. Shoven, eds., *National Saving and Economic Performance*, pp. 227–60. Chicago: University of Chicago Press.

Freeman, R. 1992. "Does Suppression of Labor Contribute to Economic Success? Labor Relations and Markets in East Asia." Background paper for the volume *The East Asian Miracle.* Harvard University, Cambridge, MA.

Freeman, R., and L. F. Katz, eds. 1995. *Differences and Changes in Wage Structures.* Chicago: University of Chicago Press.

Freeman, R., and J. Medoff. 1984. *What Do Unions Do?* New York: Basic Books.

Frenkel, S. 1993. "Variations in Patterns of Trade Unionism: A Synthesis." In S. Frenkel, ed., *Organized Labor in the Asia-Pacific Region*, pp. 309–46. Ithaca, NY: ILR Press.

Frenzen, P. P., and D. P. Hogan. 1982. "The Impact of Class, Education, and Health Care on Infant Mortality in a Developing Society: The Case of Rural Thailand." *Demography* 19: 391–408.

Fricke, T., J.-S. Chang, and L.-S. Yang. 1994. "Historical and Ethnographic Perspectives on the Chinese Family." In A. Thornton and H.-S. Lin, eds., *Social Change and the Family in Taiwan*, pp. 22–48. Chicago: University of Chicago Press.

Friend, I. 1986. "The Policy Options for Stimulating National Saving." In G. Adam and S. Wachter, eds., *Savings and Capital Formation*, pp. 224–49. Lexington, MA: D. C. Heath.

Fry, M. 1984. "Saving, Financial Intermediation, and Economic Growth in Asia." *Asian Development Review* 2: 82–91.

———. 1991. "Domestic Resource Mobilization in Developing Asia: Four Policy Issues." *Asian Development Review* 9: 15–39.

Fry, M., and L. F. Katz, eds. 1995. *Differences and Changes in Wage Structures*. Chicago: University of Chicago Press.

Fry, M., and A. Mason. 1982. "The Variable Rate-of-Growth Effect in the Life-Cycle Saving Model: Children, Capital Inflows, Interest, and Growth in a New Specification of the Life-Cycle Model Applied to Seven Asian Developing Countries." *Economic Inquiry* 20(July): 426–42.

Fuchs, V. 1989. "Women's Quest for Economic Equality." *Journal of Economic Perspectives* 3(1): 25–41.

Fuller, B. 1986. *Raising School Quality in Developing Countries: What Investments Boost Learning?* Washington, DC: World Bank.

Ghatak, S., with D. Deadman and C. Eadie. 1981. *Technology Transfer to Developing Countries: The Case of the Fertilizer Industry*. Greenwich, CT: JAI Press.

Glewwe, P., and H. Jacoby. 1994. "Student Achievement and Schooling Choice in Low-Income Countries." *Journal of Human Resources* 29(4): 843–64.

Goldberger, A. 1973. "Dependency Rates and Savings Rates: Further Comment." *American Economic Review* 63: 232–33.

Gonnot, J.-P. 1995. "Demographic Changes and the Pension Problem: Evidence from Twelve Countries." In J.-P. Gonnot, N. Keilman, and C. Prinz, eds., *Social Security, Household, and Family Dynamics in Aging Societies*, pp. 47–110. Dordrecht, the Netherlands: Kluwer Academic.

Greenhalgh, S. 1985. "Sexual Stratification: The Other Side of 'Growth with Equity' in East Asia." *Population and Development Review* 11(2): 265–314.

Gregory, P., and D. Lal. 1977. *Demand, Supply, and Structure: A Cross-Sectional Analysis of Manufacturing Wages*. Employment and Rural Development Division Working Paper. Washington, DC: World Bank.

Griliches, Z. 1979. "Sibling Models and Data in Economics: Beginnings of a Survey." *Journal of Political Economy* 87(5, part 2): S37–S64.

Gronau, R. 1982. "Inequality of Family Income: Do Wives' Earnings Matter?" In Y. Ben-Porath, ed., *Income Distribution and the Family*. Supplement to *Population and Development Review* 8: 119–36.

Guat, J. S. A. 1996. "Crime in the Foreign Community." In Singapore Police Force, ed., *Police Life Annual 1996*, pp. 88–95. Singapore: Koon Wah Lithographers.

Gullaprawit, C. 1997. *Population Policy and Programs in Thailand*. East-West Center Working Paper 88–23. Honolulu: East-West Center.

———. 2001. "Population Policy and Programs in Thailand." In A. Mason, ed. *Population Policies and Programs in East Asia*, pp. 115–34. East-West Center Occasional Papers, Population Series 123 (July). Honolulu: East-West Center.

Habakkuk, H. J. 1971. *Population Growth and Economic Development since 1750.* Leicester, England: Leicester University Press.

Hajnal, J. 1953. "Age at Marriage and Proportions Marrying." *Population Studies* 7(2): 111–36.

Hammer, J. 1986. "Population Growth and Savings in LDCs: A Survey." *World Development* 14: 579–91.

Hanushek, E. A. 1986. "The Economics of Schooling: Production and Efficiency in Public Schools." *Journal of Economic Literature* 24(3): 1141–77.

———. 1991. "When School Finance 'Reform' May Not Be Good Policy." *Harvard Journal on Legislation* 28(2): 423–56.

———. 1995. "Interpreting Recent Research on Schooling in Developing Countries." *World Bank Research Observer* 10(2): 227–46.

Harberger, A. 1996. "Reflections on Economic Growth in Asia and the Pacific." *Journal of Asian Economics* 7(3): 365–92.

———. 1997. "Evaluating Development Experiences in Latin America and East Asia." Paper prepared for the Third Senior Policy Forum for the Economic Development Management in Asia and the Pacific (EDAP) Network, East-West Center, Honolulu, 20–22 May.

Harbison, R., and E. Hanushek. 1992. *Educational Performance of the Poor: Lessons from Rural Northeast Brazil.* New York: St. Martin's Press.

Hayami, Y. 1995. *Development Economics.* Tokyo: Sobunsha (in Japanese).

———. 1997. *Development Economics: From the Poverty to the Wealth of Nations.* Oxford: Oxford University Press.

Hayami, Y., and M. Kikuchi. 1982. *Asian Village Economy at the Crossroads: An Econometric Approach to Institutional Change.* Baltimore: Johns Hopkins University Press.

Hayami, Y., and K. Otsuka. 1994. "Beyond the Green Revolution: Agricultural Development Strategy into the New Century." In J. Anderson, ed., *Agricultural Technology Issues for the International Community*, pp. 15–42. Oxford: CAB International.

Hayami, Y., and V. W. Ruttan. 1971. *Agricultural Development: An International Perspective.* Baltimore: Johns Hopkins University Press.

———. 1985. *Agricultural Development: An International Perspective*, 2d ed. Baltimore: Johns Hopkins University Press.

———. 1987. "Population Growth and Agricultural Productivity." In D. G. Johnson and R. D. Lee, eds., *Population Growth and Economic Development: Issues and Evidence.* Madison, WI: University of Wisconsin Press.

Hayami, Y., and S. Yamada, eds. 1991. *Agricultural Development in Japan: A Century's Perspective.* Tokyo: University of Tokyo Press.

Health Intelligence Service. 1994. *1991 Philippine Health Statistics.* Manila: Republic of the Philippines, Department of Health.

Hermalin, A. I., J. A. Seltzer, and C.-H. Lin. 1982. "Transitions in the Effect of Family Size on Female Educational Attainment: The Case of Taiwan." *Comparative Education Review* 29(2): 254–70.

Hernandez, D. J. 1993. *America's Children*. New York: Russell Sage Foundation.

Herrin, A. N., A. de la Paz Kraft, O. F. Picazo, O. C. Solon, M. M. Taguiwalo, and M. S. Zingapan. 1993. *Health Sector Review: Philippines*. HFDP Monograph 3. Manila: Department of Health and Health Finance Development Project.

Higgins, M. 1994. "The Demographic Determinants of Savings, Investment, and International Capital Flows." Ph.D. dissertation, Harvard University, Cambridge, MA.

———. 1998. "Demography, National Savings, and International Capital Flows." *International Economic Review* 39(2): 343–70.

Higgins, M., and J. G. Williamson. 1996. *Asian Demography and Foreign Capital Dependence*. NBER Working Paper 5560. Cambridge, MA: National Bureau of Economic Research.

———. 1997a. "Age Structure Dynamics in Asia and Dependence on Foreign Capital." *Population and Development Review* 23(2): 261–93.

———. 1997b. "Asian Demography and Foreign Capital Dependence: The Role of Demography." Background paper for the volume *Emerging Asia*. Harvard University, Cambridge, MA.

Hill, H. 1990. "Foreign Investment and East Asian Economic Development." *Asian-Pacific Economic Literature* 4(2): 21–58.

———. 1995. *Economy of Pakistan*. Lahore, Pakistan: K. A. Saeed, S. A. Salam Publications.

———. 1996. *Indonesian Economy since 1966*. Cambridge: Cambridge University Press.

Hirschman, C. 1985. "Premarital Socioeconomic Roles and the Timing of Family Formation: A Comparative Study of Five Asian Societies." *Demography* 22(1): 35–60.

Hogan, D. P., and D. T. Lichter. 1995. "Children and Youth: Living Arrangements and Welfare." In R. Farley, ed., *State of the Union: America in the 1990s*, pp. 93–141. New York: Russell Sage Foundation.

Honma, M. 1994. *Political Economy of Agricultural Problems*. Tokyo: Nihon Keizai Shimbunsha (in Japanese).

Hoon, H. T. 1991. "The Long-Run General Equilibrium Consequences of Choosing the CPF Contribution Rate in the Singapore Economy." *Singapore Economic Review* 36(1): 70–80.

Hossain, M. 1993. "Production Environments, MV Adoption, and Income Distribution in Bangladesh." In C. C. David and K. Otsuka, eds., *Modern Rice Technology and Income Distribution in Asia*, pp. 221–79. Boulder, CO: Lynne Rienner.

Hou, C.-M., and C. H. Chang. 1982. "Education and Economic Growth in Taiwan: The Mechanism of Adjustment." In Lee K. T. and T. S. Yu, eds., *Experiences and Lessons of Economic Development in Taiwan*, pp. 337–90. Taipei: Academia Sinica.

Hou, C.-M., and Y. C. Hsu. 1976. "The Supply of Labor in Taiwan." In *Proceedings of the Conference on Population and Economic Development in Taiwan*, pp. 315–62. Taipei: Institute of Economics, Academia Sinica.

Huang, F.-M. 1997. *Education, Earning, and Fertility in Taiwan*. East-West Center Working Papers, Population Series no. 88–17. Honolulu: East-West Center.

Hubbard, R. G. 1984. *"Precautionary" Saving Revisited: Social Security, Individual Welfare, and the Capital Stock.* NBER Working Papper 1430 (August). Boston: National Bureau of Economic Research.

———.1986. "Pension Wealth and Individual Saving: Some New Evidence." *Journal of Money, Credit, and Banking* 18(2): 167–78.

———. 1987. "Uncertain Lifetimes, Pensions, and Individual Savings." In Z. Bodie, J. B. Shoven, and D. A. Wise, eds., *Issues in Pension Economics*, pp. 175–210. Chicago: University of Chicago Press for the National Bureau of Economic Research.

Hughes, H. 1992. *East Asian Export Success.* Working Paper. Canberra: Research School of Pacific Studies, Australian National University.

Huguet, J. 1992. "The Future of International Migration within Asia." *Asian and Pacific Migration Journal* 1(2): 250–77.

Hui, W.-T. 1997. "Country Report: Singapore." Paper presented at the Conference on International Migration and Labour Markets in Asia, Japan Institute of Labour, Tokyo, January.

Hyodo, T. 1971. *Evolution of Japanese Industrial Relations.* Tokyo: University of Tokyo Press (in Japanese).

IAEA [Institute of Asian Economic Affairs]. 1961. *Rice Farming in Asia.* Tokyo: Institute of Asian Economic Affairs (in Japanese).

IDE [Institute of Developing Economies]. 1969. *One Hundred Years of Agricultural Statistics in Japan.* Tokyo: Institute of Developing Economics.

IIPS [International Institute for Population Sciences]. 1995. *National Family Health Survey (MCH and Family Planning), India, 1992–93.* Bombay (Mumbai): International Institute for Population Sciences.

Ikemoto, Y. n.d. "Income Distribution in Malaysia." Unpublished discussion paper of the Division of Pan Asian Economics, the Institute of Oriental Culture, University of Tokyo, Tokyo.

Ikemoto, Y., and I. Santisart. n.d. "Income Distribution in Thailand: 1962–1992." Unpublished discussion paper of the Division of Pan Asian Economics, the Institute of Oriental Culture, University of Tokyo, Tokyo.

ILO [International Labour Office]. 1990. *Statistical Report 1989: International Labour Migration from Asian Labour-Sending Countries.* Bangkok: Asian Regional Programme on International Labour Migration.

ILO, Bureau of Statistics. 1997. Economically Active Population, 1950–2010. Computer File, 4th ed. Geneva: International Labour Office.

———. Various years. *Year Book of Labour Statistics [1945–89].* Geneva: International Labour Office.

IMF [International Monetary Fund]. Selected years. *International Financial Statistics Yearbook.* Washington, DC: International Monetary Fund.

———. Undated. Data files on line at *http://migration.ucdavis.edu/Data/remit.on.www/remittances.html.*

Indonesia CBS [Central Bureau of Statistics]. 1984. *Statistical Yearbook of Indonesia, 1983.* Jakarta: Indonesia Central Bureau of Statistics.

———. Various years. *Labor Force Situation in Indonesia, September–December [1976, 1986, 1991, and 1994].* Jakarta: Indonesia Central Bureau of Statistics.

Indonesia CBS [Central Bureau of Statistics], State Ministry of Population, Ministry of Health, and Macro International. 1992. *Indonesia Demographic and Health Survey 1991*. Calverton, Maryland: Indonesia Central Bureau of Statistics and Macro International.

———. 1995. *Indonesia Demographic and Health Survey 1994*. Calverton, Maryland: Indonesia Central Bureau of Statistics and Macro International.

Inoue, S. 2001. "Population Policies and Programs in Japan." In A. Mason, ed., *Population Policies and Programs in East Asia*, pp. 23–37. East-West Center Occasional Papers, Population Series 123 (July). Honolulu: East-West Center.

IRRI [International Rice Research Institute]. 1990. *World Rice Statistics, 1989*. Los Baños, Philippines: International Rice Research Institute.

———. 1991. *World Rice Statistics, 1990*. Los Baños, Philippines: International Rice Research Institute.

———. 1995. *World Rice Statistics, 1993–94*. Los Baños, Philippines: International Rice Research Institute.

———. 1997. World Rice Statistics. Database (February). Los Baños, Philippines: International Rice Research Institute.

JAI [Japan Immigration Association]. 1991. *A Guide to Entry, Residence, and Registration Procedures in Japan for Foreign Nationals*. Tokyo: Japan Immigration Association.

James, E., E. M. King, and A. Suryadi. 1996. "Finance, Management, and Costs of Public and Private Schools in Indonesia." *Economics of Education Review* 15(4): 387–98.

James, W., S. Naya, and G. Meier. 1989. *Asian Development: Economic Success and Policy Lessons*. Madison, WI: University of Wisconsin Press.

Jamison, D., L. Lau, and J. Wang. 1998. "Health's Contribution to Economic Growth, 1965–90." In World Health Organization, *Health, Health Policy, and Economic Outcomes*, pp. 61–80. Final Report of the Health and Development Satellite WHO Director-General Transition Team. Geneva: World Health Organization.

Japan CLMHR [Committee on Labor Movement Historical Records]. 1959. *Labor Movement Historical Records in Japan*, v. 10. Tokyo: Committee on Labor Movement Historical Records.

Japan MOAFF [Ministry of Agriculture, Forestry, and Fisheries]. Various years. *Statistical Yearbook of the Ministry of Agriculture, Forestry, and Fisheries*. Tokyo: Ministry of Agriculture, Forestry, and Fisheries (in Japanese).

Japan MOL [Ministry of Labor]. 1988. *The 40-Year History of Labor Statistics*. Tokyo: Ministry of Labor.

———. 1994. *The 70-Year History of the Monthly Labor Survey*. Tokyo: Ministry of Labor.

———. 1997. *Annual Report on the Monthly Labor Survey, 1996*. Tokyo: Ministry of Labor.

———. Various years. *Annual Report on the Labor Force Survey*. Tokyo: Statistics Bureau.

———. Various years. *Monthly Labor Survey*. Tokyo: Ministry of Labor.

———. Various years. *Wage Structure Survey*. Tokyo: Ministry of Labor.

Japan SB [Statistics Bureau]. Selected years. *Employment Status Survey* [for 1982 and 1992]. Tokyo: Statistics Bureau.

————. Various years. *Population Census of Japan*. Tokyo: Statistics Bureau.

Japan Statistical Association. 1987. *Historical Statistics of Japan*, v. 1. Tokyo: Japan Statistical Association.

Jennings, P. R. 1964. "Plant Types as a Rice Breeding Goal." *Crop Science* 4(1): 13–15.

Jensen, E. R., and D. A. Ahlburg. 1998. *A Multicountry Analysis of the Impact of Unwantedness and Family Size on Child Health and Preventive and Curative Care*. Working Paper. Williamsburg, VA: College of William and Mary.

————. 1999. "Within-Family Resource Pressures and Child Health in Indonesia, Korea, and the Philippines." In A. Mason, T. Merrick, and P. Shaw, eds., *Population Economics, Demographic Transition, and Development*, pp. 143–77, with rejoinder, pp. 184–86. Washington, DC: World Bank.

Joekes, S. P. 1987. *Women in the World Economy*. An INSTRAW Study. New York: Oxford University Press.

Johnson, D. G., and R. D. Lee, eds. 1987. *Population Growth and Economic Development: Issues and Evidence*. Madison, WI: University of Wisconsin Press.

Jones, G. W. 1975. *Population Growth and Educational Planning in Developing Nations*. New York: Irvington.

————. 1990. "Fertility Transitions among Malay Populations of Southeast Asia." *Population and Development Review* 16(3): 507–37.

————. 1997. "The Demise of Universal Marriage in East and South-East Asia." In G. Jones, ed., *The Continuing Demographic Transition*, pp. 51–79. Oxford: Clarendon Press.

Jones, L. P., and I. Sakong. 1980. *Government, Business, and Entrepreneurship in Economic Development: The Case of Korea*. Cambridge, MA: Harvard University Press.

Kang, K. 1994. "Why Did Koreans Save So Little and Why Do They Now Save So Much?" *International Economic Journal* 8: 99–111.

Kang, S. D. 1996. "Typology and Conditions of Migrant Workers in South Korea." *Asian and Pacific Migration Journal* 5(2–3): 265–79.

Karunatilake, H. N. S. n.d. "Long-term Changes in Income Inequalities in Sri Lanka." Unpublished paper, Centre for Demographic and Socio-economic Studies, Colombo, Sri Lanka.

Kayo, Nobufumi, ed. 1958. *Basic Statistics of Japanese Agriculture*. Tokyo: Norin Suisangyo Seisankojokaigi (in Japanese).

Kelley, A. C. 1988a. "Economic Consequences of Population Change in the Third World." *Journal of Economic Literature* 26(4): 1685–1728.

————. 1988b. "Population Pressures, Saving, and Investment in the Third World: Some Puzzles." *Economic Development and Cultural Change* 36(3): 449–64.

————. 1996. "The Consequences of Rapid Population Growth on Human Resource Development: The Case of Education." In D. A. Ahlburg, A. C. Kelley, and K. O. Mason, eds., *The Impact of Population Growth on Well-Being in Developing Countries*, pp. 67–138. Heidelberg: Springer-Verlag.

Kelley, A. C., and R. M. Schmidt. 1996. "Saving, Dependency, and Development." *Journal of Population Economics* 9(4): 365–86.

————. 2001. "Economic and Demographic Change: A Synthesis of Models, Findings, and Perspectives." In N. Birdsall, A. C. Kelley, and S. W. Sinding, eds., *Population Does Matter: Demography, Poverty, and Economic Growth*. Oxford: Oxford University Press (in press).

Keyfitz, N. 1977. *Applied Mathematical Demography*. New York: John Wiley & Sons.

Keyfitz, N., and W. Flieger. 1968. *World Population: An Analysis of Vital Data*. Chicago: University of Chicago Press.

Kikuchi, M., and Y. Hayami. 1985. "Agricultural Growth against a Land Resource Constraint: Japan, Taiwan, Korea, and the Philippines." In K. Okhawa and G. Rani, eds., *Japan and the Developing Countries*, pp. 67–90. Oxford: Blackwell.

Kim, D.-I., and R. H. Topel. 1995. "Labor Markets and Economic Growth: Lessons from Korea's Industrialization, 1970–1990." In R. B. Freeman and L. F. Katz, eds., *Differences and Changes in Wage Structures*, pp. 227–64. Chicago: University of Chicago Press.

Kim, J.-I., and J. L. Lau. 1994. "The Sources of Economic Growth of the East Asian Newly Industrialized Countries." *Journal of the Japanese and International Economies* 8: 235–71.

———. 1995. "The Role of Human Capital in Economic Growth of the East Asian Newly Industrialized Countries." *Asia-Pacific Economic Review* 1: 3–22.

Kim, W. B. 1996. "Economic Interdependence and Migration Dynamics in Asia." *Asian and Pacific Migration Journal* 5(2–3): 303–17.

King, E. M., J. R. Peterson, S. Moertiningsih, L. J. Domingo, and S. H. Syed. 1986. *Changes in the Status of Women across Generations in Asia*. Publication R-33-99-RF. Santa Monica, CA: RAND Corporation.

King, R. G., and R. Levine. 1994. "Capital Fundamentalism, Economic Development, and Economic Growth." *Carnegie-Rochester Conference Series on Public Policy* 40: 259–92.

King, R. G., and S. Rebelo. 1993. "Transitional Dynamics and Economic Growth in the Neoclassical Model." *American Economic Review* 83: 908–31.

Kiyokawa, Y. 1988. Technical Education and Market Adaptations: The Role Played by a New Supervisor Class in Silk-Reeling Filatures of Japan. *Shakai-Keizai-Shigaku* [Socioeconomic History] 54(3): 1–33 (in Japanese).

Knodel, J., A. Chamratrithirong, and N. Debavalya. 1987a. "Societal Change and the Demand for Children." In J. Knodel, A. Chamratrithirong, and N. Debavalya, *Thailand's Reproductive Revolution*, pp. 117–54. Madison, WI: University of Wisconsin Press.

———. 1987b. "Synthesis and Conclusions: Toward an Understanding of Thailand's Rapid Fertility Decline." In J. Knodel, A. Chamratrithirong, and N. Debavalya, *Thailand's Reproductive Revolution*, pp. 193–205. Madison, WI: University of Wisconsin Press.

Knodel, J., and V. Prachuabmoh. 1973. "Desired Family Size in Thailand: Are the Responses Meaningful?" *Demography* 10: 495–506.

Koike, K. 1988. *Understanding Industrial Relations in Modern Japan*. London: Macmillan Press.

———. 1997. *Human Resource Development*. Tokyo: Japan Institute of Labour.

Koike, K., and T. Inoki, eds. 1990. *Skill Formation in Japan and Southeast Asia*. Tokyo: University of Tokyo Press.

Kong, S. K., I. H. Park, A. J. Cho, J. S. Kim, and H. S. Chang. 1987. *Family Transition in Korea*. Seoul: Korea Institute for Population and Health (in Korean).

Kono, S. 1996. "Relation between Women's Economic Activity and Child Care in Low-Fertility Countries." In United Nations, Department for Economic and Social Information and Policy Analysis, *Population and Women: Proceedings of UN Expert Group Meeting on Population and Women, Gabarone, Botswana 22–26 June 1992*. New York: United Nations, Population Division.

Korea Government-General. Various years. *Agricultural Statistics*. Seoul: Korea Government-General (in Korean).

Kotlikoff, L. 1984. "Taxation and Savings: A Neoclassical Perspective." *Journal of Economic Literature* 22(4): 1576–1629.

Kotlikoff, L., and L. H. Summers. 1981. "The Role of Intergenerational Transfers in Aggregate Capital Accumulation." *Journal of Political Economy* 89: 706–32.

Krueger, A. O. 1993. "East Asia: Lessons for Growth Theory." Paper presented at the Fourth Annual East Asian Seminar on Economics, National Bureau of Economic Research, San Francisco, June.

———. 1995. "East Asian Experience and Endogenous Growth Theory." In T. Ito and A. Krueger, eds., *Growth Theories in Light of the East Asian Experience*, pp. 9–30. NBER East Asia Seminar on Economics, v. 4. Chicago: University of Chicago Press.

Krueger, A. O., M. Schiff, and A. Valdes, eds. 1991. *Political Economy of Agricultural Pricing Policies*, 5 Vols. Baltimore: Johns Hopkins University Press.

Krugman, P. R. 1994a. "Does Third World Growth Hurt First World Prosperity?" *Harvard Business Review* 72(4): 113–21.

———. 1994b. "The Myth of Asia's Miracle." *Foreign Affairs* 73(6): 62–78.

Krugman, P. R., and M. Obstfeld. 1994. *International Economics: Theory and Policy*, 3d ed. New York: Harper Collins College Publishers.

Kuptsch, C., and N. Oishi. 1995. *Training Abroad: German and Japanese Schemes for Workers from Transition Economies or Developing Countries*. International Migration Paper 3. Geneva: International Labour Office.

Kuznets, P. W. 1988. "An East Asian Model of Economic Development: Japan, Taiwan, and South Korea." *Economic Development and Cultural Change* 36(3, April Supplement): S11–S43.

Kuznets, S. 1966. *Modern Economic Growth: Rate, Structure, and Spread*. New Haven, CT: Yale University Press.

———. 1976. "Demographic Aspects of the Size Distribution of Income: An Exploratory Essay." *Economic Development and Cultural Change* 25(1): 1–94.

———. 1979. "Growth and Structural Shifts." In W. Galenson, ed., *Economic Growth and Structural Change in Taiwan*, pp. 15–131. Ithaca, NY: Cornell University Press.

Kuznets, S., Wilbert E. Moore, and Joseph J. Spengler, eds. 1955. *Economic Growth: Brazil, India, Japan*. Durham, NC: Duke University Press.

Kwon, T.-H. 2001. "The National Family Planning Program and Fertility Transition in Korea." In A. Mason, ed., *Population Policies and Programs in East Asia*, pp. 39–64. East-West Center Occasional Papers, Population Series 123 (July). Honolulu: East-West Center.

Lam, D. 1997a. *Demographic Variables and Income Inequality.* Research Report 97–385. Ann Arbor, MI: Population Studies Center, University of Michigan.

———. 1997b. "Demographic Variables and Income Inequality." In M. R. Rosenzweig and O. Stark, eds., *Handbook of Population and Family Economics,* pp. 1015–59. Amsterdam: Elsevier Science B.V.

Lam, D., and D. Levison. 1992. "Age, Experience, and Schooling: Decomposing Earnings Inequality in the United States and Brazil." *Sociological Inquiry* 62(2): 218–45.

Lau, L. J. 1996. "The Sources of East Asian Economic Growth." Unpublished paper, Department of Economics, Stanford University, Stanford, CA.

Lee, C., and S. Haggard. 1995. "Introduction: Issues and Findings." In S. Haggard and C. Lee, eds., *Financial Systems and Economic Policy in Developing Countries,* pp. 1–27. Ithaca, NY: Cornell University Press.

Lee, J. S. 1995. "Economic Development and the Evolution of Industrial Relations in Taiwan, 1950–1993." In A. Verma, T. A. Kochan, and R. D. Lansbury, eds., *Employment Relations in the Growing Asian Economies,* pp. 88–118. London: Routledge.

Lee, J. S., and S.-W. Wang. 1996. "Recruiting and Managing of Foreign Workers in Taiwan." *Asian and Pacific Migration Journal* 5(2–3): 281–301.

Lee, K., G. Walt, L. Lush, and J. Cleland. n.d. *Population Policies and Programmes: Determinants and Consequences in Eight Developing Countries.* London: London School of Hygiene and Tropical Medicine.

Lee, R. D. 1994. "The Formal Demography of Population Aging, Transfers, and the Economic Life Cycle." In L. G. Martin and S. Preston, eds., *The Demography of Aging,* pp. 8–49. Washington, DC: National Academy Press.

———. 2000. "Intergenerational Transfers and the Economic Life Cycle: A Cross-Cultural Perspective." In A. Mason and G. Tapinos, eds., *Sharing the Wealth: Demographic Change and Economic Transfers between Generations,* pp. 17–56. Oxford: Oxford University Press.

Lee, R. D., A. Mason, and T. Miller. 2000. "Life Cycle Saving and the Demographic Transition: The Case of Taiwan." *Population and Development Review* 26: 194–219.

Lee, Y.-J., M. Brinton, and W. Parish. 1992. *Married Women's Employment in East Asia.* Population Research Center Discussion Paper 92–9. University of Chicago: Population Research Center.

Leff, N. H. 1969. "Dependency Rates and Savings Rates." *American Economic Review* 59(Dec.): 886–95.

Lehrer, E., and M. Nerlove. 1981. "The Impact of Female Work on Family Income Distribution in the United States: Black-White Differentials." *Review of Income and Wealth* 27(4): 423–31.

Leimer, D. R., and S. D. Lesnoy. 1982. "Social Security and Private Saving: New Time Series Evidence." *Journal of Political Economy* 90(3): 606–29.

Levine, R., and D. Renelt. 1992. "A Sensitivity Analysis of Cross-Country Growth Regressions." *American Economic Review* 82(4): 942–63.

Liang, C.-Y. 1995. "Productivity Growth in Asian NIEs: A Case Study of the Republic of China, 1961–93." *APO Productivity Journal* Winter: 17–40.

Lillard, L. A., and R. J. Willis. 1994. "Intergenerational Education Mobility: Effects of Family and State in Malaysia." *Journal of Human Resources* 29(4): 1126–66.

Lim, C. Y., V. C. H. Chua, K. P. Kalirajan, B. K. Kapur, J. R. Kerr, Y. S. Lee, H. G. H. Lim, L. L. S. Low, D. L. Schulze, G. Shantakumar, B. N. Tay, and P. Wiboonchutikula. 1986. "Report of the Central Provident Fund Study Group." Special issue of *Singapore Economic Review* 31(1).

Lim, L. L. 1993. "The Feminization of Labour in the Asia-Pacific Rim Countries: From Contributing to Economic Dynamism to Bearing the Brunt of Structural Adjustments." In N. Ogawa, G. Jones, and J. Williamson, eds., *Human Resources in Development along the Asia-Pacific Rim*, pp. 175–209. Singapore: Oxford University Press.

Limskul, K. 1995. "Sources of Economic Growth and Development in Thailand." *Singapore Economic Review* 40(1): 117–31.

Little, I. M. D. 1979. "An Economic Reconnaissance." In W. Galenson, ed., *Economic Growth and Structural Change in Taiwan*, pp. 448–508. Ithaca, NY: Cornell University Press.

Liu, P. K. C. 1985. "Human Resource Development and Modern Economic Growth in Taiwan." *Academia Economic Papers* 13: 367–406.

———. 2001. "Population Policies and Programs in Taiwan." In A. Mason, ed., *Population Policies and Programs in East Asia*, pp. 65–87. East-West Center Occasional Papers, Population Series 123 (July). Honolulu: East-West Center.

Liu, P. K. C., and Kuo-Shu Hwang. 1987. *Relationships between Changes in Population, Employment, and Economic Structure in Taiwan*. Studies of Modern Economy Series, no. 8. Taipei: Institute of Economics, Academia Sinica.

Liu, Y. C., and C. H. Chang. 1987. "The Impact of Wives' Earnings on Family Income Inequality: The Case of Taiwan." *Economic Essays* 15: 509–33.

Lloyd, C. B. 1994. "Investing in the Next Generation: Implications of High Fertility at the Level of the Family." In R. Cassen, ed., *Population and Development: Old Debates and New Conclusions*, pp. 181–202. Washington, DC: Overseas Development Council. Also published by Transactions Publishers, Oxford.

Lloyd, C. B., and S. Desai. 1992. "Children's Living Arrangements in Developing Countries." *Population Research and Policy Review* 11(3): 193–216.

Low, L., and T. M. Heng, eds. 1992. *Public Policies in Singapore*. Singapore: Times Academic Press.

Lucas, R. E., Jr. 1988. "On the Mechanics of Economic Development." *Journal of Monetary Economics* 22: 3–42.

———. 1990. "Why Doesn't Capital Flow from Rich Countries to Poor Countries?" *American Economic Review* 80: 92–96.

Lucas, R. E., Jr. 1993. "Making a Miracle." *Econometrica* 61(2)(March): 251–72.

Lutz, Wg. 1987. *Finnish Fertility since 1722*. Helsinki: Population Research Institute, Finnish Population and Family Welfare Federation.

Mackie, J. A. C. 1988. "Economic Growth in the ASEAN Region: The Political Underpinnings." In H. Hughes, ed., *Achieving Industrialization in East Asia*, pp. 283–326. Cambridge: Cambridge University Press.

Malaysia, Economic Planning Unit. 1993. *Mid-Term Review of the Sixth Malaysian Plan*, December. Kuala Lumpur: Economic Planning Unit.

Malthus, T. R. 1967 [1798]. *Population: The First Essay*. Ann Arbor, MI: Ann Arbor Paperbacks, University of Michigan Press.

Mankiw, N. G., D. Romer, and D. N. Weil. 1992. "A Contribution to the Empirics of Economic Growth." *Quarterly Journal of Economics* 107(2): 407–37.

Manning, C., and E. F. Pang. 1990. "Labour Market Trends and Structures in ASEAN and the East Asian NIEs." *Asian-Pacific Economic Literature* 4(2): 59–81.

Martin, P. L. 1993. *Trade and Migration: NAFTA and Agriculture*. Washington, DC: Institute for International Economics.

———. 1997. "Guest Worker Policies for the Twenty-First Century." *New Community* 23(4): 483–94.

Martin, P. L., A. Mason, and T. Nagayama, eds. 1996. *The Dynamics of Labor Migration in Asia*. Special issue of *Asian and Pacific Migration Journal* 5(2–3).

Martin, P. L., A. Mason, and C.-L. Tsay, eds. 1995. *Labor Migration in Asia*. Special issue of *ASEAN Economic Bulletin* 12(2).

Martin, P. L., and J. E. Taylor. 1996. "The Anatomy of a Migration Hump." In J. E. Taylor, ed., *Development Strategy, Employment, and Migration: Insights from Models*, pp. 43–62. Paris: Organization for Economic Cooperation and Development.

Martin, P. L., and J. Widgren. 1996. *International Migration: A Global Challenge*. Population Bulletin, v. 51, no. 1. Washington, DC: Population Reference Bureau.

Mason, A. 1981. *An Extension of the Life-Cycle Model and Its Application to Population Growth and Aggregate Saving*. East-West Population Institute Working Paper 4. Honolulu: East-West Center.

———. 1987a. *HOMES: A Household Model for Economic and Social Studies*. Papers of the East-West Population Institute, no. 106. Honolulu: East-West Center.

———. 1987b. "National Saving Rates and Population Growth: A New Model and New Evidence." In D. G. Johnson and R. D. Lee, eds., *Population Growth and Economic Development: Issues and Evidence*, pp. 523–60. Madison, WI: University of Wisconsin Press.

———. 1988. "Saving, Economic Growth, and Demographic Change." *Population and Development Review* 14(Mar.): 113–44.

———. 1993. "Demographic Change, Household Resources, and Schooling Decisions." In N. Ogawa, G. W. Jones, and J. G. Williamson, eds., *Human Resources in Development along the Asia-Pacific Rim*, pp. 259–82. Singapore: Oxford University Press.

———, ed. 2001. *Population Policies and Programs in East Asia*. East-West Center Occasional Papers, Population Series 123 (July). Honolulu: East-West Center.

Mason, A., and T. Miller. 2000. "Dynasties, Intergenerational Transfers, and Life-cycle Income." In A. Mason and G. Tapinos, eds., *Sharing the Wealth: Demographic Change and Economic Transfers between Generations*, pp. 57–84. Oxford: Oxford University Press.

Mason, K. O., with A. Cardamone, J. Holdren, and L. Retherford. 1995. *Is the Situation of Women in Asia Improving or Deteriorating?* Asia-Pacific Population Research Reports, no. 6, Honolulu: East-West Center.

Massey, D. S., J. Arango, G. Hugo, A. Kouaouci, A. Pelligrino, and J. E. Taylor. 1993. "Theories of International Migration: A Review and Appraisal." *Population and Development Review* 19(3): 431–65.

Masson, P. 1990. "Long-Term Macroeconomic Effects of Aging Populations." *Finance and Development* 27: 6–9.

Matsunaga, Y. 1993. *Labour Mobility in the Asian Region and Japan's Response.* Tokyo: Normura Research Institute.

McCusker, H. F., Jr., and H. J. Robinson. 1962. *Education and Development: The Role of Educational Planning in the Economic Development of the Republic of China.* Stanford Research Institute Project IMU-4027. Palo Alto: Stanford Research Institute.

McNamara, R. 1982. "Demographic Transition Theory." In J. A. Ross, ed., *International Encyclopedia of Population*, v. 1, pp. 146–7. New York: Free Press.

Meadows, D. H., D. L. Meadows, J. Randers, and W. W. Behrens III. 1972. *The Limits to Growth.* New York: Signet.

Meissner, D., R. Hormats, A. G. Walker, and S. Ogata. 1993. *International Migration Challenges in a New Era.* New York: Trilateral Commission.

Migration News. 1994–. Asia section.

Miller, M. J., and P. L. Martin. 1982. *Administering Foreign-Worker Programs: Lessons from Europe.* Lexington, MA: Lexington Books, D. C. Heath.

Mincer, J., and H. Ofek. 1982. "International Work Careers: Depreciation and Restoration of Human Capital." *Journal of Human Resources* 17(1): 3–24.

Mincer, J., and S. Polachek. 1974. "Family Investments in Human Capital: The Earnings of Women." *Journal of Political Economy* 82(2, part 2, March–April supplement): 76–108.

Mitchell, B. R. 1975. *European Historical Statistics, 1750–1970.* New York: Columbia University Press.

Mitchell, O. S., ed. 1993. *As the Workforce Ages: Costs, Benefits, and Policy Challenges.* Ithaca, NY: ILR Press, Cornell University.

Mizoguchi, T., and Y. Terasaki. 1992. "The Impact of Economic, Sociological, and Institutional Factors on Changes in Size Distribution of Household Income." Unpublished paper, Hitotsubashi Institute of Economics, Tokyo.

Modigliani, F. 1980. *Collected Papers of Franco Modigliani.* Cambridge, MA: MIT Press.

———. 1988. "Measuring the Contribution of Intergenerational Transfers to Total Wealth: Conceptual Issues and Empirical Findings." In D. Kessler and A. Masson, eds., *Modelling the Accumulation and Distribution of Wealth*, pp. 21–52. Oxford: Clarendon Press.

Montgomery, M. R., and A. Kouame. 1993. *Fertility and Schooling in Côte d'Ivoire: Is There a Tradeoff?* Technical Working Paper 11. Washington, DC: World Bank, Africa Technical Department.

Montgomery, M. R., A. Kouame, and R. Oliver. 1995. *The Tradeoff between the Number of Children and Their Schooling: Evidence from Côte d'Ivoire and Ghana.* Research Division Working Paper 82. New York: Population Council.

Montgomery, M. R., and C. B. Lloyd. 1996a. "Excess Fertility, Unintended Births, and Children's Schooling." Mimeograph, Population Council, New York.

———. 1996b. "Fertility and Maternal and Child Health." In D. A. Ahlburg, A. C. Kelley, and K. O. Mason, eds., *The Impact of Population Growth on Well-Being in Developing Countries*, pp. 37–66. Heidelberg: Springer-Verlag.

———. 1996c. "High Fertility, Unwanted Fertility, and Children's Schooling." Paper prepared for the National Academy of Sciences Workshop on Education and Fertility in the Developing World, Washington, DC, February 29–March 1.

Montgomery, M. R., C. B. Lloyd, P. C. Hewett, and P. Heuveline. 1997. *The Consequences of Imperfect Fertility Control for Child's Survival, Health, and Schooling.* Demographic and Health Surveys Analytical Reports, no. 7. Calverton, MD: Macro International.

Mueller, E., and K. Short. 1983. "Effects of Income and Wealth on the Demand for Children." In R. A. Bulatao and R. D. Lee, eds., *Determinants of Fertility in Developing Countries*, v. 1, pp. 590–642. New York: Academic Press.

Mundell, R. A. 1957. "International Trade and Factor Mobility." *American Economic Review* 47:321–35.

Muramatsu, M. 1966. "Japan." In B. Berelson, R. Anderson, O. Harkavy, J. Maier, W. P. Mauldin, and S. Segal, eds., *Family Planning and Population Programs: A Review of World Developments*, pp. 7–20. Chicago: University of Chicago Press.

Myhrman, A., P. Olsen, P. Rantakallio, and E. Lara. 1995. "Does the Wantedness of a Pregnancy Predict a Child's Educational Attainment?" *Family Planning Perspectives* 27(3): 116–19.

Nam, C. B., and S. G. Philliber. 1984. *Population: A Basic Orientation*, 2d ed. Englewood Cliffs, NJ: Prentice-Hall.

Naya, S. 1988. "The Role of Trade Policies in the Industrialization of Rapidly Growing Asian Developing Countries." In H. Hughes, ed., *Achieving Industrialization in East Asia*, pp. 64–94. Cambridge: Cambridge University Press.

NIEVR [National Institute of Employment and Vocational Research]. 1988. *Women Workers in Japan.* NIEVR Report 4. Tokyo: National Institute of Employment and Vocational Research.

Nimura, K. 1994. "Union Movement at the Beginning of the Postwar Society." In O. Watanabe, ed., *Japanese Modern and Contemporary History*, v. 4, *Postwar Reforms and the Formation of the Contemporary Society*, pp. 37–78. Tokyo: Iwanami Shoten (in Japanese).

Nishimizu, M., and D. W. Jorgenson. 1995. "U.S. and Japanese Economic Growth, 1952–1974: An International Comparison." In D. W. Jorgenson, ed., *Productivity*, v. 2, *International Comparisons of Economic Growth*, pp. 179–202. Cambridge, MA: MIT Press.

Nortman, D. L. 1970. *Population and Family Planning Programs: A Factbook*, 2d ed. Reports on Population/Family Planning, no. 2. New York: Population Council.

———. 1985. *Population and Family Planning Programs: A Compendium of Data through 1983*, 12th ed. New York: Population Council.

Nortman, D. L., and E. Hofstatter. 1978. *Population and Family Planning Programs*, 9th ed. New York: Population Council.

Obstfeld, M. 1986. "Capital Mobility in the World Economy: Theory and Measurement." *Carnegie-Rochester Conference Series on Public Policy* 24(Spring): 55–103.

Odaka, K. 1984. *Analysis of Labor Markets.* Tokyo: Iwanami Shoten (in Japanese).

OECD SOPEMI [Organisation for Economic Co-operation and Development, Continuous Reporting System on Migration]. 1995. *Trends in International Migration: 1994.* Paris: Organisation for Economic Co-operation and Development.

Ogaki, M., J. Ostry, and C. Reinhart. 1996. *Saving Behavior in Low- and Middle-*

Income Developing Countries: A Comparison. International Monetary Fund Staff Papers, v. 43, no. 1. Washington, DC: International Monetary Fund.

Ogawa, N., and J. Bauer. 1996. "The Impact of Married Women's Labor Supply on the Distribution of Family Income in Japan." Unpublished paper, Nihon University Population Research Institute, Tokyo.

Ogawa, N., G. Jones, and J. Williamson. 1993. "Introduction." In N. Ogawa, G. Jones, and J. Williamson, eds., *Human Resources in Development along the Asia-Pacific Rim*, pp. 1–20. Singapore: Oxford University Press.

Ogawa, N., and R. Matsukura. 1995. "Population Change, Women's Role and Status, and Development in Japan: Executive Summary." In *Population Change, Development, and Women's Role and Status in Asia*, pp. 85–115. New York: United Nations Economic and Social Commission for Asia and the Pacific.

Ohkawa, K., M. Shinohara, and M. Umemura, eds. 1996. *Long-Term Economic Statistics of Japan*, v. 9. Tokyo: Toyokeizaishimposha.

Okunishi, Y. 1993. "Internal Promotion, Wage Profiles, and Mandatory Retirement in Japan." Ph.D. dissertation, School of Industrial and Labor Relations, Cornell University, Ithaca, NY.

————. 1996. "Labor Contracting in International Migration: The Japanese Case and Implications for Asia." *Asian and Pacific Migration Journal* 5(2–3): 219–40.

————. 1997. *Changing Labor Forces and Labor Markets in Asian "Miracle" Countries*. East-West Center Working Papers, Population Series, no. 88–16. Honolulu: East-West Center.

O'Neill, J. 1985. "The Trend in the Male-Female Wage Gap in the United States." *Journal of Labor Economics* 3(1, part 2): 91–116.

Oshima, H. 1993. *Strategic Processes in Monsoon Asia's Economic Development.* Baltimore: Johns Hopkins University Press.

————. 1995. "Trends in Productivity Growth in the Economic Transition of Asia and Long-Term Prospects for the 1990s." *Asian Economic Journal* 9(2): 89–112.

Oshima, H., and J. Estudillo. n.d. "Rising Income Disparities in China under Economic Reform." Unpublished paper, East-West Center, Honolulu.

————. 1997. *Uncertain Trends and Erratic Changes in India's Income Distribution.* Honolulu: East-West Center.

Osmani, S. R., and A. Rahman. n.d. "Income Distribution in Bangladesh." Unpublished paper, Bangladesh Institute of Development Studies, Dhaka.

Pang, E. F. 1992. "Absorbing Temporary Foreign Workers: The Experience of Singapore." *Asian and Pacific Migration Journal* 1(3–4): 495–509.

Parish, W. L., and R. J. Willis. 1993. "Daughters, Education, and Family Budgets: Taiwan Experiences." *Journal of Human Resources* 28(4): 863–98.

Park, D., and C. Rhee. 1996. "Explaining Changes in Saving Rates in Korea: A Synthetic Cohort Approach." Mimeograph, Department of Economics, Harvard University, Cambridge, MA (August).

Park, Y.-B. 1990. "International Labor Migration and Labor Market Developments: Past Patterns and Emerging Issues in Korea." In W. Goonerate, P. L. Martin, and H. Sazanami, eds., *Regional Development Impacts of Labour Migration in Asia*, pp. 275–306. UNCRD Research Report Series, no. 2. Nagoya, Japan: United Nations Centre for Regional Development.

Park, Y.-B., and M. B. Lee. 1995. "Economic Development, Globalization, and Practices in Industrial Relations and Human Resource Management in Korea." In A. Verma, T. A. Kochan, and R. D. Lansbury, eds., *Employment Relations in the Growing Asian Economies*, pp. 27–61. London: Routledge.

Pasay, N. H. A., and T. S. Wongkaren. 2001. "Population and the Asian Miracle: Population Policy and Programs in Indonesia." In A. Mason, ed., *Population Policies and Programs in East Asia*. East-West Center Occasional Papers, Population Series 123 (July). Honolulu: East-West Center.

Perkins, D. H. 1994. "There Are at Least Three Models of East Asian Development." *World Development* 22(4): 655–62.

Perkins, F. 1990. *Integration of Women into Development in the Asian Region*. Working Paper 90/8. Canberra: National Center for Development Studies, Australian National University.

Perotti, R. 1996. "Growth, Income Distribution, and Democracy: What the Data Say." *Journal of Economic Growth* 1(2): 149–88.

Persson, T., and G. Tabellini. 1994. "Is Inequality Harmful for Growth?" *American Economic Review* 84(3): 600–62.

Phananiramai, M. 1993. "Women's Economic Roles in Thailand." Paper prepared for the Conference on Women and Industrialization in Asia, Seoul National University, Seoul, September.

———. 1995. *Population Change, Development, and Women's Role and Status in Thailand*. Economic and Social Commission for Asia and the Pacific [ESCAP], Population and Development, Asian Population Studies Series, no. 135. New York: United Nations.

———. 1997. *Population Changes and Economic Development in Thailand: Their Implications for Women's Status*. East-West Center Working Papers, Population Series 88-11 (August). Honolulu: East-West Center.

Phelps, E. S. 1968. "Population Increase." *Canadian Journal of Economics* 1: 497–518.

Philippines National Statistics Office and Macro International. 1994. *National Demographic Survey 1993*. Manila and Calverton, MD: National Statistical Office and Macro International.

Pillai, P. 1992. *People on the Move: An Overview of Recent Immigration and Emigration in Malaysia*. ISIS Issue Paper. Kuala Lumpur: Institute of Strategic and International Studies.

Piore, M. J., and C. F. Sabel. 1984. *The Second Industrial Divide: Possibilities for Prosperity*. New York: Basic Books.

Pitt, M. M. 1997. "Estimating the Determinants of Child Health When Fertility and Mortality Are Selective." *Journal of Human Resources* 32(1): 129–58.

Platteau, J. P. 1992. *Formulation and Privatization of Land Rights in Sub-Saharan Africa: A Critique of Current Orthodoxies and Structural Adjustment Programmes*. London School of Economics Research Programme, DEP 34, Suntory-Toyota International Centre for Economics and Related Disciplines. London: London School of Economics.

———. 1994a. "Behind the Market Stage Where Real Societies Exist. I. The Role of Public and Private Order Institutions." *Journal of Development Studies* 30(April): 533–77.

———. 1994b. "Behind the Market Stage Where Real Societies Exist. II. The Role of Moral Norms." *Journal of Development Studies* 30(July): 758–817.

Platteau, J. P., and Y. Hayami. 1996. "Resource Endowments and Agricultural Development: Africa vs. Asia." Paper presented at the International Economic Association Round Table Conference, Institutional Foundation of Economic Development in East Asia, Tokyo, December.

Polachek, S. 1981. "Occupational Self-Selection: A Human Capital Approach to Sex Differences in Occupational Structure." *Review of Economics and Statistics* 63(1): 60–69.

Pong, S.-L. 1991. "The Effect of Women's Labor on Family Income Inequality: The Case of Hong Kong." *Economic Development and Cultural Change* 40(1): 131–52.

PRB [Population Reference Bureau]. 1998. World Population Data Sheet. Washington, DC: Population Reference Bureau.

Preston, S. H., and M. Guillot. 1997. "Population Dynamics in an Age of Declining Fertility." *Genus* 53(3–4): 15–32.

Pritchett, L. 1996. *Population Growth, Factor Accumulation, and Productivity*. Policy Research Working Paper 1567. Washington, DC: Policy Research Department, World Bank.

Psacharopoulos, G. 1985. "Return to Education: A Further International Update and Implications." *Journal of Human Resources* 20(4): 583–604.

Quisumbing, A. R. 1994. "Intergenerational Transfers in Philippine Rice Villages: Gender Differences in Traditional Inheritance Customs." *Journal of Development Economics* 43(2): 167–95.

Radalet, S., J. Sachs, and J.-S. Lee. 1997. *Economic Growth in Asia*. HIID Development Discussion Papers, no. 609. Cambridge, MA: Harvard Institute for International Development.

Ram, R. 1982. "Dependency Rates and Aggregate Savings: A New International Cross-Section Study." *American Economic Review* 72: 537–44.

Ramstetter, E. 1993. "Prospects for Foreign Firms in Developing Economies of the Asian and Pacific Region." *Asian Development Review* 11(1): 151–85.

Rao, V. V. B., and C. Lee. 1995. "Sources of Growth in the Singapore Economy and Its Manufacturing and Service Sectors." *Singapore Economic Review* 40(1): 83–116.

Rebick, M. 1993. "The Japanese Approach to Finding Jobs for Older Workers." In O. S. Mitchell, ed., *As the Workforce Ages: Costs, Benefits, and Policy Challenges*, pp. 103–24. Ithaca, NY: ILR Press, Cornell University.

Ricardo, D. 1951. *On the Principle of Political Economy and Taxation*, 3d ed., P. Sraffa, ed. Cambridge: Cambridge University Press.

Riedel, J. 1988. "Economic Development in East Asia: Doing What Comes Naturally?" In H. Hughes, ed., *Achieving Industrialization in East Asia*, pp. 1–38. Cambridge: Cambridge University Press.

———. 1991. "Intra-Asian Trade and Foreign Direct Investment." *Asian Development Review* 9(1): 111–46.

Roberts, K. D. 1997. "China's 'Tidal Wave' of Migrant Labor: What Can We Learn from Mexican Undocumented Migration to the United States?" *International Migration Review* 31(2): 249–93.

Robinson, W. C. 1993. "Summary and Synthesis: Towards a Model of the Asia-

Pacific Rim Success Story and the Role of Human Resources." In N. Ogawa, G. Jones, and J. Williamson, eds., *Human Resources in Development along the Asia-Pacific Rim*, pp. 373–87. Singapore: Oxford University Press.

ROC CEPD [Republic of China, Council for Economic Planning and Development]. 1996. *Taiwan Statistical Data Book, 1996*. Taipei: Council for Economic Planning and Development.

———. 1997. *Taiwan Statistical Data Book, 1997*. Taipei: Council for Economic Planning and Development.

ROC CLA [Republic of China, Council of Labor Affairs, Executive Yuan]. Various years. *Yearbook of Labor Statistics, Taiwan Area, Republic of China*. Taiwan: Council of Labor Affairs.

ROC COEY [Republic of China, Census Office of the Executive Yuan]. 1992. *The 1990 Census of Population and Housing, Taiwan-Fukien Area, Republic of China*, v. I, Part I. Taipei: Census Office of the Executive Yuan.

ROC DGBAS [Republic of China, Directorate-General Bureau of Accounting and Statistics]. n.d. The 1978–1995 Tapes of Manpower Utilization Surveys. Taipei: Directorate-General Bureau of Accounting and Statistics.

———. 1986. *Report on Fertility and Employment of Married Women, Taiwan Area, Republic of China, 1985*. Taipei: Directorate-General Bureau of Accounting and Statistics.

———. 1994a. *Health and Vital Statistics*, v. 2. Taipei: Directorate-General Bureau of Accounting and Statistics.

———. 1994b. *Report on Fertility and Employment of Married Women, Taiwan Area, Republic of China 1993*. Taipei: Directorate-General Bureau of Accounting and Statistics.

———. Various years. *Report on the Manpower Utilization Survey*. Taipei: Directorate-General Bureau of Accounting and Statistics.

———. Various years. *Report on the Survey of Personal Income Distribution in Taiwan Area, Republic of China*. Taipei: Directorate-General Bureau of Accounting and Statistics.

———. Various years. *Statistical Yearbook of the Republic of China*. Taipei: Directorate-General Bureau of Accounting and Statistics.

———. Various years. *Yearbook of Earnings and Productivity Statistics*. Taipei: Directorate-General Bureau of Accounting and Statistics.

———. Various years. *Yearbook of Manpower Survey Statistics*. Taipei: Directorate-General Bureau of Accounting and Statistics.

ROC MOE [Republic of China, Ministry of Education]. 1995. *Educational Statistics of the Republic of China*. Taipei: Ministry of Education.

ROC MOI [Republic of China, Ministry of Interior]. Various years. *Taiwan-Fukien Demographic Fact Book of the Republic of China*. Taipei: Ministry of Interior.

ROI CBS [Republic of Indonesia, Central Bureau of Statistics]. 1992. *Statistical Yearbook of Indonesia: 1992*. Jakarta: Central Bureau of Statistics.

ROK EPB [Republic of Korea, Economic Planning Board] and NBS [National Bureau of Statistics]. Various years. *Population and Housing Census Report*. Seoul: National Bureau of Statistics.

ROK MOL [Republic of Korea, Ministry of Labor]. Various years. *Wage Structure Survey* (previously *Occupational Wage Survey*). Seoul: Ministry of Labor.

———. Various years. *Yearbook of Labor Statistics.* Seoul: Ministry of Labor.

ROK NSO [Republic of Korea, National Statistical Office]. Selected years. *Annual Report on the Economically Active Population Survey.* Seoul: National Statistical Office.

———. Selected years. *Major Statistics of Korean Economy.* Seoul: National Statistical Office.

Romer, P. M. 1986. "Increasing Returns and Long-Run Growth." *Journal of Political Economy* 94(5): 1002–37.

———. 1990. "Endogenous Technological Change." *Journal of Political Economy* 98(5): S71–S102.

———. 1994. "The Origins of Endogenous Growth." *Journal of Economic Perspectives* 8(1): 3–22.

ROS CPF [Republic of Singapore, Central Provident Fund] Board. Various years. *Annual Report.* Singapore: Ministry of Labour.

ROS DOS [Republic of Singapore, Department of Statistics]. 1983. *Economic and Social Statistics of Singapore, 1960–1982.* Singapore: Singapore National Printers.

———. 1996. *General Household Survey, 1995: Socio-Demographic and Economic Characteristics.* Singapore: Singapore National Printers.

———. Various years. *Singapore Yearbook of Statistics.* Singapore: Singapore National Printers.

ROS EDB [Republic of Singapore, Economic Development Board]. 1993a. *Regionalisation Forum Proceedings.* Singapore: Singapore National Printers.

———. 1993b. *Your Partners in Regionalisation: Singapore Government Agencies.* Singapore: Singapore National Printers.

———. 1995. *Singapore System of National Accounts.* Singapore: Singapore National Printers.

ROS MOF [Republic of Singapore, Ministry of Finance]. 1993. *Report of the Committee to Promote Enterprise Overseas.* Singapore: Singapore National Printers.

Singapore MOL [Ministry of Labor]. 1995. *Profile of the Labour Force of Singapore, 1983–1994.* Singapore: Singapore National Printers.

———. 1996. *Report on Wages in Singapore, 1995.* Singapore: Singapore National Printers.

———. 1997. *Report on the Labour Force Survey of Singapore, 1996.* Singapore: Singapore National Printers.

———. Various years. *Singapore Yearbook of Labour Statistics.* Singapore: Singapore National Printers.

ROS MOTAI [Republic of Singapore, Ministry of Trade and Industry]. 1986. *The Singapore Economy: New Directions.* Singapore: Singapore National Printers.

———. 1995. *Economic Survey of Singapore.* Singapore: Singapore National Printers.

Rosenzweig, M. R. 1990. "Population Growth and Human Capital Investment: Theory and Evidence." *Journal of Political Economy* 98(5): S38–S70.

———. 1995. "Why Are There Returns to Schooling?" *American Economic Review* 85(2): 153–58.

Rosenzweig, M. R., and T. P. Schultz. 1982. "Market Opportunities, Genetic Endowments, and Intrafamily Resource Distribution: Child Survival in Rural India." *American Economic Review* 72(4): 803–15.

———. 1987. "Fertility and Investment in Human Capital: Estimates of the Consequences of Imperfect Fertility Control in Malaysia." *Journal of Econometrics* 36(1–2): 163–84.

Rosenzweig, M. R., and K. Wolpin. 1980. "Testing the Quantity-Quality Fertility Model: The Use of Twins as a Natural Experiment." *Econometrica* 48(1): 227–40.

———. 1993. "Maternal Expectations and Ex Post Rationalization: The Usefulness of Survey Information on the Wantedness of Children." *Journal of Human Resources* 28(2): 205–29.

Ross, J., W. P. Mauldin, and V. Miller. 1993. *Family Planning and Population: A Compendium of International Statistics*. New York: Population Council.

Sachs, J., and F. Larrain. 1993. *Macroeconomics in the Global Economy*. Englewood Cliffs, NJ: Prentice Hall.

Saito, O. 1997. *Perspectives of Comparative History*. Tokyo: NTT Publishing (in Japanese).

Sala-I-Martin, X. 1997. "I Just Ran Two Million Regressions." *American Economic Review* 87(2): 178–83.

Samuelson, P. A. 1958. "An Exact Consumption-Loan Model of Interest With or Without the Social Contrivance of Money." *Journal of Political Economy* 66: 467–82.

Sassen, S. 1993. "Economic Internationalization: The New Migration in Japan and the United States." *International Migration* 31(1): 73–102.

Schmidt-Hebbel, K., L. Serven, and A. Solimano. 1996. "Saving and Investment: Paradigms, Puzzles, Policies." *World Bank Research Observer* 11(1): 87–117.

Schultz, T. P. 1982. "Family Composition and Income Inequality." *Population and Development Review* 8(supplement): 137–50.

———. 1985. *School Expenditures and Enrollments, 1960–1980: The Effect of Income, Price, and Population Growth*. Discussion Paper 487, Economic Growth Center. New Haven, CT: Yale University.

———. 1987. "School Expenditure and Enrollment, 1960–80: The Effects of Income, Prices, and Population Growth." In D. G. Johnson and R. D. Lee, eds., *Population Growth and Economic Development: Issues and Evidence*, pp. 413–76. Madison, WI: University of Wisconsin Press.

———. 1989. *Women's Changing Participation in the Labor Force: A World Perspective*. Economic Growth Center, Discussion Paper 171. New Haven, CT: Yale University.

———. 1994. "Human Capital, Family Planning, and Their Effects on Population Growth." *American Economic Review* 84(2): 255–60.

———. 1996. "Accounting for Public Expenditures on Education: An International Panel Study." In T. P. Schultz, ed., *Research in Population Economics*, v. 8, pp. 233–64. Greenwich, CT: JAI Press.

———. 1997. *Income Inequality in Taiwan, 1976–1995: Changing Family Composition, Aging, and Female Labor Force Participation*. Economic Growth Center, Discussion Paper 778. New Haven, CT: Yale University.

Schultz, T. W. 1953. *The Economic Organization of Agriculture*. New York: McGraw-Hill.

———. 1961. "Investment in Human Capital." *American Economic Review* 51(1): 1–17.

Sherraden, M., S. Nair, S. Vasoo, N. T. Liang, and M. S. Sherraden. 1995. "Social Policy Based on Assets: The Impact of Singapore Central Provident Fund." *Asian Journal of Political Science* 3(2): 112–133.

Shih, C.-S. 1976. "The Contribution of Education to Economic Development in Taiwan." In *Proceedings of the Conference on Population and Economic Development in Taiwan*, pp. 287–314. Taipei: Institute of Economics, Academia Sinica.

Shimada, Ho. 1994. *Japan's Guestworkers.* New York: Columbia University Press.

Shoven, J. B. 1984. "Saving in the U.S. Economy." In M. L. Wachter and S. M. Wachter, eds., *Removing Obstacles to Economic Growth*, pp. 187–223. Philadelphia: University of Pennsylvania Press.

Silverman, G. 1996. "Vital and Vulnerable." *Far Eastern Economic Review* 159(20): 61.

Simmons, G. B., C. Smucker, S. Bernstein, and E. Jensen. 1982. "Post-Neonatal Mortality in Rural North India: Implications of an Economic Model." *Demography* 19(3)(Aug.): 371–90.

Simon, Julian L. 1981. *The Ultimate Resource.* Princeton, NJ: Princeton University Press.

Singh, A. 1995. *How Did East Asia Grow So Fast? Slow Progress Towards an Analytical Consensus.* UNCTAD Papers, no. 97. Geneva: United Nations Conference on Trade and Development.

Skeldon, R. 1992. "International Migration within and from the East and Southeast Asian Region: A Review Essay." *Asian and Pacific Migration Journal* 1(1): 19–63.

Solow, R. M. 1956. "A Contribution to the Theory of Economic Growth." *Quarterly Journal of Economics* 70(1): 65–94.

Spencer, D. S. C. 1994. *Infrastructure and Technology Constraints to Agricultural Development in the Humid and Subhumid Tropics in Africa.* EPTD Discussion Paper 3. Washington, DC: International Food Policy Research Institute.

Srinivasan, T. N. 1985. *School Expenditures and Enrollments, 1960–1980: The Effect of Income, Price, and Population Growth.* Economic Growth Center, Discussion Paper 487. New Haven, CT: Yale University.

———. 1995. "Long-Run Growth Theories and Empirics: Anything New?" In T. Ito and A. Krueger, eds., *Growth Theories in Light of the East Asian Experience.* NBER East Asia Seminar on Economics, v. 4, pp. 37–66. Chicago: University of Chicago Press.

Srinivasan, T. N., and J. A. Robinson. 1995. *Long-Term Consequences of Population Growth: Technological Change, Natural Resources, and the Environment.* Economic Growth Center, Discussion Paper 748. New Haven, CT: Yale University.

Stiglitz, J. E. 1989. "Markets, Market Failures, and Development." *American Economic Review* 79(2): 197–203.

Stiglitz, J. E., and M. Uy. 1996. "Financial Markets, Public Policy, and the East Asian Miracle." *World Bank Research Observer* 11(2): 249–76.

Stockwell, E. G., and H. T. Groat. 1984. *World Population: An Introduction to Demography.* New York: Franklin Watts.

Straubhaar, T. 1988. *On the Economics of International Labor Migration.* Bern and Stuttgart: Paul Haupt.

Sugayama, S. 1989. The Interwar Employment System in Japan: A Comparative

Study of the Employment Conditions of White-Collar Staff and Workers. *Shakaik-Keizai-Shigaku* [Socio-Economic History] 55(4): 1–33 (in Japanese).

Summers, L. H. 1986. "Issues in National Savings Policy." In G. Adam and S. Wachter, eds., *Savings and Capital Formation*, pp. 65–88. Lexington, MA: D. C. Heath.

Summers, R., and A. Heston. 1991. "The Penn World Table (Mark 5): An Expanded Set of International Comparisons, 1950–1988. (Mark 5.6a Update, Which Includes Data to 1991.)" *Quarterly Journal of Economics* 105(2): 327–66.

Summers, R., A. Heston, B. Aten, and D. Nuxoll. n.d. Penn World Tables, Mark 5.6a. Available on diskette from the National Bureau of Economic Research, Cambridge, MA.

Taiwan Government-General. Various years. *Yearbook of Taiwan Agriculture*. Taipei: Taiwan Government-General (in Chinese).

Tan, J.-P., and A. Mingat. 1992. *Education in Asia: A Comparative Study of Cost and Financing*. Washington, DC: World Bank.

Tangri, S. S., and P. G. Gray, eds. 1967. *Capital Accumulation and Economic Development*. London: D. C. Heath.

Tay, B. N. 1992. "The Central Provident Fund: Operation and Schemes." In L. Low and T. M. Heng, eds., *Public Policies in Singapore*, pp. 264–84. Singapore: Times Academic Press.

Taylor, A. 1995. "Debt, Dependence, and the Demographic Transition: Latin America into the Next Century." *World Development* 23: 869–79.

Taylor, A., and J. G. Williamson. 1994. "Capital Flows to the New World as an Intergenerational Transfer." *Journal of Political Economy* 102: 348–69.

Thailand MOFA [Ministry of Foreign Affairs]. 1996. "Educational Policy." World Wide Web Document. URL: *http://www.nectec.or.th/bureaux/opm/pol06.htm*.

Thailand NSO [National Statistical Office]. Various years. *Report of the Labor Force Survey*. Bangkok: National Statistical Office.

Tham, S. Y. 1995. "Productivity, Growth, and Development in Malaysia." *Singapore Economic Review* 40(1): 41–64.

Thomlinson, R. 1976. *Population Dynamics: Causes and Consequences of World Demographic Change*. New York: Random House.

Tiffen, M., and M. Mortimore. 1994. "Malthus Controverted: The Role of Capital and Technology in Growth and Environment Recovery in Kenya." *World Development* 22(July): 997–1010.

Tobin, J. 1967. "Life Cycle Saving and Balanced Economic Growth." In W. Fellner, ed., *Ten Economic Studies in the Tradition of Irving Fisher*, pp. 231–56. New York: Wiley.

Toh, M. H. 1996. *A Study of the Effects of Demographic Change on Singapore Households, 1990 to 2030*. Research Paper. Singapore: Department of Business Policy, National University of Singapore.

Toyokeizaishimposha. 1967. *Price Statistics*. Tokyo: Toyokeizaishimposha (in Japanese).

Trussel, J., and K. Kost. 1987. "Contraceptive Failure in the United States: A Critical Review of the Literature." *Studies in Family Planning* 18(5): 237–83.

Tsui, A. O. 1996. *Family Planning Programs in Asia: Approaching a Half-Century of Effort*. Asia-Pacific Population Research Reports, no. 8. Honolulu: East-West Center.

Tsuya, N. O., and L. L. Bumpass. 1998. "Time Allocation between Employment and Housework in Japan, South Korea, and the United States." In K. O. Mason, N. O. Tsuya, and M. K. Choe, eds., *The Changing Family in Comparative Perspective: Asia and the United States*, pp. 83–104. Honolulu: East-West Center.

Tsuya, N. O., and M. K. Choe. 1991. *Changes in Intrafamilial Relationships and the Roles of Women in Japan and Korea*. Nihon University Population Research Institute Research Paper Series, no. 58. Tokyo: Nihon University.

———. 1999. "Investments in Children's Education, Desired Fertility, and Women's Employment." Unpublished paper, East-West Center, Honolulu.

Tyabji, A. 1996. "Financing Social Security." In M. G. Asher and A. Tyabji, eds., *Fiscal System of Singapore: Trends, Issues, and Future Directions*, pp. 82–113. Singapore: Centre of Advanced Studies, National University of Singapore.

UN [United Nations]. 1994. Unpublished data tables. Online at *http://migration .ucdavis.edu/Data/pop.on.www/foreign_pop.html*.

UN DESIPA [United Nations, Department for Economic and Social Information and Policy Analysis]. 1971. *Rapid Population Growth*. Baltimore: Johns Hopkins University Press.

———. 1991. *Global Estimates and Projections of Populations by Age and Sex*. New York: United Nations.

———. 1995a. *1993 Demographic Yearbook*. 44th issue. New York: United Nations.

———. 1995b. *World Population Prospects: The 1994 Revision*. New York: United Nations.

———. 1998. *World Population Prospects: The 1998 Revision*. New York: United Nations.

UN DIESA [United Nations, Department of International Economic and Social Affairs], Statistical Office. 1979. *Demographic Yearbook: Historical Supplement*. New York: United Nations.

UNCTAD [United Nations Conference on Trade and Development]. 1994. *Trade and Development Report*. Geneva: United Nations Conference on Trade and Development.

UNESCO [United Nations Economic, Social, and Cultural Organization]. Various years. *Statistical Yearbook*. Lanham, MD: Bernan Press.

UN FAO [United Nations Food and Agriculture Organization]. 1997. FAOSTAT Database, February. Rome: Food and Agriculture Organization.

UNHCR [United Nations High Commissioner for Refugees]. 1995. *The State of the World's Refugees*. Geneva: United Nations High Commissioner for Refugees.

US BOC [Bureau of the Census]. 1992. *1990 Census of Population*. Washington, DC: US Government Printing Office.

———. 1996. *Statistical Abstract of the United States, 1996*. Washington, DC: US Government Printing Office.

US CSIMCED [Commission for the Study of International Migration and Cooperative Economic Development]. 1990. *Unauthorized Migration: An Economic Development Response*. Washington, DC: US Government Printing Office.

US DOL [Department of Labor]. 1994. *Employment, Hours, and Earnings: United States, 1909–94*, v. 1. Washington, DC: US Government Printing Office.

US INS [Immigration and Naturalization Service]. 1997. *INS Statistical Yearbook*. Washington, DC: US Government Printing Office.

US NAS [National Academy of Science]. 1971. *Rapid Population Growth: Consequences and Policy Implications*, 2 vols. Baltimore: Johns Hopkins University Press.

US NRC [National Research Council]. 1986. *Population Growth and Economic Development: Policy Questions*. Washington, DC: National Academy Press.

US NRC [National Research Council], Committee on Population. 1995. *Resource Allocation for Family Planning in Developing Countries: Report of a Meeting*. Washington, DC: National Academy Press.

US NRC [National Research Council], Committee on Science and Public Policy. 1963. *The Growth of World Population: Analysis of the Problems and Recommendations for Research and Training*. Washington, DC: National Academy of Sciences.

US NRC [National Research Council], Working Group on Population Growth and Economic Development. 1986. *Population Growth and Economic Development: Policy Questions*. Committee on Population, Commission on Behavioral and Social Science and Education. Washington, DC: National Academy Press.

van de Ven, W. P. M. M., and B. M. S. van Praag. 1981. "The Demand for Deductibles in Private Health Insurance: A Probit Model with Sample Selection." *Journal of Econometrics* 17(2): 229–52.

Wade, R. 1990. *Governing the Market: Economic Theory and the Role of the Government in East Asian Industrialization*. Princeton, NJ: Princeton University Press.

Watson, W. B., ed. 1977. *Family Planning in the Developing World: A Review of Programs*. New York: Population Council.

Webb, S., and H. Zia. 1990. "Lower Birth Rates = Higher Saving in LDCs." *Finance and Development* 27: 12–14.

Weeks, J. R. 1989. *Population: An Introduction to Concepts and Issues*. Belmont, CA: Wadsworth.

Williamson, J. G. 1979. "Why Do Koreans Save 'So Little'?" *Journal of Development Economics* 6: 343–62.

———. 1993. "Human Capital Deepening, Inequality, and Demographic Events along the Asia-Pacific Rim." In N. Ogawa, G. Jones, and J. Williamson, eds., *Human Resources in Development along the Asia-Pacific Rim*, pp. 129–58. Singapore: Oxford University Press.

———. 1996. "Globalization, Convergence, and History." *Journal of Economic History* 56: 277–306.

Wittfogel, K. A. 1957. *Oriental Despotism: A Comparative Study of Total Power*. New Haven, CT: Yale University Press.

Wong, A. K., and S. H. K. Yeh. 1985. *Housing a Nation*. Singapore: Maruzen Asia for the Housing Development Board.

Wong, K. P. 1986. "Saving, Capital Inflow, and Capital Formation." In C. Y. Lim and P. Lloyd, eds., *Resources and Growth in Singapore*, pp. 45–78. Oxford: Oxford University Press.

World Bank. 1980. *World Development Report, 1980*. New York: Oxford University Press.

———. 1984. *World Development Report 1984*. New York: Oxford University Press.

———. 1987. *World Development Report, 1987*. New York: Oxford University Press.

———. 1990. *World Development Report, 1990*. New York: Oxford University Press.

―――. 1992. *World Development Report, 1992*. New York: Oxford University Press.

―――. 1993a. *The East Asian Miracle: Economic Growth and Public Policy*. New York: Oxford University Press.

―――. 1993b. *World Development Report, 1993*. New York: Oxford University Press.

―――. 1995. *Workers in an Integrating World*. World Development Report. Washington, DC: World Bank.

―――. 1999. *World Development Indicators*. CD-ROM. Washington, DC: World Bank.

Yang, Y.-H. 1993. "Government Policy and Strategic Industries in Taiwan." In T. Ito and A. Krueger, eds., *Trade and Protectionism*, pp. 387–408. Chicago: University of Chicago Press.

Yap, M. T. 1997. *Population Policies and Programs in Singapore*. East-West Center Working 88–22. Honolulu: East-West Center.

―――. 2001. "Population Policies and Programs in Singapore." In A. Mason, ed., *Population Policies and Programs in East Asia*, pp. 89–113. East-West Center Occasional Papers, Population Series 123 (July). Honolulu: East-West Center.

Yasukawa, M. 1977. "Demographic Transition in Japan." In Japanese Organization for International Cooperation in Family Planning (JOICFP), *Fertility and Family Planning in Japan*, pp. 3–20. Tokyo: Japanese Organization for International Cooperation in Family Planning.

Yoo, J.-H. 1990. *The Industrial Policy of the 1970s and the Evolution of the Manufacturing Sector in Korea*. KDI Working Paper 9017. Seoul: Korean Development Institute.

Young, A. 1992. "A Tale of Two Cities: Factor Accumulation and Technical Change in Hong Kong and Singapore." In J. Blanchard and S. Fischer, eds., *NBER Macroeconomics Annual, 1992*, pp. 13–56. Cambridge, MA: MIT Press.

―――. 1994. "Accumulation, Exports, and Growth in the High Performing Asian Economies: A Comment." *Carnegie-Rochester Conference Series on Public Policy* 40: 237–50.

―――. 1995. "The Tyranny of Numbers: Confronting the Statistical Realities of the East Asian Growth Experience." *Quarterly Journal of Economics* 110(3): 641–80.

Index